ROUTLEDGE HANDBOOK ON TOURISM IN THE MIDDLE EAST AND NORTH AFRICA

The *Routledge Handbook on Tourism in the Middle East and North Africa* examines the importance of tourism as a historical, economic, social, environmental, religious and political force in the Middle East and North Africa (MENA). It highlights the ecological and resource challenges related to water, desert environments, climate change and oil. It provides an in-depth analysis of the geopolitical conditions that have long determined the patterns of tourism demand and supply throughout the region and how these play out in the everyday lives of residents and destinations as they attempt to grow tourism or ignore it entirely.

While cultural heritage remains the primary tourism asset for the region as a whole, many new types of tourisms are emerging, especially in the Arabian Gulf region, where hyper-development is closely associated with the increasingly prominent role of luxury real estate and shopping, retail, medical tourism, cruises and transit tourism. The growing phenomenon of an expatriate workforce, and how its segregation from the citizenry creates a dual socio-economic system in several countries, is unmatched by other regions of the world. Many indigenous people of MENA keep themselves apart from other dominant groups in the region, although these social boundaries are becoming increasingly blurred as tourism, being one socio-economic force for change, has inspired many nomadic peoples to settle into towns and villages and rely more on tourists for their livelihoods. All of these issues and more shape the foundations of this book.

This *Handbook* is the first of its kind to examine tourism from a broad regional and inclusive perspective, surveying a broad range of social, cultural, heritage, ecological and political matters in a single volume. With a wide range of contributors, many of whom are natives of the Middle East and North Africa, this *Handbook* is a vital resource for students and scholars interested in Tourism, Middle East Studies and Geography.

Dallen J. Timothy is Professor of Community Resources and Development and Senior Sustainability Scientist at Arizona State University. He also holds visiting professorships and research associateships in China, Spain and South Africa. His research interests include cultural heritage-based tourism, religious tourism, peripheral regions, heritage cuisines and geopolitics.

ROUTLEDGE HANDBOOK ON TOURISM IN THE MIDDLE EAST AND NORTH AFRICA

Edited by Dallen J. Timothy

Routledge
Taylor & Francis Group

LONDON AND NEW YORK

First published 2019 by Routledge

2 Park Square, Milton Park, Abingdon, Oxfordshire OX14 4RN
52 Vanderbilt Avenue, New York, NY 10017

Routledge is an imprint of the Taylor & Francis Group, an informa business

First issued in paperback 2020

British Library Cataloguing-in-Publication Data
A catalogue record for this book is available from the British Library

Library of Congress Cataloging-in-Publication Data
Names: Timothy, Dallen J., editor.
Title: Routledge handbook on tourism in the Middle East
and North Africa / edited by Dallen J. Timothy.
Description: Milton Park, Abingdon, Oxon ; New York, NY : Routledge, [2019] |
Includes bibliographical references and index.
Identifiers: LCCN 2018035929 (print) | LCCN 2018039682 (ebook) |
ISBN 9781315624525 (master) | ISBN 9781317229247 (Adobe Reader) |
ISBN 9781317229230 (Epub) | ISBN 9781317229223 (Mobipocket) |
ISBN 9781138651920 (hardback) | ISBN 9781315624525 (ebook)
Subjects: LCSH: Tourism–Middle East. | Tourism–Africa, North.
Classification: LCC G155.M66 (ebook) |
LCC G155.M66 R68 2019 (print) | DDC 338.4/79156–dc23
LC record available at https://lccn.loc.gov/2018035929

ISBN: 978-1-138-65192-0 (hbk)
ISBN: 978-0-367-65970-7 (pbk)

Typeset in Bembo
by Out of House Publishing

CONTENTS

Contents

FIGURES

TABLES

NOTES ON CONTRIBUTORS

Ammar O. Abulibdeh received his PhD from the University of Waterloo in Canada in 2013 in Geography and Environmental Management. He completed two Master's degrees from the University of Waterloo, a Master of Civil Engineering in 2006 and a Master of Applied Sciences in Economic Development in 2007. Dr Abulibdeh is an assistant professor of geography and urban planning at Sultan Qaboos University in Oman. He was formerly a faculty member at the United Arab Emirates University and Qatar University. He specialises in urban planning and development, specifically in transportation and environmental planning. His research interests focus on urban sustainability and planning policies, travel behaviour, climate change and implications of sustainable transportation systems on sustainable development.

Nazia Ali is Senior Lecturer in Events and Leisure Management at the University of East London. She is a graduate in Sociology from Middlesex University; she was awarded her doctorate from the University of Bedfordshire. Her research agenda is largely qualitative, operating within an interpretive framework to investigate the role of tourism in identity formation. Nazia has published in areas of tourism, migration and researcher reflexivity.

Dhoha AlSaleh is an assistant professor at Gulf University for Science and Technology—Kuwait. She has published in several journals including *Industrial Marketing Management, Tourism Recreation Research, Journal of Business Ethics Education, Health Marketing Quarterly* and *Journal of Business Inquiry*. She received a number of research grants from Kuwait Foundation for the Advancement of Sciences. She has participated in many international conferences. Her research interests include consumer behaviour and technology, social media and cross-cultural studies. She has recently become interested in the tourism behaviour of Arab and Muslim tourists, including destination marketing and development.

Eli Avraham is Media Professor in the Department of Communication at the University of Haifa, Israel. He is the author/co-author of a number of books including *Campaigns for Promoting and Marketing Cities in Israel* (2003), *Media Strategies for Marketing Places in Crisis and Improving the Image of Cities, Countries and Tourist Destinations* (2008) and *Marketing Tourism for Developing Countries: Battling Stereotypes and Crises in Asia, Africa and the Middle East* (2016). His research interests include public relations and marketing strategies, marketing places, nation branding, advertising, image repair and crisis communication.

Susanne Becken is the Director of the Griffith Institute for Tourism and a Professor of Sustainable Tourism at Griffith University, Australia. She has widely published on the topics of sustainable tourism, climate change, energy use and greenhouse gas emissions, tourist behaviour, environmental policy and risk management. She was a contributing author to the Fourth and the Fifth Intergovernmental Panel on Climate Change Assessment Reports. She is on the editorial boards of *Annals of Tourism Research, Journal of Travel Research, Journal of Sustainable Tourism, Journal of Policy Research in Tourism, Leisure and Events, Tourism and Hospitality Prospects* (China) and the *Tourism Review.*

Richard W. Butler, a geographer by training, is Emeritus Professor in the Strathclyde Business School and Visiting Professor at NHTV University in Breda, Holland. He has published 20 books on tourism and many articles and chapters, his main research interests being destination development, island tourism and the links between tourism, war and religion. He is a past president of the International Academy for the Study of Tourism and UNWTO Ulysses Laureate (2016).

Christine N. Buzinde is an associate professor at Arizona State University. Her research focuses on two areas: community development through tourism and the politics of tourism representations. Her work on representations regards tourism texts as cultural repositories through which inclusion/exclusion, North/South and core/periphery can be understood. Her work on development adopts a grass-roots approach and aims to understand the relationship between community well-being and tourism development within marginalised communities.

Michele Carboni is currently a researcher at CRENoS, University of Cagliari and University of Sassari (Italy). His research interests are related to mobility, tourism and development in Africa. In recent years, he has published mainly on tourism and Islam in Northern Africa.

Noga Collins-Kreiner is a professor in the Department of Geography and Environmental Studies at the University of Haifa, Israel, the Head of the Haifa and Galilee Research Institute and the Vice-President of the Israeli Geographical Association (IGA). Her main research interests are pilgrimage, heritage tourism, hiking and tourism development and management. She is also a resource editor for *Annals of Tourism Research* and has published many papers on the topics of tourism and human geography.

John Connell is Professor of Human Geography in the School of Geosciences, University of Sydney. He has been a consultant to the World Health Organization and to the International Labour Organization, the South Pacific Commission, the World Bank, the Asian Development Bank, the Commonwealth Secretariat and the International Organisation of Migration. His research interests span various themes in geography and development studies, but in this century has focused on development in small island states, especially in the Pacific; the global and regional migration of health workers, the development of medical tourism and other forms of migration in the Pacific region, including temporary guestworkers and potential 'environmental migrants'. He has written more than 300 articles and over 20 books. The books include *Papua New Guinea. The Struggle for Development* (1997); *Urbanisation in the Island Pacific. Towards*

Sustainable Development (with J. Lea, 2002); *The Global Health Care Chain. From the Pacific to the World* (2008); *Migration and the Globalisation of Health Care: The Health Worker Exodus* (2010), and more recently, *Medical Tourism* (2011) and *Islands at Risk* (2013).

Harald A. Friedl is the Head of the Tourism Research Department and a Professor of Sustainability and Ethics in Tourism at the FH JOANNEUM—University of Applied Sciences, Austria. He has published on the topics of sustainable tourism, nature and health tourism, terrorism in tourism, tourism in the Greater Middle East and innovative didactics in higher tourism education.

C. Michael Hall is a professor at the University of Canterbury, New Zealand, and Visiting Professor at Linnaeus University, Kalmar, Sweden, and Docent, University of Oulu, Finland. His research interests include tourism, regional development, environmental change, food, sustainability and World Heritage.

Kevin Hannam is a professor and Dean of the Faculty of International Tourism at City University of Macau. He is also a senior research fellow at the University of Johannesburg, South Africa. He holds a PhD from the University of Portsmouth, UK. Previously he held positions as Head of Tourism & Languages at Edinburgh Napier University, Director of Doctoral Programmes at Leeds Beckett University and Associate Dean (Research) and Head of Tourism, Hospitality and Events at the University of Sunderland, UK. He has edited and authored/co-authored ten books and over 100 academic articles and book chapters. He is founding co-editor of the academic journals *Mobilities* and *Applied Mobilities*. He is also a resource editor for *Annals of Tourism Research* and serves on the editorial boards of *Tourist Studies*, the *International Journal of Tourism Anthropology*, the *Journal of Heritage Tourism* and *Tourism Geographies*.

Joan C. Henderson was Associate Professor in the Division of Marketing and International Business, specialising in tourism studies, at Nanyang Business School (Singapore) for over 20 years before her retirement from full-time employment in 2019. Prior to moving to Singapore, she lectured in travel and tourism in the United Kingdom after periods of working in the public and private tourism sectors there. She is a regular reviewer for a number of international tourism and hospitality journals and sits on the editorial board of several. She has published widely on the subject, contributed chapters to edited books and written one book. Current research interests include issues of tourism development in the Middle East and South East Asia and heritage tourism.

Rami K. Isaac was born in Palestine, did his undergraduate studies in the Netherlands, his graduate studies in the UK and has earned his PhD from the University of Groningen in the Netherlands. He is a senior lecturer in tourism, teaching at the NHTV Breda University of Applied Sciences. In addition, he is Assistant Professor at Bethlehem University, Palestine. His research interests are in the area of tourism development and management, critical theory and political aspects of tourism.

Magdalena Karolak is Associate Professor of Humanities and Social Sciences at Zayed University, UAE and has a PhD in Linguistics at the University of Silesia, Poland. Her research interests include transformations of societies in the Arabian Gulf and comparative linguistics. She has published more than 30 journal articles and book chapters on shifting gender relations, social media, culture and identity and political system transformations in the Gulf Cooperation Council countries.

Nurit Kliot is Emerita Professor in the Department of Geography and Environment Studies at the University of Haifa, Israel. Her main research areas are management of water resources, local and transboundary resources, environmental resources management, political geography and geopolitics, population migration and refugees, Middle East, terrorism, climate change, tourism and tourism management. She is the author of five books, seven edited volumes, four monographs and about 100 scientific papers and chapters in edited volumes. Her current research interests include hiking trails, refugees and human rights, and climate change effects.

Gui Lohmann is Associate Professor in Aviation Management and Head of the Aviation Discipline at Griffith University (Australia). He has authored several books, including *Tourism Theory: Concepts, Models and Systems* (2012), and peer-reviewed journal articles in English, Spanish and Portuguese on transport- and tourism-related topics. He has worked as a consultant for the Brazilian Ministry of Tourism, the World Tourism Organization and the United Nations Environment Programme, in addition to providing consulting to Adelaide Airport, Brisbane Airport Corporation and Queensland Airport Ltd. He is the founder and previous executive director of ABRATUR, the International Academy for the Development of Tourism Research in Brazil.

Asad Mohsin is Associate Professor of Tourism and Hospitality Management at the Waikato Management School. He has accumulated several years of industry and academic experience working in different countries in the Middle East, Southeast Asia and Asia Pacific region, including Australia. His main research interests and publications are in the area of Tourism & Hospitality customer perceptions and contemporary trends, human resource issues and challenges, and product and service quality assessment.

Omar Moufakkir is currently Associate Professor of Marketing and Head of the Business Administration Department at the Gulf University for Science and Technology in Kuwait. His research interests include Arab travel, politics and prejudice in tourism. He also researches the influential role of cultural differences and how these manifest in the context of tourism.

Mairna H. Mustafa is an associate professor in the Queen Rania Faculty of Tourism & Heritage at the Hashemite University-Zarqa, Jordan. Her research interests and published work are mostly in the behaviour of tourists in archaeological sites, tourism education, socio-cultural impacts of tourism and sustainable tourism development.

Daniel H. Olsen is an associate professor in the Department of Geography at Brigham Young University in Provo, Utah, US. His research interests revolve around religious and spiritual tourism, heritage tourism and the management of sacred sites, with secondary research interests in tourism in peripheral areas and tourism and disabilities. He is co-editor of *Tourism, Religion and Spiritual Journeys* (2006), and has published over 40 journal articles and book chapters.

Aylin Orbaşlı is Reader in Architectural Regeneration at Oxford Brookes University. Her research interests are focused on tourism and the conservation of historic urban districts, with a specific focus on the Islamic world. As a consultant she works across the Middle East with national and regional authorities and donor organisations supporting the conservation and management of cultural heritage, including World Heritage Sites.

Cody Morris Paris is the Deputy Director of Middlesex University Dubai and an Associate Professor in the School of Law and the Business School. He is also a Senior Research Fellow with the University of Johannesburg. He holds a PhD in Community Resource Development, an MSc in Tourism Studies and a BIS in International Geography and Political Science-International Studies with minors in Cultural Anthropology and Tourism from Arizona State University. Cody is a social scientist with varied research and teaching interests within the areas of tourism, community development, experiential learning, technology, sustainable development, mobilities, international politics and global security. He is the Editor-in-Chief of the *e-Review of Tourism Research* and serves on the boards of several leading journals, professional organisations and NGOs.

Carlo Perelli is Associate Researcher at CRENoS, University of Cagliari and University of Sassari, Italy. His interests are in geography, tourism geography and planning mainly in Sardinia (Italy), Morocco and Tunisia. He has been working on heritage tourism and halal tourism as diversification strategies in Morocco and Tunisia. In parallel to research activities he participated as a consultant in several EU-funded projects focusing on tourism, planning and environmental management in the MENA Region.

Yvette Reisinger is Professor in Marketing, College of Business Administration, Gulf University for Science and Technology (GUST), Kuwait. Prior to joining GUST she taught in the United States and Australia. She has a long-standing research interest in tourism and culture and communication, particularly in the area of cultural influences on tourist behaviour and destination marketing with a special focus on cross-cultural and behavioural analytical/quantitative studies. Her most current research interests focus on travel behaviour of Kuwaiti nationals. Her books *Cross-Cultural Behaviour in Tourism: Concepts and Analysis* (with Lindsay W. Turner, 2001), *International Tourism: Cultures and Behaviour* (2009), *Transformational Tourism: Host Perspectives* (2013) and *Transformational Tourism: Tourist Perspectives* (2016) provide a path to a very important field of tourism study in a global world.

Amos S. Ron is a senior lecturer and head of the Department of Tourism Studies at Ashkelon Academic College in Israel. A tour guide and a cultural geographer by training, he is a specialist on the geography of monotheistic religions, with an emphasis on contemporary Christian travel, religious culinary tourism, religious-themed environments, perceptions of time in pilgrimage, tour guiding in sacred space, and sacred site management. He is currently engaged in research on the landscapes of Christianity and on the ethical dilemmas of Jewish guides guiding Christian pilgrims.

Chris Ryan has been a professor at the University of Waikato since 1998, having arrived from his previous post of Professor of Tourism at the Northern Territory University. Chris is the editor of *Tourism Management* and from 2012 to 2017 was also the editor of *Tourism Management Perspectives*, which he founded in 2012. He has written well over 350 academic journal articles, book chapters and conference papers.

Bojana Spasojevic is Lecturer in Aviation Management at Griffith University, with a particular interest in the field of air transport and tourism. Her PhD topic focuses on leadership and stakeholder engagement during the process of air route development. Bojana uses innovative teaching in her courses, including the use of the Airline Online simulation as well as the AirportIS database. She has worked on consulting projects for Brisbane Airport Corporation and Adelaide Airport Ltd, in Australia.

Marcus L. Stephenson is Professor of Tourism and Hospitality Management and Dean of the School of Hospitality at Sunway University (Malaysia). Prior to this appointment in October 2017, he was Professor and Head of the School of Tourism and Hospitality Management at the University of the South Pacific (Fiji). He has published extensively on the sociology of tourism, especially concerning nationality, race, ethnicity, culture and religion. He is co-author of *Tourism and Citizenship: Rights, Freedoms and Responsibilities in the Global Order* (2014). He is also co-editor of *International Tourism Development and the Gulf Cooperation Council States: Challenges and Opportunities* (2017).

Dallen J. Timothy is Professor of Community Resources and Development and Senior Sustainability Scientist at Arizona State University. He is also a Senior Research Associate at the University of Johannesburg, South Africa, and Visiting Professor at Beijing Union University, Luoyang Normal University, and the University of Girona, Spain, in the European Master's of Tourism Management Program. He serves on 26 editorial boards and is the editor of the *Journal of Heritage Tourism*. He has ongoing research projects in the Middle East, North America, Europe and the Pacific Islands on topics related to pilgrimage/religious tourism, food heritage, souvenirs, borders and tourism, and participatory development.

Neda Torabi Farsani is Assistant Professor at the School of Tourism, Art University of Isfahan in Iran. She received her PhD degree in Tourism in 2012 from the University of Aveiro, Portugal. She also has papers in the fields of tourism published in international conferences and journals. She has been involved in writing several book chapters and she is the editor of the book titled *Geoparks and Geotourism: New Approaches to Sustainability for the 21st Century* (2011).

Alan S. Weber, PhD, teaches medical humanities, philosophy and medical ethics at Weill Cornell Medicine in Qatar, a Cornell University campus in the Middle East. His current research interests include: environmental philosophy, bioethics, and the history and philosophy of medicine. He is the co-editor with Andy Spiess and Faisal Mubarak of *Tourism Development in the GCC States: Reconciling Economic Growth, Conservation and Sustainable Development,* forthcoming in 2019.

Esmat Zaidan is Assistant Professor of Policy, Planning and Development at Qatar University. She received her PhD degree from the University of Waterloo in Canada in 2011 in Geography and Environmental Management. She holds a Master's in Urban Planning and a Master's in Applied Environmental Studies in Local Economic Development from University of Waterloo. Her research interests focus on sustainability in tourism planning and development, more specifically in economic and socio-cultural dimensions of sustainability.

Hamira Zamani-Farahani has a PhD in Tourism Management and has worked as a tourism researcher, writer, consultant and lecturer for several years. She is founder of the Astiaj Tourism Consultancy & Research Centre in Tehran. Publications include international and local journal papers, book chapters and three books. Her research interests are wide and summarised to tourist/host attitudes, religious tourism, tourism impact, event and special interest tourism, tourism development and management, rural/urban tourism, tourism marketing and entrepreneurship and train cruise tourism.

PART I

The space and place of MENA

1

INTRODUCTION

Understanding the Middle East and North Africa

Dallen J. Timothy

Remnants of prehistoric civilisations; vast deserts with nomadic peoples and green oases; the life-giving Nile, Tigris and Euphrates Rivers; the tales of Lawrence of Arabia and the Arabian Nights; the abiding cultures of Persia, Arabia, Egypt and the Maghreb; the Tower of Babel and the Land of Ur; Mesopotamia and the ancient empires of Assyria, Egypt, Babylon, Greece and Rome—these and multitudes of other quintessential representations have long conjured up images of romance, faith and fantasy, and fed the wanderlust of explorers, traders, pilgrims and tourists. The region commonly referred to today as the Middle East is home to some of the most remarkable historic localities, imposing topography and natural phenomena, richest resources, and venerated religious hearths on the planet. These have cultivated classical sagas and buttressed iconic places that have become the foundations of legends, motion pictures, novels, medieval explorations and modern day travel.

Despite its pivotal past and present, there is no consensus on the geographical extent of the Middle East and North Africa. Various organisations, international bodies, and geographical societies define the region in different ways using disparate criteria. For example, the World Bank includes Djibouti but does not include Afghanistan, Israel or Turkey. The World Tourism Organization, a UN-affiliated agency, classifies Israel and Turkey as Europe, and Iran as part of South Asia. Some international agencies include the Caucuses countries of Armenia, Azerbaijan and Georgia in their definitions, while others include Turkey, Cyprus, Sudan, South Sudan, Niger, Chad, Mali, Mauritania, Afghanistan and Pakistan as part of MENA. Thus, there are considerable geographical disparities between which countries are part of MENA and which are not, and these classifications are typically based upon the mandates of each agency involved.

Strictly in locational terms, MENA is comprised of two major areas: Southwest Asia and North Africa. Southwest Asia is frequently referred to as the Middle East and includes two sub-regions based on landforms and culture: the Arabian Peninsula and the transition zone between the Arabian Peninsula, the Mediterranean Sea and the Mountains of Iran and Turkey (Lew, Hall, & Timothy 2015). The Arabian Peninsula is dominated by a true desert landscape and Arab culture and is home to Yemen, Oman, Saudi Arabia, the United Arab Emirates, Qatar, Bahrain and Kuwait. The transition zone is comprised of highlands, smaller deserts, more water resources and fertile areas, and is more culturally diverse. It includes Iran, Turkey, Iraq, Syria, Jordan, Lebanon, Palestine and Israel.

In North Africa, Western Sahara is a stateless territory that is administered partly by Morocco and partly by the displaced government of the Sahrawi Arab Democratic Republic—considered a government in exile by much of the international community. Thousands of displaced Sahrawis, a Berber people, live in refugee camps in Algeria near the border of Western Sahara. The Maghreb (the land where the sun sets) was the traditional region that today includes Morocco, Algeria and Tunisia, although Libya is now frequently included as part of the Maghreb. Egypt and Southwest Asia have been known throughout history as Mashriq, or the land where the sun rises (Lew, Hall, & Timothy 2015). The Maghreb, together with Egypt, comprise the region of North Africa, which is characterised by desert environments, high mountains in Morocco and Algeria, Arab and Berber cultures, and Islamic religious traditions (Drysdale & Blake 1985; Heing 2017).

Geographers define regions not only by their locations but also by their boundaries, which unite areas using certain criteria that reflect a degree of homogeneity in cultural and/or physical characteristics (de Blij & Muller 2006). Thus, Southwest Asia and North Africa are defined by their cultural qualities, including their ancient role as cultural hearths or origins of great civilisations and innovations; the ubiquity of religious, cultural and ethnic conflicts; the dominance of Arabic-speaking populations; their role as the source area of three major world religions—Islam, Christianity and Judaism—and the current predominance of Islam as the main religion in every country, except Israel. The physical or natural features that also help define the realm include the dominance of hyper-arid deserts, scarce water supplies, and an abundance of oil and natural gas (Davis 2012; Downing 2007; Hobbs 2009; Longrigg 2017; Stewart 2013).

The term 'Middle East' is frequently used in popular lexicon, the media, educational spheres, and amongst government agencies to refer to Southwest Asia and North Africa, again owing largely to their association with Islam and arid environments. The term 'Middle East' was initially used by the British India Office in the mid-nineteenth century in reference to Southwest Asia. East and Southeast Asia were known as the 'Far East'; the area of the Ottoman Empire that is today Turkey was known as the 'Near East', and the 'Middle East' referred to the area of Southwest Asia that lies southeast of Turkey. The term has been widely criticised for its Eurocentric undertones and geographical imprecision (Adelson 2012; Bonine, Amanat, & Gasper 2012; de Blij & Muller 2006; Lew, Hall, & Timothy 2015) but has nonetheless become commonly used throughout the world.

For the purposes of this book, based on location and geography, climate and limited water resources, and religion, ethnicity and culture, the Middle East and North Africa includes the following countries of Southwest Asia: Bahrain, Iran, Iraq, Israel, Jordan, Kuwait, Lebanon, Oman, Palestine, Qatar, Saudi Arabia, Syria, Turkey, UAE and Yemen. In this book, North Africa is delineated as: Algeria, Egypt, Libya, Morocco and Tunisia (see Table 1.1).

In common with other world regions, MENA is a mix of affluence and poverty. Qatar's per capita GDP of US$124,900 is the second highest in the world, second only to that of Liechtenstein. Yet Yemen, a country sharing the Arabian Peninsula, has one of the world's lowest (US$2,300). In Egypt, the most populous country in the realm, less than 3 per cent of the total territory is arable land, and agriculture is overwhelmingly concentrated in a narrow strip along the banks of the Nile River, yet the country produces a significant portion of its food products. Several countries have vast oil and natural gas resources (e.g. Qatar, Saudi Arabia, Iran, Iraq, Kuwait, UAE, Egypt, Bahrain), while others have little or none. Those with few petroleum products have tended to rely much more on tourism and other service sectors than the states with vast oil wealth. Several countries have large, agriculturally productive areas fed by rainfall and plentiful groundwater (e.g. Morocco, Algeria, Turkey, Iran), while others cannot feasibly grow their own foodstuffs owing to the prohibitive cost of ocean water desalination, which

Table 1.1 The countries of MENA and their basic characteristics

Country	Capital city	Area/Size (sq. km)	Population	GDP per capita (2017 est., US$)	Largest ethnic group(s)
Algeria	Algiers	2,381,741	40,969,443	$15,100	Arab, Berber
Bahrain	Manama	760	1,410,942	$51,800	Arab, Asian
Egypt	Cairo	1,001,450	97,041,072	$13,000	Arab, Copt
Iran	Tehran	1,648,195	82,021,564	$20,000	Persian, Azeri, Kurdish
Iraq	Baghdad	438,317	39,192,111	$17,000	Arab, Kurdish
Israel	Jerusalem*	20,770	8,299,706	$36,200	Jewish, Arab
Jordan	Amman	89,342	10,248,069	$12,500	Arab, Circassian, Armenian
Kuwait	Kuwait City	17,818	2,875,422	$69,700	Arab, Asian
Lebanon	Beirut	10,400	6,229,794	$19,500	Arab, Armenian
Libya	Tripoli	1,759,540	6,653,210	$9,800	Arab, Berber
Morocco	Rabat	446,550	33,986,655	$8,600	Arab, Berber
Oman	Muscat	309,500	4,613,241	$45,500	Arab, Baluchi
Palestine	Jerusalem**/ Ramallah***	6,220	4,543,126	$4,300 (2014 est.)	Arab, Jewish
Qatar	Doha	11,586	2,314,307	$124,900	Arab, Asian
Saudi Arabia	Riyadh	2,149,690	28,571,770	$55,300	Arab, Asian
Syria	Damascus	185,180	18,028,549	$2,900 (2015 est.)	Arab, Kurdish, Armenian
Tunisia	Tunis	163,610	11,403,800	$12,000	Arab, Berber
Turkey	Ankara	783,562	80,845,215	$26,500	Turkish, Kurdish
UAE	Abu Dhabi	83,600	6,072,475	$68,200	Arab, Asian
Yemen	Sanaa	527,968	28,036,829	$2,300	Arab

Source: Compiled from data in Central Intelligence Agency (2018).

* Proclaimed capital, without universal recognition; many administrative departments and foreign emissaries are based in Tel Aviv.
** Proclaimed capital.
*** Current administrative capital during Israeli occupation.

makes them overdependent on imports. Global patterns of climate change continue to exacerbate the water scarcity in much of MENA, while a few countries, including Israel, have adapted to limited water resources by creating extremely efficient irrigation systems that enable them to limit their reliance on imported agricultural products.

MENA is endowed with vast deserts, snow-capped mountains, coastlines and beaches, rivers, forests, marine environments and many other natural attractions. It is home to a wide range of modern cultures, ancient traditions, trade routes, marketplaces, material culture and archaeology, villages and cities, colonial and indigenous architecture, labyrinths of languages, diverse religious traditions and hospitality unmatched by other cultures (Timothy 2011; Timothy & Daher 2009).

Instability and security concerns dominate the socio-political and economic landscapes of the Middle East and North Africa (Hall, Timothy & Duval 2003). Nearly every day, news headlines around the world depict the turmoil deriving from the geopolitical problems of MENA. While there were wars during the Ottoman period, those since its collapse in the 1920s have lasted longer and been more impactful on entire nations and regional development. At the time of writing (2018), Syria is embroiled in a civil war, and Islamist extremism has divided the country and spilled over into Iraq and Turkey. The recent Iran–Iraq War, while officially over, continues to overshadow contentious relations between the two large neighbours. The US invasion of Iraq had destabilised the country, giving rise to extremist elements and internal conflict, and eventually helping to empower Iraqi Kurdistan to hold an independence referendum in September 2017. Soured relations between Iran and the West have placed an otherwise resplendent destination country on many states' travel warning lists. Turkey is experiencing internal conflict between the state and the independence-minded Kurds, who are accused of terror activities throughout the country. Turkey's image has also been tainted in recent years by human rights violations against its Kurdish population and political dissidents, which has been a major stumbling block to its joining the European Union. Israel continues to occupy and control the Palestinian territories with increasing settlement encroachment in the West Bank and limitations on Palestinians' mobility. Qatar is currently under a complete trade, travel and diplomatic embargo by several of its neighbours for political reasons. Morocco continues to occupy Western Sahara, forcing most of the Sahrawi nation to live in exile in nearby Algeria. The 2011 Arab Spring affected the political, social and economic lives of several MENA countries, resulting in a failed Libyan state and an overthrow of governments in Egypt and Tunisia and persistent unrest in several countries. In addition to this, the region has suffered many high-profile terrorist attacks directly against tourists and the tourism establishment.

The long-time geopolitical hostility in the region that was exacerbated by colonial interference before and after the collapse of the Ottoman Empire, the establishment of Israel in 1948, religious conflict, territorial disputes, and contemporary Islamist extremism, have kept tourism at bay and dictated the types of tourism that have grown and developed in the region (Almuhrzi, Alriyami, & Scott 2017; Daher 2006; Hazbun 2004; Kalesar 2010). They have furthermore contributed to environmental degradation and the mass destruction of some of the world's most important historic sites. Except for Sub-Saharan Africa, there is no other region on earth that is so well endowed with cultural and natural assets yet lacks the level of tourism development commensurate with its potential (Timothy & Nyaupane 2009). For some observers in the region, this is not an entirely negative prospect. Tourism is often regarded as a corrupting influence in the conservative societies that dominate MENA, and several countries or factions within those countries have been quite vocal in their disdain for tourism and their desire to avoid it, or certain manifestations of it, where possible (Hazbun 2006).

This book

The chapters in this book address these and many other core issues facing the MENA region today. They reflect the growing importance of the Middle East and North Africa not only as a tourist destination but also as a laboratory for understanding tourism in the face of environmental, political, cultural and security challenges. Every effort was made to involve a wide range of authors from throughout MENA, as well as others with considerable research experience in the region. This proved to be challenging for a variety of reasons that shall not be enumerated here. Nevertheless, success was achieved with a balance of authors from MENA and from other parts of the globe with expertise in subjects that are directly relevant to the Middle East and North Africa.

For organisational purposes, ease of reading and based upon current trends and issues in MENA, the book is divided into the following seven parts: (I) The space and place of MENA; (II) Heritage, culture and urban space; (III) Religion and tourism; (IV) Natural and environmental challenges; (V) Tourism and geopolitics; (VI) transportation; and (VII) Contemporary trends. The chapters in Part I provide an overview of the social, cultural and environmental contexts of the region, examining the most pressing human and physical geographical issues in the region today to help set the context for the broader discussions that follow. It also provides a tourism context, looking at patterns and trends throughout the region.

Part II examines the human foundations of tourism from a cultural and heritage perspective. Mairna Mustafa describes the most prominent elements of intangible patrimony that help define MENA and sell it as an important heritage destination, including, amongst others, oral traditions and folklore, music and dance, handicrafts, festivals and community life. He also identifies several of the threats facing intangible culture in the region. Marcus Stephenson and Nazia Ali examine the cultural and theological foundations of the world-famous Arab hospitality, as well as the importance of private and public spaces of Arab hospitality. In Chapter 7, Christine Buzinde considers the concepts of deterritorialisation and reterritorialisation in the context of colonialism and indigenous knowledge in North Africa. In her chapter on urban and built heritage, Aylin Orbaşlı looks at the role of tourism in maintaining the survival of historic Arab cities, as well as how these urban spaces are depicted by locals and interpreted for commercial gain from an Orientalist perspective.

MENA's critical position as the birthplace of the Abrahamic religions, which provides the impetus for much of the region's tourism, is the focus of the third part. Daniel Olsen probes the relationship(s) between religion and tourism in the Middle East and contends that the region has unique challenges in managing pilgrim and religious tourism than the challenges facing other religious destinations. Within the broader context of Middle East tourism, Hamira Zamani-Farahani, Michele Carboni, Carlo Perelli and Neda Torabi Farsani examine the long-established but only recently studied Islam-oriented tourism, most noteworthy being the annual *Hajj* in Saudi Arabia. They consider intra-regional and global Muslim tourism and ask critical questions about cultural appropriateness and intercultural relations, religious needs, codes of conduct, and the impact of geopolitics in Muslims' travel patterns. Noga Collins-Kreiner surveys Jewish tourism in the Middle East. While obviously most Jewish travel takes place in Israel, there are other MENA localities that are home to important Jewish heritage and communities. However, given the political tensions of the region, little Jewish-oriented tourism takes place outside of Israel. She examines the growing importance of Jewish pilgrimage tourism, as well as current trends in heritage, diaspora and educational tourism. In Chapter 12, Dallen Timothy and Amos Ron assess the role of the Middle East in Christian tourism and travel patterns. They examine the places, products and dissonances that are unique to Christianity and also the denominational differences within Christianity as regards travel to the Holy Land. The chapter also draws out critical discussion points about solidarity with Palestinians or Israelis and the role of religious politics in shaping travel to the region.

Part IV delivers a critical examination of the natural and ecological challenges in MENA from a tourism perspective. Second only to geopolitical turmoil, environmental concerns are one of the most disconcerting trials facing the countries of the Middle East. Water scarcity is the focus of Nurit Kliot's chapter. She investigates water as an inadequate resource and political pawn, as well as water management challenges and alternative sources of water to meet the agricultural and tourism needs of the region, with tourism being an over-user of this meagre resource. Susanne Becken and Harald Friedl look at the region's abundance of oil and how it has been exploited during the past century to raise MENA out of economic obscurity. However, with the realisation that oil is a finite resource, some states, particularly in the Gulf region, have turned to tourism as an alternative means of economic development. Chapter 15 describes desert environments as ideal localities for tourism, especially given their unique natural and cultural environments. In this chapter, Alan Weber discusses many challenges, both natural and cultural, that confront desert tourism development—water deficiencies and cultural sensitivities being amongst the most prevalent. One of the biggest challenges facing the earth today, and raising questions about its viability as a habitat for humankind, is climate change, which has been studied in considerable detail in recent years by climate scientists and within the tourism context by social scientists. In Chapter 16, Michael Hall outlines the most prevalent climate change indicators in the Middle East and indicates how these are playing out, and will continue to play out, in the context of tourism, including rising seas, increased droughts, coral bleaching, algal blooms, and extreme weather events, to name but a few. He also points out the irony that so many of the countries facing these problems are also mass producers of natural resources (i.e. hydrocarbons) that contribute radically to global warming.

The fifth part of the book directly addresses conflict and geopolitics, although several other chapters in other parts address political discord indirectly. Rami Isaac examines the Israeli occupation of Palestinian lands and argues that tourism and urban planning are used by Israel to keep the Palestinian population of East Jerusalem in an underprivileged state of dispossession and displacement. He asserts that this is done via city planning policies that evict Palestinians and the suppression of the Old City's economy, increasing East Jerusalem as a tourist destination and a hub for Israeli high-tech industries and education. In Chapter 18, Richard Butler questions the dominant image of the Middle East as a region of conflict and how this affects tourism there. He underscores the importance of image and political tensions in the region's efforts to develop tourism but concludes that the conflicts and security challenges themselves are more important than how they manifest in tourism. Eli Avraham addresses the important question of how MENA countries can and do counter-market the effects of crises. He looks at each country's efforts to repair their broken images during and following crisis events, especially as regards their coping strategies, messaging and marketing efforts.

The focus of Part VI is transportation. MENA leads in many areas of tourist transportation but also lags behind in others. The chapters in this part examine the most pertinent of these issues. Magdalena Karolak provides a solid overview of the cruise sector, not just as a mode of transportation but also a vacation experience in the Middle East. She traces the historical development of the cruise sector in MENA and explores its current patterns and trends. Importantly, Karolak also appraises the future of cruises and how the subsector might develop or languish in the broader Middle East. Ammar Abulibdeh adopts an urban transportation and planning perspective to review the relationships between tourism and local transportation. He describes transportation trends in several major urban areas and delves into the growing areas of smart transportation and information technology in urban transport systems and informal and formal means of urban mobility. Given the escalating importance of several cities in the region as hubs of global air transportation and the development of Gulf-based mega airlines, Bojana Spasojevic and Gui Lohmann focus their attention on air transport and route development, as well as the causes of rapid network growth and transit tourism development in the Gulf States, particularly the United Arab Emirates and Qatar.

Part VII is the final part of the book and focuses on established and emerging trends in tourism in MENA. Touched upon by a few other chapters in the volume, Chapter 23 examines halal tourism in considerable depth. In their discussion of halal tourism, Asad Mohsin and Chris Ryan describe the unique needs of Muslim travellers and the requisite services that destinations should provide to cater to this increasingly lucrative market segment. Following Mohsin and Ryan's essay, Omar Moufakkir, Yvette Reisinger and Dhoha AlSaleh provide a critique of the current trend in halal tourism research. They argue that not all Muslims who travel are seeking halal experiences and that the tourism industry and academic researchers often fail to differentiate between Arabs and Muslims, and between Islamic journeys and Muslims taking vacations. The focus of Chapter 25 is migrants working in tourism in the Middle East. Kevin Hannam and Cody Paris document how the rapid growth of urban tourism in parts of the Middle East gave rise to the sponsored worker programme that was responsible for the rapid rise in expatriate populations in many Gulf States. These immigrant workers from within MENA and from outside the region support the growth of tourism both as workers and as tourists. Joan Henderson's chapter provides an overview of business tourism in the Middle East, looking at the demand for MICE tourism, the supply of MICE features, the patterns of business travel between countries of the region, and the challenges encountered by MICE developers. Medical tourism is a flourishing phenomenon throughout the world, and the Middle East is no exception. John Connell in Chapter 27 investigates many elements of supply and demand for medical tourism in MENA, both from within and without the region. He also questions the ethics and appropriateness of this lucrative form of tourism and whether or not the hype associated with this service can live up to the local political turmoil and inequitable conditions that dominate the region. Finally, Esmat Zaidan directs readers' attention to the important role of shopping as a focus of tourism development in the Middle East, in particular in the Gulf States. This is closely aligned with the patterns of urban hyper-development that accentuate retailscapes and cater to high-end local and tourist consumers. Shopping in traditional marketplaces and in hyperreal shopping centres continues to play an important role in the tourism development efforts of several MENA countries and will likely continue to do so far into the future.

This book contains many perspectives on tourism in the Middle East and North Africa, yet there are unquestionably many other topics and themes of pertinence to tourism in MENA that are not covered in detail, yet are embedded throughout the volume in several chapters. This volume brings together a wide range of scholars from throughout the world, and especially MENA, to provide a foundation from which researchers can continue to progress knowledge in a dynamic region, a region defined by its natural and cultural characteristics and a region that has yet to realise its full tourism potential.

References

Adelson, R. (2012) 'British and U.S. use and misuse of the term "Middle East"', in M.E. Bonine, A. Amanat, & M.E. Gasper (eds), *Is There a Middle East? The Evolution of a Geopolitical Concept* (pp. 36–55). Stanford, CA: Stanford University Press.

Almuhrzi, H., Alriyami, H., & Scott, N. (eds) (2017) *Tourism in the Arab World: An Industry Perspective.* Bristol: Channel View Publications.

Bonine, M.E., Amanat, A., & Gasper, M.E. (eds) (2012) *Is There a Middle East? The Evolution of a Geopolitical Concept.* Stanford, CA: Stanford University Press.

Central Intelligence Agency (2018) *World Factbook.* Available online: www.cia.gov/library/publications/the-world-factbook/ (Accessed 27 February 2018).

Daher, R.F. (ed) (2006) *Tourism in the Middle East: Continuity, Change and Transformation.* Clevedon: Channel View Publications.

Davis, D.K. (2012) 'Scorched Earth: The problematic environmental history that defines the Middle East', in M.E. Bonine, A. Amanat, & M.E. Gasper (eds), *Is There a Middle East? The Evolution of a Geopolitical Concept* (pp. 170–187). Stanford, CA: Stanford University Press.

de Blij, H.J., & Muller, P.O. (2006) *Geography: Realms, Regions, and Concepts,* 12th edn. Hoboken, NJ: Wiley.

Downing, D. (2007) *Geography and Resources of the Middle East.* Milwaukee, WI: World Almanac Library.

Drysdale, A., & Blake, G.H. (1985) *The Middle East and North Africa: A Political Geography.* Oxford: Oxford University Press.

Hall, C.M., Timothy, D.J., & Duval, D.T. (eds) (2003) *Safety and Security in Tourism: Relationships, Management and Marketing.* New York: Haworth.

Hazbun, W. (2004) 'Globalisation, reterritorialisation and the political economy of tourism development in the Middle East', *Geopolitics*, 9(2): 310–341.

Hazbun, W. (2006) 'Explaining the Arab Middle East tourism paradox', *The Arab World Geographer*, 9(3): 201–214.

Heing, B. (2017) *Geography, Government, and Conflict across the Middle East: Understanding the Cultures of the Middle East*. New York: Cavendish Square Publishing.

Hobbs, J.J. (2009) *World Regional Geography*, 6th edn. Belmont, CA: Brooks/Cole.

Kalesar, M.I. (2010) 'Developing Arab-Islamic tourism in the Middle East: An economic benefit or a cultural seclusion', *International Politics*, 3(5): 105–136.

Lew, A.A., Hall, C.M., & Timothy, D.J. (2015) *World Regional Geography: Human Mobilities, Tourism Destinations, Sustainable Environments*, 2nd edn. Dubuque, IA: Kendall-Hunt.

Longrigg, S.H. (2017) *The Geography of the Middle East*, 2nd edn. London: Routledge.

Stewart, D.J. (2013) *The Middle East Today: Political, Geographical and Cultural Perspectives*. London: Routledge.

Timothy, D.J. (2011) *Cultural Heritage and Tourism: An Introduction*. Bristol: Channel View Publications.

Timothy, D.J., & Daher, R.F. (2009) 'Heritage tourism in Southwest Asia and North Africa: Contested pasts and veiled realities', in D.J. Timothy, & G.P. Nyaupane (eds), *Cultural Heritage and Tourism in the Developing World: A Regional Perspective* (pp. 146–164). London: Routledge.

Timothy, D.J., & Nyaupane, G. (eds) (2009) *Cultural Heritage and Tourism in the Developing World: A Regional Perspective*. London: Routledge.

2

THE PHYSICAL GEOGRAPHY OF THE MIDDLE EAST IN THE ANTHROPOCENE

C. Michael Hall

Introduction

The geographical concept of the Middle East is more a political and cultural construct than a physical geography one. Nevertheless, the landscape and physical environment of the region play an important part in its attractiveness, as well as create many of the challenges tourism in the region faces. The Middle East is a meeting place of both human and physical geography. The very notion of the Middle East is usually associated with the role the region plays in being a cultural and economic crossroads between Asia and Europe, and Africa and Europe (Lew, Hall, & Timothy 2015). However, the physical geography is greatly shaped by the various tectonic plates that interact with each other and have helped contribute to the spectacular landscapes that draw tourists, as well as to the region's active geology. Indeed, the tectonic landscape is closely related to the cultural landscape, and tectonic events such as earthquakes and tsunamis have shaped the region's history, folklore and religions (Al Rabady 2013; Finkel 2014; Pappé 2014).

Mountains and deserts divide the Middle East and North Africa (MENA) into a number of geographically distinct zones that have had an enormous influence on culture and economic development. Emberling (2010) identifies these as the Nile River (Egypt); the eastern Mediterranean coastal plain (Israel, coastal Syria, Lebanon, Palestine); the Anatolian Plateau (Turkey); the Arabian Peninsula (Bahrain, southern Iraq, eastern Jordan, Kuwait, Oman, Qatar, Saudi Arabia, southeast Syria, United Arab Emirates, Yemen); Mesopotamia (the river valleys of the Tigris and Euphrates rivers that run through Turkey, Syria, Iraq and Iran into the Persian Gulf; and the Zagros Mountains that stretch from the Persian Gulf of Iran through northern Iraq (Iraqi Kurdistan) and into eastern Turkey. However, Emberling's (2010) categorisation, though useful, misses a number of other significant geographical features and distinct physiographic regions, including the Sahara Desert, through which the Nile runs; the Sinai Peninsula of Egypt; coastal western Turkey; and the mountains of Eastern Iran that stretch from the Indian Ocean through to the Caspian Sea and the Atlas Mountains in North Africa.

Saharan North Africa is a distinct geographical entity determined by the Mediterranean Sea to the north, the Atlantic Ocean to the west and the Red Sea to the east. To the south, Saharan North Africa is distinguished from the Sahel, which is a belt of semi-tropical savannah characterised by higher rainfall. The Mediterranean coast has sufficient rainfall for agriculture and urban centres, but the region's geography is dominated by the Sahara Desert, which is the largest non-polar desert on Earth. With an area of approximately 92 million km², it is more than a million km² larger than the contiguous United States and covers about 6 per cent of the land surface area of the Earth (Cook & Vizy 2015).

The Middle East has one of the driest climates in the world (Drake 1997). The area generally has a hot arid climate with the wettest part of the region being the Caspian Sea coast of northern Iran and the Black Sea coast of northern Turkey, although the influences of mountain ranges also mean that some of the desert areas of Iran may receive no rain for many years, a phenomenon that can also occur in other desert portions of the region. Coastal areas, especially in the eastern Mediterranean and northern Turkey tend to have more moderate temperatures, although lowland desert areas in the interior of the Arabian Peninsula, Iran, Iraq, Syria and Egypt have extreme summer temperatures (Fisher 2013). The Sahara Desert region, which extends into the Arabian Peninsula and Somalia, has the highest annual temperatures of any region on the planet along with very low levels of rainfall (Cook & Vizy 2015). One of the ironies of the region's physical geography is that though many of its economies are driven by oil and gas exploitation, the climate actually makes it ideal for wind and solar power generation (Nematollahi, Hoghooghi, Rasti, & Sedaghat 2016).

The aridity of MENA has shaped the pattern of human settlement which is concentrated along the eastern and southern Mediterranean coastlines and its extensions, such as the Black Sea and the Sea of Marmara, and in river valleys, such as the Nile, Tigris and Euphrates (Nematollahi et al. 2016). Snow is also found along some of the highest mountain ranges with Turkey and Iran also being dominated by mountain plateaus. Although the Sahara is often represented as consisting of ergs—sandy 'seas' of dunes—in popular culture, it is actually dominated by hamada (stone plateaus), while much of it is also mountainous. Ranges include the Adrar n Ifoghas (Adrar des Iforas) on the border of northeastern Mali and southern Algeria; the Saharan Atlas mountain range that runs from Morocco through Algeria to Tunisia; the Aïr Mountains that extend from northern Niger to the Ahaggar Mountains in southern Algeria; and the Tibesti Mountains ranging between northern Chad and southern Libya. The Eastern Desert region of Egypt, which lies to the east of the River Nile, is also relatively mountainous. In northwest Africa the Atlas mountain range also includes Middle Atlas, the Anti-Atlas and the High Atlas range; and the Tell Atlas range that lies predominantly on the Algerian coast. Also of interest is the Rif mountains in Morocco, which geologically are connected to the mountains of the southeast Iberian Peninsula bordering the Alboran Sea rather than the Atlas Range (Martínez-García, Comas, Soto, Longergan, & Watts 2013). The mountain regions are significant in terms of human settlement and tourism as they provide different climate and rainfall regimes to the far more arid desert lands, and are often focal points for ecotourism operations because of their relatively high levels of biodiversity. Also of significance for human settlement and tourism are the Saharan oases that are usually located in geological depressions, such as the Siwa Oasis in Egypt, or in wadis. Oman is also on the margin of the South Asian monsoon system (Gupta, Yuvaraja, Prakasam, Clemens, & Velu 2015) and the Dhofar Region of Oman experiences a substantially less arid climate than most of the Arabian Peninsula.

The chapter is divided into two main sections. The first section places the physical geography of the region in the context of its tectonic plates as a way of organising the different regions and main water bodies. The second section discusses issues of understanding its physical geography, given the notion of the Anthropocene as a distinct geological period, especially in relation to vegetation and landscape change.

The arrangement of the tectonic plates of the Middle East

The Middle East is a meeting point of a number of tectonic plates, the centre point of which is the Arabian Plate which broadly corresponds to the Arabian Peninsula but which also includes a small piece of Africa (the Afar Depression). The Arabian plate is bordered by the Somali Plate to the south, which runs the length of the African continent with the East Africa Rift separating the Somali Plate from the African Plate. To the west is the African Plate, the northern boundary of which borders the Eurasian, Aegean Sea and Anatolian plates. To the north of the Arabian Plate is the Anatolian Plate, which comprises most of the Anatolian peninsula (also referred to as Asia Minor). To the north of both the Anatolian Plate and the northeastern side of the Arabian Plate is the Eurasian Plate, and to the east the Indian Plate.

Arabian Plate

The Arabian Plate was part of the African Plate until the Oligocene; it began to separate approximately 25 million years ago and is moving north at the rate of 20–25 mm a year. The separation between the plates has led to the opening of the Red Sea Rift and the growth of the Red Sea, as well as the Dead Sea Fault, which runs from the southern tip of the Sinai Peninsula to southeastern Turkey. The Red Sea Rift extends from the Dead Sea Fault System to the Afar Depression on the borders of Eritrea, Djibouti and Ethiopia. The Red Sea is clearly a major geographical feature that serves as an important transport route and which is also important for tourism because of its coral reefs. Although not widely recognised, the Red Sea Rift is also an active volcanic region, including the island of Jabal al-Tair located northwest of the Bab al-Mandab passage at the mouth of the Red Sea, about halfway between Yemen and Eritrea, which erupted in September 2007 with the loss of several lives (BBC News 2007). There is also another group of active volcanic islands in the southern Red Sea, the Zubair Archipelago also between Yemen and Eritrea. In addition there are active volcanic fields in Saudi Arabia, Harrat Rahat and Harrat Khaybar, both being close to the holy city of Medina.

The Red Sea

The Red Sea (also called the Erythraean Sea), which occupies the border between the Arabian Plate and the African Plate, is underlain by the Red Sea Rift, which is a continuation of the Great Rift Valley between the African Plate and the Somali Plate. The Sea is a seawater inlet of the Indian Ocean, which is connected to the Indian Ocean by the Bab el Mandeb strait and the Gulf of Aden. The Red Sea is one of the saltiest areas of ocean water in the world with its higher than average salinity due to limited interchange of water with the Indian Ocean; few river systems draining into the sea; and high levels of evaporation. Nevertheless, the sea is biologically rich and has significant fringing coral reefs that serve as the basis for dive tourism, although they are now being threatened by climate change and coastal development (Furby, Bouwmeester, & Berumen 2013; Hall 2001; Riegl, Berumen, & Bruckner 2013).

There is no natural connection between the Red Sea and the Mediterranean Sea; however, the Suez Canal built in the mid-nineteenth century and enlarged in 2014–2016 provides a link between the two waterways. Because there are no locks on the canal, the waterway provides a sea route not only for ships but also for a number of species between the two seas. These introductions of exotic species that become invasive can have enormous impacts on the indigenous ecology (Galil 2007; Golani 1998; Goren, Galil, Diamant, & Stern

2016), even if their effects are often not immediately recognised. For example, 'The siganids [rabbitfish], successful Erythrean invasive aliens, have altered the community structure and the native food web along the Levantine rocky infralittoral' (Galil 2007: 316). Two species of siganid fish, *Siganus rivulatus* and *S. luridus*, which entered the Mediterranean from the Red Sea through the Suez Canal, were first recorded off the coast of Israel in 1924 and 1955 respectively. Both species are now found as far west as the southern Adriatic Sea, Sicily and Tunisia. The siganids comprise 80 per cent of the abundance of the herbivorous fish in shallow coastal sites in Lebanon and one third of the fish biomass in rocky habitats along the Israeli coast and have replaced native herbivorous fish in many locations in the Levantine Sea (Eastern Mediterranean) (Galil 2007). The impacts on biodiversity and coastal ecology by such invasions, of which there are many as a result of the Suez Canal, are substantial. As Galil (2007: 318) stated,

> biodiversity is not a simple arithmetic. Local population losses and niche contraction may not induce immediate extirpation, but they augur reduction of genetic diversity, loss of functions, processes, and habitat structure, increase the risk of decline and extinction, and lead to biotic homogenization.

Leading her to conclude, 'It seems that the establishment of alien biota, and the concurrent adverse changes in the native communities, are part of a catastrophic anthropogenic ecosystem shift in the Mediterranean Sea' (Galil 2007: 319).

The Dead Sea Fault

The Dead Sea Fault has a number of geographical features, known as pull-apart basins, which are important tourist attractions, including the Gulf of Aqaba, the Dead Sea, the Sea of Galilee and Lake Hula, although the entire fault region is subject to earthquakes. The Gulf of Aqaba, which lies to the east of the Sinai Peninsula and divides Egypt, Israel, Jordan and Saudi Arabia, is a major international site for coral reef diving. Taba in Egypt, Eilat in Israel, and Aqaba in Jordan are all important resort destinations.

The Dead Sea is arguably the most well-known geographical feature of the rift. With a shoreline over 400m below sea level (and continuing to fall) the Dead Sea is the Earth's lowest elevation on land. In addition, the sea is hypersaline and almost ten-times saltier than seawater, making it one of the world's saltiest large bodies of water. The sea is an attraction in its own right but is also a significant health and spa tourism destination on both the Israeli and Jordanian sides of the sea with the salts being regarded as having health benefits. Because of water abstraction from the Jordan River (the sea's only significant permanent inflow), for agriculture, industrial use and domestic supply, the sea levels have been continuing to decrease. In response, there are proposals to carry seawater from the Gulf of Aqaba to the Dead Sea for both hydroelectricity and desalination purposes and to stabilise the Dead Sea water level (World Bank 2013).

The Sea of Galilee, also known as Lake Kinneret, is the lowest freshwater lake on Earth and the second-lowest lake in the world, after the Dead Sea. However, water demand and reduced precipitation have meant that the lake has had a decreasing water level, raising concerns over its long-term sustainability as a fresh-water ecosystem. Lake Hula was a lake north of the Sea of Galilee that was drained in the 1950s, although a small part has since been reflooded in an attempt to regenerate the marshland ecosystem (Tal 2002).

The Anatolian, Iranian and Eurasian Plates

The Anatolian and Iranian/Eurasian Plates are both highly active and characterised by frequent earthquakes. The Anatolian massif with heights on average of over 400 m dominates Asian Turkey and means that lowlands are confined to the Black Sea and Mediterranean coastlines. The meeting of the Arabian Plate and the Eurasian/Iranian Plate is responsible for the mountainous terrain of most of Iran including the Zagros Mountains. These mountains roughly correspond to Iran's western border, and run from Iraqi Kurdistan/southeastern Turkey, the whole length of the western and southwestern Iranian plateau, ending at the Strait of Hormuz. The collision between the plates means that the mountains are continuing to gradually increase in height. The north–south shortening from Arabia to Eurasia is 2–2.5 cm/year, and the transition from subduction (southeast Iran at Makran opposite northern Oman) to collision (Zagros on the Persian Gulf opposite the United Arab Emirates) is very sharp and governs the different types of deformation observed in Iran. In the eastern part of Iran, most of the shortening is accommodated in the Gulf of Oman, while in the western part, the shortening is more distributed from south to north (Nilforoushan et al. 2003).

The tectonic forces operating in Iran mean that the country is very susceptible to major earthquakes, some of which have occurred with substantial loss of life and impact on heritage. For example, the Bam urban earthquake of 26 December 2003 (Magnitude (M) 6.6) hit the Kerman province of southeastern Iran killing between 31,000 and 43,000 people. The city had been a major domestic and international tourist destination primarily because of its World Heritage 2000-year-old mud-brick citadel and its association with the Silk Road. The citadel was almost totally destroyed by the earthquake but has since been partially rebuilt. Previous large urban earthquakes in Iran include the 1930 Salmas (M 7.1, approximately 2,500 deaths), the 1978 Tabas-e-Golshan (M 7.4, approximately 20,000 deaths), and the 1990 Rudbar-Tarom (M 7.3, approximately 40,000 deaths) (Berberian 2005). The Bam earthquake was also 100 km south of the destructive earthquakes of 11 June 1981 (M 6.6, approximately 3,000 deaths) and 28 July 1981 (M 7.3, approximately 1,500 deaths) (Berberian 2005). Vulnerable urban areas in Iran, in which prominent potential seismic sources have been mapped under heavily populated centres, include greater Tehran-Karaj, Tabriz, Neyshabur, Mashhad, Kashan, Natauz and Bushehr. 'All these cities are located on and/or adjacent to numerous major exposed and blind capable faults' (Berberian 2005: s80) and:

> The extent of destruction and the probable death toll in the poorly constructed and unprepared institutions of the mega-city of Tehran, covering an area of close to 900 sq km, hugging numerous active faults, with a population of greater than 7 million living in 1.5 million housing units composed of 48% old and traditional buildings, and aging infrastructure … subjected to the same level of strong ground motion recorded in Bam or Tangshan, will be disastrous.

Although the region's tectonic forces can clearly be extremely destructive, they have also contributed to spectacular mountain landscapes and highlands that are important tourism resources and sources of many of the region's major rivers. In Turkey, for example, the Taurus Mountains provide winter skiing opportunities near Antalya, which is Turkey's largest resort region. The southeastern Taurus Mountains are also the source of the iconic Euphrates and Tigris rivers.

The Persian Gulf

The Persian Gulf (also referred to as the Arabian Gulf) marks the border between the Arabian and the Eurasian/Iranian Plates. The Gulf is an extension of the Gulf of Oman in the Indian Ocean through the Strait of Hormuz and lies between Iran to the northeast and the Arabian Peninsula to the southwest. In the north is the Shatt al-Arab river delta formed by the conflu-ence of the Euphrates and the Tigris. The Gulf is an extremely recent geographical body being formed only 15,000 years ago with the present shorelines not being reached until 6,000 years ago. Because of this and its relative isolation, the Gulf hosts an ecologically significant fauna and flora although many of the ecosystems, such as coral reefs and mangroves, are under threat from coastal developments. The timing of the creation of the Persian Gulf and its basins also has implications for the early movements of people in the Middle East and the timing of the earliest settlements in lower Mesopotamia. For example, the early Gulf floor would have provided a natural route for people moving westwards from regions to the east of Iran from the late Palaeolithic to early Neolithic (Lambeck 1996). Although the Persian Gulf is extremely important as a transport route, its most well-known geology is arguably the extensive oil and gas deposits that lie both onshore and offshore and which have fuelled economic development in the region.

The Mediterranean

The Mediterranean is an arm of the Atlantic Ocean, and its coastlines are focal points for tourism development while it has also grown as a cruise location in recent years. The Mediterranean also has a number of regional seas located within it. The Levantine Sea, or the Eastern Mediterranean Sea, is bordered by Turkey in the north, Syria, Lebanon, Israel and Palestine in the east, and Egypt and Libya in the south. Coastal areas of the Levantine Sea off Israel, Palestine and Egypt have significant gas and oil deposits, as do coastal areas of Libya and Egypt. In the Western Mediterranean the main regional sea is the Alboran Sea, between Spain and Morocco. The Strait of Gibraltar at the west end of the Alboran Sea, is the narrow strait that connects the Mediterranean with the Atlantic Ocean and separates North Africa from Europe. At the narrowest point, the strait is only 14.3 km (8.9 miles) wide and is a major tourist attraction in its own right. The western coast of Morocco borders the Atlantic Ocean, which plays an extremely important role in providing moderate temperatures on the coastal plains even in summer, owing to the effect of the cold Canary Current that lies offshore. This means that coastal Morocco is significantly cooler than the high temperatures that exist in the inland Sahara at the same latitude. As a result, the climate of much of Morocco is similar to that of California and has proven to be attractive for tourism, although climate change appears to be impacting both the productivity of the marine ecosystem and the potential increases in the intensity of coastal storms (Aouiche et al. 2016).

The Aegean Sea in the northwestern part of the Eastern Mediterranean is usually regarded more as part of Europe than of the Middle East as a result of its association with European culture and the Ancient Greeks in particular, although the coastal Aegean between Greece and Turkey also represents a political and, to a certain extent, a cultural boundary as well. Many of the islands in the Aegean are volcanic and have been historically associated with major natural disasters. Similarly, the island of Cyprus in the Eastern Mediterranean Sea is also very much a cultural and political meeting point between the Middle East and Europe. However, geograph-ically it is closer to countries of the Middle East than Mediterranean Europe, and it is situated in the Eastern Basin of the Levantine Sea. Because of its climatic similarity to the countries of the region, Cyprus also shares many of their same ecological and environmental problems. The two main problems are (1) loss of the indigenous vegetation as a result of agriculture, introduced species and lack of an effective conservation programme, and (2) declining precipitation and a warming climate placing pressure on water supply (Grove & Rackham 2003; Blondel 2006).

The Mediterranean also represents the boundary between the African and Eurasian Plates (Gaina et al. 2013). In the central and eastern Mediterranean, the African Plate is subducting underneath the Eurasian Plate leading to significant mountain building and volcanic activity in the Mediterranean region. The Western Mediterranean is also geologically active and the region, including the Atlas Mountains system, represents a diffuse plate boundary in which the Atlas Mountains comprise narrow deformable zones bounding larger, relatively rigid crustal blocks (Gomez, Beauchamp, & Barazangi 2000). The tectonic convergence between the African and Eurasian plates is also responsible for the formation of the Mediterranean. One of the most significant events is the Messinian salinity crisis, believed to have begun about six million years ago, in which the Mediterranean Sea became progressively isolated as a result of a combination of tectonic uplift and variations in the level of the Atlantic Ocean. The isolation of the Mediterranean Basin from the Atlantic Ocean was established between 5.59 and 5.33 million years ago, leading to a large fall in the Mediterranean's water level of 1500–2500 metres (Gargani & Rigollet 2007). The isolation of the Mediterranean from the Atlantic is believed to have ended 5.33 million years ago when eastward regressive stream erosion opened the Gibraltar Strait with the refill of the Mediterranean Basins potentially taking less than 40 years (Blanc 2012). This event is known as the Zanclean flood. Approximately 500 km^3 of rock was eroded at the Gibraltar Strait during the flood climax (Garcia-Castellanos et al. 2009). The Messinian salinity crisis and the geomorphological characteristics of the Western Mediterranean remain important to the present-day because of their influence on the nature of the Mediterranean Sea.

Because of the limited access to the Atlantic Ocean, tides in the Mediterranean are very limited and water circulation is linked more to changes in water salinity. Overall the Mediterranean is more saline than the Atlantic because of the high rate of evaporation in relation to precipitation and inflow from rivers, as well as the limited exchange of waters between the two bodies. The marine biota of the Mediterranean is primarily derived from the Atlantic Ocean. However, growth in global shipping and the construction and enlargement of the Suez Canal have meant that many exotic marine species have now become established. The Mediterranean has also experienced previous sea level change as a result of geological and climate changes. Under the impact of present anthropogenic climate change the Mediterranean is expected to become more saline and experience substantial shifts in ecosystem change as well as sea level rise (SLR) (Marcos & Tsimplis 2008), although rates are lower than the global average. The Eastern Mediterranean will potentially have lower rates of SLR than the Western, but will be more affected by salinification as a result of reduced runoff from the Black Sea and increased evaporation (Marcos & Tsimplis 2008). Nevertheless, SLR and environmental change already appear to be having impacts on the Nile Delta and agricultural production, as well as increases in flooding of coastal urban areas. An additional element of climate change in North Africa and the Eastern Mediterranean is the potential increase in the severity of the Sirocco, a wind of sometimes hurricane speeds that originates in the Sahara and causes dusty dry conditions along the north coast of Africa with significant implications for health and comfort (D'Amato et al. 2013).

The total area of Egypt is about one million km^2, of which approximately 94 per cent is desert. The water of the Nile River represents the only renewable water resource in Egypt, as well as being a significant transport route for the country and source of national identity (Abd-Elhamid, Javadi, Abdelaty, & Sherif 2016). In the case of the Nile Delta, the coastal and estuarine landscapes are affected by land subsidence and SLR. Sušnik et al. (2015) note that for the Alexandria region of the Nile Delta, land subsidence alone is estimated at 0.4–2.0 mm per year and this is likely to cause increasing loss of low-lying coastal areas and will lead to seawater intrusion into coastal aquifers. They also suggest that an SLR of 0.5 m above land subsidence in the Nile Delta would affect approximately 3.8 million people and 1800 km^2 of agricultural land. This is also a major issue given that even though the Nile Delta aquifer is amongst the largest underground freshwater reservoirs in the world, seawater intrusion into the aquifer has already extended inland more than 100 km from the Mediterranean coast (Abd-Elhamid et al. 2016).

Another significant arm of the Mediterranean that represents a border between Europe and Asia, and hence the Middle East, is the Sea of Marmara, which is connected to the Aegean Sea by the Dardanelles strait, and to the Black Sea by the Bosphorus strait. These are known collectively as the Turkish Straits. These waterways have been regarded as a major physical and cultural border between East and West since antiquity, although the Sea of Marmara, which is a pull-apart basin, is currently an inland sea that lies entirely within the borders of Turkey. The surface salinity of the Sea of Marmara is slightly greater than that of the Black Sea but is lower than that of the Mediterranean. Geologically the region is extremely active with the North Anatolian Fault, the boundary between the Eurasian Plate and the Anatolian Plate, running under the Sea and then through northern Turkey before meeting the East Anatolian Fault in eastern Turkey and the Zagros system of faults in Iran (Rockwell 2013). Because the North Anatolian Fault runs through highly populated areas in Turkey, and especially the Istanbul metropolitan region, the fault poses a substantial seismic hazard and has an active earthquake history (Bohnhoff, Martínez-Garzón, Bulut, Stierle, & Ben-Zion 2016).

The Black Sea is also a maritime border of the Middle East. Unlike many of the other seas discussed in this chapter, the Black Sea has a positive water balance, that is, there is a greater outflow of water from the Black Sea into the Mediterranean than what flows into the Black Sea from the Mediterranean as part of the hydrological exchange between the two seas. The waters are also markedly different as the surface waters of the Black Sea are much less saline than those of the Mediterranean, thereby creating an anoxic layer of water that is depleted of dissolved oxygen with corresponding impacts on biological diversity.

In terms of geological time, the nature of the Black Sea is very much influenced by the interaction between the Eurasian, African and Arabian Plates and the smaller Anatolian Plate, and global sea levels. Geological uplift in Anatolia has, at times, isolated the Black Sea from the Mediterranean and beyond to the global ocean system, especially when combined with lower sea levels such as during ice ages and subsidence of the Black Sea basin (Nikishin, Korotaev, Ershov, & Brunet 2003). When cut off from the Mediterranean, the Black Sea becomes similar to the Caspian Sea, which is an endorheic basin (has no outflows) that borders Iran, and which became landlocked about 5.5 million years ago as a result of tectonic uplift and sea level decline. The last time the Black Sea was in this state was during the most recent Quaternary glaciation, when the Black Sea was a giant freshwater lake with levels more than 100 metres below its current outlet. Ryan et al. (1997) claimed that when the Mediterranean rose to the Bosporus sill at 7,150 years Before Present, saltwater poured through this spillway to refill the lake and submerge, catastrophically, more than 100,000 km^2 of the exposed continental shelf. They also argue that the permanent drowning of such a vast terrestrial landscape may have possibly accelerated the dispersal of early neolithic foragers and farmers into the interior of Europe at that time. These sudden geological events also potentially provide the basis for the folk memory of 'The Flood' that underlies many of the religious and historical traditions in the Middle East (Finkel 2014).

The Anthropocene: Rethinking the physical geography of the Middle East?

The concept of the Anthropocene as a distinct geological era is the notion that the impact of humans on the environment is now so great, and so distinct, as to constitute an identifiable geological period (Steffen, Grinevald, Crutzen, & McNeill 2011; Smith & Zeder 2013). The previous period, the Holocene, is the name given to the post-glacial period of the past 10,000–12,000 years. However, the Anthropocene can be distinguished by numerous factors including loss of biodiversity, ocean acidification, climate change and plastics in the environment. As Steffen, Crutzen, and McNeill (2007: 614) observe,

> Human activities have become so pervasive and profound that they rival the great forces of Nature and are pushing the Earth into planetary terra incognita. The Earth is rapidly moving into a less biologically diverse, less forested, much warmer, and probably wetter and stormier state.

In the case of the biodiversity of the Mediterranean, for example, Blondel (2006) argued that high intraspecific adaptive variation arose from natural processes of the Pleistocene, mainly from a combination of periodic refugia formation and climate dynamics. During the Holocene, the main sources of disturbance came increasingly from humans, such as the introduction of new fire regimes, specifically from the coupled cultural and natural modifications of community and landscape structure. However, in the Anthropocene human interaction with ecosystems and landscapes have become even more pronounced—e.g. introduction of new agricultural practices, urbanisation, pollution, dam construction, and creation of conservation reserves, leading to further changes in landscape dynamics (e.g. Dusar, Verstraeten, Notebaert, & Bakker 2011).

The Anthropocene forces students to reassess not only the role of tourism in global environmental change but also how we understand present day physical geographies, including those of MENA, given that much of the landscape and biodiversity has been strongly shaped by humans and now that even the very forces that help shape the landscape (Gössling & Hall 2006; Hall 2016), such as climate, are subject to anthropogenic change (see Hall, Chapter 16, this volume). The extreme diversity in space and time of both environments and human societies makes the structure and dynamics of coupled natural and human systems difficult to interpret (Harris 2012), especially when baseline conditions are difficult to assess (Tzedakis 2007). In the Middle East, the succession of peoples and societies that waxed and waned over several millennia has had great impacts on biota and ecosystems everywhere in the region (Blondel 2006; Grove & Rackham 2003). This has meant that a complex 'coevolution' has developed, which shapes the interactions between ecosystem components and human societies and the consequent landscape. This means, for example, that some seemingly 'natural landscapes' and ecosystems, many with high value from both a biodiversity and a tourism perspective, can only be maintained with human activities of particular kinds, often related to agricultural practices (Bugalho, Caldeira, Pereira, Aronson, & Pausas 2011; Geri, Amici, & Rocchini 2010; Keeley, Bond, Bradstock, Pausas, & Rundel 2012). Such a perspective also provides a substantial challenge to the two opposing schools of thought that traditionally have considered the consequences of human pressures on Mediterranean, North African and Middle Eastern ecosystems. First, the 'ruined landscape' or 'lost Eden' approach argues that human action resulted in a cumulative degradation and desertification of Mediterranean landscapes. In contrast, the second school argues that humans actually contributed to keeping Mediterranean landscapes diverse since the last glacial episode (Blondel 2006; Grove & Rackham 2003). Both approaches frame the environmental imaginaries by which people, including tourists and marketers, perceive and portray many of the destinations of the Middle East and North Africa (Davis & Burke III 2011; Mikhail 2013).

These debates are not just academic, as they have enormous influence on the ways in which ecosystems and the physical geography of a place are managed, particularly in response to tourism (Antrop 2006), and other elements of change. Interestingly, even though there is clearly a long legacy of human and natural system co-evolution in the Middle East region, more recent changes are seen as a threat to existing qualities and thus the conservation of these becomes an aim in itself and a means to achieve sustainability. The protection of heritage values (both cultural and natural) of landscapes focuses upon the sustainability of existing values and is confronted with land-use intensification, urbanisation and tourist and recreational pressure (Antrop 2006). For example, large areas of the Tunisian coast have been affected by tourism-related developments. According to De Stefano (2004), tourist areas occupied by hotels and second homes occupy approximately 35 per cent of the total urbanised linear coastal space. She suggested that this tourism and second homes development would eventually occupy about 14 per cent of the entire coastline. This is significant for coastal environmental processes, as inappropriate siting of tourist infrastructures on foredunes is accelerating the process of beach erosion and altering the water dynamics of coastal areas (De Stefano 2004).

The physical geography of MENA therefore also needs to be understood in terms of the future landscape that is emerging as a result of various economic and cultural pressures, such as tourism, and their interplay with the physical environment and the forces that shape that environment. From such a perspective, seeing the physical geography of the Middle East needs to be understood not just in passive terms—that is, how the physical geography affects tourism, but also in the reverse, such as how does tourism contribute to the region's physical geography, for example, by particular forms of coastal development, but also what sort of physical geography do we actually want in the future?

Conclusion

This chapter has provided an introduction to the physical geography of the Middle East and North Africa region. The first section of the chapter has done so in more traditional terms with respect to the extremely significant tectonic structure of the region as well as the associated marine and river systems. The second section of the chapter is more challenging and moves beyond the descriptive to try and illustrate the way in which the physical geography of the Anthropocene is a result of the interaction of cultural and natural systems in which tourism is now deeply embedded. The components and dynamics of biodiversity and landscape in the Middle East therefore cannot be understood without taking into account the history of human-induced changes with positive and negative feedback cycles between cultural practices and natural systems (Blondel 2006; see also Antrop 2006). While the underlying geological forces are unchanged, the surface geography of the region is therefore now substantially influenced by humans and, as noted, even the character of forces that shape the landscape such as climate and water are now substantially affected by anthropogenic activity.

Tourism is a part of these processes. The physical environment of MENA has proven attractive to tourists for much of the past 200 years with the climate and waters providing opportunities for the development of very specific tourist products, such as spa tourism at the Dead Sea, desert safaris, as well as more generic products such as sunbathing and beaches. Yet tourism is now also affecting the physical geography of many locations both directly in terms of tourism developments, tourism-related urbanisation and the idealisation of certain landscapes, as well as indirectly via its pollution and emissions. The challenge for tourism therefore is not just to understand present-day physical geographies of the Middle East but to image what will be desirable for the future.

References

Abd-Elhamid, H., Javadi, A., Abdelaty, I., & Sherif, M. (2016) 'Simulation of seawater intrusion in the Nile Delta aquifer under the conditions of climate change', *Hydrology Research*, 47(6): 1198–1210.

Al Rabady, R. (2013) 'Creative cities through local heritage revival: A perspective from Jordan/Madaba', *International Journal of Heritage Studies*, 19(3): 288–303.

Antrop, M. (2006) 'Sustainable landscapes: Contradiction, fiction or utopia?', *Landscape and Urban Planning*, 75(3): 187–197.

Aouiche, I., Daoudi, L., Anthony, E.J., Sedrati, M., Harti, A., & Ziane, E. (2016) 'The impact of storms in the morphodynamic evolution of a human-impacted semi-sheltered beach (Agadir Bay, Morocco)', *Journal of African Earth Sciences*, 115: 32–47.

BBC News (2007) 'Volcano erupts on Red Sea Island', BBC News. Available online: http://news.bbc. co.uk/2/hi/middle_east/7021596.stm.

Berberian, M. (2005) 'The 2003 Bam urban earthquake: A predictable seismotectonic pattern along the western margin of the rigid Lut block, southeast Iran', *Earthquake Spectra*, 21(S1): 35–99.

Blanc, P.L. (2012) 'The opening of the Plio-Quaternary Gibraltar Strait: Assessing the size of a cataclysm', *Geodinamica Acta*, 15(5–6): 303–317.

Blondel, J. (2006) 'The "design" of Mediterranean landscapes: A millennial story of humans and ecological systems during the historic period', *Human Ecology*, 34(5): 713–729.

Bohnhoff, M., Martínez-Garzón, P., Bulut, F., Stierle, E., & Ben-Zion, Y. (2016) 'Maximum earthquake magnitudes along different sections of the North Anatolian fault zone', *Tectonophysics*, 674: 147–165.

Bugalho, M.N., Caldeira, M.C., Pereira, J.S., Aronson, J., & Pausas, J.G. (2011) 'Mediterranean cork oak savannas require human use to sustain biodiversity and ecosystem services', *Frontiers in Ecology and the Environment*, 9(5): 278–286.

Cook, K.H., & Vizy, E.K. (2015) 'Detection and analysis of an amplified warming of the Sahara Desert', *Journal of Climate*, 28(16): 6560–6580.

D'Amato, G., Baena-Cagnani, C.E., Cecchi, L., Annesi-Maesano, I., Nunes, C., Ansotegui, I., D'Amato, M., Liccardi, G., Sofia, M., & Canonica, W.G. (2013) 'Climate change, air pollution and extreme events leading to increasing prevalence of allergic respiratory diseases', *Multidisciplinary Respiratory Medicine*, 8(1): 12.

Davis, D.K., & Burke III, E. (2011) *Environmental Imaginaries of the Middle East and North Africa*. Athens, OH: Ohio University Press.

De Stefano, L. (2004) *Freshwater and Tourism in the Mediterranean*. Rome: WWF Mediterranean Programme.

Drake, C. (1997) 'Water resource conflicts in the Middle East', *Journal of Geography*, 96(1): 4–12.

Dusar, B., Verstraeten, G., Notebaert, B., & Bakker, J. (2011) 'Holocene environmental change and its impact on sediment dynamics in the Eastern Mediterranean', *Earth-Science Reviews*, 108(3): 137–157.

Emberling, G. (2010) *The Geography of the Middle East, Teaching the Middle East a Resource for Educators*. Chicago: The Oriental Institute, The University of Chicago. Available online: http://teachmiddleeast. lib.uchicago.edu/foundations/geography/essay/essay-01.html.

Finkel, I. (2014) *The Ark before Noah: Decoding the Story of the Flood*. London: Hachette UK.

Fisher, W.B. (2013) *The Middle East: A Physical, Social and Regional Geography*. Abingdon: Routledge.

Furby, K.A., Bouwmeester, J., & Berumen, M. (2013) 'Susceptibility of central Red Sea corals during a major bleaching event', *Coral Reefs*, 32(2): 505–513.

Gaina, C., Torsvik, T.H., van Hinsbergen, D.J., Medvedev, S., Werner, S.C., & Labails, C. (2013) 'The African Plate: A history of oceanic crust accretion and subduction since the Jurassic', *Tectonophysics*, 604: 4–25.

Galil, B.S. (2007) 'Loss or gain? Invasive aliens and biodiversity in the Mediterranean Sea', *Marine Pollution Bulletin*, 55(7): 314–322.

Garcia-Castellanos, D., Estrada, F., Jiménez-Munt, I., Gorini, C., Fernández, M., Vergés, J., & De Vicente, R. (2009) 'Catastrophic flood of the Mediterranean after the Messinian salinity crisis', *Nature*, 462(7274): 778–781.

Gargani, J., & Rigollet, C. (2007) 'Mediterranean Sea level variations during the Messinian salinity crisis', *Geophysical Research Letters*, 34(10): L10405.

Geri, F., Amici, V., & Rocchini, D. (2010) 'Human activity impact on the heterogeneity of a Mediterranean landscape', *Applied Geography*, 30(3): 370–379.

Golani, D. (1998) 'Impact of Red Sea fish migrants through the Suez Canal on the aquatic environment of the Eastern Mediterranean', in J. Albert, M. Bernhardsson, & R. Kenna (eds), *Transformations of Middle Eastern Natural Environments: Legacies and Lessons* (pp. 375–387). New Haven, CT: Yale University.

Gomez, F., Beauchamp, W., & Barazangi, M. (2000) 'Role of the Atlas Mountains (northwest Africa) within the African–Eurasian plate-boundary zone', *Geology*, 28(9): 775–778.

Goren, M., Galil, B.S., Diamant, A., & Stern, N. (2016) 'Invading up the food web? Invasive fish in the southeastern Mediterranean Sea', *Marine Biology*, 163(8): 180.

Gössling, S., & Hall, C.M. (eds) (2006) *Tourism and Global Environmental Change*. London: Routledge.

Grove, A.T., & Rackham, O. (2003) *The Nature of Mediterranean Europe: An Ecological History*. New Haven, CT: Yale University Press.

Gupta, A.K., Yuvaraja, A., Prakasam, M., Clemens, S.C., & Velu, A. (2015) 'Evolution of the South Asian monsoon wind system since the late Middle Miocene', *Palaeogeography, Palaeoclimatology, Palaeoecology*, 438: 160–167.

Hall, C.M. (2001) 'Trends in coastal and marine tourism: The end of the last frontier?' *Ocean and Coastal Management*, 44: 601–618.

Hall, C.M. (2016) 'Loving nature to death: Tourism consumption, biodiversity loss and the Anthropocene', in M. Gren, & E.H. Huijbens (eds), *Tourism and the Anthropocene* (pp. 52–73). Abingdon: Routledge.

Harris, S.E. (2012) 'Cyprus as a degraded landscape or resilient environment in the wake of colonial intrusion', *Proceedings of the National Academy of Sciences*, 109(10): 3670–3675.

Keeley, J.E., Bond, W.J., Bradstock, R.A., Pausas, J.G., & Rundel, P.W. (2012) *Fire in Mediterranean Ecosystems: Ecology, Evolution and Management*. Cambridge: Cambridge University Press.

Lambeck, K. (1996) 'Shoreline reconstructions for the Persian Gulf since the last glacial maximum', *Earth and Planetary Science Letters*, 142(1–2): 43–57.

Lew, A.A., Hall, C.M., & Timothy, D.J. (2015) *World Regional Geography: Human Mobilities, Tourism Destinations, Sustainable Environments*, 2nd edn. Dubuque, IA: Kendall-Hunt.

Marcos, M., & Tsimplis, M.N. (2008) 'Comparison of results of AOGCMs in the Mediterranean Sea during the 21st century', *Journal of Geophysical Research: Oceans*, 113(C12): 1–21.

Martínez-García, P., Comas, M., Soto, J.I., Lonergan, L., & Watts, A.B. (2013) 'Strike-slip tectonics and basin inversion in the Western Mediterranean: The Post-Messinian evolution of the Alboran Sea', *Basin Research*, 25(4): 361–387.

Mikhail, A. (ed.) (2013) *Water on Sand: Environmental Histories of the Middle East and North Africa*. Oxford: Oxford University Press.

Nematollahi, O., Hoghooghi, H., Rasti, M., & Sedaghat, A. (2016) 'Energy demands and renewable energy resources in the Middle East', *Renewable and Sustainable Energy Reviews*, 54: 1172–1181.

Nikishin, A.M., Korotaev, M.V., Ershov, A.V., & Brunet, M.F. (2003) 'The Black Sea basin: Tectonic history and Neogene–Quaternary rapid subsidence modelling', *Sedimentary Geology*, 156: 149–168.

Nilforoushan, F., Masson, F., Vernant, P., Vigny, C., Martinod, J., Abbassi, M., Nankali, H., Hatzfeld, D., Bayer, R., Tavakoli, F., Ashtiani, A., Doerflinger, E., Daigniéres, M., Collard, P., & Chéry, J. (2003) 'GPS network monitors the Arabia-Eurasia collision deformation in Iran', *Journal of Geodesy*, 77(7–8): 411–422.

Pappé, I. (2014) *The Modern Middle East: A Social and Cultural History*. Abingdon: Routledge.

Riegl, B., Berumen, M., & Bruckner, A. (2013) 'Coral population trajectories, increased disturbance and management intervention: A sensitivity analysis', *Ecology and Evolution*, 3(4): 1050–1064.

Rockwell, T. (2013) 'North Anatolian Fault', in P.T. Bobrowsky (ed.), *Encyclopedia of Natural Hazards* (pp. 738–739). Dordrecht: Springer.

Ryan, W.B., Pitman, W.C., Major, C.O., Shimkus, K., Moskalenko, V., Jones, G.A., Dimitrov, P., Gorür, N., Sakinç, M., & Yüce, H. (1997) 'An abrupt drowning of the Black Sea shelf', *Marine Geology*, 138(1): 119–126.

Smith, B.D., & Zeder, M.A. (2013) 'The onset of the Anthropocene', *Anthropocene*, 4: 8–13.

Steffen, W., Crutzen, P.J., & McNeill, J.R. (2007) 'The Anthropocene: Are humans now overwhelming the great forces of nature', *AMBIO: A Journal of the Human Environment*, 36(8): 614–621.

Steffen, W., Grinevald, J., Crutzen, P., & McNeill, J. (2011) 'The Anthropocene: Conceptual and historical perspectives', *Philosophical Transactions of the Royal Society of London A: Mathematical, Physical and Engineering Sciences*, 369(1938): 842–867.

Sušnik, J., Vamvakeridou-Lyroudia, L.S., Gebert, N., Kloos, J., Renaud, F. La Jeunesse, I., Mabrouk, B., Savić, D.A., Kapelan, Z. Ludwig, R., Fischer, G., Roson, R., & Zografos, C. (2015) 'Interdisciplinary assessment of sea-level rise and climate change impacts on the lower Nile Delta, Egypt', *Science of the Total Environment*, 503–504: 279–288.

Tal, A. (2002) *Pollution in a Promised Land: An Environmental History of Israel*. Berkeley, CA: University of California Press.

Tzedakis, P.C. (2007) 'Seven ambiguities in the Mediterranean palaeoenvironmental narrative', *Quaternary Science Reviews*, 26: 2042–2066.

World Bank (2013) 'Red Sea—Dead Sea Water Conveyance Study Program Overview—Updated January 2013'. Available online: http://siteresources.worldbank.org/EXTREDSEADEADSEA/Resources/Overview_RDS_Jan_2013.pdf?resourceurlname=Overview_RDS_Jan_2013.pdf%26.

3

THE MIDDLE EAST AND NORTH AFRICA

A dynamic cultural realm

Dallen J. Timothy

Introduction

The Middle East and North Africa (MENA) is a vast region of many natural and cultural landscapes. It is a realm united (and divided) by physical geography, anthropogenic imprints and living cultures. It is one of the major clusters of humankind on earth and home to two ancient culture hearths (the Nile Valley and the Fertile Crescent/Mesopotamia), from which many innovations diffused to other areas of the world, including certain agricultural systems and products, written language, the lunar calendar, and the wheel. The Arabian Peninsula and the Levant later became a hearth for the diffusion of religion (Islam, Judaism and Christianity), which has touched every corner of the globe. As the previous chapter denoted, MENA is also home to an immensely diverse natural environment and varied ecosystems that make the area resilient, unique, and attractive for tourism.

This chapter describes elements of the cultural geography of MENA that have a salient bearing on the development of tourism. It briefly examines the peoples, cultures, and heritages that characterise the region and assesses the cultural and natural assets that together provide the foundations of a flourishing tourism system.

Influential empires

Throughout history, MENA has been affected tremendously by internal and external forces. It is home to some of the oldest human civilisations, particularly in the Nile Valley and along the Tigris and Euphrates Rivers which, as noted earlier, spurred the development of many innovations that the world enjoys today. Some of the earliest evidence of nomadic peoples settling into sedentary communities dates from the Levant approximately 12,000 BCE and are believed to have derived from a steady food supply and ample water. Verifiable towns and cities have been excavated from the Neolithic period around 10,000 years BCE. Some of the earliest cities were Memphis (Egypt), Uruk (in present-day Iraq), and Jericho (Palestine), which were home to sizeable populations (Anderson 2000). Today, the remnants of many Neolithic cities and towns dot the ancient landscapes of MENA.

From these earliest settlements, large empires developed, representing the forerunners of the modern concept of the state. The Sumarians dominated much of ancient Mesopotamia from 3500 to 199 BCE. The Egyptian Empire in various forms lasted from approximately 3050 BCE until being conquered by the Romans in 30 BCE. The Babylonians and Assyrians controlled much of the Middle East from 1895 BCE to 500 BCE. These were followed by periods where large swaths of MENA were under the imperial rule of the ancient Persians, Phoenicians, Greeks, Romans and Byzantines (Eastern Roman Empire) and many smaller empires. The height of the Byzantine Empire occurred in 550 CE at which time it controlled most of the lands around the Mediterranean Sea. Soon after, however, the Muslim conquests shrunk the Byzantine Empire dramatically and ushered in the Arab Empire (632–1258 CE), which became the dominant force in the region and the most influential in terms of its cultural impacts which remain today. All of the countries of MENA today, except parts of Turkey and parts of a few North African states, were under the control of the Arab Empire. The most obvious vestiges of that realm are the Arabic language, Islamic religion, and Arab architecture (Lew, Hall, & Timothy 2015). The Ottoman Empire, centred in today's Turkey, eventually became the ruling power over much of MENA from 1299 CE until its collapse in 1923 CE as a result of the First World War.

These empires all played a crucial part in the spread of ideas and innovations from their hearths to outlying areas, helping to create standardised cultural, agricultural, linguistic and religious practices. They became the hubs of invention and technology. They contributed much in the areas of medicine, philosophy, astronomy, mathematics, art, transportation, military warfare, farm tools and equipment, and travel. The invention and diffusion of wheeled carriages and sailing vessels thousands of years ago in Mesopotamia were a colossal boost for human mobility. This resulted in increased levels of trade throughout the world. Places that were accessible by sea saw the most lucrative trade, although camel and carriage caravans were an important means of travel and trade throughout Southwest Asia and North Africa. Goods from Africa, Europe and Asia criss-crossed the Middle East, resulting in established transportation corridors and trade routes and the growth of nodes of commerce that eventually became important cities. Populations grew as trade grew, and elements of culture, including language, religion, food and agricultural production, and cultural practices, were dispersed along major trading routes (Shackley 2002).

Religious dominions

Much of today's cultural landscape is directly connected to the religious heritages that dominate MENA, including those of Jews, Christians and Muslims (Sharkey 2017). The early Jewish diaspora began several hundred years BCE as many Israelites were taken captive, exiled and otherwise forced out of their homeland by various invading superpowers (e.g. Assyrians and Babylonians) and perhaps through early migration to what is now Ethiopia. During the Roman period, many Jews had spread to other parts of the empire, some of whom fled the Roman destruction of Jerusalem in 70 CE, or were taken as prisoners to Europe. The dispersion of Jews continued after the fall of Rome, during the Middle Ages and into the modern era, with millions of them living throughout Europe and other parts of MENA by the seventeenth century. After the Jewish expulsion from Spain in 1492, many ended up settling in North Africa, and other large Jewish populations settled in the Americas, Asia and Oceania from the sixteenth to the twentieth centuries, in large part through the process of European colonisation. At the time modern Israel was established in 1948, there were approximately 76,000 Jews in Palestine, although most of these had arrived from elsewhere during the previous 40 years (League of Nations 1921). The countries surrounding Palestine had sizeable Jewish populations, in particular Iraq, Morocco, Turkey, Iran, Egypt, Algeria and Tunisia (Simon, Laskier, & Reguer 2002).

Soon after the death and resurrection of Jesus, the apostles began evangelising throughout the eastern Mediterranean in areas that are today in Turkey, Malta, Greece, Cyprus and Italy. Many of them met their demise during their missionary efforts and died as martyrs for the cause, yet their efforts to spread the Christian message were not deterred. Christianity spread throughout Europe and the Caucasus rather quickly until it eventually pervaded most of Europe and various parts of the Middle East (Evans 2017). Within a few centuries after the time of Christ, Christian churches were built throughout Europe, and church shrines associated with the life and ministry of Jesus had developed throughout the lands. Pilgrimages to the lands of Jesus from Armenia, Georgia and other countries in Europe began soon after the death of Christ, and Christian pilgrimages to the Holy Land were commonplace throughout the Middle Ages, although it slowed considerably with the Protestant Reformation of the sixteenth and seventeenth centuries, as certain Christian sects began prohibiting pilgrimage travel (Ron & Timothy 2019).

After its foundation in the early seventh century, Islam spread throughout much of the Mediterranean, Southwest Asia and North Africa by means of conquests, geographic expansion of various caliphates and empires, and eventually further afield through trade. Islam replaced Christianity in parts of Europe and the Middle East, as well as Buddhism and Hinduism in areas of South and Southeast Asia. The spread of Islam is one of the most influential factors that today define the boundaries of the Middle East and North Africa. The foundation of Islam as the primary religion in the Middle East was secured with the growth of the Arab Empire and later the Ottoman Empire, which had adopted Islam as the state religion and which, by the end of the seventeenth century, had usurped much of the populated territory of today's MENA region. Islam is, perhaps more than any other cultural force, the most influential factor in regional politics, economics, education, law, social mores, tangible and intangible heritage, and tourism development (Timothy & Daher 2009).

Cultures of today

European colonialism had a crucial role to play in the development of the contemporary cultural and political landscapes of MENA. Through a series of conquests in the nineteenth and twentieth centuries, several European powers usurped land in North Africa from the Ottoman Empire. The British acquired Egypt in 1882. The French acquired Algeria in 1830, Tunisia in 1881 and most of Morocco in 1911. Spain acquired portions of Morocco and Western Sahara in 1912, and Italy took over Libya in 1911. During the mid-nineteenth century, the British gained control over much of the southeastern portion of the Arabian Peninsula (including southern Yemen, Oman and the Trucial States (now the United Arab Emirates)). These areas had not been colonised by the Ottomans, but the British intervened in the region to expand their own colonial interests.

Prior to the First World War, the Ottoman Empire continued to hold sovereignty over the areas of modern-day Palestine/Israel, Lebanon, much of Syria, coastal portions of Saudi Arabia, Bahrain, Qatar, much of Kuwait, and large portions of Iraq. With the WWI collapse of the Ottoman Empire, however, these territories were divided between French and British control. Syria and Lebanon came under French rule, while Iraq, Syria, Jordan and Palestine became British mandates/protectorates. Only Turkey and Iran remained independent throughout the European colonial period, although parts of both countries were under the heavy influence of European powers. From the 1800s, there were many efforts by several colonies to become independent states, but most only succeeded between the 1940s and 1960s. The young states of the Arabian Gulf and Arabian Peninsula emerged as independent countries from British protectorship in the 1960s and 1970s, including Bahrain, Kuwait, Oman, Qatar, the United Arab Emirates, North Yemen and South Yemen (the two Yemens united in 1990).

Perhaps the most controversial element of colonial influence was the establishment of Israel in 1948. After the British Mandate of Palestine was established in 1922, the British government, under heavy pressure from the Zionist movement, agreed to establish Palestine as a homeland for the world's diasporic Jews. In response to centuries of antisemitism, suppressed rights and intensifying persecution, especially in Europe, Zionism commenced in the late 1800s with the primary goal of reclaiming the Jewish homeland. The UK's Balfour Declaration effectively opened the mandate's borders to Jewish immigration from across the globe, often resulting in the seizure of land and communities that were already inhabited by the local Arab population. This resulted in the exodus of hundreds of thousands of Palestinians from the homes and communities they had occupied for many generations. This, of course, raised considerable tension between the repatriated Jews and the extant Arab inhabitants, leading to frequent skirmishes and attacks against the diasporic returnees. In November 1947, the United Nations proffered a plan to partition the territory into a Jewish state and a Palestinian state. The Jews accepted the resolution, but the Arabs rejected it. As a result of this rejection, the ongoing battles with their Arab neighbours, and the growing need to provide homes for the despondent refugees from devastated Europe, on 14 May 1948, Israel declared independence, which was recognised soon after by several countries and eventually by the majority of countries. Many primarily Muslim countries in Asia, the Middle East and North Africa still do not officially recognise Israel's independence. Iran initially recognised the new state but withdrew its support in 1979 at the time of the Islamic Revolution. A day after Israel's declaration of independence, the 1948 Arab–Israeli War broke out between Israel and its Arab neighbours (the Arab League) and lasted nearly ten months. The existence of the State of Israel lies at the core of many of the security problems, wars and extremist activity that dominate the region's headlines.

Religion

As noted above, one of the main legacies of the Arab Empire was the Islamisation of MENA. Today, more than 90 per cent of the region's population adheres to Islam. In some countries, the number hovers close to 100 per cent (e.g. Algeria, Morocco, Yemen). Islam is divided between two major sects: the Sunnis and the Shiites. There are other Islamic factions as well, such as Sufism, Khwarij and Ahmadiyya, but these tend not to be closely associated with the larger sects. Even within Shia and Sunni Islam there are various subsects, branches and schools of thought that differ in several doctrinal ways and according to questions of prophetic succession (e.g. Alawites, Ismailis, Zaidis). Most of the countries of MENA have a Sunni majority. The exceptions are Iran, Iraq and Bahrain, where Shia Islam dominates, but these states also have significant Sunni minorities. Yemen's population is approximately two-thirds Sunnis and one-third Shiites, and most countries in the region are home to other minority Muslim populations.

While Islam is one cultural criterion often used to define MENA, there are millions of people who adhere to other religions (see Table 3.1). Christianity is the second most populous religion in MENA (approximately 15 million adherents), followed by Judaism and several other faiths. Christians comprise approximately 41 per cent of Lebanon's population. Other countries with large Christian minorities include Egypt, Syria, Jordan, Israel, Iraq, Iran, Palestine and Turkey. The main traditional Christian denominations in the region include Maronites,

Table 3.1 Religious adherence in MENA

Country	Muslims % of population	Christians % of population	Jews % of population	Other or unaffiliated % of population
Algeria	99.0	< 0.001	< 0.001	< 1.0
Bahrain	70.3	14.5	0.6	14.6
Egypt	90.0	10.0	< 0.001	< 0.001
Iran	99.4	< 0.005	< 0.002	0.6
Iraq	99.0	0.8	< 0.001	0.2
Israel	17.7	1.0	74.7	6.6
Jordan	97.2	2.2	< 0.001	0.6
Kuwait	76.7	17.3	< 0.001	5.9
Lebanon	54.0	40.5	< 0.001	5.5
Libya	96.6	2.7	< 0.001	0.7
Morocco	99.0	< 0.002	< 0.001	1.0
Oman	85.9	6.5	< 0.001	7.6
Palestine				
West Bank	84.0	2.5	13.0	0.5
Gaza	99.0	0.5	< 0.001	0.5
Qatar	67.7	13.8	< 0.001	18.5
Saudi Arabia★	100	n/a	n/a	n/a
Syria	87.0	10.0	< 0.001	3.0
Tunisia	99.1	< 0.001	< 0.001	0.9
Turkey ★★	99.8	–	–	0.2
UAE	76.0	9.0	< 0.001	15.0
Yemen	99.1	0.2	< 0.001	0.7

Source: Compiled from data in Central Intelligence Agency (2018).

★ Saudi Arabia does not provide data on guest workers' religions; only Saudis' religious adherence is counted.

★★ Christians and adherents to other faiths in Turkey are often registered as Muslims, which may inflate this number. Other estimates suggest that Muslims comprise 80–85 per cent of the population, with Christians, Jews and other religions comprising a larger percentage of the population.

Coptic Christians, Melkites, Assyrian and Syriac Christians, Armenian Christians, Greek and Arab Christians, and various Orthodox sects. The Gulf States' expatriate and guest workforce from countries in Asia (e.g. the Philippines), Africa, Europe and North America account for the high numbers of non-traditional Middle Eastern Christians living in several Gulf States (e.g. Bahrain, Kuwait, Qatar, Saudi Arabia and the UAE).

There are nearly 6.6 million Jews living throughout MENA, with the obvious majority residing in Israel. Before the foundation of Israel in 1948, hundreds of thousands of Jews were scattered throughout North Africa and the Middle East. Today, however, owing to harassment and discrimination in many of the countries where they had lived for centuries as well as Israel's Law of Return, which gives Jews everywhere a pathway to live in Israel and receive Israeli citizenship, relatively few Jews live in the Middle East outside of Israel. Many were expelled from Arab states, while others chose to migrate to Israel and become Israelis. The exception to few Jews living in Arab states is Palestine, where thousands of Jews live in the West Bank, on land that has been appropriated from the Palestinians by the Israeli government for building Jewish settlements. Although the Jewish population in countries such as Morocco, Yemen, Tunisia, Iran and Iraq has dwindled significantly through emigration since the establishment of Israel, many Jewish historic places, such as tombs, urban neighbourhoods and synagogues, and a few Jewish strongholds with small remnant populations (e.g. Djerba Island, Tunisia) remain in a handful of countries.

Besides the three Abrahamic religions, there are other faith-based minorities in MENA. The high number of 'other' adherents in countries such as Bahrain, Qatar and the UAE is also attributable to those countries' large expatriate workforces. Hindus, Buddhists and Sikhs make up the largest portion of the other believers, who come to the region largely from India, Sri Lanka, Nepal and Thailand to work in construction, services and domestic labour.

The 'other' category also includes Druze, the Bahá'í Faith and a handful of other small groups (e.g. Samaritans). Druze is an ancient monotheistic religion from the tenth century, founded partly on Islamic teachings but including additional dogmas that are not accepted by mainstream Islam, including reincarnation, Greek philosophy and ideas borrowed from Christianity and other faiths. They speak Arabic and practise secret ceremonies and rites that are passed down through initiatory rituals. Large Druze populations are located in Syria, Lebanon, Israel and Jordan. The Bahá'í Faith was established in 1863 in Iran and Syria and is a syncretic creed that accepts the value of all religions and promotes the unity of humankind. Bahá'ís live throughout MENA but have a particularly strong presence in Iran and Israel (where the religion's headquarters is located and is a UNESCO World Heritage Site) (Collins-Kreiner & Gatrell 2006).

Ethnicity

Ethnicity in this part of the world is a social group identity, often based on language together with religion and a shared history more so than racial characteristics. It does not follow a precise definition and frequently does not adhere to state boundaries. The majority of people in North Africa and the Middle East speak Arabic, identify as Arabs and, as already noted, practise Islam. However, there are some notable exceptions to this. Several parts of the region can be classified as Islamic but not Arab (Lew, Hall, & Timothy 2015). These include Turkey, Iran, much of Morocco, and northern Iraq (Kurdistan), and of course, most Israelis would not identify as Arabs or Muslims. While Arabness dominates the cultural landscapes of North Africa and the Middle East, there is a much wider assortment of ethno-linguistic groups in MENA than only Arabs. Table 3.2 highlights several of these and outlines the countries where they are most common. The Arabs are believed to have derived from the nomadic Bedouins that have roamed the deserts of the Middle East and North Africa for millennia, herding goats and camels. Their main sources of nourishment came from these animals and centred mostly on milk products and meat. Their animal husbandry traditions and itinerant lifestyles saw the development of many cultural characteristics that remain today and have important tourism implications: camel races, camel-based transportation, poetry and oral traditions, dancing, and a strong social order. As well, the languages and dialects spoken by the Bedouins were considered the purist form of Arabic and were therefore used to standardise the language throughout the region (Holes 2004).

Fearing that the Bedouins would continue to undermine Ottoman sovereignty in the region, in the late 1800s, the Ottoman rulers began forced Bedouin sedentism into towns and villages. While this had varying degrees of success, it did begin the gradual change amongst many groups from nomadic living to sedentary living with alterative employment and livelihoods, including tourism (Falah 1985). Later, in the twentieth century, based upon pressure from the emerging states in the region to have a stable and governable population, together with growing trade and its economic influence, many nomadic peoples gave up their itinerant lifestyles and settled in

Table 3.2 Examples of the peoples of MENA

Ethno-linguistic group	MENA countries with significant population	Language family
Arabs	Bahrain, Qatar, UAE, Oman, Yemen, Saudi Arabia, Iraq, Israel, Syria, Lebanon, Jordan, Palestine, Egypt, Libya, Tunisia, Algeria, Morocco	Semitic
Jews	Israel, Iran, Morocco, Palestine	Semitic
Copts	Egypt, Libya	Semitic
Assyrians/Chaldeans	Syria, Iraq, Iran, Turkey	Semitic
Berbers	Algeria, Morocco, Libya, Tunisia, Egypt, Israel	Kemetic/Berber
Turks	Turkey, Iraq, Saudi Arabia, Syria, Lebanon, Jordan, Libya	Turkic
Kurds	Iran, Iraq, Syria, Turkey	Indo-European
Circassians	Israel, Jordan, Turkey, Egypt, Saudi Arabia, Iraq, Syria	Caucasic
Persians	Iran	Indo-European
Balochs	Iran, UAE, Oman, Saudi Arabia	Indo-European
Azeris	Iran	Turkic

Source: Author's compilation.

organised communities, adopting agriculture and commerce as a more secure livelihood. With this change, cities have grown, and many indigenous tribes and ethnic groups in MENA have become involved in the tourism sector (Abuamoud, Libbin, Green, & Al Rousan 2014; Al-Oun & Al-Homoud 2008). Today, the Bedouins continue to have a strong sense of identity. While many Bedouins now live in permanent settlements, even in urban neighbourhoods, thousands continue to roam the deserts of North Africa, the Levant and the Arabian Peninsula (Chatty 2006; Keohane 2011; Dehau & Bonte 2007).

The southern parts of Algeria, Tunisia and Libya, and much of Morocco, are sparsely populated owing to their extreme heat and aridity, but the Sahara Desert has been the abode of the Berbers for thousands of years. Berbers (or Amazigh people) are indigenous to North Africa, and live primarily in Morocco, Algeria, Libya and Tunisia but are not Arabs. Many Amazigh tribes were traditionally sedentary farmers, although some of the southern tribes practised, and continue to practise, nomadic herding and transhumance. They speak a variety of dialects of Berber—a non-Arabic language. In recent years, there has been a resurgence of the Berber identity in North Africa, including native language use (Maddy-Weitzman 2011; Sadiqi 2014). One result of their efforts towards more equitable recognition has been Berber being recognised as an official language of Morocco in 2011 and in Algeria in 2016 together with Arabic. Between one-quarter and one-third of the population of Morocco speaks Berber, and approximately one-third of Algeria's population speaks Berber. French is a common language of commerce and education in both countries as well. Hundreds of years ago, the Berbers converted to Islam through the Muslim conquests and Arab Empire, although they are known for practising a form of Islam that blends Muslim doctrines and practices with their native rites and rituals (Silverstein 2012).

The Berbers' unique culture, language, food and traditional lifestyles have started to receive considerable tourist attention during the past 20 years, and many Berber communities in North Africa have involved themselves in tourism (Hoffman & Miller 2010; Rogers 2012), with some observers voicing concerns over how the industry might change these Sahara Desert natives the way it has other people in the region (Silverstein 2010).

The Persians, Kurds, Azeris, Balochs, Copts, Turks, Assyrians and other groups have also played important roles in the development of the Middle East's cultural landscapes (Stewart

2013). They are culturally unique and speak distinct languages, occupy inimitable environments, and practise diverging forms of Islam and Christianity. As well, many of them are involved in tourism as service providers, yet they are not as intentionally sought out by tourists as an attraction as the Berbers and Bedouins are. Much of this can be attributed to the romanticised impressions of the latter that were so often the substance of travel writings and novels from the Middle Ages onward by the likes of Ibn Battuta, Leo Africanus and T.E. Lawrence (Lawrence of Arabia), and later through Hollywood-produced motion pictures.

Geopolitics

One of MENA's unfortunate impressions on the world stage is its proclivity for conflict and war. This is not a recent development. The ancient nomads of North Africa and the Middle East were known for their ferocious fighting skills and tendencies, which they demonstrated through inter-tribal warfare and hostilities against imperial and colonial invaders. Berber tribesmen were frequently engaged to protect governors and places of governance during ancient and colonial times.

Many imperial actions pitted tribe against tribe and later colonial events resulted in outright war. The 1917 Balfour Declaration, which set in motion the establishment of Israel by designating the British Mandate of Palestine as the location for a 'national home for the Jewish people', was a pivotal turning point in the relationship between the Middle East's Jewish and Arab populations. Neighbouring Arabs felt betrayed by the British, and the inhabitants of Palestine, who were Muslim and Christian Arabs with only a small Jewish minority, protested profusely. The consequences of this infamous pronouncement were the founding of a Jewish state and a persistent conflict between the Arabs and Jews of the Middle East (Watts 2008). The majority of states in MENA still have not recognised the establishment of Israel. Turkey, Egypt, Jordan and Iran are the only exceptions, although as noted previously, Iran revoked its recognition in 1979 and is one of the most hostile countries against Israel.

Following the US terror attacks of 11 September 2001, the US invaded Afghanistan, the stronghold of al-Qaeda, the terrorist organisation responsible for the attack. The US and some of its allies invaded Iraq two years later, which was ostensibly for the purpose of deposing Saddam Hussein and his support for terrorism and to destroy his stockpiles of weapons of mass destruction, which never materialised. While it achieved some of its goals, the US-led offensive contributed to the destabilisation of Iraq and much of the broader region, which allowed terrorist groups to get a foothold in Iraq. The Iraq War decimated much of the country's infrastructure, cost thousands of lives, and created a power vacuum that resulted in belligerent groups fighting amongst themselves in a domestic context. A consequence of the 2011 US troop withdrawal was increased sectarian violence and power struggles within Iraq until a full-blown civil war broke out in 2014.

In December 2010, in response to long-time authoritarian regimes and people's desire for a better life, a string of violent and non-violent protests began in Tunisia and quickly spread through North Africa and the Middle East. This 'Arab Spring' affected Tunisia, Libya, Egypt, Syria, Yemen and Bahrain more than other countries in the region and with the result that governments were overthrown, dictators were imprisoned and/or executed, and civil wars ensued (Gause 2011; Haas 2018). Following the fall of Yemen's autocratic president in 2011, insurgent groups began controlling large areas of the country, and opposing political factions began infighting. After a brief period of rest and the formation of a unity government, civil war broke out in 2015, which has tangled not only political factions within Yemen but also involved Iran and Saudi Arabia in the country's turmoil.

Another outcome of the Arab Spring was the Syrian civil war between the government forces supporting President Bashar al-Assad and various rebel organisations that had tried to overthrow the Assad regime. This also severely destabilised Syria, which led to conditions that allowed the establishment and growth of ISIS/ISIL (Islamic State), another terrorism organisation that ended up infiltrating and controlling large portions of Syria and Iraq between 2011 and 2018. The Syrian Civil War has had spillover effects into neighbouring countries, such as Turkey, which also suffered from ISIS-related insecurity between 2012 and 2018, in addition to its own internal conflicts related to the Kurdish minority and the insurrection of anti-government opposition groups (Gunter 2015). As of spring 2018, much of ISIS had been defeated by allied forces, although small pockets remained. The Arab Spring revolts also led to the overthrow of Muammar Gaddafi and the collapse of the Libyan state. At the time of writing, Libya is divided between two factions and is plagued by continued violence and insecurity, and is considered by many commentators to be a 'failed state' (Lynch 2016).

This overview provides only a glance at some of the many conflicts that have long plagued MENA. Others include the Dhofar Rebellion/Omani Civil War (1962–1976), the Arab–Israeli War (1967), the Lebanese Civil War (1975–1990), the Iran–Iraq War (1980–1988), the Turkish–Kurdish conflict (1978–present) and the Gulf War (1990–1991). Many other hostilities have lasted shorter periods of time (Davidson 2016; Heing 2017; Tucker 2010).

This troubled geopolitical history has stayed the hand of tourism development in several countries and areas of MENA (Mansfeld 1996). Tourists are especially cautious about travelling to risky destinations, which has affected the industry's growth in the region. Nevertheless, even political tensions can be tourist attractions after the fact. Some localities have capitalised on this fact where war zones (active and former), hostile borders and areas of notable conflict have drawn significant tourist attention (Gelbman & Timothy 2010). Hostility in the Middle East has also spurred the development of 'solidarity tourism' or 'justice tourism' with the most prominent case being the Palestinian and Israeli conflict. There is a growing segment of travellers who travel in solidarity with the Palestinian cause (Isaac & Hodge 2011; Ron & Timothy 2019). They visit the Palestinians in the West Bank and participate in political rallies in a show of support for their struggle with Israel. On the other side, there is a large cohort of Israel supporters whose visits are motivated in part at least for the purpose of demonstrating solidarity with the State of Israel.

Cultural heritage

Colonialism, indigeneity, religion, ethnic identity, language and geopolitics are all part of the cultural heritage of the Middle East and North Africa. Because of harsh climatic conditions that made nomadism increasingly challenging, the domestication of plants and animals through agricultural practices, and the development of long-distance trade routes, towns and cities developed in the region and became nodes of transportation, commerce and governance.

Successive empires and later European metropoles took advantage of these nascent patterns of urbanisation to establish their colonial capitals from which they could rule and tax their colonial subjects. The ancient imperial footprint in MENA manifests today in the region's vast collection of archaeological sites and ancient cities that testify of successive empires and their desires to conquer, destroy and rebuild. Cyrene, Libya, is an outstanding example of a Greek and Roman city on the Mediterranean coast. Baalbek, Lebanon, is home to one of the best-preserved Roman temples in the entire Levant. The Kasbah of Algiers is a prime example of Ottoman architecture. Iraq is home to exceptional remnants of Assyrian and Babylonian civilisations. The physical imprint of the Phoenicians, Byzantines and other superpowers is evident in many localities as well. Arab and Muslim urban design and architecture, including souqs and medinas, pervade the entire region from the time of the Arab Empire (Baker 2003; Timothy & Daher 2009). At the same time, the French, British, Italian and Spanish architectural influence on the cityscapes of MENA is unmistakable (Khirfan 2017). Much of the area's built heritage centres on religion. Some of the most monumental mosques, churches, temples and synagogues anywhere in the world are located in MENA.

Transportation systems are another legacy of the empires and colonisers. Many of the highways and roads in MENA today directly overlay or parallel the transport routes established by imperial governors. Rome established the most omnipresent road network in the Middle East, and many Roman roads were the footings of today's thoroughfares in the region. As well, some of the ancient ports dug, developed and reinforced by the Egyptians, Romans, Phoenicians and Greeks remain important seaports and harbours to the present day. Likewise, many railways established by European colonialists in the nineteenth and twentieth centuries remain part of the transport infrastructure of the modern states of the region, while others have fallen into disrepair and are seen as heritage corridors (Orbaşlı & Woodward 2008).

Beyond its enormous catalog of material culture, MENA is home to a vast intangible heritage, which often swells people's sense of identity and pride more so than the tangible past does—largely because the intangible patrimony better reflects resilience and resistance to outside forces. Languages, religious practices, music, dance, nomadic living, hunting skills and falconry, poetry and oral traditions all lay the foundation of the proud heritage of the Middle East and North Africa (Baker 2003). Regional food traditions strongly reflect this pride and the physical and social conditions that have determined people's behaviours and needs since the beginning of time. Cuisine reflects humankind's struggles with nature and environment, disease and poverty, wealth and opulence, colonialism and indigeneity. It is in essence a repository of the human story. Middle Eastern food reflects these issues well and has become one of the world's iconic foods in the Middle East and outside the region (Zubaida & Tapper 1994).

Conclusion

Together with the natural environment described in the previous chapter, the cultural landscapes of the Middle East and North Africa reflect a proud heritage of a diverse people and set the backdrop for tourism development. While the wars and turmoil that have beleaguered this region for centuries, especially since nineteenth- and twentieth-century colonial times, have inhibited the growth of tourism in some countries, this hampering effect is not seen universally as a negative issue. This is especially so where the tenets of tourism are perceived to be disharmonious with local social and religious standards (Ekiz, Öter, & Stephenson 2017; Hazbun 2006).

Successive empires that controlled most of the Middle East and much of North Africa during the past few thousand years left a significant imprint on the cultural and political landscapes. Urban design, architecture, political systems, religious traditions, and patterns of conflict are all connected to the region's imperial and colonial history. The imperialists dictated the course of history and left behind pervasive evidence of outside control and subjugation. Colonial actions resulted in political boundaries that often do not correspond to tribal, linguist or ethnic lines, and decisions made in faraway metropoles a century ago continue to perpetuate regional conflicts.

Despite all of this, MENA remains a vibrant region full of ancient cultures, historic sites, native hospitality, enigmatic places, and imposing deserts that draw seekers of 'otherness' from around the globe.

References

Abuamoud, I.N., Libbin, J., Green, J., & Al Rousan, R. (2014) 'Factors affecting the willingness of tourists to visit cultural heritage sites in Jordan', *Journal of Heritage Tourism*, 9(2): 148–165.

Al-Oun, S., & Al-Homoud, M. (2008) 'The potential for developing community-based tourism among the Bedouins in the Badia of Jordan', *Journal of Heritage Tourism*, 3(1): 36–54.

Anderson, E.W. (2000) *The Middle East: Geography and Geopolitics*. London: Routledge.

Baker, W.G. (2003) *The Cultural Heritage of Arabs, Islam, and the Middle East*. Dallas, TX: Brown Books.

Central Intelligence Agency (2018) *The World Factbook*. Washington, DC: Central Intelligence Agency. Available online: www.cia.gov/library/publications/the-world-factbook/fields/2122.html (Accessed 3 February 2018).

Chatty, D. (ed.) (2006) *Nomadic Societies in the Middle East and North Africa: Entering the 21st Century*. Leiden: Brill.

Collins-Kreiner, N., & Gatrell, J.D. (2006) 'Tourism, heritage and pilgrimage: The case of Haifa's Bahá'í Gardens', *Journal of Heritage Tourism*, 1(1): 32–50.

Davidson, C. (2016) *Shadow Wars: The Secret Struggle for the Middle East*. London: Oneworld.

Dehau, E., & Bonte, P. (2007) *Bedouin and Nomads: Peoples of the Arabian Desert*. London: Thames & Hudson.

Ekiz, E., Öter, Z., & Stephenson, M.L. (2017) 'Tourism development in the Kingdom of Saudi Arabia: Determining the problems and resolving the challenges', in M.L. Stephenson, & A. Al-Hamarneh (eds), *International Tourism Development and the Gulf Cooperation Council States: Challenges and Opportunities* (pp. 124–139). London: Routledge.

Evans, G.R. (2017) *A Short History of Medieval Christianity*. London: I.B. Tauris.

Falah, G. (1985) 'The spatial pattern of Bedouin sedentarization in Israel', *GeoJournal*, 11(4): 361–368.

Gause, F.G. (2011) 'Why Middle East studies missed the Arab Spring: The myth of authoritarian stability', *Foreign Affairs*, 90(4): 81–90.

Gelbman, A., & Timothy, D.J. (2010) 'From hostile boundaries to tourist attractions', *Current Issues in Tourism*, 13(3): 239–259.

Gunter, M.M. (2015) 'Iraq, Syria, ISIS and the Kurds: Geostrategic concerns for the US and Turkey', *Middle East Policy*, 22(1): 102–111.

Haas, M.L. (2018) *The Arab Spring: The Hope and Reality of the Uprisings*. London: Routledge.

Hazbun, W. (2006) 'Explaining the Arab Middle East tourism paradox', *The Arab World Geographer*, 9(3): 201–214.

Heing, B. (2017) *Geography, Government, and Conflict across the Middle East: Understanding the Cultures of the Middle East*. New York: Cavendish Square Publishing.

Hoffman, K.E., & Miller, S.G. (2010) 'Introduction', in K.E. Hoffman, & S.G. Miller (eds), *Berbers and Others: Beyond Tribe and Nation in the Maghrib* (pp. 1–13). Bloomington, IN: Indiana University Press.

Holes, C. (2004) *Modern Arabic: Structures, Functions and Varieties*. Washington DC: Georgetown University Press.

Isaac, R.K., & Hodge, D. (2011) 'An exploratory study: Justice tourism in controversial areas—the case of Palestine', *Tourism Planning & Development*, 8(1): 101–108.

Keohane, A. (2011) *Bedouin: Nomads of the Desert*. London: Kyle Books.

Khirfan, L. (ed.) (2017) *Order and Disorder: Urban Governance and the Making of Middle Eastern Cities*. Montreal: McGill-Queen's University Press.

League of Nations (1921) 'An Interim Report on the Civil Administration of Palestine'. Available online: https://unispal.un.org/DPA/DPR/unispal.nsf/0/349B02280A930813052565E90048ED1C (Accessed 22 January 2018).

Lew, A.A., Hall, C.M., & Timothy, D.J. (2015) *World Regional Geography: Human Mobilities, Tourism Destinations, Sustainable Environments*, 2nd edn. Dubuque, IA: Kendall-Hunt.

Lynch, M. (2016) 'Failed states and ungoverned spaces', *Annals of the American Academy of Political and Social Science*, 668(1): 24–35.

Maddy-Weitzman, B. (2011) *The Berber Identity Movement and the Challenge to North African States*. Austin, TX: University of Texas Press.

Mansfeld, Y. (1996) 'Wars, tourism and the "Middle East" factor', in A. Pizam, & Y. Mansfeld (eds), *Tourism, Crime and International Security Issues* (pp. 265–278). New York: Wiley.

Orbaşlı, A., & Woodward, S. (2008) 'A railway "route" as a linear heritage attraction: The Hijaz Railway in the Kingdom of Saudi Arabia', *Journal of Heritage Tourism*, 3(3): 159–175.

Rogers, A.E. (2012) 'La Maison de la Photographie: Tafza Berber Ecomuseum', *African Arts*, 45(2): 88–90.

Ron, A.S., & Timothy, D.J. (2019) *Contemporary Christian Travel: Pilgrimage, Practice and Place*. Bristol: Channel View Publications.

Sadiqi, F. (2014) 'Berber and language politics in the Moroccan educational system', in M. Ennaji (ed.), *Multiculturalism and Democracy in North Africa: Aftermath of the Arab Spring* (pp. 81–91). London: Routledge.

Shackley, M. (2002) 'The Frankincense Route: A proposed cultural itinerary for the Middle East', *Historic Environment*, 16(2): 12–17.

Sharkey, H.J. (2017) *A History of Muslims, Christians, and Jews in the Middle East*. Cambridge: Cambridge University Press.

Silverstein, P.A. (2010) 'The local dimensions of transnational Berberism: Racial politics, land rights, and cultural activism in southeastern Morocco', in K.E. Hoffman, & S.G. Miller (eds), *Berbers and Others: Beyond Tribe and Nation in the Maghrib* (pp. 83–102). Bloomington, IN: Indiana University Press.

Silverstein, P.A. (2012) 'In the name of culture: Berber activism and the material politics of "popular Islam" in southeastern Morocco', *Material Religion*, 8(3): 330–353.

Simon, R.S., Laskier, M.M., & Reguer, S. (eds) (2002) *Jews of the Middle East and North Africa in Modern Times*. New York: Columbia University Press.

Stewart, D.J. (2013) *The Middle East Today: Political, Geographical and Cultural Perspectives*. London: Routledge.

Timothy, D.J., & Daher, R.F. (2009) 'Heritage tourism in Southwest Asia and North Africa: Contested pasts and veiled realities', in D.J. Timothy, & G.P. Nyaupane (eds), *Cultural Heritage and Tourism in the Developing World: A Regional Perspective* (pp. 146–164). London: Routledge.

Tucker, S.C. (ed.) (2010) *The Encyclopedia of Middle East Wars: The United States in the Persian Gulf, Afghanistan and Iraq Conflicts*. Santa Barbara, CA: ABC-CLIO.

Watts, T. (2008) 'The Balfour Declaration', in S.C. Tucker, & P. Roberts (eds), *The Encyclopedia of the Arab–Israeli Conflict: A Political, Social, and Military History* (pp. 190–191). Santa Barbara, CA: ABC-CLIO.

Zubaida, S., & Tapper, R. (eds) (1994) *Culinary Cultures of the Middle East*. London: Tauris Academic Studies.

4

TOURISM TRENDS AND PATTERNS IN MENA

A resource perspective

Dallen J. Timothy

Introduction

Tourism is an extremely important part of the economic system of the Middle East and North Africa (MENA), and the region has been a significant tourist destination for centuries. For many years, Turkey has been one of the top destinations in the world and has held a strong position on the World Tourism Organization's (UNWTO) list of top destination countries (Ertugrul & Mangir 2015; Tosun, Timothy, & Öztürk 2003). However, recent terrorist activities since 2016, the spillover effects of the war next door in Syria, and political squabbles with Germany and the United States, two of Turkey's main market source countries, have resulted in significantly fewer international tourist arrivals, dislocating Turkey from the UNWTO's top ten list in 2016 and 2017. Morocco, Israel, Jordan, Egypt, Tunisia and the United Arab Emirates (UAE) have been leaders in tourism for many years, with the other countries being supporting destinations for decades.

As the previous chapters have clearly shown, MENA is rich in natural and cultural assets that wield considerable appeal for tourists. However, several countries have shied away from tourism, owing to its potential to clash with traditional beliefs and social practices, but nearly all of them have in the 2000s begun to target tourism as an economic development tool, especially those rentier states that have become wealthy based on fossil fuel resources. This chapter examines some of the most pressing tourism issues in MENA from a regional perspective, briefly examines some of the limited data available, and provides a country-by-country brief of some of the timeliest issues affecting tourism throughout the region.

Tourism patterns and trends

As Table 4.1 denotes, tourism data are sparse for MENA as a whole. This is true for various reasons. First, several countries tabulate their tourist arrivals differently. For example, some count all non-nationals arriving at border checkpoints (airports, seaports and land crossings), including day visitors, while others count only people who enter and stay overnight. Some countries distinguish between day-trippers, while others do not. Second, not all countries allow day-trippers, and many are not in a situation to receive cruise passengers, one of the most common day-visitor segments throughout the world. Third, and most obviously, are the war and conflict situations in the region. For example, while foreigners do enter Iraq for various travel purposes, the last year of arrivals data reported was 2010. Similar situations exist in Yemen, Syria and Libya. Fourth, some countries have only recently begun reporting certain types of arrivals (e.g. cruise passengers). Finally, some countries report only non-nationals who stay in hotels, resorts or other commercial lodging establishments, thereby ignoring the important segment of travellers who stay in non-commercial accommodations and with friends and relatives. Despite these complications, Table 4.1 provides a basic overview of tourist arrival patterns in MENA.

At the time of writing, tourist arrivals data for the MENA region was available for 2016 from the World Tourism Organization. That year, 110.9 million international tourists arrived in MENA, down by nearly ten million from the year before (121.1 million in 2015) (World Tourism Organization 2017b).

During the mid-2000s, the Middle East was one of the fastest growing destination regions in the world (Timothy & Nyaupane 2009). However, with the political crises that began in 2010 with the Arab Spring, followed by the Syrian, Libyan and Yemeni civil wars, overthrown governments in Egypt, Tunisia and Yemen, and the increased presence of extremist terrorist organisations throughout the region, tourism saw a notable decline up to 2018. Some countries' tourism was more heavily impacted by the political events than others, depending on the extent of conflict and public perceptions of safety. The countries that saw only minor protests during the Arab Spring and in its aftermath (e.g. Morocco, Jordan, Palestine, Kuwait, Bahrain, Oman, Saudi Arabia) saw only minor dips in arrivals in 2011–2012.

In Egypt, tourist arrivals plummeted in 2011 with the Egyptian revolution and again dropped by nearly half between 2015 and 2016, largely a result of multiple terror attacks against tourists in 2015, including the downing of a Russian passenger plane en route from Sharm el Sheikh to St Petersburg, killing everyone on board. The crash of EgyptAir flight 804 from Paris to Cairo over the Mediterranean near the coast of Egypt followed in May 2016. At the time of writing, the investigation of EgyptAir 804 was still ongoing, but many observers suspect terrorism. The 2015 crash was followed by numerous other attacks, and foiled attacks, that year near tourist resorts and hubs in Sinai and Cairo. The Arab Spring uprisings began in Tunisia in December 2010 with local protests against autocratic rule, spurred by the self-immolation of a street vendor in protest against government harassment. Soon after his death, solidarity spread throughout MENA effecting protests against autocratic regimes and perceived injustices in many countries, most notably Tunisia, Egypt, Yemen, Libya, Syria, Iraq, Lebanon, Algeria, Bahrain, Morocco, Oman, Jordan, Palestine and Kuwait. Despite the initial instability created by the Arab Spring revolt in 2011, Tunisia's tourism began to recover in 2013. However, two significant terrorist activities against tourists in 2015—the Bardo National Museum massacre on 18 March 2015, and the 26 June 2015 Sousse beach shootings—brought about a massive decline in tourist arrivals in Tunisia in 2015 and 2016, although the 2016 data show a slight increase in arrivals over 2015 with assurances from the new Tunisian government of its efforts to eradicate terrorism in the country and protect tourism interests (Selmi 2017).

While the Arab Spring movement affected most countries in the realm between 2011 and 2012, and terrorist activities and the Syrian civil war continue to influence tourism as a whole, a few countries have been successful in maintaining a steady growth in arrivals throughout this period. Iran, Kuwait, Lebanon, Oman and Qatar all saw moderately steady growth during the period of instability (2011–2016). Tourism in Israel and Palestine saw a drop in arrivals between 2014 and 2016, partly because of people's perceptions of the Syrian conflict next door, as well as localised knife attacks by Palestinians against Israelis and rocket launches from Gaza with Israel's retaliatory actions. Part of the decline, however, is ostensibly because of

Table 4.1 International tourism in MENA, 2012–2016

Country	2012 (000s)	2013 (000s)	2014 (000s)	2015 (000s)	2016 (000s)
Algeria					
Overnight	–	–	–	–	–
Same-day	–	–	–	–	–
Total	2,634	2,733	2,301	1,710	2,039
Bahrain					
Overnight	–	–	–	3,965	3,990
Same-day	–	–	–	5,706	6,168
Total	8,062	9,163	10,452	9,670	10,158
Egypt	11,196				
Overnight	336	9,174	9,628	9,139	5,258
Same-day	11,532	290	249	189	141
Total		9,464	9,878	9,328	5,399
Iran					
Overnight	–	–	–	–	–
Same-day	–	–	–	–	–
Total	3,834	4,769	4,967	5,237	4,942
Iraq					
Overnight	–	–	–	–	–
Same-day	–	–	–	–	–
Total	–	–	–	–	–
Israel					
Overnight	2,886	2,962	2,927	2,799	2,900
Same-day	635	578	324	309	170
Total	3,520	3,540	3,251	3,109	3,070
Jordan					
Overnight	4,162	3,945	3,990	3,761	3,858
Same-day	2,152	1,444	1,337	1,048	920
Total	6,314	5,389	5,327	4,809	4,779
Kuwait					
Overnight	300	307	198	182	203
Same-day	–	–	–	–	–
Total	5,729	6,217	6,528	6,941	7,055
Lebanon					
Overnight	1,366	1,274	1,355	1,518	1,688
Same-day	–	–	–	–	–
Total	–	–	–	–	–
Libya					
Overnight	–	–	–	–	–
Same-day	–	–	–	–	–
Total	–	–	–	–	–
Morocco					
Overnight	9,375	10,046	10,283	10,177	10,332
Same-day	455	303	359	365	345
Total	9,830	10,349	10,642	10,542	10,677

Table 4.1 (Cont.)

Country	2012 (000s)	2013 (000s)	2014 (000s)	2015 (000s)	2016 (000s)
Oman					
Overnight	1,241	1,392	1,611	1,909	2,292
Same-day	473	531	614	725	859
Total	1,714	1,934	2,225	2,634	3,151
Palestine					
Overnight	490	545	556	432	400
Same-day	2,561	2,661	2,527	1,907	1,175
Total	3,051	3,206	3,083	2,339	1,575
Qatar					
Overnight	2,324	2,612	2,839	2,941	2,938
Same-day	–	–	–	–	–
Total	–	–	–	–	–
Saudi Arabia					
Overnight	16,332	15,772	18,260	17,994	18,049
Same-day	3,515	4,162	4,750	3,840	2,931
Total	19,847	19,934	23,010	21,834	20,979
Syria					
Overnight	–	–	–	–	–
Same-day	–	–	–	–	–
Total	–	–	–	–	–
Tunisia					
Overnight	6,999	7,352	7,163	5,359	5,724
Same-day	–	–	–	–	–
Total	–	–	–	–	–
Turkey					
Overnight	35,698	37,795	39,811	39,478	30,289
Same-day	2,017	2,066	1,816	1,636	618
Total	37,715	39,861	41,627	41,114	30,907
UAE					
Overnight	–	–	13,200	14,200	14,910
Same-day	–	–	–	–	–
Total	–	–	–	–	–
Yemen					
Overnight	–	–	–	–	–
Same-day	–	–	–	–	–
Total	–	–	–	–	–

Source: Compiled from data in World Tourism Organization (2017b, 2018); Trading Economics (2018).

★ Same-day visitors include cruise passengers where applicable.

★★ Countries of MENA enumerate tourism differently.

the economic crisis in Russia and Eastern Europe, where many of the Holy Land's tourists originate (Shamah 2016). According to the World Tourism Organization's (2018) analysis, in 2017, North Africa saw a notable recovery with arrivals increasing by 13 per cent. The Middle East region received 5 per cent more tourists than the year before, reflecting sustained growth in some countries and a strong recovery in others. Much of this nascent recovery is a result of many MENA countries' efforts at recovery marketing and effective crisis management (Avraham 2015, 2016).

Resources and products

Regardless of the geopolitical volatility of the region, MENA is gifted with many cultural and natural assets that appeal to tourists and have the potential to attract more. As a result, there are many different types of tourism in MENA. Downhill snow skiing is available in Morocco, Lebanon, Algeria, Turkey, Iran and Israel. Nature-based tourism and ecotourism in the mountains and deserts is catching on quickly, and the long-established ethnic and cultural tourism products are gaining popularity in a region known for its ethnic diversity. The vibrant living cultures and tangible archaeological remnants of the region are vast and amongst the most recognisable heritage sites in the world (Timothy & Nyaupane 2009). There are currently 116 cultural UNESCO World Heritage Sites (WHSs), four natural WHSs, and five mixed WHSs in MENA, 22 of which are on UNESCO's list of World Heritage Sites in Danger. MENA has more WHSs on the danger list than any other region of the world, primarily because of war and terrorist destruction.

Beach and coastal resorts are increasingly popular in the UAE, Qatar, Turkey, Israel, Egypt, Morocco and Tunisia. The pervasive cruise sector calls in at various ports in the Persian Gulf, the Mediterranean, the Red Sea and the Gulf of Aqaba. While the cruise sector sees far fewer cruise ships and passenger landings than the northern Mediterranean and other heavily cruised areas of the world, it is an important sector that will likely see continued growth into the future. Although Turkey, Qatar, Egypt and the UAE are popular cruise destinations, they do not report cruise data to the World Tourism Organization. Of the countries where data are available, Morocco was the most visited in 2016, followed by Oman and Israel (Table 4.2).

Resorts and second-home clusters are being constructed rapidly in Qatar, Bahrain and the UAE, which are all leaders in the Persian Gulf trend towards hyper-development, seemingly trying to outdo one another with the utmost superlatives—the tallest, largest, busiest and most expensive. This hyperreal overdevelopment closely aligns with rising consumer classes, particularly those of Gulf citizens themselves: Qataris, Bahrainis and Emiratis. One consequence of this growing consumer class is the expansion of shopping mega-malls and amusement parks for citizens, expatriate residents and tourists.

Pilgrimage has a long history in many parts of MENA and is a very important type of tourism in Saudi Arabia and Israel, as well as in Iran, Iraq, Egypt, Turkey, Syria and Jordan. Most pilgrimages no longer resemble what they did a thousand years ago or even 30 years ago (Qurashi 2017; Ron & Timothy 2019). They are now more commercialised and profit-driven,

Table 4.2 Cruise passengers arriving in MENA countries, 2012–2016

Cruise destination country	2012	2013	2014	2015	2016
Bahrain	–	–	–	40,000	56,000
Israel	251,000	257,000	88,000	95,000	75,000
Jordan	85,000	96,000	36,000	34,000	57,000
Morocco	455,000	303,000	359,000	365,000	345,000
Oman	257,000	252,000	127,000	148,000	217,000

Source: Compiled from data in World Tourism Organization (2017a).

and according to the work of Qurashi (2017), *Hajj* pilgrimages have become overpriced to the point that they are out of reach for many poorer Muslims of the *Ummah* (the world's Islamic community). Christian tourism to the Holy Land is hardly the arduous journey that it once was and has largely taken on a pseudo-leisure characteristic in an overly touristified environment.

Tourism in the countries of MENA

Despite its vast potential, there are many concerns and issues facing tourism and its development in the MENA region (Almuhrzi, Alriyami, & Scott 2017; Daher 2007). These centre largely on natural resources and environmental challenges, cultural uniqueness and diversity, and geopolitical conditions.

Algeria

Algeria is blessed with a wide range of heritage resources—archaeological sites, historic city centres and citadels, mosques and churches with seven UNESCO World Heritage Sites as of 2018. It is also home to ten national parks and vast desert landscapes that cater to a potential nature-based tourism market. As well, there is an emerging ski industry in the Atlas Mountains in Chréa National Park. Although there is much potential for desert safaris and 4-wheel-drive activities, large areas of the Sahara are controlled by terrorist organisations and insurgency groups, and at present tourists are warned against visiting desert areas outside of cities and away from major highways.

The Western Sahara War (1975–1991) between the pro-independence Sahrawi insurgency group, Polisario, and Morocco officially ended with a ceasefire agreement in 1991, although there have been periodic skirmishes since that time. Presently, most of Western Sahara is controlled by Morocco, although about 20 per cent of the territory's area is controlled by the Sahrawi Arab Democratic Republic (SADR), which is essentially a government in exile. Several Sahrawi refugee camps were established in southwestern Algeria through the years of the war and are under the de facto administration of the SADR. Through collaboration with Algerian authorities, these refugee camps have begun to develop solidarity tourism and various other forms of 'responsible tourism' (arts and culture-based tourism), which are seen as an important tool for building support for the Sahrawi independence movement (Guia, van de Velde, & Chan 2017). This is an interesting and increasingly important manifestation of political tourism in the southern desert of Algeria.

Bahrain

Bahrain is a modern island state located in the Arabian/Persian Gulf. It is the smallest country in MENA in geographic area, but it has a range of important assets that it uses to develop its tourism industry. Like many Gulf States, Bahrain is attempting to diversify its economy away from petroleum dependence, which includes tourism development. Much of the country's tourism marketing focuses on ancient forts and castles that dot the arid landscape, some dating from 3000–4000 years ago. There are two WHSs in Bahrain, one of which commemorates the ancient civilisations of the country, while the other focuses on Bahrain's pearling industry, which formed a considerable part of the local merchant economy prior to the growth of the fossil fuels sector.

Perhaps most remarkable in tourism policy and practice is the country's physical development efforts that resemble those of the UAE and Qatar—luxury real estate and leisureplex developments (Bagaeen 2017). One example is Durrat Al Bahrain, a group of artificial islands built through land reclamation that host golf courses, luxury hotels, marinas, and residential areas. Other tourism mega-developments, including water parks and malls, are currently being built or are in the planning phase in Bahrain. Perhaps the most noteworthy architectural feature in the country, however, is the King Fahd Causeway—a 25km bridge connecting the tiny kingdom with Saudi Arabia. After decades of negotiations and planning, the causeway was opened in 1986, enabling greater cross-border travel between the two countries and facilitating thousands of car trips each day. Plans have also been underway to build the Qatar–Bahrain Causeway, construction of which was supposed to have started in 2008 or 2009, but owing to tensions between the neighbours, the project never came to fruition and is currently on hold (Timothy 2017).

Egypt

Historic records indicate that even in antiquity Egypt was a tourist destination and home to two of the Seven Wonders of the Ancient World. Egypt has traditionally been one of the most visited countries in MENA, often linked with visits to Israel as part of broader Holy Land tours amongst Christian package tourists, even since the early 1800s excursions of Thomas Cook (Ron & Timothy 2019). The Pyramids of Giza, the imposing Sphynx, and the elaborate Valley of the Kings have long exuded a heritage appeal accentuated by legendary Egyptologists, extraordinary archaeological finds (e.g. King Tutankhamen's tomb and mummified body), themed museums around the world, and motion pictures and television shows that depict the mystical life of the ancients.

Today, most of the tourism appeal of Egypt remains in the country's extraordinary ancient heritage and the reputation of the Nile River as the longest river in the world (although this is disputed with the Amazon) and the history associated with it. Supplementing the heritage element has been the growth of coastal resorts in recent years, particularly along the Red Sea and Gulf of Aqaba at Sharm El Sheikh, Hurghada, and Port Ghalib, as well as Nile River and Red Sea cruises.

In 1979, a peace treaty was signed between Egypt and Israel, which eventually opened up their common border to cross-border travel by Israelis, Egyptians and others, which found moderate success at various times between the 1980s and the 2000s. Many Israelis spent their holidays in Sinai resorts, such as Taba and Sharm El Sheikh, although this was generally a one-way flow of tourists. Since around 2007, this flow has reduced dramatically owing to an increased presence of extremist militant groups and terrorist organisations gaining a foothold in the Sinai Peninsula with the stated aim of targeting Israelis who venture across the border.

These incidents, and many others since the 1990s, have affected tourism in Egypt significantly. Several terrorist attacks have targeted tourists directly, including bombings, shootings and kidnappings. The Arab Spring of 2011, or here known as the Egyptian Revolution, led to the end of the Mubarak administration, replacing it with a handful of subsequent governments in intervening years. The current administration has made considerable strides to ensure tourist security and stability, including along the border with Israel, but the country's security environment is fragile, and tourism continues to be affected by the terror activities of, and threats by, extremist organisations (Esmail 2016).

Iran

Iran is an enormous country with a wide range of climates and physiographic regions. It has high, snow-capped mountains, arid deserts, fertile river valleys, woodlands, grasslands, and many other physiographic and vegetation regimes. This has determined how the country's cultures have thrived or diminished, how its infrastructure has been developed, and how tourism has grown or not. Perhaps more than any other force in Iran, however, has been its geopolitical relations with other countries since the Revolution of 1979 (Khodadadi 2016).

Iran is culturally different from other countries in MENA in that its population adheres overwhelmingly to Shia Islam rather than the Sunni Islam, which dominates most other countries in the realm. As well, its population is largely Persian rather than Arab. While Shiite Muslims also are required to undertake the *Hajj* at least once in their lifetime, there are many Shiite shrines and holy places in Iran that drive a thriving pilgrimage tourism market both domestically and amongst the Shiite populations in other countries. By mid-2018, Iran was home to 22 UNESCO sites and 13 elements of living culture on UNESCO's List of Intangible Cultural Heritage. Owing to its size and physical and cultural diversity, Iran's tourism resources are virtually innumerable. As a result, many types of tourism have developed and been promoted in recent years, including snow skiing, cruises and sailing, heritage and culture, medical, religious pilgrimages, shopping, food and cuisine, ecotourism, agritourism, business and educational tourism, and many others. There is even limited beachfront tourism in a few designated areas, such as Kish Island (Timothy 2017).

Despite occasional street protests, Iran is a relatively safe tourist destination, although some Western governments warn against travel there owing to risks of arbitrary arrests and detentions, especially amongst academics, dual Iranian nationals, and journalists. Sour relations between Iran and several Western countries (e.g. the United States, Canada, the UK) and economic boycotts have resulted in few travellers from these countries visiting Iran, which has had ripple effects on other nationalities visiting the country as well. Prior to the Islamic Revolution of 1979, tourism thrived and Iran had harmonious relations with most Western countries.

Iraq

At the time of writing, Iraq is still embroiled in armed conflict brought about by the US-led invasion of 2003, the subsequent establishment of ISIS, and an ongoing civil war since 2014. Although the US-led Iraq War officially ended in 2011, terrorist cells continue to operate within the country, and Iraq has been embroiled in a war against ISIS, which held large swaths of territory for many months, although its position in mid-2018 had shrunk to small pockets in Iraq and Syria. Most Western governments warn their citizens against visiting Iraq owing to continued hostility, armed conflict, kidnappings and terrorist activities. Despite these warnings, a small tourism industry has functioned throughout the 2000s, particularly fuelled by Iranian religious pilgrims, European adventure tourists, and the active promotional efforts of the Kurdish regional authorities, which is seen as the safest part of Iraq. In 2013, approximately 892,000 foreign tourists visited the country (Index Mundi 2018), although shortly thereafter the main conflict involving ISIS and the economic crisis in Iran saw tourism come to a standstill.

Iraq's primary tourist appeal is its built heritage. The country is home to a rich and varied patrimony that dates back to the earliest part of the Anthropocene. Present-day Iraq (ancient Mesopotamia (the Fertile Crescent)) is the birthplace of many innovations, including a written alphabet, the wheel and wheeled vehicles, standardised agricultural practices, sailboats, mathematics, the calendar, and much more. It hosts many of the ancient localities described in the Old Testament, including Ur (the hometown of Abraham), Nineveh, Babylon, the Tigris and Euphrates Rivers, and the location of the fabled Tower of Babel. Deriving from this rich human history are five WHSs, although three of them are on UNESCO's List of World Heritage in Danger as a result of the Iraq War, targeted destruction by ISIS, and the country's ongoing civil war.

Iraq has considerable potential for tourism owing to its vast cultural and natural heritage resources, most of which are inaccessible at present but which could become salient attractions when political tensions die down. The country is home to Shiite Muslim shrines and sacred sites that attract many visitors each year from neighbouring Iran, even during times of crisis. While the majority of the country's urban infrastructure and much of its built heritage have suffered severe destruction, there are areas of Iraq that remain open to tourist visitation (McGahey 2006).

Israel

Pilgrimage and other types of religious tourism are Israel's primary form of tourism. Israel, together with Palestine and Jordan (and sometimes Egypt), is often referred to as the Holy Land because of its important role in the development of Christianity and Judaism. While Israel is a popular destination for the world's Jewish population (Cohen Ioannides & Ioannides 2006), and a limited number of Muslim tourists when they are able to get permission from their home states to visit, Christians are especially drawn to Israel because of its central role in the life of Jesus and the development of Christianity. While Christian tours are popular year-round, Easter and Christmas are especially busy as people desire to spend their religious holidays in the places best associated with these commemorative celebrations. Religious tourists visit both Old and New Testament localities in Israel, and the country's tourism infrastructure is geared overwhelmingly to meeting the needs of this lucrative market (Ron & Timothy 2019).

Jewish diaspora-based tourism is also popular in Israel and takes several forms. The first is people visiting friends and relatives either who are from Israel originally or who have migrated there later. Second, many Jews visit important sacred and secular Jewish sites, such as the Western Wall and Masada. The third diasporic form of tourism is the return to the Jewish homeland to celebrate holidays, festivals and bar mitzvahs and bat mitzvahs. There is a growing specialised industry in Israel that caters mitzvah celebrations to the global Jewish diaspora. Volunteering on kibbutzim is another form of Jewish tourism to Israel that has gained popularity in recent years. Finally is the phenomenon known as Birthright Israel (*taglit*), which enables Jewish youth from around the world to 'discover' Israel, build solidarity with the state and enhance their Jewish identity (Abramson 2017).

In addition to religious affiliation and heritage, Israel is home to a flourishing sun, sea and sand tourism sector, especially on the Red Sea at Eilat and near Tel Aviv on the Mediterranean. Likewise, the Dead Sea has long been a popular destination for swimming and healthcare. Today, health and medical tourism are booming at the Dead Sea, and the area is home to a bustling health tourism sector with therapy centres, spas and hospitals that cater to the needs of Israeli and foreign medical tourists.

Israel has a booming domestic tourism sector, even amongst devout Orthodox Jews (*haredi*) (Cahaner & Mansfeld 2012). While Israelis frequently undertake short-haul international travel by air in the Mediterranean, domestic tourism has become popular in part because of the country's political isolation from many of its belligerent Arab neighbours, which makes travelling abroad to neighbouring states nearly impossible or difficult at best.

Jordan

Like its neighbours, Israel and Palestine, Jordan has a rich archaeological heritage that provides much of the country's tourist appeal. Jerash and Petra are the most important archaeological sites in the country. The Petra UNESCO World Heritage Site was voted one of the New Seven Wonders of the World in 2007, which increased its visibility, although it has long been a popular archaeological attraction for many decades. Petra is a popular day-trip destination from Amman, the capital, and the resort town of Aqaba, as well as from Israel. The native people near Petra are often cited as one of the premier examples of indigenous Bedouins being involved in tourism (Al-Oun & Al-Homoud 2008; Paradise 2016).

There is an important Christian tourism industry in Jordan with the Jordan River and the Baptismal Site of Jesus being important attractions, together with Mount Nebo and Madaba. Health tourism is gaining popularity on the Dead Sea, and there are a growing number of beach resorts on the Gulf of Aqaba in the far south, where scuba diving has become particularly popular. Numerous nature preserves play host to rock climbers and other outdoor enthusiasts, which is a sector the tourism authorities are beginning to hone in on more.

The 1994 Israel–Jordan peace treaty officially established bilateral relations and opened up the frontier for cross-border travel and collaboration. This has enabled more Israeli tourists to visit their neighbours to the east and foreign tourists to cross the border in both directions. It has ostensibly also opened opportunities for Jordanians to visit Israel and the West Bank, but the majority of cross-border flows have been unidirectional. While the bilateral relations are serving a significant tourism purpose, the treaty is still fragile, and many Israelis remain reluctant to visit Jordan and vice versa without joining an organised tour package.

Kuwait

Kuwait is one of the few countries in MENA that has not set its sights high on tourism as an economic development tool (Kelly 2017). As a result, tourism is quite modest. Most tourism in the country has traditionally been related to business travel in conjunction with the oil industry, and several resort hotels have been built over the past quarter century to cater to this specific market segment. Kuwait is also home to a number of large-scale amusement parks and shopping malls that cater not only to a wealthy Kuwaiti clientele but also to an increasing international cohort of visitors.

While Kuwait has several important landmarks and historic sites, such as the Kuwait Towers, the Grand Mosque and the archaeological sites on Failaka Island (Paris 2017), there is little by way of cultural heritage-based tourism development. However, with growing interest in the latent aspects of tourism in the country, authorities are contemplating building a high-capacity international airport to allow expanded growth in arrivals as the entire Gulf region becomes increasingly popular as a tourism destination; Kuwait has an interest in linking with other Gulf States to develop its tourism product.

Lebanon

Tourism has been an important part of Lebanon's economy for many years. Prior to its brutal civil war (1975–1990), Beirut was known as the 'Paris of the Middle East' owing to its wide avenues, French and Arab inspired architecture, cleanliness and visitability. The war destroyed much of the built environment of Beirut and other cities, but efforts are currently under way to rebuild and renovate the capital (Ladki & Dah 1997). The loss of life was immense (more than

125,000 killed), and several religious-cultural factions were involved in the long conflict. This caused tourism to fall drastically, although since the 1990s, it has begun to recover, albeit slowly and carefully. Growth has been slow not only because of the global image engrained by the civil war but also because of the country's ongoing conflict with Israel, the prominent presence of the Hezbollah terror organisation and, because Lebanon borders Syria, which is currently involved in its own civil war, there is potential for the conflict to spill into Lebanon.

In spite of its history of conflict, Lebanon is working hard to grow tourism and proceed with counter-marketing efforts. The country is home to many world-class archaeological sites, including Anjar, Baalbek, Byblos, Tyre and the Forest of the Cedars of God—all UNESCO WHSs. Most of Lebanon's nascent tourism is based upon its ancient heritage, modern cities, and preserves where the famed Cedars of Lebanon are protected. Beyond its cultural heritage, the country's tourism officials are continuing to emphasise natural heritage with the ecotourism, adventure tourism and mountain skiing that go along with it.

There is also an important Christian heritage that draws pilgrims from around the world, particularly from other areas of the Middle East, to visit ancient monasteries and other holy Christian sites, such as Sidon and Tyre, which were both key cities in the development of Christianity. Part of the country's famous heritage is its traditional cuisine. Lebanese food is an important part of the heritage product of Lebanon but is also one of the most popular ethnic foods throughout the world; much Middle Eastern food inside and outside the region is based upon an 'idealised' Lebanese gastronomy.

Libya

Tourism has traditionally not been an important part of the Libyan economy. Even before the country's recent civil war (2011–present), tourism did not play a major role in the economy, and fewer than 200,000 tourists visited the country each year. With the onset of the 2011 Arab Spring-inspired civil war, which overthrew the dictator Muammar Gaddafi, tourism essentially disappeared. Today, Libya is considered a no-go zone for tourists, with various factions, including an ineffective national government, ruling different parts of the country, and the country is seen as a hotbed for terrorist activity. Almost every tourist source country in the world warns its citizens against travel to Libya.

Despite the country's current security crisis, it has significant potential for tourism development in the future, if conditions improve (Lafferty & Youssef 2015). It is home to five WHSs, which are all on the Danger List owing to the ongoing civil war and the various factions' propensity to target heritage places to make a political statement. Some of the best Roman and Greek archaeological sites in the southern Mediterranean are located on the coast of Libya, but their protection has taken a back burner to security concerns. Under normal conditions, the Sahara would provide an important backdrop for ecotourism and adventure tourism, but warring factions control much of the desert region, placing it beyond the reach of tourism.

Morocco

Morocco has one of the most successful tourism industries in MENA, receiving more than 10 million tourists each year. It has a large diversity of assets and tourism products that cater to a wide market; however, Morocco is primarily a heritage tourism destination. Its ancient cities with their marketplaces and medinas have attracted traders and tourists for centuries, and the depictions of its cities such as Casablanca, Fez and Marrakesh in motion pictures have made it an important film-induced destination for many years. In addition to its historic cities, there are also a number of tourist resorts that have become important winter destinations for Europeans, for example Agadir and Tarfaya on the Atlantic coast.

Travel across the Strait of Gibraltar between Spain and Tangier has long been a popular activity. A 'side trip to Africa' is a popular addition to journeys in southern Spain and Gibraltar. Frequent ferry services between Spain and Morocco have enabled this sort of adventure that links Europe and Africa, albeit a small sampling of North Africa, to trips in southern Europe. The boat services are also a standard means of tourist transport between the two continents.

The Atlas Mountains provide several different tourism opportunities. Trekking is becoming increasingly popular in the mountains, and although few people tend to associate North Africa with skiing, winter precipitation provides adequate snowfall for a handful of ski resorts that often tout themselves as less-expensive and less-crowded alternatives to those in Europe. The mountains are also home to many unique villages and towns with thriving cultures. The Berber population is increasingly involved in tourism both as an attraction and as service providers.

Morocco's tourism success is largely a result of the country's political stability in a rather unstable region. However, it is still embroiled in a conflict with the indigenous people of Western Sahara, the Sahrawis. Morocco claims control over Western Sahara and has fought the Polisario Front (the internationally recognised representative government over the Sahrawi people) since the early 1970s. Most of Western Sahara continues to be occupied by Morocco, while the eastern portion is occupied by the Polisario Front, and there are large Sahrawi refugee camps nearby in Algeria. While the Sahrawis' main concern is an independent homeland, they are interested in developing tourism as noted earlier in the Algeria section.

Oman

Oman is a geographically fragmented state. The Musandam Peninsula on the northeasternmost point of the Arabian Peninsula and the nearby Omani exclave of Madha are separate from the main part of the country and have become salient 4-wheel drive safari and adventure tourism destinations. Tourists must pass through the UAE to get to either one of these fragmented portions of Oman, which in a sense adds to the appeal of visiting (Timothy 2017). Other parts of Oman have also developed into prominent ecotourism destinations (Alriyami, Scott, Ragam, & Jafari 2017).

Besides being physically fragmented, Oman is also one of the most stable countries of the Middle East. It is often seen as a safe haven in a difficult region. This has resulted in tourism dividends, and tourism is projected to be one of the country's primary economic sectors in the next decade or so. Several coastal areas have undergone development with resorts, and the cruise sector is becoming increasingly important at the port of Muscat (Atef & Al-Balushi 2017).

Palestine

The most pressing issue for Palestine's tourism sector is Israel's occupation of Palestinian lands and its control of tourism and the local economy in general. Owing to its occupation of the West Bank and East Jerusalem, as well as its blockade of the Gaza Strip, Israel has power over the flow of goods, services and people in and out of Palestine and the external elements of tourism supply and demand. Tourism in Palestine, thus, is entirely at the mercy of Israel's policies and military practices (Isaac 2010). For example, while Palestine itself does not require visas of foreign nationals, Israel in many cases does, and all visitors to Palestine must pass through Israel or Israeli-controlled areas of the West Bank.

Owing to the ongoing conflict between Gaza and Israel, the Gaza Strip is inaccessible to general tourists. Israelis are not allowed to enter the areas of the West Bank controlled militarily and civically by Palestinian authorities, and with few exceptions, most Palestinians who reside in Palestine are not permitted to enter Israel, especially for tourism purposes, which includes travel abroad to third countries. Approximately half of all tourists in Palestine are Palestinian domestic visitors; international visitors are comprised largely of foreign tourists who cross into Palestine on day trips to see Bethlehem, Jericho and a handful of other localities.

The main foreign market for Palestine comprises Christian tourists from North America and Europe. Their primary destination is Jerusalem, where they celebrate the life, ministry and crucifixion of Jesus; Bethlehem, where they commemorate the birth of Jesus; and Jericho, which also has significant biblical associations. For domestic visitors, the cities of Jenin, Hebron, Nablus and Ramallah are especially popular destinations as centres of culture and art, urban tourism, history and religion (Isaac, Hall, & Higgins-Desbiolles 2016). There are many cultural heritage attractions in Palestine, and the country's Ministry of Tourism and Antiquities is devoting considerable effort towards developing hiking trail-based tourism, special events and festivals and heritage cuisine-based tourism.

Qatar

Like its Persian Gulf neighbours, Qatar has a fossil fuel-dependent economy. However, officials recognise that supplies are not limitless and therefore have decided to consider other economic sectors, particularly tourism. Much of Qatar's tourism demand has originated from other Gulf Cooperation Council and MENA countries, but with the June 2017 diplomatic crisis led by Saudi Arabia in response to Qatar's ostensible support of terrorist activities and connections to Iran, several of its traditional allies in the region, including Saudi Arabia, the UAE, Yemen, Bahrain, Egypt and Libya enacted a strict embargo. This action resulted in limited trade with, and travel to and from, Qatar. To make up for the downturn in arrivals in 2017 and 2018, the country's tourism authorities are turning to other lucrative markets, including Russia and India, and expanding their cruise tourism capacity (Qatar Tribune 2017). According to a report by the Qatar Tribune (2017), approximately 21 cruise ships were scheduled to call at Doha between October 2017 and April 2018, and passenger arrivals are expected to exceed 300,000 through the 2019–2020 season, up from 47,000 just two years earlier. The embargo also saw the closing of the Qatar–Saudi Arabia border, which meant that access to Qatar was limited only to air and sea arrivals far into 2018.

Large-scale urban development, resembling some of that in Dubai and other areas of the UAE, is also occurring in Qatar (Scharfenort 2017). Luxury residential and resort areas on reclaimed land, and the development of large-scale hyperreal shopping malls, are characteristic of Qatar's tourism landscape today. Sport tourism is also now being targeted by Qatari tourism authorities as a lucrative activity, and the country has seen considerable interest in this area at the small scale with desert races and on a large scale with multinational competitions. Qatar hosted the 2006 Asian Games and also acquired the rights to host the 2022 FIFA World Cup, which has stimulated a great deal of construction and infrastructure development in and around Doha.

Saudi Arabia

Saudi Arabia's most famous tourism product is the Islamic pilgrimages in Mecca and Medina—the *Hajj* and *Umrah* (a pilgrimage in Mecca with similarities to the Hajj but which can be done at any time of the year) and other pilgrimages known as *ziarat* (Timothy & Iverson 2006).

There, during the month of *Zul-Hijja*, approximately 2.5 million people gather to participate in sacred rites and rituals. Mecca has developed far beyond the spartan pilgrim destination it once was to become a centre of urban growth and luxurious pilgrimage facilities and services (Qurashi 2017). Large, international chain hotels now dot the landscape, and plethoric tour operators provide modern packaged pilgrimage experiences for the hajjis who can afford it. There has been considerable debate in recent years about the suitability of the touristification or over-commercialisation of the religious sites in Mecca and Medina, which has even called into question Saudi Arabia's ability to be the keeper of the holy places.

Saudi Arabia still does not issue regular individual tourist visas. It issues *Hajj* visas to pilgrims, individual business travellers and people visiting friends and relatives (VFR), as well as group visas to members of organised tours. While most of the country's wealth continues to be tied to the oil sector, officials are beginning to realise the economic potential of tourism outside the realm of pilgrimage, VFR and business travel. Dune safaris in the Rub' al Khali (the Empty Quarter and largest sand desert in the world) are organised and sold, and visits to cultural sites are becoming more common.

Syria

Syria also has great potential for tourism, but because of the civil war, which was spurred by the Arab Spring in 2011 (Ali, Arifin, & Hasim 2012) and continues at the time of writing, it is currently a virtual impossibility. All Western countries have issued strong travel warnings against visiting Syria, airlines have cancelled all services, most of its borders are closed, most hotels outside Damascus have shut their doors, and ISIS and the civil war have destroyed many of the country's best historic sites and cities. Traditionally, however, Syria has been an important pilgrimage destination for Muslims and various ancient Christian denominations. The Umayyad Mosque (Great Mosque) of Damascus is considered one of the holiest Islamic shrines, and the country is home to some of the Middle East's oldest Byzantine-era churches and monasteries (Walker 2004). All six of Syria's World Heritage Sites are vitally in danger. Some of them were destroyed or heavily damaged by the Islamic State's occupation (e.g. Palmyra and Ancient Aleppo), and landmines are believed to be present throughout many archaeological areas. Despite the war, small numbers of domestic tourists have continued to visit coastal areas and historic sites in the safer parts of the country.

Tunisia

For more than 60 years, Tunisia has been an important Mediterranean destination with several resort areas having developed along the coast. Its popular beach resorts have drawn tourists from all over the world, especially from northern Europe, although its heritage sites have complemented the resort development and in fact are an important tourist attraction in their own right. The Phoenician and Roman ruins of Carthage are amongst the best-known heritage sites in North Africa and are a UNESCO World Heritage Site, together with the medinas of Sousse and Tunis. The country is host to several other WHSs, including Ichkeul National Park with its wetlands and migratory birds. As noted above, the 2011 Arab Spring, which affected most of MENA, originated in Tunisia in December 2010 and resulted in the overthrow of President Zine El Abidine Ben Ali, who had ruled for nearly a quarter of a century. Despite a few notable terror attacks aimed directly at tourists in 2015, the country's tourism industry appears to be making a slight comeback through counter-marketing efforts and an increased security presence (Esmail 2016).

Turkey

Turkey's tourism sector is the most developed and best known in MENA, and as noted earlier, Turkey attracts more tourists than any other country in the realm. The country is home to many national parks, multitudes of archaeological sites, numerous WHSs, mountain landscapes, living cultures, a diverse and well-regarded culinary heritage, and Mediterranean beach resorts in the area of Antalya (Lew, Hall, & Timothy 2015; Tosun, Timothy, & Öztürk 2003). As well, for decades, cruises have been an important element of Turkey's tourism, and several ports have actively sought cruise tourism based on the country's sunshine and beaches and its ancient heritage, much of it associated with Christian history. Owing to its connections to ancient Christianity, Turkey has also become a salient destination for New Testament-oriented package tours and biblical cruises (Ron & Timothy 2019).

Due to its large size, physical geography, varied history and the longevity of its tourism industry, Turkey is home to many different types of tourism that appeal to a wide range of visitor segments, attracting between 35 and 40 million foreign tourists each year. However, owing to the general climate of instability in the country and in neighbouring Syria, arrivals have plummeted from 41 million in 2015 to 31 million in 2016, although a slight gain was achieved in 2017 with slightly more than 32 million foreign arrivals that year (Hürriyet Daily News 2018). Several events and processes in the past few years have tainted the image of Turkey. The 2016 attempted coup d'état and President Erdogan's heavy-handed response, increased religious conservatism and nationalistic rhetoric in general, arguments with major market source countries (e.g. Germany and the US), the Syrian war spilling over the border, violent revolutionary activities by Kurdish rebels, and terrorist activities associated with ISIS, have all destabilised much of the economic sector and social life of Turkey and caused a notable decline in international arrivals.

Turkey desires to join the European Union and has been working closely with the European Commission for many years to achieve the goals needed for accession to the bloc. However, chronic financial problems, recent issues pertaining to rule of law, and concerns over human rights related to the Kurds and the failed 2016 coup and the purges that ensued have raised roadblocks to the country's moving closer to joining the union (Cornell 2018).

United Arab Emirates

Soon after their 1968 independence from the United Kingdom, the Gulf emirates, known at the time as the Trucial States, decided to merge into one country. On 2 December 1971, the emirates (principalities) of Abu Dhabi, Ajman, Dubai, Fujairah, Sharjah and Umm al-Quwain unified into a single state—the United Arab Emirates. A few months later, Ras Al Khaimah joined the others, completing the country as it is known today. With vast oil reserves, the UAE became dependent on petroleum for its livelihood and rapid development, replacing the historic traditions of fishing and pearl diving. In recent years, however, under the direction of various emirs, the country has diversified its national economy beyond oil-based rentier capitalism to include other industries, especially tourism and its subsidiary real estate development.

Although cultural heritage is important to the Emiratis and to the country's overall tourism plans, it is frequently eclipsed by the rapid urban development of Dubai and to a lesser extent Abu Dhabi. The most visited and best-known city/emirate in the country is Dubai, which, in recent years, has actively sought to develop a high-end, luxury destination brand (Lew, Hall, & Timothy 2015). Dubai is home to the world's first (self-proclaimed) seven-star hotel, the Burj

Al Arab, and the tallest building in the world, the Burj Khalifa (828 metres). Intense resort and luxury living developments (e.g. the Palm Islands, the World), ubiquitous mall construction, and airport/airline hub development have also been a trademark of Dubai's hyper-development. Dubai has become synonymous with efforts to be the most superlative (largest, tallest) in spatio-economic growth (Lawton & Weaver 2017), leading to what some observers equate with the Disneyfication of the desert (Thani & Heenan 2017). Not to be left completely behind Dubai, massive tourism developments are also currently underway in Abu Dhabi, including luxury housing areas, mega-resorts and hotels, sport facilities and theme parks. Dubai and Abu Dhabi's international airports are two of the world's busiest transit hubs, and their airlines, Emirates and Etihad, are ranked amongst the world's best.

The other emirates are much less physically developed, although they too have seen a boom in hotel and resort growth in recent years. Ajman, Fujairah, Ras Al Khaimah, Sharjah and Umm al-Quwain are considered cosier and often more authentic or traditional destinations within the UAE, free of the urban chaos and hyper-development of Dubai and Abu Dhabi.

The UAE is becoming increasingly known as a medical, shopping and sport tourism destination—all of which are closely associated with the rapid urbanisation and luxury tourism that are characteristic of Dubai and Abu Dhabi. Desert safaris and other nature-based activities are an increasingly important element of tourism in the other emirates.

Yemen

One of Yemen's strengths is its diversity of built heritage, and most of its incoming tourism has traditionally focused on this asset (Soltanzadeh & Moghaddam 2015). The country is currently home to four WHSs (even though they are on the danger list), remarkable historic cities and interesting natural environments. The Socotra Archipelago is home to some of the most intriguing endemic plant species in the world and is the part of the country least affected by the current civil war. Although Yemen has prodigious potential for tourism owing to its unique natural and cultural heritage, current hostilities have essentially halted all tourism, with the exception of a trickle of returnees from the Yemeni diaspora coming home to visit family members. As of 2018, however, it has become common for Yemenis to arrange meetings and reunions with overseas relatives in nearby third countries, such as Oman.

The current civil war (2015–present), sparked by the 2011 Arab Spring, has resulted in sections of the country being controlled by rebel forces, the official government, terrorist organisations and sundry other factions, as well as outright cross-border hostility and weaponised skirmishes with Saudi Arabia (Ali, Arifin, & Hasim 2012; Sharp 2017). Western governments routinely warn their citizens against travelling there, most hotels have shuttered their doors, and the national airline, Yemenia, has suspended normal operations since 2015, with occasional services beginning and ending unpredictably between 2015 and 2018.

Conclusion

This chapter took an inbound tourism approach from a primarily supply-side perspective. However, much could still be said about domestic tourism in the countries of MENA, as well as intra-regional and outbound travel. While not explicitly a part of this chapter, these are touched upon in other parts of the book. The diversity of supply and demand for tourism in the Middle East and North Africa in light of its geopolitical and ecological challenges, makes the region an exceptional laboratory for studying tourism and its characteristics from supply and demand perspectives, especially in terms of innovation and adaptation.

The Middle East and North Africa is home to vast and diverse cultural and natural landscapes punctuated by religious traditions, commerce and oil production, rapid urbanisation, hyperreal leisurescapes, war and malcontent, to name only a few influential stimuli. All of these forces have helped shape tourism development, or prevented it. Despite regional conflicts and deepening environmental challenges, many countries have developed successful tourism industries. Most identifiable types of tourism are present in MENA, although not every country is interested in developing them. Some countries have been reluctant to cultivate certain types of tourism (e.g. beach resorts) owing to their adverse social connotations, or even tourism at all, but the majority now realise not only its supplementary fiscal potential but also its central role in an increasingly diverse future economy. Each country's history and geography determine which ways tourism manifests and how enthusiastic the state will be to encourage tourists to come. Despite some national similarities in tourism planning, policy, and supply and services, these geographical and historical realities have resulted in 20 unique models of tourism development that reflect the dynamics of a region unlike any other.

References

Abramson, Y. (2017) 'Making a homeland, constructing a diaspora: The case of Taglit-Birthright Israel', *Political Geography*, 58: 14–23.

Ali, A., Arifin, Z., & Hasim, S. (2012) 'The challenges of tourism in the countries of the Arab spring revolutions', *Advances in Natural and Applied Sciences*, 6(7): 1162–1171.

Almuhrzi, H., Alriyami, H., & Scott, N. (eds) (2017) *Tourism in the Arab World: An Industry Perspective*. Bristol: Channel View Publications.

Al-Oun, S., & Al-Homoud, M. (2008) 'The potential for developing community-based tourism among the Bedouins in the Badia of Jordan', *Journal of Heritage Tourism*, 3(1): 36–54.

Alriyami, H., Scott, N., Ragam, A.M., & Jafari, J. (2017) 'Evaluating ecotourism challenges in Oman', in M.L. Stephenson, & A. Al-Hamarneh (eds), *International Tourism Development and the Gulf Cooperation Council States: Challenges and Opportunities* (pp. 156–168). London: Routledge.

Atef, T.M., & Al-Balushi, M. (2017) 'Cruising market in Oman: Current trends and future perspectives', *Journal of Tourism and Hospitality Management*, 5(1): 1–14.

Avraham, E. (2015) 'Destination image repair during crisis: Attracting tourism during the Arab Spring uprisings', *Tourism Management*, 47: 224–232.

Avraham, E. (2016) 'Destination marketing and image repair during tourism crises: The case of Egypt', *Journal of Hospitality and Tourism Management*, 28: 41–48.

Bagaeen, S. (2017) 'Tourism development in Bahrain: Dealing with flux and transformation', in M.L. Stephenson, & A. Al-Hamarneh (eds), *International Tourism Development and the Gulf Cooperation Council States: Challenges and Opportunities* (pp. 95–110). London: Routledge.

Cahaner, L., & Mansfeld, Y. (2012) 'A voyage from religiousness to secularity and back: A glimpse into "Haredi" tourists', *Journal of Heritage Tourism*, 7(4): 301–321.

Cornell, S.E. (2018) 'The Kurdish question in Turkish politics', in M.S. Radu (ed.), *Dangerous Neighborhood: Contemporary Issues in Turkey's Foreign Relations* (pp. 123–142). London: Routledge.

Daher, R.F. (ed.) (2007) *Tourism in the Middle East: Continuity, Change and Transformation*. Clevedon: Channel View Publications.

Ertugrul, H.M., & Mangir, F. (2015) 'The tourism-led growth hypothesis: Empirical evidence from Turkey', *Current Issues in Tourism*, 18(7): 633–646.

Esmail, H.A.H. (2016) 'Impact of terrorism and instability on the tourism industry in Egypt and Tunisia after revolution', *The Business & Management Review*, 7(5): 469–475.

Guia, J., van de Velde, S., & Chan, L. (2017) 'New forms of "responsible tourism" in refugee camps and contested regions: The case of Western Sahara', Paper presented at the BEST EN Think Tank 17, Innovation and Progress in Sustainable Tourism, University of Mauritius.

Hürriyet Daily News (2018) '32.4 mln foreigners visit Turkey in 2017: Tourism Ministry', *Hürriyet Daily News*, 21 January 2018. Available online: www.hurriyetdailynews.com/32-4-mln-foreigners-visit-turkey-in-2017-tourism-ministry-126559 (Accessed 10 February 2018).

Index Mundi (2018) 'Iraq—International tourism'. Available online: www.indexmundi.com/facts/iraq/international-tourism (Accessed 22 February 2018).

Isaac, R.K. (2010) 'Alternative tourism: New forms of tourism in Bethlehem for the Palestinian tourism industry', *Current Issues in Tourism*, 13(1): 21–36.

Isaac, R.K., Hall, C.M., & Higgins-Desbiolles, F. (eds) (2016) *The Politics and Power of Tourism in Palestine*. London: Routledge.

Kelly, M. (2017) '(No) tourism in Kuwait: Why Kuwaitis are ambivalent about developing tourism', in M.L. Stephenson, & A. Al-Hamarneh (eds), *International Tourism Development and the Gulf Cooperation Council States: Challenges and Opportunities* (pp. 111–123). London: Routledge.

Khodadadi, M. (2016) 'A new dawn? The Iran nuclear deal and the future of the Iranian tourism industry', *Tourism Management Perspectives*, 18: 6–9.

Ladki, S.M., & Dah, A. (1997) 'Challenges facing post-war tourism development: The case of Lebanon', *Journal of International Hospitality, Leisure & Tourism Management*, 1(2): 35–43.

Lafferty, G., & Youssef, J. (2015) 'Beyond the Arab Spring: Evaluating Libya's long-term tourism potential', *Tourism Management Perspectives*, 14: 55–62.

Lawton, L.J., & Weaver, D.B. (2017) 'Destination brands Dubai and Abu Dhabi: Bitter rivalry or strategic partnership?' in H. Almuhrzi, H. Alriyami, & N. Scott (eds), *Tourism in the Arab World: An Industry Perspective* (pp. 161–174). Bristol: Channel View Publications.

Lew, A.A., Hall, C.M., & Timothy, D.J. (2015) *World Regional Geography: Human Mobilities, Tourism Destinations, Sustainable Environments*, 2nd edn. Dubuque, IA: Kendall-Hunt.

McGahey, S. (2006) 'Tourism development in Iraq: The need for support from international academia', *International Journal of Tourism Research*, 8(3): 235–239.

Paradise, T. (2016) 'The Bedouins of Petra, Jordan: A geographer's life with the Bdoul', *The Arab World Geographer*, 19(3–4): 209–224.

Paris, C.M. (2017) 'A critical evaluation of the potentiality of tourism and destination development in Failaka Island', in M.L. Stephenson, & A. Al-Hamarneh (eds), *International Tourism Development and the Gulf Cooperation Council States: Challenges and Opportunities* (pp. 245–257). London: Routledge.

Qatar Tribune (2017) 'Qatar targets cruise tourism, new markets to boost growth', *Qatar Tribune*, 4 December 2017. Available online: www.qatar-tribune.com/news-details/id/99567 (Accessed 13 January 2018).

Qurashi, J. (2017) 'Commodification of Islamic religious tourism: From spiritual to touristic experience', *International Journal of Religious Tourism and Pilgrimage*, 5(1): 89–104.

Ron, A.S., & Timothy, D.J. (2019) *Contemporary Christian Travel: Pilgrimage, Practice and Place*. Bristol: Channel View Publications.

Scharfenort, N. (2017) 'Tourism development challenges in Qatar: Diversification and growth', in M.L. Stephenson, & A. Al-Hamarneh (eds), *International Tourism Development and the Gulf Cooperation Council States: Challenges and Opportunities* (pp. 140–155). London: Routledge.

Selmi, N. (2017) 'Tunisian tourism: At the eye of an Arab Spring storm', in H. Almuhrzi, H. Alriyami, & N. Scott (eds), *Tourism in the Arab World: An Industry Perspective* (pp. 145–160). Bristol: Channel View Publications.

Shamah, D. (2016) 'Where have all the tourists gone? They're right here', *The Times of Israel*, 15 February 2016. Available online: www.timesofisrael.com/where-have-all-the-tourists-gone-theyre-right-here/ (Accessed 3 February 2018).

Sharp, J.M. (2017) *Yemen: Civil War and Regional Intervention*. Washington, DC: Congressional Research Service.

Soltanzadeh, H., & Moghaddam, M.S. (2015) 'Sana'a, structure, historical form, architecture and culture', *Civil Engineering and Architecture*, 3(3): 56–67.

Thani, S., & Heenan, T. (2017) 'The UAE: A Disneyland in the desert', in H. Almuhrzi, H. Alriyami, & N. Scott (eds), *Tourism in the Arab World: An Industry Perspective* (pp. 104–117). Bristol: Channel View Publications.

Timothy, D.J. (2017) 'Tourism and geopolitics in the GCC region', in M.L. Stephenson, & A. al-Hamarneh (eds), *International Tourism Development and the Gulf Cooperation Council States: Challenges and Opportunities* (pp. 45–60). London: Routledge.

Timothy, D.J., & Iverson, T. (2006) 'Tourism and Islam: Considerations of culture and duty', in D.J. Timothy, & D.H. Olsen (eds), *Tourism, Religion and Spiritual Journeys* (pp. 186–205). London: Routledge.

Timothy, D.J., & Nyaupane, G.P. (2009) *Cultural Heritage and Tourism in the Developing World: A Regional Perspective*. London: Routledge.

Tosun, C., Timothy, D.J., & Öztürk, Y. (2003) 'Tourism growth, national development and regional inequality in Turkey', *Journal of Sustainable Tourism*, 11(2): 31–49.

Trading Economics (2018) 'Palestine tourist arrivals'. Available online: https://tradingeconomics.com/palestine/tourist-arrivals (Accessed 30 January 2018).

UNWTO (United Nations World Tourism Organization) (2017a) UNWTO eLibrary. Available online: www.e-unwto.org/action/doSearch?ConceptID=2469&target=topic (Accessed 2 February 2018).

UNWTO (2017b) 'UNWTO Tourism Highlights'. Madrid: World Tourism Organization.

UNWTO (2018) '2017 International Tourism results: The highest in seven years', Press Release 18003, 15 January 2018. Available online: http://media.unwto.org/press-release/2018-01-15/2017-international-tourism-results-highest-seven-years (Accessed 3 February 2018).

Walker, B.J. (2004) 'Commemorating the sacred spaces of the past: The Mamluks and the Umayyad mosque at Damascus', *Near Eastern Archaeology*, 67(1): 26–39.

PART II

Heritage, culture and urban space

5

INTANGIBLE HERITAGE AND CULTURAL PROTECTION IN THE MIDDLE EAST

Mairna H. Mustafa

Introduction

When the New Imperialist expansion of the European metropoles started in the eighteenth century, spelling the beginning of the end of the Ottoman Empire, a new type of travel emerged. It entailed intellectual travellers, funded by European scientific societies, visiting Africa and Southwest Asia (known to them at that time as the Near East) to encounter Arabs, Druze, Circassians, Turks, Armenians and many other groups (Qala'aji 2004). The purpose of these journeys was to gather information about the geography, cultures, and lives of Middle Eastern and African peoples. In their diaries were recorded many observations about the daily lives of these people, including village chiefdoms, nomadic practices, hospitality customs, funeral rites, settlements patterns, marriage celebrations, mythologies and worship places and ceremonies. These travel records showed the variation and richness of the heritage of different groups in the Middle East and North Africa. Amongst the most famous of these explorers were Burckhardt (1822, 1831), Conder (1889), Musil (1928), Bell (2000), Lawrence of Arabia (1925), and Oppenheim (1929).

These journeys were in large part undertaken for political purposes. For example, Gertrude Bell and T.E. Lawrence (Lawrence of Arabia) were sent by the British Ministry of Foreign Affairs to document details about Middle Easterners' lifestyles to gather intelligence about the political situation in Arabia and its tribes. Despite their geopolitical origins, these accounts detailed much about the living cultures of the Bedouin tribes and other peoples, including their migratory patterns, tent designs, religious beliefs, language, settlement patterns, urban centres and water and food sources (Howell 2006). These early records reveal much about traditional lifestyles and elements of culture throughout the Middle East and North Africa (MENA) and contributed to the Western romanticisation of the region.

The Middle East is diverse and complex in terms of its historical, political, religious, cultural, developmental and ethnic characteristics. It is a cradle of ancient civilisation with a human settlement that stretches back 1.5 million years and is located at the crossroads between Europe, Africa and Asia (the Old World). The region also occupies the remains of great empires, kingdoms and dynasties from which hundreds of thousands of archaeological sites derive, where Hittites, Sumerians, Assyrians, Babylonians, Persians, Egyptians, Canaanites, Hebrews, Greeks, Romans,

Nabataeans, Byzantines and Islamic Caliphates left their legacies of cultural achievement and heritage treasures (Adams 2008; Pritchard 1958). The Middle East is also the hub of three major world religions—Judaism, Christianity and Islam. This history has made the Middle East a significant heritage tourism destination.

MENA's vast cultural treasures are not only apparent in the number of archaeological sites and historic areas, and material culture archived in museums. It is also rich in intangible heritage related to different ethnic and religious groups, including oral traditions, performing arts, social practices, rituals, festivals, handicrafts and practices related to nature and the universe (UNESCO 2006). In common with many other parts of the world, MENA's tangible cultural heritage has received much more conservation and tourism attention compared to its intangible patrimony. Local regulations and international laws and conventions have overwhelmingly concentrated on protecting the material heritage against theft, illegal excavations, destruction and trafficking, leaving the intangible heritage in a state of disregard in documentation, conservation and interpretation (Mursi 2008). Intangible heritage faces the constant threat of slow accumulative changes through globalisation, media invasion, predominance of tourism development, political turbulence, and cultural appropriation. All of these lead to a state of cultural erosion, and nowhere is this more evident than in the Middle East. This chapter describes several types of intangible heritage in MENA and discusses the current situation of these resources, including many of the threats that hinder their sustainable use and protection. To conclude, recommendations are offered regarding what is needed to ensure better protection and the sustainable use of these irreplaceable resources.

Intangible heritage in MENA

Besides the 125 UNESCO World Heritage Sites (as of 2018) in MENA, there are 58 forms of intangible heritage listed by the same organisation in the countries defining MENA in this book. A sample of these is listed in Table 5.1, although it should be noted that such a list covers only a small part of the vast diversity of intangible heritage forms in the region. Following is a brief description of some of these forms of heritage and different issues concerning their development and conditions surrounding them.

Storytelling

The Arabian Peninsula and its surrounding neighbours have long been the places of legends and tales of prophets, saints, kings and warriors. Being the cradle of Judaism, Christianity and Islam, MENA was the scene of events mentioned in the holy books. It was also the location of famous wars amongst Arab tribes from which great Arab poets derived—poets who described epic tales and love stories through their craft, not least of which were the tales of the Arabian Nights (One Thousand and One Nights). These literary works generated the splendid sagas of Arab lore repeated throughout history and passed down through generations.

One of the most popular historical elements of the cultural landscape of the urban Middle East was the ubiquitous Arab cafés and street scenes. Here, until the mid-twentieth century, storytellers (*hakawati*) used to perform their narrations of the sagas while sometimes playing a musical instrument, such as the *rababa* (a two-string spike fiddle). Amongst the most famous of these sagas are the chivalry of Antar, the hero Abu Zayd, the migration of the Banu Hilal tribe, the warrior-princess Dhat al-Himmah, and 'Ali Zaybaq (Sheppard 2012). Unfortunately, this practice has diminished.

Table 5.1 Examples of MENA's intangible heritage on UNESCO's List of Intangible Cultural Heritage

Form of heritage	Year of inscription by UNESCO	MENA countries in which the form of heritage is practised
Taskiwin, martial dances of the western High Atlas	2017	Morocco
Whistled language	2017	Turkey
Nawrouz	2016	Iran, Iraq, Turkey
Al-Razfa, a traditional performing art	2015	Oman, UAE
Alardah Alnajdiyah, dance, drumming and poetry	2015	Saudi Arabia
Arabic coffee, a symbol of generosity	2015	UAE, Saudi Arabia, Oman, Qatar
Majlis, a cultural and social space	2015	UAE, Saudi Arabia, Oman, Qatar
Al-Ayyala, a traditional performing art of the Sultanate of Oman and the United Arab Emirates	2014	Oman, UAE
Al-Zajal, recited or sung poetry	2014	Lebanon
Ebru, Turkish art of marbling	2014	Turkey
Turkish coffee culture and tradition	2013	Turkey
Falconry	2012	UAE, Morocco, Qatar, Saudi Arabia, Syria
Mesir Macunu festival	2012	Turkey
Qālišuyān rituals of Mašhad-e Ardehāl in Kāšān	2012	Iran
Kırkpınar oil wrestling festival	2011	Turkey
Music of the Bakhshis of Khorasan	2011	Iran
Pahlevani and Zoorkhanei rituals	2011	Iran
Sema, Alevi-Bektaşi ritual	2010	Turkey
Traditional skills of carpet weaving in Fars and Kashan	2010	Iran
Âşıklık (minstrelsy) tradition	2009	Turkey
Karagöz	2009	Turkey
Radif of Iranian music	2009	Iran
Al-Sirah Al-Hilaliyyah epic	2008	Egypt
Arts of the Meddah, public storytellers	2008	Turkey
Cultural space of the Bedu in Petra and Wadi Rum	2008	Jordan
Iraqi Maqam	2008	Iraq
Palestinian Hikaye	2008	Palestine
Song of Sana'a	2008	Yemen

Source: Compiled from UNESCO (2018).

A remaining storytelling form, however, is the Palestinian *hikaye* (hikaye is the Arabic word for story). This narration is usually practised by elderly women and originated from their telling stories to their children and grandchildren. They recite fictional stories about people from their own societies, most commonly during winter evenings. The stories are narrated in the Palestinian dialects *fallahi* (rural) or *madani* (urban), and in some cases, young children tell the tales for fun (UNESCO 2006). In Lebanon, similar children's stories are told by the Druze women of the mountain areas (Tohmé-Tabet 2001).

Another form of storytelling with a poetic prose is the Hilali epic, which narrates the migration of a Bedouin tribe known as Banī Hilāl from the Arabian Peninsula to North Africa in the tenth century. Stories of the Banī Hilāl tribe have been recorded across the Arab world from

Morocco to Oman and as far away as Nigeria, Chad and Sudan, deep in Sub-Saharan Africa (Reynolds 1989). This epic is the only one of its kind that is still performed in its pure musical form. Despite being widespread throughout the Middle East since the fourteenth century, this art is now performed only in Egypt where poets (usually at weddings, circumcision ceremonies, and private gatherings) sing the verses while playing a rababa (UNESCO 2006). In Turkey and Turkic-speaking countries, a popular theatre storytelling method known as *meddahlik* was traditionally performed in cafés and public areas. The storyteller (*meddah*) selects songs and tales from popular romances, legends and epics (UNESCO 2016a).

Traditional stories and their delivery methods are facing significant threats from the mass media, which frequently convinces younger generations to see their ancestors' native customs as backward traditions. In some instances, this has caused elderly women storytellers to change the original narrations in content and form to be more interesting to the youth of today. Moreover, the turbulent political situation in some areas of MENA is causing a disruption in local social life, which is also recognised as a salient threat to continuing this form of heritage (UNESCO 2006). Because these stories are transmitted orally rather than through official educational channels, they may eventually disappear (Mursi 2008).

Musical traditions and expressions

The Middle East and North Africa is home to a heterogeneous array of oral and musical traditions that for centuries have helped to create tribal and national identities. One distinguished form of musical performance is the Iraqi *maqam*, which generally takes place at private gatherings and in coffeehouses and theatres. These strophic songs are basically composed of classical and colloquial Arabic poetry recited in a melodic fashion (UNESCO 2006). A similar tradition can be found in Turkey in the form of *Âşıklık*, which is performed by wandering poet-singers known as *âşıks*, who perform at weddings, coffeehouses and during public festivals, wearing traditional clothes and plucking a stringed *saz* (UNESCO 2016b).

Zajal is a well-known musical expression in Lebanon that entails oral vernacular poetry being sung with the accompaniment of music; the poetry comes in the standard Arabic language, *fuṣḥā*. The zajal performer is called *zajjāl*, *qawwāl*, or *shācir zajal*. This music form consists of different styles: *al-muhmal* (a form without diacritical marks), *al-marṣūd* (where the first hemistich starts with a particular obligatory letter), *al-mujazzam* (where every line in the successive stanzas rhymes with the others, except for the last line whose rhyme is a return to the rhyme of the opening line or lines), and *al-alifiyyāt*, in which the first letter of every line follows the order of the Arabic alphabet. Similar performances are known in Saudi Arabia, the Gulf countries, Syria and Jordan (Haydar 1989).

There is a similar art in Palestine known as *hidā*, which is a colloquial poetry sung by native Palestinian poets at weddings, baptisms, private parties, public festivals and other important social occasions (Sbait 1989). In Oman, this art form is known as *Al 'azi*—a genre of sung poetry punctuated by sword and step movements and poetic exchanges between a singer and a choir comprised of villagers or tribe members (UNESCO 2016e). In Yemen, a musical tradition known as the Song of Sana'a, or al-*Ghina al-San'ani*, dates to the fourteenth century and is still practised in the *samra* marriage evenings and the *magyal* (daily afternoon gathering with friends) (UNESCO 2006).

A very basic type of poetry recited by Bedouin tribes all over the Middle East is *Nabaṭī*, which comes with or without a *rababa* accompaniment. It has three main forms: *Hjīnī*, belonging to the *Ḥadū* traditional genre, *cArḍa* (war song), and *Sāmrī*, which includes syllabic songs performed by sedentarised Bedouins at their weddings or other special occasions (Jargy 1989).

These musical heritage performances are threatened by competition from contemporary media, especially amongst the younger generations, who seem to be more attracted to modern styles of music and singing. The number of performers of poetic and musical arts is dwindling, with fewer young people being willing to commit to practising these traditional arts. Moreover, most original poems are too long to be fully performed in folklore shows held as part of tourist programmes. As such, they are frequently shortened to meet the time constraints and interest levels of tourists, and there is a danger of these changes becoming permanent as a result of tourism, much the same way intangible cultural heritage has been enduringly modified in other parts of the world (Timothy 2011).

Dancing

There are many forms of traditional dances in the Middle East, including the following:

- Awalim—a professional style of oriental belly dancing in which a group of trained dancers and musicians perform together; this is well known in Egypt.
- The Bedouin dance, which differs in name and movements from one country to another.
- Bamboutiyeh—an Egyptian traditional dance where women imitate boatmen.
- Ghawazi—a dance performed by gypsies in the southern parts of Egypt.
- Dabkeh—mostly performed in the Levant, this fast-paced dance is based on foot stomping movements out of beat. Groups of men (or men and women) perform this dance in a line or a circle.
- Fellahi is a form of belly dance performed in rural areas of Egypt and Iraq.
- Khaliji or Samri is performed by women in Arabian Gulf countries.

(Janan 2005)

The *Tahteeb* in Egypt is performed in public, wherein a brief, non-violent exchange occurs between two dancers wielding long sticks while folk music plays in the background; no striking is allowed (UNESCO 2016d). *Al-Razfa* is a traditional dance in the United Arab Emirates (UAE) and Oman, performed during weddings and national festivals, where dancers move in two facing lines with others filling the spaces between. Led by the main singer, the dancers repeat his words to the accompaniment of drums and other instruments (UNESCO 2016c). Similar to this is *Alardah*, a traditional dance in Saudi Arabia whose performers include drummers, dancers and poets. Dancers carry light swords and stand shoulder to shoulder in two lines, leaving space in between for drummers. A poet chants verses in a loud voice, which are then sung antiphonally by the dancers (UNESCO 2016j).

Another form of dancing takes on more religious significance. This Turkish pirouette is perhaps the most famous dance routine in all of MENA. An ascetic Sufi order founded in 1273 in Konya, Turkey, regularly performs this *Mevleviye* (whirling dervish) movement for tourist audiences (Özdemir 2016). Although it has been shortened and simplified to meet commercial tourism requirements, this art form used to be performed all over the Ottoman Empire, which brought it considerable fame (Uyar & Beşiroğlu 2012). However, with the Ottoman rule diminishing throughout the Mediterranean region in the late nineteenth and early twentieth centuries, and with restrictions on this spiritually-oriented dance by the 1925 secularisation policies of Atatürk and the new Republic of Turkey, it almost disappeared until it was once again allowed in public performances in the 1950s. Since the 1990s, the whirling dervish dance has been practised by Turkish communities worldwide, but the most active centres are in Konya and Istanbul (UNESCO 2006).

Many of the dances described above have been negatively affected by the lucrative tourism industry. Some traditional shows are performed as brief excerpts meant to entertain tourists. This applies particularly to the case of the Turkish *sema*, which is no longer performed in its original religious context; it was simplified and shortened to meet the needs of tourism (UNESCO 2016h), the same way traditional shows have changed in other parts of the world (Timothy 2011).

Handicrafts

Handcrafted objects hold both tangibility in their components and intangibility in their crafts-manship and cultural meaning (Swanson & Timothy 2012). Exploiting these resources for tourism is of great economic significance in most parts of the world. Communities embody their social, cultural and spiritual values in these objects, which are then transmitted not only to tourists but also to future generations (Robinson & Picard 2006). In the Middle East, each country has its own unique artistic details related to motifs and colours, although some common types of handicrafts are popular throughout the region, as observed by the author (see Table 5.2). In many Middle Eastern countries, the handicraft sector is crippled by a variety of issues. Comprehensive national plans that unify the efforts of diverse stakeholders in this sector are lacking. There is also unfair competition between locally produced goods and imported crafts, which are bought in bulk and sold to tourists at deep discounts. Pashmina shawls and scarves, inexpensive rayon and cotton dresses from India and Pakistan, and cheap shells, jewellery, clothing and toys from China appeal to tourists because of their low cost compared to locally made products of higher quality and cultural significance.

The high prices of local handicrafts is also a problem caused by a casual and low volume production system, poor management, and lack of proper financial management skills. Moreover, guidebooks and websites that describe the heritage of the Middle East lack sufficient information about handicrafts, their meaning and value, or about the best places for purchasing higher quality, locally made crafts (Mustafa 2011).

Festivals

Many folklore and other traditional festivals take place regularly in the Middle East. These events help sustain and raise awareness of different aspects of heritage such as performed arts, handicrafts, cuisines, horse and camel racing, folk poetry, costumes, popular markets, book fairs, falconry, sports and local communities. While it is not possible to mention all of the region's festivals, there are many representative examples, including Nawrouz, a two-week celebration beginning in March that marks the new year in several countries, including Iran, Iraq and Turkey (UNESCO 2016g). The popular Kırkpınar oil wrestling festival in Edirne, Turkey, hosts thousands of people every year to see wrestlers (*pehlivan*) fight for the Kırkpınar Golden Belt and title of Chief Pehlivan (UNESCO 2016i). Falconry festivals are especially popular in the Gulf States, where traditional dress, food, music, poetry and dance are all part of the celebration in company with hunting carried out by trained falcons (UNESCO 2016f). Added to these events is the Beiteddine Festival in Lebanon, the Konya International Mystic Music Festival in Konya, Turkey, the Muscat Festival in Oman, the Palmyra Tourism Festival in Syria, the al-Janadriyah Festival in Saudi Arabia, the Jerash Festival of Culture and Arts in Jordan, and many others.

Most cultural festivals in the Middle East have been rather successful in sustaining heritage practices, though some of them have focused disproportionately on music, thereby marginalising

Table 5.2 A sample of unique handicrafts in the MENA region

Craft type	Comments
Weaving	This technique is used to make wool products. After shearing the sheep, the raw wool is washed, carded and spun into yarn. It is then dyed and attached to looms to create carpets, cushions, wall-hangings and saddle bags. This is a common Bedouin craft all over the region. Another form is weaving carpets from silk, a very distinguished art in Iran.
Embroidery	The cross-stitch is usually used to decorate different fabrics for dresses, shawls, cushions, bags and furniture. Each area of the Middle East has its own combinations of designs and colours.
Handmade glass	Different coloured vessels are made by blowing raw glass. Hebron, Palestine and Egypt are especially known for this art form.
Mosaics	Mosaics are still made with traditional techniques. Pieces of ceramic, glass or stone are cut with hammers, tile cutters or tile snippers. These pieces are inserted into the mosaic design and attached with an adhesive material. Jordan is known for its Mosaic School and local crafters in Madaba City.
Sand bottles	Bottles of different shapes are filled with layers of coloured sand into different shapes and designs, such as animals, flowers and geometric elements.
Ceramics	Ceramics are used to create different vessels, marbles and figurines from earthenware. Turkey is a famous producer for ceramic glazed and coloured tiles.
Metalwork	Metal pieces include incised and/or jewelled weapons such as daggers and swords, as well as vessels, all of which are common throughout the region.
Leatherwork	Leatherwork is common in saddles, bags, purses and shoes.
Mother of pearl	This is a common decorative material for wooden boxes, frames and furniture. Egypt, Syria and Palestine are especially known for these items.
Gold and silver	Gold and silver ornaments and jewellery with precious and semiprecious stones are routinely created in many parts of MENA.
Wood carving	Wood carvings are common in the form of boxes, tiles, picture frames, figurines, furniture and vessels.

Source: Author's compilation.

other elements of living culture. Thus, in many cases, they have become an occasion for entertainment rather than for promoting local heritage (Na'amneh 2009).

Cultural spaces and local communities

Very few studies have discussed the cultural spaces of Middle Eastern communities involved in tourism development. These include communities around the sites of Um Qais, a Greco-Roman archaeological site in Jordan; Wadi Rum and Petra (a Nabataean site) in Jordan; and Luxor, Egypt, where historic nearby villages were transformed through private investment into luxury facilities and museums. In Lebanon, some extended families have transformed their cultural properties into well-known museums as is the case in Sidon (Saida) where the Debbane family restored their residence into the Debbane Palace and History Museum, and the Audi family adapted their home into a Soap Museum (Daher 2006).

In Um Qais and Petra, Jordan, and Luxor, Egypt, rural villages were uprooted and relocated to new locales where the people were marginalised and worked in low-paying jobs (Mustafa & Abu Tayeh 2011). According to Daher (2006), inadequate planning ordinances and excessive government overreach into villagers' social life spurred this problem where heritage and its commercialisation took precedence over the well-being of the communities. This situation led to the impoverishment of many rural areas, and extensive migration to urban areas destroyed the ancestral equilibrium of those populations. The promise of new lifestyles and more consumption-oriented lives caused them to move to cities, abandoning the rural areas, causing them to become isolated and ignored (Boumedine 2008).

Another issue related to native peoples is the commoditisation of Bedouin life and culture. There are plentiful examples of this in the Negev, Sinai and Badia deserts where many Bedouins started to sell their traditional hospitality to tourists who were lured by the mystical Bedouin lifestyle (Abuamoud, Libbin, Green, & Al Rousan 2014; Al-Oun & Al-Homoud 2008). In doing so, the indigenous desert dwellers built and rented out fake villages, and the community itself became an exotic and romanticised attraction to be commodified for Western tourists (Dinero 2002).

One of the most distinguishable cases in the Middle East is the Bedouins in the southern part of Jordan, most particularly in Petra, Wadi Rum and the Feynan Eco-lodge where the Bdul, Ammarin and the Sa'idiyyin tribes live in semi-arid lands and continue to practise traditional ways of life. Their practices include pastoral culture and preserving knowledge related to flora and fauna, traditional medicine, camel husbandry, tent-making artisanship, tracking and climbing skills, in addition to moral and social codes expressed and transmitted orally through poetry, folktales and songs (Na'amneh, Shunnaq, & Tasbasi 2008). Over the last 50 years, more and more Bedouins have settled in permanent communities where the provision of education, housing, health care, and sanitation provide social benefits, although this has led to the erosion of skills and customs developed over hundreds of years and many generations (Mustafa & Abu Tayeh 2011; UNESCO 2006).

Wadi Rum is well known for significant geological formations and sand dunes, as well as being the filming location of *Lawrence of Arabia* in the early 1960s. Several outdoor activities take place there, such as hiking, rock climbing, camel riding, sand surfing, jeep tours, and camping. Tourists visit Wadi Feynan to appreciate its unique ecosystem and ancient sites related to copper metallurgy, which dates back to the fourth millennium BC (Teller 2006). Despite tourism's positive economic contribution to the Bedouin tribes in these areas through job opportunities as guides, lodge staff and handicrafters, some undesired cultural changes have occurred. Abuamoud, Alrousan and Bader (2015) argue that most of the younger generation ignores their heritage lifestyle and tend to adopt a more modern existence by way of the clothes they wear, their use of technology and language. Many have left their customary employment as herders and shepherds to work as tourist guides.

Since its rediscovery on 22 August 1812, by the Swiss traveller J. Burckhardt, (Burckhardt 1822), the ancient Nabataean city of Petra has lured explorers and tourists. The city's magnificently carved architectural features and the customary Bedouin lifestyle of the area's traditional inhabitants combined to attract tourism development and facilities since the early 1920s, in which locals from the Liyathnah and Bedul tribes found employment (Shoup 1985). When Petra was inscribed as a World Heritage Site in 1985, the Bedouins who had settled the ancient city were forced to leave the caves and edifices they used as homes (Lubick 2004). Even with the growth of tourism, the Bedul continued goat herding and dry-farming wheat and barley. Their residences included black tents made of goat hair, masonry structures in natural rock shelters, and empty Nabataean tombs within and around Petra.

The village of Umm Siehoun was built by the government to replace the Petra dwellings, which the Bedul had been using for centuries (Mustafa & Abu Tayeh 2011). There, better education and health care were available, but their access to traditional pastoral lands and agricultural areas was limited. Many people became involved in the tourist trade to compensate for the economic losses in other areas and to support a growing population (Kooring & Simms 1996).

Even with tourism's economic benefits, some undesirable impacts have manifested (Mustafa & Balaawi 2013). One frequently mentioned outcome is the commercialisation of Bedouin culture. Tribesmen realised the appeal that their traditional dwelling tents and nomadic practices exuded to tourists, so they began to set up mock Bedouin camps where they built refreshment stands and where women started to sell Bedouin items to tourists. This process of commercialisation brought about changes in values: young Bedouins now imitate Westerners' dress and mannerisms, despite the general perception amongst older generations that Westerners share corrupted values, such as alcoholism and immoral relationships. This has caused conflict between Western 'values' and the strength of ties to Bedouin culture amongst many locals (Mustafa & Abu Tayeh 2011).

Cultural changes that took place after the expansion of tourism are evident in the decline of traditional handicrafts. Since the 1950s, most women stopped weaving carpets and making their own tents. However, tourists' interest in these processes and products helped revive some of these arts, and as a result, some women started to make small bags, carpets, miniature looms with partially finished panels still on them, and spindle whorls in order to help support their families (Shoup 1985).

Other threats to intangible heritage in the Middle East

Despite the deep economic need for tourism by many Middle Eastern countries, the lack of awareness about the benefits of tourism by some segments of Arab societies leads to negative perceptions of, and reaction towards, tourists. This was behind a number of calamities in the region, such as the kidnapping of Western tourists by tribesmen in the interior highlands of Yemen, terrorist attacks on tourists during the 1990s in Egypt (Boniface & Cooper 2001), and more recent attacks on tourists at resorts in Tunisia and on flights to and from Egypt. These events were followed by a continuous string of unstable political situations in addition to the already contentious Palestinian–Israeli conflict, several wars (e.g. the Iraqi–Iranian War (1980–1988), the Gulf War (1990–1991) and the Iraq War since 2003), and finally the Arab Spring, where a series of revolts and protests took place from December 2010. All of these had dramatic influences on the performance of tourism (Masetti & Körner 2013), as indicated by the decline in international arrivals to the Arab states, a decrease in hotel occupancy rates, and a reduction in tourism revenue. In addition, many Arab countries were replaced with alternative destinations, such as Turkey, Malaysia, Thailand and Indonesia (OECD 2011).

More importantly for this discussion, however, was the loss of heritage in all of its forms. Besides the destruction of archaeological sites and museums, and the theft of antiquities and their illicit trade by terrorist groups, the intangible heritage has also faced serious threats during these times of crisis. Tangible and intangible heritage have suffered, especially those heritages that have been targeted deliberately by warring parties as part of their cultural cleansing campaigns. This situation is ongoing and resembles the older cases of Armenians, Kurds and Palestinians.

The displacement of communities in such situations causes a disruption in social ties and a radical separation of people from their places of origin, eventually weakening people's bonds with their heritage. Issues of identity loss, cultural transformation and reconstructed collective memory amongst refugees are salient consequences of human displacement and detachment from place (Bajalan 2016). Such disturbing political situations also deeply affect performing arts, since holding public concerts is necessarily limited for security reasons, which is clearly visible now in the case of Iraqi Maqam (UNESCO 2006).

The collective identity and social memory of communities (and individuals) are threatened by migration from the countryside to the city, leading to a deterioration of rural cultural environments (Mursi 2008). Even when people remain in their original settlements (usually located near tourism attractions), cultural erosion takes place due to the need to adapt living heritage to the needs of tourists. As well, many people, primarily youth, exhibit a certain degree of admiration for foreign cultures vis-à-vis the tourists; young people in host destinations tend to be attracted to tourists' lifestyles, which, according to the tenets of the 'demonstration effect', can degrade their own cultural heritage as it is usurped by outside influences (Fisher 2004).

In some cases, the reverse can occur when the sense of community increases as local heritage is highlighted in order to attract tourists, but these are very rare cases in the Middle East. Another obstacle is the limited ability of local NGOs to protect and document heritage, which largely results from insufficient funds and support. The uprooted populations suffering from war displacement, including Palestinians, Armenians, Kurds and Assyrians, put a lot of effort into safeguarding their group identity to prevent younger generations from forgetting their country and culture. Older generations (mainly women) try to pass down different elements of folklore, including songs, stories, dances and music. There are a few NGOs with limited resources that document these elements of living culture, publish their findings in books and integrate them into youth club activities (Tohmé-Tabet 2001).

For educational establishments, most heritage museums in MENA focus mainly on storing and displaying archaeological objects and artefacts. Even if intangible heritage exists, most museums only devote a small portion of their space and efforts to its preservation and interpretation. The same applies to tourist brochures and guidebooks, both of which lack sufficient information about the region's intangible cultural heritage. There is a related problem in higher educational programmes that specialise in cultural resource management and conservation. Overwhelmingly they offer courses focusing on conservation and management techniques for archaeological sites and historic buildings, while largely ignoring intangible cultural heritage at both the theoretical and practical levels. As a result, graduates often lack the knowledge and skills needed to document, protect, encourage and interpret the immaterial culture of the region (Na'amneh 2009).

Conclusion

UNESCO's 2003 Convention for the Safeguarding of Intangible Cultural Heritage stipulates that intangible heritage comprises the 'practices, representations, expressions, knowledge, skills—as well as the instruments, objects, artifacts and cultural spaces associated therewith—that communities, groups and, in some cases, individuals recognize as part of their cultural heritage' (UNESCO 2017: n.p.). This sort of patrimony is extremely fragile. In addition to its importance in maintaining cultural diversity in the face of growing globalisation, it helps create intercultural dialogue and encourages mutual respect for others' way of life. It also transmits knowledge and skills to new generations (UNESCO 2017). The protection of material heritage is meaningless without the conservation of living culture and the social expressions that bring it to life (Selicato 2016).

While extremely important, conserving and managing intangible heritage is complicated. This is evident in UNESCO's use of the word 'safeguarding' intangible culture rather than 'preserving' it. The latter word indicates freezing cultural practices in time rather than allowing them to adapt to changing circumstances. The truth is that cultures constantly evolve by means of many exogenous and endogenous forces; interpreting culture and transmitting it to future generations must be adaptable and recognise the fact that conditions do change (Rio Tinto 2011). The main problem occurs when changes are unnaturally incurred through crises or an overwhelming commoditisation by tourism and media coverage.

Wars and manifestations of globalisation (e.g. travel, the Internet and social media) erode cultures through acts of dominance and hegemony, which tend to be boundless. The role of intangible cultural heritage here becomes apparent, as it becomes the keeper of ancestral traditions, forming the line of defence between preservation and extinction. Concentrated efforts must be made to protect living culture from melting into other cultures by instilling within younger generations a desire to protect and practise ancestral customs in a way that guarantees their survival, continuity and influence (Mursi 2008). As Boumedine (2008) states, such realities initiate the need to develop educational programmes to raise awareness about the significance and values of heritage, especially amongst local communities involved in tourism. Such programmes should promote respect for the past and encourage community members to take responsibility for protecting their own heritage. This can be supported by establishing scientific national databases or archives that focus on collecting, documenting and classifying intangible elements of the cultural past. More effort by governments, educational establishments, and NGOs is needed to train experts who will help safeguard all forms and manifestations of human heritage.

Another issue concerns the cultural rights of indigenous people or traditional communities; many are dissatisfied about the ways in which knowledge about them and their cultures is presented, interpreted and used by outsiders (Johnston 2003). Some fear that recording and making traditional cultural expressions available to the outside world might expose them to misappropriation and misuse by other parties. This raises concerns about a lack of legal protection and intellectual property rights (Johnston 2003; Skrydstrup & Wendland 2006). Governments should provide legal protections, both locally and internationally, for people's heritage and intellectual rights. Despite plethoric international efforts to establish legal mechanisms for protecting heritage, national legislation is lacking in looking after intangible heritage. Instead, most legislation focuses on built environments and material culture. This is inadequate in addressing the need for safeguarding intangible heritage, which is equally important in sustaining and enhancing a nation's cultural identity.

References

Abuamoud, I., Alrousan, R., & Bader, M. (2015) 'Impacts of ecotourism in Jordan: Wadi Rum', *European Journal of Social Sciences*, 5(1): 119–129.

Abuamoud, I., Libbin, J., Green, J., & Al Rousan, R. (2014) 'Factors affecting the willingness of tourists to visit cultural heritage sites in Jordan', *Journal of Heritage Tourism*, 9(2): 148–165.

Adams, R. (2008) *Jordan: An Archaeological Reader*. London: Equinox.

Al-Oun S., & Al-Homoud, M. (2008) 'The potential for developing community-based tourism among the Bedouins in the Badia of Jordan', *Journal of Heritage Tourism*, 3(1): 36–54.

Bajalan, S. (2016) 'Conflict and living heritage in the Middle East: Researching the politics of cultural heritage and identities in times of war and displacement'. Available online: https://networks.hnet.org/node/73374/announcements/113908/conflict-and-living-heritage-middle-east-researching-politics (Accessed 3 November 2017).

Bell, G. (2000) *Gertrude Bell: The Arabian Diaries, 1913–1914*. Syracuse, NY: Syracuse University Press.

Boniface, B., & Cooper, C. (2001) *Worldwide Destinations: The Geography of Travel and Tourism*, 3rd edn. Oxford: Butterworth-Heinemann.

Boumedine, R. (2008) 'Sustainable development of Saharan tourism and heritage', in F. Hassan, A. de Trafford, & M. Youssef (eds), *Cultural Heritage and Development in the Arab World* (pp. 205–228). Alexandria: Bibliotheca Alexandrina.

Burckhardt, J. (1822) *Travels in Syria and the Holy Land.* London: Association for Promoting the Discovering of the Interior Parts of Africa.

Burckhardt, J. (1831) *Notes on the Bedouins and Wahabys.* London: Henry Colburn and Richard Bentley.

Conder, C. (1889) *The Survey of Eastern Palestine: Memoirs of the Topography, Orography, Hydrography, Archaeology, etc. Volume 1, The 'Adwân Country.* London: The Committee of the Palestine Exploration Fund.

Daher, R. (2006) 'Reconceptualising tourism in the Middle East: Place, heritage, mobility and competitiveness', in R. Daher (ed.), *Tourism in the Middle East: Continuity, Change and Transformation* (pp. 1–69). Bristol: Channel View Publications.

Dinero, S. (2002) 'Image is everything: The development of the Negev Bedouins as a tourist attraction', *Nomadic Peoples*, 6(1): 69–94.

Fisher, D. (2004) 'The demonstration effect revisited', *Annals of Tourism Research*, 31(2): 428–446.

Haydar, A. (1989) 'The development of Lebanese Zajal: Genre, meter, and verbal duel', *Oral Tradition*, 4(1–2): 189–212.

Howell, G. (2006) *Gertrude Bell: Queen of the Desert, Shaper of Nations.* New York: Farrar, Straus & Giroux.

Janan, M. (2005) 'An overview of the dances of the Middle East: Relation to current American belly dance', Bameda, 6 November. Available online: http://mahsati-janan.com/ArticlesbyMJ/MahsatiJanan-DanceOverview.pdf (Accessed 3 June 2017).

Jargy, S. (1989) 'Sung poetry in the oral tradition the Gulf region and the Arabian Peninsula', *Oral Tradition*, 4(1–2): 174–88.

Johnston, A.M. (2003) 'Self-determination: Exercising indigenous rights in tourism', in S. Singh, D.J. Timothy, & R.K. Dowling (eds), *Tourism in Destination Communities* (pp. 115–133). Wallingford: CAB International.

Kooring, D., & Simms, S. (1996) 'The Bedul Bedouin of Petra, Jordan: Traditions, tourism and an uncertain future', *Cultural Survival Quarterly*, 19(4). Available online: www.culturalsurvival.org/ourpublications/csq/article/the-bedul-bedouin-petra-jordan-traditionstourism-and-uncertain-future (Accessed 21 December 2010).

Lawrence, T.E. (1925) *Seven Pillars of Wisdom.* Middlesex: Doubleday.

Lubick, N. (2004) 'Petra: An eroding ancient city', *Geotimes*, June 2004. Available online: www.geotimes. org/june04/feature_petra.html (Accessed 21 December 2010).

Masetti, O., & Körner, K. (2013) 'Two years of Arab Spring: Where are we now? What's next?', *Deutsche Bank Research, Current Issues: Emerging Markets*, 25 January 2013. Available online: www.dbresearch. com/PROD/RPS_EN-PROD/PROD0000000000451962/Two_years_of_Arab_Spring%3A_Where_are_we_now%3F_What%E2%80%99s.pdf (Accessed 2 December 2017).

Mursi, A. (2008) 'Identification, domains and safeguarding intangible cultural heritage', in F. Hassan, A. de Trafford, & M. Youssef (eds), Cultural Heritage and Development in the Arab World, (pp. 243–252). Alexandria: Bibliotheca Alexandrina.

Musil, A. (1928) *The Manners and Customs of the Rwala Bedouins.* New York: American Geographical Society.

Mustafa, M.H. (2011) 'Potential of sustaining handicrafts as a tourism product in Jordan', *International Journal of Business and Social Science*, 2(2): 145–152.

Mustafa, M.H., & Abu Tayeh, S.N. (2011) 'The impact of tourism development on the archaeological site of Petra and local communities in surrounding villages', *Asian Social Science*, 7(8): 88–96.

Mustafa, M.H., & Balaawi, F.A. (2013) 'Evaluating visitor management at the archaeological site of Petra', *Mediterranean Archaeology and Archaeometry*, 13(1): 77–87.

Na'amneh, M. (2009) 'Cultural heritage and collective identity: The status of intangible heritage in Jordan from an anthropological perspective', *Al-Manarah*, 15(3): 1–8.

Na'amneh, M., Shunnaq, M., & Tasbasi, A. (2008) 'The modern sociocultural significance of the Jordanian Bedouin tent', *Nomadic Peoples*, 12(1): 149–163).

OECD (2011) *Socio-Economic Context and Impact of the 2011 Events in the Middle East and North Africa Region.* Paris: MENA-OECD Investment Programme.

Oppenheim, M. (1929) *Travel in the Land of Schummer and North of al-Jazireh.* (Trans. to Arabic by Mohammad Kbibo, 2009). Amman: al-Warraq Press.

Özdemir, G. (2016) 'Festivals as a short-duration tourism attraction in Turkey', in I. Egresi (ed.), *Alternative Tourism in Turkey* (pp. 141–150). Cham, Switzerland: Springer.

Pritchard, J. (1958) *Ancient Near East, Volume 1: An Anthology of Texts and Pictures*. Princeton, NJ: Princeton University Press.

Qala'aji, Q. (2004) *Discovering the Arabian Peninsula: Five Centuries of Adventures and Science*. Cairo: Madboli.

Reynolds, D. (1989) 'Sīrat Banī Hilāl: Introduction and notes to an Arab oral epic tradition', *Oral Tradition*, 4(1–2): 80–100.

Rio Tinto (2011) *Why Cultural Heritage Matters: A Resource Guide for Integrating Cultural Heritage Management into Communities Work at Rio Tinto*. Melbourne: Rio Tinto Ltd.

Robinson, M., & Picard, D. (2006) *Culture, Tourism and Development, the Division of Cultural Policies and Intercultural Dialogue*. Paris: UNESCO, Culture and Development Section.

Sbait, D. (1989) 'Palestinian improvised-sung poetry: The genres of Ḥidā and Qarrādī—performance and transmission', *Oral Tradition*, 4(1–2): 213–35.

Selicato, F. (2016) 'The concept of heritage', in F. Rotondo, F. Selicato, V. Marin, & J. López Galdeano (eds), *Cultural Territorial Systems: Landscape and Cultural Heritage as a Key to Sustainable and Local Development in Eastern Europe* (pp. 7–12). Cham, Switzerland: Springer.

Sheppard, T. (2012) 'Traditional storytelling in Asia and the Middle East'. Available online: www.timsheppard.co.uk/story/,dir/traditions/asiamiddleast.html (Accessed 16 March 2017).

Shoup, J. (1985) 'The impact of tourism on the Bedouin of Petra', *The Middle East Journal*, 39(2): 277–291.

Skrydstrup, M., & Wendland, W. (2006) 'Protecting intangible cultural heritage: From ethical dilemmas to best practice', *ICOM News*, No. 2, 2006. Available online: http://icom.museum/resources/publications-database/publication/protecting-intangible-cultural-heritage-from-ethical-dilemmas-to-best-practice-1/ (Accessed 18 February 2017).

Swanson, K.K., & Timothy, D.J. (2012) 'Souvenirs: Icons of meaning, commercialisation, and commoditisation', *Tourism Management*, 33(3): 489–499.

Teller, M. (2006) *The Rough Guide to Jordan*. New York: Rough Guides.

Timothy, D.J. (2011) *Cultural Heritage and Tourism: An Introduction*. Bristol: Channel View Publications.

Tohmé-Tabet, A. (2001) 'Women, intangible heritage and development in the Arab World', Unpublished manuscript. Available online: www.unesco.org/culture/ich/doc/src/00161-EN.pdf (Accessed 20 December 2017).

UNESCO (2006) 'Masterpieces of the oral and intangible heritage of humanity, Proclamations 2001, 2003 & 2005', UNESCO. Available online: http://unesdoc.unesco.org/images/0014/001473/147344e.pdf (Accessed 22 April 2017).

UNESCO (2016a) 'Alardah Alnajdiyah, dance, drumming and poetry in Saudi Arabia'. Available online: www.unesco.org/culture/ich/en/RL/alardah-alnajdiyah-dance-drumming-and-poetry-in-saudi-arabia-01196 (Accessed 5 September 2017).

UNESCO (2016b) 'Al 'azi, elegy, processional march and poetry'. Available online: www.unesco.org/culture/ich/en/RL/al-azi-elegy-processional-march-and-poetry-00850 (Accessed 5 September 2017).

UNESCO (2016c) 'A-Razfa: A traditional performing art'. Available online: www.unesco.org/culture/ich/en/RL/al-razfa-a-traditional-performing-art-01078 (Accessed 5 September 2017).

UNESCO (2016d) 'Arts of the Meddah: Public story tellers'. Available online: www.unesco.org/culture/ich/en/RL/arts-of-the-meddah-public-storytellers-00037 (Accessed 5 September 2017).

UNESCO (2016e) 'Âşıklık (Minstrelsy) tradition'. Available online: www.unesco.org/culture/ich/en/RL/asklk-minstrelsy-tradition-00179 (Accessed 5 September 2017).

UNESCO (2016f) 'Falconry: A living human heritage'. Available online: www.unesco.org/culture/ich/en/RL/falconry-a-living-human-heritage-00732 (Accessed 5 September 2017).

UNESCO (2016g) 'Kırkpınar Oil Wrestling Festival'. Available online: www.unesco.org/culture/ich/en/RL/krkpnar-oil-wrestling-festival-00386 (Accessed 5 September 2017).

UNESCO (2016h) 'Lists of intangible cultural heritage and the Register of Best Safeguarding Practices'. Available online: www.unesco.org/culture/ich/en/lists (Accessed 5 September 2017).

UNESCO (2016i) 'Novruz, Nowrouz, Nooruz, Navruz, Nauroz, Nevruz'. Available online: www.unesco.org/culture/ich/en/RL/nawrouz-novruz-nowrouz-nowrouz-nawrouz-nauryz-nooruz-nowruz-navruz-nevruz-nowruz-navruz-01161 (Accessed 5 September 2017).

UNESCO (2016j) 'Tahteeb Stick Game'. Available online: www.unesco.org/culture/ich/en/RL/tahteeb-stick-game-01189 (Accessed 5 September 2017).

UNESCO (2017) 'What is Intangible Cultural Heritage'. Available online: https://ich.unesco.org/en/convention#art2 (Accessed 18 November 2017).

UNESCO (2018) 'Intangible Cultural Heritage'. Available online: https://ich.unesco.org/en/lists (Accessed 10 January 2018).

Uyar, Y.M., & Beşiroğlu, Ş.Ş. (2012) 'Recent representations of the music of the Mevlevi Order of Sufism', *Journal of Interdisciplinary Music Studies*, 6(2): 137–150.

6

DECIPHERING 'ARAB HOSPITALITY'

Identifying key characteristics and concerns

Marcus L. Stephenson and Nazia Ali

Introduction

Hospitality is deeply embedded in the cultural, economic, historical, political, social, theological and traditional landscapes of people and populations of Arab civilisations and nations. These embodiments in hospitality are also perceived necessary to sustain the development of tourism in the Arab nations, service the tourist gaze, and fuel the hospitality industry in the Arab world. In fact, the omnipresent role of hospitality across this region is well documented, particularly in such countries as Iraq (Fernea Warnock 1989), Jordan (Al-Oun & Al-Homoud 2008; Shryock 2004), Morocco (Fernea Warnock 1975), Oman (Eickelman 1984) and Yemen (Meneley 1996).

Crucially, hospitality is seen as being synonymous with the Arab world because Arabs are 'famed' for the hospitality they show to their guests (Barnes 2013). Unfortunately, however, these perceptions have been increasingly confounded by socio-political constructions of the 'Arab other', agitated by the global phenomenon of Islamophobia (see Stephenson & Ali 2010). The spaces of hospitality where the (Arab) host comes into contact with the (Arab and non-Arab) guest to deliver the Arab hospitality experience in the private, commercial and social domains are examined within this chapter. Based upon Lashley's (2000: 4) conceptualisation of such hospitality domains as the private realm, the assessment considers the role of the home in the Arab world because it often determines the primary socialisation of hosts into conducting hospitable practices. This is in contrast to the commercial domain, which focuses on the provision of hospitality as a formalised service encounter and economic exchange. Therefore, the social focus is directed to dealing and communicating with strangers who are paying customers.

The work acknowledges critical aspects of (in)hospitality in the Arab world, associated with formal and informal practices and provisions. The formal dimension inspects how Arab hospitality is personified, symbolised and represented in the hospitality industries, and therefore examined in the context of the commercial (or commodified) domain. The informal aspect is examined by interpreting the roots of Arab hospitality in view of Bedouin rituals and cultures to comprehend how *karam* (hospitality) has been traditionally communicated to strangers within (and beyond) the private and social domains. Karam, however, is generally interpreted as 'generosity' or 'hospitality', though it can denote 'nobility', 'grace' and 'refinement' (Shryock 2004: 36).

Therefore, the chapter begins by reviewing the roots of Arab hospitality, particularly in the context of pre-Islamic and Islamic societies and cultures. The Bedouin, prominent in the Abrahamic (e.g. Christian, Jewish and Islamic) theological narrative, continue to exert an influence on Arab hospitality. The spaces of hospitality—the private, commercial and social domains—are observed to comprehend host–guest relationships in non-Western settings. Moreover, within the context of both the informal and formal provisions and practices of Arab hospitality, there is a paradox whereby the inhospitable and hostile climate towards Arabs and Muslims actually nullifies pre-modern perceptions of Arab (or Bedouin) hospitality. As the Arab world, including countries in the Middle East and North Africa, accommodates 93 per cent (approximately 341 million) of the world's Muslims (De Silver & Masci 2017), this chapter draws upon the theology of Islam to analyse the commercial, private and social spaces of hospitality.

Arab hospitality: Pre-Islamic and Islamic attributes

The theology of hospitality in an Arab context can be located in the three Abrahamic (monotheistic) faiths—Christianity, Islam and Judaism. Therefore, an 'Abrahamic legacy' can be interpreted as a 'shared and second language', that is, an expression (and extension to others) of human kindness (Shryock 2012: 21). In theological teachings, Abraham's act of kindness and generosity is representational, where he invited three travellers into his tent, not knowing they were angels in the guise of humans, and provided them with food, rest and shelter. This narrative is a marker of the virtue of hospitality in monotheistic religions, indicating the role ethics plays in hospitality, particularly towards strangers. The socio-symbolic importance associated with greeting the guest (the traveller or stranger) in the Arab world and welcoming him/her into one's abode is rooted in pre-Islamic cultures and rituals associated with 'Bedouin Arab hospitality' (Al-Oun & Al-Homoud 2008; Barnes 2013; Sobh, Belk, & Wilson 2013). Consequently, Arab hospitality is symbolically associated with narratives that can be traced back to the pre-Islamic era, mythologised through such legendary characters as Hatim al-Tai, who was a poet from Ha'il in the northwest region of Saudi Arabia and who died in 578 AD. He has been famed in the Arab world for his extreme generosity to others (see Stetkevych 2000). Arab hospitality has been popularised by historians and social analysts as having the ability to progressively influence the future status of the guest. According to Attar (2005: 19):

> For the ancient Arabs, hospitality, in its general and wider sense, also means that it was possible for a stranger to become part of the tribe. If one shared a meal with his hosts, or tasted a few drops of the host's blood he would become part of the family and the group.

However, Bravmann (1962) associated generosity of the pre-Islamic period with charity of the Islamic era, as expressed in the Qur'an (1997) (Chapter 57, Verse 7) in terms of spending one's wealth through focusing on charitable deeds, for instance:

> Believe in Allah and His Messenger and spend out of that in which He has made you successors. For those who have believed among you and spent, there will be a great reward.

Therefore, generosity continued to manifest itself in many ways in Islam. Informatively, the illustrious Moroccan traveller Ibn Battuta (2004: 4) travelled throughout parts of the Islamic world from Asia to West Africa from 1325 to 1354CE, noting ways in which hospitality was situated and presented. He thus observed that travellers were 'entertained' and 'hospitably welcomed' at resthouses and hospices, often maintained by 'generations of benefactors'. Siddiqui (2017) links the virtue of hospitality with the theology of Islam to highlight the ethical relationship between the host and guest/traveller, which suppresses the potential for hosts to experience inhospitable or hostile encounters with people viewed as strangers. Sobh et al. (2013: 446) note that there is a 'general consensus among Muslim scholars that hospitality and generosity toward guests are an integral part of faith in Islam'.

Charles Montagu Doughty, an English writer travelling through the Arabian Peninsula during the 1870s and living amongst Bedouin communities, often indicated how he was positively received by others in hospitable ways. These experiences encouraged him to view Arab hospitality in a genuine and organic way, despite disagreement from other fellow Europeans. Doughty (1921: 152, 257) states:

> In the hospitality of the Arabs is kinship and assurance, in their insecure countries. This is the piety of the Arab life, this is the sanctity of the Arabian religion, where we may not look for other. Returning one day, in Syria, from a journey, I enquired the way of a countryman in the road. It was noon; the young man, who went by eating bread and cheese, paused and cut a piece of his girdle-cake, with a pleasant look, and presented it to the stranger: when I shook the head, he cut a rasher of cheese and put it silently to my mouth; and only then he thought it a time to speak. Also if a stranger enter vine-yard or orchard, he is a guest of that field; and, in the summer months, the goodman, if he be there, will bring some of his fruits to refresh him … I speak many times of the Arabian hospitality, since this I have been often questioned in Europe and for a memorial of worthy persons.

Nonetheless, there is a point at which it is necessary to acknowledge the persistence of 'regimes of hospitality' often determining the way in which hospitality is constructed, conveyed and negotiated. The commercial hospitality and tourism industries are arguably proactive in such a determination. Shryock's (2004) ethnography of the Balga Bedouin living in the suburbs of Amman, Jordan, illustrates the application of regimes of hospitality in relation to gender dimensions. Opportunities for unmarried females to work in heritage sites socially compromise traditional values, as they are used as 'bait to attract tourists' (2004: 46), thus representing a social risk, especially if they play a direct role in commercial transactions and activities deemed to be culturally inappropriate (e.g. serving coffee to male tourists). Understandably, the spatial difference between the male guest and the Arab woman has also been a significant defining factor of Arab hospitality within private space. This has been influenced at varying degrees by socio-cultural notions of 'honour and shame', particularly within the context of the more traditional societies (Young 2007: 49). Accordingly, Young's (2007: 50) study concerning the Rashaayda Bedouin of eastern Sudan, indicated that it should not be always assumed that men are fundamentally the 'dispensers of generous hospitality' and women are the 'mere bystanders', as this would underestimate the crucial role of women in the 'exchange of food and shelter'. The modernisation of gendered roles and responsibilities challenges the degree to which Arab hospitality can fully retain its conventional elements and customary features.

Indeed, the boundaries of the theology of Islam are being challenged, especially in the context of the impacts of modernity and globalisation. Faith is often 'tested' through problematic ways in receiving others in modern times, especially in the context of economic migration and urban development. This is apparent by the ways in which guests, particularly Asian immigrant workers, do not always consistently receive hospitality and hospitable relations in Arab countries. As discussed later, this could thus indicate that conformity to Arab principles and legacies of hospitality are not always pervasive. Nonetheless, in terms of regimes of hospitality, one system of Arab hospitality concerns the fact that, in a non-particularistic way, hospitality is culturally and spatially determined. Accordingly, individuals across the Arab diaspora can share with one another through mobility and migration a discourse of hospitality based on pan-Arab notions of hospitality, induced by a common language and religion (though not entirely), as well as similar cultural idiosyncrasies (Stephenson 2014). This may manifest in such activities as pan-Arab cultural and sporting events, or even at a micro-level of interaction in terms of mutual affinities with one another within the context of common places and spaces in everyday life.

Feghali (1997) observes that hospitality thus predates the third Pillar of Islam: *Zakat* (giving alms or charity). Arab societies place heavy emphasis on hospitality as a core value, which contains undertones of Bedouin traditions that have retained their importance in Islam. Nonetheless, in terms of Islamic doctrine the importance of karam (hospitality) persists. Shryock (2009: 34) emphasises that 'it is a compliment to say of a man who forgets his prayers, but treats his guests well that "hospitality is his religion"'. There are several references in the Qur'an which emphasise the importance of looking after guests well and welcoming them in 'God's name' (Siddiqui 2017). In the Qur'an (1997), *Surah Hud* (Chapter 11) states:

> And certainly did Our messenger (i.e. angels) come to Abraham with good tidying; they said 'Peace'. He said, 'Peace', and did not delay in bringing (them) a roasted calf (Verse 69) ... So fear Allah and do not disgrace me concerning my guests. Is there not among you a man of reason (Verse 78).

Surah adh-Dhariyat (Chapter 51, Verse 24–27) indicates the theological narrative of hospitality:

> Has there reached you the story of the honoured guests of Abraham (Verse 24). When they entered upon him and said, '[We greet you with] peace.' He answered, '[And upon you] peace; [you are] a people unknown' (Verse 25). Then he went to his family and came with a fat [roasted] calf (Verse 26). And placed it near them; he said, 'Will you not eat?' (Verse 27)

The above quotations from the Qur'an underscore the prominence of hospitality, generosity and kindness towards guests. Islamic hospitality is thus entrenched within other forms of Islamic scripture. Vukonić (2010: 40) observes that the Prophet's Hadith (146) states that: 'There is no wellbeing in a family which does not welcome and treat guests well.' Subsequently, being hospitable to others is seen in the Hadith as a pathway to paradise ('Jannah') (2010: 40). These principles underpinning Arab hospitality further echo the theology of Islam, which promotes the importance of duty and obligations to others rather than self-indulgence. Hence, as noted in the Qur'an (1997) (Chapter 4, Verse 36):

> Worship Allah and associate nothing with Him, and to parents do good, and to relatives, orphans, the needy, the near neighbor, the neighbor farther away, the companion at your side, the traveler, and those whom your right hands possess. Indeed, Allah does not like those who are self-deluding and boastful.

Private spaces of Arab hospitality

The social and symbolic function and structure of the family home in Islamic communities are indicative of Arab hospitality and the Islamic elements of hospitality (Memarian, Toghr-oljerdi, & Ranjbar-Kermani 2011; Othman, Arid, & Buys 2015; Sobh & Belk 2011). Hospitality can be operationalised in terms of family gatherings and events, but modesty is integral to the production of hospitable activities. As Othman et al. (2015: 21) express:

> Maintaining physical modesty through dress code becomes an integral part of protecting the females' body privacy while allowing hospitable activities to continue within a home.

Although houses in the Arab world can be very welcoming to guests, they often serve to 'safeguard their own integrity, which is often described as *hurma*, as "sacredness" or "inviolability"' (Shryock 2004: 36). Therefore, the domestic area or the home of the host, represents private space that guests and extended kin, friends and strangers enter to receive basic hospitality provision of food, rest and shelter. The private space is an embodiment of theological and philosophical forces of duty, obligations to others, and ethical relations between hosts and guests. However, Siddiqui's (2017) interpretation of hospitality within the context of private domains in Islam and Christianity suggests that religion precedes philosophy, especially as hosts are aware of the presence of God. Therefore, it can be argued that hospitable relations are triadic (i.e. God–host–guest). As Siddiqui (2017: n.p.) suggests:

> We ourselves are all guests of God's hospitality and have an obligation to show hospitality to others. Thus, our hospitality to others is a sign of our love for God as God is always present when guests are present at the table.

From a young age, children in Arab homes are socialised into the importance of hospitality as both a personal quality and a symbol of status (Feghali 1997). There is a symbolic relationship between hospitality and status, which extends to honour, reputation and sovereignty (Young 2007; Shryock 2009, 2012; Sobh et al. 2013). Moreover, in terms of status it is clear that power relations surface in private spaces as hosts strive to preserve their honour, reputation and sovereignty. At the same time, however, guests 'judge' the quality of their Arab hospitality experience. Accordingly, one significant concern for the host is that if she/he fails to provide (or be seen to provide) a hospitable encounter or experience, this could trigger the guest to later speak ill of the host to fellow kin. The host's character, honour and reputation could thus be tarnished and her/his sovereignty weakened (Shryock 2012).

The laws of hospitality are arguably meaningless without the symbolic performance of rituals, which are also central to the construction of Arab identities. Moreover, the hospitality rituals are symbolic of Bedouin pasts and continue to exert their influence over Arabs in the domestic sphere (Sobh et al. 2013). In private space, or what Sobh et al. (2013) refer to as 'home hospitality', the Arab host–guest relationship is secured through the ritualised drinking of Arabic coffee. The preparation, serving and drinking of Arabic coffee (*ghahwa*) in the Arab home helps the host to earn a reputation for generosity, or karam (Young 2007), thus shielding the host from being demonised and shamed by a guest. In Jordan, for instance, a cup of coffee is shared with guests to secure the status and sovereignty of the host (Shryock 2004, 2012). The coffee ritual is a sequential act and is essential in assimilating the guest as a stranger (in the home) into the private space of hospitality (Sobh et al. 2013). In addition to sharing coffee, the host and guest consume food together, which is a customary and ritualised act attached to Arab food culture. Food is symbolic in hospitality because it is perceived as an embodiment of God. In Islam and Christianity, when one is near food she/he is in God's presence (Siddiqui 2017). Sobh et al. explain the gastronomic culture of Qataris:

> After serving coffee and dates, the host typically brings a range of local snacks and desserts called *fualah*. The variety and amount of *fualah* will vary based on the status of the guest, the occasion of the visit, and whether the guest is expected or the visit is improvised. *Fualah* is generally followed by a traditional dinner for men (rice and lamb) and increasingly a modern banquet for women. Display is very important and there should be more food than the party could possibly eat.
>
> *(2013: 452, authors' emphasis)*

The challenges concerning such forms of hospitality relate to the social pressure for guests to conform to the consumption of generous offerings and not offend the host. In a lifestyle study of Qatari women, Donnelly et al. (2011) found that as social courtesy and hospitality were central features in the social interaction of women during social gatherings and home events, women would often feel obliged to eat types of food that were knowingly unhealthy food choices. Food is thus inextricably linked to conceptions of Arab hospitality, which was also a popular perceived attribute prior to the modernisation of the Arab world. Doughty (1921) recalled the worthiness of the hospitality that he received in his Arabian Peninsula travels, especially in terms of being presented with a variety of food and beverage when he visited various camps and villages: a sacrificed yearling lamb (1921: 235), rice and steaming mutton (1921: 236), sacrificed bull (1921: 210), dates and coffee (1921: 60), buttermilk (1921: 309) and tamarind (1921: 358). The presentation of high quality food to guests is also characteristic of Arab hospitality in pre-Islamic times. According to Stetkevych (2000: 98):

> for hospitality in the quintessential Bedouin sense implies also offering the guest meat: the camel breeder slaughters a camel and the huntsman brings in the best of his kill. Within this ethos, generosity was thus held as the Bedouin's emblematic virtue.

Eating and drinking rituals associated with Arab hospitality have been subjected to Orientalist (visual and verbal) constructions, popularly portraying Arabs eating in an uncivilised manner. These textual images of Arabs performing hospitality in terms of sitting together and feasting, and eating large quantities of food with their hands are presented to the West as an uncivilised performance. Thus, the 'Othering' of Arab hospitality in the private space takes place through the 'Western' gaze as the Orient is Orientalised because gastronomic cultures are aligned to notions of the 'savage body', which contain undertones of animality (Steet 2000: 86). Steet argues that *National Geographic* photographs and captions in the 1930s and 1940s demonised representations of Arab hospitality in a non-Western, exotic and non-European context. The images captured Arabs as undertaking hospitality and thus contributing to the Orientalisation of Arab hospitality for the Western gaze. For instance, in response to a photographic caption: *Bedouins of the Author's Escort Enjoy a Meal of Rice and Dried Shark (October 1932)*, Steet (2000: 86–87) infers that Arab hospitality was perceived to be undesirable and undomesticated, stating:

> The caption to a 1932 picture of Arabs sitting on the ground eating … read: 'Using no knife or fork, the Arab takes rice in his right hand, squeezes it into a ball, and bolts it. If fowl or mutton is served, the leader of the party tears it to pieces and tosses a

portion to each diner, who deftly catches it in mid-air.' [...] These were not pictures of men sitting in a huddle on the ground; these were pictures of non-Europeans eating, and more specifically, Arabs who ate like animals. This framing changed everything. Viewers looked for and at difference; the photographs, therefore, became interesting and could reveal much more than they did at first glance.

Said's (1978) work on Orientalism is pertinent in realising how hospitality has historically been portrayed by the West, where art and literature have aided the construction of stereotypes of the Orient (the 'East') and in this case the Arab world (see also Kabbani 1986). Culture and daily life has been depicted as static, uncivilised and inferior—irrespective of the fact that Bedouin hospitality has been portrayed and characterised as 'legendary' (Withey 1998: 256). Nonetheless, hospitality is not something which is stationary in time and space. Fattah and Eddy-U (2017) examine ways in which Egyptian Bedouin are represented in English-language tourist brochures and how tour operators wish to preserve the traditional images of Bedouin life, irrespective of the fact that these communities have been socio-culturally and economically transformed through modernisation. This is acknowledged by the way in which 'warm hospitality' and the willingness of hosts to respond to tourist activities are projected and constructed (Fattah & Eddy-U 2017: 201). However, in some Arab states (UAE and Qatar, for instance) there have been significant capital investments in the development of destinations that are highly sophisticated, technologically advanced and innovatively driven (see Scharfenort 2017; Stephenson 2014; Wakefield 2017). Subsequently, it could be argued that there is an attempt in parts of the Arab world (intentional or otherwise) to disassociate from traditional elements of social life and authentic representations of the past through a process of de-orientalisation. Indeed, the way in which hospitality has been artificialised and impersonalised represented key elements of the postmodernisation of hospitality in parts of the Arab world.

Commercial spaces of Arab hospitality

The Bedouin desert has been transformed into an urban landscape where the 'old' has merged with the 'new' to deliver the Arab hospitality experience (Al-Oun & Al Homoud 2008). Commercial spaces of hospitality occupy a tangible and an intangible presence in Arab cities, where there is often no perceivable alternative than to develop the hospitality and tourism industries. The depletion of oil over the next century in the Gulf Cooperation Council (GCC) region, for instance, indicates the crucial importance of these industries in strengthening economic buoyancy (Stephenson 2017). As Stephenson (2017: 6) reaffirmed: 'As the oil sector is not labour intensive, the need for states to diversify and create more labour-intensive industries is imperative.' Ironically, however, for members of the GCC region, notably UAE, Qatar and Saudi Arabia, there have been challenges in terms of encouraging nationals to work in the tourism and hospitality industries (Sadi and Henderson 2005; Stephenson et al. 2010), which affect the extent to which Arab hospitality products are actually grounded by the geo-cultural idiosyncrasies and attributes of the region. Subsequently, limitations in the availability of cultural ambassadors of hospitality in parts of the Arab world could threaten the long-term survival of Arab forms of formal hospitality within a regional context.

Therefore, the non-Arab host is often a perpetual reality in terms of welcoming and servicing the new non-Arab guest, which proliferates as the hospitalities industries expand to respond to market demands resulting in 'the actual practice of non-Arab hospitality' (Sobh et al. 2013: 456). Moreover, the 'new' extends to the arrival of guests from non-Arab nations as these have been the target markets for businesses in Arab cities, despite the fact that such 'new' people and populations 'do not subscribe to the same culture of hospitality' (Barnes 2013: n.p.). However, non-Arabs serving and servicing hospitality in commercial spaces could also potentially challenge Oriental discourses and representations, as well as romanticised imagery of the exotic 'Arab Other'. This reflects Sardar's (1998: 165) position that there has been a common movement or indeed a digression from the 'quest for cultural authenticity'. For instance, Dubai had to 'forfeit the true principles of Arabian/Bedouin hospitality' with its ambition to become a neo-global (tourism) city, consequently staging hospitality which is detached from the past in terms of location (e.g. desert) and oral narratives (e.g. stories) (Barnes 2013).

Despite the commercial spaces of hospitality, where economically driven exchanges or transactions take place between the host and guest in the Arab world, theological and philosophical principles and practices have not been eradicated altogether. In fact, the religious obligation to take care of guests and the philosophical duty to offer hospitality are embedded within commercialised Arab hospitality products, services and experiences (Friese 2004; Siddiqui 2017; Zamani-Farahani & Henderson 2010). In some Arab countries, Islam retains its governance within hospitality-related commercial activities (e.g. tourism) and cannot necessarily be fully compromised. Saudi Arabia, for instance, already has the 'Islamic resources and infrastructure in place' to help develop Islamic forms of hospitality and tourism beyond the pilgrimage product (Ekiz, Öter, & Stephenson 2017: 133). Also, the Emirate of Sharjah in the United Arab Emirates has the potential to become a central hub in the region for Islamic tourism (Ashill, Williams, & Chathoth 2017). These authors acknowledge that the destination has an abundance of services, activities and attractions that can cater for Muslim (and non-Muslim) travellers. Sharjah thus embodies a form of hospitality that is family oriented and associated with Islamic traditions.

Traditional Arab hospitality can still be found in many forms across the Arab nations. Kan Zaman at the Abu Jaber Estate in Amman, Jordan, for instance, is a tourist village home to a large restaurant and coffee shop, souk and array of shops selling glassware, jewellery and ceramics (Teller 2013). For Shryock (2004: 43), the Kan Zaman is a place where Orientalist images of 'traditional hospitality' thrive as karam retains its symbolic and spiritual value in the ritual of preparing and serving coffee. This form of hospitality can also publicly represent heritage. The 'traditional village of al-Saha', located in a southern suburb of Beirut, is an illustration of how hospitality can be a touristic event though based on inherent elements of Islamic and cultural forms of hospitality. Alcohol is not available to visitors and Islamic principles underpin entertainment, along with the demonstration of Islamic and Arabic architecture, art, music and poetry. The profit accrued from this enterprise is donated to the Al-Mabarrat, a philanthropic body administering charities for people in need (Mona 2006).

One of the significant challenges relates to the extent to which it is really possible to differentiate between authentic and inauthentic forms of Arab hospitality, and also between traditional and non-traditional forms of hospitality. To contextualise commercialised notions of Arab hospitality within a more contemporary post-Bedu context would indeed be historically misplaced. The traditional trade routes themselves fuelled commercial hospitality across the Middle East region, where caravanserais, teahouses, guesthouses and wakalahs fostered capitalist development (Rodinson 2007). Arab cities and towns are as global and cosmopolitan as those in the West, witnessing the mass immigration of people and populations from both developed and developing worlds. As a result, Arab nationals have often found themselves to be the minority population, whereas migrants are the majority. In the UAE, for instance, 11.5 per cent of the total population represents Arab nationals, which means that 88.5 per cent are foreign nationals. In Qatar, 10.1 per cent represents Arab nationals, while 89.9 per cent are foreign nationals (Gulf

Labour Markets and Migration 2016). Labour-led migration from developed and developing countries to the Gulf Cooperation Council (GCC) states played a major role in changing the demographic landscape of particular Arab nations.

Hospitality experiences of (labour) migrants (as non-Arabs) differ from that of the hosts (Arabs), which could be seen to undermine the theological virtues and philosophical morals embedded in Arab hospitality. The extension of private forms of Arab hospitality to migrant 'guests' (considered as foreigners by their Arab hosts) is not always forthcoming, though commercial Arab hospitality may well extend to the wealthy migrants (e.g. from Western countries). In Qatar, for instance, such hospitality is provided by a non-Arab (e.g. non-Qataris) labour force (Sobh et al. 2013), which is not uncommon in such states as Kuwait and the UAE.

Nonetheless, given that Islam is the dominant religion in the region, Arab hospitality is inextricably tied to Islamic forms of hospitality. This form of hospitality is becoming increasingly visible. Stephenson (2014) argues that Islamic hotels and Shari'a-compliant products and services have significant scope for future development. However, he observes that given the movement towards establishing ultra-modernised places and destinations, Islamic traditions could be endangered. He states:

> Nevertheless, grandiose plans that place significant emphasis on extravagance and luxury could be counterproductive to the expansion of self-effacing forms of hospitality pertinent to Islamic hotel sector development. Consequently, the fundamental objective would be to produce moderate developments, which focus more on the essence of Islam and at the same time reflect a sense of community pride and value.
>
> *(Stephenson 2014: 159)*

Indeed, there are forms of public and commercial hospitality based on various gradations and perceptions of Islamic purity, which would always need to be contextualised in relation to both liberal and conservative interpretations of Islamic forms of hospitality across Arab states.

Hospitality and inhospitality in social spaces

Nonetheless, if migrant workers from low socio-economic backgrounds confront inhospitable and hostile climates in the host destination, where they have little access to spaces of hospitality, then this could indicate that elements of Arab hospitality have profoundly changed. Accordingly, there may well be a dialectical relationship between inhospitality and hostility manifested in particular ways. A critical issue in the discussion of hospitality is hostility, as Derrida (2000: 45) raises in his essay on the *Foreigner Question*: 'the foreigner (*hostis*) welcomed as guest or as enemy. Hospitality, hostility, *hospitality*'. Although the kafala (sponsorship) system, established to meet labour demands in particular nations such as those on the Arabian Peninsula, welcomed low-skilled migrant workers, they too faced socio-economic inequalities (Coates Ulrichsen 2016).

The long-term challenges faced by unpretentious forms of hospitality, whether linked to Islamic teachings or cultural idiosyncrasies, concern the extent to which perceptions of Islamic hospitality are overshadowed by socio-political constructions of hostility, imbued by Islamophobia. Following the 9/11 terrorist attacks on the World Trade Centre, the international Muslim (and Arab) community has become susceptible to public distrust and anti-Muslim sentiment. Islamophobia compromises the perception of Islamic communities as being hospitable, civilised and safe (Stephenson 2014: 162). Therefore, this fear can affect hospitable exchanges, relations and experiences. Said (1997: iv) notes how Islam is incriminated on a number of conjectures, stating:

> Yet there is a consensus on 'Islam' as a kind of scapegoat for everything we do not happen to like about the world's new political, social and economic patterns. For the right, Islam represents barbarism; for the left, medieval theocracy; for the centre, a kind of distasteful exoticism.

Contemporary representational concerns over popularised perceptions of Arabs as being hostile to others, or outsiders, challenges traditional and Islamic conceptions of hospitality and hospitableness. Such persistence in the long-term will no doubt counteract the positive attributes of Arab hospitality that have prevailed, though in various forms, since the pre-Islamic era.

Conclusion

The role that Arab hospitality plays in private, commercial and social spaces is inherently complex, especially as Arab nations transcend from the pre-modern to modern and postmodern times: in this transition deconstructions of hospitality are often caught up in the trajectories of Orientalism and de-Orientalism. Despite contextualising Arab hospitality, it should be noted that the social space of hospitality does not exist in isolation but is located within private and commercial spaces and domains.

It is clear that pre-Islamic values and virtues of hospitable relations are still prevalent in the Islamic era. The 'old' Arab hospitality is a tourist attraction and there are attempts to stage the authentic 'old' hospitality in the commercial domain, but by non-Arabs working in the hospitality industry. The stranger (e.g. tourist and/or immigrant) as a guest cannot always successfully reach the 'back stage', or the private space where the laws of hospitality stemming from pre-Islamic and Islamic theologies authenticate Arab hospitality—or gaze upon the fantasised visuals of Orientalist representations of Arab Bedouin hospitality.

Future theoretical and conceptual interpretations of Arab hospitality should persist in examining the role of the guest in view of private, commercial and social spaces of hospitality. Future research agendas could aim to investigate the contribution women make to hosting and staging the Arab hospitality experience. This would advance our understanding of patriarchal ideologies underlying the preservation of male honour, reputation and sovereignty in Arab homes and in public spaces too. There is potential to pursue a case study approach on how socio-economic power across the Arab world, social class and strata-based inequalities characterise and determine Arab hospitality. This could therefore be contrasted to looking at cases concerning how hospitality intersects with, and is defined by, excessive wealth and conspicuous consumption.

Although there is a need to be aware of the boundaries of Arab hospitality based on disposable income and economic power, it would also be crucial to distinguish how this form of hospitality interconnects with religious groups beyond Islam, most notably amongst the Arab Christians. Such positioning would encourage a more multi-dimensional approach to deciphering Arab hospitality to develop. Moreover, as this chapter inspected hospitality in the Arab world there is potential to research the Arab diaspora in non-Arab nations (e.g. Argentina, Brazil, France and the US), especially to comprehend the transitionary nature of Arab hospitality in the context of migration studies. In view of the above, future researchers deconstructing the theories, philosophies and theologies of Arab hospitality could thus look in more depth in relation to national boundaries, rural and urban distinctions, deeper cultural idiosyncrasies and gender differentials.

References

Al-Oun, S., & Al-Homoud, M. (2008) 'The potential for developing community-based tourism among the Bedouins in the Badia of Jordan', *Journal of Heritage Tourism*, 3(1): 36–54.

Ashill, N.J. Williams, P., & Chathoth, P. (2017) 'Examining the marketing opportunities of Sharjah as an Islamic tourism destination', in M.L. Stephenson, & Ala Al-Hamarneh, *International Tourism Development and the Gulf Cooperation Council States: Challenges and Opportunities* (pp. 171–184). London: Routledge.

Attar, S. (2005) 'Conflicting accounts on the fear of strangers: Muslim and Arab perceptions of Europeans in Medieval geographical literature', *Arab Studies Quarterly*, 27(4): 17–29.

Barnes, J. (2013) 'Bedouin' hospitality in the neo-global city of Dubai', *E-International Relations*. Available online: www.e-ir.info/2013/10/16/bedouin-hospitality-in-the-neo-global-city-of-dubai/ (Accessed 2 July 2017).

Battuta, I. (2004) *Travels in Asia and Africa: 1325e1354* (H.A.R. Gibb, Trans.). Oxon: Routledge Curzon.

Bravmann, M.M. (1962) 'The surplus of property—an early Arab social concept', *Der Islam*, (Berlin), 38(62): 28–50

Coates Ulrichsen, K. (2016) *The Gulf States in International Political Economy*. New York: Palgrave Macmillan.

De Silver, D., & Masci, D. (2017) 'World's Muslim population more widespread than you might think'. Pew Research Centre. Available online: www.pewresearch.org/fact-tank/2017/01/31/worlds-muslim-population-more-widespread-than-you-might-think/ (Accessed 12 July 2017).

Derrida, J. (1997/2000) *Of Hospitality*. Stanford, CA: Stanford University Press.

Donnelly, T.T., Al Suwaidi, J., Al Bulushi, A., Al Enazi, N., Yassin, K., Rehman, A.M., Hassan, A.A., & Idris, Z. (2011) 'The influence of cultural and social factors on healthy lifestyle of Arabic women', *Avicenna*, 3: 1–13.

Doughty, C.M. (1921) *Travels in Arabia Deserta, Volume 2*. London: Philip Lee Warner.

Eickelman, C. (1984) *Women and Community in Oman*. New York: New York University Press.

Ekiz, E. Öter, Z., & Stephenson, M.L. (2017) 'Tourism development in the Kingdom of Saudi Arabia: Determining the problems and resolving the challenges', in M.L. Stephenson, & A. Al-Hamarneh, *International Tourism Development and the Gulf Cooperation Council States: Challenges and Opportunities* (pp. 124–139). London: Routledge.

Fattah, A.A., & Eddy-U, M. (2017) 'Representation of Egyptian Bedouins in English-language tourist brochures', in H. Almuhrzi, H. Alriyami, & N. Scott (eds), *Tourism in the Arab World* (pp. 188–206). Bristol: Channel View Publications.

Feghali, E. (1997) 'Arab cultural communication patterns', *International Journal of Intercultural Relations*, 21(3): 345–378.

Fernea Warnock, E. (1975) *A Street in Marrakech: A Personal View of Urban Women in Morocco*. New York: Doubleday.

Fernea Warnock, E. (1989) *Guests of the Sheik: An Ethnography of an Iraqi Village*. New York: Doubleday.

Friese, H. (2004) 'Spaces of hospitality', *Journal of the Theoretical Humanities*, 9(2): 67–79.

Gulf Labour Markets and Migration (2016) 'GCC: total population and percentage of nationals and foreign nationals in GCC countries'. Demographic and economic database. Available online: http:// gulfmigration.eu/gcc-total-population-percentage-nationals-foreign-nationals-gcc-countries-national-statistics-2010-2016-numbers/ (Accessed 21 July 2017).

Kabbani, R. (1986) *Europe's Myths of Orient*. London: Pandora.

Lashley, C. (2000) 'Towards a theoretical understanding', in C. Lashley, & A. Morrison (eds), *In Search of Hospitality: Theoretical Perspectives and Debates* (pp. 1–17). London: Routledge.

Memarian, G.H, Toghr-oljerdi, S.M.H., & Ranjbar-Kermani, A.M. (2011) 'Privacy of house in Islamic culture: A comparative study of pattern of privacy in houses in Kerman', *International Journal of Architecture and Urban Planning*, 21(2): 69–77.

Meneley, A. (1996) *Tournaments of Value: Sociability and Hierarchy in a Yemeni Town*. Toronto: University of Toronto Press.

Mona, H. (2006) 'Pious entertainment in Beirut: Al-Saha traditional village', *ISIM Review 'Popular Piety'*, 17: 10–11.

Othman, Z., Arid R., & Buys L. (2015) 'Privacy, modesty, hospitality, and the design of Muslims homes: A literature review', *Frontiers of Architectural Research*, 4: 12–23.

Qur'an, The (1997) *Arabic Text with Corresponding English Meanings*. Jeddah, Saudi Arabia: Abul Qasim Publishing House.

Rodinson, M. (2007) *Islam and Capitalism*. London: Saqi.

Sadi M., & Henderson, J.C. (2005) 'Local versus foreign workers in the hospitality and tourism industry: A Saudi Arabian perspective', *Cornell Hotel and Restaurant Administration Quarterly*, 46(2): 247–257.

Said, E.W. (1978) *Orientalism*. London: Routledge & Kegan Paul.

Said, E.W. (1997) *Covering Islam: How the Media and Experts Determine How We See the Rest of the World*. New York: Vintage Books.

Sardar, Z. (1998) *Postmodernism and the Other: The New Imperialism of Western Culture*. London: Pluto Press.

Scharfenort, N. (2017) 'Tourism development challenges in Qatar: Diversification and growth', in M.L. Stephenson, & A. Al-Hamarneh (eds), *International Tourism Development and the Gulf Cooperation Council States: Challenges and Opportunities* (pp. 140–155). London: Routledge.

Shryock, A. (2004) 'The new Jordanian hospitality: House, host and guest in the culture of public display', *Comparative Studies in Society and History*, 46(1): 35–62.

Shryock, A. (2009) 'Hospitality lessons: Learning the shared language of Derrida and the Balga Bedouin', *Paragraph*, 32(1): 32–50.

Shryock, A. (2012) 'Breaking hospitality apart: Bad hosts, bad guest, and the problem of sovereignty', *Journal of the Royal Anthropological Institute*, 18: 20–23.

Siddiqui, M. (2017) 'Welcoming in God's name: Hospitality in Islam and Christianity', Religion and Ethics. Available online: www.abc.net.au/religion/welcoming-in-gods-name-hospitality-in-islam-and-christianity/10096180 (Accessed 9 March 2017).

Sobh, R., & Belk, R. (2011) 'Domains of privacy and hospitality in Arab Gulf homes', in Z. Yi, J.J. Xiao, J. Cotte, & L. Price (eds), *Asia-Pacific Advances in Consumer Research, Volume 9* (pp. 88–90). Duluth, MN: Association for Consumer Research.

Sobh, R., Belk, R.W., & Wilson, J.A.J. (2013) 'Islamic Arab hospitality and multiculturalism', *Marketing Theory*, 13(4): 443–463.

Steet, L. (2000) *Veils and Daggers: A Century of National Geographic's Representation of the Arab World*. Philadelphia, PA: Temple University Press.

Stephenson, M. L. (2014) 'Deciphering "Islamic hospitality": Developments, challenges and opportunities', *Tourism Management*, 40: 155–164.

Stephenson, M. L. (2017) 'Deciphering international tourism development in the GCC region', in M.L. Stephenson, & A. Al-Hamarneh (eds), *International Tourism Development and the Gulf Cooperation Council States: Challenges and Opportunities* (pp. 1–25). London: Routledge.

Stephenson, M.L., & Ali, N. (2010) 'Tourism, travel and Islamophobia: Post 9/11 journeys of Muslims in non-Muslim states', in N. Scott, & J. Jafari (eds), *Tourism in the Muslim World* (pp. 235–251). Bingley: Emerald.

Stephenson, M.L., Russell, K.A., & Edgar, D. (2010) 'Islamic hospitality in the UAE: indigenisation of products and human capital', *Journal of Islamic Marketing*, 1(1): 9–24.

Stetkevych, J. (2000) 'Sacrifice and redemption in early Islamic poetry: Al-Ḥuṭay'ah's Wretched Hunter', *Journal of Arabic Literature*, 31(2): 89–120.

Teller, M. (2013) *The Rough Guide to Jordan*, 5th edn. London: Rough Guides.

Vukonić, B. (2010) 'Do we all understand each other?', in N. Scott, & J. Jafari (eds), *Tourism in the Muslim World: Bridging Tourism Theory and Practice* (pp. 31–45). Bingley: Emerald.

Wakefield, S. (2017) 'Transnational heritage in Abu Dhabi: Power, politics and identity', in M.L. Stephenson, & A. Al-Hamarneh (eds), *International Tourism Development and the Gulf Cooperation Council States: Challenges and Opportunities* (pp. 235–244). London: Routledge.

Withey, L. (1998) *Grand Tours and Cook's Tours: A History of Leisure Travel, 1750 to 1915*. London: Arum Press.

Young, W.C. (2007) 'Arab hospitality as a rite of incorporation: The case of the Rashaayda Bedouin of Eastern Sudan', *Anthropos*, 102: 47–69.

Zamani-Farahani, H., & Henderson, J.C. (2010) 'Islamic tourism and managing tourism development in Islamic societies: The cases of Iran and Saudi Arabia', *International Journal of Tourism Research*, 12: 79–89.

7

TOURISM AND INDIGENOUS COMMUNITIES

Linking reterritorialisation and decolonisation in North Africa

Christine N. Buzinde

Introduction

Tourism research on the Middle East has generally adopted a macro development lens. For instance, research on perceptions of risks involved in travel to the Middle East aims to equip local destination management organisations (DMOs) with knowledge related to how destinations are perceived and how such perceptions can inform changes to marketing campaigns. According to Long (2003), macro-approaches to development often draw on modernisation theory and they highlight large-scale structures. The predominant focus on risk perceptions related to Middle Eastern DMOs invariably regards the region via the lens of globalisation, which more often than not focuses on transnational mobility of capital and nations' ability to regulate economic activity/development. Globalisation is often characterised and measured by the concept of deterritorialisation, which 'implies that as distances and national barriers become easier and cheaper to traverse, location comes to matter less to economic activity, resulting in the detachment of production systems and consumer markets from specific (national) territories' (Hazbun 2004: 311–312).

Deterritorialisation is characteristic of modernity, an era in which dominant society has sought universal reason and 'to disengage from the past and immediate surroundings' (Bar-on 2015: 787). Drawing on Short's (2001) work, Hazbun (2004) states that globalisation tends to be solely associated with space when it should be regarded as having a dialectical relationship: *space* and *place*. Hazbun (2004: 312) argues that globalisation results not only in the homogenisation of spatiality but also inspires 'increased relevance of location and characteristics of place for global economic activity', a process he refers to as *reterritorialisation* because it highlights ways in which nation states and local social agents 'exert control over territorial assets'.

This approach to viewing society is not unique to Hazbun (2004), as many critical social theorists have long argued for similar views. For instance, a phrase similar to reterritorialisation utilised by some development scholars is the notion of micro approaches to development. Micro approaches focus on 'the level of operating or acting units' and the various experiences that characterise social actors' 'responses to [the] structural conditions' that define their societal existence (Long 2003: 10). Within the context of MENA, few studies have examined tourism from a micro development lens to highlight the actions of social actors, and there has been even less focus on North Africa and the Middle East. As communities in MENA increasingly engage in tourism development, it becomes paramount for tourism scholars to explore the varying ways in which tourism-involved communities negotiate the impacts of modernity.

Explicating the role of academia in understanding and remedying the impact of modernity on various communities, Bar-on (2015: 787) states that factions such as

> the ecological movement and its social counterpart, the human rights movement, riding on the destabilising and often destructive forces modernity brings on, are calling for a new strategy. No longer should we use the social and technological sciences to exploit the social and natural world. Instead, we must use them to exist with and to help improve the world.

This call to action is more pronounced and relevant in the global south where societies, particularly those comprised of indigenous communities, struggle to sustain themselves and to absolve themselves of the enduring effects of colonialism that have relegated them to their current compromising circumstances. Critical scholarship that examines such phenomena moves away from assumptions that constituents of the global south are victims and towards a view of these communities associated with agency and resistance.

It is important for tourism scholars researching the Middle East to go beyond deterritorialisation to allow for an understanding of new articulations of place informed by reterritorialisation. Drawing on Hazbun's (2004) work, this chapter is premised on the argument that there is a need for more tourism research on MENA in particular, which adopts a micro approach to focus on the process of reterritorialisation. A framework of reterritorialisation or a micro approach to development facilitates scholarly discussions on the various ways in which local communities, especially indigenous groups, are (re)articulating territorial particulars in the wake of globalisation. Furthermore, such an approach to examining tourism development can shed light on the various ways in which indigenous groups in the region are drawing on indigenous knowledge to navigate structural conditions in a way that allows them to use tourism as a tool that contributes to community well-being.

The term 'community well-being' refers to enhancing the social, economic and environmental dimensions associated with a given community. The enhancement of community well-being can be an outcome of community tourism development efforts. Within indigenous communities, the conceptualisation of development, as well as perceptions of indicators of well-being, are often informed by indigenous knowledge. But one might ask: what is indigenous knowledge and how is it related to North Africa? How is indigenous knowledge related to development in general and to tourism development in particular? How do researchers engage differently with indigenous communities in an attempt to understand how communities negotiate reterritorialisation? The subsequent sections of this chapter offer responses to these questions.

A synopsis of indigeneity and MENA

The nations of North Africa are often classified as Middle Eastern simply because they are, to a great extent, Arabic-speaking and Islam-observant countries. It is, however, important to note that there are many dialects spoken in North Africa, and most of them are associated with indigenous groups such as the Imazighen or Berber, the Tuareg, the Sahrawi or the Haratin, to name a few. The United Nations estimates that there are 400 million indigenous groups worldwide residing in over 90 nations (First Peoples Worldwide 2016).

Some 5 million indigenous people reside in North Africa and other Middle Eastern countries (Stephens, Nettleton, Porter, Willis, & Clark 2005). Within North Africa and the Middle East, these indigenous groups (e.g. Imazighen, Tuareg, Sahrawi and Haratin) are varyingly spread across a vast (hyper)arid landscape. Their dispersion can be attributed to arbitrary boundaries drawn by colonialists during the genesis of nation states, nomadic lifestyles, economic and environmental hardships, and/or political instability. Many of these peoples are moving to permanent settlements and are becoming increasingly involved in tourism (Al-Oun & Al-Homoud 2008; Chatelard 2005; Fattah & Eddy-U 2017; Kohl 2002; Shoup 1985).

Critical examinations of the many histories associated with indigenous populations unfortunately often indicate experiences of depravity imposed by colonialistic regimes and other forms of control over the people and their lands. Poignantly, the effects of decades of control over indigenous communities are still evident today in many parts of the world (Hall & Tucker 2004), including MENA

(Neo)colonialism is far from over; it exists in tandem with ubiquitous fascinations, by dominant society, with the lifestyles and traditions of indigenous groups. In fact, it can be argued that indigenous culture has long captivated Western imagination and in many cases has fuelled the development of cultural tourism enterprises within indigenous communities. Critics have bemoaned the proliferation of acculturation resulting from increased encounters between indigenous communities and tourists as well as the frequency of cultural commodification undertaken by communities. By the same token, a counter argument maintains that indigenous communities often obtain financial benefit from commodifying their culture. Settling this deliberation is not the goal intended for this section but rather the aim is to highlight an interesting lacuna in tourism literature that has ignored the fact that indigenous communities' engagement in tourism is often informed by local ways of knowing, otherwise referred to as indigenous knowledge (IK). So, for instance, a four-day package tour involving Bedouin culture may incorporate traditional gastronomy, modes of transportation (e.g. by camel), specific ways of engaging tourists in performances, all of which complexly draw on the intergenerational transference of IK.

Indigenous knowledge and development: An odyssey

Indigenous knowledge is the knowledge systems created by a given community and often used in decision-making processes. IK is local and geographically bound. According to Warren and Rajasekaran (1993: 8), IK is considered

> the information base for a society, which facilitates communication and decision-making. IK is the systematic body of knowledge acquired by local people through the accumulation of experiences, informal experiments, and intimate understanding of the environment in a given culture.

There are many examples of indigenous knowledge within contemporary society. Some examples outlined by Ocholla (2007: 2) include:

> medicine (e.g. Fulani treatment of cattle ticks using euphoria herbs); community development (e.g. communality or the *Ubuntu* support system); farming practices; ...

nutrition (e.g. hoodia stem/cactus used by San people to stave off hunger on hunting trips); politics (conflict resolution through *indaba, baraza, imbizo, kgotla,* etc.).

Certainly the arts, including cultural performances celebrating dance, singing and storytelling all draw on intergenerational transference of indigenous knowledge (Kalavar, Buzinde, Melubo, & Simon 2014).

Warren and Rajasekaran (1993: 9) state that '[a] growing number of case studies conducted in recent years have shown that IK systems can play an important facilitating role in establishing a dialogue between rural populations and development workers'. But how is IK connected to development? After all, postcolonial researchers and critical tourism scholars alike have criticised the role enacted by modernity and its globalisation engine in silencing the subaltern, resultantly committing what Spivak (1988) refers to as *epistemic violence.* Thus, given the history of (neo) colonialism alongside the silencing of the Other, how then is the subaltern's voice heard, if at all, in the context of development, whether tourism related or not?

Many scholars have discussed the link between indigenous knowledge and development (see Briggs, Sharp, Yacoub, Hamed, & Roe 2007; Castiano & Mkabela 2016; Johnston 2000, 2003; Sillitoe 1998). Furthermore, practitioners, including multinational development agencies like the World Bank, have highlighted the important role indigenous knowledge enacts in informing development in emerging economies. In fact, the World Bank has created a database of the various ways indigenous knowledge has been applied to development related contexts.

IK scholars have endeavoured to document the many content-related examples that show-case the copious recapitulations of indigenous knowledge systems that inform the daily lives of native communities. These efforts undertaken by IK scholars are laudable given that they have propelled IK to the forefront. However, it would be remiss to overlook the fact that this par-ticular journey is fraught with challenges related to the fight to legitimise IK (Sillitoe 2010). In the past, development agencies sought to impose knowledge on the communities they were tasked to help and such approaches were often neither successful nor sustainable because the top-down mechanisms employed precluded local involvement (Fraser, Dougill, Mabee, Reed, & McAlpine 2006; Timothy 1999). Describing the *modus operandi* employed in top-down approaches to development, Briggs and Sharp (2004: 662) state that

> [t]ypically 'development experts' from the West are brought to analyze a development problem and to offer a solution based on scientific method. Just as in the colonial period, an assumption dominates that either Western science and rationality are more advanced or refined than other positions or, more simply, that they are the norm— 'knowledge' in the singular form—from which others deviate in their fallibility.

Perceptions regarding the superiority of Western knowledge, such as those espoused by the practitioners described by Briggs and Sharp (2004), are perpetuated within many scientific communities, which more often than not favour top-down approaches, rely on the applicability of universal reason, and the superiority of scientific knowledge (Escobar 1995).

Poignantly, when contrasted to Western knowledge, IK is at times viewed as inferior, and it is often subjected to validity experiments to substantiate its legitimacy (see Varisco (2000) on IK validity related to indigenous irrigation and water harvesting in Yemeni communities). IK has indeed been rendered valid in a plethora of cases, particularly in agronomy where, for instance, PH and other soil tests have been used to verify IK approaches to soil assessment. Many have, however, critiqued efforts to ascertain the validity of IK because such endeavours are inevit-ably underpinned by assumptions regarding the superiority of Western ways of knowing and by so doing they focus solely on technical aspects of IK that can be applied to development solutions. Furthermore, as articulately mentioned by Agrawal (1995: 6), when IK is compared to Western or scientific knowledge the latter is often regarded as the 'arbiter of knowledge'. In support of Agrawal's (1995) comments, Horsthemke (2004: 38) states that such views are redundant because they are based on the argument that 'knowledge is necessarily valid, legitimate, warranted. There simply could be no *other* knowledge, i.e., knowledge that is invalid, illegitimate or unwarranted. It would not be *knowledge* then.'

Increasingly, development agencies, such as the World Bank example offered earlier in this chapter, are beginning to understand and appreciate the pivotal role IK plays in development. This outcome is in part attributable to the fact that '[t]he transfer of Western science and technology, often uncritically, [has] failed to transform the lives of the majority of people in the global south' particularly in Africa (Briggs 2013: 232). There is thus recognition of the fact that a new approach, which involves the indigenous communities for whom development efforts are targeted, is necessary. Additionally, society has come to the realisation that IK 'has value not only for the culture in which it develops, but also for scientists and entrepreneurs seeking solutions to community problems' (Mehta, Semali, Fleishman, & Maretzki 2011: 1). Resultantly, with the help of the copious body of literature produced by scholars in the field of IK, development agencies have come to appreciate the role of creating development agendas, be they tourism-related or not, which respect, incorporate and build upon local knowledge systems.

From this vantage point, IK-centred approaches to development 'take greater account for the specificities of local conditions, [and] draw on the knowledge of a population who have lived experience of the environments in question' (Briggs & Sharp 2004: 661). In 2006, and in acknowledgement of this aforementioned fact, the UN Permanent Forum on Indigenous Issues recommended that 'agencies and bodies of the United Nations and other inter-governmental organisations' should

> rethink the concept of development, with the full participation of indigenous peoples in development processes, taking into account the rights of indigenous peoples and the practices of their traditional knowledge.
>
> *(E/C.19/2003/22, Para. 26)*

Suffice it to mention that the forum bemoaned the exclusion of indigenous groups in the formulation of the millennium development goals (MDGs), and their vocal opposition was to a great extent accounted for and the problem 'remedied' in the new development agenda, the sustainable development goals (SDGs). The moral of this odyssey is that when dealing with the global south one inevitably has to account for IK. For scholars embarking on such a scholarly journey, I propose that there are certainly lessons to be gleaned from extant IK scholarship; however, such lessons have to be complemented by insights from literature on decolonisation in order to overcome the *impasse* in which IK scholars find themselves. Discussions on the IK *impasse*, as well as elaborations on decolonisation, are detailed in the subsequent section.

A path forward: IK and decolonising approaches to indigenous research

IK scholars have celebrated the fact that their work over the years has resulted in the resonance of the term 'indigenous knowledge' for academics and practitioners. They have strived to showcase 'the importance and relevance of indigenous knowledge repertoires, and the ways in which local people in communities have been able to develop and use knowledge in their everyday practices' (Briggs 2013: 240). However, IK scholars bemoan the fact that their work, which has predominantly focused on demonstrating the numerous examples of IK-related *content*, has failed to inform development (Sillitoe 2010). In fact, Sillitoe's (2010) seminal piece elaborates on this problem and calls for the formulation of viable solutions. Similarly, Briggs and Sharp (2004: 661) state that IK was 'heralded as seemingly offering a way out of the development impasse' and this is a 'contrast to the past, when traditional knowledges were typically seen as obstacles to development'. One of the underlying problems identified by IK scholars is the fact that IK content is context specific yet development practitioners are often in search of generalisable (beyond the knowledge-producing community) information.

One response to Sillitoe's (2010) treatise is Briggs' (2013) work, which proposes that IK scholarship should shift away from a focus on *content* to one on *practice*. According to Briggs (2013: 237), practice features

> ways of observing, discussing, questioning, analyzing and making sense of information, whether it is new or received. That is, the focus now becomes indigenous ways of knowing, with a sharper focus on the epistemology of indigenous knowledge systems.

Briggs' (2013) discussion of practice as entailing a focus on epistemology is indeed a welcome change and one that critical theorists of indigenous origins have long argued for. But what Briggs (2013) offers by way of much-needed direction is lacking in terms of depth, particularly as it relates to discussions on what indigenous epistemologies and methodologies mean and entail. Suffice it to mention that according to Briggs (2013), IK as practice is anchored in the local context, but it is not bound by it. Such a conceptualisation of IK enables Briggs (2013) not only to respond to Sillitoe (2010) but also to make IK useful to development practitioners. I respectfully argue that by anchoring IK's success to its extensive use by development practitioners, scholars have inadvertently led *themselves* to the IK impasse described by Sillitoe (2010). That is, are development practitioners then not wrongfully assigned the title of 'new arbiters of knowledge' because their use of IK determines whether IK is valid or not in Western development agendas? In my opinion the IK impasse is a result of IK scholars focusing on practice, as relates to how such information helps development practitioners *generalise* IK to other contexts beyond the knowledge-producing communities, rather than focusing on IK as a practice complexly undertaken by communities negotiating reterritorialisation.

Additionally, the emphasis on influencing the mindsets of development practitioners, who tend to want quick and generalisable information, relegates IK to a utilitarian and positivistic framework that results in the deterritorialisation of IK and ignores the pervasive power dynamics embedded in such knowledge exchanges. As will be discussed later in this section, the absence of concerted discussions of power is also reflected within extant critical tourism research (see Bianchi 2009; Higgins-Desbiolles & Powys Whyte 2013). Recently, this lacuna has been addressed through discussions of *decolonising* research which, as is argued in the subsequent section, is useful in guiding IK scholarship, be it tourism-related or not, towards a sustainable research agenda for and by indigenous communities.

Decolonisation inquiry

In her seminal text, *Decolonizing Methodologies*, indigenous scholar, Linda Tuhiwai Smith (1999) states that research has been used to colonise indigenous peoples who, through this process, are regarded as objects of Western research; indigenous knowledge is taken away by researchers and very little is given back to the indigenous communities. Accordingly, a radically different approach, a decolonial approach to indigenous research is needed—one that allows indigenous peoples to make important decisions about research. This does not mean that only indigenous peoples should engage in indigenous research, in part because there are many insider perspectives within any given community. The key issue is that the adoption of indigenous methodologies has to be one that critically thinks about the research processes undertaken and has to ensure that the indigenous community's interests are what drive the research methodology and the construction of knowledge related to the indigenous community in question (Rigney 1999).

From this vantage point, the term indigenous methodologies can be described as 'research by and for indigenous peoples, using techniques and methods drawn from the traditions and knowledges of those peoples' (Evan, Hole, Berg, Hutchinson, & Sookraj 2009: 894). Smith (1999: 143) alerts scholars to the significance of focusing on methodology in working on indigenous research because 'it frames the questions being asked, determines the set of instruments and methods to be employed and shapes the analysis'. Indigenous methodologies are aligned with decolonising inquiry, which comprises 'the performance of counterhegemonic theories that disrupt the colonial and the postcolonial' (Denzin & Lincoln 2008: xi). Decolonising research problematises 'imperialism, colonialism, and postcoloniality' while drawing on 'indigenous epistemologies and critical interpretive practices' designed by and for the indigenous communities in which research is taking place (Denzin & Lincoln 2008: xi). The decolonising project is underpinned by a moral ethic that aims to rebuild communities while celebrating survival, remembering, claiming, revitalising, reframing, restoring, protecting, negotiating, sharing, returning, democratising, naming (Smith 1999). Denzin and Lincoln (2008: 22) offer a clear synopsis of what a decolonising research approach to indigenous research entails in terms of its delineation of ethics, methodology, ontology and epistemology:

> Decolonising ethics ask, what does it mean to be a moral person in an indigenous, decolonised world? Decolonising epistemology asks, how do we, in a decolonising framework, know the world? What is the relationship between inquirer and the known? Every epistemology implies an ethical, moral stance between the world and the self of the researcher. Decolonising ontology raises basic questions about the nature of reality and the nature of the human being in the world.

The decolonising framework allows scholars to account for, and be sensitive to, the socio-political dynamics that shape indigenous communities and their encounters with outsiders. It also allows scholars to articulate a moral ethic that resonates with indigenous people's lived experiences and centres their voices to ensure that research is by and for them. Thus, adopting a decolonising lens to inquiry on indigenous communities facilitates a space within which scholars can begin to problematise how these communities are varying negotiating reterritorialisation, particularly in the context of community tourism development in North Africa. Given the foundation laid thus far in the chapter via discussions on links between IK and decolonising inquiry, the focus of the subsequent and penultimate section centres on suggestions for research trajectories that tourism scholars interested in indigenous community tourism in MENA, particularly North Africa, can pursue.

Envisioning tourism research in MENA through reterritorialisation and decolonisation

Critical tourism scholars recognise that extant knowledge regarding tourism is euro-centric and as such has ignored the existence of other knowledges, especially those associated with marginalised and indigenous communities (Hollinshead 1992; Tribe 2007). It should be noted that recent tourism studies have experienced a '*critical turn*' that aims 'to disrupt the dominance of Western ways of thinking, knowing and being to argue for the privileging of indigenous knowledges' (Chambers & Buzinde 2015: 2). Although useful, the critical turn has been criticised for its occlusion of discussions on power and indigeneity. Following Smith's (1999) prolegomenon, tourism scholars are calling for the decolonisation of tourism scholarship (Chambers & Buzinde 2015), which 'is about the process in both research and performance of valuing, reclaiming, and foregrounding indigenous voices and epistemologies' (Swadener & Mutua 2008: 31).

As outlined in the previous section, tourism research related to indigenous communities should adopt indigenous methodologies and should be underpinned by a restorative and emancipatory ethic. The research agenda should be co-created by and with the indigenous community and should focus on issues of interest to them. For instance, a reterritorialisation study focused on tourism development in a Bedouin community should be an outcome of collaborative efforts between the researcher and the community to ensure the process is addressing issues of relevance to the community members who are equal partners in the inquiry. Such collaborations do not preclude non-indigenous scholars, but rather they highlight the importance of ensuring that the indigenous community and not outsiders drive the research.

Researchers have to prevent themselves from falling into the trap of wanting to enter an indigenous community and, within a specified short timeframe, exit with a wealth of information. Such a trap is befitting of Smith's (1999) characterisation and admonition of research (in indigenous communities) that perpetuates the colonialistic mentality and violates indigenous ethics. Articulating a viable and ethical alternative, Smith (1999) proposes that scholars team up with communities that have requested research assistance and then take the time needed to acquaint themselves with the community and, through this encounter, uncover local indigenous methodologies. Similarly, Lakota scholar Cheryl Crazy Bull (1997: 19), states that 'knowledge would be external rather than integrated into [indigenous peoples'] lives if [they] do not put [their] own tribal mark on research'. Consequently, tourism scholars undertaking research agendas in North Africa have to find ways of working with communities in placing a tribal mark on research. For instance, in Maori culture, a tribal mark has been placed on research through the creation of an indigenous methodological frame referred to as *whanaungatanga*, which assumes a reciprocal relationship between the researcher and the indigenous community (see Bishop (1996) for further details). Similarly, in Africa there are many indigenous approaches to obtain information, regarding the role of those involved in information provision but also determining how the shared information is disseminated (see Ocholla 2007 for more information). Some of these approaches undoubtedly influence community decisions related to community-led indigenous tourism. However, until scholars begin to dedicate more scholarly attention to this phenomenon, knowledge of it will not be readily available and an opportunity to learn how communities negotiate reterritorialisation in tourism-related contexts will continue to elude us.

It is important to revisit the notion of the reciprocal relationship mentioned by Bishop (1996) because it requires the researcher to view the indigenous community not as objects but rather as equal participants in the research process. Additionally, the reciprocal relationship also requires the researcher to appreciate the value of IK and look for areas in which IK and Western knowledge intersect without prioritising the latter nor regarding the former as fixed. Certainly, indigenous knowledge systems interact with Western knowledge, so from this vantage point one has to recognise that indigenous knowledge is neither static nor unchangeable. For instance, in the context of North Africa, one can plausibly argue that the IK has been influenced by encounters with missionaries, traders and colonisers but also by the socio-ecological, as well as the micro- and macro-economic circumstances experienced by indigenous communities in the region. Indigenous knowledge producers frequently update IK systems based on experience, and they also examine and contrast them to Western knowledge systems based on attempts to uncover the most feasible solutions (Berkes 2009; Briggs & Moyo 2012; Moyo & Moyo 2014). It is important to note that a decolonising framework does not obviate the possible emergence of hybrid knowledges. Some scholars suggest that the merging of indigenous knowledge and Western knowledge would 'produce a more realistic and sensitive understanding and management of [for instance] natural resources for sustainable development' (Lado 2004: 281). As one focuses on North Africa, a region characterised to a great extent by hyperaridity, knowledge of best practices that draw on hybrid knowledges (Western and indigenous) that help communities engage in environmental stewardship while benefiting from sustainable tourism development can be vital.

There are certain questions that researchers undertaking research in indigenous communities, be they located in MENA or elsewhere, should account for:

> Whose research is this? Who owns it? Whose interests does it serve? Who will benefit from it? Who has designed its questions and framed its scope? Who will carry it out? Who will write it up? How will the results be disseminated?
>
> *(Smith 1999: 10)*

A concerted effort on the part of the researcher to respond to the above questions while abiding by a decolonising framework is a necessary step in any indigenous-related research endeavour. One way to accomplish the research criteria mentioned above is through participatory approaches to collaborations with indigenous communities (Semali et al. 2007). The voices and experiences of indigenous groups are of particular interest because their unique life ways are often commodified in the process of reterritorialisation. Commodification in such instances is not to be examined from a victimisation perspective because doing so would render subliminal the numerous acts of agency and resistance undertaken by indigenous communities through reterritorialisation processes.

In an effort to augment tourism research on the Middle East and North Africa, this chapter proposes a focus on indigenous communities in the region as a way of understanding how they are negotiating reterritorialisation processes as they varyingly engage with tourism development. There is a need for more research, on the Middle East in general and North Africa in particular, that showcases the plurality of issues that indigenous communities tackle and the varying ways in which they draw on IK to make tourism development-related decisions. Foregrounded in this chapter are the ethical and methodological considerations that can inform forays into indigenous research in MENA. It is hoped that the provided philosophical discussion will help researchers better engage in collaborative endeavours with indigenous communities.

Conclusion

Tourism scholars charting new avenues that include reterritorialisation within the context of MENA cannot ignore indigenous communities, as many are varyingly involved in tourism development. By the same token, any analysis of indigenous communities requires scholars to account for the various ways in which indigenous knowledge is at play. IK aids in the comprehension of local epistemologies, local theories of knowledge that inform perceptions of tourism development, ways of engaging in tourism, but also local interpretations of what development entails. These local ways of knowing invariably differ from location to location; what works in one locale may not necessarily function in another. From this perspective, the role of tourism scholars operating in such contexts is not simply to gather content, as doing so has prematurely led to the stagnation of IK research, as articulated by Sillitoe (2010). Rather, tourism scholars should adopt indigenous methodologies informed by a decolonising framework and aim to understand, document and (re)analyse the constantly evolving practices associated with IK. The focus can be on the process through which IK is enacted, practised, embodied and/or manifested. A key element is the involvement of the community as key decision makers in the research process. As scholars adopt indigenous methodologies informed by a decolonising framework they have to be conscious not to contrast IK to Western knowledge but rather to work with the community to co-create solutions that draw from both spheres of knowledge. Such a practice would likely yield a type of endogenous approach to development that is characterised by empowerment through ownership of the knowledge-production process.

References

Agrawal, A. (1995) 'Indigenous and scientific knowledge: Some critical comments', *Indigenous Knowledge Monitor*, 3(3): 1–6.

Al-Oun, S., & Al-Homoud, M. (2008) 'The potential for developing community-based tourism among the Bedouins in the Badia of Jordan', *Journal of Heritage Tourism*, 3(1): 36–54.

Bar-On, A. (2015) 'Indigenous knowledge: Ends or means?' *International Social Work*, 58(6): 780–789.

Berkes, F. (2009) 'Indigenous ways of knowing and the study of environmental change', *Journal of the Royal Society of New Zealand*, 39: 151–156.

Bianchi, R. (2009) 'The 'Critical Turn' in tourism studies: A radical critique', *Tourism Geographies*, 11(4): 484–504.

Bishop, R. (1996) *Collaborative Research Stories: Whakawhanaungatanga*. Palmerston North, NZ: Dunmore Press.

Briggs, J. (2013) 'Indigenous knowledge: A false dawn for development theory and practice?' *Progress in Development Studies*, 13(3): 231–243.

Briggs, J., & Moyo, B. (2012) 'The resilience of indigenous knowledge in small-scale African agriculture: Key drivers', *Scottish Geographical Journal*, 128: 64–80.

Briggs, J., & Sharp, J. (2004) 'Indigenous knowledges and development: A postcolonial caution', *Third World Quarterly*, 25(4): 661–676.

Briggs J., Sharp J., Yacoub H., Hamed N. & Roe, A. (2007) 'Environmental knowledge production: Evidence from Bedouin communities in Southern Egypt', *Journal of International Development*, 19: 239–51.

Castiano, J.P., & Mkabela, Q.N. (2016) 'Indigenous knowledge systems and development', *Indilinga African Journal of Indigenous Knowledge Systems*, 15(3): v–viii.

Chambers, D., & Buzinde, C. (2015) 'Tourism and decolonisation: Locating research and self', *Annals of Tourism Research*, 51: 1–16.

Chatelard, G. (2005) 'Desert tourism as a substitute for pastoralism? Tuareg in Algeria and Bedouin in Jordan', in Archives-Ouvertes (eds), *Nomadic Societies in the Middle East and North Africa: Entering the 21st Century* (pp. 710–736). Leiden: Brill.

Crazy Bull, C. (1997) 'A native conversation about research and scholarship', *Tribal College: Journal of American Indian Higher Education*, 9(1): 16–24.

Denzin, N.K., & Lincoln, Y.S. (2008) 'Preface', in N.K. Denzin, Y.S. Lincoln, & L.T. Smith (eds), *Handbook of Critical and Indigenous Methodologies* (pp. ix–xv). London: Sage.

Escobar, A. (1995) *Encountering Development: The Making and Unmaking of the Third World*. Princeton, NJ: Princeton University Press.

Evans, M., Hole, R., Berg, L.D., Hutchinson, P., & Sookraj, D. (2009) 'Common insights, differing methodologies: Toward a fusion of indigenous methodologies, participatory action research, and white studies in an urban aboriginal research agenda', *Qualitative Inquiry*, 15(5): 893–910.

Fattah, A.A., & Eddy-U, M. (2017) 'Representation of Egyptian Bedouins in English-language tourist brochures', in H. Almuhrzi, H. Alriyami, & N. Scott (eds), *Tourism in the Arab World: An Industry Perspective*, pp. 188–206. Bristol: Channel View Publications.

First Peoples Worldwide (2016) 'Who are indigenous peoples'. Available online: www.firstpeoples.org/who-are-indigenous-peoples (Accessed 1 August 2016).

Fraser, E.D., Dougill, A.J., Mabee, W.E., Reed, M., & McAlpine, P. (2006) 'Bottom up and top down: Analysis of participatory processes for sustainability indicators identification as a pathway to community empowerment and sustainable environmental management', *Journal of Environmental Management*, 78(2): 114–127.

Hall, C.M., & Tucker, H. (eds) (2004) *Tourism and Postcolonialism: Contested Discourses, Identities and Representations*. London: Routledge.

Hazbun, W. (2004) 'Globalisation, reterritorialisation and the political economy of tourism development in the Middle East', *Geopolitics*, 9(2): 310–341.

Higgins-Desbiolles, F., & Powys Whyte, K. (2013) 'No high hopes for hopeful tourism: A critical comment', *Annals of Tourism Research*, 40: 428–433.

Hollinshead, K. (1992) '"White" gaze, "red" people—shadow visions: The disidentification of "Indians" in cultural tourism', *Leisure Studies*, 11: 43–64.

Horsthemke, K. (2004) 'Indigenous knowledge: Conceptions and misconceptions', *Journal of Education*, 32: 31–48.

Johnston, A.M. (2000) 'Indigenous peoples and ecotourism: Bringing indigenous knowledge and rights into the sustainability equation', *Tourism Recreation Research*, 25(2): 86–96.

Johnston, A.M. (2003) 'Self-determination: Exercising indigenous rights in tourism', in S. Singh, D.J. Timothy, & R.K. Dowling (eds), *Tourism in Destination Communities* (pp. 115–134). Wallingford: CAB International.

Kalavar, J.M., Buzinde, C.N., Melubo, K., & Simon, J. (2014) 'Intergenerational differences in perceptions of heritage tourism among the Maasai of Tanzania', *Journal of Cross-Cultural Gerontology*, 29(1): 53–67.

Kohl, I. (2002) 'The lure of the Sahara: Implications of Libya's desert tourism', *Journal of Libyan Studies*, 3(2): 56–69.

Lado, C. (2004) 'Sustainable environmental resource utilisation: A case study of farmers' ethnobotanical knowledge and rural change in Bungoma District, Kenya', *Applied Geography*, 24(4): 281–302.

Long, N. (2003) *Development Sociology: Actor Perspectives*. New York: Routledge.

Mehta, K., Semali, L., Fleishman, A., & Maretzki, A. (2011, January). 'Leveraging indigenous knowledge to foster developmental entrepreneurship', in *Venture Well. Proceedings of Open, the Annual Conference* (p. 1). National Collegiate Inventors & Innovators Alliance.

Moyo, B.H.Z., & Moyo, D.Z. (2014) 'Indigenous knowledge perceptions and development practice in northern Malawi', *The Geographical Journal*, 180(4): 392–401.

Ocholla, D. (2007) 'Marginalised knowledge: An agenda for indigenous knowledge development and integration with other forms of knowledge', *International Review of Information Ethics*, 7(9): 1–10.

Rigney, L.I. (1999) 'Internationalisation of an indigenous anti-colonial cultural critique of research methodologies: A guide to indigenist research methodology and its principles', *Wicazo Sa Review*, 14(2): 109–121.

Semali, L.M., Ackerman, R.M., Bradley, S.G., Buzinde, C.N., Jaksch, M.L., Kalavar, J.M., Montecinos, V., & Chinoy, M.R. (2007) 'Developing excellence in indigenously-informed research', *AlterNative: An International Journal of Indigenous Scholarship*, 3(2): 8–23.

Short, J.R. (2001) *Global Dimensions: Space, Place and the Contemporary World*. London: Reaktion Books.

Shoup, J. (1985) 'The impact of tourism on the Bedouin of Petra', *Middle East Journal*, 39(2): 277–291.

Sillitoe, P. (1998) 'The development of indigenous knowledge: A new applied anthropology', *Current Anthropology*, 39: 223–52.

Sillitoe, P. (2010) 'Trust in development: Some implications of knowing in indigenous knowledge', *Journal of the Royal Anthropological Institute*, 16: 12–30.

Smith, L.T. (1999) *Decolonising Methodologies: Research and Indigenous Peoples*. London: Zed Books Ltd.

Spivak, G.C. (1988) 'Can the subaltern speak?', in C. Nelson, & L. Grossberg (eds), *Marxism and the Interpretation of Culture* (pp. 271–313). Chicago, IL: University of Illinois Press.

Stephens, C., Nettleton, C., Porter, J., Willis, R., & Clark, S. (2005) 'Indigenous peoples' health—why are they behind everyone, everywhere?', *The Lancet*, 366(9479): 10–13.

Swadener, B.B., & Mutua, K. (2008) 'Decolonising performances: Deconstructing the global postcolonial', in N.K. Denzin, Y.S. Lincoln, & L. Tuhiwai-Smith (eds), *Handbook of Critical and Indigenous Methodologies* (pp. 31–44). Thousand Oaks, CA: Sage.

Timothy, D.J. (1999) 'Participatory planning: A view of tourism in Indonesia', *Annals of Tourism Research*, 26(2): 371–391.

Tribe, J. (2007) 'Critical tourism: Rules and resistance', in I. Ateljevic, A. Pritchard, & N. Morgan (eds), *The Critical Turn in Tourism Studies: Innovative Research Methodologies* (pp. 29–39). London: Elsevier.

UN Permanent Forum on Indigenous Issues (2006) *Millennium Development Goals and Indigenous Peoples E/C.19/2003/22, Report on the Second Session of the UNPFII*, Para. 26: United Nations.

Varisco, D. (2000) 'Indigenous knowledge and development', *Anthropology New*, 41(8): 14–15.

Warren, D.M., & Rajasekaran, B. (1993) 'Putting local knowledge to good use', *International Agricultural Development*, 13(4): 8–10.

8

URBAN HERITAGE IN THE MIDDLE EAST

Heritage, tourism and the shaping of new identities

Aylin Orbaşlı

Introduction

The Middle East is home to some of the world's oldest cities dating back to the early civilisations of the fertile crescent (Mesopotamia) and the Nile valley. It is the centre of the old world order where trade routes intertwined and collided with one another, and where not only goods, but also ideas, ideologies and interventions were traded, and settlements grew and thrived at the major intersections up until modern times. Today, some of these once great cities have turned to dust, others into major archaeological sites, and some of them into small settlements that are a distant shadow of their former glory. Others, on the other hand, are now embedded into the fabric of buzzing twenty-first-century metropolises such as Cairo and Istanbul in an uneasy juxtaposition of historic layers with development pressures fuelled as much by lucrative real estate propositions as by need.

No two of these cities are the same, yet somehow in their own way they each intrigue travellers with the sense of the exotic shrouded in an oriental mystique. Stimulated by a newfound engagement with the Orient, the great centres of Islamic civilisation and scholarship emerged on the European consciousness as destinations to be visited from the eighteenth century onwards. Thus, gentlemen visitors mingled with traders in the *souqs* and bazaars of Cairo, Istanbul, Aleppo and Jerusalem, sketched mosques, fountains and public baths and further fuelled an orientalist allure and an appetite for it back home. Edward Said's (1978) concept of Orientalism has been much debated, but still continues to manifest itself in the expectations of the modern-day tourist to the region, though often through a series of carefully assembled visual cues that build on preconceived narratives.

Many of the early travel destinations of the region have continued to feature as tourist destinations in different ways and guises up to the present. Many of them, having survived intact up until the middle of the twentieth century, have experienced profound and seismic changes to their economic, political and social structures. Several unfortunately have fallen victim to the many conflicts that have enveloped the region over the past century, while others continue to do so. All of these factors influence the ways in which they are perceived by tourists today and how city authorities have started to shape their historic districts to specifically serve a growing tourism market. No two of these cities are the same and each and every one has experienced a different trajectory of growth, stability and conflict and an equally different engagement with history and heritage. Meanwhile, the larger forces of globalisation, neo-liberal economic policies and investor and consumer interests are shaping cityscapes across the region.

This chapter examines urban heritage tourism, which constitutes a growth market for MENA. It specifically considers influences that can often be traced back to the aftermath of the 1974 oil crisis and the neo-liberal economic practices that followed. But it has not only been global economic developments and local geopolitics, but also worldwide shifts in conservation theory and worldview, not least by postmodernism, that also influences the ways in which urban heritage is preserved, presented and packaged for tourism consumption (Orbaşlı 2017).

The predominant form of cultural tourism to the region was borne around its ancient sites, fuelled by nineteenth-century European antiquarian interests. To this day countries like Jordan, Egypt and Israel focus much of their tourism promotion offers on their ancient built heritages (Timothy 2014; Timothy & Daher 2009). Nonetheless, a growing recognition that historic settlements are also of tourism interest has played a significant role in safeguarding and supporting the conservation of historic urban quarters and traditional settlements.

A review of literature from the 1980s and 1990s illustrates a collective concern for the future of urban heritage in the Islamic World under pressures of development and ambitions of modernisation (see, for example, Abu Lughod 1980; Lewcock 1978; Rghei & Nelson 1994; The Aga Khan Trust for Culture 1990). Tourism makes a rare appearance in many of the discussions where the condition of the built fabric and the livelihood needs of local communities take centre stage. Furthermore, it was being argued that the urban form and the social networks that were at the heart of the eponymous 'Islamic' city generated different conservation challenges and required different approaches (Antoniou 1981). Most commonly, campaigns for conservation have had to contend with forces of rapid urban development and a general social ambivalence towards historic urban quarters associated with a past and more 'primitive' era (Warren & Fethi 1984).

In the same way that not all so-called 'Islamic cities' have developed in the same way, so does each geographical sub-region face its own specific challenges when it comes to urban conservation. As the protection of historic urban neighbourhoods has become accepted over time, a number of distinct trends are, however, emerging in the way they embrace tourism. By identifying and elaborating on a number of typical scenarios of urban heritage tourism in the Middle East, the chapter aims to capture the essence of urban tourism in a fast-moving and often volatile region. These are presented under a number of overarching headings, but many of these situations and scenarios are often interwoven or overlap. Many of these cities are anything but socially homogeneous, and politics, minorities, representation and identity are often very closely linked to what is preserved, how it is preserved and moreover how cultural heritage is presented to tourism.

The chapter evolves around two theoretical standpoints: first, that although the survival of historic urban quarters cannot be solely attributed to tourism, tourism is increasingly shaping the ways in which urban heritage is preserved and constructed; the second is a continuing Orientalist narrative that is evident both in the visitors' expectations when travelling to the region (Bryce 2007) and in the way that cultural heritage is presented and interpreted by local actors in recognition of commercial opportunity. It further emphasises the inherent conflict between various notions of privacy that determine the urban form and character of many Islamic cities with expanding commercial activity that alters the physical character and counteracts the meaning of place (Orbaşlı 2007).

There are inevitably some generalisations in this text, given the constraints of a single chapter to adequately cover a large geographical area and to address the timeframe that is necessary to understand and contextualise current developments. The chapter has also deliberately omitted the great cities of pilgrimage that also characterise the region, from the two great holy cities of Makkah and Madinah to others such as Jerusalem, Mahshad, Karbala or Najaf.[1]

The changing face of the Medina

In the latter half of the twentieth century when there were heated discussions on how to save the historic quarters of the Islamic world that were being threatened by loss of interest, general dilapidation and development pressures, the various *medina*, or historic walled cities of North Africa, became forerunners and standard bearers for an emergent conservation movement. Holistic approaches, sensitive revitalisation projects and local community-centred approaches resulted in a number of award-winning projects with a social conscience. The medinas of Fez in Morocco and Tunis in Tunisia stand out in particular. In both cases, the formulation of two organisations, ADER-Fès and the *Association de Sauvegarde de la Medina de Tunis* (ASM), played an important role in developing and implementing regeneration projects within the old towns. Although both organisations continue to play an important part in the conservation and management of their respective cities, their focus has markedly shifted to fostering tourism growth.

Depending heavily on external funding from the likes of the World Bank or the EU, the ASM is rare for the region for its continuity and for acting as a knowledge bank for the various and often external programmes (Nardella & Cidre 2016). The early achievements of the ASM were recognised by two Aga Khan awards for the regeneration projects it instigated in the Medina. However, over time there has been a very definitive shift towards tourism, observed in a growth of tourism related businesses but also in the way in which ASM and its funders have been prioritising projects. Sanitation and beautification programmes for designated 'tourist' routes have included urban realm improvements that go beyond recognised conservation practices to promote embellishments to building façades to emphasise historic character.

For the walled city of Fez, the World Heritage Site listing of 1981 also marked the start of a three-decade-long rehabilitation process that was driven by local need and an understanding that the city was a dynamic place that would continue to evolve within its medieval structure (Radoine 2003). A World Bank loan in 1993 was notably not only a game changer for the old town of Fez, but also marked a shift in World Bank funding policy in that cultural heritage was recognised as having development value, though one that was exclusively linked to tourism. The outcome, according to one observer was that:

> many places with great archaeological and historical value are now nothing more than a zoo for tourists to visit [...] the original inhabitants have been replaced by bazaars and Ali Baba's adventures to build up a new façade based on 'extraordinary' or exotic scenes.
>
> *(Radoine 2003: 473)*

The same pattern is repeated through many other examples from Salt in Jordan to Tripoli in Libya where World Bank and other donor funds for conservation have singularly focused on increasing the appeal of these often secondary towns to tourism as an economic development vehicle (Daher 2007).

Tourism undoubtedly provides opportunities to reuse buildings that would otherwise be redundant and establish ways in which their rich heritage and characteristics can be preserved and to an extent remain accessible, whilst also providing visitors with unique experiences (Orbaşlı 2000). The conversion of North African *riads*, or Damascene courtyard houses, into exquisite hotels and restaurants became a common trend and a sought-after visitor experience. Popularised in Cairo, Egypt, since the 1980s as historic hotels, often with romantic associations, old palaces were revived and converted into boutique hotels; in some areas an influx of Gulf investors has resulted in the rapid transformation of old properties into objects of intense property speculation (Salamandra 2004). So popular have these types of hotels been that in Istanbul's historic peninsula there has been a proliferation of fake heritage hotels hoping to capture the market's appetite for this type of accommodation. In Morocco, too, an increasing flow of foreign capital attracted to cultural tourism returns is driving a boom in the construction of new *riads* alongside conservation projects (Lee 2008).

Some visitors, finding that staying in a historic *riad* was not enough, started to restore historic houses in the old medinas as second homes and holiday accommodation. The growing trend of foreign home ownership, initially popularised in Marakesh, has spread to places like Fez and in the early years of the millennium also extended to cities like Aleppo and Damascus, often depicted in lavishly illustrated articles in magazines such as *Interiors Today*. While foreigners arrive with ready capital to restore the old houses, local and incomer perceptions and expectations of the historic quarters have to be carefully balanced for these neighbourhoods to maintain their urban dynamic (McGuinness & Mouhli 2012). The common morphological character of the Islamic city regularly sets apart marketplaces and commercial town centres from residential neighbourhoods, which are seen as places of privacy for their tight-knit communities. The presence of foreigners in their midst, or even tourists milling around has further diminished the appeal of older quarters as living environments for locals (Orbaşlı 2007).

The declining and reinvented urban quarter

The *medinas* of Fez and Tunis still remain exceptions compared to the dilapidation and development pressures many other historic towns in the region have suffered over the past 40 years. For many it has been a case of gradual decline. As middle-class inhabitants frequently moved out to better housing in newly developing city and suburban areas, the older neighbourhoods became home to immigrants, many of them attracted from rural areas to seek better work opportunities in the burgeoning cities. This often led to multiple occupancies and sublets with very little incentive to maintain the buildings that were being considered out of fashion (Lewcock 1978).

Warren and Fethi (1984) succinctly explain the predicament of the old quarters of Baghdad, Iraq, where the old houses and quarters neither served the purposes of the smaller modern family nor did they fit the image of modern and contemporary lifestyles. In their dilapidated condition and often inherited by numerous siblings and cousins, they had become more burden than asset. Inheritance plays an important role as, in the Islamic system, all property is divided amongst offspring, resulting in joint ownerships that within two generations can escalate to a substantial number of shareholders. This fuels a loss of interest and abandonment and makes redevelopment into modern and higher apartments that afford each stakeholder an independent unit an attractive proposition.

Across the region, as the old urban quarters became redundant, pressures to demolish and rebuild also prevailed and continues to do so in many instances. Where heated campaigns—often spearheaded by academics—have been successful, area-based conservation legislation has been introduced and attitudes towards the protection and conservation of historic urban areas has started to change. The added benefits of tourism, though, have certainly played a role in accelerating conservation efforts (Khirfan 2014; Rghei & Nelson 1994; Timothy

& Daher 2009). From the 1990s onwards a growing focus on urban heritage as a tourism product alongside ancient sites in countries like Jordan, Lebanon and Turkey often started with a small number of prominent houses being conserved to function as museums, as was the case in Salt, Jordan (Khirfan 2014) and Saida, Lebanon, for example (Daher 2007). Consequently, cities across the region are also competing to obtain the coveted designation of UNESCO World Heritage Site.

However, where tourism development has been the primary driver, the emphasis has been on streetscape beautification rather than a holistic approach to the urban fabric, thus jeopardising environmental and social values of places. Growing commercial interest generated by tourism also impacts on surrounding land value and loss of traditionally residential uses to the expansion of, often unregulated, commercial activity that can negatively impact the heritage value. Located at the heart of a thriving coastal tourism destination on Turkey's south coast, Antalya is just one example of a historic quarter that has become fully transformed into a tourism playground. Even conservation area status and well-meant urban planning efforts to protect the historic walled town could not stop residential areas becoming taken over by commercial activity as private money and developers flooded into the area and rapidly displaced the locals (Orbaşlı 2000).

A similar trend is recorded in Egypt, where

> many state-led schemes focus on superficial conservation, of a kind concerned mainly with sanitizing the old fabric. In pursuit of tourist dollars, such schemes appropriate the urban fabric and permit heavy traffic through it, overlooking some important subjective qualities, such as community well-being.
>
> *(Sedky 2009: xix)*

This is also the experience of Eskişehir's Odunpazarı district in Turkey where a street sanitisation project instigated by the local municipality has created a remodelled destination filled with souvenir shops, though in this example largely serving the domestic tourism market. Interestingly, with a new generation now attaching nostalgia value to these quarters, their growth as tourism destinations is also being supported by growing domestic markets of day and weekend visitors. In pre-conflict Damascus, the conversion of old courtyard houses into restaurants also had an appeal to the local Damascene audience, as many were local and family run businesses closely linked to the area (Daher 2007).

A more organised tourism-led urban conservation approach was that taken for Old Acre in Israel, where a master plan deliberately aimed at turning the World Heritage City with its Crusader heritage into a managed tourism attraction (Khirfan 2015). The development process that followed focused very specifically on the physical infrastructure of the city and visitor management measures and facilities, whilst little attention was placed on social services or the economic development needs of its local, predominantly Arab, population (Shoval 2013). Khirfan (2015) notes that although the initial plans took little notice of the Arab inhabitants of the old quarter, it is the Arab markets that are amongst the most popular attraction for many visitors because it is a means of engaging with the real life of the place, which for most visitors is actually what makes these places interesting.

In Cairo, it is the government authorities who are pushing through major projects to restore historic buildings in the old quarter and sanitise their environment. This is also seen by some commentators as a deliberate intent to 'refashion the historic centre', clearing it of the 'merchants, artisans, and residents who live in—and give life to—this nucleus of Cairo so that large groups of tourists [...] will be able to traverse it along designated paths as quickly and summarily as possible' (Williams 2006: 270). To this end, businesses have been moved and livelihoods and social networks lost. Ironically of course, just as in Fez, Tunis and Acre, it is this 'life' and activity, which the visitors are really interested in seeing, that is being obliterated.

As these historic quarters transform into tourism destinations they also go against the inherent character of the Islamic city with its distinct separation of public and private spaces. As the social meaning and value attached to privacy is eroded, the spatial organisation that is presented to visitors takes on new characteristics. 'Where residential gives way to commercial then the social balance, the spatial characteristics and most importantly the sought after character will be lost' (Orbaşlı 2007: 174). And once commercial and entertainment venues are introduced into a neighbourhood, then locals living nearby leave as it becomes culturally problematic to share residential life with such functions and the influx of outsiders they attract. In Najaf, Iraq, hotels being built to house pilgrims have become a deterrent to locals who feel that the privacy afforded by the traditional neighbourhood structure is compromised (Abid 2016). Williams (2006) also points out that the creation of open spaces within the tightly-knit medieval heart of Cairo overlooks the fact that traditionally open spaces were provided in the inner courtyards and were private family spaces.

As cultural tourism becomes a bigger economic sector, the beneficiaries of this economic growth in historic towns often end up being a small select number of players with access to capital and political backing, and it empowers only some interests (Daher 2007); for a majority of local inhabitants the growth of tourism has resulted in displacement or further marginalisation. The promised socio-economic development at times highlighted in regeneration schemes is barely realised, whilst at the same time the much sought-after living city aspects are also irreversibly lost.

Hip and trendy urban quarters

A comparison is often made that in Western societies a longer period of industrialisation has resulted in a nostalgia for the past, which in turn has led not only to the protection of historic buildings but an active desire to live in them. The argument is that with time a sense of nostalgia and a sufficient distancing from the past and any associations of 'backwardness' will see them being revived. This has indeed been the case in several metropolitan areas in MENA as art quarters are shaped and popularised by a middle-class intellectual elite. What often starts as an alternative to commercialised mainstream living and the coming together of like-minded 'creatives' quite soon develops into areas with natural appeal to the tourism market.

The Ortaköy neighbourhood in Istanbul, Turkey, first attracted the attention of a small group of writers and architects who could see the potential of the run-down buildings which they started to renovate. With its attractive location on the shores of the Bosphorous, before long the area became a popular destination with its waterfront cafés and arty vibe. In an era where places also become rapidly popularised via social media, these types of areas became attractive to tourists seeking supposedly 'alternative' experiences beyond the more monumental heritage attractions.

A similar pattern is observed in Amman, Jordan, where one of the older neighbourhoods linked to its historic downtown has started to become popular with affluent residents from West Amman. Amman, by comparison a city lacking the elevated historic past of places such as Damascus or Aleppo, has turned to a more recent colonial heritage for both identity and tourism attraction, making the architectural heritage of the 1930s to the 1950s the focus of conservation and reuse (Jacobs 2010). Starting around Rainbow Street and the conservation of the modernist Rainbow Cinema, old houses have been converted to restaurants or other cultural and linked retail uses. The once middle-class area is in part being re-discovered and in part romanticised. While the initial attraction was a mingling with residents of the area, gentrification is gradually turning the area into an entertainment district with a 'a new social identity for the upper middle class' (Daher 2007: 39). In contrast to the car-dominated city, it notably creates a rare public walkable environment.

Meanwhile in Ortaköy, demand has outstripped supply, and the area has become overcrowded and the art/souvenir products mass-produced with reviews that now refer to the area as a 'tourist trap'—crowded, noisy and overpriced—especially by those who remember its earlier appeal. Meanwhile, long-forgotten areas such as the historic Fener neighbourhood are rapidly transforming with cafés, restaurants and antique shops into new destinations. This is not only a story of growing tourism interest in historic neighbourhoods, but one of gentrification and the displacement of local residents.

For many of these cities, the gentrification of older districts into hip urban destinations, initially for local consumption but with growing tourism appeal, is also a notable shift in the tourism narrative from major monuments of antiquity and the Islamic period, to a much more recent social history and a domestic scale of architecture.

The repackaged heritage quarters of the Arabian Gulf

The countries of the Arabian Gulf region (UAE, Saudi Arabia, Qatar, Bahrain, Kuwait, Yemen and Oman) have been relative latecomers to the recognition of the heritage value of historic urban quarters and their tourism potential. This growing interest in urban heritage conservation often combines tourism interests with a means for defining and celebrating local 'identity'. For a culture where 'cultural heritage' is more likely to be transmitted between generations through intangible heritage in the form of beliefs, traditions and pastimes, there is an emerging recognition that culture and identity may also be embedded in historic fabric, including that of the urban vernacular heritage.

The rapid urbanisation and modernism that followed the oil boom that enriched the region often resulted in a swift shift from traditional neighbourhood to modern villa and high-rise living. The character of the old towns was quickly eroded as they were surrounded by new high-rise buildings that sharply contrasted with the horizontal layout of the historic buildings to an extent that they engulf them. The reclamation of the shoreline, as seen in Manama, Bahrain, has also deprived many historic areas of their connection to the sea and essential character (Ben Hamouche 2008). Like Sharjah, UAE, or even Jeddah's Al Balad district in Saudi Arabia, they have become isolated islands within the modern cityscape, surrounded by heavy traffic arteries.

The conservation of Dubai's Bastakiya quarter set an example for a number of conservation and development projects that would have a defined agenda of appealing to cultural tourism. A largely abandoned residential quarter, Bastakiya houses were renovated and adapted to new cultural uses ranging from institutional headquarters to art galleries and cafés (Coles & Jackson 2007). Bastakiya today exemplifies many of the problems faced by tourism in the private–public urban form traditionally favoured in Islamic cultures. Each of the buildings as originally serving residential purposes clearly face inwards to open courtyards with deliberately blank external walls. The streets, once the domain of playing youngsters, are eerily quiet with only small openings through which the new functions have a means of engaging with a passing public. This not only makes it difficult for tourists to navigate, but is equally frustrating to traders in attracting business. Yet to open up the façades would run contrary to the traditional character of the area.

Perhaps for this reason, many other initiatives in the region have started off by focusing on their traditional *souq* and commercial areas. In Doha, Qatar, the Souq Waqif has been sanitised, largely rebuilt and transformed as a 'showcase for Doha's past'. The project went beyond the removal of modern additions and through renovations created 'an original that never existed' in which the past is idealised so as to appeal to tourists (Adham 2008: 240). The conservation of Manama Souk in Bahrain has been similarly criticised as being a 'simplistic' project, which has ignored the socio-economic fabric in favour of 'the visual effects of design' that 'recalls some symbols of the oriental city' (Ben Hamouche 2008).

These two projects highlight a growing ease in the region for carefully managed heritage tourism projects that are more concerned with a singular narrative than authenticity (Orbaşlı 2015). Heritage is thus readjusted to conform to a specific narrative or destination ideal. Sharjah's old quarter, for example, is largely rebuilt with altered plot boundaries to serve the purpose of a tourism district used for festivals with the additional advantage of adequate space for car access and parking.

Unlike historic urban districts noted elsewhere, displacement of local populations has rarely been the case in the Gulf region, as many of these districts already lay abandoned. Though far from an advantage, this abandonment has also meant that these places are devoid of the social structures and networks that have made many other historic settlements in the wider region attractive to tourism. Thus, what is presented to visitors becomes a carefully selected and curated narrative in a somewhat sterile and artificial environment, though one that is innately safe.

Constructing the new heritage

These reformulated historic quarters of the Gulf region are not the only narratives that are changing or being deliberately reworked. In both Istanbul and Cairo, predominantly Western style and colonial neighbourhoods from the early twentieth century are now the focus of conservation efforts and are seen to be adding value to real estate developments. However, preservation efforts often compete with real estate developments that randomly replicate historic styles to serve a growing tourism-linked commercial demand. Consequently, in these more complex cities, reconstruction and imagined or replicated heritage is not just a case of seeking simpler past roots and vernacular style, but a replication and reconfiguring of more sophisticated semi-colonial styles that are just as much about generating and portraying new identities as they are about celebrating the past.

Most profound, in this respect, is the redevelopment of central Beirut following 15 years of civil war. A multi-million-dollar reconstruction project spearheaded by a development company vehicle known as Solidere drew on public and private investment to reshape the city centre. Both the intensions and the outcomes of the project are seen from different perspectives as sound financial investments, identity-building and creating a tourism destination. Nagel (2002) considers part of the aim to generate a new collective memory of the once cosmopolitan Beirut following a bloody civil war, although this act of nation-building was simultaneously delivering financial benefits to the city's elite. Ultimately the rubble of the conflict was replaced with a carefully planned new quarter, of open public spaces, some of them incorporating archaeological sites as part of the tourist attractiveness. However, what remained of the old *souqs* was demolished to make way for a car park, with a new reimagined *souq* on top of it, which is in effect a modern shopping mall (Makdisi 1997). Whilst many of the new landmark buildings were high-rise towers, old *khans* were reconstructed and a select number of buildings restored, many of them only following a public outcry (Sawalha 2010). The work of Solidere in Beirut is derided by its critics as a vulgar neo-liberal restructuring (Daher 2007), the re-writing of history (Nagel 2002), and creating a new type of space that lacks any form of historical depth or meaning (Makdisi 1997), erasing memories in doing so.

The Solidere approach notably provides a solution for overcoming the complicated web of ownership and fragmented property rights in Islamic inheritance (Gavin & Maluf 1996)—an approach that is gaining ground in other large cities and already evident in several of Istanbul's historic districts where redevelopment through land amalgamation under the name of urban regeneration is proving lucrative to developers. At the time of writing there are already unconfirmed rumours that similar 'grand development' plans may already be on the table for cities like Aleppo, Syria, where hundreds of years and layers of history have been badly damaged in recent atrocities.

Prior to the conflicts, Aleppo had become a popular tourist destination. The city's growing tourism sector focused on the world-famous *souqs* in the commercial centre, which meant a higher prioritisation of conservation projects there, with tourism-related outcomes (Khirfan 2015). How the reconstruction of Aleppo will play out will also have wider implications for the reconstruction and reinterpretation of urban heritage in a much wider region. Whether driven by investment value or the need to re-establish an urban identity, tourism as a lucrative beneficiary will undoubtedly play a role in shaping the outcome. Reconstruction, whether for an urban or for a monument/archaeological site, creates a singular narrative; and it will be this singular narrative that tourists will experience, as they do in Beirut or in Dubai's Bastakiya.

Conclusion

Today tourism in the region is also marked by regular volatility caused by economic cycles and political unrest and uncertainty, a shift in visitor profile from European and Western to Gulf State and Asian markets, and finally direct mandates for heritage to deliver a profit as a driver of development. Some of these are a reflection of international trends, others markedly specific to the region.

This chapter has illustrated how tourism to the cities of MENA has changed significantly over the course of the last century. While an element of the 'exotic' and the flavour of the Orient is still upheld, this is now largely in the imagination of the travellers and the deliberate packaging and representation of the destination by the locals. Even in the vast expanse of Istanbul's Grand Bazaar or the Walled City of Jerusalem, the everyday hustle and bustle is being replaced by souvenir businesses exclusively intended for the tourism market.

For the rich urban heritage of the region, war is not the only threat; the genuine article is rapidly disappearing and under threat like never before. Although the urban heritage is now more widely being acknowledged, not least due to tourism, the levels of abandonment seen in the Gulf region are also widely spreading. This may partly be due to the fact that the older buildings and quarters are seen to be too far removed from modern-day amenities and living standards. However, gentrification and a notable shift from residential to commercial uses spearheaded by tourism development are also having a significant influence in depopulation. Historic neighbourhoods are thus evolving from once lived in places to reimagined and increasingly re-produced environments being served up for tourism consumption. While selected methods of preservation and presentation are said to blur the distinction between what is genuine and what is fake (Orbaşlı 2015), further consideration is needed as to how 'genuine' an urban place can be without its social infrastructure and ultimately what this signifies in terms of the visitor experience.

Note

1 There is much debate on whether pilgrimage is also a form of tourism and in many of these cities pilgrimage visits are also combined with visitation of a more touristic nature. However, it was felt that the specific conditions of the pilgrimages and the impacts on the historic fabric, organisation and presentations of the cities would warrant a chapter in their own right. This phenomenon is discussed in other chapters in this book.

References

Abid, S. (2016) 'Representing Najaf: An investigation into the current pressure on the physical and social fabric of Najaf's old town', *International Planning History Society Proceedings*, 17(1): 171–172.

Abu Lughod, J.L. (1980) 'Preserving the living heritage of Islamic cities', in R. Holod (ed.), *Toward an Architecture in the Spirit of Islam* (pp. 61–75). Philadelphia, PA: The Aga Khan Awards.

Adham, K. (2008) 'Rediscovering the island: Doha's urbanity from pearls to spectacle', in Y. Elsheshtawy (ed.), *The Evolving Arab City: Tradition, Modernity and Urban Development* (pp. 218–258). London: Routledge.

Aga Khan Trust for Culture (AKTC) (1990) *Architectural and Urban Conservation in the Islamic World*. Geneva: The Aga Khan Trust for Culture.

Antoniou, J. (1981) *Islamic Cities and Conservation*. Geneva: UNESCO Press.

Ben Hamouche, M. (2008) 'Manama: The metamorphosis of an Arab Gulf city', in Y. Elsheshtawy (ed.), *The Evolving Arab City: Tradition, Modernity and Urban Development* (pp. 184–217). London: Routledge.

Bryce, D. (2007) 'Repackaging Orientalism: Discourses on Egypt and Turkey in British outbound tourism', *Tourist Studies*, 7(2): 165–191.

Cole, A., & Jackson, P. (2007) *Wind Tower*. London: Stacey International.

Daher, R. (2007) 'Reconceptualising tourism in the Middle East: Place, heritage, mobility and competitiveness', in R. Daher (ed.), *Tourism in the Middle East: Continuity, Change and Transformation* (pp. 1–69). Clevedon: Channel View Publications.

Gavin, A., & Maluf, R. (1996) *Beirut Reborn: The Restoration and Development of the Central District*. Chichester: Wiley.

Jacobs, J. (2010) 'Re-branding the Levant: Contested heritage and colonial modernities in Amman and Damascus', *Journal of Tourism and Cultural Change*, 8(4): 325–336.

Khirfan, L. (2014) *World Heritage, Urban Design and Tourism: Three Cities in the Middle East*. London: Routledge.

Khirfan, L. (2015) 'Place making and experience in World Heritage Cities', in L. Bourdeau, M. Gravari-Barbas, & M. Robinson (eds), *World Heritage, Tourism and Identity: Inscription and Co-production* (pp. 157–172). Surrey: Ashgate.

Lee, J. (2008) 'Riad fever: Heritage tourism, urban renewal and the Médina property boom in old cities of Morocco', *E Review of Tourism Research*, 6(4): 66–78.

Lewcock, R. (1978) 'Three problems in conservation: Egypt, Oman, Yemen', in R. Holod (ed.), *Conservation as Cultural Survival* (pp. 66–76). Istanbul: Aga Khan Awards.

Makdisi, S. (1997) 'Laying claim to Beirut: Urban narrative and spatial identity in the age of Solidere', *Critical Inquiry*, 23(3): 660–705.

McGuinness, J., & Mouhli, Z. (2012) 'Restoration dramas: Home refurbishment in historic Fès (Morocco), 2000–2009', *Journal of North African Studies*, 17(4): 697–708.

Nagel, C. (2002) 'Reconstructing space, re-creating memory: Sectarian politics and urban development in post-war Beirut', *Political Geography*, 21: 717–725.

Nardella, B.M and Cidre, E. (2016) 'Interrogating the "implementation" of international policies of urban conservation in the medina of Tunis', in S. Labadi, & W. Logan (eds), *Urban Heritage, Development and Sustainability* (pp. 57–79). London: Routledge.

Orbaşlı, A. (2000) *Tourists in Historic Towns: Urban Conservation and Heritage Management*. London: Spon Press.

Orbaşlı, A. (2007) 'The "Islamic" city and tourism: Managing conservation and tourism in traditional neighbourhoods', in R. Daher (ed.), *Tourism in the Middle East: Continuity, Change and Transformation* (pp. 161–187). Clevedon: Channel View Publications.

Orbaşlı, A. (2015) 'Nara+20: A theory and practice perspective', *Heritage & Society*, 8(2): 178–188.

Orbaşlı, A. (2017) 'Conservation theory in the twenty-first century: Slow evolution or a paradigm shift?', *Journal of Architectural Conservation*, 23(3): 157–170.

Radoine, H. (2003) 'Conservation-based cultural, environmental, and economic development: The case of the walled city of Fez', in L. Fusco Girard (ed.), *The Human Sustainable City: Challenges and Perspectives from the Habitat Agenda* (pp. 457–477). Aldershot: Ashgate.

Rghei, A.S., & Nelson, J.G. (1994) 'The conservation and use of the walled city of Tripoli', *Geographical Journal*, 160: 143–158.

Said, E.W. (1978) *Orientalism*. London: Routledge and Kegan Paul.

Salamandra, C. (2004) *A New Old Damascus: Authenticity and Distinction in Urban Syria*. Bloomington, IN: Indiana University Press.

Sawalha, A. (2010) *Reconstructing Beirut: Memory and Space in a Postwar Arab City*. Austin, TX: University of Texas Press.

Sedky, A. (2009) *Living with Heritage in Cairo: Area Conservation in the Arab-Islamic City*. Cairo: The American University of Cairo Press.

Shoval, N. (2013) 'Street-naming, tourism development and cultural conflict: The case of the Old City of Acre/Akki/Akka', *Transactions of the Institute of British Geographers*, 38(4): 612–626.

Timothy, D.J. (2014) 'Contemporary cultural heritage and tourism: Development issues and emerging trends', *Public Archaeology*, 13(1–3): 30–47.

Timothy, D.J., & Daher, R.F. (2009) 'Heritage tourism in Southwest Asia and North Africa: Contested pasts and veiled realities', in D.J. Timothy, & G.P. Nyaupane (eds), *Cultural Heritage and Tourism in the Developing World: A Regional Perspective* (pp. 146–164). London: Routledge.

Warren, J., & Fethi, I. (1984) *Conservation of Traditional Houses, Amanat al-Assima, Baghdad*. Sussex: Coach Publishing.

Williams, C. (2006) 'Reconstructing Islamic Cairo', in D. Singerman, & P. Amar (eds), *Cairo Cosmopolitan: Politics, Culture and Urban Space in the New Globalised Middle East* (pp. 269–294). Cairo: American University of Cairo Press.

PART III

Religion and tourism

9

RELIGION, PILGRIMAGE AND TOURISM IN THE MIDDLE EAST

Daniel H. Olsen

Introduction

Religious tourism and pilgrimage have become big business. While exact numbers of people travelling for religious or spiritual purposes, and the economic impact of this niche market, are unclear and speculative at best, the World Tourism Organization (UNWTO 2011) estimates that there are over 600 million national and international religious trips every year, with between 300 and 330 million people visiting a religious site or engaging in a religious activity. These religious trips, however, are not evenly spread across the globe, as an estimated 40 per cent of those travelling for religious purposes travel to Europe, with another approximately 50 per cent travelling to Asia (UNWTO 2011: xxv). Economically, there is little in the way of estimating the economic impact of religious tourism. The only semi-credible number available stems from Wright's (2008) declaration that the global religious travel market is a US$18 billion a year industry. Others have estimated the economic impact of religious tourism for individual countries, such as Saudi Arabia (US$16 billion) (Derhally 2013) and Italy (€4.5 billion) (Trono 2017). Dated estimates suggest that the sale of religious souvenirs reaches more than US$200 million a year in Italy alone (Fleischer 2000). These numbers, however, are probably very low, considering that the religious tourism market consists of travellers from all economic classes, and not just low-budget travellers (Olsen 2013).

The Middle East and North Africa (MENA) has a long and rich history of pilgrimage and religious tourism, having attracted pilgrims from both within and without the region for centuries. Faith traditions related to Christianity, Judaism and Islam in particular, have long established holy places in this region, including St. Catherine's Monastery in Egypt, the Al Masjid Al Haram and the Masjid al-Qiblatayn in Saudi Arabia, Mount Nebo and Bethabara in Jordan, the Imam Ali Mosque and Imam Reza Shrine in Iran, the Baha'i Holy Shrine and Gardens in Haifa, Ephesus in Turkey, and the Western Wall, the Al Aqsa Mosque, the Church of the Holy Sepulchre and the Via Dolorosa in Jerusalem, to name a few. The Middle East serves as the axis mundi for Muslims and Jews, with the sites and ceremonies related to the Hajj and the Western Wall, respectively, serving as preeminent pilgrimage destinations for these groups. For Christians, the Middle East is where Jesus Christ ministered and where his disciples preached during the founding of the early Christian church.

While pilgrimage and religious tourism are probably more pervasive and socio-economically important to this region than anywhere else in the world (Timothy & Daher 2009), the Middle East is also characterised as having strong socio-cultural and political tensions that affect the flows and management of these types of 'population mobilit[ies]' (Collins-Kreiner 2010). In this vein, the purpose of this chapter is to discuss the relationships, key issues, and challenges regarding pilgrimage and religious tourism in MENA. While pilgrimage and religious tourism take place throughout this region, Al-Hamarneh and Steiner (2004) suggest that different countries have come to specialise in different tourist niche markets, with Saudi Arabia, Yemen, Syria and Palestine being the Arab countries that dominate the multi-ethnic cultural and religious tourism market. As such, most of the discussion here focuses on these countries within MENA.

As other chapters in this volume focus more on religion-specific pilgrimages, including Islam, Christianity and Judaism, this discussion remains at a macro-level for the region. More particularly, this chapter begins by discussing the similarities and differences between pilgrimage and religious tourism, and how scholars and the tourism industry have tried to differentiate between those who travel for religious reasons and those who engage with religious culture for leisure and educational purposes. Then, themes and challenges related to the economic, political and social issues in this region that affect pilgrimage and religious tourism will be discussed.

Defining and (de)differentiating religious tourism and pilgrimage

Pilgrimage is one of the oldest forms of travel. From its prehistoric and Palaeolithic roots to the present day, pilgrimage has motivated millions of people to travel to places of religious or spiritual significance, or *loca sancta*, for many reasons, including curiosity, worship, healing, to fulfil vows or promises, recreation, education and participation in initiatory or cleansing rituals (Morinis 1992). Many of the oldest cities in the world have acted as foci of pilgrimage travel, as have sacred mountains, groves, rivers, religious buildings, shrines, festivals, and holy men and women (Adler 2002; Leppäkari & Griffin 2017; Rutte 2011; Verschuuren, Wild, McNeely, & Oviedo 2010). In many of the world's major religions, including Islam, Buddhism, Hinduism, Christianity and Shintoism, formal and informal pilgrimage is an important ritual that strengthens individual and collective religious identity and faith as well as helps maintain socio-religious boundaries (Barbato 2013).

While modernity and secularisation have led to the belief that religion has lost its importance in the public sphere, religion has been resilient in the face of this secularisation, with public displays of religious belief, like pilgrimage, being more common in many regions of the world (Davidsson Bremborg 2013; Olsen 2017; Reader 2007). Indeed, since the Second World War, religious groups have sought to use pilgrimage as a vehicle to revitalise cultural, religious, and spiritual values and identities (Barbato 2013; Reader 2007). This pilgrimage-cum-revitalisation strategy has benefited from improvements and innovations in transportation, hospitality management, telecommunications, as well as general increases in discretionary time and money amongst the world's middle class. These changes have led to less dangerous and less physically demanding travel, and have allowed many pilgrims to engage in pilgrimage without the traditional element of sacrifice.

These changes, however, have also led to the democratisation of travel (Richter 2003: 340), where travel during leisure time is a more accessible option for a larger portion of the world's population. With this popularisation of travel, the number of people visiting religious sites and attending religious cultural festivals and events has increased dramatically, spurred in part by government and tourism officials, and religious groups in some cases, who are increasingly using religious cultural heritage to market and promote destinations (e.g. Olsen 2003; Tilson 2005).

This has led to a more diverse visitor base at religious cultural heritage sites, with many people seeking leisure and educational experiences in addition to, or instead of, religious or spiritual experiences (Hughes, Bond, & Ballantyne 2013; Olsen 2013). However, this blending of religious and tourist space, in addition to increasing inter-religious and pilgrim-tourist encounters (Bremer 2014; Guter & Feldman 2006), has also led to several concerns related to the management of tourism at religious sites and destinations (e.g. Olsen 2006; Shackley 2001; Wiltshier & Griffiths 2016; Woodward 2004).

Traditionally, pilgrimage has been viewed as a religious act—with religious piety and belief motivating believers to travel to sites deemed sacred by a socio-religious group to participate in religious rituals and events. As Barber (1993: 1) posits, pilgrimage is 'a journey resulting from religious causes, externally to a holy site, and internally for spiritual purposes and internal understanding'. Globally, every year millions of people engage in pilgrimage as a strictly religious act (Reader 2007). However, in recent years, the practice and ideological nature of pilgrimage has shifted, at least on an epistemological level, to where any 'journey undertaken by a person in quest of a place or a state that he or she believes to embody a valued ideal' (Morinis 1992: 2) can be considered a pilgrimage. For example, travel to sporting events, the homes of famous persons, government buildings, as well as any form of hedonistic and corporate travel, have been labelled pilgrimages (e.g. Campo 1998; Gammon 2004; Thompson & Smith 2001; Vikan 2012).

This blurring of lines between pilgrimage and religious tourism (Kaelber 2006) has led to several academic discussions regarding whether pilgrimage is different from religious tourism. From a broader perspective, some tourism scholars argue that modern tourism is structurally and metaphorically akin to a 'sacred journey' or pilgrimage (Graburn 1989; MacCannell 1976). They contend that mediaeval pilgrimage was the forerunner of modern tourism, and travel solely for religious reasons began to give way to more multi-functional and multi-motivational trips after the Second World War (Jackowski & Smith 1992). For many people, travel marks a break or a transition in their lives, a process of transformation through which they can escape from daily life and find their 'authentic self' (MacCannell 1973, 1976). Like pilgrims, contemporary tourists, when travelling, separate themselves from ordinary life, enter a realm of 'non-ordinary flotation' (Jafari 1987) or a state of hyper-reality (Holmberg 1993), experience a non-ordinary sacred 'high' (Graburn 1989), and then return to their profane life—an experience akin to Turner's (1973) ideas of liminality and communitas in the context of religiously motivated pilgrimage. This makes the tourist journey, then, a part of a 'nonordinary sphere of existence', making the goals of tourists 'symbolically sacred and morally on a higher plane than the regards of the ordinary workday world' (Graburn 1989: 28).

From an industry perspective, the importance of segmenting different aspects of the tourism market has led to a focus on differentiating tourist motivations and activities to maximise profit and provide quality experiences. While modern pilgrimage travel may be distinct from other forms of pilgrimage (see the next section), it is generally considered a sub-niche market of religious tourism, particularly as modern pilgrims tend to use the same transportation and service infrastructure such as lodging, meals, washrooms, and in some areas parking and banking/ ATM access, as tourists (Gupta 1999). As noted by Timothy and Olsen (2006: 272), the tourism industry tends to define tourist types based on the activities in which they engage rather than motivations for travel. As such, pilgrims are treated as a type of religious tourist who travels to sites of religious and/or spiritual significance, regardless of whether religion is the primary motive to travel. At the same time, to differentiate the tourist who is interested in religious cultural heritage from the tourist who is motivated by religion to visit religious places and events,

Russell (1999: 40) distinguishes between *religious tourists*, 'who set out to visit a destination of religious significance for a specifically religious purpose', and *religious heritage tourists*, who visit the same sites for educational and leisure purposes. Other attempts to note this motivational difference include those by scholars and tourism promoters, who utilise terms such as *pilgrimage tourism, spiritual tourism, religious tourism, tourism pilgrimage*, and *faith tourism* to describe modern pilgrimage travel (Cassar & Munro 2016; Hudman & Jackson 1992; Olsen 2011).

From a theological perspective, tourism is a form of escapism from daily life, and lacks the deeper cultural and spiritual significance that pilgrimage entails. As such, tourism does not lead to a 'substantial' change or a transformation in a person's life, but rather is undertaken for diversionary purposes (Kotler 1997: 103). Although there is a close historical relationship between Christian pilgrimage and tourism, instead of pilgrimage being a forerunner of tourism, modern tourism development occurred through the Grand Tour, not from religious pilgrimage traditions (Bremer 2005). Considering the negative socio-cultural and ethical/moral impacts that tourism causes, suggestions that pilgrimage is a type of tourism would make pilgrimage and pilgrim activity equal with more hedonistic forms of tourism activity such as wine tourism or sex tourism (Ostrowski 2000). Therefore, religious pilgrimage is seen by some observers as being very different from religious tourism. These views would suggest that the utilisation of religion for tourist commodification and consumption would be inherently bad, as this is connected to processes that lead to the 'aestheticization, exoticization, folklorization, fossilization, musealization, Orientalizing, and/or romanticization' of religion (Stausberg 2011: 222). However, many religious groups have long commodified their religious sites, ceremonies, and relics for profit (Hung et al. 2017; Olsen 2003; Reader 2014), with formal and informal theological reflections encouraging tourism visitation to fulfil religious goals related to outreach, pastoral care and proselytisation (Cohen 1998; Olsen 2016; Vukonić 1996, 2000).

While in some ways the above discussion may seem abstract and banal, the type of visitor to the Middle East that engages with religious culture has changed over time (Bar & Cohen-Hattab 2003). While pilgrimage has shaped the tangible and intangible cultural landscape of this region for centuries, and pilgrimage is still an important travel motivation to the region, the ideal of the 'pure pilgrim' does not necessarily exist in the modern era (Olsen 2010). Tourism and its related practices influence practically every region of the world (Bremer 2004), including the practice of pilgrimage. In fact, because of the aforementioned structural similarities, both metaphorically and practically, it is difficult to discuss pilgrimage outside of the lens of tourism promotion and development. Indeed, in the Middle East, as in other world regions, Christian pilgrims demand air-conditioned buses, and pilgrims participating in the hajj are increasingly expecting modern conveniences and comforts (Cohen-Hattab & Shoval 2014; Green 2014; Ron & Timothy 2019). As well, many Jewish travellers to the Middle East and elsewhere seek out hotels that offer kosher food and Sabbath day elevators (Cohen Ioannides & Ioannides 2006), while Muslim travellers seek Shariah-compliant lodging (Battour, Ismail, & Battor 2010a; Henderson 2010), and as such, seek to have their religious needs and comforts met when using available tourism infrastructures to cater to their travel wants and needs. Therefore, while the Latin word for pilgrim—*peregrinus*—implied a person leaving the comfort of their home to wander (Maddrell, Della Dora, Scafi, & Walton 2014: 3), in the present era, the element of sacrifice and suffering seems to mainly take place when a person enters a specific religious site or region rather than throughout the course of an entire pilgrimage journey.

As well, like the pilgrim of old, modern pilgrim-tourists combine a number of motivations and activities while journeying (Olsen 2010). Rather than just visiting religious sites on their way to their final destination, these travellers may also engage in sightseeing, gambling, recreational activities, and visit other cultural attractions during their trip. Also, pilgrim motivations can gradually change over the course of a journey. As Post, Pieper and van Uden (1998: 47) note, 'One can set out for purely recreational reasons, but come to be spiritually touched after arriving at the pilgrimage site. The next time that person may then go on pilgrimage out of the motivation of deepening their faith.' This can also be the reverse, where a person travelling for purely religious reasons can become more recreationally minded during their travels (Olsen 2010). Therefore, a journey purely motivated by religious causes and participation only in holy activities is something that is more of an ideal than a practicality (Olsen 2010). However, this has not stopped scholars from attempting to differentiate tourist motivations based on religious intensity or fervour and their religious travel needs and activities (e.g. Kamenidou & Vourou 2015; Olsen 2013; Öter & Çetinkaya 2016; Nyaupane, Timothy, & Poudel 2015; Ron 2009).

Because of the increasing numbers of people engaging in pilgrimage travel and visiting religious sites, several businesses have arisen to cater to the wants and needs of both visitors who are travelling for religious purposes and those who visit religious sites for educational or curiosity reasons (Timothy & Olsen 2006). These businesses range from tour operators offering religious-themed package tours to helping pilgrims negotiate a pilgrimage route and process, creating themed hotels with religious motifs and menus, apps that help spiritual and religious pilgrims find restaurants and hotels along their pilgrimage route, and other such services. In addition, many pilgrims and religious tourists who seek a more structured trip seem to prefer guides that reflect their theological views, and prefer to travel to places that have similar religious affinities (Wilkinson 1998).

Themes and challenges related to pilgrimage and religious tourism in MENA

Today, holy places in the Middle East attract millions of international and domestic visitors, with a high percentage of them coming to engage with religious heritage. While many of these sacred sites can be accessed only by pious believers, others are open to visitors of all nationalities, creeds, and motivations. The demand for religious sites, ceremonies, and other aspects of religious cultural heritage as a part of tourist itineraries has increased in the past few decades, and may continue to grow in the near future. However, this interest is tempered by a number of micro- and macro-level factors and challenges, which has inhibited pilgrimage and religious tourism visitation rates. As such, this section focuses on some of the research related to pilgrimage and religious tourism in the region, and focuses more specifically on the challenges that affect pilgrimage and religious tourism development and growth.

The potential for religious tourism development

Considering the long tradition of pilgrimage and tourism to this region, it may seem strange to discuss the potential for religious tourism in this region. However, the majority of countries in MENA have not seen the same numbers of travellers for pilgrimage and religious tourism purposes as Israel and Saudi Arabia have. Therefore, there is a growing body of literature examining the potential of religious tourism development in different countries and at specific sites, as well as in terms of religious tourism infrastructure. For example, regarding Turkey, a few studies have discussed the potential economic importance of religious tourism and the types of religious supply that could be incorporated into non-religious tour itineraries (Aktas & Ekin 2007; Duman 2012; Egresi, Kara, & Bayram 2014; Tosun 2001), with some scholars recommending a number of regions within Turkey with the potential for increased incorporation of religious culture with tourism development, including Istanbul, Marmara and the Aegean Coast amongst others (Egresi, Bayram, Kara, & Kesik 2012). Likewise, Egresi,

Bayram and Kara (2012) focus on the motivations of visitors to Mardin, Turkey, and Ozdemir and Met (2012) discuss the religious needs of Muslim tourists in the country with a specific focus on the accommodations industry. More broadly, Battour, Ismail and Battor (2010b) note that while Turkey is a more liberal Muslim country, the tourism industry is cognisant of the religious needs of conservative Muslim tourists, and have set spaces aside for these travellers to practise their faith.

Iran has also been the focus of several studies on religious tourism. Some of these have included Iran in broader discussions of the development and management of tourism in Islamic societies (Aziz 2001; Din 1989; Timothy & Iverson 2006; Zamani-Farahani & Henderson 2010), while others have focused on the current situation, development potential, management issues, and cultural impacts related to pilgrimage and religious tourism in the country (Alipour & Heydari 2005; Ghaderi & Henderson 2012; Khaksari, Lee, & Lee 2014; Morakabati 2011; Zamani-Farahani & Musa 2012). Other publications have examined pilgrimage and religious tourism management in Iran in a comparative manner (Pinto 2007; Zamani-Farahani & Henderson 2010). While research on pilgrimage and religious tourism has not been as pervasive in other Middle Eastern countries, there is a small literature focusing on a few of these countries, including Syria (Pinto 2007) and Lebanon (Farra-Haddad 2015).

Internal geopolitical conflicts

For the tourism industry to succeed several elements need to be in place, including political stability, security, peace and intercultural dialogue (Al-Hamarneh & Steiner 2004). In MENA, the biggest challenge to maintaining pilgrimage and religious tourism growth is internal geopolitical conflicts that are inherent to one of the historically most conflict-riddled regions in the world (Timothy & Daher 2009). Pilgrimage and religious tourism do not exist in a socio-political and spatial vacuum, as they are affected by the politics and social trends of the area where they take place. Shackley (2001: 7–8), for example, suggests that national, regional and local political and social instability can heighten management problems and disrupt visitor flows, arguing that 'the easiest sites to manage are those where [socio-political] stability is high even if visitor numbers are high … since this stability and control permits the development and implementation of effective visitor management systems'.

While pilgrimage and religious tourism seem to be 'recession-proof', in that pilgrimage and religious tourism destinations do not see the same levels of visitor decline due to war, terrorism, social instability and economic recession (Singh, 1998), this region has not been immune from decreasing numbers of religious visitors during times of war and conflict. For example, the presence of ISIL and its destruction of religious monuments and buildings, in part to eradicate incompatible religious beliefs and institute religious absolutism over the region (Turku 2017), not only limits the locations where pilgrims and religious tourism can take place, but destroys the spiritual link locals and international visitors have with this religious heritage (Al-Marashi 2017; Harmanşah 2015). As well, in instances of religious civil war, which seem to be increasing in frequency in MENA (Feliu & Grasa 2013; Svensson 2013), religious heritage sites that are viewed as important to one side have been targeted by opposing sides (Naccache 1998; Timothy & Daher 2009). In the case of Syria's civil war and the ISIL conflict, extensive damage to all six World Heritage Sites and other ancient and religious monuments and archaeological sites has occurred (Perini & Guidetti 2015). The Arab Spring, starting in 2010, also led to a decline in tourist visitation rates in MENA because of violent confrontations between protestors and government militias (Morakabati 2013).

The conflict between, and political debates surrounding, Israel and Palestine have also led to a decrease in pilgrim and religious tourist visitation rates. During the second Intifada (2000–2005), tourism to Israel declined by two-thirds, including pilgrims and religious tourists (Gelbman 2016). In addition, the conflict between Israel and Palestine has led to a systematic destruction of tourism infrastructure in Palestine, which has made it difficult for pilgrims and religious tourists to visit and find the services they need in the Palestinian territories (Isaac 2010b). As well, the security/segregation wall, which acts as a dark tourism tourist attraction in its own right, functions as a barrier to pilgrims and religious tourists who wish to visit Bethlehem. However, because of Christians' desire to visit Bethlehem, both sides of this conflict have made special efforts to ensure the quick movement of tour buses through the barrier (Gelbman 2016).

Terrorism and political conflict tend to lead to the development of negative destination images in and around where these events take place (Baker 2014). For example, after the 9/11 attacks in the United States in 2001 and the subsequent US-led war in Afghanistan, tourism visitation to MENA declined 20–30 per cent, and in countries such as Turkey, Egypt, Jordan and throughout North Africa, tour operators reported that fears of reprisals against Western tourists led to cancellation rates reaching 60 to 70 per cent (Hazbun 2006). In Iran, tourism development, including pilgrimage and religious tourism, has been limited because of the threat of inter-regional instability and conflict in surrounding countries (Morakabati 2011). As well, terror attacks against tourists to this region have occurred because of the terrorists' beliefs that certain tourist behaviours are incompatible with local cultural and religious values (Aziz 1995; Sönmez 1998). This has affected the risk perception of potential tourists regarding MENA (Ahlfeldt, Franke, & Maennig 2009), as well as long-term foreign investments in tourism (Morakabati 2013; Steiner 2010). As such, conflict in some countries projects an image of war and terrorism on other countries in the region, decreasing pilgrim and religious tourist arrivals region-wide.

Contested sacred space

As noted earlier, MENA is one of the world's premier pilgrimage and religious tourism destinations because of its importance to the faith traditions of Christianity, Judaism and Islam. In particular, Jerusalem is generally viewed as the world's foremost holy city, with hundreds of thousands of people every year visiting for religio-political purposes (Timothy & Emmett 2014). Jerusalem is the prototypical case study for issues related to contested religious heritage and contested sacred space, in part because it is the centre of 'supraregional hierarchies of power' (Heing 2012) and has garnered global attention because of its contested nature as the capital of two nations (Shachar & Shoval 1999).

Indeed, conflict is always a part of a particular space or place because of its role in politico-social relations between different cultural, ethnic and religious groups. Religious groups typically hold certain places and landscapes as inherently sacred or holy because supernatural or divine manifestations have occurred there, and subsequently mark those places and landscapes through a process of signification and sacralisation (Chidester & Linenthal 1995). As a part of controlling a social space, those in power tend to delineate and solidify their cultural (and religious) ideologies and legitimacy through representing the meanings of sacred spaces as fixed, bounded and static, and defining their places and landscapes as being in opposition to other ideologies and places (Massey 1995). In doing so, they may practise a politics of exclusion, where dominant discourses and decision makers dictate what is considered appropriate behaviour through regulation and surveillance. This behaviour includes a decision about what is 'in-place' and what is 'out-of-place' (i.e. what is considered to be appropriate behaviour) and who is included or excluded from entering/performing in this space (Cresswell 1996; Sibley 1995; Trudeau 2006). However, other social groups or individuals may have different views of the meaning of that space and how it is represented, and contest those meanings and representations through counter-hegemonic opposition to dominant ideologies through resistance and struggle (Graham, Ashworth, & Tunbridge 2000: 76). This contest over meaning and representation can give rise to multiple cultural and political discourses relating to issues over what cultural/religious ideologies are represented and who has the power to represent them (Olsen & Guelke 2004).

The city of Jerusalem is contested at multiple scales. For example, at the international level, there is conflict between followers and representatives of the Abrahamic religions; at a regional level, there is conflict between Israel and the surrounding Arab states; at the national level is the conflict between Israelis and Palestinians; and at the local level, conflicts exist between competing visions of Jerusalem's development by different stakeholder groups (Albin 2005). This contestation has affected pilgrimage and tourism development in Jerusalem in multiple ways. For example, there are different viewpoints regarding the development of modern tourism infrastructure in Jerusalem and maintaining the spiritual, Orientalist and picturesque look and feel of Jerusalem, free from any type of modernisation (Olsen & Ron 2013). While there have been some compromises regarding the physical development of Jerusalem (Albin 2005), these viewpoints have been further intensified by the fact that most stakeholders see tourism development as a zero-sum game, in which the advantage to one stakeholder group means other stakeholder groups are automatically disadvantaged (Olsen & Guelke 2004). As such, any attempts to develop tourism infrastructure or attractions involves a delicate balance between maintaining the status quo and the need to improve pilgrimage and tourism-related spaces (Olsen & Ron 2013). However, at the local level, cooperation between stakeholders seems to be easier than at broader scales.

The politics of pilgrimage and religious tourism

While tourism as a field of research has typically been apolitical (outside of the study of local, regional, and national politics in tourism management and policymaking), calls have been made in recent years for tourism scholars to move beyond tourism as an economic practice and 'apply more critical and deconstructed analyses of the moral, cultural, and social dimensions of tourism within wider global trends, including increases in technological, political, and trans-local cultural exchanges' (Olsen & Timothy 2017: 7061). As Hall (2011: 39) argues, 'what we do in tourism is inherently political, or has political implications in terms of who gets what, why, and where.' As such, in critically studying tourism, scholars have turned to issues related to cultural appropriation, neo-colonialism, commodification and authenticity, the ethics of cultural and ethnic encounters, and the embodied, reflexive, and multi-sensory nature of 'geographies of encounter' (Valentine 2008).

Within this context, while pilgrimage is generally viewed as being apolitical in nature, being motivated solely by religious intentions, some scholars have suggested that these religious forms of travel are contested in terms of the meaning of these journeys, the discourses given at religious sites, and the contested views and performances between pilgrims and tourists (Coleman & Elsner 1995; Digance 2003; Di Giovine 2011; Eade & Sallnow 1991). Religious landscapes and sites are also used to promote particular sides of inter-governmental or ethno-religious conflict (Breger, Reiter, & Hammer 2012; Philip & Mercer 1999; Winter 2007) or act as the background for photo-ops by government leaders who wish to cater to a particular group of religious voters in their home country during official visits (Olsen 2017). Even visits by the Pope are generally couched in the context of geopolitics (Katz 2003).

This has been the case regarding pilgrimage and religious tourism to the Middle East, where travel is used as a political tool to promote different discourses regarding the identity and proper ownership of land. For example, pilgrimage to the Holy Land is generally viewed as being filled with theo-political symbolism (Belhassen 2009; Belhassen & Ebel 2009). This is the case with American 'Zionist tourism' to Israel, where Evangelical tourists travel to Israel to show solidary with God's 'chosen people' (Belhassen 2009: 135) as well as support for the state of Israel and Jewish sovereignty (Belhassen & Ebel 2009; Ron & Timothy 2019). To appeal to these Zionist tourists, tours are carefully scripted to cater to their theological and political viewpoints, and are designed to promote a pro-Israel message (Belhassen 2009; Belhassen & Ebel 2009; Belhassen & Santos 2006; Brin & Noy 2010; Cohen-Hattab 2004; Feldman 2007; Kaell 2010, 2014; Smith 2010). At the same time, the Zionist tourism discourse is contested by those engaged in developing 'Palestinian tourism', who promote and tell both the Palestinian side of the Israeli/Palestinian conflict and the political colonisation of Palestinian lands by Israel (Al-Rimmawi 2003; Isaac 2009, 2010a, 2010b, 2013; Isaac, Hall, & Higgins-Desbiolles 2016; Nasser 2009). While Israelis and Palestinians compete for Christian pilgrims and religious tourists to promote their vision of this region (Brin 2006; Cohen-Hattab 2004), there have also been calls for tourists to the Holy Land to be more socially and politically aware regarding social justice for Palestinians (Isaac 2010a; Kassis 2004) as well as greater consideration for the daily struggles of Christian Palestinians, who have traditionally been ignored by Christian pilgrims and religious tourists (Sizer 1999).

Congestion, sacred space and management challenges

The popularity of pilgrimage and religious tourism to this region, in particular to the Holy Land, has led to a number of studies examining the logistics of moving religious visitors around cities and sacred sites. As noted earlier, scholars have examined several management issues related to religious heritage sites. More broadly, some of these issues include the theft of artefacts, vandalism, graffiti, accidental damage and wear and tear, pollution (noise, litter, fouling), microclimatic change and crowding (Olsen 2006; Shackley 2001; Woodward 2004). These issues affect various aspects of pilgrimage and religious tourism management from the city level to the specific site level. For example, overcrowding is a major issue in many urban spaces, particularly where it is difficult to expand tourism spaces due to existing historical infrastructural constraints. This is why in Mecca and Medina, authorities enforce strict quotas on the number of religious visitors to keep them at a manageable level (Zamani-Farahani & Henderson 2010). At the site level, the Church of the Holy Sepulchre experiences severe overcrowding because there is only one small entrance to the church, which results in long lines of people trying to enter and exit through the same doorway (Olsen & Ron 2013).

Events related to religious calendars, holy years or special one-off religious events, such as the religious connotations associated with the turn of the new millennium or the visit of the Pope to the Holy Land (Katz 2003; Olsen & Timothy 1999), can exacerbate overcrowding at different times of the year. As Olsen and Ron (2013: 61) note, the three Abrahamic religions use at least five different religious calendars, each with different feast days, and 'The simultaneous use of several calendars with moveable and unmovable feast days is a great managerial challenge for authorities, sites and visitors to Jerusalem'. This is in part because ordinary guidebooks are unable to list all the different times of the year when a particular religious site might be inundated with pilgrims. This is particularly acute in Islam, where certain religious holidays are celebrated based on a lunar calendar, and so the exact day of the celebration is not known until the night before, further adding to confusion regarding visitor flows within the city.

Historically, the contestation at these various scales has led to the development of segregated tourist spaces, which include holy sites (Shachar & Shoval 1999) with different religio-cultural groups owning and maintaining different areas of Jerusalem as well as parts of specific buildings. As noted earlier, considering that religious sites in MENA are couched in the politics and social trends of the area in which they take place, it can be difficult to manage pilgrims and religious tourists effectively at these sites, particularly in the context of multi-faith locales (Timothy & Emmett 2014). As a case in point, the Church of the Holy Sepulchre experiences management difficulties because of the inter-faith 'turf-war' (Bowman 2011) that takes place in the Church. Since the site is controlled by several Christian groups, with each given 'possessory rights' over certain parts of the building, it is difficult to make changes to the interior of the church, as well as changes in visitor management protocols, since all parties must agree to any modifications, and clashes have been known to occur when one group transgresses the spatial status quo (Bowman 2011; Cohen 2008).

The contested nature of land ownership in Jerusalem also influenced the management of the Temple Mount in Jerusalem, which is viewed as holy to all three Abrahamic religions. For example, because of the impossibility of sharing sacred space throughout most of Jerusalem (Hassner 2003), particular dynamics exist regarding visitation to both the Western Wall and the Al-Aqsa Mosque. While Muslim visitors are welcome to visit the Al-Aqsa Mosque, non-Muslim visitors must enter a specific gate after passing through security, and only at specific times of the day so as not to interfere with prayer times. Understandably, visitors must also adhere to a specific code of conduct and dress. While Jewish visitors are welcome, Orthodox Jews do not visit the Mosque because of the religious prohibition to enter the Temple Mount in case they inadvertently walk through the site of the Holy of Holies. As well, since the city of Jerusalem is technically responsible for the maintenance of the Temple Mount, workers can only enter at certain times and only walk around its edges. As such, seemingly simple things are complicated by overarching religious and political issues (Olsen & Ron 2013).

Conclusion

MENA has a long history of pilgrims traversing difficult terrain to visit holy sites. In recent years, in conjunction with the rise in tourism and corresponding infrastructural advancements, people combining both religious and recreational motives have begun to visit this region. However, the region continues to deal with strong socio-cultural and political tensions that affect the flows and management of pilgrims and religious tourists. Terrorism, intra-regional conflict, strongly contested sacred space, the use of pilgrimage and religious tourism to promote ideological perspectives, and the difficulties of managing increasing visitors to sacred sites, have affected the flows of pilgrims and religious tourists to and throughout this region. While the Holy Land is a major pilgrimage destination, and most research on pilgrimage and religious tourism has focused on this region and the Hajj in Saudi Arabia, religious tourism is a growing sector of the economy in MENA, with countries such as Turkey and Iran exploring and investing in this tourism niche market. As pilgrimage and religious tourism continue to grow in the Middle East, and as government tourism officials utilise religious sites for economic gain, it will be interesting to see how the governments of different states engage with religious tourists and with other countries to ensure the safety and positive experiences of these visitors while addressing the broader political issues of the region.

References

Adler, J. (2002) 'The holy man as traveler and travel attraction: Early Christian asceticism and the moral problem of modernity', in W.H. Swatos Jr., & L. Tomasi (eds), *From Medieval Pilgrimage to Religious Tourism* (pp. 25–50). London: Praeger.

Ahlfeldt, H., Franke, B., & Maennig, W. (2009) 'Terrorism and the regional and religious risk perception of foreigners: The case of German tourists', *Hamburg Contemporary Economic Discussions*, No. 24. Available online: http://ideas.repec.org/p/hce/wpaper/024.html (Accessed 15 October 2017).

Aktas, A., & Ekin, Y. (2007) 'The importance and the role of faith (religious) tourism in the alternative tourism resources in Turkey', in R. Raj, & N.D. Morpeth (eds), *Religious Tourism and Pilgrimage Management: An International Perspective* (pp. 170–183). Wallingford: CAB International.

Albin, C. (2005) 'Explaining conflict transformation: How Jerusalem became negotiable', *Cambridge Review of International Affairs*, 18(3): 339–355.

Al-Hamarneh, A., & Steiner, C. (2004) 'Islamic tourism: Rethinking the strategies of tourism development in the Arab world after September 11, 2001', *Comparative Studies of South Asia, Africa and the Middle East*, 24(1): 173–182.

Alipour, H., & Heydari, R. (2005) 'Tourism revival and planning in Islamic Republic of Iran: Challenges and prospects', *Anatolia*, 16(1): 39–61.

Al-Marashi, I. (2017) 'The impact of the Islamic State of Iraq and Syria's campaign on Yezidi religious structures and pilgrimage practices', in Leppäkari, M., & Griffin, K. (eds), *Pilgrimage and Tourism to Holy Cities: Ideological and Management Perspectives* (pp. 144–155). Wallingford: CAB International.

Al-Rimmawi, H.A. (2003) 'Palestinian tourism: A period of transition', *International Journal of Contemporary Hospitality Management*, 15(2): 76–85.

Aziz, H. (1995) 'Understanding attacks on tourists in Egypt', *Tourism Management*, 16(2): 91–95.

Aziz, H. (2001) 'The journey: An overview of tourism and travel in the Arab/Islamic context', in D. Harrison (ed.), *Tourism and the Less Developed World: Issues and Case Studies* (pp. 151–160). Wallingford: CAB International.

Baker, D.M.A. (2014) 'The effects of terrorism on the travel and tourism industry', *International Journal of Religious Tourism and Pilgrimage*, 2(1): 58–67.

Bar, D., & Cohen-Hattab, K. (2003) 'A new kind of pilgrimage: The modern tourism pilgrim of nineteenth-century and early twentieth century Palestine', *Middle Eastern Studies*, 39(2): 131–148.

Barbato, M. (2013) *Pilgrimage, Politics, and International Relations: Religious Semantics for World Politics*. New York: Palgrave-MacMillan.

Barber, R. (1993) *Pilgrimages*. London: Boydell.

Battour, M.M., Ismail, M.N., & Battor, M. (2010a) 'Toward a halal tourism market', *Tourism Analysis*, 15(4): 461–470.

Battour, M.M., Ismail, M.N., & Battor, M. (2010b) 'The impact of destination attributes on Muslim tourist's choice', *International Journal of Tourism Research*, 13(6): 527–540.

Belhassen, Y. (2009) 'Fundamentalist Christian pilgrimages as a political and cultural force', *Journal of Heritage Tourism*, 4(2): 131–144.

Belhassen, Y., & Ebel, J. (2009) 'Tourism, faith and politics in the Holy Land: An ideological analysis of evangelical pilgrimage', *Current Issues in Tourism*, 12(4): 359–378.

Belhassen, Y., & Santos, C.A. (2006) 'An American evangelical pilgrimage to Israel: A case study on politics and triangulation', *Journal of Travel Research*, 44(4): 431–441.

Bowman, G. (2011) 'In dubious battle on the Plains of Heav'n: The politics of possession in Jerusalem's Holy Sepulchre', *History and Anthropology*, 22(3): 371–399.

Breger, M. J., Reiter, Y., & Hammer, L. (eds) (2012) *Sacred Space in Israel and Palestine*. London: Routledge.

Bremer, T.S. (2004) *Blessed with Tourists: The Borderlands of Religion and Tourism in San Antonio*. Chapel Hill, NC: University of North Carolina Press.

Bremer, T.S. (2005) 'Tourism and religion', in L. Jones (ed.), *Encyclopedia of Religion* (pp. 9260–9264). Detroit, MI: Macmillan.

Bremer, T.S. (2014) 'A touristic angle of vision: Tourist studies as a methodological approach for the study of religions', *Religion Compass*, 8(12): 371–397.

Brin, E. (2006) 'Politically-oriented tourism in Jerusalem', *Tourist Studies*, 6(3): 215–243.

Brin, E., & Noy, C. (2010) 'The said and the unsaid: Performative guiding in a Jerusalem Neighbourhood', *Tourist Studies*, 19(1): 19–33.

Campo, J.E. (1998) 'American pilgrimage landscapes', *Annals of the American Academy of Political and Social Sciences*, 55(840): 40–56.

Cassar, G., & Munro, D. (2016) 'Malta: A differentiated approach to the pilgrim-tourist dichotomy', *International Journal of Religious Tourism and Pilgrimage*, 4(4): 67–78.

Chidester, D., & Linenthal, E.T. (1995) 'Introduction', in D. Chidester, & E.T. Linenthal (eds), *American Sacred Space* (pp. 1–42). Bloomington, IN: Indiana University Press.

Cohen, E. (1998) 'Tourism and religion: A comparative perspective', *Pacific Tourism Review*, 2: 1–10.

Cohen, R. (2008) *Saving the Holy Sepulchre: How Rival Christians Came Together to Rescue their Holiest Shrine.* New York: Oxford University Press.

Cohen-Hattab, K. (2004) 'Zionism, tourism, and the battle for Palestine: Tourism as a political-propaganda tool', *Israeli Studies*, 9(1): 61–85.

Cohen-Hattab, K., & Shoval, N. (2014) *Tourism, Religion and Pilgrimage in Jerusalem*. London: Routledge.

Cohen Ioannides, M.W., & Ioannides, D. (2006) 'Global Jewish tourism', in D.J. Timothy, & D.H. Olsen (eds), *Tourism, Religion and Spiritual Journeys* (pp. 156–171). London: Routledge.

Coleman, S., & Elsner, J. (1995) *Pilgrimage: Past and Present in the World Religions*. Cambridge, MA: Harvard University Press.

Collins-Kreiner, N. (2010) 'Researching pilgrimage: Continuity and transformations', *Annals of Tourism Research*, 37(2): 440–456.

Cresswell, T. (1996) *In Place/Out of Place: Geography, Ideology, and Transgression*. Minneapolis, MN: University of Minnesota Press.

Davidsson Bremborg, A. (2013) 'Creating sacred space by walking in silence: Pilgrimage in a late modern Lutheran context', *Social Compass*, 60(4): 544–560.

Derhally, M.A. (2013) 'Saudi reaps \$16.5bn from religious tourism'. *Arabian Business*. Available online: www.arabianbusiness.com/saudi-reaps-16-5bn-from-religious-tourism-484586.html (Accessed 26 September 2017).

Di Giovine, M.A. (2011) 'Pilgrimage: Communitas and contestation, unity and difference—an introduction', *Tourism*, 59(3): 247–259.

Digance, J. (2003) 'Pilgrimage at contested sites', *Annals of Tourism Research*, 30(1): 143–159.

Din, K.H. (1989) 'Islam and tourism: Patterns, issues, and options', *Annals of Tourism Research*, 16(4): 542–563.

Duman, T. (2012) 'The value of Islamic tourism: Perspectives from the Turkish experience', *Islam and Civilisational Renewal*, 3(4): 718–739.

Eade, J., & Sallnow, M.J. (eds) (1991) *Contesting the Sacred: The Anthropology of Pilgrimage*. London: Routledge.

Egresi, I., Bayram, B., & Kara, F. (2012) 'Tourism at religious sites: A case from Mardin, Turkey', *Geographica Timisiensis*, 21(1): 5–15.

Egresi, I., Bayram, B., Kara, F., & Kesik, O.A. (2012) 'Unlocking the potential of religious tourism in Turkey', *GeoJournal of Tourism and Geosites*, 5(1): 63–80.

Egresi, I., Kara, F., & Bayram, B. (2014) 'Economic impact of religious tourism in Mardin, Turkey', *Journal of Economics and Business Research*, 18(2): 7–22.

Farra-Haddad, N. (2015) 'Pilgrimages toward South Lebanon: Holy places relocating Lebanon as a part of the Holy Land', in R. Raj, & K. Griffin (eds), *Religious Tourism and Pilgrimage Management: An International Perspective*, 2nd edn. (pp. 279–296). Wallingford: CAB International.

Feldman, J. (2007) 'Constructing a shared Bible land: Jewish Israeli guiding performances for Protestant pilgrims', *American Ethnologist*, 34: 351–374.

Feliu, L., & Grasa, R. (2013) 'Armed conflicts and religious factors: The need for synthesised conceptual frameworks and new empirical analyses—the case of the MENA region', *Civil Wars*, 15(4): 431–453.

Fleischer, A. (2000) 'The tourist behind the pilgrim in the Holy Land', *International Journal of Hospitality Management*, 19: 311–326.

Gammon, S. (2004) 'Secular pilgrimage and sport tourism', in B.W. Ritchie, & D. Adair (eds), *Sport Tourism: Interrelationships, Impacts and Issues* (pp. 30–45). Clevedon: Channel View Publications.

Gelbman, A. (2016) 'Tourism along the geopolitical barrier: Implications of the Holy Land fence', *GeoJournal*, 81(5): 671–680.

Ghaderi, Z., & Henderson, J.C. (2012) 'Sustainable rural tourism in Iran: A perspective from Hawraman Village', *Tourism Management Perspectives*, 2: 47–54.

Graburn, N.H.H. (1989) 'Tourism: The sacred journey', in V.L. Smith (ed.), *Hosts and Guests: The Anthropology of Tourism* (pp. 21–36). Philadelphia, PA: University of Pennsylvania Press.

Graham, B., Ashworth, G.J., & Tunbridge, J.E. (2000) *A Geography of Heritage: Power, Culture, and Economy*. London: Arnold.

Green, N. (2014) 'The Hajj as its own undoing: Infrastructure and integration on the Muslim journey to Mecca', *Past & Present*, 226(1): 193–226.

Gupta, V. (1999) 'Sustainable tourism: Learning from Indian religious traditions', *International Journal of Contemporary Hospitality Management*, 11(2–3): 91–95.

Guter, Y., & Feldman, J. (2006) 'Holy Land pilgrimage as a site of inter-religious encounter', *Studia Hebraica*, 6: 87–93.

Hall, M.C. (2011) 'Researching the political in tourism: Where knowledge meets power', in C.M. Hall (ed.), *Fieldwork in Tourism Methods: Issues and Reflections* (pp. 39–54). London: Routledge.

Harmanşah, Ö. (2015) 'ISIS, heritage, and the spectacles of destruction in the global media', *Near Eastern Archaeology*, 78(3): 170–177.

Hassner, R.E. (2003) '"To halve and to hold": Conflicts over sacred space and the problem of indivisibility', *Security Studies*, 12(4): 1–33.

Hazbun, W. (2006) 'Explaining the Arab Middle East tourism paradox', *The Arab World Geographer*, 9(3): 201–214.

Heing, D. (2012) '"This is our little Hajj": Muslim holy sites and reappropriation of the sacred landscape in contemporary Bosnia', *American Ethnologist*, 39(4): 751–765.

Henderson, J.C. (2010) 'Sharia-compliant hotels', *Tourism and Hospitality Research*, 10(3): 246–254.

Holmberg, C.B. (1993) 'Spiritual pilgrimages: Traditional and hyperreal motivations for travel and tourism', *Visions of Leisure and Business*, 12(2): 18–27.

Hudman, L.E., & Jackson, R.H. (1992) 'Mormon pilgrimage and tourism', *Annals of Tourism Research*, 19: 107–121.

Hughes, K., Bond, N., & Ballantyne, R. (2013) 'Designing and managing interpretive experiences at religious sites: Visitors' perceptions of Canterbury Cathedral', *Tourism Management*, 36: 210–220.

Hung, K., Yang, X., Wassler, P., Wang, D., Lin, P., & Liu, Z. (2017) Contesting the commercialisation and sanctity of religious tourism in the Shaolin Monastery, China', *International Journal of Tourism Research*, 19(2): 145–159.

Isaac, R.K. (2009) 'Alternative tourism: Can the Segregation Wall in Bethlehem be a tourist attraction?', *Tourism and Hospitality Planning & Development*, 6(3): 247–254.

Isaac, R.K. (2010a) 'Palestinian tourism in transition: Hope, aspiration, or Reality?', *The Journal of Tourism and Peace Research*, 1(1): 16–26.

Isaac, R.K. (2010b) 'Alternative tourism: New forms of tourism in Bethlehem for the Palestinian tourism industry', *Current Issues in Tourism*, 13(1): 21–36.

Isaac, R.K. (2013) 'Palestine: Tourism under occupation', in R. Butler, & W. Suntikul (eds), *Tourism and War* (pp. 143–158). London: Routledge.

Isaac, R.K., Hall, C.M., & Higgins-Desbiolles, F. (eds) (2016) *The Politics and Power of Tourism in Palestine*. London: Routledge.

Jackowski, A., & Smith, V.L. (1992) 'Polish pilgrim-tourists', *Annals of Tourism Research*, 19: 92–106.

Jafari, J. (1987) 'Tourism models: The sociocultural aspects', *Tourism Management*, 8: 151–159.

Kaelber, L. (2006) 'Paradigms of travel: From medieval pilgrimage to the postmodern virtual tour', in D.J. Timothy, & D.H. Olsen (eds), *Tourism, Religion and Spiritual Journeys* (pp. 49–63). London: Routledge.

Kaell, H. (2010) 'Pilgrimage in the jet age: The development of the American Evangelical Holy Land travel industry, 1948–1978', *Journal of Tourism History*, 2(1): 23–38.

Kaell, H. (2014) *Walking Where Jesus Walked: American Christians and Holy Land Pilgrimage*. New York: New York University Press.

Kamenidou, I., & Vourou, R. (2015) 'Motivation factors for visiting religious sites: The case of Lesvos Island', *European Journal of Tourism Research*, 9: 78–91.

Kassis, R. (2004) 'The Palestinians and justice tourism', *Contours*, 14(2/3): 18–21.

Katz, K. (2003) 'Legitimising Jordan as the Holy Land: Papal pilgrimages—1964, 2000', *Comparative Studies of South Asia, Africa and the Middle East*, 23(1): 181–189.

Khaksari, A., Lee, T.J., & Lee, C.K. (2014) 'Religious perceptions and hegemony on tourism development: The case of the Islamic Republic of Iran', *International Journal of Tourism Research*, 16(1): 97–103.

Kotler, J.A. (1997) *Travel That Can Change Your Life: How to Create a Transformative Experience*. San Francisco, CA: Jossey-Bass Publishers.

Leppäkari, M., & Griffin, K.A. (eds) (2017) *Pilgrimage and Tourism to Holy Cities: Ideological and Management Perspectives*. Wallingford: CAB International.

MacCannell, D. (1973) 'Staged authenticity: Arrangements of social space in tourist settings', *American Sociological Review*, 79: 589–603.

MacCannell, D. (1976) *The Tourist: A New Theory of the Leisure Class.* New York: Schocken.

Maddrell, A., Della Dora, V., Scafi, A., & Walton, H. (2014) *Christian Pilgrimage, Landscape and Heritage: Journeying to the Sacred.* London: Routledge.

Massey, D. (1995) 'The conceptualisation of place', in D. Massey, & P. Jess (eds), *A Place in the World? Place, Cultures and Globalisation* (pp. 45–86). Oxford: Open University/Oxford University Press.

Morakabati, Y. (2011) 'Deterrents to tourism development in Iran', *International Journal of Tourism Research,* 13(2): 103–123.

Morakabati, Y. (2013) 'Tourism in the Middle East: Conflicts, crises and economic diversification, some critical issues', *International Journal of Tourism Research,* 15(4): 375–387.

Morinis, A. (1992) 'Introduction: The territory of the anthropology of pilgrimage', in A. Morinis (ed.), *Sacred Journeys: The Anthropology of Pilgrimage* (pp. 1–28). Westport, CT: Greenwood Press.

Naccache, A. (1998) 'Beirut's memorycide: Hear no evil, see no evil', in L. Meskell (ed.), *Archaeology Under Fire: Nationalism, Politics and Heritage in the Eastern Mediterranean and Middle East* (pp. 140–158). London: Routledge.

Nasser, C. (2009) 'Silenced voices in the development of Palestinian tourism', in R. Isaac, V. Platenkamp, & A. Protegies (eds), *Voices in Tourism Development: Creating Spaces for Tacit Knowledge and Innovation* (pp. 132–150). Amsterdam: NHTV Expertise Series.

Nyaupane, G.P., Timothy, D.J., & Poudel, S. (2015) 'Understanding tourists in religious destinations: A social distance perspective', *Tourism Management,* 48: 343–353.

Olsen, D.H. (2003) 'Heritage, tourism, and the commodification of religion', *Tourism Recreation Research,* 28(3): 99–104.

Olsen, D.H. (2006) 'Management issues for religious heritage attractions', in D.J. Timothy, & D.H. Olsen (eds), *Tourism, Religion and Spiritual Journeys* (pp. 104–118). London: Routledge.

Olsen, D.H. (2010) 'Pilgrims, tourists, and Weber's "ideal types"', *Annals of Tourism Research,* 37(3): 848–851.

Olsen, D.H. (2011) 'Towards a religious view of tourism: Negotiating faith perspectives on tourism', *Journal of Tourism, Culture and Communication,* 11(1): 17–30.

Olsen, D.H. (2013) 'A scalar comparison of motivations and expectations of experience within the religious tourism market', *International Journal of Religious Tourism and Pilgrimage,* 1(1): 41–61.

Olsen, D.H. (2016) 'The Church of Jesus Christ of Latter-day Saints, their "three-fold mission," and practical and pastoral theology', *Practical Matters,* 9. Available online: http://practicalmattersjournal.org/2016/06/29/lds-three-fold-mission/.

Olsen, D.H. (2017) 'Social politics on the move: The case of the Marian Ocean to Ocean pilgrimage', in M.S.C. Mariani, & A. Trono (eds), *The Ways of Mercy: Arts, Culture and Marian Routes between East and West* (pp. 405–430). Galatina, Italy: Mario Congedo.

Olsen, D.H., & Guelke, J.K. (2004) 'Spatial transgression and the BYU Jerusalem Center controversy', *The Professional Geographer,* 56(4): 503–515.

Olsen, D.H., & Ron, A.S. (2013) 'Managing religious heritage attractions: The case of Jerusalem', in B. Garrod, & A. Fyall (eds), *Contemporary Cases in Heritage, Volume 1* (pp. 51–78). Oxford: Goodfellow.

Olsen, D.H., & Timothy, D.J. (1999) 'Tourism 2000: Selling the millennium', *Tourism Management,* 20(4): 389–392.

Olsen, D.H., & Timothy, D.J. (2017) 'Tourism', in D. Richardson, N. Castree, M. Goodchild, W. Liu, A. Kobayashi, & R. Marston (eds), *The International Encyclopedia of Geography: People, the Earth, Environment, and Technology* (pp. 7058–7063). Malden, MA: Wiley/AAG.

Ostrowski, M. (2000) 'Pilgrimages or religious tourism', in A. Jackowski (ed.), *Peregrinus Cracoviensis* (pp. 53–61). Krakow: Institute of Geography, Jagiellonian University.

Öter, Z., & Çetinkaya, M.Y. (2016) 'Interfaith tourist behaviour at religious heritage sites: House of the Virgin Mary case in Turkey', *International Journal of Religious Tourism and Pilgrimage,* 4(4): 1–18.

Ozdemir, I., & Met, O. (2012) 'The expectations of Muslim religious customers in the lodging industry: The case of Turkey', in A. Zainal, S.M. Radzi, R. Hashim, C.T. Chik, & R. Abu (eds), *Current Issues in Hospitality and Tourism Research and Innovation* (pp. 323–328). London: CRC Press.

Perini, S., & Guidetti, M. (2015) 'Civil war and cultural heritage in Syria, 2011–2015', *Syrian Studies Association Bulletin,* 20(1). Available online: https://ojcs.siue.edu/ojs/index.php/ssa/article/view/3115/1128.

Philip, J., & Mercer, D. (1999) 'Commodification of Buddhism in contemporary Burma', *Annals of Tourism Research,* 26(1): 31–54.

Pinto, P.G. (2007) 'Pilgrimage, commodities, and religious objectification: The making of trans-national Shiism between Iran and Syria', *Comparative Studies of South Asia, Africa and the Middle East*, 27(1): 109–125.

Post, P., Pieper, J., & van Uden, M. (1998) *The Modern Pilgrim: Multidisciplinary Explorations of Christian Pilgrimage*. Leuven: Uitgeverij Peeters.

Reader, I. (2007) 'Pilgrimage growth in the modern world: Meanings and implications', *Religion*, 37(3): 210–229.

Reader, I. (2014) *Pilgrimage in the Marketplace*. London: Routledge.

Richter, L.K. (2003) 'International tourism and its global public health consequences', *Journal of Travel Research*, 41(4): 340–347.

Ron, A.S. 2009 'Towards a typological model of contemporary Christian travel', *Journal of Heritage Tourism*, 4(4): 287–297.

Ron, A.S., & Timothy, D.J. (2019) *Contemporary Christian Travel: Pilgrimage, Practice and Place*. Bristol: Channel View Publications.

Russell, P. (1999) 'Religious travel in the new millennium', *Travel & Tourism Analyst*, 5: 39–68.

Rutte, C. (2011) 'The sacred commons: Conflicts and solutions of resource management in sacred natural sites', *Biological Conservation*, 144(10): 2387–2394.

Shachar, A., & Shoval, N. (1999) 'Tourism in Jerusalem: A place to pray', in D.R. Judd, & S.S. Fainstein (eds), *The Tourist City* (pp. 198–214). New Haven, CT: Yale University Press.

Shackley, M. (2001) *Managing Sacred Sites: Service Provision and Visitor Experience*. London: Continuum.

Sibley, D. (1995) *Geographies of Exclusion: Society and Difference in the West*. London: Routledge.

Singh, S. (1998) 'Probing the product life cycle further', *Tourism Recreation Research*, 23(2): 61–63.

Sizer, S.R. (1999) 'The ethical challenges of managing pilgrimages to the Holy Land', *International Journal of Contemporary Hospitality Management*, 11(2/3): 85–90.

Smith, D.O. (2010) 'Hotel design in British Mandate Palestine: Modernism and the Zionist vision', *The Journal of Israeli History*, 29(1): 99–123.

Sönmez, S.F. (1998) 'Tourism, terrorism, and political instability', *Annals of Tourism Research*, 25(2): 416–456.

Stausberg, M. (2011) *Religion and Tourism: Crossroads, Destinations, and Encounters*. London: Routledge.

Steiner, C. (2010) 'An overestimated relationship? Violent political unrest and tourism foreign direct investment in the Middle East', *International Journal of Tourism Research*, 12(6): 726–738.

Svensson, I. (2013) 'One God, many wars: Religious dimensions of armed conflict in the Middle East and North Africa', *Civil Wars*, 15(4): 411–430.

Thompson, R.B., & Smith, D.G. (2001) 'Towards a new theory of the shareholder role: "Sacred space" in corporate transactions', *Texas Law Review*, 80(261): 261–326.

Tilson, D.J. (2005) 'Religious–spiritual tourism and promotional campaiging: A church-state partnership for St. James and Spain', *Journal of Hospitality & Leisure Marketing*, 12(1–2): 9–40.

Timothy, D.J., & Daher, R.F. (2009) 'Heritage tourism in Southwest Asia and North Africa', in D.J. Timothy, & G.P. Nyaupane (eds), *Cultural Heritage and Tourism in the Developing World: A Regional Perspective* (pp. 146–164). London: Routledge.

Timothy, D.J., & Emmett, C.F. (2014) 'Jerusalem, tourism, and the politics of heritage', in M. Adelman, & M.F. Elman (eds), *Jerusalem: Conflict and Cooperation in a Contested City* (pp. 276–292). Syracuse, NY: Syracuse University Press.

Timothy, D.J., & Iverson, T. (2006) 'Tourism and Islam: Considerations of culture and duty', in D.J. Timothy, & D.H. Olsen (eds), *Tourism, Religion, and Spiritual Journeys* (pp. 186–205). London: Routledge.

Timothy, D.J., & Olsen, D.H. (2006) 'Conclusion: Whither religious tourism?', in D.J. Timothy, & D.H. Olsen (eds), *Tourism, Religion and Spiritual Journeys* (pp. 271–278). London: Routledge.

Tosun, C. (2001) 'Challenges of sustainable tourism development in the developing world: The case of Turkey', *Tourism Management*, 22(3): 289–303.

Trono, A. (2017) 'Logistics at holy sites', in M. Leppäkari, & K.A. Griffin (eds), *Pilgrimage and Tourism to Holy Cities: Ideological and Management Perspectives* (pp. 113–128). Wallingford: CAB International.

Trudeau, D. (2006) 'Politics of belonging in the construction of landscapes: Place-making, boundary-drawing and exclusion', *Cultural Geographies*, 13(3): 421–443.

Turku, H. (2017) *The Destruction of Cultural Property as a Weapon of War: ISIS in Syria and Iraq*. Cham, Switzerland: Springer.

Turner, V. (1973) 'The center out there: Pilgrim's goal', *History of Religions*, 12(3): 191–230.

UNWTO (2011) *Religious Tourism in Asia and the Pacific*. Madrid: World Tourism Organization.

Valentine, G. (2008) 'Living with difference: Reflections on geographies of encounter', *Progress in Human Geography*, 32: 323–37.

Verschuuren, B., Wild, R., McNeely, J., & Oviedo, G. (eds) (2010) *Sacred Natural Sites: Conserving Nature and Culture*. London: Earthscan.

Vikan, G. (2012) *From the Holy Land to Graceland: Sacred People, Places and Things in Our Lives*. Washington, DC: The AAM Press.

Vukonić, B. (1996) *Tourism and Religion*. Oxford: Elsevier.

Vukonić, B. (2000) 'Pastoral care', in J. Jafari (ed.), *Encyclopedia of Tourism* (p. 429). New York: Routledge.

Wilkinson, J. (1998) 'In search of holy places: Then and now', in J.M. Fladmark (ed.), *In Search of Heritage as Pilgrim or Tourist?* (pp. 15–24). Shaftesbury: Donhead.

Wiltshier, P., & Griffiths, M. (2016) 'Management practices for the development of religious tourism sacred sites: Managing expectations through sacred and secular aims in site development; Report, store and access', *International Journal of Religious Tourism and Pilgrimage*, 4(7): 1–8.

Winter, T. (2007) *Post-Conflict Heritage, Postcolonial Tourism: Culture, Politics and Development at Angkor*. London: Routledge.

Woodward, S.C. (2004) 'Faith and tourism: Planning tourism in relation to places of worship', *Tourism and Hospitality Planning & Development*, 1(2): 173–186.

Wright, K. (2008) *The Christian Travel Planner*. Nashville, TN: Thomas Nelson.

Zamani-Farahani, H., & Henderson, J.C. (2010) 'Islamic tourism and managing tourism development in Islamic societies: The cases of Iran and Saudi Arabia', *International Journal of Tourism Research*, 12(1): 79–89.

Zamani-Farahani, H., & Musa, G. (2012) 'The relationship between Islamic religiosity and residents' perceptions of socio-cultural impacts of tourism in Iran: Case studies of Sare'in and Masooleh', *Tourism Management*, 33(4): 802–814.

10

ISLAMIC TOURISM IN THE MIDDLE EAST

*Hamira Zamani-Farahani, Michele Carboni, Carlo Perelli
and Neda Torabi Farsani*

Introduction

The Middle East, known also as the land of the great Abrahamic religions (Bourke 2008; Worldatlas 2016), is the birthplace and spiritual centre of various religions/faiths such as Zoroastrianism, Mandeanism, Mithraism, Manicheanism, Judaism, Christianity, Islam, Yezidi, Druze, Yarsan and the Bahá'í. Consequently, the region is home to some of the most important pilgrimage sites in the world. The Temple of Anahita in Iran; the Saint Stepanos Monastery in Iran; Jerusalem; the Tomb of Esther and Mordecha, Hamadān (Iran); Chak Chak, Yazd (Iran); Mashhad (Iran); Najaf, Karbala, Samarra and Kadhimiya in Iraq; and Mecca and Medina in Saudi Arabia are good examples of holy cities and religious destinations in the region.

The Muslim faith, including its various sects (e.g. Sunni, Shi'a, Druze, Ibadh, Isma'ilite, Alawite, Zaydi, Sufism, Nusayri), is the prominent religion in the Middle East and North Africa (MENA) with an approximate population of 604 million (PRB 2015). The most populous countries in the region are Egypt (89.1 million), Iran (78.5 million), and Turkey (78.2 million); contrariwise, the least populated ones are Bahrain (1.4 million), Qatar (2.4 million), and Kuwait (3.8 million) (PRB 2015). The highest population countries in the region with Sunnite and Shiite majorities are Turkey and Iran respectively, both with non-Arab populations. The top five languages, in terms of numbers of speakers are Arabic, Persian, Turkish, Hebrew and Kurdish with a wide variety of minority languages. However, Arabic is the most common language. Arabs, Azeris, Egyptians, Kurds, Persians, Turks and Berbers constitute the largest ethnic groups in the region by population. While religion, shared history, and a common political fate play an important role in the identification of the region (Younesian 2006), Islam is the main link between the people of MENA (Kovjanic 2014).

Iran's Islamic Revolution in 1979 led to the establishment of an Islamic republic (Axworthy 2013). It was followed by the growth of Islamist tendencies, and developments in the region and in the Arab countries such as the success of Islamists in Tunisia and Egypt in the first elections after the fall of those countries' dictators, might indicate that the tendency towards Islam and Islamic values is much stronger than observers in the West originally thought (Abzar Moaser Tehran Institute 2011). In the Republic of Turkey—a democratic, laic and social state governed by the rule of law—there has recently been a re-awakening of Islamic identity as a component of Turkish identity (Doganyilmaz 2013).

The Middle East is located in a strategic and geopolitical position, which has transformed it into the centre of gravity in international politics. Middle Eastern countries have great natural, historical and cultural attractions, as well as the potential for tourism, but for political, cultural and economic reasons they have not been well exploited (Kovjanic 2014). Moreover, because of its status as the epicentre of Muslim culture, the region cannot be neglected in terms of the relationship between tourism and Islam. Besides, as most of the countries in the region have a Muslim majority population, new Muslim-friendly tourism products have the potential to attract and to be favourably received by their populations.

Owing to the diversity and unique characteristics of the countries in MENA, the World Tourism Organization (UNWTO) classified these countries into four regional groups. These are the Middle East region (Bahrain, Egypt, Iraq, Jordan, Kuwait, Lebanon, Libya, Oman, Qatar, Saudi Arabia, Syrian Arab Republic, United Arab Emirates, Yemen and Palestine), the South Asia region (Afghanistan and Iran), the Europe Region (Israel and Turkey), and the Africa region (Algeria, Morocco and Tunisia) (UNWTO 2016).

The present chapter aims to provide a regional overview of key issues and implications in the area of Islamic pilgrimage and tourism in the Middle East. The chapter begins with an introduction to the recent development of tourism in the region, followed by a section dedicated to Islamic tourism and pilgrimages.

Tourism in Middle Eastern countries

The Middle East is diverse and extremely rich in attractions and 'can reasonably be referred to as one of the world's original and most significant tourist attractions' (Morakabati 2011: 106). Despite this potential, considered by many academics as the competitive advantage of the Middle East (Mansfeld & Winckler 2004), for decades the region has struggled to attract a significant share of the international tourism market. However, particularly since the new millennium, the industry has started growing at unprecedented rates. Tourism in the Middle East has changed a lot over the decades, and the process of transformation continues. Such deep change and the region's extreme dynamism have not necessarily been perceived or understood, above all by Westerners.

The dynamics of tourism destinations have differed remarkably across MENA. Pioneers in developing the sector were a number of Arab non-oil-producing countries. Tunisia was one of the first countries to promote tourism after independence in 1956, developing a 'sun-sea-sand' offer to accommodate primarily Western tourists (Poirier 1995). Other Arab countries, concentrated on the commodification of their heritage sites, such as in the Nile Valley in Egypt or the ruins of Petra in Jordan, established themselves as main heritage destinations (Gregory 1999; Hazbun 2008). This resulted in tourism becoming the largest private-sector employer in countries like Tunisia, Morocco, Egypt and Jordan.

Nevertheless, most countries of the region, despite their huge potential, for a long time pursued a rejectionist or isolationist policy and adopted political strategies to discourage tourism development (Din 1989; Timothy & Iverson 2006). Several countries have been reluctant recipients of tourists, afraid of the negative social impacts that international tourism could bring with it (Timothy & Iverson 2006). However, the situation started changing in the mid-1980s when more countries began to enhance their leisure and beach tourism offers. Egypt itself diversified its tourism products, for instance, and new countries entered the market (Steiner 2009). Turkey made tourism a national priority in the early 1980s and in 1990 hosted less than 5 million international tourists; in 2011 that number surpassed 31 million (Lanquar 2013). Within two decades, Turkey had become one of the top ten world destinations, although political instability and terrorist activity and war in neighbouring Syria have diminished Turkey's tourism industry since 2015.

During the 1990s, tourist arrivals in the region more than doubled. Even if most of the arrivals were directed to a few destinations, notably Egypt, Tunisia, Morocco and Turkey, the attitude towards the sector deeply modified. From 1990 to 2010, the countries of the southern and eastern Mediterranean (Algeria, Egypt, Israel, Jordan, Lebanon, Libya, Morocco, Palestine, Syria, Tunisia and Turkey) had the highest growth rates of inbound world tourism (Lanquar 2013). Tourism has emerged as a relevant sector even in countries like Syria, which until the end of the 1980s did not really promote the industry. In 2010, Syria's tourism industry accounted for 12 per cent of the GDP and was responsible for 11 per cent of the employment opportunities (Ibrahim & Razzouk 2011). Unfortunately, Syria acquired a reputation as an unsafe destination due to the recent war. In Libya, where tourism, before the fall of Gaddafi and the current crisis, could only be described as emerging and underdeveloped (Jones 2010), the growth in international arrivals was estimated to be more than 180 per cent between 1990 and 2010 (Lanquar 2013).

In the oil-rich Arab countries, with the remarkable exception of the Hajj in Saudi Arabia, tourism as a modern industry almost did not exist until recently (Mansfeld & Winckler 2015). The aversion of these countries concerning the possible negative impacts related to tourism development was abandoned by the United Arab Emirates (UAE) (especially Dubai) and Bahrain during the 1980s. Oman and Abu Dhabi followed in the 1990s, and Saudi Arabia and Qatar in 2000. In recent years, investments in tourism have massively increased and several oil-producing countries have demonstrated a strong determination in becoming worldwide tourism destinations. Dubai's tourism vision is to increase the number of tourists to 20 million in 2020 and to triple the sector's contribution to GDP to more than US$81 billion (MEED 2013). Qatar aims at hosting 7 million tourists by 2030 when the industry is hoped to contribute 5.1 per cent of GDP (Mansfeld & Winckler 2015; QTA 2014). Similarly, the total contribution of tourism to Oman's GDP is expected to grow from 6.7 per cent in 2010 to 9.2 per cent in 2020 (Gutcher 2013). Amongst Middle Eastern countries, tourism as an economic driver is most observable in countries such as Turkey, UAE, Lebanon, Tunisia, Morocco and Egypt. In recent years, political conflict and terrorism have affected the position of Egypt as one of the Islamic world's most visited countries.

Hazbun (2010a: 226) argues that 'A shift in the global discourse about tourism in the ME/NA is overdue'. Underlining the existence of long-lasting Orientalist views, Hazbun calls for a deeper reflection of the stereotypical view shared by many academics, the international media and the tourism industry itself about MENA, its culture and its tourism industry. Viewed through an Orientalist lens, the region continues to be depicted as unchanging and exotic, the only 'tourists' taken into consideration being the Western ones and the success of a destination (and of the broader region) is measured 'in terms of how it appeals to Western cultural perceptions and desires' (Hazbun 2010a: 226). Based upon such a limited and distorted perspective, tourism in the Middle East is having a hard time escaping its 'natural' condition of underdevelopment because of conflict and extremism, but also because of the local population's anti-Western attitude.

This view does not match reality on the ground because it does not take into account the extreme diversity of countries in the region and, above all, because tourism in several countries is far from being unsuccessful or discouraged. On the contrary, the sector—above all since 2000—has experienced a profound process of transformation.

Issues of stability and subsequent perceptions of insecurity have always characterised the region. Several tourism crises experienced by MENA have been related to a long list of terrorist attacks or induced by civil, bilateral or regional wars. The traditional realm of Islamic civilisation, oil and energy resources, geopolitical importance, and lately the universal suffering of long conflicts in the region, such as the Israeli–Palestinian and Lebanon conflicts, Iraq's invasion of Kuwait and Iran, the civil war in Syria, the current war between Yemen and Saudi Arabia, and the rise of ISIS can be considered key issues that define the Middle East. The ongoing conflict between Saudi Arabia and Iran should also be included. It is worth noting that these two actors play an important role in tourism safety and security throughout the region. Tourism marketing in MENA is highly influenced by revolutions, wars, nuclear negotiations, sanctions, oil prices and local currency values against the dollar (Farsani & Shafiei 2015). Local safety, terrorism and terrorist attacks, political crises, human rights issues, local regulations and management are other influential factors. Because of this, considerable efforts have been deployed to deal with negative images and stereotypes of violence and wars by means of national tourism marketing strategies (Avraham 2013).

Several authors have questioned the direct links between violent political unrest and tourism investment behaviour in the Middle East. Steiner (2010a), focusing on the Egyptian and other Middle Eastern cases, showed that the relationship between stability and security, and tourism foreign direct investments has been overestimated in the past. Indeed, other variables, such as the institutional and business environment, a high level of local and regional dependence between investors, and other long-lasting factors, seem to be able to reduce the impact of single events.

Nevertheless, whilst in the past the tourism industry has always been able to recover relatively quickly, the crisis resulting from the Arab Spring in some countries seems to be deeper and more profound. Since 2011, tourism in Tunisia and Egypt, for instance, has lost a remarkable part of its importance. The effects of the Arab Spring have dramatically affected some countries, but tourism in other destinations, on the contrary, has recovered soon or even increased. In Dubai the number of hotel guest nights increased from 20.5 million in 2007 to over 41 million in 2013 (Mansfeld & Winckler 2015). The number of hotel guest nights in Bahrain decreased in 2011 but two years later amounted to two million, a number higher than ever before. The sector expanded in the same years also in Oman and Qatar, two other countries not affected by the consequences of the Arab Spring.

The spatial development of tourism in the region has shown some very interesting patterns. A relevant ongoing process as imagined by Steiner (2010b) is the 'Dubaisation' of some destinations. Even if questionable by global financial and economic standards, the 'Dubai model' (waterfront projects, malls and mega hotels, etc.) adopted also by other Middle Eastern countries (see, for example, Barthel (2014) on Morocco and Tunisia), has emerged as one of the region's new models of tourism development.

MENA has a rich historical and cultural heritage. Except for Kuwait, all Middle Eastern countries have UNESCO World Heritage Sites (UNESCO 2016a). Nevertheless, in recent decades, the idea of 'outstanding universal value' as supported by UNESCO and its World Heritage discourse and listing has attracted growing criticism (for an overview see di Giovine 2009). In particular, criticism has emerged about UNESCO's Eurocentric approach (Labadi 2013). As remarked by several authors, in many Middle Eastern countries the Islamic heritage has not received due attention, and policies regarding heritage tourism have been affected by efforts to meet Western tourists' expectations. For example, Addison (2004) notes the complete absence of tourist signs for Muslim holy sites on Jordanian main roads. Such a choice not to have these signs, probably motivated by the will to project the image of a safe and Westernised country, has inhibited the development of domestic and intra-Arab tourism and obscured a relevant part of Jordan's national heritage. Similar concerns have emerged with heritage tourism in Palestine; on the bias against non-Christian heritage see De Cesari (2010), the city of Jerusalem

(Dumper & Larkin 2012), Turkey (Tucker & Carnegie 2014), Tunisia (Perelli & Sistu 2014), Morocco (Wagner & Minca 2014) and colonial nostalgia in the Syrian and Jordanian Levant (Jacobs 2010).

One of the main problems in studying tourism in the Middle East is the lack of accurate information and regular and reliable tourism statistics. Additionally, as previously mentioned, the sector in the Middle East has been experiencing a deep transformation; its evolution is still ongoing and affects several aspects that certainly need more research.

Islamic tourism and the Middle East

In recent years, the growth of tourism in the Middle East has been accompanied by a growing worldwide interest in the relationship between tourism and Islam by the industry itself and by academics. With the exception of pilgrimages, this relationship has long been neglected by researchers (Battour, Ismail, & Battor 2011; Din 1989; Henderson 2003; Zamani-Farahani & Henderson 2010). Similarly, for a long time the tourism industry did not sufficiently consider the needs of Muslim tourists and Islamic prescriptions when developing tourism products (Carboni, Perelli, & Sistu 2014). Only recently have these issues received increasing attention, especially as relates to sharia-compliant hotels (Henderson 2010a), Muslim tourism (Scott & Jafari 2010), halal tourism (Mohsin, Ramli, & Alkhulayfi 2016; WTM 2007) and Islamic tourism (Battour, Ismail, Battor, & Awais 2014), which are growing in popularity as research topics and industry foci even if often surrounded by a certain vagueness (Hamza, Chouhoud, & Tantawi 2012; Henderson 2010b).

Muslim-oriented tourism is undeniably a customer segment that has been attracting increasing interest over the past few years (Jafari & Scott 2014; Scott & Jafari 2010). There are several reasons behind this increasing interest. Demography plays a salient role; the number of Muslims is supposed to reach 2.2 billion by 2030 (Pew Forum 2015). This demographic change has coupled with an increase in the number of Muslim tourists, as a consequence of Muslims' growing spending power (Sandikci 2011; Stephenson, Russell, & Edgar 2010).

The 9/11 attacks impacted global tourism in several ways. One of the consequences has been a partial re-orientation of tourism flows. A growing number of Muslim tourists, instead of visiting Europe or North America, where new rules have limited their mobility and an increasing Islamophobia has made them feel uncomfortable, have opted for geographically and culturally closer destinations (Kalesar 2010; Stephenson & Ali 2010).

Intra-regional tourism in the Middle East flourished and certain countries succeeded in attracting more Muslim tourists. One of the implemented strategies was to offer halal travel services like accommodation, halal-certified cuisine and a non-alcoholic environment, prayer rooms, gender separation of recreation and leisure facilities, trained staff observing the halal traditional lifestyle, and services for the Muslim community that have been specially created to ensure the comfort and well-being of Muslim tourists.

To assist this process, some Halal booking sites (i.e. HalalBooking, VoyagesHalal, VacancesHalal, MuslimBreak, HalalTrip and HalalVilla) have become established as leading global online platforms for halal-conscious travellers to search for and book quality halal accommodations, leisure holidays and Islamic heritage tours, mainly in the Middle East. Iran as an Islamic theocracy has been the only country in the region to provide an entirely halal tourism experience to its guests by default. However, because of strict regulations, the West's negative propaganda against Iran, and a lack of proper tourism planning, marketing and appropriate tourism management, the country remains a long shot for developing into a top halal tourism destination.

A recent study by Crescent Rating (2015) revealed that the value of the Muslim travel market was approximately US$145 billion, with 108 million Muslim travellers representing 10 per cent of the entire travel economy in 2014. This is forecasted to grow to 150 million visitors by 2020 and 11 per cent of the market with an expenditure projected to grow to US$200 billion. Muslim travel will likely continue to be one of the fastest growing travel sectors in the world as places become more halal-oriented and as numbers of Muslim tourists continue to grow. Iran, Saudi Arabia, Turkey and the UAE are the main countries competing for Islamic tourism leadership in the region. However, it seems that Turkey and the UAE have become the most popular destinations for Muslim travellers, offering Islamic-friendly recreational, leisure and shopping facilities and resources.

In connection with Islamic/halal tourism, Saudi Arabia, Iran and Iraq are the most important destinations for Islamic pilgrimages (Zamani-Farahani & Eid 2015). Saudi Arabia is known as the birthplace of Islam and home of the Prophet Mohammed. The most important Islamic travels by Muslims around the world are Hajj and Umrah pilgrimages, which are both hosted and managed by Saudi Arabia where about two million Muslims gather for one of world's largest annual pilgrimages. Revenues from both Hajj and Umrah are estimated to be more than US$18.6 billion (Mangla 2014), which in company with oil, makes this form of tourism one of Saudi Arabia's largest earners (Sardar 2014). In spite of Islam's mandate for simplicity, nowadays the pilgrimages have become big business (Mangla 2014), and pilgrimage services have become more luxurious, with pilgrims now having to spend much more for the experience (Qurashi 2017).

The Hajj, one of the world's largest gatherings (a 5–6 day annual Islamic pilgrimage to Mecca), is a duty for Muslims to be carried out at least once in their lifetime, as long as they are physically able to take this journey and afford it (Timothy & Iverson 2006). Hajj begins on the eighth day of the Dhu al-Hijjah lunar month and finishes on the 13th day. The Hajj re-enacts the actions of the Prophet Muhammed in his farewell pilgrimage in AD632, and is a central pillar of the Islamic faith meant to bring Muslims from all nationalities together and cleanse the faithful of sin and bring them closer to God (Aljazeera 2016a). The Umrah pilgrimage (which means to visit an important place) is recommended but not required in Islam (Bhardwaj 1998). It can be performed at any time of the year along with Hajj or otherwise.

During the Hajj, Muslims visit the Ka'bah at the centre of the Sacred Mosque of Mecca (*Masjid al-Haram*), performing *tawaaf* (circumambulation) around it, walking between Safaa and Marwah seven times. Putting on the *ihram* clothing (men's and women's garments worn by pilgrims during the Ihram pilgrimage (Hajj or Umrah)). Having their hair shaved or cut completes the rite and ends the restriction of Ihram. In some years the Hajj and Umrah pilgrimages are disrupted by tragic accidents and crises (i.e. 1975, 1979, 1987, 1990, 1994, 1997, 1998, 2001, 2004, 2006 and 2015 (IRIB 2015)).

Iran boycotted the Hajj for three years between 1988 and 1990 after clashes between Iranian pilgrims and Saudi police in 1987 left around 400 people dead (Aljazeera 2017). Throughout the 2015 Hajj, over 2,000 pilgrims were trampled to death in a stampede owing to overcrowding and mismanagement in *Masjid al-Haram* and in Medina. Saudi authorities were blamed for the deaths during this stampede. Iran's supreme leader urged Muslims around the world to reconsider Saudi Arabia's custodianship and management of Islam's holiest sites in Mecca and Medina. The Saudi state accused Iran of politicising the pilgrimage (Aljazeera 2016b). These socio-political tensions between the two countries affected Iranian pilgrims' travel to Saudi Arabia for the Hajj and Umrah in 2016. Nevertheless, Iranian pilgrims took part in 2017's annual pilgrimage after officials from the two countries completed the necessary measures to ensure Iranian pilgrims were allowed to perform Hajj 1438 (2017) (Aljazeera 2017).

Apart from the important Islamic sites in Mecca, Medina and Jerusalem, which are acceptable by all Muslims, the places, mosques and tombs associated with the Prophet Muhammed, his family members and descendants, prophets and their companions are considered holy places by different Islamic schools of thought. Pilgrimages to them are known as ziyarat (Zamani-Farahani 2010). The shrines of Shia Islam can be found throughout the Middle East, but there are a number of sites and events deemed holy by Shia pilgrimages found mainly in Iran (e.g. Mashhad, Qom and Shiraz), Iraq (Karbala, Najaf, Samarra and Kadhimiya), and Syria (Damascus) (Zamani-Farahani 2010). Most Shia holy places in the region are renovated and maintained with funding from Iranian authorities.

Islamic events, festivals, rituals, and traditions may also be viewed as tourist attractions in Muslim countries. Muharram (the first month of the Islamic calendar) ceremonies, Tasua and Ashura, (Khavarian-Garmsir, Zare, & Mostofiolmamalek 2014), are famous events held across the world, especially in the Middle East by both Sunnis and Shias. These are celebrated on the ninth and tenth day of Muharram in the Islamic calendar, which marks a day of remembrance of Hussain's martyrdom (the Prophet Muhammed's grandson and third Shiite imam). On the day of Ashura, millions of Muslims across the globe commemorate the martyrdom of the Imam Hussain, and all his companions at the Battle of Karbala. The day before Ashura is called Tasua (UNESCO 2015). For Shia Muslims in particular, this is a day of mourning, expressed in a more dramatic fashion than amongst Sunnis (CIOGC 2013).

Ta'azyeh (an Intangible Cultural Heritage form inscribed on the UNESCO list in 2010) is a ritual dramatic art that recounts religious events, historical and mythical stories and folk tales during Ashura and Arbaeen (fortieth Hosseini condolences). Its performances help promote and reinforce religious and spiritual values. Despite the serious threat of terrorism in Iraq, Arbaeen is becoming the world's largest annual pilgrimage gathering, with the number of pilgrims far exceeding the two million visitors who descend on Mecca for the Hajj. Each year, a few days before Arbaeen, millions of pilgrims from all over the world travel to Iraq to walk to the holy shrine of Imam Hussein and his half-brother Abbas in the holy city of Karbala (where their shrines are located), southwest of Baghdad, to mark the end of the 40-day mourning period. Shia Islamic tradition dictates that a mourning period should last 40 days. Imam Hussein is highly cherished and commemorated amongst Shiites for his battle against the thousands of troops dispatched by the second Umayyad caliph Yazid to confront him and his 72 companions in AD 680 (Cusack 2016; Faghihi 2016; Sim 2016).

Arbaeen's performance has been cancelled several times owing to political crises. For nearly 30 years under Saddam Hussein's regime, it was forbidden to celebrate Arbaeen in Iraq, extended further by the 2003 invasion of Iraq. In recent years, travel agencies across the world have been offering Arbaeen, Ashura and Arafah full package tours accompanied by spiritual guides, visiting Karbala, Najaf and Kazmain for a duration of two to three weeks. Some travel agencies have used attractive slogans such as 'It is said that Ziaarat of Imam Hussain on the day of Arbaeen is the sign of a true momin [one who believes in God] and its sawaab [reward for good deeds] is equal to 70 Hajjs' (Al Mehdi Tours 2016). However, Iranian authorities claim that no fatwa (an Islamic religious ruling, a scholarly opinion on a matter of Islamic law) has ever been made about the substitution of this pilgrimage to Karbala for the Hajj rituals in Mecca (Cusack 2016).

Another Islamic event recognised as world intangible cultural heritage by UNESCO is the Qalishuyan rituals of Mashad-e Ardehal, which has been practised for more than a thousand years to honour the memory of Soltān Ali (the son of Muḥammad al-Bāqir, the fifth Shia Imam), a holy figure amongst the people of Kashan and Fin in Iran. It takes place on the nearest Friday to the 17th day of the Persian month of Mehr (September), according to the solar-agricultural calendar (UNESCO 2012).

Many other celebrations in the region give rise to religious-oriented festivals and travel. The Turkish ceremonial Keşkek tradition, for instance, focuses on a local food called Keşkek for religious holidays. Also important are the Semah, Alevi-Bektaşi ritual religious practices and Mevlevi Sema ceremony in Konya and Istanbul, Turkey. All of these religious events and rituals are inscribed on the List of the Intangible Cultural Heritage of Humanity by UNESCO (UNESCO 2016b). Eid-ul-Fitr (fast-breaking at the end of Ramadan) and Eid-ul-Adha (Festival of the Sacrifice)—which occurs 70 days after Eid-ul-Fitr and memorialises the Prophet Ibrahim's (Abraham's) willingness to sacrifice his son Ismail (Ishmael) for Allah)—Mawlid an-Nabi (Birth of the Prophet) and Islamic New Year on the 1st of Muharram are some of the many religious celebrations (Eid) throughout MENA that provide motives for festivities and travel to be with friends and relatives.

Conclusion

This chapter describes ongoing debates and several important issues related to Islamic tourism and culture in the Middle East. Despite the growing role of the Middle East as a traditional destination and all of MENA as an emerging destination on the world tourism stage, there is still a certain resistance to introducing new discourses and perspectives when it comes to approaching the topic and describing the region. Further research is needed on themes that are still underdeveloped and which can help in better understanding Muslim tourism demand in the area. As an example, recent research has emerged on the tourism consumption experience and value from the perspectives of Muslim customers (Al-Hamarneh & Steiner 2004; Eid & El-Gohary 2015) and more generally the debate over tourism and hospitality products meeting Muslim tourists' needs, from hotels to mosques to food services (Kessler 2015). Nevertheless, little research at this stage exists, for instance, on the personal meaning of travelling for Muslim tourists, especially from the more conservative Muslim countries (for a recent overview starting from communication theory see Oktadiana, Pearce, & Chon 2016). The same limits are observable in research on Western Muslims' experiences in performing Hajj or other pilgrimages (for a relevant contribution on the UK see McLoughlin (2015)). Furthermore, as observed by Afifi (2015), by analysing UNWTO codes of ethics there appears to be a certain hesitation in including Islamic principles when developing tourism codes of conduct.

Recently Cohen and Cohen (2015a, 2015b) provided a valid contribution to the debate focusing on the call for a paradigm shift in Middle East tourism studies in light of Eurocentric biases and the need for re-orienting tourism studies towards evolving mobilities paradigms. A dynamic perspective on tourism phenomena dealing with complex boundaries between mobilities, tourism and pilgrimage in emerging non-European regions can help make sense of traditional centre-periphery perspectives (on markets, products and travel motivations). Furthermore, such a perspective can provide relevant support to those observers calling for a deeper understanding of neglected domestic and regional tourism practices in emerging tourism regions (see Al-Hamarneh & Steiner 2004; Berriane 1990; Cohen & Cohen 2015a; Hazbun 2010a; Khaled Magableh, & Kharabsheh 2013; Ladki, Mikdashi, Fahed, & Abbas 2002; Prayag & Hosany 2014).

Hazbun's (2010a, 2010b) work underlines the role of tourism in consolidating transnational, hybrid knowledges of globalisation in the Middle East and North Africa. He calls for an increased understanding of the contribution of local tourism systems (tourists' practices, the role of the state, tourism firms' development, local communities) in shaping contemporary tourism development in the area. As shown by Carboni and Idrissi Janati (2016), pilgrimage in Fez, Morocco, is the driver of local development for local communities and at the same time the opportunity to capture globalised tourism flows. The Ziyarates Fès project created a new tourism product based on spirituality and culture, and from the beginning the project was declared to foster intercultural dialogue between Western tourists, pilgrims and hosts by sharing some common spaces and spending time together. Similarly, cosmopolitan tourism practices in the Middle East should be better investigated as a negotiated meeting space between tourism from different religious and cultural backgrounds.

The Middle East is far from being homogeneous. The fact that Islam is the largest and most widespread religion in this region does not make the area any more homogeneous, the Muslim world being extremely diverse itself. Nevertheless, also because of this diversity, MENA certainly has the potential to establish itself as a major destination for the Islamic faithful from all over the world. The Muslim universe is bigger than the Middle East, which makes the region an attractive destination for Muslims from all over the world. Indeed, despite extant safety and security concerns, the Middle East is the cradle of religious tourism and has seen the rapid development of spiritual, Islamic and halal tourism in recent decades. Finally, promoting religious, spiritual, Islamic and halal tourism in the MENA region can be a strategy for overcoming the challenges of mono-product economies, especially those overly dependent on oil.

References

Abzar Moaser Tehran Institute (2011) *Middle East 8 (Special Islamism and Islamic Awakening in the Middle East)*. Tehran: Abzar Moaser.

Addison, E. (2004) 'The roads to ruins: Accessing Islamic heritage in Jordan', in Y. Rowan, & U. Baram (eds), *Marketing Heritage Archaeology and the Consumption of the Past* (pp. 229–247). Walnut Creek, CA: AltaMira.

Afifi, G.M.H. (2015) 'Benchmarking the UNWTO Practical Tips for the Global Traveller: An Islamic preview', *AlmaTourism*, 6(12): 18–34.

Al-Hamarneh, A., & Steiner, C. (2004) 'Islamic tourism: Rethinking the strategies of tourism development in the Arab World after September 11, 2001', *Comparative Studies of South Asia, Africa and the Middle East*, 24(1): 18–27.

Al Mehdi Tours (2016) 'Tour packages'. Available online: www.almehditours.com/tours.html (Accessed 30 April 2017).

Aljazeera (2016a) 'Hajj 2016: Five-day ritual begins on September 10'. *Aljazeera*, 16 September. Available online: www.aljazeera.com/news/2016/09/hajj-2016-day-ritual-begins-september-9-1609 01180331137.html (Accessed 30 May 2017).

Aljazeera (2016b) 'Saudi Arabia and Iran spar over Hajj pilgrimage'. *Aljazeera*, 6 September. Available online: www.aljazeera.com/news/2016/09/saudi-arabia-iran-spar-hajj-pilgrimage-160906143744475.html (Accessed 30 May 2017).

Aljazeera (2017) 'Iran pilgrims to join this year's Hajj: Saudi Arabia'. *Aljazeera*, 18 March. Available online: www.aljazeera.com/news/2017/03/iran-pilgrims-join-year-hajj-saudi-arabia-170317124931718. html (Accessed 30 May 2017).

Avraham, E. (2013) 'Crisis communication, image restoration, and battling stereotypes of terror and wars: Media strategies for attracting tourism to Middle Eastern countries', *American Behavioral Scientist*, 57(9): 1350–1367.

Axworthy, M. (2013) *Revolutionary Iran: A History of the Islamic Republic*. New York: Oxford University Press.

Barthel, P.A. (2014) 'Global waterfronts in the Maghreb: A mere replication of Dubai? Study cases from Morocco and Tunisia', in B. Krawietz, K. Bromber, & S. Wippel (eds), *Under Construction: The Material and Symbolic Meaning of Architecture and Infrastructure in the Gulf Region* (pp. 56–79). Aldershot: Ashgate.

Battour, M., Ismail, M.N., & Battor, M. (2011) 'The impact of destination attributes on Muslim tourists' choice', *International Journal of Tourism Research*, 13(6): 527–540.

Battour, M., Ismail, M.N., Battor, M., & Awais, M. (2014) 'Islamic tourism: An empirical examination of travel motivation and satisfaction in Malaysia', *Current Issues in Tourism*, 20(1): 50–67.

Berriane, M. (1990) 'Tourisme national et migration de loisirs au Maroc: Etude geographique'. Unpublished thesis, University of Tours, France.

Bhardwaj, S.M. (1998) 'Non-hajj pilgrimage in Islam: A neglected dimension of religious circulation', *Journal of Cultural Geography*, 17(2): 69–87.

Bourke, S. (2008) *Ancient Civilizations, The Middle East: The Cradle of Civilization Revealed.* London: Thames & Hudsons.

Carboni, M., & Idrissi Janati, M. (2016) 'Halal tourism de facto: A case from Fez', *Tourism Management Perspectives*, 19: 155–159.

Carboni, M., Perelli, C., & Sistu, G. (2014) 'Is Islamic tourism a viable option for Tunisian tourism? Insights from Djerba', *Tourism Management Perspectives*, 11: 1–9.

CIOGC (2013) 'Islam 101 by the Council of Islamic Organizations of Greater Chicago (CIOGC)'. Available online: www.ciogc.org/index.php/aboutislam/islam-101/67-muslim-celebrations (Accessed 3 June 2017).

Cohen, E., & Cohen, S.A. (2015a) 'Beyond eurocentrism in tourism: A paradigm shift to mobilities', *Tourism Recreation Research*, 40(2): 157–168.

Cohen, E., & Cohen, S.A. (2015b) 'A mobilities approach to tourism from emerging world regions', *Current Issues in Tourism*, 18(1): 11–43.

Crescent Rating (2015) 'Global Muslim Travel Index 2015 (GMTI 2015)'. Available online: http://gmti.crescentrating.com/imgtemp/GMTI_report.pdf (Accessed 10 May 2017).

Cusack, R. (2016) 'Iraq prepares for biggest Shia-Muslim Arbaeen gathering in history'. Available online: www.alaraby.co.uk/english/news/2016/11/16/iraq-prepares-for-biggest-shia-muslim-arbaeen-gathering-in-history (Accessed 30 May 2017).

De Cesari, C. (2010) 'World Heritage and mosaic universalism: A view from Palestine', *Journal of Social Archaeology*, 10: 299–324.

di Giovine, M. (2009) *The Heritage-scape: UNESCO, World Heritage, and Tourism.* Lanham, MD: Lexington Books.

Din, K. (1989) 'Islam and tourism: Patterns, issues, and options', *Annals of Tourism Research*, 16(4): 542–563.

Doganyilmaz, D. (2013) 'Religion in Laic Turkey: The case of Alevis', *Quaderns de la Mediterrània*, 18(19): 191–202.

Dumper, M., & Larkin, C. (2012) 'The politics of heritage and the limitations of international agency in contested cities: A study of the role of UNESCO in Jerusalem's Old City', *Review of International Studies*, 38(1): 25–52.

Eid, R., & El-Gohary, H. (2015) 'Muslim tourist perceived value in the hospitality and tourism industry', *Journal of Travel Research*, 54: 774–787.

Faghihi, R. (2016) 'Are Shiites substituting Arbaeen for hajj?'. Available online: www.al-monitor.com/pulse/originals/2016/11/iran-pilgrims-arbaeen-khamenei-fatwa-hajj.html (Accessed 4 May 2017).

Farsani, N.T., & Shafiei, Z. (2015) 'Tourism: A solution for economic growth in developing countries (Case Study: IRAN)', in A. Tavidze (ed.), *Progress in Economics Research, Volume 32.* Hauppauge, NY: Nova.

Gregory, D. (1999) 'Scripting Egypt: Orientalism and the cultures of travel', in J. Duncan, & D. Gregory (eds), *Writes of Passage: Reading Travel Writing* (pp. 114–151). London: Routledge.

Gutcher, L. (2013) 'Oman's grand vision for tourism'. *The National*, 22 March. Available online: www.thenational.ae/business/industry-insights/the-life/omans-grand-vision-for-tourism (Accessed 3 April 2017).

Hamza, I.M., Chouhoud, R., & Tantawi, P. (2012) 'Islamic tourism: Exploring perceptions & possibilities in Egypt', *African Journal of Business and Economic Research*, 7(1): 85–98.

Hazbun, W. (2008) *Beaches, Ruins, Resorts: The Politics of Tourism in the Arab World.* Minneapolis, MN: University of Minnesota Press.

Hazbun, W. (2010a) 'Revising itineraries of tourism and tourism studies in the Middle East and North Africa', *Journal of Tourism and Cultural Change*, 8(4): 225–239.

Hazbun, W. (2010b) 'Modernity on the beach: A postcolonial reading from southern shores', *Tourist Studies*, 9(3): 203–222.

Henderson, J.C. (2003) 'Managing tourism and Islam in Peninsular Malaysia', *Tourism Management*, 24(4): 447–456.

Henderson, J.C. (2010a) 'Sharia-compliant hotels', *Tourism and Hospitality Research*, 10(3): 246–254.

Henderson, J.C. (2010b) 'Islam and tourism: Brunei, Indonesia, Malaysia, and Singapore', in N. Scott, & J. Jafari (eds), *Tourism in the Muslim World* (pp. 75–90). Bingley: Emerald.

Ibrahim, L., & Razzouk, N. (2011) 'Syria generated $8.3 billion in revenue from tourism last year'. *Bloomberg*, 23 January. Available online: www.bloomberg.com/news/articles/2011-01-23/syria-generated-8-3-billion-in-revenue-from-tourism-last-year (Accessed 5 April 2017).

IRIB (2015) 'Saudi Arabia's sinister record of Hajj mismanagement'. Available online: http://english.irib. ir/news/item/216926-saudi-arabia%E2%80%99s-sinister-record-of-hajj-mismanagement (Accessed 8 May 2017).

Jacobs, J. (2010) 'Re-branding the Levant: Contested heritage and colonial modernities in Amman and Damascus', *Journal of Tourism and Cultural Change*, 8(4): 316–326.

Jafari, J., & Scott, N. (2014) 'Muslim World and its tourisms', *Annals of Tourism Research*, 44: 1–19.

Jones, E. (2010) 'Arab politics and tourism: Political change and tourism in the great socialist people's Libyan Arab Jamahiriya', in R. Butler, & W. Suntikul (eds), *Tourism and Political Change* (pp. 108–119). Oxford: Goodfellow.

Kalesar, M.I. (2010) 'Developing Arab-Islamic tourism in the Middle East: An economic benefit or a cultural seclusion? *International Politics*, 3: 105–136.

Kessler, K. (2015) 'Conceptualizing mosque tourism: A central feature of Islamic and religious tourism', *International Journal of Religious Tourism and Pilgrimage*, 3(2): 11–32.

Khaled Magableh, I., & Kharabsheh, R. (2013) 'Antecedents of local demand for domestic tourism in Jordan', *International Journal of Culture, Tourism and Hospitality Research*, 7(1): 78–92.

Khavarian-Garmsir, A.R., Zare, S.M., & Mostofiolmamalek, R. (2014) 'Tasua and Ashura ceremonies as tourist attractions in Iran: A case study of the town of Taft', *International Journal of Religious Tourism and Pilgrimage*, 2(2): 90–102.

Kovjanic, G. (2014) 'Islamic tourism as a factor of the Middle East regional development', *Tourism*, 18(1): 33–43.

Labadi, S. (2013) *UNESCO, Cultural Heritage and Outstanding Universal Value*. Lanham, MD: AltaMira Press.

Ladki, S.M., Mikdashi, T.S., Fahed, W., & Abbas, H. (2002) 'Arab tourists and the Lebanese vacation ownership industry: A quality of life perspective', *International Journal of Hospitality Management*, 21(3): 257–265.

Lanquar, R. (2013) 'Tourism in the Mediterranean: Scenarios up to 2030. MEDPRO Report No. 1/July 2011'. (Updated May 2013).

Mansfeld, Y., & Winckler, O. (2004) 'Options for viable economic development through tourism among the non-oil Arab countries: The Egyptian case', *Tourism Economics*, 10(4): 365–388.

Mansfeld, Y., & Winckler, O. (2015) 'Can this be Spring? Assessing the impact of the "Arab Spring" on the Arab tourism industry', *Tourism*, 63(2): 205–223.

Mangla, I.S. (2014) 'Hajj 2014: For Saudi Arabia, the Muslim pilgrimage is big business'. *International Business Times*, 7 October. Available online: www.ibtimes.com/hajj-2014-saudi-arabia-muslim-pilgrimage-big-business-1700108 (Accessed 3 June 2017).

McLoughlin, S. (2015) 'Pilgrimage, performativity, and British Muslims: Scripted and unscripted accounts of the Hajj and Umra', in L. Mols, & M.W. Buitelaar (eds), *Hajj: Global Interactions through Pilgrimage* (pp. 41–64). Leiden: Sidestone Press.

MEED (2013) MEED *(Middle East Economist Digest)* 31 May to 6 June 2013. London: Weekly.

Mohsin, A., Ramli, N., & Alkhulayfi, B.A. (2016) 'Halal tourism: Emerging opportunities', *Tourism Management Perspectives*, 19: 137–143.

Morakabati, Y. (2011) 'Deterrents to tourism development in Iran', *International Journal of Tourism Research*, 13(2): 103–123.

Oktadiana, H., Pearce, P.L., & Chon, K. (2016) 'Muslim travellers' needs: What don't we know?', *Tourism Management Perspectives*, 20: 124–130.

Perelli, C., & Sistu, G. (2014) 'Jasmines for tourists: Heritage policies in Tunisia', in J. Kaminski, A.M. Benson, & D. Arnold (eds), *Contemporary Issues in Cultural Heritage Tourism* (pp. 71–87). London: Routledge.

Pew Forum (2015) 'The Future of World Religions: Population Growth Projections, 2010–2050'. Available online: www.pewforum.org/files/2015/03/PF_15.04.02_ProjectionsFullReport.pdf. (Accessed 22 April 2017).

Poirier, R. (1995) 'Tourism and development in Tunisia', *Annals of Tourism Research*, 22(1): 157–171.

PRB (2015) *Population Reference Bureau*. Available online: www.prb.org/pdf15/2015-world-population-data-sheet_eng.pdf (Accessed 4 April 2017).

Prayag, G., & Hosany, S. (2014) 'When Middle East meets West: Understanding the motives and perceptions of young tourists from United Arab Emirates', *Tourism Management*, 40: 35–45.

QTA (2014) 'Press Release: Qatar Tourism Authority Leads Qatari delegation at Arabian Travel Market'. Available online: arabiantravelmarket.wtm.com/__novadocuments/92253?v=635721270379500000 (Accessed 14 May 2017).

Qurashi, J. (2017) 'Commodification of Islamic religious tourism: From spiritual to touristic experience', *International Journal of Religious Tourism and Pilgrimage*, 5(1): 89–104.

Sandikci, Ö. (2011) 'Researching Islamic marketing: Past and future perspectives', *Journal of Islamic Marketing*, 2(3): 246–258.

Sardar, Z. (2014) *Mecca, The Sacred City*. London: Bloomsbury Publishing.

Scott, N., & Jafari, J (2010) 'Islam and tourism', in N. Scott, & J. Jafari (eds), *Tourism in the Muslim World* (pp. 1–13). Bingley: Emerald.

Sim, D. (2016) 'Arbaeen: Millions of Shia Muslims gather in Karbala in world's largest annual pilgrimage'. *International Business Times*, 22 November. Available online: www.ibtimes.co.uk/arbaeen-millions-shia-muslims-gather-karbala-worlds-largest-annual-pilgrimage-1592600 (Accessed 3 May 2017).

Steiner, C. (2009) 'From heritage to hyperreality? Prospects for tourism development in the Middle East between Petra and the Palm'. Paper presented at the Conference Traditions and Transformations: Tourism, Heritage and Cultural Change in the Middle East and North Africa Region, Amman, Jordan, 4–7 April.

Steiner, C. (2010a) 'An overestimated relationship? Violent political unrest and tourism foreign direct investment in the Middle East', *International Journal of Tourism Research*, 12: 726–738.

Steiner, C. (2010b) 'From heritage to hyper-reality? Tourism destination development in the Middle East between Petra and the Palm', *Journal of Tourism and Cultural Change*, 8(4): 240–253.

Stephenson, M.L., & Ali, N. (2010) 'Tourism and Islamophobia in non-Muslim states', in N. Scott, & J. Jafari (eds), *Tourism in the Muslim World* (pp. 235–251). Bingley: Emerald.

Stephenson, M.L., Russell, K., & Edgar, D. (2010) 'Islamic hospitality in the UAE: Indigenisation of products and human capital', *Journal of Islamic Marketing*, 1(1): 9–24.

Timothy, D.J., & Iverson, T. (2006) 'Tourism and Islam: Considerations of culture and duty', in D.J. Timothy, & D.H. Olsen (eds), *Tourism, Religion and Spiritual Journeys* (pp. 168–205). London: Routledge.

Tucker, H., & Carnegie, E. (2014) 'World Heritage and the contradictions of "universal value"', *Annals of Tourism Research*, 47: 63–76.

UNESCO (2012) 'Qālišuyān rituals of Mašhad-e Ardehāl in Kāšān'. Available online: https://ich.unesco.org/en/RL/qalisuyan-rituals-of-mashad-e-ardehal-in-kasan-00580 (Accessed 5 May 2017).

UNESCO (2015) 'UNESCO representative attends Ashura ceremonies in Semnan'. Available online: www.unesco.org/new/en/tehran/about-this-office/single-view/news/unesco_representative_attends_ashura_ceremonies_in_semnan (Accessed 5 May 2017).

UNESCO (2016a) 'World Heritage List'. Available online: http://whc.unesco.org/en/list/?delisted=1 (Accessed 15 December 2016).

UNESCO (2016b) 'Browse the lists of intangible cultural heritage and the register of best safeguarding practices'. Available online: www.unesco.org/culture/ich/en/lists (Accessed 15 December 2016).

UNWTO (2016) *Member States / World Tourism Organization UNWTO*. Available online: www2.unwto.org/members/states (Accessed 15 December 2016).

Wagner, L.B., & Minca, C. (2014) 'Rabat retrospective: Colonial heritage in a Moroccan urban laboratory', *Urban Studies*, 5: 3011–3025.

Worldatlas (2016) 'Middle East'. Available online: www.worldatlas.com/webimage/countrys/me.htm (Accessed 5 December 2016).

WTM (World Travel Market) (2007) 'The World Travel Market Global Trend Report 2007'.

Younesian, M. (2006) *Middle East 5 (Especially Reforms in the Middle East)*. Tehran: Abzar Moaser.

Zamani-Farahani, H. (2010) 'Iran: Tourism, heritage, & religion', in J. Jafari, & N. Scott (eds), *Bridging Tourism Theory & Practice (Volume 2): Tourism in the Muslim* (pp. 207–222). Bingley: Emerald.

Zamani-Farahani, H., & Eid, R. (2015) 'Muslim world: A study of tourism and pilgrimage among OIC member states', *Tourism Management Perspectives*, 19: 144–149.

Zamani-Farahani, H., & Henderson, J.C. (2010) 'Islamic tourism and managing tourism development in Islamic societies: The cases of Iran and Saudi Arabia', *International Journal of Tourism Research*, 12(1): 79–89.

11

CONTEMPORARY JEWISH TOURISM

Pilgrimage, religious heritage and educational tourism

Noga Collins-Kreiner

Introduction

What is the relationship between visiting Jerusalem as a religious obligation and visiting sites related to the Holocaust and youth summer trips to Israel? Can a religious duty that has existed for thousands of years truly be discussed in the same breath as popular visits to graves of hallowed saintly figures and the visitation of friends and relatives in Israel? These are the major questions that concerned me before starting to write the following assessment of contemporary Jewish tourism.

This chapter explores the connections between Judaism and tourism in the Middle East from historical and contemporary perspectives. The analysis it offers holds particular relevance for efforts to understand current trends in Jewish tourism and their relationship with religion and religiosity in the context of modernity. The discussion, however, is limited to Jewish tourism to and within Israel, as the current political climate in the Middle East precludes Jewish tourism to other countries. Jewish visitation to most MENA countries, including Libya, Syria, Lebanon, Iran, Iraq and many others, is either not possible at the moment or is not recommended for safety reasons (for more details, see the Israeli government travel warnings website at http://nsc.gov.il/he/Travel-Warnings/Pages/allwarnings.aspx). It should be noted, however, that there are Jewish heritage places scattered throughout the Middle East and North Africa, as will be described later, which could potentially be attractions if the political climate were different (Levy 1997).

As a result of this situation, virtually all Jewish tourism in the Middle East occurs to and within Israel. In 2015, 27 per cent of all tourists to Israel were Jewish (Israel Ministry of Tourism 2015), amounting to 839,322 visitors in total. In the last few decades, between one-quarter and one-third of all tourists to Israel have been Jewish, whereas most (approximately two-thirds) have been Christian. According to the Israel Ministry of Tourism (2015), adherents of other faiths seldom visit Israel.

Estimates for Jews in North Africa and the Middle East acknowledge the practical end of the Jewish presence in most countries and the ongoing reduction in size of the small Jewish communities remaining mainly in Morocco and Tunisia, which were estimated in 2013 to have a population of 3,300 (Dashefsky, Della Pergola, & Sheskin 2013). Those indigent Jews' travel patterns have been barely researched, and the results are of little significance owing to the low numbers of samples involved.

This chapter aims to contribute to the literature by investigating a topic that has thus far evaded thorough exploration: the sensitive and complex relationship amongst Judaism, tourism, pilgrimage, heritage, culture and politics. Understanding the context in which these elements have developed and interacted within Jewish culture enables us to understand better the complex relationship between Judaism and tourism in both the past and the present.

This analysis is based on Smith's (1992) continuum of travel and the theory of de-differentiation that has come to be widely used in recent years (Collins-Kreiner 2010). According to Smith's model, pilgrims and tourists are distinct actors situated at the opposite poles of the pilgrimage–tourism axis, which ranges from *sacred* to *secular*. This axis traverses an almost endless range of possible sacred-secular combinations, with a central region that has come to be referred to generally as 'religious tourism'. These combinations reflect the multiple changing motivations of travellers, whose interests and activities may shift—consciously or subconsciously—from tourism to pilgrimage and vice versa. Smith (1992) understands the possible variations as stemming from differences in individual beliefs and worldviews.

Badone and Roseman (2004) have been more explicit, positing that rigid dichotomies between pilgrimage and tourism or pilgrims and tourists no longer seem tenable in the shifting world of postmodern travel, and, elsewhere, I maintain that the de-differentiation between different kinds of tourism has stemmed from the increasing difficulty of distinguishing between them (Collins-Kreiner 2010), as will also be explained in this chapter.

Each of the chapter's three sections is devoted to a different segment of Jewish tourism, deriving from a different type of relationship between the Jewish religion and tourism, as well as to different historical periods: pilgrimage travel in Judaism in the pre-modern era, Jewish pilgrimage tourism in the modern period, and current Jewish heritage tourism. It is based on the premise that Jewish pilgrimage constituted the initial building block of Jewish tourism and for this reason must be the first element considered by any analysis. Broadening our understanding also requires consideration of the ways in which Jewish tourism has developed over the years, from a religion-based obligation to heritage-focused popular visitation. Whereas past research on Jewish tourism has typically considered Jewish pilgrimage solely from a religious perspective, it is now clear that the phenomenon must also be explored in the context of heritage, culture and politics.

The chapter's first section contextualises the concept of Jewish pilgrimage, the centrality of the Jewish Temple to the development of Jewish perceptions of pilgrimage, and the consequences of the demise of this centre (Luz & Collins-Kreiner 2015). The second section considers the main attributes and sites of Jewish pilgrimage in the pre-modern period and the emergence of a more nuanced and complex Jewish hagiographic map. It also discusses the dramatic changes in Jewish pilgrimage that have occurred during the modern period, particularly as part of the emergence of Jewish society within the state of Israel. The third section examines Jewish heritage, educational and diaspora tourism in an effort to understand tourism in Judaism not solely from a religious point of view but also from the perspective of the mixed motives of culture and heritage that are characteristic of the current period.

The chapter concludes with a discussion and summary that draws out the chapter's main insights and brings together its different sections. My main argument is that, just as scholars of tourism (e.g. Badone & Roseman 2004; Bilu 1998) argue that rigid dichotomies between pilgrimage and tourism are no longer tenable in the shifting world of postmodern travel, the case of Jewish tourism is well suited to more fluid theorisations of the conceptual boundaries between 'sacred' and 'profane', as the sacred increasingly comes to encompass practices and sites that are not at all religious.

Pilgrimage travel in Judaism

Pilgrimage, as movement towards a sacred centre aimed at being exposed to God's presence (Coleman & Elsner 1995), lies at the very core of the Jewish faith. The biblical text is unequivocal about the importance of this journey and the religious imperative of performing it on both physical and metaphorical levels (Luz & Collins-Kreiner 2015):

> Three times a year all your men must appear before the Lord your God at the place he will choose: at the Festival of Unleavened Bread, the Festival of Weeks and the Festival of Tabernacles. No one should appear before the Lord empty-handed: Each of you must bring a gift in proportion to the way the Lord your God has blessed you.
>
> *(Deuteronomy 16: 16–17)*

Following the ascendancy of Davidic traditions, Jerusalem and its religious centre (the Jewish Temple) became supreme and all other existing pilgrimage centres were shunned. The end of Jewish autonomy, reflected primarily in the destruction of this sacred site in 70 CE, only intensified Jerusalem's symbolic role in this context (Luz & Collins-Kreiner 2015).

Like those of other religions, Jewish perspectives towards pilgrimage have changed over time. As noted, Jews were expected to 'appear before the Lord…at the place he will choose'. According to the prevailing Jewish narrative constructed by canonised texts that largely follow Judean literature, the Jerusalem Temple—after its inauguration by King Solomon in 970 BCE—became the most important and revered Jewish pilgrimage site. Although this narrative has come under increasing scrutiny in recent years (Eliav 2005, 2008; Finkelstein & Silberman 2001), there is ample evidence reflecting the growing role of the Jerusalemite temple as the focal point of Jewish pilgrimage (in Hebrew, *'aliyah la-regel*) during the Second Temple period (Eliav 2005). Under King Herod (37–34 BCE), the compound underwent an extensive and highly ambitious renovation and refurbishment project, which, amongst other things, involved the construction of four massive retaining walls. This construction project transformed the temple into a separate urban entity, which since then has been known as the Temple Mount. Following the Temple's destruction by the Romans, the western retaining wall emerged as the most iconic Jewish pilgrimage site.

Over time, the city in general and the Western Wall, or Wailing Wall (as the most important relic of the former temple) in particular, regained its mythic and central importance. Jews continued to undertake pilgrimages to Jerusalem, culminating—political circumstances permitting—in a visit to the Wailing Wall (Prawer 1988). Thus, through a convoluted and meandering historical process that originated in biblical times, intensified during the Second Temple period, and finalised after the Roman conquest in 70 CE, Jerusalem and its temple were transformed from ideas that symbolised the Jewish presence in the Holy Land into spiritual and metaphysical symbols that came to constitute the very essence of Jewish existence. Hence, from Late Antiquity (between the fourth and sixth centuries CE) onward, Jewish pilgrims were no longer engaged in the canonical 'Aliya La-regel' but rather performed rituals which can be better translated as, and bear a greater semblance to, the Latin term 'peregrination', or pilgrimage (Reiner 2014).

Arguably, the Wailing Wall and its environs have constituted the most iconic landmark and the fulcrum of processes that have played a role in the increasing importance of the religious sphere in contemporary Israel. Jews yearned for and venerated the site for centuries before it once again became accessible to Jewish pilgrims after the 1967 Arab–Israeli War. The state played an active role in transforming the site by altering its spatiality. The changes were designed not only to produce a central pilgrimage site for Jews but also to reflect an emergent religious nationalist understanding (Nitzan-Shiftan 2011). The centrality of this site and its canonical status as the most important national and pilgrimage icon must also be understood in the context of everyday Jewish Israeli attitudes towards a mythologised past, manifested in the geographical concept of Eretz Israel as the 'historical' foundation of modern-day Israel. Each year, millions of international and domestic visitors make their way to Jerusalem in general and to the Wailing Wall in particular (Luz & Collins-Kreiner 2015).

Current Jewish pilgrimage tourism

A new phase in Jewish pilgrimage tourism emerged out of the socio-political changes that ultimately led to the emergence of Israel as a Jewish state within the geographical setting of the biblical Holy Land. The twentieth century, particularly following the creation of Israel in 1948, witnessed a dramatic growth in pilgrimage sites (whether old, new or renewed) and a soaring increase in the volume of Jewish pilgrims, along with significant trends of religious radicalisation and religious resurgence (D. Bar 2004, 2009, 2010; G. Bar 2008; Bilu 1998, 2010; Collins-Kreiner 2004, 2007, 2010; Epstein 1995; Sered 1986, 1989, 1991, 1998; Sasson 2002).

Today, the holy sites dating from historical periods consist primarily of the burial places of saintly figures (Cohen Ioannides & Ioannides 2006; Collins-Kreiner 1999; Sered 1998), including, amongst others, the Tomb of Rachel the Matriarch in Bethlehem, the tomb of Maimonides in Tiberias, and the Cave of the Patriarchs in Hebron. It must be noted, however, that most of these sites are recognised as saintly graves based on later traditions and do not necessarily mark the saintly figure's (*zaddik*) exact burial location.

After the destruction of the Second Temple in 70 CE, the Galilee region in general and, more specifically, the Upper Galilee city of Safed, where new lunar months (*Roshei Hodashim*) were announced, became the main Jewish centre. Tiberias, on the shore of Lake Kinneret (Sea of Galilee), was also an important spiritual centre in Mishnaic and Talmudic times, and the Sanhedrin (an assembly of 71 ordained scholars, which served as both a legislature and a supreme court) was relocated there from Yavne. During this period, the Galilee also emerged as an important centre for Jewish sages and poets, and Safed and Tiberias took their place as two of the four Jewish holy cities.

For example, one of the most important of these major peripheral centres in Israel is the tomb of Rabbi Shimon Bar-Yochai, located on Mount Meron near Safed. Shimon Bar-Yochai lived during the second century and preached against the Romans, from whom he lived in hiding in a cave for 13 years. He is believed to have written the *Zohar* (The Book of Splendor), the most important book of Jewish mysticism (Levy 1997) and to have performed miracles. Pilgrims visit the site throughout the year, but mass visitation occurs only on the festival of *Lag Ba'omer* (the 33rd day after Passover), which is the site's major day of celebration. On this single day, an estimated 250,000 people visit the locale, representing approximately 5 per cent of all Israeli citizens, whereas the site's estimated annual number of visitors stands at approximately 1.5 million. The site is a major attraction of domestic tourism in Israel, drawing members of all segments of Jewish society in the country and imbuing the place with a largely popular character. Other major peripherally located pilgrimage centres of a popular character include the tombs of Rabbi Yonatan Ben-Oziel near Safed, Rabbi Meir Ba'al Hanes near Tiberias, Rabbi Akiva in Tiberias, Honi Hameagel at Hatzor Haglilit in the Galilee, Rabbi Yehuda Bar-Elaee near Safed and many more.

Most if not all of these sites are located in peripheral areas. According to the Israel Ministry of Tourism, the number of annual visitors to each of these locations is estimated in the tens of thousands. At the sites themselves, religion, folk beliefs and customs mix freely. Each locale is believed to have its own special properties, and, on this basis, pilgrims come to pray, to ask for personal favours and blessings (*brachot*), and to seek assistance related to marriage, health and fertility. People also visit the sites to meet up with family members, friends and others, and to eat, talk and even dance.

Since the 1980s, new sacred sites for Jewish saints have been established or 'discovered' in several Israeli development towns. Several studies, such as those of Weingrod (1990, 1998) and Ben-Ari and Bilu (1997) and Bilu and Ben-Ari (1992), reflect on the reasons for this new kind of peripheral site and find that the socio-cultural and political characteristics of Israeli society, in conjunction with the new Jewish immigrants who arrived in the country in the 1950s, primarily from Muslim North Africa, were major factors in their emergence. These immigrants brought with them the popular Muslim tradition of '*ziyara*', or visitation of the sacred graves of holy figures. About ten such minor centres currently exist throughout the country and their number is growing. Most have only a limited hinterland, but some are popular throughout the entire country and enjoy a large number of visitors throughout the year, especially on Jewish holidays and the *hillulot*, marked by a gathering at the grave of the saintly figure on the anniversary of his death.

The major reason for visits by these Jewish 'traditional' (*masorti*) believers is their faith in the holy persons themselves and in what they have to gain from the visit. Most traditional visitors are women of all ages from throughout the country, usually of low to medium socio-economic status. Most of them are of Sephardic origin, and many typically visit the sites as part of an organised group, asking for assistance relating to fertility, health, marriage, or some other personal need. The women place their written supplications on the gravestone of the saintly figure, light candles, and tie coloured cloths around the branches of a 'wishing tree' in hopes of having their wishes granted.

The most popular site of this kind is the Tomb of the Baba Sali in the town of Netivot in the Negev Desert region of southern Israel. Another pilgrimage site of this kind is Rabbi Chaim Chouri's tomb in Beer Sheva (Weingrod 1990). Many tombs located in North Africa—in Morocco, Tunisia and Egypt, in particular—also attract visitors from Israel, who visit them as pilgrims.

The number of pilgrims/tourists to these sites has continued to increase, and new platforms are being used to increase public knowledge and awareness about this burgeoning practice. Social media, Internet forums, general information websites, and websites of specific sites are becoming increasingly widespread, reflecting not only a proliferation and an increase in the number of sites but also the more general religious resurgence that is currently underway throughout Israel.

Heritage, educational and diaspora Jewish tourism

The term 'heritage tourism' has been used to denote the interest of large numbers of visitors in aspects of a nation's history, archaeology, culture, religion, art and natural landscape (Prentice 1993; Timothy 2011). This meaning is consistent with Boniface and Fowler's (1993: 150) definition of heritage as 'the cultural expression of what makes us what we are, our spiritual DNA'.

Jewish heritage tourism (JHT) is defined as the supply of, and demand for, sites and activities connected to the Jewish faith, culture and tradition, including both relics of the past and products of the present (Krakover 2012, 2013, 2017).

Overall, in the category of 'roots tourism', 'diaspora tourism', 'pilgrimage to memorial sites and concentrations camps', 'pilgrimage of nostalgia', and 'heritage tours', JHT has been on the rise since the turn of the millennium and has been the focus of many different studies (Biran, Poria, & Oren 2011; Cohen 2016; Kidron 2013; Krakover 2012, 2013, 2017; Russo & Romagosa 2010; Stone 2006; Stone & Sharpley 2008). Most research on Jewish diaspora tourism relates to Holocaust sites around the world but also to sites and experiences in Israel (Feldman 1995, 2001, 2002, 2005; Gruber 2002, 2007; Kirshenblatt-Gimblett 1998). Collins-Kreiner and Olsen (2004) have offered a comprehensive segmentation of the element of demand, spanning heritage tours, interaction tours, solidarity missions and ritual tours.

Jewish heritage tourism is a complex segment combining different visitors with different motives that all relate to their Jewish identity and are therefore addressed in this chapter. Some can be classified as 'roots tourism', meaning Jewish visitors trying to find their identity while visiting Israel, while others can be classified as 'event tourism', as in the case of Jewish families coming to Israel to celebrate a 'Bar-Mitzvah' (a Jewish boy's 13th birthday) (http://barmitzvah-in-israel.co.il). Such an event is partially religious in nature and partially heritage-oriented, and the differing levels of each element, depending largely on the religiosity of the family, provides a good example not only of how such a visit could be located at different locations along Smith's 1992 continuum, but also of the difficulty of differentiating amongst different activities, motivations and characteristics.

Another interesting market within JHT is the 'educational tourism' segment, which also includes a variety of programmes. Some of these programmes are intended for high school and college students and young adults, and others are open to all ages (www.jewishagency.org). However, they all have one thing in common: their aim of strengthening the Jewish identity and connection to Israel of Jews living outside the country (Cohen 2016).

Numerous researchers have examined other patterns of Jewish tourism, including Cohen Ioannides and Ioannides (2006), Ioannides and Cohen Ioannides (2002) and Kugelmass (1993), who investigated patterns of Jewish travel in the United States. Other researchers have written about aspects of Jewish summer youth trips to Israel, and especially the impact of 'Taglit-Birthright Israel', which provides young adults between the ages of 18 and 26 with a free educational trip to Israel (see, for example, Chazan 1992, 1997; Cohen 2016; Kelner et al. 2000). Other works include Goldberg's (1995) ethnographic perspective on visits to Israel, Shapiro's (2001) study of the three-month *Livnot u'lehibanot* work-study program, Heilman's (1995) study on the visits of members of the Young Judea youth movement, and Cohen's (1999) work on the 'Israel Experience'.

The year 2000 witnessed the launching of the above-mentioned Taglit-Birthright program, which quickly came to have a significant impact on the world of Jewish educational tourism. Within a decade, this programme had several hundred thousand alumni, primarily but not exclusively from North America (Cohen 2016). Another initiative launched around this time was the MASA Israel Journey program, which provided a cohesive umbrella organisation to match young adults with long-term study programmes lasting from several months to several years. Available programmes cover a wide range of areas of interest such as archaeology, ecology, history, religious studies, Hebrew language, community service and more. Between 2004 and 2011, some 55,000 individuals joined study programmes via MASA. The growth in participation in these three main branches of organised educational tourism—Israel Experience,

Taglit-Birthright Israel and MASA—is notable, with around 10,000 to 13,000 people participating in each one in 2011 (Cohen 2016).

Solidarity tours of Jewish visitors and interaction tours are also part of the heritage tourism market and are currently offered by different organisations in Israel. There are also currently numerous international projects with different itineraries that bring youngsters to Israel for short visits (Cohen 2016).

Conclusion

This chapter has considered the primary aspects that have characterised the varied and diverse relationship between Judaism and tourism over time. First is the fact that pilgrimage to holy sites in general, and to Jerusalem in particular, was the most prominent feature of Jewish tourism in the past and remains so today. Second is the fact that there appear to be several motives, and different combinations of religious, heritage and cultural reasons, for travel in the context of Jewish tourism. Whether or not Jews feel a personal affinity with Israel or Judaism, current Jewish travel patterns suggest that their cultural and religious identity have a strong influence on their touristic activities.

Third, it is clear that this trend is consistent with the current literature (Badone & Roseman 2004; Collins-Kreiner 2010; Smith 1992) regarding the growing de-differentiation amongst pilgrimage, religious tourism and heritage tourism, as well as between the sacred and the profane. A good example of this continuum and the growing de-differentiation is the case of Jewish Ultra-Orthodox Jews, known in Hebrew as 'Haredim'. This group's population in Israel stands at approximately 700,000, constituting some 10 per cent of the country's overall population. Studies have postulated that because each subgroup within this unique population is different in its socio-economic, cultural and religious attributes, they each display a significantly different set of travel expectations and consumer behaviour patterns, from totally religious travel, motives and behaviours to almost secular forms of travel, focused primarily on leisure and enjoyment (Cahaner & Mansfeld 2012).

The fourth conclusion is that the commodification of national identity and ethnicity has been one of the most distinctive features of Jewish tourism development over the past decade. One motivation for this process has been increased interest, amongst Jewish communities and individuals, in learning more about their collective pasts and identities by discovering family roots and expanding their awareness of past historical events and places.

In conclusion, Jewish tourism today is a complex term that brings together a wide variety of sites, motives, visitors, meanings, worldviews and identities and appears to be well suited to more fluid theorisations of the conceptual boundaries between sacred and profane, as the sacred comes increasingly to encompass practices and sites that are not necessarily religious at all.

References

Badone, E., & Roseman, S. (eds) (2004) *Intersecting Journeys: The Anthropology of Pilgrimage and Tourism*. Champaign, IL: University of Illinois Press.

Bar, D. (2004) 'Re-creating Jewish sanctity in Jerusalem: The case of Mount Zion and David's Tomb between 1948–1967', *The Journal of Israeli History*, 23(2): 233–251.

Bar, D. (2009) 'Mizrahim and the development of sacred space in the state of Israel, 1948–1968', *Journal of Modern Jewish Studies*, 8(3): 267–285.

Bar, D. (2010) 'Jewish holy places in Israel: Continuity and change', *Zmanim*, 110: 92–103.

Bar, G. (2008) 'Reconstructing the past: The creation of Jewish sacred space in the State of Israel, 1948–1967', *Israel Studies*, 13(3): 1–21.

Ben-Ari, E., & Bilu, Y. (1997) *Grasping Land: Space and Place in Contemporary Israeli Discourse and Experience.* New York: State University of New York.

Bilu, Y. (1998) 'Divine worship and pilgrimage to holy sites as universal phenomena', in R. Gonen (ed.), *To the Holy Graves: Pilgrimage to the Holy Graves and Hillulot in Israel* (pp. 11–26). Jerusalem: The Israel Museum.

Bilu, Y. (2010) *The Saints' Impresarios: Dreamers, Healers, and Holy Men in Israel's Urban Periphery.* Tel Aviv: Academic Studies Press.

Bilu, Y., & Ben-Ari, E. (1992) 'The making of modern saints: Manufactured charisma and the Abu-Hatseiras of Israel', *American Ethnologist*, 19(4): 672–687.

Biran, A., Poria, Y., & Oren, G. (2011) 'Sought experiences at (dark) heritage sites', *Annals of Tourism Research*, 38(3): 820–841.

Boniface, P., & Fowler, P.J. (1993) *Heritage and Tourism in 'the Global Village'.* Chicago, IL: Routledge.

Cahaner, L., & Mansfeld, Y. (2012) 'A voyage from religiousness to secularity and back: A glimpse into "Haredi" tourists', *Journal of Heritage Tourism*, 7(4): 301–321.

Chazan, B. (1992) 'The Israel trip as Jewish education', *Agenda*, 1(Fall): 30–34.

Chazan, B. (1997) *Does the Teen Israel Experience Make a Difference?* New York: Israel Experience Inc.

Cohen, E. (1999) 'Informal marketing of Israel Experience educational tours', *Journal of Travel Research*, 37(3): 238–243.

Cohen, E.H. (2016) 'Towards a social history of Jewish educational tourism research', *Hagira—Israel Journal of Migration*, 5: 41–49.

Cohen Ioannides, M., & Ioannides, D. (2006) 'Global Jewish tourism: Pilgrimages and remembrance', in D.J. Timothy, & D.H. Olsen (eds), *Tourism, Religion & Spiritual Journeys* (pp. 156–171). London: Routledge.

Coleman, S., & Elsner, J. (eds) (1995) *Pilgrimage: Past and Present in the World Religions.* Cambridge, MA: Harvard University Press.

Collins-Kreiner, N. (1999) 'Pilgrimage holy sites: A classification of Jewish holy sites in Israel', *Journal of Cultural Geography*, 18(3): 57–78.

Collins-Kreiner, N. (2004) 'Jewish pilgrimage tourism in Israel: Holy tombs as tourist attractions', *Horizons in Geography*, 60/61: 267–278.

Collins-Kreiner, N. (2007) Graves as attractions: Pilgrimage-tourism to Jewish holy graves in Israel. *Journal of Cultural Geography*, 24(1), 67–89.

Collins-Kreiner, N. (2010) 'Researching pilgrimage: Continuity and transformations', *Annals of Tourism Research*, 37(2): 440–456.

Collins-Kreiner, N., & Olsen, D.H. (2004) 'Selling diaspora: Producing and segmenting the Jewish diaspora tourism market', in T. Coles, & D.J. Timothy (eds), *Tourism, Diasporas and Space* (pp. 279–290). London: Routledge.

Dashefsky, A., Della Pergola, S., & Sheskin, I. (2013) *Current Jewish Population Reports.* Jerusalem: Berman Jewish Data Bank in cooperation with The Association for the Social Scientific Study of Jewry.

Eliav, Y. (2005) *God's Mountain: The Temple Mount in Time, Space, and Memory,* Baltimore, MD: Johns Hopkins University Press.

Eliav, Y. (2008) 'The Temple Mount in Jewish and early Christian traditions: A new look', in T. Mayer, & S. Mourad (eds), *Jerusalem: Idea and Reality* (pp. 47–66). London: Routledge.

Epstein, S. (1995) 'Inventing a pilgrimage: Ritual, love and politics on the Road to Amuka', *Jewish Folklore and Ethnology Review*, 17(1–2): 25–32.

Feldman J. (1995) '"It is my brothers whom I am seeking": Israeli youth pilgrimages to Holocaust Poland', *Jewish Folklore and Ethnology Review*, 17(1–2): 33–36.

Feldman J. (2001) 'In the footsteps of the Israeli Holocaust survivor: Youth voyages to Poland and Israeli identity', *Theory and Criticism*, 19: 167–190.

Feldman J. (2002) 'Marking the boundaries of the enclave: Defining the Israeli collective through the Poland "experience"', *Israel Studies*, 7(2): 84–114.

Feldman, J. (2005) 'In search of the beautiful land of Israel: Youth voyages to Poland', in E. Cohen, & H. Noy (eds), *Israeli Backpackers and their Society: From Tourism to Rite of Passage* (pp. 217–250). New York: State University of New York Press.

Finkelstein, I., & Silberman, N. (2001) *The Bible Unearthed: Archaeology's New Vision of Ancient Israel and the Origin of Its Sacred Texts.* New York: Simon and Schuster.

Goldberg, H. (1995) *A Summer on a NFTY Safari, 1994: An Ethnographic Perspective.* Montreal and Jerusalem: CRB Foundation.

Gruber, R.E. (2002) *Virtually Jewish: Reinventing Jewish Culture in Europe.* Berkeley, CA: University of California Press.

Gruber, R.E. (2007) *Jewish Heritage Travel: A Guide to Eastern Europe.* Washington, DC: National Geographic Society

Heilman, S.C. (1995) *A Young Judea Israel Discovery Tour: The View from the Inside.* Montreal and Jerusalem: CRB Foundation.

Ioannides, D., & Cohen Ioannides, M.W. (2002) 'Pilgrimages of nostalgia: Patterns of Jewish travel in the United States', *Tourism Recreation Research*, 27(2): 17–25.

Israel Ministry of Tourism (2015) *Tourism to Israel.* Jerusalem: Ministry of Tourism.

Kelner, S., Saxe, L., Kadushin, C., Canar, R., Lindholm, M., Ossman, H., Perloff, J., Phillips, B., Teres, R., Wolf, M., & Woocher, M. (2000) *Making Meaning: Participants' Experience of Birthright Israel.* Waltham, MA: Brandeis University, Maurice and Marilyn Cohen Center for Modern Jewish Studies.

Kidron, C. (2013) 'Being there together: Dark family tourism and the emotive experience of co-presence in the Holocaust past', *Annals of Tourism Research*, 4(1): 175–194.

Kirshenblatt-Gimblett, B. (1998) *Destination Culture: Tourism, Museums, and Heritage.* Berkeley, CA: University of California Press.

Krakover, S. (2012) 'Coordinated marketing and dissemination of knowledge: Jewish heritage tourism in Serra da Estrela, Portugal', *Revista Turismo & Desenvolvimento*, 17: 11–16.

Krakover, S. (2013) 'Generation of a tourism product: Jewish heritage tourism in Spain', *Enlightening Tourism*, 3(2): 142–168.

Krakover, S. (2017) 'A heritage site development model: Jewish heritage product formation in south-central Europe', *Journal of Heritage Tourism*, 12(1): 81–101.

Kugelmass, J. (1993) 'The rites of the tribe: The meaning of Poland for American Jewish tourists', *Going Home: YIVO*, 21: 395–454.

Levy, A. (1997) 'To Morocco and back: Tourism and pilgrimage among Moroccan-born Israelis', in E. Ben-Ari, & Y. Bilu (eds), *Grasping Land: Space and Place in Contemporary Israeli Discourse and Experience* (pp. 25–46). Albany, NY: State University of New York.

Luz N., & Collins-Kreiner N. (2015) 'Exploring Jewish pilgrimage in Israel', in J. Eade, & A. Dionigi (eds), *International Perspectives on Pilgrimage Studies: Itineraries, Gaps and Obstacles* (pp. 134–151). New York: Routledge.

Nitzan-Shiftan, N. (2011) 'Stones with a human heart: On monuments, modernism and preservation at the Western Wall', *Theory and Criticism*, 38: 65–100.

Prawer, J. (1988) *The History of the Jews in the Latin Kingdom.* Oxford: Oxford University Press.

Prentice, R. (1993) *Tourism and Heritage Attractions.* London: Routledge.

Reiner, E. (2014) 'Jewish pilgrimage to Jerusalem in Late Antiquity and the Middle Ages', in O. Limor, E. Reiner, & M. Frenkel (eds), *Pilgrimage: Jews, Christians, Muslims* (pp. 46–130). Rananna: The Open University of Israel Press.

Russo, A.P., & Romagosa, F. (2010) The network of Spanish Jewries: In praise of connecting and sharing heritage. *Journal of Heritage Tourism*, 5(2): 141–156.

Sasson A. (2002) 'Movement of graves: The passage of the hegemony of holy graves from North to South', in M. Cohen (ed.), *Sedot-Negev: Man, Environment and Heritage* (pp. 117–134). Jerusalem: The regional Council Sdot-Negev & Makom.

Sered, S. (1986) 'Rachel's Tomb and the Milk Grotto of the Virgin Mary: Two women's shrines in Bethlehem', *Journal of Feminist Studies in Religion*, 2(2): 7–22.

Sered, S. (1989) 'Rachel's Tomb: Societal liminality and the revitalisation of a shrine', *Religion*, 19: 27–40.

Sered, S. (1991) 'Rachel, Mary, and Fatima', *Cultural Anthropology*, 6(2): 131–146.

Sered, S. (1998) 'A tale of three Rachel's, or the cultural history of a symbol', *Nashim: A Journal of Jewish Women's Studies & Gender Issues*, 1: 5–41.

Shapiro, F.L. (2001) 'Learning to be a diaspora Jew through the Israel experience', *Studies in Religion*, 30(1): 23–24.

Smith V.L. (1992) 'Introduction: The quest in guest', *Annals of Tourism Research*, 19(1): 1–17.

Stone, P.R. (2006) 'A dark tourism spectrum: Towards a typology of death and macabre related tourist sites, attractions and exhibitions', *Tourism*, 52(2): 145–160.

Stone, P.R., & Sharpley, R. (2008) 'Consuming dark tourism: A thanatolological perspective', *Annals of Tourism Research*, 35(2): 574–595.

Timothy, D.J. (2011) *Cultural Heritage and Tourism: An Introduction*. Bristol: Channel View Publications.

Weingrod, A. (1990) *The Saint of Beersheba*. New York: State University of New York Press.

Weingrod, A. (1998) 'The Saints go marching on', in O. Abuhab et al. (eds), *Local Anthropology*, Tel Aviv: Cherikover (in Hebrew).

12

CHRISTIAN TOURISM IN THE MIDDLE EAST

Holy Land and Mediterranean perspectives

Dallen J. Timothy and Amos S. Ron

Introduction

More than two billion people on the earth consider themselves Christians. They look to Jesus Christ as the son of God and saviour of the world. His birth, life, death and resurrection were pivotal points in his earthly ministry and recorded by his contemporaries in writings that became the New Testament. During his ministry, he called apostles to assist in ministering, healing and evangelising. After Jesus' death and resurrection, the apostles continued their missionary efforts, travelling throughout the Levant and Mediterranean Europe, preaching the doctrines of Christ and ministering to converts. Many of Jesus' original apostles died as martyrs for the cause, thereby sealing their own fates as heroes of Christendom. Beginning with the birth of Jesus, through his ministry, to his death and resurrection, and including the work of the apostles, certain places in the Holy Land and broader Mediterranean region have become inextricably linked to Jesus and his early followers.

Within a few hundred years after the death of Christ, several countries in Europe, Asia Minor and the Caucasus had become Christianised. Their populations began visiting the Holy Land and venerating the sacred landscapes there, building shrines and churches on spots which, according to local traditions, were the scenes of sacred Christian events. During the intervening 2,000 years, these sites as recorded in the Bible have become nodes of Christian worship and pilgrimage (Harpur 2002; Trono & Imperiale 2018; Turner & Turner 1978). For centuries, followers of Christ have travelled to the Holy Land and other places associated with his life and the ministry of the apostles in Italy, Greece, Malta, Turkey, Cyprus, Lebanon, Syria, Palestine, Israel, Jordan and Egypt. This has created a unique and lucrative tourist market for several Mediterranean countries, primarily those in the Middle East. Christian pilgrims comprise approximately 53 per cent of annual arrivals in Israel. For Palestine, the number is even higher—nearly 70 per cent of all tours in the Palestinian territories are comprised of Christian pilgrims.

The socio-economic importance of this religious travel niche in several countries of MENA, especially Israel and Palestine, cannot be overstated. This chapter examines travel patterns that are unique to the Christian market, including denominational differences in supply and demand, destination preferences, the Christian tourism products of the region, and the elements of dissonance that manifest from overlapping spaces and doctrinal differences between sects.

Christian tourism in MENA

Three primary themes were identified as a conceptual framework for this discussion (Table 12.1). Most elements of Christian tourism in MENA fit within this three-part classification. The three themes are destinations, products and dissonance.

Destinations

As the cradle of the Abrahamic religions, the Middle East and North Africa is a significant destination for travellers seeking to fulfil religious obligations, supplicate God for mercy, visit important religious shrines, or 'walk in the footsteps of Jesus'. As noted above, Christianity began in what is today Israel and Palestine and spread quickly throughout the Levant and eastern Mediterranean with the evangelising efforts of Jesus' apostles and other disciples. The primary attractions and destinations amongst Christian tourists in the Holy Land are New Testament sites—those localities mentioned in the New Testament as being part of the ministry of Jesus and later his missionary apostles. Christians revere the Old Testament as sacred scripture as well, so its stories and events also play a prominent role in the faith. From a Christian perspective, the term 'Holy Land' refers to Israel and Palestine at its core, but also includes Jordan and sometimes Egypt. These four countries correspond with important biblical events and are frequently included in general Holy Land tours. Biblical sites from the Old Testament are located primarily in Egypt, Jordan, Palestine, Israel, Syria, Lebanon and Iraq. In spite of the considerable potential for Christian tourism in Iraq and Syria (Poujeau 2012), for obvious current security reasons, few Western tourists visit the two countries, and most European and North American Christians avoid travel to Lebanon, owing to its enduring conflict with Israel and ongoing internal strife. Thus, the vehement political tensions of the region severely limit the geographical extent of the visitable Holy Land, which in practical terms equally limits the boundaries of the Holy Land.

The most visited cities in Israel by Christians are Jerusalem, Nazareth and Tiberias. Much of Jesus' life and ministry took place in the Galilee region and the Golan Heights, so much Christian tourism focuses on this region, particularly around Nazareth and various localities

Table 12.1 Patterns of Christian tourism in the Middle East and North Africa

Products	Destinations	Dissonance
Tours	Old Testament sites	Denominational differences
Cruises	Egypt	Conflicts
Themed spaces	Jordan	Solidarity
Food experiences	Israel	
Baptisms	Palestine	
Holy trails	Lebanon	
Volunteer experiences	Syria	
	Iraq	
	New Testament sites	
	Israel	
	Palestine	
	Turkey	
	Jordan	

around the Sea of Galilee. Jerusalem is deemed most important as it was the location of the last days of Jesus' life—his final entry into the city, betrayal, judgment, crucifixion and resurrection.

Within Palestine, Jerusalem is the most visited location, followed by Bethlehem—the birthplace of Jesus—with its nearby 'Shepherds' Fields'. Bethlehem and the fields are usually a day-trip destination from Jerusalem. There are several other key attractions in the West Bank, including Jacob's Well in Nablus, the Mount of Temptation in Jericho, the Cave of the Patriarchs in Hebron, the baptismal site of Jesus, and the representative Inn of the Good Samaritan. While the areas under Palestinian control, particularly Bethlehem and Jericho, see some benefits from tourism, several important locations see relatively few Christian tourists, owing to security concerns and Israeli restrictions placed upon travel to large swaths of the Palestinian lands (Isaac 2013, 2016). The West Bank's Christian holy sites are found primarily in Area A (under civil and security control of the Palestinian authorities) and Area C (under the civil and security control of Israeli authorities). Those in Area C (e.g. the Inn of the Good Samaritan and the baptismal site) are administered by the Israeli Ministry of Tourism, while those in Area A fall under the authority of the Palestinian Ministry of Tourism and Antiquities.

Jordan is home to Al-Maghtas (Bethany beyond the Jordan), which is believed to be the location of Jesus' baptism at the Jordan River (Mustafa 2014). This event is celebrated and marked on both sides of the border with Qaser el-Yahud (on the West Bank side) being a major Christian destination as well. Mount Nebo of the Old Testament and various localities associated with Jesus' ministry are also located in Jordan. Egypt is home to several Old Testament places, including Ramesses and variously representative localities in the Sinai Desert (Hobbs 1992; Shackley 1998). Turkey, the main country of the eastern Mediterranean included in MENA, has become a popular Christian destination also, owing to its association with the missionary work of Paul the Apostle. Popular Turkish destinations include Antakya, Antalya, Ephesus, Tarsus, Troy and other cities noted in the New Testament (Egresi, Bayram, & Kara 2012).

Products

Given the importance of the Middle East as a Christian destination, many different products have developed over the centuries to cater to the needs and desires of this market. The most pervasive product is tour packages. Themed environments, volunteer opportunities, and Bible-centred hiking trails are other related products and will be discussed in greater detail below.

Organised tour packages and cruises

The commonest mode of today's Christian pilgrimage travel to the Holy Land is organised group packages, although independent travel is becoming increasingly popular. Tour companies in the Middle East or in the countries from which the tourists arrive typically assemble these package tours. This is often done in collaboration with religious organisations, ministers and evangelists to cater to the specific needs and interests of their groups. Most New Testament-focused tours include sites in Israel and Palestine, and sometimes Jordan. Others focus on combining Old Testament sites in Egypt and Jordan with New Testament localities in Israel and Palestine. Some tours stay only within Israel but focus on Old and New Testament spaces. A common distinction in the industry is 'in the footsteps of Jesus' and 'in the footsteps of Paul' tours. The first category focuses on sites and events depicted in the four gospels and to a certain extent the Book of Acts. The second category focuses on the life of the apostles and the places noted in the Book of Acts and the various 'Letter' books of the New Testament.

The popularity of package tours in the Holy Land indicates a few different things. First, organised group tours provide a certain level of security and safety that independent travel does not. This is especially pertinent in a politically fragile region such as the Middle East (Collins-Kreiner, Kliot, Mansfeld, & Sagi 2006; Kaell 2014). Second, package tours provide in-depth interpretation by local guides from an Israeli or Palestinian perspective that would not be available for people travelling on their own. Finally, as some groups are escorted by well-known Christian authors or church leaders, including tele-evangelists, the experience also provides a unique gospel perspective in line with biblical principles and encourages the development of fellowship and camaraderie amongst fellow church members.

Several unique experiences also characterise some Holy Land tours. Many Christians seek to be baptised or re-baptised in the Jordan River. This is a common activity amongst groups on both the Jordanian and Israeli/Palestinian side of the river. Second, many people seek opportunities to celebrate Jewish holidays in Israel and eat biblical meals that are based upon the traditional and 'authentic' foods of the Bible. Biblical meal suppliers work with tour operators to organise these Bible-based feasts, which are typically accompanied by commentary and culinary interpretation from the scriptures (Ron & Timothy 2013; Timothy & Ron 2016).

Bible-oriented cruises are also gaining popularity in the Mediterranean. These are primarily of two types. The first type is comprised of specific 'In the Footsteps of Paul' cruises that take in locations in Turkey, Greece, Cyprus, Malta and Italy to commemorate the journeys of Paul. In Turkey, the cruises typically call in at Izmir and Ephesus. The second type are general Mediterranean cruises that are less Bible-themed but allow passengers time in Israel at ports of call in Ashdod and Haifa. From Ashdod, Christian shore excursions can be arranged to Jerusalem and Bethlehem. From Haifa they can be purchased for the Galilee region or Jerusalem. This category of cruises provides Christians with spiritual opportunities on shore in the Holy Land during an otherwise secular vacation.

Themed spaces

Theming has been a significant tourism trend for decades. Shopping malls, amusement parks, restaurants, festivals, resorts and other tourism spaces have found theming to be an effective way of making spaces of consumption more attractive, titillating, and entertaining for tourists (Hannam & Halewood 2006; Hung, Wang, & Tang 2015; Shaw & Williams 2004). Themed environments or spaces are locations that have been intentionally planned and designed according to a specific subject matter as a way of creating a unique selling proposition that will draw visitors and other consumers. There are jail-themed restaurants, outer space-themed hotels, family fun theme parks (e.g. Disney), and traditional marketplace-themed shopping centres, to name but a few examples. This has also crept into the realm of religious tourism and is most prevalent in Christianity (Rivera, Shani, & Severt 2009; Ron & Feldman 2009; Shoval 2000).

There are more than 200 Bible-themed attractions throughout the world—in North America, Asia, Latin America and Europe (Bielo 2016). In Israel, two notable establishments have led the way for biblical theming in the Middle East and were intentionally developed to attract the lucrative Christian tourist market (Shoval 2000): the Biblical Resources Museum (Jerusalem) and Nazareth Village (Nazareth). Since its establishment more than 25 years ago, the Biblical Resources Museum (BRM) has changed locations a few times, most recently from the Jerusalem neighbourhood of Ein Kerem to its current location in LaGrange, Georgia (US), known there as the Biblical History Center. In Ein Kerem, the remaining institution is now referred to as the Bible Times Center. At the BRM, tourists visited staged examples of New Testament-period life, including agricultural practices, replicas of a crucifixion site and tomb of Jesus, as well as a simulated Last Supper, in which tour groups could participate (Ron & Timothy 2013).

To enhance the appeal of Nazareth for Protestant pilgrims, who typically stay less than two hours and only visit the Catholic Basilica of the Annunciation and the Arab bazaar, the Israeli government undertook efforts to gentrify the old Arab city, particularly in the main tourist areas (Cohen-Hattab & Shoval 2007; Gelbman & Laven 2016). This was undertaken in large part owing to the expectation of a rapid increase in Christian arrivals after the 2000 turn of the millennium (Olsen & Timothy 1999). In anticipation of the 1999–2000 millennial event and owing to the need to increase tourists' length of stay in Nazareth, Nazareth Village (NV) was founded in 2000 by a Mennonite non-profit organisation under the leadership of a local Protestant Arab (Shoval 2000). NV would become a themed Galilean village ostensibly based upon archaeological evidence of what such a place might have looked like during the time of Christ. At the staged village, tourists interact with costumed actors who herd sheep, press olive oil or winnow grain; walk along reconstructed streets; enter period buildings; visit a reconstructed synagogue; and handle replica artefacts. Visitors may also purchase a biblical meal (Ron & Timothy 2019; Shoval 2000). As Shoval (2000) predicted at the outset of the project, the majority of visitors are evangelical Protestants from the United States, with a smaller proportion coming from Europe and other areas of the world. While both BRM and NV provide 'staged' experiences that seem to satisfy the more natural needs of Protestant tourists outside the garish and alienating churchscapes of the Catholic and Orthodox shrines in Nazareth and Jerusalem, there has been considerable debate about their inauthentic representations of New Testament heritage (Ron & Timothy 2019; Shoval 2000).

While most examples of tourism theming entail deliberate efforts to theme or brand a place or activity, in the case of Israel, a unique organic landscape has developed into a kind of spontaneous 'themed environment': biblical foodscapes. Food is mentioned many times in the Bible and is in many cases a romanticised part of the holy writ—manna from heaven, turning water to wine, and the Last Supper. Research by Ron and Timothy (2013) examined a unique biblical foodscape in the Holy Land comprised of restaurants, menus, souvenirs and symbols that all depict gastronomy related to the Bible. Israel's biblical foodscape centres on the themes of the Holy Land as the Promised Land (e.g. multiple gastronomical references to the Land of Milk and Honey), obedience to the word and will of God (e.g. commodified Passover meals), the miracles and ministry of Jesus (e.g. water to wine and St Peter's fish), the Passion of Christ (e.g. Last Supper re-enactments), and the spirit of the Holy Land (e.g. Jewish foodways and ancient herbs).

Volunteering

Serving humankind is a Bible-derived principle of Christianity. Many practising Christians spend many hours each month volunteering for a variety of causes in their home communities. This frequently translates into travel specifically for volunteer purposes. Christian volunteer tourism is becoming increasingly popular in the Middle East. There are several types and contexts of Christian volunteer tourism, but only two are examined here. The first is volunteering at archaeological sites of biblical importance. This essentially started in the 1960s with the Masada excavations, which involved hundreds of volunteer tourists, some of whom were Christians who appreciated the opportunity to get 'their hands dirty' in the Holy Land (Yadin 1966). Many other excavations have begun and concluded in the intervening years, and there are several archaeological digs currently under way in Israel, Palestine, Jordan, Cyprus and Turkey that are connected to the Bible directly or indirectly. Archaeological teams actively seek volunteer participants and know that Christians are especially keen to assist in Bible-related projects. A current example is the excavation at Shiloh in Palestine, which was a site of ancient Hebrew worship and home to the famed tabernacle for a time. For many participants, digging, sifting, cleaning, organising and cataloguing are important contributions to creating new knowledge and discovering archaeological evidence of the veracity of the Bible (Ron & Timothy 2019). Volunteers pay their own travel and living expenses, as well as a programme fee, in exchange for the opportunity to work alongside archaeologists and their fellow believers (Timothy 2018a).

Staffing at Christian attractions is the other volunteer experience that is most salient in the MENA context. Working at the themed locales described above is an opportunity in which Christians share an interest. Volunteer duties range from guides and actors to behind-the-scenes maintenance and research. Nazareth Village is very dependent on short-term Christian volunteers (typically Mennonites) from Europe and North America who spend weeks or in some cases months volunteering (Ron 2009). While Nazareth Village is not considered a sacred site by most Christian visitors, it is a venue where sacred experiences can occur but is more likely to be seen as a place of learning in an 'edutaining' sort of environment that aims to depict what life might have been like in Nazareth at the time of Christ. Volunteers play a key role in delivering this message and fulfilling these goals.

Church-owned sites in MENA tend to be less dependent on volunteer tourists because they are usually staffed by church employees or local volunteers. Sites owned and operated by NGOs or private enterprises usually require more assistance by volunteer tourists. Perhaps the best example in the Holy Land is the Garden Tomb in Jerusalem. The Garden Tomb (Jerusalem) Association owns and operates this sacred place, which most Protestants revere as the site of Jesus' crucifixion, burial and resurrection. Although the Garden Tomb does have paid employees, most staff members are volunteers from Europe, particularly the United Kingdom, from a few different Christian denominations (Ron & Timothy 2019). Guiding at the garden is done exclusively by volunteers rather than outside paid guides, except in situations where an unfamiliar language is required (Ron & Feldman 2009). The guides spend weeks or months volunteering in an environment that enables their spiritual growth and satisfies their own need for a personal pilgrimage (Engberg 2017). Many of them have ministerial experience, and their main goal is to evangelise and bear witness of Christ and the Bible to other visitors (Chadwick 2003).

Hiking trails

The final product in this section is the increasingly popular trails that crisscross various parts of the Middle East (Trono & Imperiale 2018). There are many long-distance trade routes throughout the Middle East, as well as several long-distance walking trails, but the Gospel Trail and the Jesus Trail are the two most geared towards a Christian market (Collins-Kreiner & Kliot 2016). The 63km Gospel Trail was launched in 2011 by Israel's Ministry of Tourism after many years of planning. This hiking path emphasises the life of Jesus and focuses on the natural landscapes of the Galilee region, and economic development and tourism for the communities it traverses (Timothy 2018b; Timothy & Boyd 2015). During the time the Gospel Trail was being planned, the 65km Jesus Trail was established in 2007 by a non-profit partnership in Nazareth. While it also focuses on the ministry of Jesus and passes through very important New Testament localities in Galilee, it embraces a deeper ecotourism ethos, emphasising not just the natural landscapes but also the cultures and peoples encountered along the way and the social benefits of meeting locals (Dintaman & Landis 2013).

The routes begin at different localities in Nazareth and parallel one another in several spots, but they both focus on important Christian sites, even if their narrative is slightly different. The two trails have not been without controversy. Most criticism has been levelled at the Ministry of Tourism for inaugurating a Gospel Trail ostensibly as a competitor to the Jesus Trail, which was already functioning successfully (Mansfeld 2012; Timothy & Boyd 2015). Segments of the Jesus Trail pass through Arab towns and villages, while the Gospel Trail tends to avoid these, which hints at the political orientations of the two trails (Ron & Timothy 2019). More Christians utilise the Jesus Trail because it encompasses more sacred sites than the Gospel Trail (Troen & Rabineau 2014).

A third route with important associations for Christians is the Abraham Path (*Masar Ibrahim al Khalil* in Arabic), which currently extends slightly more than 1,000km through the ancient Abrahamic landscapes of several Middle Eastern countries, although only 400km have been developed and demarcated in Palestine, Israel, Jordan, Syria and Turkey (Weiss 2011). The long-distance hiking trail connects a multitude of locations that Abraham is believed to have lived in and visited. In Palestine alone, there are 266km of walking trails associated with this route (Kutulas & Awad 2016). This cultural route

> retraces the remembered journey of Abraham and his family through the cradle of civilization 4,000 years ago. Abraham's Path connects many of the world's most fabled and cherished destinations … [and] is at once a network of ancient walking paths, a place of courageous encounter across cultures, and an open-air university where people, young and old, can rediscover what connects us all.
>
> *(Weiss 2011: 529)*

The path was established in 2007, based largely on the concept of the long-distance walking route of Camino de Santiago in Europe (Weiss 2011). The Abraham Path Initiative is spearheaded by a US-based non-profit and non-religious organisation and supported by the UN Alliance of Civilizations and the World Tourism Organization. It aims to encourage walking, the appreciation of the Abraham-associated multi-religious heritage of the Middle East, to promote the native hospitality of the region, develop networks of regional partners, provide employment and encourage economic development through sustainable tourism, and create a linear space where different peoples can meet and learn from one another (Isaac 2018; Kutulas & Awad 2016). Owing to safety concerns and political instability at the time of writing, many areas of the route (e.g. in Syria and Iraq) are off-limits to tourists and other hikers. However, the trail has considerable tourism potential amongst Christians in Palestine, Israel, Jordan and Turkey.

Dissonance

Dissonance reflects a lack of harmony between players or stakeholders and is inherently connected to human heritage (Hartmann 2014; Timothy 2011; Timothy & Boyd 2003; Tunbridge & Ashworth 1996), including religion (Collins-Kreiner, Shmueli, & Ben Gal 2013; Ben Gal, Collins-Kreiner, & Shmueli 2015). Heritage dissonance in religious contexts is manifested in a wide variety of ways as regards tourism in the Middle East. In this chapter, however, it is examined within the context of denominational differences, conflicts in sacred space, and solidary tourism.

Denominational differences

Christianity is comprised of hundreds of different denominations or sects, each one varying slightly or significantly, based upon doctrinal differences and diverging interpretations of the Bible. These denominational variations translate into different travel patterns and preferences regarding the Holy Land and broader Middle East. While Christians of all denominations tend to visit various anchor sites in the Holy Land, including the Church of the Nativity in Bethlehem, the Church of the Holy Sepulchre in Jerusalem, and various sites around the Sea of Galilee, several individual denominations have their own sacred spaces throughout the Middle East that they prefer to visit but which might not attract Christians of other denominations. Some believers feel that sites of other churches are inauthentic or unholy. As well, the ornateness of many Catholic and Orthodox churches in the Holy Land deters many Protestant and neoteric Christian denominations, who prefer simpler, more natural locations that are much less developed (Belhassen, Caton, & Stewart 2008; Collins-Kreiner & Kliot 2000; Feldman & Ron 2011; Ron & Feldman 2009).

There are several places in Israel and Palestine where Orthodox churches and the Catholic Church 'compete' for authentic localities. In Nazareth, for example, there are three churches of the annunciation—the Catholic Basilica of the Annunciation, the Greek Orthodox Church of the Annunciation, and the Maronite Church of the Annunciation. In addition to these pilgrimage sites, several other denominations have built representative churches, including the Christ Anglican Church, the Greek Catholic Church, and the Upper Nazareth Baptist Church. The most prominent of these as a tourist attraction is the Basilica, but Baptists, Maronites and Greek Catholics are equally likely to visit their own churches in the same city.

Eastern Orthodox Christians commonly visit Jerusalem, Bethlehem, Istanbul, Antioch, Meteora, Mount Athos and Mount Sinai, and pay particular homage at the various Orthodox churches in these locations. Saint Catherine's Monastery in Egypt is one of the earliest operational Christian monasteries in the world and is heavily venerated by all of the various Eastern Orthodox Churches (Shackley 1998, 2001). Many national Orthodox churches (e.g. Greek Orthodox, Georgian Orthodox and Russian Orthodox) have their own establishments in Jerusalem, which become the centres of pilgrimage for people of those national faiths.

Like their Eastern Orthodox counterparts, Oriental Orthodox Christians (Armenian, Coptic, Ethiopian and Syrian Orthodox) are also keen Holy Land visitors, although the Copts of Egypt rarely visit sites in Israel owing to travel restrictions and security concerns. They are avid pilgrims within their own country, however, and regularly visit sacred shrines in Cairo and throughout the Nile Valley. The same is true of Orthodox Iraqi and Syrian Christians who tend to travel within their own countries, occasionally visiting Israel and Palestine when they are permitted to do so.

There are some significant differences between Roman Catholic and Orthodox pilgrimages to the Middle East. Catholics tend to focus more on the act of pilgrimage—the way and means of getting to their sacred destination—while Orthodox pilgrims focus more on the destination with its shrines, relics and place-bound spiritual powers (Della Dora, Maddrell, & Scafi 2015). Catholics and Protestant groups regularly participate in 'In the Footsteps of Jesus' tours in the Holy Land, and many Protestant groups participate in 'In the Footsteps of Paul' tours and cruises that take in various sites in Turkey and Greece. Evangelical Protestant groups frequently seek re-baptism in the Jordan River, while many other sects do not.

In common with other Christians, members of the Church of Jesus Christ of Latter-day Saints (LDS or Mormons) actively travel to the Holy Land to walk in the footsteps of Jesus and to feel the spirit of the places associated with his life and ministry (Guter 2006; Olsen 2006).

Members of the Church of Jesus Christ of Latter-day Saints visit all of the core Christian sites in Israel and Palestine, and many in Jordan and Egypt. However, like some Protestant churches, there are a few unique Latter-day Saint localities that other denominations have little interest in visiting. The most important of these is the Brigham Young University Jerusalem campus where students study Hebrew, Arabic, biblical history and Middle East History (Olsen & Guelke 2004). Some church-specific tour packages also include visits to the Orson Hyde Memorial Garden on the Mount of Olives, where in 1841, the church leader dedicated the country for the gathering of Israel; the Orson Hyde Square in Netanya; the graves of nineteenth-century missionaries who died in Haifa; and the Lehi Cave in Judea, which some scholars maintain may be related to early accounts in the Book of Mormon (Chadwick 2009; Ron & Timothy 2019).

Christian spatial cacophony in Jerusalem

As several chapters in this book have made perfectly clear, conflict is a part of everyday life in parts of MENA. It is no less so within the bounds of Christianity. Two intra-Christian spaces of discord are described here. The first of these is the dissonance between the two localities defined as the place of crucifixion and entombment of Jesus Christ. The second is the conflicted sacred space within the Church of the Holy Sepulchre.

While it does not present a great deal of contention on the ground, two locations in Jerusalem are considered possible sites of Jesus' crucifixion and entombment. The first is an area of rocky outcrops over which the Church of the Holy Sepulchre was built originally in the fourth century CE but was destroyed in 1009 and reconstructed in the same location in 1048. The church remains much as it did in the eleventh century and is venerated by Catholics and Eastern Orthodox faithful as the location of Golgotha and Tomb of Joseph of Arimathea, which is where Jesus is believed to have been laid to rest and from which he resurrected (Biddle, Avni, Seligman, & Winter 2000). Not far away (approximately 600 metres) from the Church of the Holy Sepulchre is the Garden Tomb, which is considered by most Protestant and neoteric Christian groups to be the more authentic location of these events. Most Protestant tour groups visit both locations, although Roman Catholics and Orthodox Christians rarely visit the Garden Tomb. While they visit the Church of the Holy Sepulchre, many Protestants are displeased with the flamboyant style of the church and prefer the more unspoiled and natural area of the Garden Tomb and nearby Golgotha (Ron 2010).

Even within the single space of the Church of the Holy Sepulchre, there are underlying spatially oriented tensions between denominations, particularly between Ethiopian and Coptic Christians. Jurisdiction over the building is shared between several sects—Coptic Orthodox, Syriac Orthodox, Greek Orthodox, Roman Catholic, Ethiopian Tewahedo Orthodox and Armenian Apostolic churches—with each one being responsible for the upkeep of specific areas and shrines inside the building and various liturgical elements in its own space (Biddle, Avni, Seligman, & Winter 2000). This multi-sectoral control model has resulted in years of conflict between the sects, with some blocking access by others and physical fights breaking out due to perceptions of encroachment (Cohen-Hattab & Shoval 2015; Emmett 1997; Timothy & Emmett 2014; Tsourous 2018).

Solidarity visits

Solidarity tourism entails people or groups of people travelling to demonstrate unity for a cause and to visit the people whom they support. Palestine and Israel provide a rich laboratory for the development of politically and religiously motivated solidarity tourism. In the context of

MENA, the most salient show of solidarity is between various Christian organisations and the Palestinians or the Israelis (Brin 2006; Isaac 2013; Troen & Rabineau 2014). Many evangelical Christians from North America and Europe support the cause of Israel and Zionism. These are known as Christian Zionists, and they see their Holy Land tours not only as a pilgrimage of faith but also as outward support for the State of Israel (Feldman 2011; Leppäkari 2015; Timothy & Emmett 2014). In their minds, the foundation of Israel in 1948 was a miraculous fulfilment of biblical prophecy, which they espouse and support through their activities and tour itineraries (Bajc 2007; Belhassen 2009; Shapiro 2008). Evangelical unity with Israel deepens even further during times of political calamities, when visits by solidarity Christians increase while other tourist arrivals decline (Collins-Kreiner, Kliot, Mansfeld, & Sagi 2006; Ron & Timothy 2019).

Other Christian factions are more supportive of the Christian Palestinians of Jerusalem and Bethlehem. These factions tend to be more associated with traditional Protestant denominations, such as Lutherans, Anglicans and Presbyterians. They seek to meet with and support the 'Living Stones' of Palestine (Ron 2009). The term 'Living Stones' refers to the Christian Arabs who are detained behind the security walls and whom Israeli security and human mobility policies have disadvantaged. 'Meet the stones' itineraries give supportive Christians occasions to interact with the Arab Christians of Palestine, worship with them, and provide moral and financial support (Kassis, Solomon, & Higgins-Desbiolles 2016).

Conclusion

Despite prevailing security concerns, Christian tourism in MENA continues to thrive. This can be explained in several ways. First, there are no other feasible alternatives elsewhere. While the Christian market is expanding its horizons into other products, such as biblical cruises and package tours in Turkey, Greece and Italy, as well as solidarity tours in places such as China, the Holy Land is irreplaceable as the fulcrum of Christianity. Second, the region has learned to be resilient in the face of conflict. Many countries have established methods for a quick recovery (Avraham 2015). Third, there is a strong commitment to this religious niche by individuals, service providers, companies and national governments. Finally, the distinction between safe and unsafe destinations is less relevant today than it was in the past. Security concerns are more normative and commonplace in more places today, so travellers realise they might encounter unsafe situations anywhere, not just in the Middle East.

What will the face of Christian tourism in MENA look like in the near future? According to all standard indicators, it will continue to grow, but it will likely evolve to adapt to changing markets and destination situations. Package tours will combine disparate regions with the Holy Land. For instance, many tour operators are already planning to combine the famous Oberammergau Passion Play in 2020 in Germany with visits to the Holy Land. It is also likely that numbers of FIT (foreign independent travellers or free independent travellers) tourists will continue to rise in Israel and Palestine, as will traditional package tours. The competitive environment of the aviation sector also has a bearing on Christian travel and will play an important role in its growth. The airlines of Turkey, Greece and Italy are reaching out to North American Christian groups and offering layovers in non-Holy Land biblical destinations such as Rome and Athens.

Many localities in MENA are sacred amongst Christians. From a tourism perspective, these are primarily in Israel, Palestine, Jordan, Egypt and Turkey, which are visited regularly. However, Lebanon, Iraq and Syria are also part of the broader Bible-based Holy Land. The latter three countries have considerable potential for Christian tourism development because they possess biblical assets that would attract the Christian market and the narratives to go with it. Civil unrest in Lebanon, terrorist threats, and the ongoing wars in Iraq and Syria, however, presently preclude the development of tourism in these countries (Farra-Haddad 2015; Poujeau 2012).

Christian tourism in the Middle East is simultaneously simple and complex. It involves specific destinations and products common to most denominations. However, it is also characterised by inter-sectoral dissonance that is manifested in denominational spatial and experiential differences, spatial disharmony, and solidary either with the Palestinians or the Israelis but rarely both.

References

Avraham, E. (2015) 'Destination image repair during crisis: Attracting tourism during the Arab Spring uprisings', *Tourism Management*, 47: 224–232.

Bajc, V. (2007) 'Creating ritual through narrative, place and performance in Evangelical Protestant pilgrimage in the Holy Land', *Mobilities*, 2(3): 395–412.

Belhassen, Y. (2009) 'Fundamentalist Christian pilgrimages as a political and cultural force', *Journal of Heritage Tourism*, 4(2): 131–144.

Belhassen, Y., Caton, K., & Stewart, W.P. (2008) 'The search for authenticity in the pilgrim experience', *Annals of Tourism Research*, 35(3): 668–689.

Ben Gal, M., Collins-Kreiner, N., & Shmueli, D. F. (2015) 'Framing spatial-religious conflicts: The case of Mormon development in Jerusalem', *Tijdschrift voor Economische en Sociale Geografie*, 106(5): 588–607.

Biddle, M., Avni, G., Seligman, J., & Winter, T. (2000) *The Church of the Holy Sepulchre*. New York: Rizzoli.

Bielo, J.S. (2016) 'Materialising the Bible: Ethnographic methods for the consumption process', *Practical Matters Journal*, 9: 54–69.

Brin, E. (2006) 'Politically-oriented tourism in Jerusalem', *Tourist Studies*, 6(3): 215–243.

Chadwick, J.R. (2003) 'Revisiting Golgotha and the Garden Tomb', *The Religious Educator*, 4(1): 13–48.

Chadwick, J.R. (2009) 'Khirbet Beit Lei and the Book of Mormon: An archaeologist's evaluation', *The Religious Educator*, 10(3): 17–48.

Cohen-Hattab, K., & Shoval, N. (2007) 'Tourism development and cultural conflict: The case of "Nazareth 2000"', *Social & Cultural Geography*, 8(5): 701–717.

Cohen-Hattab, K., & Shoval, N. (2015) *Tourism, Religion and Pilgrimage in Jerusalem*. London: Routledge.

Collins-Kreiner, N., & Kliot, N. (2000) 'Pilgrimage tourism in the Holy Land: The behavioral characteristics of Christian pilgrims', *GeoJournal*, 50: 55–67.

Collins-Kreiner, N., & Kliot, N. (2016) 'Particularism vs. universalism in hiking tourism', *Annals of Tourism Research*, 56: 132–137.

Collins-Kreiner, N., Kliot, N., Mansfeld, Y., & Sagi, K. (2006) *Christian Tourism to the Holy Land: Pilgrimage During Security Crisis*. Aldershot: Ashgate.

Collins-Kreiner, N., Shmueli, D. F., & Ben Gal, M. (2013) 'Spatial transgression of new religious sites in Israel', *Applied Geography*, 40: 103–114.

Della Dora, V., Maddrell, A., & Scafi, A. (2015) 'Sacred crossroads: Landscape and aesthetics in contemporary Christian pilgrimage', in S. Brunn (ed.), *The Changing World Religious Map: Sacred Places, Identities, Practices and Politics* (pp. 745–765). Dordrecht: Springer.

Dintaman, A., & Landis, D. (2013) *Hiking the Jesus Trail and Other Biblical Walks in the Galilee*, 2nd edn. Harleysville, PA: Village to Village Press.

Egresi, I., Bayram, B., & Kara, F. (2012) 'Tourism at religious sites: A case from Mardin, Turkey', *Geographica Timisiensis*, 21(1): 5–15.

Emmett, C.F. (1997) 'The status quo solution for Jerusalem', *Journal of Palestine Studies*, 26(2): 16–28.

Engberg, A. (2017) 'Ambassadors for the kingdom: Evangelical volunteers in Israel as long-term pilgrims', in M. Leppäkari, & K. Griffin (eds), *Pilgrimage and Tourism to Holy Cities* (pp. 156–170). Wallingford: CAB International.

Farra-Haddad, N. (2015) 'Pilgrimage toward south Lebanon: Holy places relocating Lebanon as part of the Holy Land', in R. Raj, & K. Griffin (eds), *Religious Tourism and Pilgrimage Management*, 2nd edn (pp. 279–298). Wallingford: CAB International.

Feldman, J. (2011) 'Abraham the settler, Jesus the refugee: Contemporary conflict and Christianity on the road to Bethlehem', *History & Memory*, 23(1): 62–95.

Feldman, J., & Ron, A.S. (2011) 'American Holy Land: Orientalism, Disneyization, and the Evangelical gaze', in B. Schnepel, G. Brands, & H. Schönig (eds), *Orient-Orientalistik–Orientalismus: Geschichte und Aktualität einer Debatte* (pp. 151–176). Bielefeld: Verlag.

Gelbman, A., & Laven, D. (2016) 'Re-envisioning community-based heritage tourism in the old city of Nazareth', *Journal of Heritage Tourism*, 11(2): 105–125.

Guter, Y. (2006) 'Pilgrims "Communitas" in the Holy Land: The case of Mormon pilgrimage', in M. Poorthuis, & J. Schwartz (eds), *A Holy People: Jewish and Christian Perspectives on Religious Community* (pp. 337–348). Leiden: Brill.

Hannam, K., & Halewood, C. (2006) 'European Viking themed festivals: An expression of identity', *Journal of Heritage Tourism*, 1(1): 17–31.

Harpur, J. (2002) *Sacred Tracks: 2000 Years of Christian Pilgrimage*. Berkeley, CA: University of California Press.

Hartmann, R. (2014) 'Dark tourism, thanatourism, and dissonance in heritage tourism management: New directions in contemporary tourism research', *Journal of Heritage Tourism*, 9(2): 166–182.

Hobbs, J.J. (1992) 'Sacred space and touristic development at Jebel Musa (Mt Sinai), Egypt', *Journal of Cultural Geography*, 12(2): 99–113.

Hung, K., Wang, S., & Tang, C. (2015) 'Understanding the normative expectations of customers toward Buddhism-themed hotels: A revisit of service quality', *International Journal of Contemporary Hospitality Management*, 27(7): 1409–1441.

Isaac, R.K. (2013) 'Palestine tourism under occupation', in R. Butler, & W. Suntikul (eds), *Tourism and War* (pp. 143–157). London: Routledge.

Isaac, R.K. (2016) 'Pilgrimage tourism to Palestine', in R.K. Isaac, C.M. Hall, & F. Higgins-Desbiolles (eds), *The Politics and Power of Tourism in Palestine* (pp. 124–136). London: Routledge.

Isaac, R.K. (2018) 'Taking you home: The Masar Ibrahim Al-Khalil in Palestine', in C.M. Hall, Y. Ram, & N. Shoval (eds), *The Routledge International Handbook of Walking* (pp. 712–183). London: Routledge.

Kaell, H. (2014) *Walking Where Jesus Walked: American Christians and Holy Land Pilgrimage*. New York: New York University Press.

Kassis, R., Solomon, R., & Higgins-Desbiolles, F. (2016) 'Solidarity tourism in Palestine: The alternative tourism group of Palestine as a catalyzing instrument of resistance', in R.K. Isaac, C.M. Hall, & F. Higgins-Desbiolles (eds), *The Politics and Power of Tourism in Palestine* (pp. 37–53). London: Routledge.

Kutulas, Y., & Awad, M. (2016) 'Bike and hike in Palestine', in R.K. Isaac, C.M. Hall, & F. Higgins-Desbiolles (eds), *The Politics and Power of Tourism in Palestine* (pp. 53–62). London: Routledge.

Leppäkari, M. (2015) 'Nordic pilgrimage to Israel: A case of Christian Zionism', in R. Raj, & K. Griffin (eds), *Religious Tourism and Pilgrimage Management*, 2nd edn (pp. 205–217). Wallingford: CAB International.

Mansfeld, Y. (2012) 'The role of religious institutions in sustainable tourism development and operation'. Paper presented at the Second International Conference on Sustainable Religious Tourism: Commandments, Obstacles and Challenges, 28 October Lecce, Italy.

Mustafa, M.H. (2014) 'Tourism development at the Baptism Site of Jesus Christ, Jordan: Residents' perspectives', *Journal of Heritage Tourism*, 9(1): 75–83.

Olsen, D.H. (2006) 'Tourism and informal pilgrimage among the Latter-day Saints', in D.J. Timothy, & D.H. Olsen (eds), *Tourism, Religion and Spiritual Journeys* (pp. 256–270). London: Routledge.

Olsen, D.H., & Guelke, J.K. (2004) 'Spatial transgression and the BYU Jerusalem Center controversy', *The Professional Geographer*, 56(4): 503–515.

Olsen, D.H., & Timothy, D.J. (1999) 'Tourism 2000: Selling the millennium', *Tourism Management*, 20(4): 389–392.

Poujeau, A. (2012) 'Sharing the *Baraka* of the saints: Pluridenominational visits to the Christian monasteries in Syria', in D. Albera, & M. Couroueli (eds), *Sharing Sacred Spaces in the Mediterranean: Christians, Muslims, and Jews at Shrines and Sanctuaries* (pp. 202–218). Bloomington, IN: Indiana University Press.

Rivera, M.A., Shani, A., & Severt, D. (2009) 'Perceptions of service attributes in a religious theme site: An importance-satisfaction analysis', *Journal of Heritage Tourism*, 4(3): 227–243.

Ron, A.S. (2009) 'Towards a typological model of contemporary Christian travel', *Journal of Heritage Tourism*, 4(4): 287–297.

Ron, A.S. (2010) 'Holy Land Protestant themed environments and the spiritual experience', in J. Schlehe, M. Uike-Bormann, C. Oesterle, & W. Hochbruck (eds), *Staging the Past: Themed Environments in Transcultural Perspectives* (pp. 111–133). Bielefeld, Germany: Verlag.

Ron, A.S., & Feldman, J. (2009) 'From spots to themed sites—the evolution of the Protestant Holy Land', *Journal of Heritage Tourism*, 4(3): 201–216.

Ron, A.S., & Timothy, D.J. (2013) 'The Land of Milk and Honey: Biblical foods, heritage and Holy Land tourism', *Journal of Heritage Tourism*, 8(2–3): 234–247.

Ron, A.S., & Timothy, D.J. (2019) *Contemporary Christian Travel: Pilgrimage, Practice, and Place*. Bristol: Channel View Publications.

Shackley, M. (1998) 'A golden calf in sacred space? The future of St Katherine's Monastery, Mount Sinai (Egypt)', *International Journal of Heritage Studies*, 4(3–4): 124–134.

Shackley, M. (2001) *Managing Sacred Sites: Service Provision and Visitor Experience*. London: Continuum.

Shapiro, F.L. (2008) 'To the apple of God's eye: Christian Zionist travel to Israel', *Journal of Contemporary Religion*, 23(3): 307–320.

Shaw, G., & Williams, A.M. (2004) *Tourism and Tourism Spaces*. London: Sage.

Shoval, N. (2000) 'Commodification and theming of the sacred: Changing patterns of tourist consumption in the "Holy Land"', in M. Gottdiener (ed.), *New Forms of Consumption: Consumers, Culture and Commodification* (pp. 251–263). Boulder, CO: Rowman and Littlefield.

Timothy, D.J. (2011) *Cultural Heritage and Tourism: An Introduction*. Bristol: Channel View Publications.

Timothy, D.J. (2018a) 'Producing and consuming heritage tourism: Recent trends', in S. Gmelch, & A. Kaul (eds), *Tourists and Tourism: A Reader*, 3rd edn (pp. 167–178). Long Grove, IL: Waveland Press.

Timothy, D.J. (2018b) 'Cultural routes: Tourist destinations and tools for development', in D.H. Olsen & A. Trono (eds), *Religious Pilgrimage Routes and Trails: Sustainable Development and Management* (pp. 27–37). Wallingford: CAB International.

Timothy, D.J., & Boyd, S.W. (2003) *Heritage Tourism*. Harlow: Prentice Hall.

Timothy, D.J., & Boyd, S.W. (2015) *Tourism and Trails: Cultural, Ecological and Management Issues*. Bristol: Channel View Publications.

Timothy, D.J., & Emmett, C.F. (2014) 'Jerusalem, tourism, and the politics of heritage', in M. Adelman, & M.F. Elman (eds), *Jerusalem: Conflict & Cooperation in a Contested City* (pp. 276–290). Syracuse, NY: Syracuse University Press.

Timothy, D.J., & Ron, A.S. (2016) 'Religious heritage, spiritual aliment and food for the soul', in D.J. Timothy (ed.), *Heritage Cuisines: Traditions, Identities and Tourism* (pp. 104–118). London: Routledge.

Troen, I., & Rabineau, S. (2014) 'Competing concepts of land in Eretz Israel', *Israel Studies*, 19(2): 162–186.

Trono, A., & Imperiale, M.L. (2018) 'The ways to Jerusalem: Maritime cultural and pilgrimage routes', in D.H. Olsen, & A. Trono (eds), *Religious Pilgrimage Routes and Trails: Sustainable Development and Management* (pp. 138–149). Wallingford: CAB International.

Tsourous, G. (2018) 'Boundaries and borders: Choreographies among the Rum Orthodox of Old City Jerusalem'. Unpublished PhD thesis, University of Kent, United Kingdom.

Tunbridge, J.E., & Ashworth, G.J. (1996) *Dissonant Heritage: The Management of the Past as a Resource in Conflict*. Chichester: Wiley.

Turner, V.W., & Turner, E. (1978) *Image and Pilgrimage in Christian Culture: Anthropological Perspective*. New York: Columbia University Press.

Weiss, J. (2011) 'Abraham's Path: The path of a thousand negotiations', in S.A. Nan, Z.C. Mampilly, & A. Bartoli (eds), *Peacemaking: From Practice to Theory, Volume 1* (pp. 529–543). Santa Barbara, CA: Praeger.

Yadin, Y. (1966) *Masada: Herod's Fortress and the Zealots' Last Stand*. London: Widenfeld and Nicolson.

PART IV

Natural and environmental challenges

13

MENA AS A CRITICAL MEETING POINT BETWEEN TOURISM AND WATER RESOURCES

Nurit Kliot

Introduction

The Middle East and North Africa covers a surface area of approximately 11.1 million km^2 or about 8 per cent of the Earth's area, and as of 2015 is home to 411 million people. Eighty-five per cent of the area is desert, and the region has about 0.7 per cent of the world's available fresh water resources. MENA is classified as a water-scarce region and with forthcoming climate changes, it will become even drier (Droogers et al. 2012; World Bank 2007).

Water scarcity in MENA is not solely an outcome of poor supply. It is largely shaped by socio-economic factors and is related to the region's politics and decision-making processes. The most important factor affecting present and future MENA societies, economies and water challenges is high population growth. The average annual population growth for MENA was 2.08 per cent or 8,371,000 people during 2013–2014. Population growth and the need to provide water to all sectors of the economy to meet their basic requirements has led to the depletion of renewable water resources at the alarming rate of over 338 per cent of available water (World Bank 2012). Water is still allocated for low-value uses, even as higher-value needs remain unmet (World Bank 2007). The region's countries are challenged to increase agricultural production to sustain fast-growing population rates; about 81 per cent of total water resources are apportioned to agriculture. Inefficiencies in agriculture, with significant water losses and with subsidies obscure the true value of water as a commodity (World Bank 2012). Non-sustainable uses of water are also prevalent in the domestic sector (9 per cent of water use) and industry (7 per cent of water use).

Tourism is a relative newcomer to MENA and its importance is expanding rapidly, with 70 million tourists having visited the region in 2014 (UNWTO 2015). The region's share of total international tourism is 6 per cent (MENA Tourism and Hospitality Report 2014), and the total contribution of tourism to the GDP was 7.4 per cent for the Middle East and 11.1 per cent for North Africa in 2014. However, MENA experiences inordinate fluctuations in tourism as a result of political instability, and the level of the sector's contribution to the economy depends ultimately on peace and stability in the region (UNWTO 2015).

This chapter is divided into two major sections: water resources and tourism and water resources. The conceptual framework adopted is broad and integrates social, economic and political factors that affect the water–tourism relationship. The water resources section examines water shortages, use and options for increasing the supply. The tourism and water resources section focuses on how tourism utilises hydro resources and the ways in which it impacts the supply and demand in the region.

Water resources in MENA

Some 86 per cent of MENA's area is desert, and the region has about 0.7 per cent of the world's available fresh water resources. All countries in MENA fall into a group that is defined by highly variable and/or low rainfall (World Bank 2007), both temporally and geographically (Droogers et al. 2012: 3103). Based on climatic changes, precipitation in the region is expected to decrease by between 5 and 30 per cent in the near future. Temperatures are expected to rise, leading to an increase in evaporation and evapotranspiration. The projected trends indicate increases in floods and droughts, and increased frequency of weather-related natural disasters (Farajallah 2012; Gregoire 2012; World Bank 2012). However, Droogers et al. (2012) show that 22 per cent of the water shortage (based on climate projections for 2001–2010 and 2041–2050) can be attributed to climate change and 78 per cent to changes in socio-economic factors (Droogers et al. 2012).

Water scarcity

In 1976, Falkenmark and Lind first defined quantitative indicators of water scarcity. Water stress prevails when annual water supplies drop below 1,700 m^3 per person per year. At levels between 1,700 and 1,000 m^3 of water per person per year, periodic or limited water shortages can be expected. When a country falls below 1,000 m^3 per person per year, it then faces water scarcity (Falkenmark & Lind 1976). It is often extremely difficult to assess whether water scarcity is caused by insufficient supply or excessive demand (Hadjikakou, Chenoweth, & Miller 2013: 548). The former is conceptualised as a physical scarcity (first order scarcity), while the latter is a scarcity of organisational capacity, namely lack of adaptive capacity including infrastructure and water management with which to manage and distribute water resources effectively (second order scarcity) (Tapper, Hadjikakou, Noble, & Jenkinson 2011: 8).

As noted above, MENA has about 0.7 per cent of the world's available fresh water resources (FAO 2016). Today's average per capita water availability in the region is slightly above the physical water scarcity limit, at about 1,076 m^3 per person per year, compared to the world average of approximately 8,500 m^3 per person per year (Droogers et al. 2012). The amount of fresh water available to citizens of MENA was halved from 3,000 m^3 per capita in 1975 to 1,500 m^3 per capita in 2001 and then to 1,000 m^3 per capita in 2010. Predictions indicate it will drop to 550 m^3 per capita by 2050 (World Bank 2007).

One explanation for this process of degradation of water resources can be found in the following alarming data. The World Bank reported that the average national percentage of total renewable water resources withdrawn in MENA was nearly 338 per cent for the period 1998–2002 (Farajallah 2012; World Bank 2007). The severity of the water situation is reflected in the data presented in Table 13.1.

The table indicates that more than half of the countries in MENA withdraw their renewable water resources at the alarming rate of well over 1,000 per cent of available water, on average (Arab Sustainable Development Report 2015). As a result of excess water use, many countries in MENA experience both water stress and water scarcity which, as noted above, will be

Table 13.1 Water resources in MENA: Supply and demand

Countries	Total water withdrawal million m³	Year	Water withdrawal as % of total actual renewable water resources	Year	Per capita withdrawal, m³ per year	Year	Average water stress 2020–2030 per capita per person, m³
Algeria	8.425	2012	67%		161	2001	200–500
Bahrain	357.400	2003	219.8%	2003	442	2003	< 200
Egypt	78.000	2010	127.0%	2010	809	2000	200–500
Iran	93.300	2004	67.7%	2004	1243	2004	
Iraq	66.000	2000	87.3%	2000	2097	2000	< 200
Israel	1.954	2004	102%	2004	268	2004	200–500
Jordan	0.940.900	2005	99.4%	2005	145	2005	< 200
Kuwait	913.200	2002	2465%	2002	299	2002	< 200
Lebanon	1.310	2005	28%	2005	308	2005	
Libya	5.830	2012	N.A.	N.A.	657	2000	501–1000
Morocco	10.500	2010	36%	2010	389	2000	< 200
Oman	1.321	2003	87%		455	2003	< 200
Palestinian Authority					> 95	2005	
West Bank	0.157	2000	20.5%	2000			
Gaza	10.071	2005	187%	2000			
Qatar	444.000	2005	455%	2005	294	2005	< 200
Saudi Arabia	23.666	2006	943%	2006	902	2006	< 200
Syria	16.690	2003	99%	2003	746	2005	501–1000
Tunisia	3.305	2011	70%	2011	275	2000	< 200
Turkey	40.100	2003	19%	2003	530	2003	
UAE	3.998	2005	2032%	2003			< 200
Yemen	3.400	2000	161%	2000			< 200

Sources: Compiled from data in FAO-AQUASTAT 2016; The Pacific Institute 2014; World Bank 2012.

exacerbated in the near future. The FAO regards renewable water availability levels of less than 1,000 m³ per person per year as a severe constraint to socio-economic development and environmental sustainability.

Likewise, climate change will affect MENA water resources. For the period 2010–2050, it is clear that total internal renewable water and recharge will show a significant decline. This comes from the combined effect of changes in precipitation and evapotranspiration (Droogers et al. 2012: 3107). Declines in the average total of renewable MENA water resources is calculated at a rate of 0.6 km³ per year until 2050. The largest decreases are seen in Jordan (-98 per cent), Oman (-46 per cent), Saudi Arabia (-36 per cent) and Morocco (-33 per cent) (Droogers et al. 2012: 3108). Altogether, precipitation in MENA is expected to decrease between 5 and 30 per cent by 2050. These projected trends indicate increases in floods and droughts and increased frequency of weather-related natural disasters (Farajallah 2012; Gregoire 2012; World Bank 2012).

Politics and water resources policies

In a situation of extreme water scarcity, political decision-making in MENA impacts both the supply of, and demand for, water resources. However, as Hadjikakou et al. (2013) note, it is often extremely difficult to assess whether water scarcity is caused by insufficient supply or excess demand (Hadjikakou et al. 2013: 548). In this chapter, the definition of 'political decision-making' is very broad and includes the inability, reluctance or refusal of governments to take affirmative action and implement policies such as water pricing, policies to curtail water losses and inefficiencies in water use and allocation. MENA national policies or absence of policies correspond well to Becken's (2014: 19) observation about whether water is 'common' or a 'commodity'.

Management of water resources

The first political issue in the management of MENA water resources arises from the World Bank's statement that 'water is very poorly managed in MENA' (World Bank 2012: xiii). Inefficiencies are notorious in agriculture, where irrigation consumes up to 81 per cent of extracted water (with water loss of 50–60 per cent). Similarly, municipal and industrial water supply systems have abnormally high losses (30–50 per cent), and most utilities are financially unsustainable (World Bank 2012).

Poor governance and other political issues affect the natural water scarcity in the North African states (Tapper et al. 2011). Far-reaching efficiency measures are required in all MENA countries if they want to maintain food-security policies to feed their growing populations (Droogers et al. 2012). As mentioned above, many MENA countries have adopted policies of over-extraction of their renewable water resources, a process which destroys those resources beyond repair (FAO 2013; Farajallah 2012; World Bank 2007).

Over-extraction of water and allocating most of the water for irrigation are political policies in all MENA countries in which a significant portion of the labour force engages in agriculture. Various observers agree about the policies MENA countries need to adopt. First, economic reforms are needed outside the water sector. This refers to policies that control water use such as agricultural pricing, trade, energy and public finance (World Bank 2007). The region needs integrated water management, such as the use of aquifer storage and recovery technology to increase reliability, and an increase in wastewater treatment and reuse, which are currently almost negligible. Most importantly, proper water pricing is the most effective way to manage water demand, reduce losses in distribution, and even reduce the cost of desalination. Improved investments in the water sector, and a preference for better management, should place greater emphasis on the demand for water than on investments in engineering projects and more desalination capacity to produce water that is costlier than water from natural sources or by reducing water losses.

Competition over scarce water resources: Sectoral demand and supply

Competition for scarce water resources and conflicts that result from this competition are already observable in MENA (Dolatyar & Gray 2000; Hall, Timothy, & Duval 2004). Currently, nearly 75 per cent of the water resources in MENA are allocated to agriculture, 22 per cent to domestic use and 3.5 per cent to industry (FAO 2013). Water use in tourism is included in domestic use. In 2000, the water demand–supply gap for MENA was 50 km^3 and it is expected to grow to 150 km^3 in 2050 (Droogers et al. 2012: 3102).

Conflicts and disputes over water use can occur in three spatio-geographical levels: between countries, amongst sectors (agriculture, domestic, industry and tourism) and locally—often between local communities and tourism developments. This is related to the disparity in water allocation to different users (Becken 2014; Gössling et al. 2012; Eurostat European Commission

2009). The combination of growing populations, demand for water for industry and tourism, and an increasingly unpredictable water supply, combined with pre-existing political and religious tensions, makes the Middle East particularly vulnerable to water security issues (Dolatyar & Gray 2000; Gössling et al. 2012; Hall et al. 2004).

In high season (peak water use season—mostly during the summer) conflicts can arise between the different sectors using water resources, such as agriculture, hydroelectric production and household consumption (Eurostat European Commission 2009). In coastal areas, a general decrease in water availability, risks of increased evaporation, depletion of resources and the salinity of coastal aquifers may lead to possible conflicts between the local population and the tourism sector over access to water (Eurostat European Commission 2009). Becken (2014: 19) shows that the potential for conflict over water access and in areas where it is scarce could be favourably biased towards commercial consumers, such as hotels, at the expense of smaller operators or the local community. Similarly, Gössling et al. (2012: 10) observed that where tourism-related fresh water demand is significant, the sector can add considerable pressure on available fresh water resources, particularly when those are concentrated in regions with few or no fossil water resources, low aquifer renewal rates and few or no surface water resources. In such areas, tourism-related water consumption may also compete with local demand. Another consideration within the framework of water resource competition is economic factors such as tourism as a source of foreign exchange revenue and a contributor to employment and GDP. Table 13.2 presents the economic performance of two competing sectors in MENA: agriculture and tourism.

The contribution of tourism to total exports in the MENA states is significant: 9.7 per cent in Bahrain, 20.7 per cent in Egypt, 6.5 per cent in Israel, 21.2 per cent in Morocco, 3.7 per cent in Saudi Arabia, 9.1 per cent in Tunisia, 17.7 per cent in Turkey and 6.7 per cent in UAE (UNWTO Yearbook 2016; World Travel and Tourism Council 2015). For the very small amount of water it uses, tourism in MENA is highly profitable economically as reflected in its contribution to GDP, employment and foreign exchange. Agriculture is undoubtedly an

Table 13.2 Economic indicators of agriculture and tourism sectors in selected MENA countries

Countries	Contribution of sector to GDP		Contribution to employment		Water withdrawal as % of total water use		
	Agriculture	Tourism	Agriculture	Tourism	Agriculture	Tourism	MCM*
Bahrain	0.3%	10.6%	1%	10.2%	45%	0.22%	(18.70)
Egypt	14.6%	11.4%	29.6%	10.5%	86%	0.03%	(19.79)
Israel	2.4%	7.0%	1.1%	7.4%	58%	0.04%	(8.56)
Morocco	14.0%	17.5%	39.1%	15.6%	88%	0.08%	(0.52)
Saudi Arabia	2.3%	8.0%	6.7%	11.4%	88%	0.09%	(14.74)
Tunisia	8.7%	12.6%	14.8%	11.5%	80%	0.69%	(18.76)
Turkey	8.2%	5.0%	25.5%	8.3%	74%	0.12%	(81.09)
UAE	0.6%	8.7%	7.0%	9.6%	83%	0.27%	(6.33)

Source: Compiled from data in Human Development Report (2015); CIA World Fact Book (2015); FAO-AQUASTAT (2016); Gössling et al. (2012: 2–3, 5); UNWTO Yearbook (2016).

★ Water consumption in million MCM.

important factor in the employment market but its contribution to the national GDP is relatively lower than that of tourism in the countries listed above. It is also an extremely important source of foreign exchange in MENA countries.

Expansion of water supply in MENA

As already noted, enlargement of the water supply in MENA could be achieved by improved management of hydro resources to reduce water losses and allocate water resources in a more economical manner. Two methods to increase water supply require technological capacity and are energy intensive: wastewater treatment and reuse, and the desalination of sea and brackish water. The latter is successfully practised in MENA, but the former is rarely used, which is quite surprising as treated wastewater could be used in agriculture and in tourism.

As regards wastewater treatment and use, approximately 60–70 per cent of fresh water ends up becoming effluent. There are different levels of sewerage treatment, and in the most advanced stage of tertiary treatment the water is suitable for irrigation of all crops and for irrigating parks, gardens and lawns in municipal areas and tourism sites. Unfortunately, this source of water is rarely used in MENA, and when it is employed, only very small amounts of treated wastewater are reused. This is particularly disappointing as all MENA countries allocate most of their fresh water to agricultural irrigation. As treated wastewater has been reused for irrigation in agriculture successfully in other locations, this is a missed opportunity for the Middle East and North Africa. Treated wastewater's relative contribution to total water resources in percentages indicates the extent to which this source is neglected. For example, treated reused wastewater constitutes only 0.1 per cent of Algeria's total water resources—in Egypt 1.9 per cent, Lebanon 0.2 per cent, Libya 0.7 per cent and Saudi Arabia 0.7 per cent (data for 2010, 2002, 2008, 2006 respectively). Modest reuse of treated wastewater is found in Bahrain (5 per cent of total water resources—2005), Jordan (9 per cent—2005), Gaza (8 per cent—2004), Qatar (10 per cent), UAE (6 per cent), and Yemen (6 per cent) (FAO 2016). Israel is the exception amongst MENA countries. Of all its wastewater produced, 75 per cent is treated and reused. Treated wastewater comprises 31 per cent of the total water supply for agriculture, and its share in the total water resources in Israel is 18 per cent (Government of Israel, Water Authority 2017).

The FAO data point to poor effluent management. In most MENA countries, only a portion of the wastewater is treated. For example, in Turkey, 2.770 million m^3 of wastewater is produced, but only 1.680 million m^3 is treated. In the UAE, 500 million m^3 of wastewater is produced while only 289 million m^3 is treated. Untreated wastewater ends up in the environment, polluting soil, water resources and the sea. With the water scarcity that prevails in MENA, there should be no option but to treat and reuse wastewater. Failure to do so can also be attributed to the political environment. The sporadic use of wastewater in tourism will be discussed later in the chapter.

By 2007, over 50 per cent of the world's desalination potential was installed in MENA, primarily in the Gulf Region (World Bank 2012: 9). Although in 2007 desalination satisfied only slightly more than 3 per cent of total regional water demand, some MENA countries depend on desalination to supply 50–99 per cent of their municipal water use (e.g. Bahrain, Kuwait, Qatar, UAE, Oman) (World Bank 2012). Moreover, about 60 per cent of the world's desalination market is located in MENA; altogether, MENA's desalination capacity was 10.2 km^3 in 2010 and was expected to increase to 32.7 km^3 in 2016 (World Bank 2012: 54). Almost all of the countries in the region are now considering desalination as a potential option for potable water. This growth is driven by chronic water shortages due to persistent droughts (Mahamed

& Al Mualla 2010), severe scarcities of fresh water, industrialisation and economic development (Drouiche et al. 2011). As most MENA countries are currently water stressed, desalination is one of very few options, particularly in the oil-rich countries of the Persian Gulf and North Africa (Drouid & Ghaffour 2011). Desalination is feasible owing to the region's access to seawater and brackish water, and to the fact that most of the population (where demand is high) is concentrated on the coast. This also happens to be the location of most tourism infrastructure.

Advances in technology are also crucial in the region's efforts to desalinise, as more desalinated water is produced per unit of energy (Einav, Harussi, & Perry 2002; El-Sadek 2010; Ghaffour, Missimer, & Amy 2013). The greatest progress in the desalination sector is the cost to produce 1 m^3 of potable water, which has through time dropped from US$ 4 per m^3 to US$ 1 per m^3 (Drouiche et al. 2011; Ghaffour et al. 2013). Israel was quoted recently as successfully reducing the costs in its desalination plants to US$ 0.31–0.63 per 1 m^3 (Ghaffour et al. 2013; Government of Israel, Water Authority 2017).

Ghaffour et al. (2013) correctly noted that desalinated seawater is truly a 'new' water source and has essentially unlimited capacity, not being subject to strict sustainability criteria, although it is limited by the energy needed for the process. It is, at present, a secure supply. However, the production of desalinated water also adversely impacts the environment through its intensive use of energy and output of air pollution and emission of GHG (Einav et al. 2002; World Bank 2012). Other negative impacts of desalination include its exploitation of large areas of coastlines, noise pollution, and its effect on coastal aquifers and on the marine environment as a result of the concentrated brine, a waste product of the process that is returned to the sea (Einav et al. 2002: 144–145).

Table 13.3 demonstrates the relatively high dependence of certain MENA countries on desalinated water. Fossil fuel-based desalination as practised in MENA is unsustainable. In addition to the strong spatial features of desalination plants, the process has a considerable localised impact on areas of intensive tourism development and scarce water resources. Egypt is using seawater and brackish water for desalination along the Red Sea to supply tourist villages and resorts, since the economic value of a unit of water through tourism is calculated to be high enough to cover desalination costs (El-Sadek 2010). Seawater desalination is used in southern Sinai and in the Gulf of Aqaba for the same purposes (Abou Rayan, Djebedjian, & Khaled 2001; El-Kady & El-Shibini 2001). Desalination plants are of two categories: units owned by the government and those belonging to the private sector, mainly hotels. Altogether, Egypt now produces about 50 million m^3 per year of desalinated water. Similar development can be found in Aqaba's tourism resorts. In the Gulf countries, desalinated water is channelled for domestic uses including tourism and industry. Desalination will continue to play a critical role in MENA's future water supply (World Bank 2012) or as El Sadek puts it, 'Water desalination as a conventional water resource should be considered as an imperative measure for water security in Egypt' (El-Sadek 2010: 884). This applies to all MENA countries.

Tourism and water in MENA

Compared to other regions of the world, tourism in MENA is underdeveloped, although it is beginning to flourish. For a long time, Arab governments considered tourism, other than pilgrimage, to be undesirable and economically unnecessary (Kovjanic 2014). Din (1989) presented several factors that likely account for the lack of popularity of tourism in Muslim countries. One is the prevailing socio-economic underdevelopment in many Muslim countries, which creates an environment of poverty and destitution that is less attractive to international tourists. In addition, problems of access and a lack of personnel affect planning

Table 13.3 Desalination capacity and contribution to water resources

Countries	Desalinated water produced (millions m³)		Desalinated water withdrawal as % of total supply	
Algeria	615		7.3%	(2012)
Bahrain	357.4		29%	(2003)
Egypt	200		0.3%	(2010)
Iran	0.2	(2004)		
Iraq	7.4	(1994)	0.01%	(2000)
Israel	519	(2015)	7.0%	(2004)
Jordan	0.9	(2005)	1.0%	(2005)
Kuwait	420.2	(2002)	46%	(2002)
Lebanon	10	(2006)	3.6%	(2005)
Libya	0.70	(2012)	1.2%	(2012)
Morocco	NA		NA	
Oman	109	(2006)	8%	(2006)
Palestinian Authority				
West Bank	None		None	
Gaza	None		None	
Qatar	180	(2005)	41%	(2005)
Saudi Arabia	166	(2006)	4.4%	(2006)
Syria	NA		NA	
Tunisia	0.020	(2011)	1%	(2011)
Turkey	0.5	(1890)		
UAE	950	(2005)	24%	
Yemen	25.1	(2006)	0.3%	

Sources: Compiled from data in FAO-AQUASTAT (2016); Koschikowsky (2011); World Bank (2012).

and advisory services (Din 1989: 545). The development of tourism in MENA was and is evolving under a political and religious climate that dictates the fortunes of tourism. Political instability, warfare and theocratic regimes are major forces of the 'push and pull' matrix of tourism in MENA.

The Middle East and North Africa are endowed with a wide variety of assets that should make it an ideal region for the development of tourism—pleasant climate, nice beaches and unique historical monuments and archaeological sites (Morakabati 2013). This underdevelopment has changed dramatically with the growth of the oil economy, which transformed the Gulf States into some of the richest countries in the world. Tourist infrastructure and general infrastructure, liberalisation of air transportation, trade and services, communications technology, and the spread of information have all contributed to a flourishing tourism industry in MENA (Hussein-Mustafa 2010; Saleh, Assaf, Ihalanayake, & Lung 2015).

There are many factors shaping tourism in MENA. First is its geographical location. MENA is close enough to the European markets in general and is situated at the crossroads where Europe, Asia and Africa meet (Hussein-Mustafa 2010). The location is attractive both for interregional and intra-regional inbound tourism. Second, the economic rewards of foreign exchange earnings and the contribution to MENA countries' exports are vast; tourism comprises 20.7 per cent of the exports of Egypt, 35.5 per cent of Jordan, 21.2 per cent of

Morocco, 17.7 per cent of Turkey, 9.7 per cent of Bahrain and 51.9 per cent of Lebanon. Saleh et al. (2015) found a long-term relationship between tourism development and GDP development. Third, tourism contributes to employment growth. It is a crucial generator of employment in a region where unemployment is high, mainly amongst youth. Fourth, many countries, particularly in the Persian Gulf, are trying to reduce their dependence on oil revenues and to diversify their economies (Battour, Ismail, & Battor 2011; Hussein-Mustafa 2010; Saleh et al. 2015). Finally, in the specific context of water resource use, all of the above achievements 'cost' very little in terms of water resources in a water-scarce region. However, politics probably constitutes the most influential factor in the development of tourism, or lack thereof, in the Middle East and North Africa.

MENA is one of the most politically unstable regions of the world. The region is rife with wars, terrorism and civil strife, which make its image unattractive to many visitors and tourism investors. Within the region, wars in Afghanistan, Lebanon, Syria, Iran, Iraq, Kuwait, Yemen, the Palestinian Authority and Israel all have contributed to the decline of inbound tourism (Din 1989; Morakabati 2013). The Arab Spring of 2010 affected MENA destinations drastically, and inbound tourism fell by 9.1 per cent in North Africa and 8.0 per cent in the Middle East (Kovjanic 2014: 34; Pillmayer & Scherle 2013; Montgomery 2014). Following the 11 September 2001, terror attack in New York and Washington, intra-regional tourism flourished in MENA as never before because the region's residents, fearful of a backlash to 9/11, deserted European and American destinations, booking regional holidays instead (Battour et al. 2011; Kovjanic 2014). Simultaneously, tourists from the US and Europe largely abandoned MENA as a destination.

Another political impact on inbound tourism is the traditional Muslim character of the MENA region, which does not welcome Western tourists whose appearance and behaviour are perceived as threats to Islamic traditions (especially Saudi Arabia, Libya and Iran) (Farahani-Zamani & Henderson 2010; Kovjanic 2014). Other countries in the region tend to concentrate tourism in isolated enclaves away from residents (e.g. Egypt, Jordan, Morocco and Tunisia) as a way of protecting their citizens from the demoralised effects of tourism. Political instability continues to shape tourism in MENA in the form of wars and, currently, ISIS terror attacks.

Tourism and water relationships

These trends in tourism and politics have a significant bearing on tourism's water use. The demand for water varies from place to place, as it is a factor of development, societal values and human behaviour (Hadjikakou et al. 2013). Although international tourism accounts for less than one per cent of national water use in MENA, it is a spatially and temporally concentrated activity and hence may be responsible for water stress in certain areas, such as the Sinai in Egypt and Bodrum in Turkey. The tourism sector poses some very specific problems in terms of water consumption. These include the spatial concentration on coastlines and on sites already characterised by a scarcity of local water resources, often at sensitive natural sites, and seasonal concentration, where visitor peak periods coincide with the periods of scarcest water supply (summer) (Eurostat European Commission 2009).

The major obstacle to presenting a picture of MENA's tourism-related water consumption is the quality of data. Statistics are not available for water use specifically by the tourism sector, and very limited research is available on water demand for tourism compared to other uses (Gössling et al. 2012; Eurostat European Commission 2009; Tapper et al. 2011; Tortella & Tirado 2011). Collecting more comprehensive information is currently difficult or even impossible due to the absence of any precise national and international classification and documented identification of the tourism sector (Eurostat European Commission 2009). Tortella and Tirado (2011) suggest this is due to the apparently negligible tourism demand for water compared to other uses. The few data that are available are often old, contradictory and applicable to different years and periods, making comparisons and analyses very difficult. Nonetheless, within the framework of these limitations, this section examines tourism and water use issues.

Tourism's use of water: Aspects of supply and demand

Water shortages intensify competition amongst water consumers, especially agriculture, hydro-electric production, household consumption and tourism (Eurostat European Commission 2009). Competition also develops between tourists and local communities. The disparity between water use by tourists and the local population is typically in the order of a factor of three to eight (Becken 2014: 18). Where water demand is significant, the tourism sector can apply considerable pressure on available fresh water resources and compete with local demand. The supply of water often needs additional infrastructure to transfer the product from water-rich areas in the interior to coastal areas and also to transport unconventional hydro-resources, such as desalinated water or treated effluent, to tourist centres (Eurostat European Commission 2009). Supply often deals not with the quantity of available water but with its quality; polluted water resources are obviously not suitable for human use. Tourism can contribute to improving water quality, for instance, when sewage treatment systems are built that can also process untreated local wastewater (Gössling et al. 2012: 10). Tourism may provide an incentive for keeping water quality high, but as Gössling et al. (2012) point out, tourism appears to contribute to declining water quality. The quantities of sewage and wastewater generated by tourism can be large; approximately 40–50 per cent of the water actually drawn is returned to the sewage system (Gössling et al. 2012: 10).

The total annual consumption of water in the global tourism industry was calculated by Gössling et al. (2012) to be 1,398 km^3 which is approximately 1–2 per cent of the world's total water withdrawal (Gössling at al. 2015). The demand for water by tourism depends on many factors and influences, such as the location of hotels and resorts, climate, facilities and activities offered by the destination, and the length and timing of the tourist season (Gössling et al. 2012). This varies according to different tourism products that cater to many tastes and budgets, from packaged mass tourism to luxury tourism (Hadjikakou, Miller, Chenoweth, Druckman, & Zoumides 2015).

Tourism's use of water can be divided into two main categories: direct use and indirect use. Direct consumption of water is typically associated with hotels and resorts involving showers, toilets, gardens, pools, wellness areas, kitchens, laundries, golf courses and cooling systems. Indirect water consumption is usually related to food production, fossil fuels (for transport and energy use), biofuels and infrastructure construction (Gössling et al. 2012, 2013, 2015).

Typically, direct water uses, particularly for food preparation and fuel use, appear to be completely consumptive, that is, lost to regional water cycles and unavailable for reuse (Gössling et al. 2012). Hadjikakou et al. (2015) supported the findings of previous studies, suggesting that indirect water use exceeds direct water use in the context of tourism (Hadjikakou et al. 2015: 21). Gössling et al. (2012, 2013, 2015) and Eurostat European Commission (2009) reached the same conclusions.

Both the demand and supply of water for and by tourism entail great losses of water through inefficiency. Tourist facilities could save substantial amounts of water; hotels can reduce indoor water consumption by 30 per cent by installing water-efficient fixtures (Cooley,

Hutchens-Cabibi, Cohen, & Gleick 2007, cited in Gössling et al. 2012: 11). Smith, Hargroves, Desha, & Stasinopoulos (2009) suggest that minimising water consumption in landscaping can reduce water use by 30–50 per cent (Gössling et al. 2012: 11). Water can be saved in swimming pools, and treated wastewater can be used to irrigate golf courses and hotel gardens. From the supply side, good management, recycling water, preventing pollution and salinity of water resources, desalination and adopting brave decisions to price water according to its real value are necessary steps that would improve water supply for the tourism sector.

Quantified estimates of water consumption in tourism

Gössling and his colleagues have undertaken monumental work about water consumption in tourism. Table 13.4 presents estimated and calculated water use, direct and indirect, for all categories of water use according to their research.

Hadjikakou et al. (2013) explored water use in Cyprus using the water footprint concept and found quantitative data similar to those of Gössling and his colleagues. The daily water footprint was found to be 5,790–8,940 litres per guest. The food water footprint comprised 75–95 per cent of the total water footprint, and the water footprint of accommodation was only 1–7 per cent of total tourism water use (Hadjikakou 2013: 552). Gössling and Peeters (2015) illuminate the importance of water consumption related to indirect tourism use, compared to direct use. Also, considerably greater uncertainty in relation to water use exists with regard to food, fossil fuel, energy use in hotels, biofuels or the construction of tourism-related infrastructure. Indirect tourism-related water consumption is creating 'water hinterlands', or regions from which 'virtual water' must be imported, for example in the form of agricultural products, cement for construction in tourism or fuel for energy production in hotels. Water use values for energy consumed in hotels is estimated to be on average 75 litres per tourist per day (Gössling & Peeters 2015; Gössling et al. 2012). A 14-day holiday may involve 70 m^3 of water use for

Table 13.4 Water use categories for various tourism uses

	Min–max water use in litre per guest night	Estimated average litre per guest night
Direct		
Accommodation	84–2,425	350
Activities	10–875	20
Indirect		
Infrastructure	0.2	0.2
Fossil fuels transport	5–2,500	130
Energy use at hotels	1–220	75
Biofuels	2,500	–
Food	4,500–8,000	6,000
Other consumption	N.A.	N.A.
Total per guest per night	4,600–12,000	6,575
Direct and Indirect		
Total per tourist per trip	19,500–50,750	27,800
Total global annual consumption tourism 2010		138 km^3

Sources: Compiled from data in Gössling (2001, 2002, 2006, 2013); Gössling et al. (2012); Gössling & Peeters (2015).

Table 13.5 Empirical data on water use in tourism in the MENA region

Country	Tourism water consumption in million m³	Water consumption litres/bed night	Supply total	
			%	Year
Jordan	4.3 (Hotel & Restaurant)			
Israel	12.0 (Hotels)			2009
Tunisia	17.5 (Hotels)	466 litres (2002)	1.0–2.0% (0.73)	2009
Morocco		600 (Luxury)	0.15%	2006
		500 (5 star)		
		400 (4 star)		2006
		300 (3 star)		2006
		180 (apartment)		2006
Egypt			0.65%	
Sharm el sheikh		400–500		2012
Turkey			0.13%	
Cyprus		215–900		2013

Source: Compiled from data in Eurostat European Commission (2009); Gössling 2013; Hadjikakou et al. (2015), Tapper et al. (2011).

food alone (Gössling 2013). There are various linkages between tourism, water production, building materials and energy use, with perhaps the most important mode to be researched being tourism's use of hydro resources. Table 13.5 provides empirical data about water use in tourism in MENA.

Some information is also available about golf course irrigation. In Morocco, 3,500 m³ is used for an average 18-hole course; in Tunisia, golf course water use ranges from 600 to 3,456 m³. The Tunisian water authority estimates that watering hotel gardens and green areas accounts for 22 per cent of their total consumption (Eurostat European Commission 2009). Eurostat European Commission (2009) provides general categories for overnight water consumption as a share of demand: high—4.5 per cent (e.g. Malta and Cyprus); medium—2.0 per cent in major destinations (Greece and Tunisia); low—1 per cent to 0.1 per cent in Syria and 0.5 per cent in Israel.

These partial data show only direct use of water in MENA's tourism and the broader Mediterranean. Moreover, the data are only based on official abstraction of water for tourism. The tourism industry in North Africa and the Middle East also has unofficial, non-metered wells whose water is not included or measured. The direct use of water in MENA does not deviate from the common values of consumption. However, there are no data on indirect water use, particularly in food and energy production.

Even though farming utilises most of the scarce water resources of MENA, all countries must import food. Hadjikakou et al. (2013) note that attempts to boost local agricultural production and reduce economic leakage may also contribute to water shortages in the destination. Destinations in arid regions can maximise economic returns in certain cases by importing water-intensive agricultural products from abroad for use in tourism. As for energy, most MENA countries are rich in oil and gas, and even with recent drops in oil revenues, they can afford the widespread use of energy in tourism. This is not the case for fuel resource-limited Jordan, Syria, Lebanon, Morocco and Tunisia, which either have no energy sources or have sources too small to meet their needs.

Table 13.6 MENA's water consumption

Country	Water consumption in tourism (2011–2014)	Data by Gössling (2006)
Algeria	6.3 million m^3	
Bahrain	28.9 million m^3	1.88 million m^3
Egypt	26.7 million m^3	19.79 million m^3
Iran	13.4 million m^3	
Iraq	2.4 million m^3	
Israel	8.1 million m^3	8.56 million m^3
Jordan	11.1 million m^3	
Kuwait	0.86 million m^3	
Lebanon	3.6 million m^3	
Morocco	27.5 million m^3	10.52 million m^3
Oman	4.1 million m^3	
Qatar	7.8 million m^3	
Saudi Arabia	50.6 million m^3	14.74 million m^3
Syria	14.0 million m^3	
Tunisia	16.8 million m^3	18.76 million m^3
Turkey	107.9 million m^3	81.09 million m^3
UAE	19.8 million m^3	6.33 million m^3
Yemen	2.7 million m^3	

Source: Compiled and calculated by the author, some data sourced from Gössling (2006).

To include both direct and indirect uses of water in the tourism industry, this chapter uses Gössling and Peeters' (2015) estimate of average water consumption per tourist per 14-day trip, which is 27,800 litres, or 27.8 m^3 of water. This is multiplied by the number of tourists in each country for 2012–2014 and is compared with the data of Gössling et al. (2012) whenever available. The total water use in MENA's tourism industry is 265.5 million m^3 which is a fraction of the renewable water resources of MENA for the years 2000–2009, which were 250 km^3 (Table 13.6).

Conclusion

This chapter addresses the tourism–water nexus in a very broad framework where the complex linkages between tourism and water resources are presented. The relationship between tourism and water in MENA is decidedly impacted by climate and physical geography, Islamic traditions, politics and policies, which are considerably more powerful than in other regions of the world. Political decision-making is very influential on resource management, particularly as regards water resources but also related to other resources such as oil and gas, land, environmental resources and the sea.

Policies shaped by religion play a role in both water resources and tourism management. By treating water as a 'common-pool' resource rather than a consumable commodity, MENA governments are depleting their water resources. For the tourism industry it appears that a state religion and regional conflict can be serious hindrances to tourism development (Zamani-Farahani & Henderson 2010). Politics in relation to water resource use is linked to the most important societal factors in MENA: large population growth and people who need food and employment. The current agricultural sector in MENA is not particularly successful when judged by most economic indicators, and especially when compared to tourism. While it has its limitations, tourism is a successful industry in MENA, and water scarcity is not crucial for its success, as it consumes relatively small quantities of the resource compared to other economic sectors. Tourism fortunes in MENA depend less on water resource availability than on political stability and peace in the region.

References

Abou Rayan, M., Djebedjian, B., & Khaled, I. (2001) 'Water supply and demand and a desalination option for Sinai, Egypt', *Desalination*, 136: 73–81.

Aranca MENA (2014) *Tourism and Hospitality Report 04*. New York: Aranca MENA.

Battour, M., Ismail, M.N., & Battor, M. (2011) 'The impact of destination attributes on Muslim tourist's choice', *International Journal of Tourism Research*, 13(6): 527–540.

Becken, S. (2014) 'Water equity—contrasting tourism water use with that of the local community', *Water Resources and Industry*, 7–8: 9–22.

CIA (2015) *The World Factbook*. Washington, DC: Central Intelligence Agency.

Cooley, H., Hutchens-Cabibi, T., Cohen, M.J., & Gleick, P.H. (2007) *Hidden Oasis: Water Conservation and Efficiency in Las Vegas*. Oakland, CA: Pacific Institute.

Din, K.H. (1989) 'Islam and tourism: Patterns, issues and options', *Annals of Tourism Research*, 16: 542–563.

Dolatyar, M., & Gray, T.S. (2000) 'The politics of water security in the Middle East', *Environmental Politics*, 9(3): 65–88.

Droogers, P., Immerzeel, W.W., Terink, W., Hoogeveen, J., Bierkens, M.F.P., van Beek, L.P.H., & Debele, B. (2012) 'Water resources trends in Middle-East and North Africa towards 2050', *Hydrology and Earth System Sciences*, 16: 3101–3114.

Drouiche, N., & Ghaffour, N. (2011) 'Reasons for the fast growing seawater desalination capacity in Algeria', *Water Resources Management*, 25: 2743–2754.

Einav, R., Harussi, K., & Perry, D. (2002) 'The footprint of the desalination processes on the environment', *Desalination*, 152: 141–154.

El-Kady, M., & El-Shibini, F. (2001) 'Desalination in Egypt and the future application in supplementary irrigation', *Desalination*, 136: 63–72.

El-Sadek, A. (2010) 'Water desalination: An imperative measure for water security in Egypt', *Desalination*, 250: 876–884.

ESCWA, UNEP, UN (2015) *Arab Sustainable Development Report*. Beirut: UNEP, ESCWA.

Eurostat European Commission (2009) *MEDSTAT II: 'Water and Tourism' Pilot Study*. Luxemburg: European Commission.

Falkenmark M., & Lindh, G. (1976) *Water for a Starving World*. Boulder, CO: Westview.

FAO (2016) *AQUASTAT*. Rome: Food and Agriculture Organisation of the United Nations.

FAO–Water Development and Management Unit (2013) *Near East and North Africa Water Days 2013*. Rome: Food and Agriculture Organisation.

Farajallah, N. (2012) 'The Middle East and North Africa's water resources in changing climate'. Heinrich Böll Stiftung. Available online: www.boell.de/en/2012/10/31/middle-east-and-north-africas-water-resources-changing-climate (Accessed 18 March 2017).

Ghaffour, N., Missimer, T., & Amy, G. (2013) 'Technical review and evaluation of the economics of water desalination: Current and future challenges for better water supply sustainability', *Desalination*, 309: 197–207.

Gössling, S. (2001) 'The consequences of tourism for sustainable water use on a tropical island: Zanzibar, Tanzania', *Journal of Environmental Management*, 61(2): 179–191.

Gössling, S. (2002) 'Global environmental consequences of tourism', *Global Environmental Change*, 12(4): 293–302.

Gössling, S. (2006) 'Tourism and water', in S. Gössling, & C.M. Hall (eds), *Tourism and Global Environmental Change: Ecological, Social, Economic and Political Interrelationships* (pp. 180–194). London: Routledge.

Gössling, S. (2013) 'Tourism and water: Interrelationships and management', *Global Water Forum UNESCO*, 16 July 2013. Available online: www.globalwaterforum.org/2013/07/16/tourism-and-water-interrelationships-and-management/ (Accessed 30 March 2017).

Gössling, S., & Peeters, P. (2015) 'Assessing tourism's global environmental impact 1900–2050', *Journal of Sustainable Tourism*, 23(5): 639–659.

Gössling, S., Peeters, P. Hall, C.M., Ceron, J-P., Dubois, G., Lehmann, L., & Scott, D. (2012) 'Tourism and water use: Supply, demand and security. An international review', *Tourism Management*, 33(1): 1–15.

Government of Israel, Water Authority (2017) 'Water Authority information'. Available online: www.water.gov.il/Hebrew/Pages/Water-Authority-Info.aspx. (Accessed 8 May 2017).

Gregoire, G. (2012) 'Climate change adaptation in the water sector in the Middle East and North Africa: A review of main issues'. Available online: www.FAO.ORG/fileadmin/user-upload/rome/2007/docs/climate_Change_Adaptation (Accessed 30 March 2017).

Hadjikakou, M., Chenoweth, J., & Miller, G. (2013) 'Estimating the direct and indirect use of tourism in the Eastern Mediterranean', *Journal of Environmental Management*, 114: 548–556.

Hadjikakou, M., Miller, G., Chenoweth, J., Druckman, A., & Zoumides, C. (2015) 'A comprehensive framework for comparing water use intensity across different tourist types', *Journal of Sustainable Tourism*, 23(10): 1445–1467.

Hall, C.M., Timothy, D.J., & Duval, D.T. (2004) 'Security and tourism: Towards a new understanding?' *Journal of Travel & Tourism Marketing*, 15(2–3): 1–18.

Henderson, J.C. (2010) 'Religious tourism and its management: The Hajj in Saudi Arabia', *International Journal of Tourism Research*, 13: 541–552.

Hussein-Mustafa, M. (2010) 'Tourism and globalisation in the Arab World', *International Journal of Business and Social Science*, 1(1): 37–48.

Koschikowsky, J. (2011) *Desalination in MENA*. Freiburg, Germany: Fraunhofer Institute for Solar Energy Systems.

Kovjanic, G. (2014) 'Islamic tourism as a factor of the Middle-East regional development', *Tourism*, 18(1): 33–43.

Mohamed, M.M., & Al-Mualla, A.A. (2010) 'Water demand forecasting in Umm al- Quwain (UAE) using the IWR-Main Specify Forecasting Model', *Water Resources Management*, 24(14): 4092–4120.

Montgomery, R. (2014) 'Tourism statistics—North Africa and Eastern Mediterranean', *Statistics in Focus*, March 2014.

Morakabati, Y. (2013) 'Tourism in the Middle East: Conflicts, crises and economic diversification, some critical issues', *International Journal of Tourism Research*, 15: 375–387.

Pillmayer, M., & Scherle, N. (2013) 'The tourism industry and the process of internationalisation in the Middle East: The example of Jordan', *International Journal of Tourism Research*, 16: 329–339.

Saleh, A.S., Assaf, A.G., Ihalanayake, R., & Lung, S. (2015) 'A panel cointegration analysis of the impact of tourism on economic growth: Evidence from the Middle East region', *International Journal of Tourism Research*, 17: 209–220.

Smith, M., Hargroves, K., Desha, C., & Stasinopoulos, P. (2009) *Water Transformed: Sustainable Water Solutions for Climate Change Adaptation*. Nathan, Australia: The Natural Edge Project.

Tapper, R., Hadjikakou, M., Noble, R., & Jenkinson, J. (2011) *The Impact of the Tourism Industry on Freshwater Resources in Countries in the Caribbean, Mediterranean, North Africa and Other Regions*. London: Tourism Concern.

The Pacific Institute (2014) *The World's Water, Volume 8*. Oakland, CA: The Pacific Institute.

Tortella, B.D., & Tirado, D. (2011) 'Hotel water consumption at a seasonal mass tourist destination: The case of the island of Mallorca', *Journal of Environmental Management*, 92(10): 2568–2579.

UN Development Program (2015) *Human Development Report 2015*. New York: UNDP.

UNWTO (2015) 'Middle East & North Africa: Tourism adapts to challenges and gains new momentum'. Press Release, 5 February 2015. Madrid: World Tourism Organization.

UNWTO (2016) *Yearbook of Tourism Statistics–Annual Report 2015*. Madrid: World Tourism Organization.

World Bank (2007) 'Making the most of scarcity: Accountability for better management results in the Middle-East and North Africa'. Washington, DC: World Bank.

World Bank (2012) 'MENA Development Report Renewable Energy Desalination—An Emerging Solution to Close MENA's Water Gap'. Washington, DC: World Bank.

World Travel and Tourism Council (2015) *TRAVEL and Tourism Economic Impact 2015 Middle-East*. London: World Travel and Tourism Council.

Zamani-Farahani, H., & J. Henderson (2010) 'Islamic tourism and managing tourism development in Islamic societies: The cases of Iran and Saudi Arabia', *International Journal of Tourism Research*, 12: 79–89.

14

OIL IN THE MIDDLE EAST

A critical resource for tourism

Susanne Becken and Harald A. Friedl

Introduction

Recent years have seen very high levels of oil price volatility. From a price of about US$151 per barrel in June 2008 to a low of US$47 per barrel in January 2009, with an increase back to US$120 in April 2011, and a temporary low price of US$29 in January 2016, prices have varied by a factor of over four. At the time of writing, the oil price is still comparatively low at about US$47 per barrel, but a recent decision amongst Organization of the Petroleum Exporting Countries (OPEC) members to reduce production is likely to lead to an increase in prices (Krauss & Reed 2016). Despite low oil prices in more recent years, demand for oil has remained relatively stable, with the International Energy Agency projecting annual growth in the order of 1.1 per cent (IEA 2016). Avoiding 'rebound' effects where low oil prices encourage excessive consumption and investment into fossil fuel-intensive technologies is important in light of urgently needed decarbonisation of the global economy to achieve reductions in greenhouse gas emissions towards net-zero emissions by 2050. Furthermore, temporarily low oil prices do not change the fact that 'cheap oil' has reached a peak, and future demand will inevitably lead to rising prices (on 'peak oil and tourism' see, for example, Becken 2015).

Low oil prices have many consequences. For oil-importing nations, in particular European countries and Japan, the low prices are a welcome relief as they reduce production costs, keep inflation low and correlate with increases in Gross Domestic Product (GDP), at least in the short term (Peersman & Robays 2009). Lower oil prices also correlate positively with increased travel from these nations (Lennox 2012). On the other hand, oil-exporting economies are negatively affected by low oil export prices, especially when oil production costs exceed the global market price. This is the case for much of the American oil production from fracking, which has become competitive under the 2008 oil prices of well over US$100 per barrel (Heinberg 2013). Even Saudi Arabia, the world's largest oil producer, requires oil prices to be above US$85 per barrel in the long term to balance its budget (Bowler 2015). Low prices, however, signify risks for investors, leading to a reduction in necessary infrastructure investment and exploration. The effects are already felt with the cancellation of major new oil and gas projects up until 2014 amounting to a total value of about US$380 billion (Wood Mackenzie 2016).

Meanwhile, global tourism continues to grow at very high rates. The World Tourism Organization (UNWTO 2016) reported a total of 1.186 billion international arrivals in 2015, an increase of 4.6 per cent compared with the previous year. In addition to international tourism, domestic tourism contributes substantially to global tourist flows—and energy demand. For example, in China alone in 2014 there were 3.6 billion domestic trips and 128 million international tourists (UNWTO, 2016 and personal communication with Dr Ma, China Tourism Administration). The main driver of tourism's energy use is transportation at about three-quarters of total demand (Scott et al. 2008). In 2005, for example, it was estimated that tourist transport consumed the equivalent of about 2.346 billion barrels. Becken (2015) calculated that this corresponds to about 10 per cent of global oil consumption. The oil intensity of tourism is nowhere more evident than in aviation. According to IATA's statistics, the global aviation industry consumed 1.857 billion barrels in 2014 (IATA 2016). With projections of aviation growth in the order of 3–6 per cent annually (Airbus 2018; IATA 2016), and the Middle East's heavy reliance on aviation, both in terms of inter-continental and intra-regional travel, air travel is therefore central to the arguments presented in this chapter.

Tourism growth, and in particular aviation growth, is highly problematic against the background of peak oil. The global expansion of the Western-style (and neo-liberally supported) consumption has embraced travel and tourism as a key mechanism to mobilise consumption into ever more remote regions of planet Earth. Global economic growth necessitates the integration of an increasing number of previously marginalised or under-privileged groups, who aspire to follow established patterns of consumption that form part of the experience economy and 'guarantee' personal fulfilment (Friedl 2015). China, for example, is proactively stimulating tourism, both domestic and international, as a golden solution to a structural crisis that stems from the current transition from a producer to a service-based consumer economy (Prantner 2016). With this in mind, it is highly plausible that a considerable and growing proportion of the 121 million barrels consumed per day in 2040 (IEA 2016) will be for travel and tourism. This poses several challenges. The tourism sector will face increasing pressure to 'deliver dividends' for its disproportional share of oil consumption, whilst at the same time it will be more vulnerable than other sectors to oil price increases and volatility. Investment into tourism as a diversification strategy can therefore only be a short-term Band-Aid for struggling economies, and may even exacerbate exposure to oil prices.

The Middle East plays a particularly important role in the context of both oil and tourism (Friedl 2010), although it is important to understand that the countries in the Middle East are highly diverse in terms of oil resources, tourism sector development, social systems and stability. Having said this, a number of Middle Eastern countries, and in particular the Gulf States on the Arabian Peninsula, form the core of OPEC and account for the majority of global oil reserves. The global tourism industry depends on this oil—and also on political stability that enables the extraction of this critical resource. Second, and in the face of dwindling resources and low prices, several Middle Eastern countries are now aggressively developing their tourism sectors to diversify the economy. This has had mixed success, with UNWTO (2016) statistics[1] showing slower-than-average growth in arrivals in the region (1.7 per cent between 2014 and 2015). Growth has slowed due to political tensions in several countries, which in themselves are caused, amongst others, by national economic crises that constrain the Middle Eastern governments' ability to maintain social order by means of subsidy and social support systems. Third, and somewhat related to the second point, the Middle East represents a region of political instability, causing disruption and tragedy to many people's lives and inadvertently undermining global security. Peace, however, is a core ingredient for a successful tourism industry (Friedl 2010; Wohlmuther & Wintersteiner 2014). At the same time, evidence from a global tourism-conflict model shows that the reverse causality is also true. Tourism has the potential to stabilise countries after periods of conflict (Becken & Carmignani 2016), indicating that to some extent tourism development could be an important peace- and stability-building tool in MENA. A careful balance of these partially conflicting drivers is required to achieve long-term sustainable outcomes.

The relationship between oil and tourism is clearly complex and multifaceted (Becken 2011; Friedl 2010). First and foremost, tourism inherently depends on oil due to its heavy transport component. Second, and as discussed in detail by Becken and Lennox (2012) and Becken (2015), outbound tourism is determined by the economic situation in originating countries (in particular income, as for example, measured through GDP), which in turn depends significantly on global oil prices. High oil prices may lead to recession and suppressed demand for travel. Third, a proportion of global tourism is driven by 'oil wealth'. Outbound travel from oil-exporting countries, such as Saudi Arabia, is closely related to income generated from oil production. Fourth, tourism and oil compete for land resources with multiple conflicts being observed, in particular around protected and/or pristine natural areas (Becken & Job 2014). Fifth, oil-induced conflict—either within the country seeking to position itself as a tourist destination or in a neighbouring state—has a detrimental effect on tourist arrivals. The nexus of oil and tourism is therefore exposed to crises of various kinds, chiefly of an economic nature, but also increasingly social, political, and environmental. Ethical considerations exacerbate the precariousness of the relationship.

This chapter aims to critically discuss the role that oil plays in the development of tourism in the Middle East, and in particular the Gulf States. The importance of oil resources from the Arabian Peninsula is briefly summarised before assessing attempts to diversify national economies of oil-exporting countries, using the case study of Dubai in the United Arab Emirates. This is followed by an overview of outbound tourism from the Middle East, and a critical synopsis of the macro-level implications of the oil–tourism nexus in this region and beyond.

Oil resources in the Middle East

Most oil resources are concentrated in a small number of large fields that were discovered relatively early between the 1940s and 1960s. No more than 100 fields worldwide make up about half of the global oil production, and about 500 fields account for three-quarters of production (Aleklett 2012). The largest fields are in Saudi Arabia (Ghawar with an estimated Ultimately Recoverable Resource of between 66 and 150 billion barrels) and Kuwait (Greater Burgan with between 32 to 75 billion barrels). In the past, the world has particularly depended on the production policies and adjustments of Saudi Arabia. More recently, global production has extended to unconventional resources, in particular deep sea and hydraulic fracturing, or 'fracking'. Heavy investment in the oil industry in the United States, and resulting increases in production, is one reason for the global oversupply in liquid fuel, and currently low prices.[2] As noted by the IEA (2016), in previous situations of oversupply, OPEC members have reduced their production to stabilise prices. However, in recent years Saudi Arabia in particular is no longer willing to act as a 'swing state' and forego revenue by cutting production. As a result, OPEC production has remained, even increased slightly, as OPEC countries seek to maintain revenue and market share.

The landscape of global oil production is convoluted and often blurred by different definitions and accounting frames of oil, lack of credible statistics, vested interests by oil companies and oil-exporting nations alike, and complex geopolitical factors (Becken 2015). In fact, OPEC oil data are majorly disputed (Owen, Inderwildi, & King 2010), because of the system in which

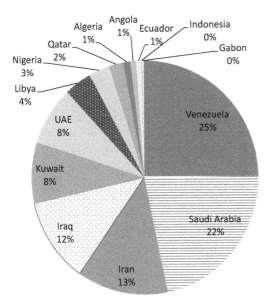

Figure 14.1 OPEC countries' share of OPEC oil reserves in 2015

Note: According to its own statistics from the OPEC Annual Statistical Bulletin.

Source: Based on data from OPEC (2016).

member countries are allocated export quotas depending on their reserves. Thus, the higher the reported reserve, the higher will be the quota. Reserve figures are not audited externally. Despite a lot of uncertainty, there is an understanding amongst key players that conventional oil peaked in about 2009. In 2010, the IEA announced a peak in conventional oil production, and highlighted the need to grow unconventional resources to ensure adequate supply to meet growing energy demand. Notwithstanding the global outlook, the Middle Eastern countries (see Figure 14.1) continue to be the key suppliers of 'cheaper' conventional oil, and as such are of critical importance to the global tourism industry.

As outlined in detail by Becken (2015), tourism is a growth-focused industry that aligns well with the neo-liberal framing of global energy resources, where increasing demand will generally be (attempted to be) satisfied with technologically facilitated enhancement of supply (Becken 2014). Aviation in particular is projected to grow at above-average rates, resulting in a doubling of air travel every 15 years (Airbus 2018). By 2036, there will be 34,900 new aircraft of which 60 per cent are purchased to satisfy new growth. The remainder will replace older aircraft. Despite some inherent improvements in fuel efficiency, due to substantial and consistent growth, travel and tourism are a thirsty industry that, in the absence of large-scale fuel alternatives, continues to depend on the supply of fossil liquid fuel (Bows-Larkin 2015).

Diversification strategies

Oil-exporting countries are seeking to diversify their economies. The last decades saw major socio-economic changes for the member countries of the Cooperation Council of the Arab States of the Gulf (GCC): Bahrain, Kuwait, Oman, Qatar, Saudi Arabia and the United Arab Emirates (UAE). Following a range of economic transformation policies, the standard of living (including health, literacy and other social indicators) has increased substantially, despite continued heavy dependence on (volatile) oil prices. The GCC economies are relatively strong and, for most of them, debt levels are low by global standards. Much of the oil revenue is collected by governments and then redistributed to the population via welfare systems and subsidies. In the meantime, however, high population growth and growing demand for participation of women in the workforce require the creation of new employment opportunities, beyond the use of expatriate workers (both low and high skilled) who currently make up much of the labour force. Investment in non-oil industries, along with investment in human capital and other institutional reforms, is therefore seen as necessary (Fasano & Iqbal 2003), in particular to bridge the gap between increasing levels of education amongst women and actual involvement in the workforce (World Bank 2013). Tourism provides one avenue to encourage the development of a private sector, foreign investment and entrepreneurship by members of the population, and most Middle Eastern countries have seen substantial growth in tourism revenue (Figure 14.2). Note that a considerable proportion of tourism in Middle Eastern countries is pilgrimage tourism. The Hajj, for example, brings now over 3 million visitors to Saudi Arabia each year and thanks to the development of air travel, the number of pilgrims (especially from Southeast Asia) has grown rapidly (Jafari & Scott 2014).

The United Arab Emirates represents a particularly interesting case study for understanding the very difficult move from an oil-based economy to a more mixed model. The UAE's proven oil reserves are about 98 billion barrels, although the resources are not equally distributed across the seven emirates. Abu Dhabi holds over 92 billion barrels, followed by Dubai (4 billion barrels), Sharjah (1.5 billion barrels) and Ras al Khaimah (500 million barrels) (OPEC 2016). It has been estimated that about 40 per cent of the UAE's GDP is related to the oil and gas industries, with about 25 per cent being directly attributed to the export of crude oil (Embassy of the United Arab Emirates 2016). Oil production in the UAE is not without challenges and relies heavily on the reinjection of carbon dioxide to avoid declining production through enhanced recovery. In addition, and in response to the fast-growing domestic energy demand of its 9.5 million people, the UAE is importing natural gas from Qatar and exploring nuclear energy.

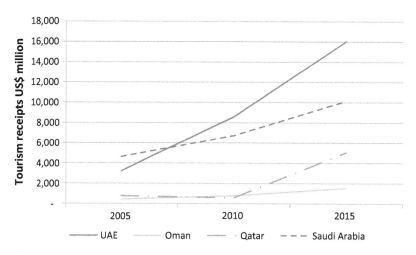

Figure 14.2 Increase in tourism receipts from international arrivals
Source: Based on data from UNWTO (2016).

Due to the differences in natural resource endowments, the emirates have chosen quite different development pathways. Dubai, in particular, reached its maximum oil production in 1991 (at 410,000 barrels per day) and is now only producing 70,000 barrels per day (Pacione 2005). Being situated strategically between Europe and Asia, Dubai has invested heavily in its development as a trading and financial hub. Following liberal real estate policies and the construction of spectacular 'superlative' structures, in combination with massive airport investment, Dubai is firmly established as a major global tourist destination (Friedl & Becken 2015). As a result, oil exports now only make up 5 per cent of GDP in Dubai—evidence of successful diversification (Hvidt 2009). Dubai's tourism infrastructure is substantial, with two large airports, a globally leading airline (Emirates), well over 500 hotels of which over 60 are of a luxury standard, and a large number of man-made attractions, such as the world's largest shopping mall (Dubai Mall), the world's tallest building (Burj Khalifa), and several ambitious land reclamation projects, including the 'Palm Jumeirah'. As a result, tourism now contributes 11 per cent to Dubai's GDP (Kumar 2012). One critical success factor is Dubai's heavy investment into the aviation sector. Already, every fifth job in Dubai depends on aviation, and further expansions of the Dubai World Central airport will only cement the central role of this sector (Friedl & Becken 2015). Other Middle Eastern countries follow similar strategies of opening their economies to global trade and travel by investing heavily in the development of airports (see Table 14.1) and 'aerotropolis', where airports become cities and cities become airports.

The Dubai case also shows that economic diversification is not without challenges. Some of these relate to environmental pressures: most notably, increasing amounts of water are being consumed as a result of tourism growth. This water is largely produced through desalination—in itself a highly energy-intensive activity further putting pressure on oil or gas resources. Some challenges relate to the economic structure and performance. Despite high growth rates in Dubai, productivity has not grown, which is explained by low labour productivity associated with tourism, retail trade and construction (Callen, Cherif, Hasanov, Hegazy, & Khandelwal 2014). The concentration of exports in the oil industry has now shifted to a dependency on exports from gold and jewellery, tourism and transportation. At the same time, these sectors

Table 14.1 Airport development in Middle Eastern countries

City	Airline operating base	Cost (US$ billions)	Planned capacity (million pax)	Details
Dubai	Emirates	$7.8	90	Expansion: Terminal 3
Dubai	Emirates	$32.0	120	Dubai World Central
Doha	Qatar Airways	$15.5	53	Expansion and upgrades
Ajman UAE	–	$0.6	1	New eco-friendly airport
Sharjah UAE	Air Arabia	$0.2	25	Upgrades and expansion
Abu Dhabi	Etihad Airways	$9.4	40	Expansion: Runway, New Terminal
Jeddah	Saudi Arabian	$4.8	25	2 new terminals and upgrade
Kuwait	Kuwait Airways	$2.1	12	Double current capacity
Muscat, Oman	Oman Air	$1.0	48	Upgrades and new terminal
Bahrain	Gulf Air	$0.5	12	Upgrades and expansion
Baghdad	Iraqi Airways	$2.0	15	3 new terminals and upgrades

Source: Adapted and updated from Friedl and Becken (2015).

are vulnerable to changes in the global economy. The ongoing need for foreign investment, and increasing competition between Gulf countries, forced the emirate to relax investment and planning policies to continuously attract much needed investment for ever-more-daring designs and structures. In the meantime, and following the recent Global Financial Crisis, construction plans were stalling and investor confidence was low. Now, with the 2020 World Expo on the horizon, and following the introduction of a tourist bed tax, business activity has been reactivated (Friedl & Becken 2015). Sustainability is one of four themes of the Dubai Expo and this provides a chance to integrate green building design, resource efficiency and sustainable practices into new developments and urban planning.

Callen et al. (2014) and Friedl and Becken (2015) point out that the Dubai model cannot necessarily be repeated across the region, and several scenarios of 'boom and bust', 'green economy', or 'de-growth' are possible (Friedl 2015). In the meantime, it is likely that oil continues to be a central pillar of the Middle Eastern economies—not least to fuel the very tourism and aviation industries that have been created as a means of reducing dependency.

Oil-fuelled tourism

As noted by the UNWTO (2012), the Middle East region comprises some of the wealthiest countries in the world, whose citizens have very high average incomes, led by Qatar (over US$98,000 in 2015). Indeed, the six GCC states rank amongst the top 40 countries globally in terms of their GDP per capita. It is not surprising that the global tourism industry and its associated organisations, such as the World Tourism Organization (UNWTO), show great interest in this region and assess current crises through an optimistic lens.

> The Middle East is one of the smallest, yet fastest growing, tourist generating regions in the world, with outbound travel quadrupling in the last 20 years. Despite the negative impact of the socio-political unrest in the Middle East on tourism flows, prospects for the sector remain positive.
>
> *(UNWTO 2012: n.p.)*

The Arabian market has seen considerable growth in outbound tourism. In particular at times of high oil prices, international departures, for example from the UAE, increased in the order of 20 to 30 per cent annually (European Travel Commission 2007). Whilst the majority of travel is regional (including for shopping), that is, between Middle Eastern nations, a growing number of consumers are travelling further afield. Europe is the most popular destination, capturing 49 per cent of all extra-regional travel (UNWTO 2012). One key driver is the desire to escape the hot climate and long summers of their home countries. The preferred type of accommodation is luxury hotels, and city environments are the preferred destinations. In their 2007 Market Intelligence report of the UAE, the European Travel Commission recognised the intricate relationship between oil wealth and travel. They noted that '… international oil prices are likely to remain high for the foreseeable future […], it implies that the prosperity, and appetite for travel, in the UAE will also be sustained' (p. 13). Whilst increasing economic pressure in key source countries of the Middle East might challenge established trends of luxury travel by the elites, the desire to practise Western life- and consumption styles that rely heavily on status symbols (e.g. luxury cars, fashion brands) for differentiation from the masses continues to be a key driver of outbound tourism. At the same time, there is potential for growing discontent with such behaviours on the part of the local populations of the Middle East, bearing a risk that the increasingly vulnerable elites see themselves pushed to re-establish legitimisation through religious justifications. This could act as a catalyst to extremism, which then would increasingly deter international tourism, thus compromising the diversification strategies discussed earlier.

Not surprisingly and following the above argument, outbound travel has slowed down in response to dropping oil prices and the Global Financial Crisis. The UNWTO (2016) data show, for example, that international expenditures by tourists from the UAE stagnated at US$13.2 billion per annum in each of 2011 and 2012, with a slim increase in 2013 to US$13.8 billion and US$14.4 billion in 2014. The latest data show a total of outbound expenditure of US$15.1 billion in 2015, indicating ongoing recovery. A similar trend of recovery could be observed for Saudi Arabia (with zero or negative growth in 2011, 2012 and 2013), although 2015 saw a decrease in expenditures by 14 per cent to a level of US$20.7 billion. Despite the drop, Saudi Arabia is the world's 13th most important tourism spender. Some destinations have completely specialised in this lucrative market (e.g. Zell am See, Austria), meaning that the vulnerability of Middle Eastern outbound tourism could also be transferred to these destinations, depending on risk mitigation strategies. Unprecedented influxes of Arab tourists into European countries have not been without problems, prompting Austrian organisations, for example, to release a pamphlet targeted at visitors from Arab countries with some key 'behavioural codes' (Al Maeena 2015). In addition to community backlash against visitors (as witnessed many times in history with other visitor groups), growing negative sentiment in European countries against Islamic groups and visitors poses an additional risk factor to the long-term sustainability of concentrated Arabic tourism in some communities.

Conclusion

This chapter touched on several interconnected challenges. Foremost, and in light of a peaking of conventional oil resources that will largely affect Middle Eastern countries, the core proposition is that oil-exporting countries are increasingly seeking to diversify away from fossil fuels and into tourism. Whilst on the surface this seems like a logical move, especially considering the global boom in tourism, the realities are more complex and bear multiple risks.

Oil-rich countries have for a long time used some of their resource wealth to 'buy' social stability by means of extensive public sector programmes, including employment, housing and health. When government budgets become tighter and these expensive programmes can no longer be maintained, the potential for social dissatisfaction and unrest increases. This is currently witnessed in several countries. Saudi Arabia, for example, recently announced substantial reductions in government spending, including pay cuts for employees and reduced subsidies for fuel (BBC 2016). Power structures can be supported by military forces, but past experiences, such as the oil crises in the 1980s, have shown that substantial crises can trigger social upheaval. Conflict or war further compromise oil exploration (e.g. civil war in Algeria in the 1990s), and also lead to a collapse in tourism, resulting in a downward spiral of destabilisation. Thus, oil income, power structures and social stability are intricately interwoven, and changes in one are likely to trigger changes in the others. At the same time, tourism in the Middle East (and elsewhere) depends on cheap oil, socio-political stability and investment. The old elites seamlessly morph into the new ones. In other words, the political and economic elites of the oil era are likely to work hand in hand (or are the same) with the emerging tourism oligarchs who own and operate key assets in Middle Eastern tourist destinations.

The ongoing success of these elites rests on similar principles. Wealth is accumulated through exclusion of broad parts of the population, and meaningful political participation is minimal or non-existent. Stability continues to depend on the effective mechanism of redistribution of benefits; however, as populations grow and income becomes relatively less, the social time bomb is ticking. This is particularly precarious, and different to similar situations in the past (e.g. civil war in Algeria in the 1990s), because members of the population now have wide access to social media, which enables them to draw on a broader global context for comparing domestic conditions with those in other (similar) countries. As a result, the deteriorating prospect of development is now coupled with a growing recognition of the constraints that the lack of a democratic system poses on ordinary citizens. Social media, then, not only offer a new source of information but also a platform for organising the masses in a system parallel to the ruling government. The collapse of socio-political systems in Libya, Syria and Yemen (in particular the loss of trust in the existing systems and elites), as well as instability in Egypt, can be seen as possible precursors of what might happen to other countries in the region, should income from oil (and tourism) decrease rapidly. Such declines may then progressively lead to social as well as political disintegration. Growing support of extremist groups and brotherhoods adds momentum to this development (Celso & Nalbandov 2016). Some of the movements are organically driven from the bottom, whilst other forms of extremism are supported by the state, for example through specific investment into Islamic schools that accelerate the de-secularisation of society.

The key question for the region, therefore, is how to prepare economically and in particular socio-politically for a post-fossil fuel world, and at the same time maintain domestic or even regional stability, and reconcile opposing social groups through targeted education and integration programmes. Political reforms are necessary and urgent. As such, the currently low oil price could also be interpreted as an opportunity to adjust government budgets, develop new policies and open up markets towards broader inclusion of the population in the workforce and the political system (in particular women). Tourism could then, indeed, become a pillar of these new economies, especially when it is planned in a way that minimises other vulnerabilities discussed in this chapter.

One Achilles heel is tourism's oil dependence. To address this major risk-heavy investment into renewable energy sources, high-speed rail networks and domestic or intra-regional tourism will be necessary. Currently low oil prices present a critical window of opportunity to initiate innovative forms of economic, socio-political and energetic reforms. A long-term approach to economic planning, including tourism, would then also avoid duplication and the high risk of substitutability (see Friedl & Becken 2015), as currently observed in several tourist cities (e.g. Dubai, Abu Dhabi, Doha). Lack of a unique tourism offer and investment into ethically and environmentally questionable mega-events, such as the FIFA 2022 football world cup in Doha, can further exacerbate the vulnerability of tourism to crisis (Weber 2016).

Notes

1 Note that the UNWTO defines the Middle East region to comprise 14 countries, namely Bahrain, Egypt, Iraq, Jordan, Kuwait, Lebanon, Libya, Oman, Palestine, Qatar, Saudi Arabia, Syrian Arab Republic, United Arab Emirates and Yemen.
2 Another reason is slowing global economic growth, in particular from China, increases in gas production, and heavy investment in renewable energy sources, in particular in European countries that seek to reduce their dependency on imported oil from geopolitically unstable regions and at the same time minimise fossil fuel-related greenhouse gas emissions.

References

Airbus (2018) 'Growing Horizons: 2017–2036. Global Market Forecast'. Available online: www.airbus. com/aircraft/market/global-market-forecast.html (Accessed 20 February 2018).

Al Maeena, T. (2015) 'The ugly side of Arab tourists'. *Gulf News*, 22 August 2015. Available online: http://gulfnews.com/opinion/thinkers/the-ugly-side-of-arab-tourists-1.1571015 (Accessed 2 August 2016).

Aleklett, K. (2012) *Peeking at Peak Oil*. Dordrecht: Springer.

BBC (2016) 'Saudi Arabia unveils first public sector pay cuts'. Middle East, 27 September 2016. Available online: www.bbc.com/news/world-middle-east-37482690 (Accessed 6 October 2016).

Becken, S. (2011) 'A critical review of tourism and oil', *Annals of Tourism Research*, 38(2): 359–379.

Becken, S. (2014) 'Oil depletion or a market problem? A framing analysis of peak oil in the Economist News Magazine', *Energy Research and Social Science*, 2: 125–134.

Becken, S. (2015) *Tourism and Oil: Preparing for the Challenge*. Bristol: Channel View Publications.

Becken, S., & Carmignani, F. (2016) 'Does tourism lead to Peace?', *Annals of Tourism Research*, 61: 63–79.

Becken, S., & Job, H. (2014) 'Protected areas in an era of global-local change', *Journal of Sustainable Tourism*, 22(4): 507–527.

Becken, S., & Lennox, J. (2012) 'Implications of a long term increase in oil prices for tourism', *Tourism Management*, 33(1): 133–142.

Bowler, T. (2015) 'Falling oil prices: Who are the winners and losers?'. January 2015, *BBC News*. Available online: www.bbc.com/news/business-29643612 (Accessed 11 September 2018).

Bows-Larkin, A. (2015) 'All adrift: Aviation, shipping, and climate change policy', *Climate Policy*, 15(6): 681–702.

Callen, T., Cherif, R., Hasanov, F., Hegazy, A., & Khandelwal, P. (2014) 'Economic diversification in the GCC: Past, present, and future'. IMF Staff Discussion Note. SDN/14/12. Available online: www.imf.org/external/pubs/ft/sdn/2014/sdn1412.pdf (Accessed 11 September 2018).

Celso, A., & Nalbandov, R. (eds) (2016) *The Crisis of the African State in the 21st Century: Globalisation, Tribalism and Jihadism Unbound*. Quantico: Marine Corps University Press.

Embassy of the United Arab Emirates (2016) 'The UAE and global oil supply'. Available online: www.uae-embassy.org/about-uae/energy/uae-and-global-oil-supply (Accessed 11 September 2018).

European Travel Commission (2007) 'Market insights'. United Arab Emirates, December. Available online: file:///C:/Users/s2825673/Downloads/ETCProfile+UAE12-07.%20(1).pdf

Fasano, U., & Iqbal, Z. (2003) 'GCC Countries: From oil dependence to diversification'. International Monetary Fund. Available online: www.imf.org/external/pubs/ft/med/2003/eng/fasano/ (Accessed 11 September 2018).

Friedl, H. (2010) 'Freiheit—limitation: Peak oil and anti-terror-Krieg', in R. Egger, & T. Herdin (eds), *Tourismus im Spannungsfeld von Polaritäten* (pp. 275–292). Vienna: Verlag.

Friedl, H. (2015) 'Degrowth', in C. Cater, B. Garrod, & T. Low (eds), *The Encyclopedia of Sustainable Tourism* (p. 136). Wallingford: CAB International.

Friedl, H., & Becken, S. (2015) 'Dubai–die letzte Erfolgsstory fossiler Wachstumsträume?', in R. Egger, & K. Luger (eds), *Tourismus und mobile Freizeit–Lebensformen, Trends, Herausforderungen* (pp. 367–394). Vienna: Studien Verlag.

Heinberg, R. (2013) *Snake Oil: How Fracking's False Promise of Plenty Imperils our Future*. Santa Rosa, CA: Post Carbon Institute.

Hvidt, M. (2009) 'The Dubai Model: An outline of key development-process elements in Dubai', *International Journal of Middle East Studies*, 41: 397–418.

IATA (International Air Transport Association) (2016) 'Fact sheet industry statistics'. June 2016. IATA: Geneva.

IEA (International Energy Agency) (2010) World Energy Outlook 2010. Paris. Available online: www.iea.org/publications/freepublications/publication/weo2010.pdf (Accessed 1 March 2013).

IEA (2016) International Energy Outlook 2016. Available online: www.eia.gov/forecasts/ieo/exec_summ.cfm (Accessed 20 July 2016).

Jafari, J., & Scott, N. (2014) Muslim world and its tourisms. *Annals of Tourism Research*, 44: 1–19.

Krauss, C., & Reed, S. (2016) 'OPEC agrees to cut production, sending oil prices soaring'. *New York Times*, 28 September 2016. Available online: www.nytimes.com/2016/09/29/business/energy-environment/opec-agreement-oil-prices.html?_r=0 (Accessed 4 October 2016).

Kumar, R. (2012) 'Tourism in Dubai: The Sunrise sector', *Middle East Journal of Business*, 7(1): 15–16.

Lennox, J. (2012) 'Impacts of high oil prices on tourism in New Zealand', *Tourism Economics*, 18(4): 781–800.

Organization of the Petroleum Exporting Countries (OPEC) (2016) 'OPEC Share of World Oil Reserves, 2015'. Available online: www.opec.org/opec_web/en/data_graphs/330.htm (Accessed 11 September 2018).

Owen, N.A., Inderwildi, O.R., & King, D.A. (2010) 'The status of conventional world oil reserves—Hype or cause for concern?' *Energy Policy*, 38: 4743–4749.

Pacione, M. (2005) 'City profile Dubai', *Cities*, 22(3): 255–265.

Peersman, G., & Robays, I. (2009) 'The economic consequences of oil shocks—A cross-country analysis'. Available online: www.wlu.ca/viessmann/rba09/Peersman.pdf (Accessed 12 November 2012).

Prantner, C. (2016, 2 October) 'Langer Marsch zum chinesischen Traum'. *The Standard*, p. 6. Available online: http://derstandard.at/2000045186659/Langer-Marsch-zum-chinesischen-Traum (Accessed 2 October 2016).

Scott, D., Amelung, B., Becken, S., Ceron, J.P., Dubois, G., Gössling, S., Peeters, P., & Simpson, M. (2008) *Climate Change and Tourism: Responding to Global Challenges*. Madrid/Paris: World Tourism Organization and United Nations Environment Programme.

UNWTO (United Nations World Tourism Organization) (2012) *The Middle East Outbound Travel Market with Special Insight into the Image of Europe as a Destination*. Madrid: UNWTO.

UNWTO (2016) *World Tourism Barometer, Volume 14*. July 2016. Madrid: UNWTO.

Weber, C. (2016) *Die ethische Vertretbarkeit von Mega-Sport-Events, untersucht am Beispiel der FIFA-WM 2022 in Katar*. Masterarbeit zur Erlangung des akademischen Grades einer Master of Arts in Business, Fachhochschul-Master-Studiengang Gesundheitsmanagement im Tourismus. FH Johanneum, Bad Gleichenberg, Austria.

Wohlmuther, C., & Wintersteiner, W. (eds) (2014) *International Handbook on Tourism and Peace*. Klagenfurt: Drava Verlag.

Wood Mackenzie (2016) 'Deferred upstream projects tally reaches 68'. News release, January. Available online: www.woodmac.com/media-centre/12530462 (Accessed 11 September 2018).

World Bank (2013) 'Opening doors. Gender equality and development in the Middle East and North Africa'. MENA Development Report. Available online: https://openknowledge.worldbank.org/bit-stream/handle/10986/12552/751810PUB0EPI002060130Opening0doors.pdf?sequence=1 (Accessed 5 October 2016).

15

DESERT LANDSCAPES AND TOURISM IN THE MIDDLE EAST AND NORTH AFRICA

Alan S. Weber

Introduction

Before the rise of ecotourism, arid deserts were relatively neglected as tourist destinations. Some of the reasons for this were the lack of infrastructure, poverty of local inhabitants, harsh and sometimes life-threatening environmental conditions and the negative misconceptions of deserts as wasteland, lifeless, and inhospitable. Before the 1940s and 1950s, when trucks capable of negotiating difficult terrain, including sand dunes, became widely available to local inhabitants, few people would venture into an arid desert without a highly experienced local guide knowledgeable about water sources, wayfinding and survival techniques. Wilfred Thesiger's *Arabian Sands* (1959) describes the first crossing of the hyper-arid Rub al 'Khali Desert between Oman and Abu Dhabi in 1946 during which his group suffered near disaster from shortages of water and food. Even some of his Bedouin guides from the local Rashid tribe were unwilling to proceed further into the desert.

However, with the advent of cell and satellite phones, GPS, reliable maps, and other modern technologies, remote desert areas can now be visited with much greater safety with proper planning and precautions. Consequently, deserts have become increasingly popular as tourist destinations owing to their natural beauty, serenity, remoteness ('off the beaten track'), and the hint of danger still attached to these extreme environments. Due to their fragility and limited ability to regenerate from human impacts, however, these ecosystems must above all be managed sustainably. This chapter examines the potential of desert landscapes in the Middle East for tourism, and the challenges that must be overcome, including long-term environmental and water resource management, equitable distribution of tourist revenues amongst local stakeholders, and preventing undesirable cultural disruption.

Desert biomes, tourism and cultural experiences

Deserts are areas of low precipitation (aridity) and account for almost 30–50 per cent of the earth's surface when including the polar regions. There is no agreed upon and strict definition of deserts, however. It is therefore best to consider deserts as a continuum of environments ranging from almost lifeless regions to areas capable of supporting various forms of agriculture.

Deserts and drylands can be defined by using various aridity indices, such as the ratio between annual precipitation and potential evapotranspiration (evaporation + transpiration) or AI = P/PET. Desert environments include hyperarid (AI < 0.05) and arid (AI = 0.05–0.20) lands, while semi-arid lands (typified by the Sub-Saharan Sahel) which support permanent grasslands, trees and shrubs are referred to as steppes, dry grasslands or dry savannahs (Middleton & Thomas 1997; Rakhecha & Singh 2009: 327). Semi-arid lands comprise approximately 20 per cent of the earth's land mass. Rainfall in desert regions usually amounts to less than 200 mm per annum (Weber 2013, 2014: 150). A large portion of the Middle East and North Africa consists of hyperarid and arid lands primarily due to the enormous Sahara Desert, which stretches across North Africa into the Arabian Peninsula, and extensive deserts are located in Iran, Pakistan and Afghanistan.

Deserts form as the result of constant warm tradewinds (Sahara Desert in North Africa), distance from large water bodies and rain-bearing clouds (Sonoran Desert in the US), offshore cold ocean currents (Atacama Desert of Chile), and rain shadow deserts when clouds drop their moisture as they rise over mountain ranges (Tibetan Plateau). Desert landscapes can consist of loose gravel, hard-packed pavements, rocky mountains and hills, canyons, sand dunes, rocky outcrops, dry lake beds and salt pans (deposits), with occasional areas of lush vegetation (oases) from underground water, springs or depressions. These varied geological features can often be found within the same desert region, providing a variety of landscapes for aesthetic enjoyment. Deserts exist in both hot and cold climates. Due to the sparse rainfall and vegetation that can only support a limited number of agricultural activities, such as date farming and nomadic animal herding, deserts generally have a low population density, although the major urban areas of Dubai (UAE), Doha (Qatar) and Riyadh (Saudi Arabia) flourish in arid deserts due to groundwater resources and seawater desalination. Without soil, plant cover, cloud cover or large bodies of tempering water, rocky deserts depending on their latitude can experience extreme temperatures ranging from -50°C to +55°C.

Desert areas, especially hyperarid regions, are underutilised and untapped as tourist destinations specifically, because they are often not suitable for mass tourism, but rather for niche activities such as adventure tourism, ecotourism and extreme tourism. Barriers to mass tourism include the fact that deserts are generally in remote or inaccessible areas with minimal infrastructure, which results in a lack of amenities such as electricity, Internet and cell phone services and creates discomforts like dust, extreme heat or cold, and unpaved roads requiring special vehicles. As evidenced by studies carried out in the Wadi Rum and Petra areas in Jordan, mass tourism places unique stress on desert biomes, which are fragile and delicately balanced (Reid & Schwab 2006). Litter, damage to the natural environment through human activity, and buildings that do not harmonise with the landscape can quickly destroy the original visual value of the destination. Desert tourist practice must therefore be governed by sustainable tourism principles.

The desert regions of MENA, with the exception of internationally renowned archaeological sites, including Petra in Jordan, the Pyramids of Egypt, Palmyra in Syria, Carthage in Tunisia and Persepolis in Iran, and coastal resorts on the Mediterranean, Red Sea and Persian Gulf, have been neglected in tourist development strategies both at the national and local policy level (Krakover 1985). Resorts along the Red Sea, Dead Sea and Mediterranean often simply provide a standard mass tourism beach holiday experience, and although located within desert regions, deserts are not necessarily part of the tourism product. The neglect of truly desert destinations is related to the current and historical challenges detailed in the section below on sustainable desert tourism. Thus, ecotourism (the sustainable appreciation of natural environments) is the main draw of deserts along with cultural tourism (appreciating archaeology, history and the traditional cultures of modern desert dwellers).

Although sometimes difficult to access by land vehicles, the lack of vegetation in some desert regions creates natural flat landing strips for small aircraft (salt pans and gravel deserts) so that regional airports do not need to be constructed. In addition, salt flats are suitable for such recreational activities as high-speed car racing (the Bonneville Speedway in Utah) and land yachting (sail-equipped wheeled vehicles), although motorised vehicles can have negative environmental impacts if not regulated. Modern off-road vehicles, helicopters, four-wheel drive trucks, and boats can also provide access in addition to well-adapted traditional means of transport such as camels, the 'Ships of the Deserts', which are particularly suited to Slow Travel and cultural immersion experiences (camping, desert safaris and homestays with camel herders).

The unique geomorphology (landscapes, geology and topography) of deserts is a major draw for visitors, and desert regions are often described as 'other-worldly' by newcomers (Eshraghi, Ahmad, & Toriman 2012). Certain desert features such as barchan sand dunes, salt flats and ventifacts only exist in drylands. Ventifacts or yardangs are statue-like rocks that have been sculpted into aesthetically pleasing forms by wind erosion. A striking example is 'Lot's Wife', a pillar of almost pure salt on Mount Sodom, Israel. Flash flooding in addition creates patterns of erosion resulting in canyons, wadis (arroyos), mesas and buttes not found in temperate climates or obscured by soil and vegetation. The lack of vegetation in deserts reveals the colours and patterns of underlying rocks. Differently coloured bands of granite, sandstones, siltstones, limestones, and volcanic ash form dramatic patterns, especially when folded by tectonic forces or uplifting. Along the Dead Sea area of Jordan and Israel, the completely exposed rock, salt and mineral deposits display pure whites from phosphates and salts, blacks, greys and browns from bitumen, pure yellow from sulphur, and a range of reddish hues from iron-bearing minerals. Thus 'geological tourism', or geotourism, based on topographical features such as shapes, colours, vistas and views, is gaining more attention in tourist strategies and represents a unique aspect of desert destinations (Allan 2016; Dowling & Newsome 2006).

Another unique experience related to the physics of sand dune movement are the 'singing sands' in some deserts. Through wind action or by walking on the surface, sand dunes under certain dry conditions produce a range of wailing, thumping, screeching and singing noises that Bedouins attributed to djinn (genies). The experience of hearing a singing sand dune is highly unique and unforgettable, a key tourist asset where they occur. Xerophytic and halophytic plants uniquely adapted to the desert, such as Saguaro cacti, and ephemeral grasses and flowers, which must rapidly bloom and produce seed after sporadic rainfalls, can transform deserts into dense, colourful landscapes. Through conservation efforts, large animals such as oryx, jackals, Thomson's gazelle, ibex, hyenas and sand cats are returning to areas that are off limits to human hunting.

Sand-skiing and sandboarding are other low-impact desert activities that complement hiking and other nature-related activities such as bird and animal watching, since these sports take place on moving sand which quickly erases human traces. Dune bashing, driving up and down dunes at high speeds and executing turns and vehicular acrobatics, is popular throughout the Arabian Peninsula, but this is a very high-risk sport with frequent injuries and fatalities from overturned cars. Also, destruction of natural dune-anchoring vegetation can cause dunes to advance rapidly, potentially aiding in desertification and the invasion of populated areas by sand. Thus, all sand dune-related recreational activities should be monitored and regulated and preferably restricted to specific areas away from protected natural parks.

As some deserts border areas of salt or fresh water, water sports and water activities including swimming, boating, jet skiing, bird watching, water animal safaris, and fishing can be combined with desert recreation. Large endorheic lakes and basins (water bodies with no outlet) surrounded by desert include the Caspian Sea, Chad Lake Basin in North Africa, whose northern region borders on the Djurab and Ténéré deserts, and the Aral Sea of Uzbekistan (once the world's fourth largest lake and a popular tourist attraction, which has now shrunk to 10 per cent of its former size since the 1960s). The green delta and snaking green ribbon of the Nile River valley of Egypt are striking when seen from space, surrounded completely by the brown, hyper-arid Sahara Desert and Qattara Depression to the west. Nile River cruises generate substantial tourism-based income, and the Red Sea, also completely bordered by desert, remains relatively unpolluted, with healthy coral reefs and marine animal abundance for snorkelling, fishing and diving. The Red Sea can be contrasted with the Persian Gulf, which is suffering severe environmental damage from tourist infrastructure projects, such as removal of protective mangrove trees and mass mortality of coral from dredging to build artificial tourist islands and resorts (Gladstone, Curley, & Shokri 2013). The entire coast of North Africa borders the Mediterranean Sea, with the western portion bordering on the Atlantic; the areas closest to the sea are generally more temperate, mild and humid, offering a more hospitable climate for northern tourists than the extremely hot and dry interiors of Algeria, Tunisia, Morocco and Libya, which are sparsely populated.

Due to low moisture in deserts, archaeological ruins suffer much less erosion than in temperate climates, especially when they have been covered by windblown sand and later excavated or are protected by caves. Prehistoric rock art from the Neolithic period has survived in Figuig, Oran, Djelfa, Ennedi and Tassili n'Ajjer across the Sahara, rivalling the Lascaux paintings in France. The Nabataean, Roman, Achaemenid, Sassanian, Egyptian and Babylonian empires have left behind significant desert ruins preserved by the dry climate. In addition, many tens of thousands of less flashy ruins, built heritage sites, geological oddities and aesthetically pleasing environments exist throughout the MENA deserts, but they must compete with iconic offerings such as the Pyramids. Tarawneh and Wray (2017) discuss the difficulties in developing tourist strategies for lesser-known Jordanian desert attractions such as Neolithic village sites, which have significant scientific, historical, cultural and archaeological value, but which also must compete with the visually stunning and well-marketed Nabataean rock sculptures.

Although most of North Africa, the Arabian Peninsula, Iran, Pakistan and Afghanistan consists of Muslim-majority nations, the Middle East boasts a surprising diversity of peoples for visitors interested in experiencing different cultures: followers of Abrahamic religions (Jews, Christians and Muslims), Indo-Iranians, Pashtun, Balochis and indigenous nomadic peoples such as Bedouin, Tuareg and Berbers. Dialect, language, foods, music and customs differ greatly amongst the major Middle Eastern desert regions—Maghreb (western Sahara), Egypt and Libya, Levant, Persian Gulf, Iranian plateau, Balochistan, and the Thar and Cholistan regions. Even within Islamic cultures, Shias, Sunnis, Ibadis, Sufis, Ismailis and Alawites follow different practices. Desert cultures tend to be highly hospitable (reciprocal altruism), even offering aid to enemies and potential enemies, since they expect similar treatment if a life-threatening situation arises such as being lost without water. Thus, native norms of guest-welcoming are valuable assets for tourism industries that respect and integrate local customs, a cornerstone of sustainable tourism practices.

A significant number of MENA countries are major oil and gas producers, and the Gulf countries (Kuwait, Qatar, UAE, Saudi Arabia, Iran, Iraq) in particular derive the majority of their GDP from oil export revenues. Thus, these countries suffer boom and bust economic cycles as their growth is governed by the rising and falling of oil prices. Many Middle Eastern countries have therefore embarked on economic diversification strategies, with national governments targeting tourism (including meetings, incentives, conferences and exhibitions (MICE)) as a major sector for state support and development (Stephenson 2017). Coastal resort and international residential development has therefore accelerated in desert regions such as Egypt (Red

Sea coast resorts), Qatar (The Pearl), UAE (Palm Jumeira, The World, Palm Deira), and Jordan and Israel (Dead Sea resorts). Developments such as the indoor ski slope Ski Dubai in the Mall of the Emirates have specifically been designed with an international clientele in mind, whose interests may lie in the warm climate, shopping and entertainment and liberal tax environment, and not necessarily in the desert location. These tourism strategies linked to economic diversification not only directly attract tourist dollars but also foreign direct investment in tourism infrastructure, such as hotels and residential compounds.

Challenges in sustainable desert tourism

A growing number of international organisations, most notably the World Tourism Organization (UNWTO), have embraced sustainable tourism principles for all sectors and markets of the tourism industry. Desert environments are fragile and do not recover from human impacts as rapidly as humid and tropical environments do, which can erase human impacts through new plant growth, erosion and bacterial and fungicidal decomposition of organic wastes, which desiccate in deserts instead of rotting. For example, tyre tracks in the desert can remain visible for decades. According to the UNWTO (2006: 11–12), sustainable tourism in deserts should:

1. **Make optimal use of environmental resources** that constitute a key element in tourism development, maintaining essential ecological processes and helping to conserve natural heritage and biodiversity.
2. **Respect the socio-cultural authenticity of host communities**, conserve their built and living cultural heritage and traditional values, and contribute to inter-cultural understanding and tolerance.
3. **Ensure viable, long-term economic operations**, providing socio-economic benefits to all stakeholders that are fairly distributed, including stable employment and income-earning opportunities and social services to host communities, and contributing to poverty alleviation.

The origin of the word desert from Latin 'desertum' or 'abandoned place' reminds us how stereotypes of these regions still persist in Western thought. Non-Middle Eastern tourists often hold two stereotypical views of these destinations: hostile and forbidding places suitable only for professional adventurers; or exotic and erotic orientalist locales, an image fostered by nineteenth- and twentieth-century colonial tourism to Algeria, Morocco and Tunisia (Al-Mahadin & Burns 2007: 138). Both of these preconceived notions can be the basis of marketing campaigns for these regions, but tourism officials should also consider the other dimensions of these locales discussed earlier, particularly since orientalist attitudes—most importantly, the stereotype that oriental peoples are governed by passion and not reason—are viewed as offensive throughout the Middle East.

Deserts can be subject to extreme and uncomfortable conditions during the hot season. The deserts of Libya, Iran and the Arabian Gulf can reach temperatures of 50–52°C (122–125.6°F) in the summer, which are at the outer limits of human survivability. Emergency services must therefore form part of tourist services—can guides treat heat exhaustion and the potentially deadly heatstroke? Both are serious medical emergencies. These temperatures can limit tourist activities to indoor attractions or to wintertime (when temperatures are comfortable) in the hot climate deserts, reducing the length of the tourist season. Dubai, a top tourist destination in the Middle East, has adapted to these potentially off-putting conditions by developing extensive indoor malls for shopping, an indoor ski slope, international dining options and entertainment, such as concerts, shows and bars serving alcohol, which are illegal or tightly regulated in the more conservative Muslim-majority countries.

Several desert regions are suffering from internal political turmoils exacerbated by international superpowers. Major armed conflicts are ongoing in Syria, Iraq, Libya, Afghanistan and Yemen. All of these countries with substantial desert regions are unsafe for Western tourists and the origin of these conflicts may be indirectly or partially related to interference by foreign powers, water conflicts, overpopulation, wealth disparity and the divide between conservative and traditional ways of life in the desert and the more cosmopolitan lifestyles of city dwellers. An insurgency in Egypt's Sinai Peninsula desert is rooted in the marginalisation of Bedouin tribes. Tourism is therefore intertwined with conflict, as violence can drive away tourists, but resolving conflicts on the other hand can establish equity with desert peoples by providing them with small business opportunities if governments assist them in providing infrastructure such as roads, airports, dams, wells and business loans. Also, since tourism is one of the world's largest industries, unresolved nation-wide and regional conflicts can severely reduce the national GDP (Avraham & Ketter 2016; Timothy & Daher 2009: 151–152).

Water is essential for understanding Middle Eastern politics, social and economic structure, and the migrations of peoples. Desert regions are not devoid of water: the large Nubian Sandstone Aquifer System lies beneath Libya, Chad, Sudan and Egypt and has been exploited by The Great Man-Made River (GMM, which supplies Sirte, Tripoli and Benghazi) developed by former Libyan leader Muammar Gaddafi. The GMM is the world's largest water delivery system. Access to water has been a source of conflict both on a local (tribal skirmishes over oases) and national scale, both historically and in modern times. The collapse of the Ma'rib Dam, which supported the irrigation of 25,000 acres of farmland, between 570–575 AD in Yemen caused a mass migration of upwards of 50,000 people into the northern Arabian Peninsula. An earlier dam breach and migration may have included the powerful and influential Ghassanids, Christian Arabs who entered Syria and allied themselves with the Roman Empire. Thus, water issues have played a central role in Middle Eastern demographic shifts and will continue to do so in the future, especially in areas of increasing population density such as the Jordan–Israel region and large North African cities (Al-Alawi 2008; Dłuzewska 2008).

Tourism development in deserts not only requires extra water for tourist arrivals, but also water for the construction of buildings, roads and attractions and water for imported construction workers. For example, arid desert regions of low population density have manual labour shortages, and therefore tourist development increases the local population (Weber 2019). Historically, water withdrawals were limited by technology and although they lack surface and running water, some deserts in Namibia and Saudi Arabia have significant underground reserves. However, these are fossil water reservoirs, the remnants of glaciation or earlier wetter periods. Many are not replaceable when withdrawals exceed recharge rates from infrequent rains. With continuous mechanised pumping of underground water, water tables drop, causing land subsidence; aquifers become contaminated with salt water layers, and continued use of groundwater for agriculture can cause salination of soils which become increasingly toxic to plants (Hussain 2005). Saudi Arabia's aquifer system, once estimated to hold about the same amount of water as Lake Erie, has been depleted in a matter of decades by an estimated two-thirds to four-fifths of its former volume (Elhadj 2004: 27) due to unrestrained withdrawals for wheat production encouraged by government subsidies. Tens of thousands of years must pass before this water can regenerate. One solution for water shortages—the desalination of salt water carried out in many Middle Eastern countries that border oceans—is extremely costly.

Another negative environmental impact associated with increased use of deserts for tourist activity includes anthropogenic desertification, in which land through human activity becomes more arid and vegetation and wildlife disappear. Although deserts pre-date the arrival of humankind, people's ability to manipulate their own environment since the invention of the steam and internal combustion engines has been unprecedented and humans may represent a major cause of desertification, primarily in the destruction of ground cover and the permanent removal of fossil fresh water with motorised pumps. This extracted water evaporates rapidly in dry regions without returning to the water table and cannot be replenished (Imeson 2012). Processes such as desertification and man's potential role in the creation of deserts, including climate change, is still not well understood due to the lack of scientific research and data gathering in remote regions. Many environmentalists, given the potential catastrophic consequences of desertification, take a cautionary 'better safe than sorry' approach and argue for limiting the worst and well-established human causes of desertification, such as slash-and-burn agriculture in drylands.

Although desert Bedouins developed ecologically sound practices such as *hima* (grassland management), their cultures have been disrupted by forced government sedentarisation policies and modernity. Living in harmony with their environment is becoming increasingly difficult, for example, when former nomadic people accustomed to searching for ephemeral grasslands after desert rains were forced to settle in one area where their domestic animal density caused severe land degradation from soil impaction and the denuding of plant cover. Thus, a rational strategy would be to combine the scientific evidence base for desertification mitigation with traditional local knowledge on how to preserve water, soil and food supplies (Davies & Holcombe 2009).

Indigenous peoples in arid deserts are sometimes poor and marginalised, existing on subsistence agriculture or nomadic pastoralism. The removal of the B'dul tribe from the Petra, Jordan, Nabataean monuments demonstrates the difficulties that can arise when competing commercial, indigenous and government forces clash over valuable tourist resources. The B'dul have lived in the Petra Park monuments for centuries and sold artefacts and provided guide and donkey transport services. They were forcibly removed by the Jordanian government in the 1980s to the government-built town of Umm Sayhoun near the park, and although many left willingly for the new amenities of electricity and running water, the eviction led to some minor armed skirmishes with officials (Al-Haija 2011; Chaouni 2014: 30–31; Comer 2012: 1–28). Using the monuments as living spaces was causing rapid deterioration of the buildings, and the continued touching of walls and the humidity from the breath of tourists has caused additional serious damage (Mustafa 2011). With very large fees charged for entrance—90 Jordanian dinars (US$127) for non-accommodated visitors—the obvious question is how much of this wealth is returned back to the local communities such as the B'dul and Layathnah? Also, international tourism experts, UNESCO, and Jordanian officials became concerned about how employment of Bedouins in the tourism industry was creating a 'neo-Bedouinism', a distorted version of traditional cultural practices which evolved to please non-Arab visitors, fulfilling their romantic preconceived notions of desert life. The UNESCO Proclamation of Masterpieces of the Oral and Intangible Heritage of Humanity placed the Bedouin culture of the Petra region and another popular tourist area, Wadi Rum, on their protected list. According to UNESCO (2005), 'the increase of desert tourism and its demand for "authentic Bedu culture" may lead to its distortion'. Bedouin culture is rapidly being subsumed by modern, urbanised culture throughout the Middle East, and cultural heritage tourism aims to preserve traditional ways of life not only to attract tourists interested in experiencing other customs, foods, language and music, but also to aid local inhabitants themselves to derive employment by simultaneously pursuing age-old patterns of living. However, some Bedouin leaders do not support this form of livelihood, fearing 'loss of traditional cultures, inflated prices, behaviour among youth that mimics tourists' behaviour, water and air pollution, and declining moral values' (Al-Oun & Al-Hamoud 2008: 37). This issue is particularly complex since a major cultural attribute of Bedouins historically has been their adaptability to changes in environmental, social and political conditions (Hobbs & Tsunemi 2007).

Conclusion

All potential uses of deserts, including tourism, mining, grazing and wildlife management should be accompanied by environmental impact assessments as well as studies on the possible economic and cultural impacts to local inhabitants. Key issues that should be resolved in desert tourism planning and management include such questions as: Are local water withdrawals from fossil (non-renewable) water supplies sustainable for future generations? What other water capture or production strategies are viable? Will pollution including human sewage compromise potable water sources? Will extinctions of key species in vulnerable desert food chains (only a small number of species are adapted to hyperarid conditions) cause the collapse of other species, degrading the environment further? Will potentially valuable medicinal plants perish permanently from unregulated collection, off-road vehicle traffic, and walking and animal riding in the desert? Do permanent or temporary exclusion zones need to be established during migration or breeding periods of birds and animals? Will increased human activity harm current aesthetics or built heritage making them less attractive to visitors? Will local inhabitants be included in tourism policy planning and management and will they share in profits? Will indigenous cultural practices be protected from exposure to tourists? Without a solid evidence base to answer these fundamental questions, all human activities in deserts have the potential to render these regions eventually unsuitable for tourism. Table 15.1 summarises these varied challenges and suggests strategies for mitigation.

Table 15.1 Desert tourism challenges and recommended mitigation strategies

Desert tourism problem	Recommended mitigation strategies
Flora and fauna fragility	Off-limits and protected zones; restrict travel to marked trails and roads only; rotate fallow regions; temporary off-limits zones during breeding; patrols and fines for hunting or damaging wildlife; artificial breeding and reintroduction of indigenous plants and animals
Slow biome regeneration	Fallow areas; limited entrance; permits; environmental education; required video viewing on responsible tourist behaviours before entering parks
Landscape destruction	Initial environmental impact assessment, including natural aesthetics; ban or limit activities such as camping, open fires, collection of natural objects
Water scarcity	Desalination, pumped ground water, rain water collection, dams; limit entrance to day trips or water carried in by tourists; building codes requiring water-saving technologies; research into renewable energy desalination
Water competition	Engage farmers, ranchers, government agencies, and tourist developers in discussions on equitable water distribution
Local culture change	Engage local leaders; education on tourist impacts on culture; government subsidy of traditional local cultural activities

Source: Compiled from information in Weber (2014).

Sustainable tourism management avoids what is alien and non-natural. For example, non-indigenous ornamental plants at hotels and parks often require more water than native plants and can compete for habitat. Artificial water instalments in deserts like ponds and swimming pools evaporate and reduce fresh water supplies. Due to its sometimes non-renewable nature, water access, use and distribution must be negotiated with local stakeholders during tourism development so that the benefits of the industry can continue for future generations. Simple and effective sustainable practices for desert use include building practices using local materials and traditional knowledge for heating and cooling, such as adobe and mud-brick construction and the wind towers and underground canals developed for cooling in Iran and the Arabian Peninsula (*barjeel* and *qanat*). These practices are often less costly, more effective than modern technologies, and they validate indigenous knowledge systems that have evolved for maximum efficiency through millennia of human trial and error.

References

Al-Alawi, M. (2008) 'Desertification in Jordan: A security issue', in P.H. Liotta, D.A. Mouat, W.G. Kepner, & J.M. Lancaster (eds), *Environmental Change and Human Security* (pp. 81–102). Dordrecht: Springer.

Al Haija, A.A. (2011) 'Jordan: Tourism and conflict with local communities', *Habitat International*, 35: 93–100.

Allan, M. (2016) 'Place attachment and tourist experience in the context of desert tourism—the case of Wadi Rum', *Czech Journal of Tourism*, 5(1): 35–52.

Al-Mahadin, S., & Burns, P. (2007) 'Visitors, visions, and veils: The portrayal of the Arab world in tourism advertising', in R.F. Daher (ed.), *Tourism in the Middle East: Continuity, Change and Transformation* (pp. 137–160). Clevedon: Channel View Publications.

Al-Oun, S., & Al-Hamoud, M. (2008) 'The potential for developing community-based tourism among the Bedouins in the Badia of Jordan', *Journal of Heritage Tourism*, 3(1): 36–54.

Avraham, E., & Ketter, E. (2016) 'Marketing Middle East destinations', in E. Avraham, & E. Ketter (eds), *Tourism Marketing for Developing Countries: Battling Stereotypes and Crises in Asia, Africa and the Middle East* (pp. 83–107). London: Palgrave Macmillan.

Chaouni, A. (ed.) (2014) *Ecotourism, Nature Conservation, and Development: Reimagining Jordan's Shobak Arid Region*. Basel: Birkhäuser.

Comer, D.C. (2012) *Tourism and Archaeological Heritage Management at Petra*. New York: Springer.

Davies, J., & Holcombe, S. (2009) 'Desert knowledge: Integrating knowledge and development in arid and semi-arid drylands', *GeoJournal*, 74: 363–375.

Dłuzewska, A. (2008) 'Direct and indirect impact of the tourism industry on drylands: The tourism industry example of southern Tunisia', *Management of Environmental Quality: An International Journal*, 19(6): 661–669.

Dowling, R.K., & Newsome, D. (2006) *Geotourism*. Oxford: Elsevier.

Elhadj, E. (2004) 'Camels don't fly, deserts don't bloom: An assessment of Saudi Arabia's experiment in Desert Agriculture'. Occasional Paper No. 48. London: School of Oriental and African Studies.

Eshraghi, M., Ahmad, H., & Toriman, M.E. (2012) 'Contribution of geomorphological assessment for sustainable geotourism: A case of Iran's desert', *Advances in Environmental Biology*, 6(3): 1188–1195.

Gladstone, W., Curley, B., & Shokri, M.A. (2013) 'Environmental impacts of tourism in the Gulf and the Red Sea', *Marine Pollution Bulletin*, 72: 375–388.

Hobbs, J.J., & Tsunemi, F. (2007) 'Soft sedentarization: Bedouin tourist stations as a response to drought in Egypt's eastern desert', *Human Ecology*, 35: 209–222.

Hussain, N. (2005) *Strategic Plan for Combating Water and Soil Salinity in Sultanate of Oman for 2005–2015*. Muscat: Ministry of Agriculture and Fisheries.

Imeson, A. (2012) *Desertification, Land Degradation and Sustainability*. Oxford: Wiley-Blackwell.

Krakover, S. (1985) 'Development of tourism resort areas in arid regions', in Y. Gradus (ed.), *Desert Development: Man and Technology in Sparselands* (pp. 271–284). Dordrecht: D. Reidel Publishing.

Middleton, N.J., & Thomas, D.S.G. (eds) (1997) *World Atlas of Desertification*, 2nd edn. London: United Nations Environment Program.

Mustafa, M.H. (2011) 'The impacts of tourism development on the archaeological site of Petra and local communities in surrounding villages', *Asian Social Science*, 7(8): 88–96.

Rakhecha, P.R., & Singh, V.P. (2009) *Applied Hydrometeorology*. New York: Springer.

Reid, M., & Schwab, W. (2006) 'Barriers to sustainable development: Jordan's sustainable tourism strategy', *Journal of Asian and African Studies*, 41(5/6): 439–457.

Stephenson, M.L. (2017) 'Introduction: Deciphering international tourism development in the GCC region', in M.L. Stephenson, & A. Al-Hamarneh (eds), *International Tourism Development and the Gulf Cooperation Council States: Challenges and Opportunities* (pp. 1–25). London: Routledge.

Tarawneh, M.S. & Wray, M. (2017) 'Incorporating Neolithic villages at Petra, Jordan: An integrated approach to sustainable tourism', *Journal of Heritage Tourism*, 12(2): 155–171.

Thesiger, W. (1959) *Arabian Sands*. London: Longman.

Timothy, D., & Daher, R.F. (2009) 'Heritage tourism in Southwest Asia and North Africa', in D.J. Timothy, & G.P. Nyaupane (eds), *Cultural Heritage and Tourism in the Developing World: A Regional Perspective* (pp. 146–164). Abingdon: Routledge.

UNESCO (2005) *Third Proclamation of Masterpieces of the Oral and Intangible Heritage of Humanity*. New York: UNESCO.

UNWTO (2006) *Sustainable Development of Tourism in Deserts: Guidelines for Decision Makers*. Madrid: World Tourism Organization.

Weber, A.S. (2013) 'Sustainable tourism in extreme environments: Lessons from desert regions', in *Tourism in Southern and Eastern Europe: Crisis—A Challenge of Sustainable Tourism Development?* (pp. 430–431). Opatija, Croatia: University of Rijeka, Faculty of Tourism and Hospitality Management.

Weber, A.S. (2014) 'Desert and drylands extreme tourist development', *Service Management*, 3(14): 149–58.

Weber, A.S. (2019) 'Mega-projects and microstates, Bedouins and businessmen: Qatar's tourism vision in revolution', in A. Spiess, F. Al-Mubarak, & A.S. Weber (eds), *Tourism Development in the GCC States: Reconciling Economic Growth, Conservation and Sustainable Development*. New York: Springer.

Zekri, S., Mbaga, M., Fouzai, A., & Al-Shaqsi, S. (2011) 'Recreational value of an oasis in Oman', *Environmental Management*, 48: 81–88.

16

TOURISM AND CLIMATE CHANGE IN THE MIDDLE EAST

C. Michael Hall

Introduction

The reality of climate change is no longer open to scientific dispute. The most recent Intergovernmental Panel on Climate Change (IPCC) report on the physical science of climate change concluded in its summary for policy makers that

> warming of the climate system is unequivocal, and since the 1950s, many of the observed changes are unprecedented over decades to millennia. The atmosphere and ocean have warmed, the amounts of snow and ice have diminished, sea level has risen, and the concentrations of greenhouse gases have increased.
>
> *(IPCC 2013a: 2)*

The IPCC also emphasises that 'human influence on the climate system is clear. This is evident from the increasing greenhouse gas concentrations in the atmosphere, positive radiative forcing, observed warming, and understanding of the climate system' (IPCC 2013a:13).

The Middle East is the first region of the world to have effectively run out of water (Allan 2001). Not surprisingly, the Middle East is therefore widely regarded as one of the world's regions that appears most at risk from current anthropogenic climate change (Evans 2009; Lelieveld et al. 2012, 2014). With the effects of climate change already regarded as having an impact on security in the region (Brown & Crawford 2009; Gleick 2014; Kelley, Mohtadi, Cane, Seager, & Kushnir 2015; Mason, Zeitoun, & Mimi 2012), including water and food security (Ludwig & Roson 2016; Misra 2014), flow-on effects on tourism are inevitable (Hall, Timothy, & Duval 2004). Undoubtedly, the relationship between tourism and climate change reflects some of the issues faced by other industries and economic sectors (Scott, Hall, & Gössling 2016b, 2016c; Scott, Gössling, Hall, & Peeters 2016a). However, as Scott et al. (2012b; Scott, Gössling, & Hall 2012a) identified, tourism has particular characteristics and vulnerabilities that necessitate specific mitigation and adaptation responses. These include tourism's disproportionate economic significance in developing countries (Gössling, Hall, & Scott 2009; Hall, Scott, & Gössling 2013); its use as a justification for biodiversity conservation (Hall 2010; Hall, Scott, & Gössling 2011); the climate change-related factors of weather, environmental change, natural disaster, risk and security in influencing tourist travel patterns (Gössling, Scott, Hall, Ceron, &

199

Dubois 2012; Hall 2013); and the extent to which tourism is especially exposed to carbon governance regimes (Scott et al. 2016b, 2016c).

Tourism, like other sectors, also contributes to, and is affected by, climate change. It is estimated that at a global scale tourism contributes between 5 and 9 per cent of anthropogenic emissions, depending on radiative forcings (World Tourism Organization, United Nations Environment Programme, and World Meteorological Organisation 2008; World Economic Forum 2009; Scott et al. 2012b), although this figure is increasing, given that the rate of tourism growth per year is greater than any efficiency gains (Scott et al. 2016a, 2016b). However, tourism is also regarded as being amongst the more vulnerable sectors because of its dependence on the environment as a factor in the attractiveness of destinations as well as its high level of carbon dependency for travel (Scott et al. 2012b), although the long-term effects of climate change on tourist decision-making is relatively unknown, given the adaptive capacity of tourists (Gössling et al. 2012).

Although its proportional share of international tourism by region is relatively low, a number of countries and regions in the Middle East are increasingly relying on tourism as a means of economic diversification, especially away from dependence on oil and gas production. Nevertheless, in 2012 it was estimated that 33 per cent of the world's total oil supply came from the Middle East (Bruckner et al. 2014). Although for some countries, such as Egypt, Israel and Jordan, tourism has long been an important source of foreign income, the implications of climate change for tourism in the region have only received extremely limited coverage in IPCC reports (Hall 2008; Scott et al. 2016b), even though the impacts of climate change in the region are already being experienced (Hartmann et al. 2013). Nevertheless, a number of studies have identified the Middle East as being a highly vulnerable tourism region with respect to climate change (Gössling & Hall 2006; World Tourism Organization et al. 2008). This chapter seeks to identify key issues in the implications of climate change for tourism in the region. It is divided into two main sections. The first defines how the terms 'climate' and 'climate change' are used, and should be understood. The second section identifies some of the main issues associated with climate change in the region and outlines some of the potential implications for tourism.

Defining climate and climate change

'Climate' is generally defined as the weather averaged over a period of time, and effectively represents the conditions one would anticipate experiencing at a specific location and time of the year (Scott, Hall, & Gössling 2012b; Intergovernmental Panel on Climate Change (IPCC) 2013a). The term can be used in both a narrow and a broader sense. According to the IPCC (2013b, glossary), in a narrow sense, climate is

> usually defined as the average weather, or more rigorously, as the statistical description in terms of the mean and variability of relevant quantities over a period of time ranging from months to thousands or millions of years. The classical period for averaging these variables is 30 years, as defined by the World Meteorological Organization [WMO]. The relevant quantities are most often surface variables such as temperature, precipitation and wind. Climate in a wider sense is the state, including a statistical description, of the climate system.

Changes in climate are described by the IPCC (2013b: glossary) in terms of either *climate variability*, variations in the mean state and other statistics (e.g. standard deviations, the occurrence of extremes) of the climate on all temporal and spatial scales beyond that of individual weather events. *Climate change* refers to a change in the state of the climate that can be identified (e.g. by using statistical tests) by changes in the mean and/or the variability of its properties, and that persists for an extended period, typically decades or longer. Climate change may be due to natural internal processes or external forcings such as modulations of the solar cycles, volcanic eruptions and persistent anthropogenic changes in the composition of the atmosphere or in land use.

The United Nations Framework Convention on Climate Change (UNFCCC), the lead international forum for developing an international response to climate change, defines climate change as 'a change of climate which is attributed directly or indirectly to human activity that alters the composition of the global atmosphere and which is in addition to natural climate variability observed over comparable time periods' (UN, 1992: Article 1).

Climate change in the Middle East

Descriptions of climate and related change are specific to a time and a location and are defined over various scales from the local to the global, and over varying degrees of time. This is an important consideration in an area as large as the Middle East and in seeking to provide assessments of specific locations within the wider region. Importantly, given the nature of assessments of past and future climate change, the degree of specificity with respect to forecasting depends on locations and the size of the area. This is because of the unevenness of previous research and the availability of data. Nevertheless, over large areas the reliability of forecasts and assessments of change are good and increasingly accurate as more data comes to hand.

Table 16.1 provides an outline of changes in a number of climate indices in the Middle East that have been observed since the middle of the twentieth century. With respect to more extreme events, Zhang et al. (2005) report that significant, increasing trends have been found in the annual maximum of daily maximum and minimum temperature, the annual minimum of daily maximum and minimum temperature, the number of summer nights, and the number of days where daily temperature has exceeded its 90th percentile. Significant negative trends have been found in the number of days when daily temperature is below its 10th percentile and daily temperature range. The reduction in the number of cold days is gradual and started in the 1970s, but the increase in warm days exhibited a sudden increase towards the 1990s. However, precipitation measures, including the number of days with precipitation, the average precipitation

Table 16.1 Observed changes in a range of climate indices since the middle of the twentieth century

Indices	Change	Confidence level
Warm Days	Increase	Medium
Cold Days	Decrease	Medium
Warm Nights	Increase	Medium
Cold Nights/Frosts	Decrease	Medium
Heatwaves/Warm Spells	Increase	Medium
Extreme Precipitation	Insufficient evidence and spatially varying trends	Low
Dryness	Increase	Medium

Note: In IPCC reports, a level of confidence is expressed using five qualifiers: very low, low, medium, high and very high.

Source: Based upon data in Zhang et al. (2005); Hartmann et al. (2013).

intensity, and maximum daily precipitation events, are characterised by strong inter-annual variability without any significant trend and do not show spatial coherence.

One of the difficulties in establishing both simulating historical and future climate change and variability for the Middle East is that it is at the fringes of the influence of different drivers of European, Asian and African climates and remains poorly analysed in the peer-reviewed literature with respect to climate model performances (Christensen et al. 2013). Model projections for this century suggest the high likelihood that further warming will occur throughout the year, while there is medium confidence in an overall reduction in precipitation in the region, though projections show some distinct sub-regional and seasonally dependent changes. In both winter (October to March) and summer (April to September) precipitation in general is projected to decrease. However, Christensen et al. (2013: 1271) do urge caution, noting 'the various interacting dynamical influences on precipitation of the region (that models have varying success in capturing in the current climate) results in uncertainty in both the patterns and magnitude of future precipitation change'. This means that although the Mediterranean side of the Middle East appears likely to become drier (Dai 2011; Evans 2009), the likely precipitation changes for the interior land masses are less clear and the intensified and northward shifting Inter Tropical Convergence Zone (ITCZ), where the northeast and southeast trade winds come together, may imply an increase in precipitation in the southernmost part of the Arabian Peninsula.

There is also evidence that the intensity of weather events in the region appear to be increasing (Yosef, Saaroni, & Alpert 2009). As Zhang et al. (2005: para. 2) note, 'Any change in the frequency or severity of extreme climate events could have profound impacts on nature and society'. However, such events can also have significant impacts on tourism infrastructure, as well as tourist experiences in and perceptions of destinations, and it is to these issues that we will now turn.

Implications of climate change for tourism

Water

The Middle East is largely arid to semi-arid, and fresh water is often a scarce and precious resource. The combination of already stressed fresh water resources and rapid population growth substantially increases the vulnerability of the region to future climate change (Chenoweth et al. 2011; Evans 2009). Reductions in water availability as a result of climate change, industry and population pressures, is of the extent that, by 2025, there could be 30 to 70 per cent less per person (Sowers, Vengosh, & Weinthal 2011). This can be expected to create increased tensions between tourism and other sectors for available water resources. According to Chenoweth et al. (2011), the countries where the required adaptation is likely to be particularly challenging include Turkey and Syria because of agriculture, Iraq because of the magnitude of the change and its downstream location from its main water sources, and Jordan because of its meagre per capita water resources coupled with limited options for desalination. This situation will mean an even greater long-term reliance on desalination for other countries in the region. Chenoweth et al. (2011) observed that if the internal water footprint of the region declines in line with precipitation but the total water footprint of the region increases in line with population, then by 2050, as much as half the total water needs of the region may need to be provided through desalination and importation as virtual water.

Direct and indirect water use by tourism may be substantial. For example, estimates of tourist use of water at Sharm El Sheikh in Egypt range from 400 litres per tourist per day, to

1,410–2,190 litres per room in five-star hotels, which reflects that tourist use of water in Egypt is more than twice that of locals (Gössling, Hall, & Scott 2015). Such already high water use in MENA may be exacerbated by climate change, given water's role in swimming pools and cooling systems, as well as bathroom facilities. However, a further critical issue in relation to water and climate change is with respect to wastewater. Bdour, Hamdi and Tarawneh (2009) argue that conventional wastewater systems may be technologically inadequate to handle the locally produced sewage in arid areas. In the Middle East, domestic wastewater is up to five times more concentrated in the amount of biochemical and/or chemical oxygen demand per volume of sewage in comparison with Europe, thereby resulting in large amounts of sludge production. This is a major issue in an area that is trying as much as possible to conserve and reuse scarce water resources. Potential solutions are possible, such as hybrid reactors, soil aquifer treatment, approaches based on pathogens treatment, and reuse of the treated effluent for agricultural purposes, as well as utilising new toilet designs with low flows or composting toilets. Nevertheless, the adoption of new technologies will require infrastructure investments, modifications to hotel designs and, in some cases, the willingness of tourism businesses and consumers to accept different technologies and waste strategies.

Sea level rise

Sea level rise (SLR) in the Eastern Mediterranean is expected to be 0.5m by 2050 and a metre by 2100 (Ministry of Environmental Protection 2010). The impacts of SLR are clearly going to be greatest on river estuaries and coastal settlements, the latter often being significant for tourism. In the case of Israel, for example, a 10 cm increase in sea level (assuming a slope of 1–5 per cent in the Israeli coast) is forecast to lead to a coastal retreat of 2–10 metres, resulting in a loss of 0.4–2 km^2 every ten years. A one-metre increase in sea level would flood a 50–100-metre-wide belt on the sandy beaches, which constitutes more than half the length of the Israeli coastline. One scenario in which such an increase will occur until 2060, predicts that 8.4 km^2 of beaches will have been lost by then, with an economic damage of 4–5 billion shekels, much of which results from the impacts on coastal tourism and recreation (Ministry of Environmental Protection 2010).

Given that 70 km out of Israel's 190 km coastline are characterised by a coastal cliff, measuring 30–40 metres in height, SLR is expected to have a significant impact on cliff retreat processes (Hall & Ram 2017). The economic costs of damage to existing buildings as a result of a cliff retreat rate of an average of 0.5 metres per year has been estimated at between NIS 67 and NIS 90 million. If the retreat rate reaches an average of one metre per year the cost may reach up to NIS 276 million (Ministry of Environmental Protection 2010). In addition, there are potentially significant effects on the market value of properties in areas affected by severe cliff erosion.

Sea level rise not only affects coastal resort areas but can also have a significant impact on tourism resources, especially cultural heritage, while other aspects of climate change such as extreme weather events and changes in humidity are also significant (Hall, Baird, James, & Ram 2016). Nevertheless, coastal cultural landscapes and built environments are particularly at risk.

Coral bleaching

Coral reef bleaching is a growing problem in the Red Sea and the Persian Gulf (Furby, Bouwmeester, & Berumen 2013). In 2006, the reef area of the two seas was estimated at 11,771 hectares, of which 35 per cent was living. Projections for 2100 with respect to what percentage of the 2006 live reef area will still be living range from 4 per cent (lower emissions pathway) to 32 per cent living (higher emissions) (Speers, Besedin, Palardy, & Moore 2016). A no-further-coral-loss scenario is unlikely. Cantin, Cohen, Karnauskas, Tarrant and McCorkle (2010) estimated that 20 to 35 per cent of coral reefs in the Red Sea would be decimated by 2030 and that 50 to 80 per cent of coral reefs would be lost by 2060. It is expected that the degradation of the coral reef by the synergistic effect of pollution and climate change will have a strong negative impact on tourism. For example, the Gulf of Eilat's international appeal is partly due to dive tourism on the coral reef (Pe'er and Safriel 2000). Stress and degradation are easily detectable on a high proportion of reefs in the area, even those remote from human usage, but increased modifications in disturbance frequency and severity are expected in step with climate (increased heat content as a trigger for bleaching events) and environmental (higher nutrient input due to increased coastal population) changes (Riegl, Berumen, & Bruckner 2013).

Algal blooms

One potential impact on both coastal and inland waters as a result of climate change and increased urban and agricultural run-off is an increase in algal blooms that may not only be unsightly but can also cause skin irritations and harm fish populations. For example, since the mid-1990s, Lake Kinneret has been invaded by two species of nitrogen-fixing cyanobacteria that appear every summer and, in some years, form a massive summer bloom, the likes of which were never observed in the lake in the past. One of these invasive species produces toxins that have a detrimental effect on water quality, including for drinking (Sternberg et al. 2014). Coastal waters have also been affected in the region, which can affect the attractiveness of coastal resorts and sea bathing (Alkawri 2016; Balkis, Balci, Giannakourou, Venetsanopoulou, & Mudie 2016), as well as marine resources that may be used for tourism, such as fishing or scuba diving. Warming of surface waters, for example of the order of 1.2°C over the last five decades in the Sea of Oman, has increased the probability and frequency of blooms (Harrison, Piontkovski, & Al-Hashmi 2017).

Extreme events

Extreme weather and climatic events such as floods, heatwaves and droughts can also impact tourists directly as well as affect a destination's image (Kostopoulou et al. 2014). Kuglitsch et al. (2010) demonstrated increases in the number, intensity and length of heatwaves in the eastern Mediterranean. The annual number of heatwave days may increase drastically in the region by the end of the twenty-first century. Based on climate change modelling, Lelieveld et al. (2014) and Zittis, Hadjinicolaou, Fnais, and Lelieveld (2016) found that heatwaves, as defined by present-day standards, will have extraordinary duration of several weeks to months with much hotter heat events being expected by the end of the century. Changes in the severity of heatwaves in terms of peak temperatures will probably exceed by far the projected mean summer temperature increases. Lelieveld et al. (2014) forecast that summer temperatures are expected to increase by 5°–7°C by the end of the century, and in some cities increases up to 10°C may occur, associated with very high numbers of heatwave days. Atmospheric conditions in the region will also become conducive for photochemical air pollution. The 8-hourly EU air quality standard of about 60 ppbv is already exceeded regularly in many cities of MENA—e.g. Beirut, Ankara and Tehran. Peak ozone levels in excess of 100 ppbv and high concentrations of particulates by desert dust and anthropogenic aerosols, are expected to greatly reduce air quality during heatwave conditions by 2050, while in Kuwait, for example, very high mixing ratios up to 200 ppbv are projected (Lelieveld et al. 2014).

Kalkstein and Tan (1995) estimated increases in summertime daily mortality in Cairo under climate change. They reported that the mortality rate was at 4.45/100,000 persons, and a 2° and 4°C rise in temperature increased the rate to 10.23 and 19.32 respectively. Their estimates of the increases in heat stress mortality from climate change appear to be similar to those of Takahashi, Honda, and Emori (2007). However, these mortality rates are based on what now appear to be conservative measures of temperature increases in many cities of the region. As Lelieveld et al. (1947; 2014) observe, 'Considering the multiple environmental stresses in metropolitan areas, including confounding factors such as the urban heat island effect and growing air pollution, the cities in this region will become true hot spots of climate change'.

Economic impact of climate change

Forecasts on the economic impact of climate change on tourism in MENA are limited, although the likely negative impacts are well recognised. Onofri, Nunes and Bosello (2013) estimated the coefficients relating to tourism demand according to different biodiversity proxies. From this they estimated that the loss of 1 per cent of a biodiversity-rich area would impose losses of 0.6 per cent of domestic and 1.65 per cent of international tourism demand. These figures were then used by Bosello and Eboli (2013) to examine the impacts of climate change. In general, GDP losses linked to tourism activity are greater than those related to agriculture in the region. High losses (-0.13 per cent/-0.36 per cent of GDP in 2050) are highlighted for Jordan, Syria, Palestine, Lebanon and Israel, with climate change-related decline in demand for tourism services estimated to be of the order of -1.32 per cent in the Middle East by 2050 (Bosello & Eboli 2013).

In a study of Egypt, Smith et al. (2014) observed that climate change is likely to have profound economic consequences for the country. This study evaluated the potential economic impacts resulting from changes in water supplies, agriculture, air quality, heat stress and tourism, although water pollution, energy consumption and biodiversity were not assessed. They noted that human health in Cairo could be adversely affected by increased particulate matter and heat stress, potentially leading to thousands of deaths valued at tens of billions of Egyptian pounds per year. Annual tourist revenues were forecast to decrease as well. Total economic losses for tourism were estimated to be 18 to 23.4 billion Egyptian pounds by 2030 and 81.6 to 106 billion Egyptian pounds by 2060, which is equivalent to approximately 2–3 per cent of future gross domestic product. Of these losses, about 15–20 per cent was derived from the expected decline in recreation expenditure because of the loss of coral reef. However, the overall impacts of global environmental change are hard to measure in just economic terms, especially over the longer term. The synergistic nature of environmental change means that the social and political implications are also enormous and will also have repercussions throughout the region with consequent impacts on security for tourism and in a wider context.

Conclusion

As this brief overview of the implications of climate change for tourism in the region has shown, the changing climate will have an enormous effect on tourists, infrastructure, destination image and, of course, the local people. Reduced precipitation and increased temperatures in particular will pose a major challenge for adaptation. Potential measures may involve urban and regional planning, changes to the built environment, use of air conditioning and behavioural and social factors. However, some of these measures, such as air conditioning and desalination, will have implications for energy use and potentially contribute to an increase in emissions. Indeed, one of the great ironies, if not difficulties, for climate change adaptation in MENA is the extent to which so many countries' economies are currently carbon-dependent as a result of oil and gas reserves. Sowers et al. (2011) also argue that, in the Middle East, the largely centralised systems of planning, taxation and revenue distribution lead to a focus on supply-side issues with little consideration of climate change and demand management, which renders their populations vulnerable to climate-induced impacts, for example on water resources or coastal loss, due to weak integration with local constituencies (Noble et al. 2014).

The region does also have tremendous potential for renewable energy, especially solar and wind (Keyhani, Ghasemi-Varnamkhasti, Khanali, & Abbaszadeh 2010; Ilkılıç, Aydın, & Behçet 2011), although the severe water scarcity makes large-scale bioenergy production unlikely. These could potentially be extremely useful for increasing use of public and electric private transport which could assist in reducing the amount of particulate matter in the air in major urban centres, as well as supporting the development of new rail services (Hall, Le-Klähn, & Ram 2017), measures that would be beneficial for domestic and international tourism. Van der Zwaan, Carmona and Kober (2013) show that renewable sources of power generation could account for about 155,000 direct and 115,000 indirect jobs in the Middle East by 2050. However, despite the interests of government to promote tourism in the region and encourage diversification, there is no matching attention to encourage tourism-related adaptation and mitigation. 'In a future that is full of technological, political, social, and economic uncertainty, climate change is a relative certainty that can be considered and planned for by policy makers' (Chenoweth et al. 2011: 17). This situation is perhaps even more perverse given that some of the major attractions in the region, such as coral reefs, and coastal heritage resources, will likely cease to exist functionally by the end of the century, while inter-regional conflicts that are connected to issues of water and food security will likely serve to severely impact destination marketing of the region as the impacts of climate change increase in the future.

References

Alkawri, A. (2016) 'Seasonal variation in composition and abundance of harmful dinoflagellates in Yemeni waters, southern Red Sea', *Marine Pollution Bulletin*, 112(1): 225–234.

Allan, J.A. (2001) *The Middle East Water Question: Hydropolitics and the Global Economy*. London: I.B. Tauris.

Balkis, N., Balci, M., Giannakourou, A., Venetsanopoulou, A., & Mudie, P. (2016) 'Dinoflagellate resting cysts in recent marine sediments from the Gulf of Gemlik (Marmara Sea, Turkey) and seasonal harmful algal blooms', *Phycologia*, 55(2): 187–209.

Bdour A.N., Hamdi, M.R., & Tarawneh, Z. (2009) 'Perspectives on sustainable wastewater treatment technologies and reuse options in the urban areas of the Mediterranean region', *Desalination*, 237: 162–174.

Bosello, F., & Eboli, F. (2013) *Economic Impacts of Climate Change in the Southern Mediterranean*. Brussels: Centre for European Policy Studies.

Brown, O., & Crawford, A. (2009) *Rising Temperatures, Rising Tensions: Climate Change and the Risk of Violent Conflict in the Middle East*. Winnipeg: International Institute for Sustainable Development.

Bruckner T., Bashmakov, I.A., Mulugetta, Y., Chum, H., de la Vega Navarro, A., Edmonds, J., Faaij, A., Fungtammasan, B., Garg, A., Hertwich, E., Honnery, D., Infield, D., Kainuma, M., Khennas, S., Kim, S., Nimir, H.B., Riahi, K., Strachan, N., Wiser, R., & Zhang, X. (2014) 'Energy systems', in O. Edenhofer, R. Pichs-Madruga, Y. Sokona, E. Farahani, S. Kadner, K. Seyboth, A. Adler, I. Baum, S. Brunner, P. Eickemeier, B. Kriemann, J. Savolainen, S. Schlömer, C. von Stechow, T. Zwickel, & J.C. Minx (eds), *Climate Change 2014: Mitigation of Climate Change: Contribution of Working Group III to the Fifth Assessment Report of the Intergovernmental Panel on Climate Change* (pp. 511–598). Cambridge: Cambridge University Press.

Cantin, N.E., Cohen, A.L., Karnauskas, K.B., Tarrant, A.M., & McCorkle, D.C. (2010) 'Ocean warming slows coral growth in the central Red Sea', *Science*, 329: 322–325.

Chenoweth, J., Hadjinicolaou, P., Bruggeman, A., Lelieveld, J., Levin, Z., Lange, M.A., Xoplaki, E., & Hadjikakou, M. (2011) 'Impact of climate change on the water resources of the eastern Mediterranean and Middle East region: Modelled 21st century changes and implications', *Water Resources Research*, 47: W06506.

Christensen, J.H., Krishna Kumar, K. Aldrian, E. An, S.I., Cavalcanti, I.F.A., de Castro, M., Dong, W., Goswami, P., Hall, A., Kanyanga, J.K., Kitoh, A., Kossin, J., Lau, N., Renwick, J., Stephenson, D.B, Xie, S.P., & Zhou, T. (2013) 'Climate phenomena and their relevance for future regional climate change', in T.F. Stocker, D. Qin, G.-K. Plattner, M. Tignor, S.K. Allen, J. Boschung, A. Nauels, Y. Xia, V. Bex, & P.M. Midgley (eds), *Climate Change 2013: The Physical Science Basis: Contribution of Working Group I to the Fifth Assessment Report of the Intergovernmental Panel on Climate Change* (pp. 1217–1310). Cambridge: Cambridge University Press.

Dai, A. (2011) 'Drought under global warming: A review', *WIREs Climate Change*, 2: 45–65.

Evans, J.P. (2009) '21st century climate change in the Middle East', *Climatic Change*, 92: 417–432.

Furby, K.A., Bouwmeester, J., & Berumen, M. (2013) 'Susceptibility of central Red Sea corals during a major bleaching event', *Coral Reefs*, 32(2): 505–513.

Gleick, P.H. (2014) 'Water, drought, climate change, and conflict in Syria', *Weather, Climate, and Society*, 6(3): 331–340.

Gössling, S., & Hall, C.M. (2006) 'Conclusion: "Wake up-this is serious"', in S. Gössling, & C.M. Hall (eds), *Tourism and Global Environmental Change* (pp. 305–320). London: Routledge.

Gössling, S., Hall, C.M., & Scott, D. (2009) 'The challenges of tourism as a development strategy in an era of global climate change', in E. Palosou (ed.), *Rethinking Development in a Carbon-Constrained World: Development Cooperation and Climate Change* (pp. 100–119). Helsinki: Ministry of Foreign Affairs.

Gössling, S., Hall, C.M., & Scott, D. (2015) *Tourism and Water*. Bristol: Channel View Publications.

Gössling, S., Scott, D., Hall, C.M., Ceron, J-P., & Dubois, G. (2012) 'Consumer behaviour and demand response of tourists to climate change', *Annals of Tourism Research*, 39: 36–58.

Hall, C.M. (2008) 'Tourism and climate change: Knowledge gaps and issues. *Tourism Recreation Research*, 33: 339–350.

Hall, C.M. (2010) 'Tourism and biodiversity: More significant than climate change?' *Journal of Heritage Tourism*, 5: 253–266.

Hall, C.M., & Ram, Y. (2017) 'Israel: Coastal tourism, coastal planning and climate change in Israel', in A. Jones, & M. Phillips (eds), *Climate Change and Coastal Tourism: A Global Perspective*. Wallingford: CAB International.

Hall, C.M., Baird, T., James, M., & Ram, Y. (2016) 'Climate change and cultural heritage: Conservation and heritage tourism in the Anthropocene', *Journal of Heritage Tourism*, 11: 10–24.

Hall, C.M., Le-Klähn, D.-T., & Ram, Y. (2017) *Tourism, Public Transport and Sustainable Mobility*. Bristol: Channel View Publications.

Hall, C.M., Scott, D., & Gössling, S. (2011) 'Forests, climate change and tourism', *Journal of Heritage Tourism*, 6: 353–363.

Hall, C.M., Scott, D., & Gössling, S. (2013) 'The primacy of climate change for sustainable international tourism', *Sustainable Development*, 21(2): 112–121.

Hall, C.M., Timothy, D.J., & Duval, D.T. (2004) 'Security and tourism: Towards a new understanding?' *Journal of Travel & Tourism Marketing*, 15(2–3): 1–18.

Harrison, P.J., Piontkovski, S., & Al-Hashmi, K. (2017) 'Understanding how physical-biological coupling influences harmful algal blooms, low oxygen and fish kills in the Sea of Oman and the Western Arabian Sea', *Marine Pollution Bulletin*, 114(1): 25–34.

Hartmann, D.L., Klein Tank, A.M.G., Rusticucci, M., Alexander, L.V., Brönnimann, S., Charabi, Y., Dentener, F.J., Dlugokencky, E.J., Easterling, D.R., Kaplan, A., Soden, B.J., Thorne, P.W., Wild, M., & Zhai, P.M. (2013) 'Observations: Atmosphere and surface', in T.F. Stocker, D. Qin, G.-K. Plattner, M. Tignor, S. K. Allen, J. Boschung, A. Nauels, Y. Xia, V. Bex, & P.M. Midgley (eds), *Climate Change 2013: The Physical Science Basis: Contribution of Working Group I to the Fifth Assessment Report of the Intergovernmental Panel on Climate Change* (pp. 159–254). Cambridge: Cambridge University Press.

Ilkılıç C., Aydın, H., & Behçet, R. (2011) 'The current status of wind energy in Turkey and in the world', *Energy Policy*, 39: 961–967.

IPCC (Intergovernmental Panel on Climate Change) (2013a) 'Summary for policymakers', in T.F. Stocker, D. Qin, G.-K. Plattner, M. Tignor, S. K. Allen, J. Boschung, A. Nauels, Y. Xia, V. Bex, & P.M. Midgley (eds), *Climate Change 2013: The Physical Science Basis: Contribution of Working Group I to the Fifth*

Assessment Report of the Intergovernmental Panel on Climate Change (pp. 3–32). Cambridge: Cambridge University Press.

IPCC (2013b) *Working Group I Contribution to the IPCC Fifth Assessment Report Climate Change 2013: The Physical Science Basis.* Geneva: IPCC.

Kalkstein, L., & Tan, G. (1995) 'Human health', in K.M. Strzepek, & J.B. Smith (eds), *As Climate Changes: International Impacts and Implications* (pp. 124–145). New York: Cambridge University Press.

Kelley, C.P., Mohtadi, S., Cane, M.A., Seager, R., & Kushnir, Y. (2015) 'Climate change in the Fertile Crescent and implications of the recent Syrian drought', *Proceedings of the National Academy of Sciences,* 112(11): 3241–3246.

Keyhani A., Ghasemi-Varnamkhasti, M., Khanali, M., & Abbaszadeh, R. (2010) 'An assessment of wind energy potential as a power generation source in the capital of Iran, Tehran', *Energy,* 35: 188–201.

Kostopoulou, E., Giannakopoulos, C., Hatzaki, M., Karali, A., Hadjinicolaou, P., Lelieveld, J., & Lange, M.A. (2014) 'Spatio-temporal patterns of recent and future climate extremes in the eastern Mediterranean and Middle East region', *Natural Hazards and Earth System Sciences,* 14(6): 1565–1577.

Kuglitsch, F.G., Toreti, A., Xoplaki, E., Della-Marta, P.M., Zerefos, C.S., Türkes, M., & Luterbacher, J. (2010) 'Heat wave changes in the eastern Mediterranean since 1960', *Geophysical Research Letters,* 37: L04802.

Lelieveld, J., Hadjinicolaou, P., Kostopoulou, E., Chenoweth, J., El Maayar, M., Giannakopoulos, C., Hannides, C., Lange, M.A., Tanarhte, M., Tyrlis, E., & Xoplaki, E. (2012) 'Climate change and impacts in the Eastern Mediterranean and the Middle East', *Climatic Change,* 114(3–4): 667–687.

Lelieveld, J., Hadjinicolaou, P., Kostopoulou, E., Giannakopoulos, C., Pozzer, A., Tanarhte, M., & Tyrlis, E. (2014) 'Model projected heat extremes and air pollution in the eastern Mediterranean and Middle East in the twenty-first century', *Regional Environmental Change,* 14(5): 1937–1949.

Ludwig, R., & Roson, R. (2016) 'Climate change, water and security in the Mediterranean: Introduction to the special issue', *The Science of the Total Environment,* 543(Pt B): 847–850.

Mason, M., Zeitoun, M., & Mimi, Z. (2012) 'Compounding vulnerability: Impacts of climate change on Palestinians in Gaza and the West Bank', *Journal of Palestine Studies,* 41(3): 1–16.

Ministry of Environmental Protection (2010) *Israel's Second National Communication on Climate Change Submitted under the United Nations Framework Convention on Climate Change.* Jerusalem: Ministry of Environmental Protection.

Misra, A.K. (2014) 'Climate change and challenges of water and food security', *International Journal of Sustainable Built Environment,* 3(1): 153–165.

Noble, I.R., Huq, S., Anokhin, Y.A., Carmin, J., Goudou, D., Lansigan, F.P., Osman-Elasha, B., & Villamizar, A. (2014) 'Adaptation needs and options', in C.B. Field, V.R. Barros, D.J. Dokken, K.J. Mach, M.D. Mastrandrea, T.E. Bilir, M. Chatterjee, K.L. Ebi, Y.O. Estrada, R.C. Genova, B. Girma, E.S. Kissel, A.N. Levy, S. MacCracken, P.R. Mastrandrea, & L.L. White (eds), *Climate Change 2014: Impacts, Adaptation, and Vulnerability. Part A: Global and sectoral aspects. Contribution of Working Group II to the Fifth Assessment Report of the Intergovernmental Panel on Climate Change* (pp. 833–868). Cambridge: Cambridge University Press.

Onofri, L., Nunes, P., & Bosello, F. (2013) *Economic and Climate Change Pressures on Biodiversity in Southern Mediterranean Coastal Areas.* Brussels: Centre for European Policy Studies.

Pe'er, G., & Safriel, U.N. (2000) *Climate Change: Israel National Report under The United Nations Framework Convention on Climate Change Impact, Vulnerability and Adaptation.* Jerusalem: Ministry of Environmental Protection.

Riegl, B., Berumen, M., & Bruckner, A. (2013) 'Coral population trajectories, increased disturbance and management intervention: A sensitivity analysis', *Ecology and Evolution,* 3(4): 1050–1064.

Scott, D., Gössling, S., & Hall, C.M. (2012a) 'International tourism and climate change', *WIRES Climate Change,* 3(3): 213–232.

Scott, D., Hall, C.M., & Gössling, S. (2012b) *Tourism and Climate Change: Impacts, Mitigation and Adaptation.* London: Routledge.

Scott, D., Gössling, S., Hall, C.M., & Peeters, P. (2016a) 'Can tourism be part of the decarbonized global economy? The costs and risks of carbon reduction pathways', *Journal of Sustainable Tourism,* 24(1): 52–72.

Scott, D., Hall, C.M., & Gössling, S. (2016b) 'A review of the IPCC 5th Assessment and implications for tourism sector climate resilience and decarbonization', *Journal of Sustainable Tourism,* 24: 8–30.

Scott, D., Hall, C.M., & Gössling, S. (2016c) 'A report on the Paris Climate Change Agreement and its implications for tourism: Why we will always have Paris', *Journal of Sustainable Tourism,* 24: 933–948.

Smith, J.B., McCarl, B.A., Kirshen, P., Jones, R., Deck, L., Abdrabo, M.A., Borhan, M., El-Ganzori, A., El-Shamy, M., Hassan, M., El-Shinnawy, I., Abrabou, M., Kotb Hassanein, M., El-Agizy, M., Bayoumi,

M., & Hynninen, R. (2014) 'Egypt's economic vulnerability to climate change', *Climate Research*, 62(1): 59–70.

Sowers, J., Vengosh, A., & Weinthal, E. (2011) 'Climate change, water resources, and the politics of adaptation in the Middle East and North Africa', *Climatic Change*, 104: 599–627.

Speers, A.E., Besedin, E.Y., Palardy, J.E., & Moore, C. (2016) 'Impacts of climate change and ocean acidification on coral reef fisheries: An integrated ecological–economic model', *Ecological Economics*, 128: 33–43.

Sternberg, M., Gabay, O., Angel, D., Barneah, O., Gafny, S., Gasith, A., Grünzweig, J., Hershkovitz, Y., Israel, A., Milstein, D., Rilov, G., Steinberger, Y., & Zohary, T. (2014) 'Impacts of climate change on biodiversity in Israel: An expert assessment approach', *Regional Environmental Change*, 15(5): 895–906.

Takahashi, K., Honda, Y., & Emori, S. (2007) 'Assessing mortality risk from heat stress due to global warming', *Journal of Risk Research*, 10(3): 339–354.

United Nations (1992) *United Nations Framework Convention on Climate Change*. New York: United Nations.

Van der Zwaan B., Carmona, L., & Kober, T. (2013) 'Potential for renewable energy jobs in the Middle East', *Energy Policy*, 60: 296–304.

World Economic Forum (2009) *Towards a Low Carbon Travel & Tourism Sector*. Davos, Switzerland: World Economic Forum.

World Tourism Organization, United Nations Environment Programme, and World Meteorological Organization (2008) *Climate Change and Tourism: Responding to Global Challenges*. Madrid: UNWTO.

Yosef, Y., Saaroni, H., & Alpert, P. (2009) 'Trends in daily rainfall intensity over Israel 1950/1–2003/4', *Open Atmospheric Science Journal*, 3: 196–203.

Zhang, X., Aguilar, E., Sensoy, S., Melkonyan, H., Tagiyeva, U., Ahmed, N., Kutaladze, N., Rahimzadeh, F., Taghipour, A., Hantosh, T.H., & Albert, P. (2005) 'Trends in Middle East climate extreme indices from 1950 to 2003', *Journal of Geophysical Research: Atmospheres*, 110: (D22).

Zittis, G., Hadjinicolaou, P., Fnais, M., & Lelieveld, J. (2016) 'Projected changes in heat wave characteristics in the eastern Mediterranean and the Middle East', *Regional Environmental Change*, 16(7): 1863–1876.

PART V

Tourism and geopolitics

17

TOURISM AS A TOOL FOR COLONISATION, SEGREGATION, DISPLACEMENT AND DISPOSSESSION

The case of East Jerusalem, Palestine

Rami K. Isaac

Introduction

Although ethnically based segregation is by no means a new phenomenon in cities (Nightingale 2012), the urban studies literature in recent decades has paid specific attention to class-based segregation corresponding to the worldwide neo-liberal turn (Castells 1996; Davis 2007). Enclaves are often subject to special governance regimes and access and movement restrictions, their etymological root in the Latin word *clavis* (key) pointing to the fact that their closed-off perimeter is a defining characteristic. Therefore, the emergence of rich gated communities alongside marginal areas is understood to have created new forms of inclusion and exclusion in post-industrial cities and towns (Douglas, Wissink, & van Kempen 2012). Despite the recent 'mobilities turn' (Sheller 2004; Urry 2007), the literature on urban segregation, borders and enclaves has paid scant attention to activities and im/mobilities, focusing its analyses mainly on residential patterns (Kwan 2009, 2013). In this context, Palestine has experienced division and occupation for several decades with severe effects on its tourism, particularly to the holy cities of Bethlehem, Jericho, Nablus, Ramallah and East Jerusalem (Isaac, Hall, & Higgins-Desbiolles 2016).

Since the beginning of the twentieth century, Palestine has seen complicated changes in its political circumstances. These have included the creation of Israel in 1948 and the 1967 war. Consequent to the latter, Israel occupied the West Bank, including East Jerusalem and the Gaza Strip. These events have created catastrophic political, economic, psychological and social impacts that have deeply affected the lives of Palestinians, many of whom became refugees dislocated to neighbouring countries and indeed throughout the world as part of the Palestinian diaspora. In many ways, Palestine itself was wiped off the map (Isaac 2010a, 2010b), with much of historic Palestine becoming known as Israel. In this context, tourism became a political tool in the supremacy and domination of the Israeli establishment over land and people, and an instrument for preventing Palestinians from enjoying the fruits of the cultural and human exchanges that tourism provides.

Edward Said (1995: 7) noted that 'only by first projecting an idea of Jerusalem could Israel then proceed to the changes on the ground [which] would then correspond to the images and projections'. Israel's idea of Jerusalem, as elaborated in its master plans—for ethnic cleansing—involves maximising the number of Jews and reducing the number of Palestinians through a gradual process of colonisation, displacement and dispossession. Therefore, this chapter examines how Israeli master plans for Jerusalem aim to shape the city into a tourism and high-tech centre, and the ways in which urban planning is used to reshape the city's demography. It also sheds light on Israel's deliberate economic breakdown of East Jerusalem, which renders the city essentially unliveable for Palestinians to ensure Jewish control over it. Tourism in this context is used as a tool to control the narrative and ensure the projection of Jerusalem in the outside world as a 'Jewish city'.

Illegal settlements

For Israel, the settlement enterprise, as many refer to it, is about the appropriation of land and legitimising the covertness that characterises it. Israel's expansionist scheme aims to cement its colonialist designs on the Palestinians. Wikipedia defines settler colonialism as '… a form of colonial formation whereby foreign people move into a region. An imperial power oversees the immigration of these settlers who consent, often only temporarily, to government by that authority.' This colonisation sometimes leads, by a variety of means, to depopulation of the previous inhabitants, and the settlers take over the land left vacant by the previous residents. Unlike other forms of colonialism, the 'colonising authority' (the imperial power) is not always the same nationality as the 'colonising workforce' (the settlers) in cases of settler colonialism. The settlers are, however, generally viewed by the colonising authority as 'racially superior to the previous inhabitants, giving their social movements and political demands greater legitimacy than those of colonised peoples in the eyes of the home government'.

Israel's occupation of Palestine remains one of the few settler–colonial occupations on earth today. Ali Jarbawi, a former Palestinian Authority ministry official (cited in Solomon 2017: n.p.) noted that

> Centuries of European colonialism have provided the world with certain basic lessons about subjugating colonized peoples: The longer any colonial occupation endures, the greater the settlers' racism and extremism tends to grow. This is especially true if the occupiers encounter resistance; at that point, the occupied population becomes an obstacle that must either be forced to submit or removed through expulsion or murder … In the eyes of an occupying power, the humanity of those under its thumb depends on the degree of their submission to, or collaboration with, the occupation. If the occupied population chooses to stand in the way of the occupier's goals, then they are demonized, which allows the occupier the supposed moral excuse of confronting them with all possible means, no matter how harsh.

The beginning of the Trump administration appears to have emboldened Israeli settlement expansion into the West Bank, with announcements of new settlements coming close on the heels of each other (Hughes 2017). Reckless politics will always have a boomerang effect.

Despite threats, the US veto at the UN Security Council in December 2016 did not deter the rest of the world from determining that it would no longer brook the illegal Israeli settlements.

Israel's settlements are a threat to viable peace. Should peace be brokered under some unusual circumstances, and a two-state solution ever take hold, what would the fate of the settlers be? They now live on land occupied since 1967. Being forced to surrender their homes and leave under international law would leave the Israeli polity virtually dismembered, for the settlers are, after all, the most placated population cohort in Israeli politics. They truly believe they live in Israel and are unwilling to recognise that their colonies were built on purloined land, and most now view their status as one of entitlement (Isaac, J. 2017). Israel has placed itself in a 'catch 22 situation'. To realise peace, Israel must surrender what it has deprived the Palestinians of, if a two-state solution is to be realised. The other option is a one-party state where Israel rules but where Arabs would be the majority, thereby establishing an apartheid state.

If, in the near future, a robust boycott, divestment and sanctions (BDS) movement comes into force, Israel will have to surrender. The Israeli empire will likely crumble from its present form. According to Solomon (2017), the warning signs are clear. Israel must find a just solution sooner rather than later, because despite its continued building of settlements, in the end, these are constructed on occupied land that belongs to the Palestinians.

Jerusalem present and future

It is almost impossible to discuss the land discourse debate in the Israeli–Palestinian conflict without recalling the Zionist slogan 'a land with no people for a people without land' (see Khalidi 1997: 101). According to some observers, such as Falah (2003), a logical reading of this ideology suggests that nothing but full annihilation of the Palestinian-Arabs is the final, covert goal, erasing them in one way or another from the region and replacing them by another population in line with what some political geographers have termed Israel's 'ethnocratic' policies (Yiftachel 1999, 2002). The founding mythology of the State of Israel involved a systematic reworking of Palestinian history, legitimising Jewish claims to the land and denying Palestinians' counter claims. 'One of the most successful propaganda campaigns in modern history has achieved in masking the fact that the creation of the State of Israel resulted in the dispossession, displacement and dispersion of another people' (Prior 1997: 186).

The situation of the Palestinian people of Jerusalem, who live in 19 neighbourhoods in the eastern part of the city, differs significantly in many ways from the situation of the Palestinians in the West Bank and Gaza Strip. East Jerusalem was occupied, annexed and controlled by Israel since 1967. Since then, Israel has made East Jerusalem's Palestinian inhabitants 'permanent residents' but not 'permanent citizens' (blue card holders). With this status, the Palestinians of East Jerusalem, who live inside what Israel unilaterally and illegally declared the municipality of Jerusalem, can routinely work and travel in Israel. They are assumed to receive the same national health care, retirement, unemployment and disability benefits received by Israeli citizens, but in practice many of them do not enjoy these benefits. They also have the right to vote in Jerusalem municipal elections, although in practice few of them do, but not in national elections (Farah & Bakr 2015). Being residents but not citizens of Israel, Jerusalem's Palestinians do not have equal rights with the Israelis and are prevented by Israel from receiving the services of the Palestinian Authority.

There are various political, economic and social problems, obstacles and challenges facing the Palestinian people who live in Jerusalem. The political challenges are reflected in two main issues: the illegal Israeli settlements and the Israeli strategy of the Judaisation of the city. The continuously expanding illegal Israeli settlements in Jerusalem and other parts of the West Bank are part of a long-standing Israeli policy of encircling the Old City of East Jerusalem and other parts of the area so as to have full authority over the entire city, including the eastern part where the Palestinians reside. The Judaisation of Palestinian land is particularly evident in East Jerusalem and has been accelerated in recent years through home evictions, home demolitions and residency revocations (Jadallah 2014)

As for the economic challenges, Israel has vigorously isolated East Jerusalem from its natural integration with the Palestinian economy in the West Bank and Gaza and other neighbouring Arab countries, while ensuring that it does not develop at the same levels as the Israeli side (Al-Haq 2015). In doing so, the effect has been to make living conditions in East Jerusalem tougher and tougher while cutting economic linkages with the rest of the Palestinian economy. In addition to the political and economic challenges, there are many social problems facing the Palestinian people. The Israeli legal, political and economic measures against the city's Palestinians lead to social problems and family-related issues particularly for youth who do not envision a bright future and are often forced to leave the city. In fact, one of the occupier's goals is to undermine the viability and resistance of East Jerusalem by forcing the Palestinian population to migrate out of the city, so that they can be replaced by Israeli settlers (Organisation of Islamic Cooperation 2014).

Recently, UNESCO's executive board passed a resolution that criticises Israel's actions in occupied Jerusalem and the Gaza Strip (Aljazeera 2017). It calls on Israel as the 'occupying power' to cease persistent excavations, tunnelling, works and projects in East Jerusalem, which the Palestinians see as the capital of their future state. UNESCO's resolution reaffirms the importance of the Old City of Jerusalem and its walls for the three monotheistic religions, while accusing Israel of taking actions that have 'altered' or purported to alter the character and status of the Holy City.

Population and land use

The primary goal and strategy of the Zionists since East Jerusalem's 1967 annexation and occupation has been to create a demographic and geographic situation that undermines the physical or spiritual traces of Palestinians in the city so that any future claims to rights over the city and challenges to the permeation of Israel will be categorised as baseless (Whitelam 2013). To realise this goal, the Israeli government has implemented numerous policies and measures to impede the natural growth of the Palestinians of East Jerusalem, most recently through the apartheid wall, revocation of residency rights, discriminatory family unification policies and disadvantageous allocation of the municipal budget and services between East and West Jerusalem. One of the first people to use the word apartheid in relation to Israel was Israel's first prime minister, David Ben Gurion who, following the 1967 war, warned of Israel becoming an 'apartheid state' if it retained control of the occupied territory.

Demography dictates Israeli policy in Jerusalem. The majority of East Jerusalem-related policy (where some 220,000 Palestinians reside) at the very least aims to maintain the demographic balance that existed in 1967: 28 per cent Palestinians to 72 per cent Jews. Isaac and Platenkamp (2012: 181) argue that

> All government policies have been formulated with the following objectives: First to assure a Jewish majority; second, to prevent contiguity between Palestinians of East Jerusalem and those in West Bank; and finally to reduce, at all costs, the number of Palestinians living in the city.

> *(See also Strickland 2015)*

In recent years, regulations stipulate the abrogation of the rights of the city's Palestinian residents who move away from the city for a period of more than seven years, whereas citizens of Israel can leave the country for any length of time without repercussions (Frykberg 2011). Likewise, Jews who migrate from other countries and who have no relationship to the land, can reside (on occupied Palestinian land) and become Israeli citizens.

A complex system involving the partisan use of planning and zoning mechanisms, land expropriation and house demolitions, combined with policies of revoking Palestinians' legal residency in Jerusalem for a myriad of reasons, ensures the 'Jewish character' of the city. For example, Amir Cheshin, the advisor on Arab affairs for the Jerusalem municipality, for a time under Ehud Olmert, said

> Israel turned urban planning into a tool of the government to be used to help pre-vent the expansion of the city's non-Jewish population. It was a ruthless policy, if only for the fact that the needs (to say nothing about the rights) of Palestinian residents were ignored. Israel saw the adoption of strict zoning plans as a way of limiting the number of new homes built in Arab neighborhoods and thereby ensuring that the Arab percentage of the city's population 28% in 1967—did not grow beyond this level. Allowing 'too many' new homes in Arab neighborhoods would mean 'too many' Arab Palestinian residents in the city. The idea was to move as many Jews as possible into East Jerusalem and move as many Palestinians out of the city entirely. Israeli housing policy in East Jerusalem was all about this numbers game.
>
> *(Cheshin, Bill, & Avi 1999: 31–32)*

This policy is still in effect.

According to the United Nations Committee on Economic, Social and Cultural Rights (United Nations 1998), the adverse impact of the growing exclusion of Palestinians in East Jerusalem from the enjoyment of their economic, social and cultural rights is deeply concerning. The committee is also concerned about the continued Israeli policies of building settlements that expand the boundaries of East Jerusalem and of transferring Jewish residents into East Jerusalem, which results in Jews outnumbering the Palestinians.

Discrimination

The United Nations (1998) also expressed concern that excessive emphasis upon the state as a Jewish State encourages discrimination and relegates its non-Jewish inhabitants to second-class citizens. The organisation notes with concern that the government of Israel does not accord equal rights to its Arab citizens, although they comprise over 19 per cent of the total popula-tion. This record of discrimination is apparent in the lower standards of living amongst Israeli Arabs as a result of, inter alia, a lack of access to housing, water, electricity and health care, and their lower level of education. The UN also noted concern that, despite the fact that the Arabic language has official status in law, it is not given equal importance in practice.

Furthermore, the UN notes with grave concern that the Status Law of 1952 authorises the World Zionist Organization/Jewish Agency and its subsidiaries, including the Jewish National Fund, control most of the land in Israel, since these institutions are chartered to benefit Jews exclusively. Despite the fact that the institutions are chartered under private law, the State of Israel nevertheless has a significant say in their policies and thereby remains responsible for their activities. A state party cannot divest itself of its obligations under the law by privatising gov-ernmental functions. The UN committee views the large-scale and systematic confiscation of

Palestinian land and property by the state and the transfer of that property to these agencies as constituting an institutionalised form of discrimination because these agencies, by definition, would deny non-Jews from using these properties. These practices, therefore, constitute a breach of Israel's obligations under the covenant.

Economy

Due to a set of specific constraints and obstacles imposed by the occupying Israeli military, Jerusalem struggles to utilise all of its available human and economic resources. These obstacles restrict key macroeconomic development. Moreover, the economy has experienced a distortion in the pattern of development, in which services account for a higher share of gross domestic product (GDP) than was the case 15 years ago, while manufacturing and agriculture account for a much smaller share (Organization of Islamic Cooperation 2014). In general, the pace of macroeconomic growth has slowed considerably since 2012. With respect to robust population growth and particularly rapid growth in the working age population, the labour market suffered from low workforce and employment opportunities, resulting in higher unemployment rates.

Tourism

Jerusalem is regularly referred to as divided (Klein 2005), segregated (Thawaba & Al-Rimmawi 2013), fragmented (Pullan 2011) or even 'many bordered' (Dumper 2014). While communal borders in Jerusalem were defined by *Mahallat* neighbourhood units during the Ottoman period, the clear segmentation of the Old City into four confessional quarters was only implemented during the British Mandate, when Jerusalem was rebuilt as a 'divided' city on the basis of the principle of 'unmixing' the people (Roberts 2013), though, despite the Mandate authorities' persistence in ethnic segregation, there were significant zones of mixing, particularly in commercial areas (Abowd 2014). While Palestinians continue to conceive of the city as the capital of their future state, Israeli urban planning, as discussed previously, reflects the goal of avoiding any future partition of the city (Bollens 1998). Since 1967, numerous Israeli settlements have been constructed and a significant increase in settlements has occurred since the Oslo Agreements in 1993. These settlements house approximately 200,000 Jews (UNOCH 2014) and range in size from large-scale neighbourhoods to individual securitised houses in the heart of Palestinian communities (Dumper 1997). The major settlements in East Jerusalem are closely linked to the west portion of the city, annexing large swathes of Palestinian land and conceptually shifting the Green Line (the pre-1967 border) far into East Jerusalem and even beyond the municipal boundaries (Allegra 2013; Shaly & Rosen 2010). The Green Line remains the internationally recognised boundary despite the fact that Israel has occupied East Jerusalem for 50 years.

Bauman (2016: 175) states

> the mobility infrastructure simultaneously enhances Israeli mobility, while restraining Palestinian movement. Major thoroughfares connecting Israeli settlements cut through Palestinian neighborhoods without serving them, dividing them into isolated enclaves, disturbing the urban fabric, and stifling local life and social exchange throughout the eastern part of the city.

Israeli settlements are strategically built colonies of Israel that are connected by a network of by-pass roads (Selwyn 2011) that separate each Palestinian community/city from the next, and constrain their ability to expand. These are all armed illegal settlements, around 200 of them located in occupied Palestinian territories, and their purpose today is foremost to continue control and domination of the occupied Palestinian territories to force out the Palestinians entirely (Isaac, R. 2017). This spatial disparity brought about by this imposed immobility is accentuated by the lack of investment in Palestinian areas of East Jerusalem. As a result of decades of abandonment, Baumann (2016: 175) states 'even middle-class Palestinian neighbourhoods lack basic amenities, including functional roads and pavements, connection to the sewage system, reliable garbage removal, community facilities, public parks and postal service'.

The apartheid wall is one of the manifestations of Israeli occupation and has cut off at least 55,000 Jerusalem residents—a quarter of the city's Palestinian population—from the city centre and the economic, educational (Harker 2009), medical and social resources located there (Bauman 2016). The obstruction of movement in, and access to, Palestinian neighbourhoods by means of walls, checkpoints, roadblocks and a complex system of permits is one of the Israeli occupation's main tools for spatio-social control (Ophir, Givoni, & Hanafi 2009; Weizman 2007). These mobility restrictions stifle Palestinians' free movement and affect everyday life in many ways (Hammami 2004, 2010).

Following the Israeli occupation and illegal annexation of East Jerusalem, the tourism sector began to deteriorate. For example, there was a radical change in the distribution of hotel rooms between the western and eastern parts of the city. Between 1968 and 1979, the percentage of hotel rooms located in East Jerusalem declined from 60 per cent to 40 per cent. While there was a 20 per cent increase in income for East Jerusalem's tourism sector between 1969 and 1973, the Israeli sector witnessed an 80 per cent rise over the same period. By the mid-1980s, 80 per cent of tourist bookings were in the Israeli sector.

According to the Palestinian Central Bureau of Statistics, in 2012 there were 41 hotels in East Jerusalem and 1,633 rooms with an average occupancy rate of 35 per cent, representing a significant increase compared to only 19.7 per cent occupancy rate in 2011. It is estimated that tourism enterprises such as hotels and restaurants account for 25 per cent of the employed labour in the city of Jerusalem, amounting to around 6,674 people, second to other services, which employed around 32 per cent of the labour force in 2010 (Organisation of Islamic Cooperation 2014). However, albeit the contribution of hotels and restaurants to the economy of the East Jerusalem declined in the post-second Intifada (uprising) period, it has seen some recovery during the past few years.

A recent bill sponsored by Minister Gideon Ezra and seven other members of the Israeli parliament proposes banning residents of East Jerusalem from serving as tour guides in the city, potentially putting hundreds out of work. He stated that the city's Palestinians should not be certified guides because they did not represent Israel's national interests well enough. The bill suggested that a guide leading a group of over 11 people or travelling in more than one vehicle, must be a citizen of Israel. Most Palestinian residents of East Jerusalem have residency status, as previously mentioned, but not citizenship and would therefore be banned from guiding the most lucrative tourist groups (Hasson 2010). Sami Bahbah, chairman of the association of East Jerusalem tour guides told *Haaretz* (an Israeli newspaper) that there are some 300 Palestinian tour guides holding certification from Israel's Ministry of Tourism. All of them could become casualties of this bill if passed. The Jerusalem NGO Ir Ammim, which works to promote Jewish–Arab–Palestinian coexistence in the city, condemned the bill, saying

> We know all too well which states attach state-sponsored guides to foreign tourists. This bill is just another one bringing us closer to this kind of state. This is not only a dangerous political suppression, but a desperate economic blow to the tourism resource, possibly the only resource still available to East Jerusalemites.
>
> *(Hasson 2010: 2)*

Currently, Israel is also using tourist sites to assert control over East Jerusalem. The state is quietly extending control over East Jerusalem in alliance with rightwing Jewish settler groups, by developing parks and tourist sites that would bring drastic change in the status quo of occupied East Jerusalem. According to McCarthy (2009), this 'confidential' plan aimed to link several areas of East Jerusalem surrounding the Old City with the goal of asserting Israeli control and strengthening its claim to Jerusalem as its capital—a move not recognised by the international community. Under an eight-year plan, a series of nine national parks, trails and tourist sites on apparent Jewish historic sites would be established, most under the control of settler groups working together with the Israeli government. The sites are also creating a link to Jewish illegal settlements in East Jerusalem and the West Bank. These parks would become a 'biblical playground' built on public and private Palestinian land and would be fenced in (McCarthy 2009).

Israeli punishments during the first and second Intifada (uprising), such as curfews and tax raids, further hampered the development of East Jerusalem's tourism sector. Moreover, Israel's construction of the Segregation Wall in 2002 (Isaac 2009) and its subsequent intensification of restrictions on East Jerusalem's development particularly damaged the tourism sector, because such actions isolated the city from the rest of the occupied territories of Palestine. Obstacles have included difficult licensing procedures for constructing new hotels or converting old buildings into hotels, high municipal taxes, weak physical and economic infrastructure, and land scarcity. Furthermore, while the development of the Israeli tourism industry enjoys considerable government support, the Palestinian tourism sector is largely run by insufficient private investments and lacks meaningful support from the Palestinian government (Arafeh 2016a).

The number of active hotels in East Jerusalem has thus been in decline. Between 2009 and 2016, the number of hotels in East Jerusalem Governorate decreased by 41 per cent, from 34 hotels in 2009 to 20 during the second quarter of 2016. The share of tourists staying in East Jerusalem hotels was 12 per cent in 2013 versus 88 per cent in West Jerusalem hotels. Further, while 34 per cent of hotels in the occupied territories were located in East Jerusalem in 2009, less than 18 per cent of hotels in Palestinian territories were in East Jerusalem by June 2016. The stifled development of the Palestinian tourism industry, combined with the negative perceptions of travel to Palestine, has led to an increasing number of tourists staying in West Jerusalem lodgings.

The suffocation of the Old City economy

The Old City of Jerusalem was a strong part of East Jerusalem's economy, attracting Arab and Palestinian customers, as well as tourists. Its current collapse serves as a potent example of the economic marginalisation that has weakened the economy and rendered life in East Jerusalem gradually more and more difficult for Palestinians. The decline of the commercial markets in the Old City has been closely linked to the falling of tourism in East Jerusalem. In the 1970s and 1980s, business activities in the Old City became progressively reliant on tourism with a surge in visitor numbers. With this shift also came a change in the nature of the markets. Though the Old City was known for its traditional industries and markets, for instance, the Souq al-Attareen (spices) and Souq al-Lahameen (meat), etc., it gradually lost their niche appeal as merchants turned their businesses into souvenir shops, which were seen as more lucrative ventures at the time. The consequent economic downgrading of East Jerusalem and the decline in tourism businesses fuelled the decline of commercial activity in the Old City. The situation was definitely compounded further by the heavy taxes imposed by Israeli authorities to stifle Palestinian commerce as part of Israel's purposely engineered economic collapse of East Jerusalem. Palestinian merchants are obligated to pay six taxes: *Arnona* (property tax), value added tax, income tax, national insurance, payroll tax and licence tax. The Palestinian traders are unable to pay these taxes given that the deterioration in their businesses has put many of them into debt. Israeli occupation has lately offered merchants substantial incentives to sell their stores if they cannot pay their taxes. Thus, taxation is another instrument used to appropriate Palestinian property and enlarge Jewish colonisation over the Old City (Arafeh 2016a).

The following damage of a competitive advantage has been accompanied by the emergence of new business centres in other areas in Jerusalem, Beit Hanina, Al-Ram and Ramallah, which have become easier to reach and therefore more attractive to Palestinians, particularly after the construction of the Segregation Wall and the obstruction of travel imposed by the Israeli military.

The mixture of new business centres, heavy tax burdens, the declining tourism sector, and the weak purchasing power of Palestinians in East Jerusalem has suffocated the economy of the Old City. According to the Jerusalem Arab Chamber of Commerce and Industry (cited in Arafeh 2016a: 4),

> more than 200 shops are currently closed in the Old City. Shops that remain open cannot stay open for longer hours at night because of their inability to cover operating costs. This has led to a 'Jerusalem sleeps early' phenomenon whereby Jerusalem residents spend their evenings and weekends in Bethlehem or Ramallah instead of the city itself.

In early 2015, Israel erected concrete roadblocks and checkpoints in several Jerusalem neighbourhoods, as well as barriers inside and outside the Old City. According to a report by Al-Haq (cited in Arafeh 2016a: 4), 'the Israeli military set up more than 30 checkpoints and observation points in the Old city, including four electronic detectors, severely constraining the movement of Palestinians and tourists'.

Israel's arrangement of the Old City's economic downturn, together with its other policies such as house demolitions; a discriminatory provision of services, which provides Palestinian residents a smaller amount of services but requires them to pay the same taxes as their Jewish counterparts; and the revocation of residency cards, purposefully render life increasingly difficult for the city's Palestinians. This process has gone hand in hand with Israel's continued efforts to fast-track its colonisation of East Jerusalem, including the Old City, by expanding its illegal settlements. Illegal settlement expansion and the colonisation of East Jerusalem are supported by right-wing organisations, potentially financed by American Jews, such as Ateret Cohanim, within the heart of Palestinian neighbourhoods, as their main aim to create a Jewish majority in the Old City and in the wider East Jerusalem. These organisations benefit from considerable assistance from the State of Israel, which provides private security services to protect settlers, especially during the expropriation of Palestinian properties. Israel similarly funds development projects in the illegal settlement and eases the transfer of Palestinian properties to right-wing organisations through bodies such as the Jewish National Fund and the Custodian of Absentee Property (Arafeh 2016b).

Figure 17.1 laments the difficult situation of younger generations of Arab Jerusalemites. These children have no legal status because their parents hold different types of ID cards. When a Palestinian with a West Bank ID and a Palestinian with a Jerusalem ID have a child together in the West Bank, that child is considered to be 'born abroad' and is therefore not granted permanent legal status in Jerusalem. Notably, no such restrictions apply to Israeli Jews; an Israeli child born in a West Bank settlement can live legally in Jerusalem or any part of present-day Israel. The policy of refusing to grant residency to Palestinian children in Jerusalem is ultimately

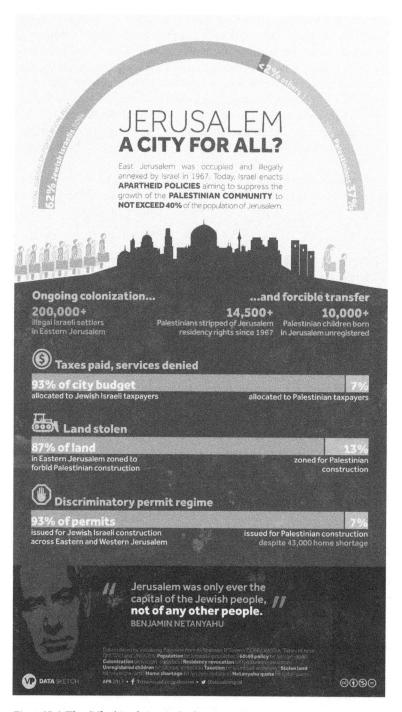

Figure 17.1 The difficulties facing Arabs from Jerusalem

intended to encourage families to move elsewhere. It is part of the Israeli government's goal of displacing Palestinians from the city, to maintain a Jewish demographic majority.

In spite of intensive illegal settlement expansion, Jews account for about 10 per cent of the inhabitants of the Old City. Hitherto, there has been a growth in the development of Jewish religious and educational institutions in the area. Particular efforts have been made to encircle the Al-Aqsa complex inside and outside the Old City with Jewish sites in an attempt to Judaise the touristic landscape. Settlers' key success has been the building of the so-called biblical theme park 'City of David', which surrounds the Old City walls and includes most of the Wadi Hilwa neighbourhood in Silwan to the south (Arafeh 2016b). According to Arafeh (2016a: 5)

> The settler group El-Ad runs the park, which is one of the most visited tourist attractions in Jerusalem. Israeli authorities and settlers use the park to project their desired narratives and images of Jerusalem as a 'Jewish city', which includes erasing the Palestinians' physical presence and history.

This is not at all a new process, but rather a continuation of the original goals of the Zionist movement, which were to manufacture a connection between Jews around the world to this land where the overwhelming majority have no actual roots. This process of heritage production and construction is very well acknowledged and analysed by many historians, including Israeli historians, and always contains appropriation of Palestinian sites and heritage, claiming them as exclusively Jewish (Ibrahim 2011; Isaac 2014).

Within this strategy, Palestine became a playground on which the space, the sphere and the symbols were reformulated so that Palestine fitted into the Zionist narrative. In other words, a specific cultural heritage had to be constructed to harmonise with the religious narrative that tries to build legitimacy in order to justify the acquisition and control of space with the aim of enhancing the project in the Jewish consciousness and creating an international supportive movement. The history and the culture of an entire population were erased and replaced by another that aimed to ensure the containment of the memory of the space and its history (Whitelam 2013). Within this narrative, the implementation of Israeli policies has taken two paths. The first is to destroy, mutilate, and neglect those elements that confirm or remind of a Palestinian existence, Palestinian rights or Palestinian history. The millennia-long history of Palestine is portrayed as though it started with the emergence of the Jewish religion when, in fact, Palestine and its people existed long before there was ever a Jewish presence. The magnitude of this policy culminated in the destruction of over 450 Palestinian villages in 1948 after their inhabitants were expelled. The stones of these homes were stolen to be reused in the construction of Jewish homes as a sign of originality and genuineness. The second path regards the implementation of Israeli policies and has included rebuilding the symbols, names and culture of specific places in order to confirm and prove the credibility and historicity of the Israeli narrative (Ibrahim 2011).

Some of the evidence of this strategy is supported by the British media. Recently, the BBC has admitted to producing a misleading map of Israel in which Jerusalem is included, the occupied West Bank is annexed to Jordan, and Gaza no longer exists. The map was produced as a graphic for a TV show. In the map, used at the beginning of an episode to illustrate where two bikers went, the West Bank was incorporated into Jordan, while Gaza was depicted as part of Israel. The Israeli flag was stamped over where Gaza used to be, while an enlarged Jordan is coloured in green. After a few seconds, Jerusalem appeared as a unified city in Israel. In this made-up BBC map, the new Jerusalem is nowhere near its actual location, divided by the armistice line between the West Bank and Israel. Instead, an illustration indicating the location of the city hovers over the Dead Sea. The BBC's message to its viewers appears to be that Jerusalem, all of it, belongs to Israel, and there is no such thing as Palestine or Palestinian lands (Saleem 2017).

A Jewish destination for tourism, higher education and high-tech

The vision in 2050 for Jerusalem has clear aims and objectives. Visitors and tourists will see a largely Jewish high-tech centre amid a sea of tourists, which includes an elimination of the Palestinian physical presence and history. To realise this vision, Israel is working on three master plans for Jerusalem. One of these master plans is the 2020 Master Plan, which has not been deposited for public scrutiny even though it was first published in 2004. The least known are the so-called 'Marom Plans'—a government-commissioned plan for the development of Jerusalem, and the 'Jerusalem 5800' Plan, also known as Jerusalem 2050, which is the result of a private initiative and is presented as a 'transformational' master plan for the city. In her policy brief, Arafeh (2016b) scrutinises all three master plans, explaining how Israel intends to shape the city into a tourism and high-tech centre, and the ways in which they use urban planning to reshape the city's demography. The bottom line of all these plans is to re-energise and advance Israel's control of the city. It should also be noted, once again, that Israel's annexation of East Jerusalem is illegal under international law and is not recognised by the international community. In addition, Israel's declaration that Jerusalem is its capital, both West and East, has no international legal standing, which is why there are no diplomatic representations in Jerusalem, not even from Israel's biggest supporter, the United States.

To make Jerusalem 'the Middle East's anchor tourist attraction' (Arafeh 2016b: 3), the Jerusalem 5800 plan aims to raise private investments and hotel construction, build rooftop gardens and parks, and change the area surrounding the Old City into an accommodations quarter whilst prohibiting the use of vehicles. The plan, in addition, envisages the construction of high-quality transportation itineraries including a high-speed national rail line; an extensive network of buses and public transportation; the addition of numerous highways and the expansion of existing roads; and an express superhighway that transverses the country from north to south. The strategy also endorses the construction of an airport in the Horkania Valley between Jerusalem and the Dead Sea to serve 35 million passengers each year. The airport would be linked through access roads and rail to Jerusalem, Ben Gurion Airport and other city centres. It is comparable to Israel's vision of the construction of illegal settlements in Palestine (Arafeh 2016b).

According to Arafeh (2016b: 3), even though the Jerusalem 5800 plan presents itself as an apolitical document that

> promotes 'peace through economic prosperity', it has demographic goals that prove otherwise. In fact, it envisages that the $120 billion of total added value from the implementation of the plan, together with 75,000–85,000 additional full-time jobs in hotels plus 300,000 additional jobs in related industries would all reduce poverty and attract more Jews to Jerusalem, increasing the number of Jews living in Jerusalem and further tilting the Jewish–Palestinian demographic balance in their favor.

While tourism is not only seen as an engine for economic development to attract Jews into Jerusalem, Israel's development of, and domination over, the city's tourism sector, is a tool to control the narratives and ensure the projection of Jerusalem to the outside world as a united (East and West) Jewish city. Israel has strict rules over who can serve as tour guides, and the narrative and history that the tourists are told. These plans to market Israeli tourism have gone hand in hand with the various Israeli-imposed actions and restrictions on the development and growth of the Palestinian tourism industry in East Jerusalem, which include the following: the isolation of East Jerusalem from the rest of Palestine, especially after the construction of the Segregation Wall; a shortage of land and the resulting high costs; weak physical infrastructure; high taxes; and restrictions on the release of permits to build hotels, or covert buildings into hotels. These impediments, even as millions of dollars are being poured into the Israeli tourism sector, ensure that Palestinian tourism has no hope of competing with Israel's. This is the dominant strategy during the occupation of the West Bank. Israeli leaders have taken actions to 'de-develop' the Palestinian economy, undermining potential growth and rendering the Palestinian economy dependent on Israel.

One additional common goal of the three plans is to attract Jews from all over the world by developing two advanced industries: high-tech and higher education. To promote higher education, the objective of the 2020 Master Plan is to launch an international university in the city centre with English as the main language of instruction. Marom Plan also seeks to make Jerusalem a 'leading academic city' (Arafeh 2016b: 4) that is attractive both to Jews and international students, who will be stimulated to settle in Jerusalem once they have finished their studies. In the same context, the Jerusalem 5800 plan sees an opening to generate jobs and achieve economic growth through 'extended-stay educational tourism'—another of the colonisation goals for the city (Arafeh 2016b).

Evicting Palestinians using urban planning and the law

Although Israel is working on making Jerusalem a business and high-tech hub that will attract Jews and offer them employment, the problems facing East Jerusalem are massive. They include squeezing Palestinian businesses and trade, weakening the education sector and hampering infrastructure and services. The results can be seen in the high rates of poverty, with 75 per cent of all Palestinians in East Jerusalem—including approximately 84 per cent of these Palestinians being children—living below the poverty line in 2015 (Arafeh 2016b).

The Segregation Wall is one of the most impactful measures Israel has put in place to ensure a Jewish majority in Jerusalem and implement the country's de facto borders of Jerusalem, thereby transforming it into the largest city of the state of Israel (see Cook 2015). Arafeh (2016b: 5) notes that

> the Segregation Wall is built in a way that enables Israel to annex an additional 160km^2 of occupied Palestine, while physically separating more than 55,000 Jerusalemites from the city centre. Planning and development in the area and districts that are now beyond the wall is extremely poor, and municipal services are virtually absent, in spite of the fact that the Palestinians living in these areas continue to pay the property taxes.

Urban planning is an additional major geopolitical and strategic instrument Israel uses to tighten its grip over Jerusalem and constrain the urban extension of Palestinians as part of its efforts to Judaise the city. As Cook (2015: 151) states

> the key policy debate in Israel—though one till now conducted mainly behind doors—is whether the apartheid system of rule over the Palestinian minority can be maintained without considering again some form of ethnic cleansing or 'transfer', possibly through an imposed peace agreement.

Urban planning is one of the major elements of the 2020 Master Plan, which views Jerusalem as one conurbation, a metropolitan centre and eventually the capital of Israel (Arafeh 2016b). The bottom line of this strategy is to sustain a solid Jewish majority by heartening Jewish illegal settlements in East Jerusalem, while at the same time reducing Jewish out-migration. The intrinsic plan is to build affordable housing units in some existing Jewish neighbourhoods and establish new districts. As mentioned earlier, the plan is to connect Israeli settlements in the West Bank geographically through a network of roads, economically and socially, to Jerusalem and Tel Aviv.

The Ir David Foundation, a non-profit group that seeks to increase Jewish settlement in the City of David and whose heads are close associates of the mayor, has in recent years bought houses near the Old City in an effort to 'Judaise' the area. In 2010, the Jerusalem municipality's planning and building committee approved a controversial plan for the Silwan neighbourhood, which calls for razing 22 Palestinian homes built without permits and constructing a tourism centre in their place. It is said the illegal construction in the area is preventing the municipality from building a tourism centre, which would include restaurants and boutique hotels (Eldar and Hasson 2010)

The Palestinian presence in Jerusalem and the development of Palestinian neighbourhoods is also severely constrained by the plan's commitment to 'a strict enforcement of the laws of planning and building … to impede the phenomenon of illegal building' (Arafeh 2016b: 6). Nevertheless, only 7 per cent of building permits in Jerusalem were issued to Palestinians in the past few years. Israel's discrimination in issuing building permits to Palestinians, combined with the high cost of the permits, has forced many Palestinians to build illegally. They also face discrimination when it comes to the execution of regulations. According to a report by the International Peace and Cooperation Center (Arafeh 2016b), 78.4 per cent of building violations took place in West Jerusalem between 2004 and 2008, compared to 21.5 per cent in East Jerusalem.

In conclusion, the 2020 master plan is thus a political plan that uses urban planning as a covert tool to ensure Jewish demographic and territorial control of the city. The plan supports the 'spatial segregation of the various population groups in the city' and considers it a real advantage. Its primary objective is to divide Jerusalem into various planning districts based on ethnic affiliation in which no area would combine both Palestinians and (Israeli/European) Jews. Therefore, Israel has also been using its laws as a tactic to expel Palestinians and appropriate their land and houses to ensure its sovereignty and control over Jerusalem. In fact, as recently as 15 March 2015, the Israeli Supreme Court activated the Absentee Property Law, which was issued in 1950 with the aim of confiscating the property of Palestinians who were expelled during the 1948 Nakba catastrophe. It was used as the 'legal basis' for transferring the property of displaced Palestinians to the newly established State of Israel. After 1967, Israel applied the law to East Jerusalem, allowing it to appropriate the property of Jerusalemites whose residence was found to be outside the boundaries of Palestine.

On 6 December 2017, the world witnessed a repeat of history as the White House declared Jerusalem to be the capital of Israel. This time, however, it was not Arthur Balfour making this decision but rather Donald Trump, the US President. His pronouncement will go down in history, together with the Balfour Declaration, as an immoral act of granting one people's land to a completely different people, reversing decades of US policy towards the city of Jerusalem. Trump's declaration is fundamentally in violation of international law and denies Palestinians' rights to the city they call home. This will certainly encourage Israeli policies to target Palestinians further, especially those living under tremendous pressure and occupation conditions in Jerusalem.

Qumsiyeh (2004) explains why and how the 'two-state' public relations campaign is not a solution but was a creation of Ben Gurion in the 1920s to convince the world that Zionists were seeking peace, while at the same time consolidating their occupation and power, and extended their control geographically and politically. Ben Gurion wrote (cited in Qumsiyeh 2017: n.p.),

> it must be clear that there is no room in the country for both peoples … If the Arabs leave it, the county will become wide and spacious for us … The only solution is a Land for Israel, at least a western land for Israel [i.e. Palestine], without Arabs. There is no room here for comprises … There is no way but to transfer the Arabs from here to the neighboring countries, to transfer all of them, save perhaps for Bethlehem, Nazareth and the old Jerusalem … Not one village must be left, not one tribe. The transfer must be directed at Iraq, Syria and even Transjordan.

He continued,

> We are presently involved not only on a conflict with Arabs neighbors, but to some extent, with most of mankind as it is organized in the United Nations—because of Jerusalem. Only a blind man does not see that the sources of this conflict are not political, economic or military alone, but also ideological.

The ideology he referred to is Zionism—a form of colonialism incompatible with the native interest.

Conclusion

This chapter has examined how Israeli master plans for Jerusalem aim to shape the city into a tourism and high-tech centre, and the ways in which urban planning is used to reshape the city's demography. It sheds light on Israel's deliberately engineered economic disintegration of East Jerusalem to make the city essentially unliveable for Palestinians in order to ensure Jewish control over it. Tourism in this context is used as a tool to control (and rewrite) the narrative and ensure the projection of Jerusalem to the outside world as a Jewish city. In essence, tourism is used as a tool for colonisation, segregation, displacement and dispossession. In support of this conclusion, the Israeli President was reported by some (e.g. AWD 2017) to have stated recently at a conference that 'it's time to admit that Israel is a sick society, the Israeli Holocaust against the Palestinians is worse than Nazis'. Both Rivlin and Professor Ruth Arnon, president of the Israel Academy of Sciences and Humanities, which organised the conference at its premises on the capital's Jabotinsky Street, spoke of the painful and bloody summer, and the resultant resurgence of animosity between Palestinians and Jews that had escalated to new heights. He was also quoted in the Israeli press on 12 February 2017 as saying that Israel's newly passed 'Regularisation Law', which formally expropriates several tracts of Palestinian land, 'will cause Israel to be seen as an apartheid state'. As Edward Said stated in one of his essays,

> one has to keep telling the Palestinian story in as many ways as possible, as insistently as possible, and in as compelling a way as possible, to keep attention to it, because there is always the fear that it might just disappear.

References

Abowd, T. (2014) *Colonial Jerusalem: The Spatial Construction of Identity and Difference in a City of Myth, 1948–2012*. Syracuse, NY: Syracuse University Press.

Al-Haq (2015) 'Israel's retaliatory seizure of tax: A war crime to punish Palestinians ICC membership'. Available online: www.alhaq.org/publications/publications-index/item/the-unlawful-seizure-of-palestinian-taxes-israel-s-collective-punishment-of-a-people (Accessed 1 December 2017).

Aljazeera (2017) 'UNESCO passes Jerusalem resolution critical of Israel'. Available online: www.aljazeera.com/news/2017/05/unesco-passes-jerusalem-resolution-critical-israel-170502160841594.html (Accessed 1 December 2017).

Allegra, M. (2013) 'The politics of suburbia: Israel settlement policy and the production of space in the metropolitan area of Jerusalem', *Environment and Planning*, A, 45: 497–516.

Arafeh, N. (2016a) *Economic Collapse in East Jerusalem: Strategies for Recovery*. Washington, DC: AlShabaka, the Palestinian Policy Network.

Arafeh, N. (2016b) *Which Jerusalem? Israel's Little Known Master Plans*. Washington, DC: AlShabaka, the Palestinian Policy Network.

AWD (2017) 'Time to admit that Israel is a sick society, the Israeli Holocaust against the Palestinians is worse than Nazis'. Available online: http://awdnews.com/political/israeli-president-time-to-admit-that-israel-is-a-sick-society,the-israeli-holocaust-against-the-palestinians-is-worse-than-nazis (Accessed 2 June 2017).

Baumann, H. (2016) 'Enclaves, borders, and everyday movements: Palestinian marginal mobility in East Jerusalem', *Cities*, 59: 173–182.

Bollens, S.A. (1998) 'Urban planning amidst ethnic conflict: Jerusalem and Johannesburg', *Urban Studies*, 35(4): 729–750.

Castells, M. (1996) *The Rise of Network Society*. Oxford: Blackwell.

Cheshin, A., Bill, H., & Avi, M. (1999) *Separate and Unequal: The Inside Story of Israeli Rule in East Jerusalem*. Cambridge, MA: Harvard University Press.

Cook, J. (2015) 'Visible equality as a confidence trick', in I. Pappé (ed.), *Israel and South Africa: The Many Faces of Apartheid* (pp. 123–159). London: Zed Books.

Davis, M. (2007) *Planet of the Slums*. London: Verso.

Douglass, M., Wissink, B., & van Kempen, R. (2012) 'Enclave urbanism in China: Consequences and interpretations', *Urban Geography*, 33(2): 167–182.

Dumper, M. (1997) *The Politics of Jerusalem since 1967*. New York: Columbia University Press.

Dumper, M. (2014) *Jerusalem Unbound: Geography, History and the Future of the Holy City*. New York: Columbia University Press.

Eldar, A., & Hasson, N. (2010) 'Jerusalem master plan: Expansion of the Jewish enclaves across the city'. Available online: www.haaretz.com/jerusalem-master-plan-expansion-of-jewish-enclaves-across-the-city-1.298651 (Accessed 1 December 2017).

Falah, G.W. (2003) 'Dynamics and patterns of the shrinking of Arab lands of Palestine', *Political Geography*, 22: 179–209.

Farah, M., & Bakr, A.A. (2015) *East Jerusalem: Exploiting Instability to Deepen the Occupation*. Ramallah, Palestine: Al-Haq Organisation.

Frykberg, M. (2011) 'Legal experts warn of ethnic cleansing in Jerusalem'. Available online: http://electronicintifada.net/content/legal-expert-warns-ethnic-cleansing-jerusalem/928 (Accessed 16 February 2017).

Hammami, R. (2004) 'On the importance of thugs: The moral economy of a checkpoint', *Jerusalem Quarterly*, 6: 16–28.

Hammami, R, (2010) 'Qalandia: Jerusalem's Tora Bora and the frontiers of global inequality', *Jerusalem Quarterly*, 41: 29–51.

Harker, C. (2009) 'Student im/mobility in Birzeit, Palestine', *Mobilities*, 4(1): 11–35.

Hasson, N. (2010) 'MKs seen to ban East Jerusalem Arabs guiding in the city'. Available online: www.haaretz.com/mks-seek-ban-on-east-jerusalem-arabs-guiding-in-the-city-1.319890 (Accessed 15 February 2017).

Hughes, S. (2017) 'With a wink and a nod: Settlement growth through construction as commemoration in the occupied West Bank', *Geopolitics*, 22(2): 360–382.

Ibrahim, N. (2011) 'The politics of heritage in Palestine: A conflict of two narratives', *This Week in Palestine*, Volume 155. Available online: www.thisweekinpalestine.com/details.php?id=3358&ed=192&edid=192# (Accessed 11 February 2017).

Isaac, J. (2017) 'Jewish settlements in the Israeli occupied State of Palestine: Undermining authentic resolution of the Israeli–Palestinian conflict', *Palestine-Israel Journal of Politics, Economics and Culture*, 22(2/3): 85–91.

Isaac, R.K. (2009) 'Can the segregation wall in Bethlehem be a tourist attraction?', *Tourism, Hospitality, Planning & Development*, 6: 221–228.

Isaac, R.K. (2010a) 'Alternative tourism: New forms of tourism in Bethlehem for the Palestinian tourism industry', *Current Issues in Tourism*, 13(1): 21–36.

Isaac, R.K. (2010b) 'Moving from pilgrimage to responsible tourism: The case of Palestine', *Current Issues in Tourism*, 13(6): 579–590.

Isaac, R.K. (2014) 'Israel's going to destroy my birth place Battir'. Paper presented at the International Critical Tourism Studies (CTS) Conference, Sarajevo, 21–26 June.

Isaac, R.K. (2017) 'Transformational host communities: Justice tourism and the water regime in Palestine', *Tourism, Culture and Communication*, 17: 139–158.

Isaac, R.K., & Platenkamp, V. (2012) 'Ethnography of hope in extreme places: Arendt's agora in controversial tourism destinations', *Tourism, Culture and Communication*, 12: 173–186.

Isaac, R.K., Hall, C.M., & Higgins-Desbiolles, F. (2016) *The Politics and Power of Tourism in Palestine*. London: Routledge.

Jadallah, D. (2014) 'Colonialist construction in the urban space of Jerusalem', *The Middle East Journal*, 68(1): 77–98.

Khalidi, R. (1997) *Palestinian Entity: The Construction of Modern National Consciousness*. New York: Columbia University Press.

Klein, M. (2005) 'Old and new walls in Jerusalem', *Political Geography*, 24(1): 53–76.

Kwan, M.P. (2009) 'From place-based to people-based exposure measures', *Social Science & Medicine*, 69(9): 1311–1213.

Kwan, M.P. (2013) 'Beyond space (as we knew it): Towards temporary integrated geographies of segregation, health and accessibility', *Annals of the Association of American Geographers*, 103(5): 1078–1086.

McCarthy, R. (2009) 'Israel using tourist sites to assert control over East Jerusalem'. Available online: www.theguardian.com/world/2009/may/10/israel-expansion-east-jerusalem (Accessed 12 February 2017).

Nightingale, C. (2012) *Segregation: A Global History of Divided Cities*. Chicago, IL: University of Chicago Press.

Ophir, A., Givoni, M., & Hanafi, S. (2009) *The Power of Inclusive Exclusion: Anatomy of Israeli Rule in the Occupied Palestinian Territories*. New York: Zone Books.

Organisation of Islamic Cooperation (2014) *Recommendations and Proposals for Supporting the Palestinian People in East Jerusalem City*. Ankara: SESRIC.

Prior, M. (1997) *The Bible and Colonialism: A Moral Critique*: Sheffield: Sheffield Academic Press.

Pullan, W. (2011) 'Frontier urbanism: The periphery at the center of contested cities', *The Journal of Architecture*, 16: 15–35.

Qumsiyeh, M. (2004) *Sharing the Land of Canaan: Human Rights and the Israeli–Palestinian Struggle*. London: Pluto Press.

Qumsiyeh, M. (2017) 'Last Straw'. Available online: http://popular-resistance.blogspot.nl/2017/12/last-straw.html (Accessed 5 January 2018).

Roberts, N.E. (2013) 'Divided Jerusalem: British urban planning in the holy city', *Journal of Palestine Studies*, 42(4): 7–26.

Said, E. (1995) 'Projecting Jerusalem', *Journal of Palestine Studies*, 25(1): 5–14.

Saleem, A. (2017) 'Israel map raises questions about BBC's impartiality'. Available online: https://electronic intifada.net/blogs/amena-saleem/israel-map-raises-questions-about-bbc-impartiality?utm_source=EI+readers&utm_campaign=52c742c783-RSS_EMAIL_CAMPAIGN&utm_medium=email&utm_term=0_e802a7602d-52c742c783-290666173 (Accessed 20 February 2017).

Selwyn, T. (2011) 'Landscapes of separation: Reflections on symbolism of by-pass roads in Palestine', in B. Bender, & M. Winer (eds), *Contested Landscapes: Movements, Exile and Place*. Oxford: Berg.

Shaly, A., & Rosen, G. (2010) 'Making places: The shifting green line and the development of greater metropolitan Jerusalem', *City and Community*, 9(4): 358–389.

Sheller, M. (2004) 'Mobile publics: Beyond the network perspectives', *Environment and Planning* D, 22(1): 39–52.

Solomon, R. (2017) 'Settlements will be Israel's downfall'. Available online: http://palestineupdates.com/settlements-will-be-israels-downfall/ (Accessed 2 February 2017).

Strickland, P. (2015) 'Israel to revoke Jerusalem residency of Palestinians'. Available online: www.aljazeera.com/news/2015/10/israel-revoke-jerusalem-residency-palestinians-151015125531507.html (Accessed 16 August 2017).

Thawaba, S. & Al-Rimmawi, H. (2013) 'Spatial transformations of Jerusalem: 1967–present', *Journal of Planning History*, 12(1): 63–77.

United Nations (1998) 'Concluding observations of the Committee on Economic, Social and Cultural Rights'. Available online: https://unispal.un.org/DPA/DPR/unispal.nsf/0/0BC7883100A957308525 69AF00575179 (Accessed 12 March 2017).

UNOCH (2014) *East Jerusalem: Key Humanitarian Concerns, Update August 2014.* Jerusalem: Office for the Coordination of Humanitarian Affairs.

Urry, J. (2007) *Mobilities.* Cambridge: Polity Press.

Weizman, E. (2007) *Hollow Land: Israel's Architecture of Occupation.* London: Verso.

Whitelam, K.W. (2013) *The Invention of Ancient Israel: The Silencing of Palestinian History.* London: Routledge.

Yiftachel, O. (1999) 'Ethnocracy: The politics of Judaizing Israel/Palestine', *Constellations*, 6(3): 364–390.

Yiftachel, O. (2002) 'The shrinking space of citizenship: Ethnocratic politics in Israel', *Middle East Report*, No. 223 (Summer).

18

TOURISM AND CONFLICT IN THE MIDDLE EAST

Richard W. Butler

Introduction

War, terrorism and conflict, rather than tourism, would appear to have become terms synonymous with the Middle East, at least in the mindset of many people living outside that region. The media is regularly dominated by stories of death and destruction, refugees, and armed forces in conflict when covering the Middle East. It is not surprising, therefore, that tourism to this region, which is incredibly rich in both cultural and natural heritage, has declined significantly in recent years, and that as a result, many communities are experiencing great hardship from the loss of tourist expenditure (UNWTO 2016a). It is scant comfort to note that in future years the scars and artefacts from the recent conflicts in this region may in turn become tourist attractions, as has been the pattern in other regions, where evidence and artefacts of past wars are current major tourist attractions (Butler & Suntikul 2013; Fyall, Prideaux, & Timothy 2006). One has to wonder, however, if the evidence of current scenes of violence in this region will be as attractive to tourists in the future as the First World War battlefields and cemeteries, the tunnels of the Viet Cong in Vietnam, Pearl Harbor in Hawaii, or the beaches of Normandy have proved to be to today's tourists. It may well be that the nature and length of the period of conflict will so scar the image of the Middle East that potential tourists will be repulsed by the horrors for many years to come.

In recent decades the Middle East has experienced violent regime changes, coups, civil wars, international conflicts, foreign invasions and occupation, the rise of terrorist groups such as the Taliban, Al Qaeda and ISIS, the exporting of terrorism and religious extremism, the large-scale killing of non-combatants and the destruction of non-military structures, including some ancient heritage sites (Bauer 2015; Hamadeh & Bassil 2017). This cycle of violence and conflict in modern times began with the downfall of the Shah of Persia in 1979 and continues in many of the countries in the region. Regime change has not brought respite, rather the contrary in most cases. Foreign interventions have not restored peace, coups have been followed by repression and violence, and civilians throughout the region are suffering in vast numbers, with several million now being refugees in their own and neighbouring countries and in Europe. It would be remarkable if such a pattern of violence and conflict had not had major repercussions on tourism to and within the region (Steiner 2007). In several countries tourism has disappeared entirely and almost completely in others. In most of the others, it has been reduced to a small remnant of the level it used to be.

This is a depressing beginning to a review and discussion of the situation in which this region we call the 'Middle East' now finds itself. It is, after all, a region that has attracted tourists for many centuries, possessing in the past the original Seven Wonders of the World, and currently containing the only remaining such wonder: the Pyramids of Egypt. O'Gorman (2010: 3) notes that tourism to these sites began at least as early as 1500 BC, citing Yoyotte (1960: 57), who recorded graffiti inside one of the Pyramids to the effect that 'Hadnakhte, scribe of the treasury … came to make an excursion and amuse himself on the west of Memphis'. The significance of the region to so much of the rest of the world, in terms of being the contact zone between east and west many centuries ago as the end of the Silk Road, the birthplace of three major religions whose followers span the world, and more prosaically, the source of much of the world's oil resources, has meant that it has rarely been an unnoticed part of the world. Few people are unaware of its great deserts, its cultural significance and its archaeological remains. It has always, therefore, been a region of tourism even if, at times, both the environment and the inhabitants have not always been welcoming to strangers.

While a broader discussion on tourism in the Middle East was presented earlier in the book, this chapter reviews the origins and rationale for tourism in this region to set the context for examining conflict. This is followed by an examination of the nature of the conflicts and terrorism that now engulf the area, and the ongoing and likely future relationships between these elements.

Tourism in the Middle East

Tourists visit their destinations for a multitude of reasons, some personal, some economic, some out of curiosity and interest, some out of obligation, and some are drawn to a location by its inherent appeal, reflecting the characteristics and attributes of that place. MENA draws tourists for all of the above reasons with various degrees of strength, depending on the characteristics and mindsets of the visitors themselves. In the modern era we think of tourism as being primarily a Western phenomenon, perhaps reflecting the dominance of Western academic research, more than reality. While most international tourists came initially from what are known as 'Western' countries, domestic tourism and regional tourism have a longer history and are far larger in volume.

The origins of tourism in the Middle East

The link between religion and tourism has been well established (see for example Sigaux 1966; Timothy & Olsen 2006; Vukonić 1996), and religious tourism has been argued to be as old as religion itself and is, thus, perceived by some academics as being the oldest form of travel (Kaelber 2006). Religion and tourism are historically related through the institution of pilgrimage, and thus one may argue that the Middle East represents the spiritual home of tourism, in that it is the site of the first recorded pilgrimages in the Abrahamic religions. The Middle East is the home of the birthplace of Jesus Christ, and the travels of the Magi (the Three Wise Men, or Kings of the East) perhaps present the first example of religious tourism or pilgrimage in the region. They set a pattern for visits to the Holy Land (as that part of the Middle East is described in Christian terms), a pattern that has continued over the next two millennia and which has presented a model for religious visitation to many other Christian sites of worship such as Rome, Fatima, Lourdes, Santiago de Compostela and countless other smaller and less significant shrines, churches and grave sites.

Similarly, the great Muslim pilgrimage to Mecca, the Hajj, a visit of obligation for all Muslims capable of making the journey, has continued unbroken for over a thousand years and increases in size each year. As with Christianity, Islam has many holy sites, not least the Dome of the Rock and Al Aqsa Mosque in Jerusalem, and visitation to this and other locations involves millions of religious tourists each year. The third great religion whose origin lies in this region is Judaism, and the remains of its holiest site, the Temple of Solomon, in the form of the Wailing Wall, also in Jerusalem, explains why this city is so important to adherents of all three faiths. Unfortunately, far from being a reason for religious tolerance and mutual acceptance, the proximity of such sites to each other within one city that has known more than its fair share of conflict over its history, has meant a continual state of tension and near conflict for many years (Timothy & Emmett 2014). Cline (2005) has recorded that Jerusalem has been destroyed twice, besieged 23 times, sacked 52 times and captured and recaptured 44 times in its long history. Despite this, Jerusalem, like many other locations within the Middle East, remains a major tourist destination, drawing tourists for reasons of obligation, faith and support for their fellow believers from around the world.

In the medieval period, visitation by Christians to the Holy Land took the form of armed excursions, namely the Crusades, aimed not only at visiting the holy sites but taking command of them to ensure they remained open to pilgrims and free from the control of other religions, particularly Islam. Beveridge and O'Gorman (2013: 39), argue that the Crusades 'were not a tourist endeavour, but rather religious-sponsored wars intertwined with elements of conquest and occupation'. However, they go on to point out the role of the Crusades in contributing to the development of tourism facilities and thus enabling the spread of tourist travel to the Middle East and elsewhere. This was achieved through the efforts of the Knights Templar and Hospitaller, with the development of accommodation for travellers and the organisation of financial services and security for pilgrims and others during their travels

Arrangements to aid travellers, not just pilgrims, were already established throughout the Middle East well before the Crusades began. Beveridge and O'Gorman (2013: 39) note that the governor of Samarkand (a major stop on one of the Silk Routes) was ordered to 'Establish caravanserai in your lands so that whenever a Muslim passes by you will put him up for a day and a night' and go on to note 'there was a well-established record of hospitable works for travellers in Bukhara, Uzbekistan' and in western Iran 'three thousand mosques and inns for travellers' (Beveridge & O'Gorman 2013: 40). Thus the presence of travellers for a variety of purposes has been well established in this region for many centuries, with specific provision being made for their accommodation and well-being. Obligations to host guests and travellers is central to Islamic teachings (O'Gorman, Baxter, & Scott 2007) but is predated by several centuries as shown by writings such as the Code of Hammurabi (Hammurabi became king of Babylon in 1792 BC), who established laws governing commercial hospitality and the protection of travellers. Writers (e.g. Pritchard 1954) quote from similar texts of road improvements and large safe establishments for travellers. Thus, the practice of travel for commercial, religious and family reasons has been common and managed within the Middle East for many centuries. The tourism seen in MENA today has clear precedents in travel many centuries ago, to holy places, to sites of historic significance and wonder, and to major cities and centres of commerce, and owes a great deal to the early pioneers in the business of protecting and serving travellers.

Modern tourism in the Middle East

The modern era of tourism likely began in the middle of the nineteenth century with the development of organised tours to the region (Larson 2000) and reflected the improved means of access to and within the Middle East (Nance 2007) and the ongoing appeal of its attractions (Cohen-Hattab & Katz 2001). The initial attractions were the Pyramids and other ancient monuments of Egypt, stimulated by the discovery of the tomb of Tutankhamun in the Valley of the Kings in 1923, the ruins of Petra, Jordan, and the continued fascination with the Holy Land sites. Other major attractions included archaeological sites, such as Leptis Magna in Libya; Palmyra and surrounding remains in Syria; the Topkapi Palace and the Hagia Sofia in Istanbul; the architecture of Damascus, Baghdad, Morocco's cities and Tehran; and the desert landscapes of Arabia and North Africa. The smaller predecessors of modern-day cruise liners made many Mediterranean ports much more accessible than previously, thus Alexandria, Jaffa, Beirut, Tripoli and other cities developed hotels and facilities for visitors. The opening of the Suez Canal also meant greatly increased marine traffic, including tourist liners to the eastern Mediterranean and beyond. Tourism to North Africa tended to begin in the coastal cities and initially ventured little distance inland, reflecting the area's harsh desert environment and limited transportation and facilities for visitors. Interior travel was more in the nature of expeditions until recent years when escorted tours have become much more widely available after the establishment of more specialised facilities and services. The political situation still limits travel in some parts of the interior of North Africa, particularly in recent years following the rise of ISIS and other terrorist groups in Libya, Tunisia and Egypt. Further east, in recent years, efforts by the World Tourism Organization (UNWTO 2016b) have resulted in increased interest in the traditional routes of the Silk Road and cities such as Tashkent and Samarkand. The UNWTO has previously organised four meetings (Samarkand 1994, Tehran 1997, Tbilisi 1997 and Bukhara 2002) on the promotion of the Silk Routes, and tourism generally has been welcomed as a financial pillar for many of the economies of the countries along that route.

The largest segment of the tourist market to the Middle East in recent decades in terms of volume has been mass tourism focusing heavily upon beach resorts and taking advantage of the tradition of hospitality and the appeal of the 'other' of the indigenous cultures. Thus, resort development now stretches completely around the Mediterranean, having begun in France and Italy, spreading then to Spain and beyond to Portugal, and eastwards to Greece, the former Yugoslavia, and then Turkey, followed by Egypt (Sinai and Red Sea coasts), Libya, Tunisia and westward to Morocco. These resort developments began in the 1960s and grew rapidly and extensively from the 1980s with the growth of budget airlines and the deregulation of European airspace in particular. Lastly, Russian tourists have added large numbers of visitors to resorts in Turkey and Egypt during the past decade.

The impact of war, terrorism and conflict on tourism

A vivid example of the rapid change brought about in tourism by conflict is in the context of the last point made above. The inflow of Russian tourists to Egypt in particular and Turkey to a lesser degree was abruptly ended in 2015. That year a Russian airliner was shot down by a terrorist group near Sharm el Sheikh in the Sinai Peninsula. This and related terrorist activities led to a prohibition of flights to Egypt from Russia and several European countries, a ban only recently lifted by some of those countries (UNWTO 2016a). Egyptian tourist numbers declined to less than half their level in 2014 as a result, despite efforts by the Egyptian government to mitigate the situation and restore confidence in the country as a safe destination

(Tomazos 2017). Russian relations with Turkey also deteriorated equally rapidly after Turkish forces shot down a Russian warplane involved in the Syrian conflict, with Russian tourists avoiding Turkey in subsequent months. Tunisian resorts suffered a similar fate in terms of a massive decline in tourist visits following the massacre of 39 people, mostly British tourists, on a beach in June 2015, and Libya has had no tourism to speak of since the fall of Muammar Gaddafi. Libya had not adopted tourism as enthusiastically as Egypt or Tunisia, reflecting the complex machinations of its leader of four decades, and the difficulties of accepting Western tourism into a conservative (if socialist) Arab Islamic nation. Tourism, which was seen as integral to the modernisation of the country, had remained very underdeveloped during Gaddafi's reign (Jones 2010). His demise was not the reason for the disappearance of tourism to Libya, but it did lead directly to the civil strife and terrorism that followed his downfall.

The conflicts that have affected MENA over the past few decades have a number of causes, one of which is regime change. The downfall of two dictators, Saddam Hussein in Iraq and Gaddafi in Libya (Jones 2010), along with the earlier deposition of the Shah of Iran (1979) and his replacement with Ayatollah Khomeini (Baum & O'Gorman 2010), brought about massive upheaval and change in these countries, along with a subsequent decline in, or disappearance of, tourism. The ongoing attempt to unseat President Assad in Syria has seen conflict in that country for several years and now involves not only Syrian combatants but Iraq, Iran, Russia, US, France, the UK and Turkey, as well as Kurds and many volunteers from other countries fighting for or against Assad's forces and ISIS. The demise of strong leaders in MENA through the 'Arab Spring' movement has caused power vacuums that have led to instability, unrest, and in many cases, uprising and civil, and often military, conflict. The impacts of these conflicts on tourism to the affected countries can be seen in visitation figures (UNWTO 2016c), in airlines and tour companies closing operations in those countries and moving customers to other areas, and the massive loss of employment and income in thousands of communities. Even countries where tourism was not a major economic sector, such as Afghanistan, saw the end of tourist visitation except for those very few with a penchant for thrills and risk-taking (Laderman 2013).

Turkey had experienced massive tourism growth in the last two decades, with many inclusive resorts being developed in Antalya in particular, as elsewhere, served particularly by tour companies and budget airlines from Western Europe. The low cost of living in Turkey gave its resorts a salient cost advantage over destinations in other countries, and the lower end of the tourist market responded enthusiastically to the combination of relatively short, cheap flights, low-priced accommodations and meals, very attractive climate, magnificent beaches and an intriguing culture and history. Much of this advantage has been lost since 2015 by a combination of negative images and perceptions of Turkey amongst Western tourist markets. Causes include the presence of refugees from Syria and elsewhere passing through Turkey en route to Greece and other European Union countries, serving as a reminder of the proximity of conflict in Syria and elsewhere in the Middle East; the sporadic terrorist acts of violence in Istanbul and other tourist destinations in 2015 and 2016; and the resulting increasingly harsh security regime being imposed in Turkey both before and after the attempted coup in 2016, with a subsequent deterioration of relations with the European Union. The rapid decline in tourist numbers to Turkey forced tour companies and airlines to change their destinations and schedules, creating major financial difficulties for some companies, and a boost in numbers to resorts in Greece, Spain and Portugal, viewed as relatively low-cost alternatives to Turkish and North African resorts. Turkey has responded by trying to attract more Islamic tourists, encouraging halal vacations and a more Islamic setting with segregated areas for men and women and no alcohol in some resorts (Smith 2016).

Relatively fewer secular tourists venture into the interior of Arabia, reflecting a combination of difficulty of access, limited facilities regarded as suitable for Western tourists and the extremes of the climate, as well as some limitations on their movement and activities. The Holy City of Mecca remains off-limits to non-Muslims but began to receive an increasing number of Hajj pilgrims as modern transportation meant Islamic populations from beyond Arabia could gain relatively easy access to Mecca. Numbers of foreign pilgrims have increased from around 50,000 in the 1920s to 100,000 in 1950, to over a million by 1995 and almost 3 million in total in 2011 (Saudi Embassy 2011). As noted below, the massive numbers of pilgrims have resulted in changes in arrangements for the Hajj, including restrictions on numbers, and have provoked strong disagreements amongst the countries involved. There have been a number of reports in the mass media and elsewhere about the increasing commercialisation of the Hajj and Mecca (Qurashi 2017; Sardar 2014; *The Times* 2014), the construction of luxury hotels and shopping malls overlooking the Kaaba (www.emaar.com), and the widespread use of mobile phones being used for taking 'selfies' by the pilgrims (*The Times* 2015). Religious disagreements between Shia and Sunni clerics over the operation of the Hajj have become proxy incentives in the political conflict between Saudi Arabia and Iran, with the former banning and restricting numbers of pilgrims from the latter (Coghlan 2016a). Despite these issues, compounded by dangerous climate conditions causing a rise in deaths amongst those participating in the Hajj (Trew 2016), it remains one of the largest pilgrimages and single movements of religious tourists in the world. Improved standards of living and accessibility mean it is likely to grow even more in the future and remain the predominant single feature of tourism in the region. So far the regional conflicts have had little apparent effect upon the Hajj, although inevitably potential pilgrims from conflict areas such as Libya and Syria, for example, may be unable to travel at the present time. One has to hope that the religious discord and conflict between factions of Islam does not slip into armed conflict over the Hajj, although recent pronouncements are not optimistic in this regard (Coghlan 2016b).

Regime change and religious issues have been traumatic for tourism to Egypt, when it was hoped that the Arab Spring might have the opposite effect. The overthrow of former President Mubarek and subsequently his successor, Musi, combined with severe reactions from police and military forces, and some terrorist incidents, appear to have finally overcome the great resilience that Egypt has shown over past decades to problems of terrorism and violence. Tomazos (2017) notes how Egypt had been more successful than many countries at restoring its tourism industry and tourist numbers to ever higher levels despite an almost regular occurrence of terrorist incidents over the last three decades and headlines in the Western media such as 'Jihadists target Egypt tourist trade with suicide attack on Luxor temple' (Trew 2015). In all cases until recently, tourist numbers had recovered quickly after incidents, but it would appear that the severity of the recent unrest and violence, combined with two coups, and the shooting down of an airliner have proved too much, and Egyptian tourist numbers halved from 2014 to 2015 and again in 2016 (Tomazos 2017). Although the Egyptian government has taken steps to improve the image of the country, tourists are still avoiding Egypt and until there is convincing evidence of political stability and internal security, this situation is likely to continue. Tunisia, another state which experienced the Arab Spring, has still not recovered from two major terrorist attacks on tourists in recent years and seems to be viewed in the same way as many of the other Arab states as regards being an unsafe destination for Western tourists.

Only Morocco to the west and the Gulf States to the east appear to have escaped the problems of conflict and violence, in the case of Morocco, perhaps because it is geographically far from the popular conception of the Middle East and has had few incidents of unrest. In the Gulf, the emirates of Abu Dhabi and Dubai have been a successful part of this region, which has seen continuous growth in tourism so far with no disruption from conflict or religious extremism. This may be due to a combination of factors, one being the accommodation of tourists and their activities within enclaves (open ones it has to be admitted) within the states, another being strong security with immediate suppression of opposition or conflict, and three, the creation of very popular state airlines (Emirates, Gulf Air and Etihad), which have been extremely successful both as airlines and as promoters of tourism in their home states. The airports they have developed, such as in Dubai, have become global hubs and a high level of luxury at relatively reasonable prices has attracted large numbers of tourists and other developments. The UAE and other Gulf states demonstrate that it is possible to develop tourism in the Middle East if security is ensured, and also that attractions can be developed that draw tourists, in the absence of inherent local attributes apart from warm weather. Despite issues over bribery and corruption in connection with the hosting of mega events such as the forthcoming World Cup and appalling working conditions for many immigrant labourers, the Gulf States have created an image of oases of calm, luxury and spectacle in an otherwise rather mundane landscape a great distance from their tourist markets (Stephenson & Al-Hamarneh 2017).

Israel presents something of a unique case in terms of tourism in the Middle East. Newly created amid controversy and opposition in 1948 as a homeland for the Jews, it has been a scene of conflict and terrorism ever since. Despite a permanent risk of terrorism, and a history of three wars with neighbours in recent decades, Israel has developed a strong tourism industry, receiving over 3 million visitors annually. Many of its international visitors are Jews from Europe and North America, and evangelical Christians, mostly from the same areas, and they visit Israel in considerable numbers almost regardless of the political and security conditions. Timothy (2013: 19) has described some of the latter as 'solidarity tourists', there to support the state of Israel, much as the Crusaders came to enforce the right of Christian pilgrims to access their holy sites. Israeli Zionists have built on this tourism appeal, using it as a propaganda tool, appealing to the Jewish diaspora throughout the world to visit and thus endorse the state of Israel (Cohen-Hattab 2004). Krakover (2013) noted that while numbers of tourists to Israel declined during and immediately following the three wars (1956, 1967 and 1973), they recovered quickly and continued to rise. Over half of visitors to Israel in 2010 were Jewish and another quarter Christian, indicating the strong links in this case between religion and visitation. This link is one of the causes of so many problems relating to tourism in this part of the world, as illustrated by opposition to Palestine being recognised by UNESCO and rival claims over the origin and control of religious sites by the three Abrahamic faiths (Hider 2011). Ongoing terrorist attacks in Israel have a similar effect to war on tourism numbers, with small declines in numbers of visitors on each occasion, followed by quick recovery, perhaps because of considerable faith in Israeli security forces. However, the Second Intifada of 2000–2002 resulted in a drop of 50 per cent in foreign visitor numbers over three years (Krakover 2013: 138). Israel has developed its tourism industry beyond the religious focus, with conventional beach resorts such as Eilat on the Red Sea coast and the spa resorts on the Dead Sea. Eilat, along with Jordanian and Egyptian resorts in close proximity, has not experienced terrorist attacks and is marketed separately from other Israeli destinations, although it too suffers from the periodic declines in general visitation to Israel due to security issues (Mansfield 1999).

As a counterpart to tourism in Israel, one might note the more limited growth and relative weakness of tourism to Palestine, which in effect, is under the control of, and at least partial occupation by, Israel. While Jerusalem was the goal of the Crusaders, to many later Christian tourists, particularly at Christmas, Bethlehem has been the focus of their visits and the primary destinations in Palestine (Collins-Kreiner, Kliot, Mansfield, & Sagie 2006; Isaac, Hall, and Higgins-Desbiolles 2016). Tourism constitutes around 14 per cent of Palestine's GDP (Isaac

2018), and the Christian religious pilgrim market is the largest segment in Palestinian tourism. The current political and security arrangements in Israel make such visits difficult, as Isaac (2013: 145) notes 'All access points (air, sea and land) to the West Bank and the Gaza Strip are controlled by Israel. Hence international visitors and pilgrims wishing to visit Palestine must first pass through the Israeli borders.' Access can be complicated, slow, and even prohibited at times by Israeli security forces, a reflection of Israeli concerns over internal security and prevention of terrorist attacks. The effects of violent outbreaks are generally felt more severely in Palestine than in Israel because of closures of access points following such incidents. Visitation to Palestine dropped from over 800,000 in 2000 to 8,000 in 2002, during the Second Intifada, with negative impacts on local craftsmen and tourism enterprises (Frenkel 2010). It has been argued that deliberate efforts have been made by Israeli authorities to steer tourists away from Palestinian destinations and to make it increasingly difficult for Palestinian tourism operators to conduct business in Israel and attract visitors to Palestinian destinations (Isaac 2013). Regardless of the merits of any particular position in this troubled area, it is clear that tourism to Palestine faces unique and major difficulties because of the security problems created by war, terrorism and conflict in and around Israel. A recent growth in numbers of Muslim tourists to visit religious sites in Palestine may indicate a new market for the region and also be indicative of a desire by such visitors to show solidarity and support for Palestine as noted above in the case of Jewish visitors to Israel. This segment may also serve as somewhat of a replacement for declining numbers of Christian tourists unable or unwilling to make the increasingly difficult journey to Bethlehem and other destinations in Palestine.

Conclusion

It will never be easy to accommodate tourism and the desires and activities of tourists in the Middle East with the strong religious constraints that Islam can require and impose on residents and visitors alike. The tenets of community-based tourism and sustainable tourism, which argue that tourism should recognise and accept the patterns of behaviour of resident culture and society, do not fit easily with the behaviour and desires of many tourists, which often include alcohol consumption, brief clothing, overt expressions of affection, sexual activity and disregard for local religious beliefs. Extremist and fundamentalist reactions to tourism and Western attitudes and behaviour in general mean that tourism will not be welcome in all parts of the region, and local communities should be able to withdraw from tourism if they really wish to do so. However, central governments or religious leaders enforcing such restrictions may not always fit well with local preferences where the need for employment and income is critical. Regardless of the difficulties of having two radically different cultures co-existing in a shared space, the reliance of tourism on stability and a conflict-free environment is clearly paramount. This security is dependent on the political power structure in destination countries wherever they are located, but in the Middle East this is complicated by religious factors. Baum and O'Gorman (2010: 183), writing about Iran in the post-Shah era, may well have been writing about the Middle East in general when they commented:

> The future of tourism in Iran depends on the tenor of the government, whether it be Islamic traditionalist or Islamic liberalist … religion and politics are inescapably intertwined and inseparable, with the priority of religion over politics … Anti-Israeli rhetoric, Holocaust denial, uncertain nuclear aims and ambitions, pollution, traffic, false imprisonment, hangings, and stonings, all serve to undermine the attractiveness

of Iran as a destination and have their origins in the political and religious changes that have taken place in Iran in recent times.

With minor variations, those comments could still apply to most, if not all of the countries in the Middle East with respect to the present and future strength of tourism there. Until the two major problems of political and religious conflicts are resolved, the outstanding tourist attractions of this region will not realise their full potential and most of the inhabitants of the region will remain deprived of a major agent of economic growth. Even more serious is the fact that conflict, violence and terrorism will remain in this region into the foreseeable future, which makes the troubles of tourism seem relatively insignificant.

References

Bauer, A.A. (2015) 'The destruction of heritage in Syria and Iraq and its implications', *International Journal of Cultural Property*, 22(1): 1–6.

Baum, T.G., & O'Gorman, K.D. (2010) 'Iran or Persia: What's in a name? The decline and fall of a tourism industry', in R.W. Butler, & W. Suntikul (eds), *Tourism and Political Change* (pp. 175–186). London: Routledge.

Beveridge, E., & O'Gorman, K. (2013) 'The Crusades, the Knights Templar, and Hospitaller', in R.W. Butler, & W. Suntikul (eds), *Tourism and War* (pp. 39–48). London: Routledge.

Butler, R.W., & Suntikul, W. (2013) *Tourism and War*. London: Routledge

Cline, E.H. (2005) *Jerusalem Besieged: From Ancient Canaan to Modern Israel*. Ann Arbor, MI: University of Michigan Press.

Coghlan, T. (2016a) 'Saudis tell Iranians: You are not proper Muslims', *The Times*, 8 September, p. 34.

Coghlan, T. (2016b) 'We're ready to fight Iran, Saudis say in haj [sic] row', *The Times*, 16 September, p. 44.

Cohen-Hattab, K. (2004) 'Zionism, tourism, and the battle for Palestine: Tourism as a political-propaganda tool', *Israel Studies*, 9(1): 61–85.

Cohen-Hattab, K., & Katz, Y. (2001) 'The attraction of Palestine: Tourism in the years 1850–1948', *Journal of Historical Geography*, 27: 166–177.

Collins-Kreiner, N., Kliot, N., Mansfeld, Y., & Sagie, K. (2006) *Tourism in the Holy Land: Christian Pilgrimage During Security Crisis*. London: Ashgate.

Frenkel, S. (2010) 'Holy city's carpenters lament loss of trade as Christian residents are whittled away', *The Times*, 21 December, p. 29.

Fyall, A., Prideaux, B., & Timothy, D.J. (2006) 'War and tourism: An introduction', *International Journal of Tourism Research*, 8(3): 153–155.

Hamadeh, M., & Bassil, C. (2017) 'Terrorism, war, and volatility in tourist arrivals: The case of Lebanon', *Tourism Analysis*, 22(4): 537–550.

Hider, J. (2011) 'UNESCO decision to give Palestinians membership ignites row over holy sites', *The Times*, 7 October, p. 47.

Isaac, R. (2013) 'Palestine: Tourism under occupation', in R.W. Butler, & W. Suntikul (eds), *Tourism and War* (pp. 143–158). London: Routledge.

Isaac, R. (2018) 'Religious tourism in Palestine: Challenges and opportunities', in R.W. Butler, & W. Suntikul (eds), *Tourism and Religion: Issues and Implications* (pp. 143–160). Bristol: Channel View Publications.

Isaac, R.K., Hall, C.M., & Higgins-Desbiolles, F. (2016) 'Palestine as a tourism Destination', in R.K. Isaac, C.M. Hall, & F. Higgins-Desbiolles (eds), *The Politics and Power of Tourism in Palestine* (pp. 15–34). London: Routledge.

Jones, E. (2010) 'Arab politics and tourism: Political change and tourism in the Great Socialist Peoples' Libyan Arab Jamahiriya', in R.W. Butler, & W. Suntikul (eds), *Tourism and Political Change*, pp. 108–119. Oxford: Goodfellow.

Kaelber, L. (2006) 'Place and pilgrimage: Real and imagined', in W.H. Swatos (ed.), *On the Road to Being There: Studies in Pilgrimage and Tourism* (pp. 277–295). Leiden: Brill.

Krakover, S. (2013) 'Developing tourism alongside threats of war and atrocities', in R.W. Butler, & W. Suntikul (eds), *Tourism and War* (pp. 232–242). London: Routledge.

Laderman, S. (2013) 'From the Vietnam War to the "war on terror": Tourism and the martial fascination', in R.W. Butler, & W. Suntikul (eds), *Tourism and War* (pp. 26–35). London: Routledge.

Larson, T. (2000) 'Thomas Cook, Holy Land pilgrims, and the dawn of the modern tourist industry', in R.N. Swanson (ed.), *Holy Land, Holy Lands and Christian History* (pp. 329–342). Woodbridge: Boydell Press for the Ecclesiastical History Society.

Mansfield, Y. (1999) 'Tourism industry, cycles of war, terror and peace: Determinants and management of crisis and recovery of the Israeli tourism industry', *Journal of Travel Research*, 38: 30–36.

Nance, S. (2007) 'A facilitated access model and Ottoman empire tourism', *Annals of Tourism Research*, 34(4): 1056–1077.

O'Gorman, K.D. (2010) 'Historical giants: Forefathers of modern hospitality and tourism', in R.W. Butler, & R.A. Russell (eds), *Giants of Tourism* (pp. 3–17). Wallingford: CAB International.

O'Gorman, K.D., Baxter, I., & Scott, B. (2007) 'Exploring Pompeii: Discovering hospitality through research synergy', *Tourism and Hospitality Research*, 7(2): 89–99.

Pritchard, J.B. (1954) *The Ancient Near East in Pictures Relating to the Old Testament*. Princeton, NJ: Princeton University Press.

Qurashi, J. (2017) 'Commodification of Islamic religious tourism: From spiritual to touristic experience', *International Journal of Religious Tourism and Pilgrimage*, 5(1): 89–104.

Sardar, Z. (2014) *Mecca: The Sacred City*. London: Bloomsbury.

Sigaux, J. (1966) *History of Tourism*. London: Leisure Arts.

Smith, L.H. (2016) 'Turks boost tourism with halal holidays', *The Times*, 9 September, p. 34.

Steiner, C. (2007) 'Political instability, transnational tourist companies and destination recovery in the Middle East after 9/11', *Tourism Hospitality Planning and Development*, 4(3): 169–190.

Stephenson, M.L., & Al-Hamarneh, A. (eds) (2017) *International Tourism Development and the Gulf Cooperation Council States: Challenges and Opportunities*. London: Routledge.

The Times (2014) 'Cleric calls for Prophet's tomb to be destroyed', *The Times*, 2 September, p. 34.

The Times (2015) 'Pilgrims chastised over selfies at Mecca', *The Times*, 3 February, p. 33.

Timothy, D.J. (2013) 'Tourism, war, and political instability: Territorial and religious perspectives', in R.W. Butler, & W. Suntikul (eds), *Tourism and War* (pp. 12–25). London: Routledge.

Timothy, D.J., & Emmett, C.F. (2014) 'Jerusalem, tourism, and the politics of heritage', in M. Adelman, & M.F. Elman (eds), *Jerusalem: Conflict & Cooperation in a Contested City* (pp. 276–290). Syracuse, NY: Syracuse University Press.

Timothy, D.J., & Olsen, D.H. (eds) (2006) *Tourism, Religion and Spiritual Journeys*. London: Routledge.

Tomazos, K. (2017) 'Egypt's tourism industry and the Arab Spring', in R.W. Butler, & W. Suntikul (eds), *Tourism and Political Change* (pp. 214–229). Oxford: Goodfellow.

Trew, B. (2015) 'Jihadists target Egypt's tourist trade with suicide attack on Luxor temple', *The Times*, 11 June, p. 33.

Trew, B. (2016) 'Haj parasols fitted with solar-powered fans', *The Times*, 26 August, p. 34.

UNWTO (World Tourism Organization) (2016a) *Compilation of UNWTO Declarations 1980–2016*. Madrid: UNWTO.

UNWTO (2016b) *WTTC and UNWTO urge UK government to lift air ban to Sharm el Sheikh*. Madrid: UNWTO.

UNWTO (2016c) *Yearbook of Tourism Statistics 2010–2014*, 2016 edn. Madrid: UNWTO.

Vukonić, B. (1996) *Tourism and Religion*. Oxford: Elsevier.

Yoyotte, J. (1960) *Les Pelerinages dans l'Egypte Ancienne: Les Pelerinages en Sources Orientales*. Paris: Seuil.

Websites

www.emaar.com/Makkah Reside in proximity to the Holy Mosque

Saudi Embassy (2011) '2,927,717 pilgrims in 2011'. Available online: www.saudiembassy.net/latest_news/news11061102.aspx (Accessed 11 September 2018).

19

IMAGE REPAIR STRATEGIES ADOPTED BY MENA NATIONAL TOURISM BOARDS DURING AND FOLLOWING CRISES

Eli Avraham

Introduction

Marketing tourism to countries and regions suffering from a prolonged image crisis is considered quite challenging; here the marketer's task is to convince potential tourists to visit places that appeared in the global media primarily in the negative context of wars, terrorist incidents, conflicts and political instability, and this is not a simple matter. Naturally, tourists are afraid to visit such places and marketers need to find creative strategies and techniques to 'prove' that the place is safe and unique in the attractions and experiences that only it can offer. Despite this challenge, it is surprising to see that there are only a few studies that deal with strategies used by tourism organisations in areas of conflict around the world. One of the least developed geographical areas of research is the Middle East; the purpose of this chapter is to fill this lacuna. Analysing statements, press releases and campaigns, and by using the 'multi-step model for altering place image' (Avraham & Ketter 2008) this study analyses how national tourism organisations in the Middle East have tried to restore their countries' images in times of crisis.

Tourism marketing and destination branding

Due to the competition between places over tourists (Uysal, Harrill, & Woo 2011), decision makers have begun paying more attention to their destination's image over the years. It is now widely recognised that a negative or weak image can be a barrier to attracting visitors (Muhwezi, Baum, & Nyakaana 2016). One central concept in improving destination image comes from the field of destination marketing. Murphy and Murphy (2004) claim that the primary goal of destination marketing is to position the place favourably. Most researchers note the complexity of destination marketing, which requires a holistic and systematic approach, involves various factors and stakeholders, and relates to different environments. These environments and stakeholders include the destination, the customers and the competitors (Muhwezi et al. 2016;

Uyzal et al. 2011). The contemporary discourse on destination marketing has advanced since the 1990s to deal with 'destination branding' (Tasci 2011). This discourse uses concepts such as identity, unique benefits and experience, brand equity, brand values, brand design and brand personality (Michelson & Paadam 2016). Many destinations invest much effort into branding themselves as the leading brand for specific market segments. Anholt (2010) argues that destination brand development has a direct and positive effect on attracting resources in general and inbound tourism in particular. Nevertheless, after analysing 1,172 academic articles in the field of place marketing and branding between 1976–2016, Vuignier (2016) claims that the field has not yet reached maturity. In his words, 'the field suffers from lack of conceptual clarity, diverging definitions and weak theoretical foundation' (Vuignier 2016: 2).

Combatting a destination's image crisis and image repair theories

Evident from worldwide experience, place marketing and branding can effect positive changes for destinations (Dinnie 2015). However, experience has limited effect when a destination is endemically associated with risks of terror, crime, political violence or a general lack of security (Taylor 2006). Crises cause serious image problems for destinations, and visitors in most cases stop arriving (Avraham 2015; Mair, Ritchie, & Walters 2016). As a result, destinations that face such crises need to take restorative measures to repair their public image. Efforts to repair organisational, corporate or brand reputations have been termed variously 'reputation repair', 'crisis communication strategies', 'reputation management', 'image restoration' and 'recovery marketing' (Coombs 2015). Research in the field has tended to focus on 'situational crisis communication theory' (SCCT) (Coombs 2015) and the 'theory of image repair' (Avery, Lariscy, Kim, & Hocke 2010), the latter of which is adopted in this study. According to Benoit (2015: 3), image repair theory focuses 'exclusively on messages designed to improve images tarnished by criticism and suspicion'. Coombs (2015) claims that reputation repair strategies can be organised into four basic groups: denial, reducing offensiveness, bolstering and redress. Benoit (2015) highlights common crisis-response strategies that include denial (simple denial, shifting the blame), evasion of responsibility (provocation, defeasibility, accident, good intentions), reduction of offensiveness (bolstering, minimisation, differentiation, transcendence, attack accuser, compensation), corrective action and mortification (Harlow, Brantley, & Harlow 2011).

The restoration techniques and solutions offered in the image repair models have been helpful for organisations, brands and companies but less suitable for tourist destinations that encounter crises. Places cannot, for example, apologise or compensate for events over which destination managers and marketers have no control; the outbreak of disease, terror attacks, war or natural disasters are not events for which apologies/compensation make sense, although these two strategies have been offered over the years in many image repair models (Benoit 2015; Coombs 2015). Therefore, in these instances, it behoves destinations to follow a specific recovery model that is place-appropriate. Adler-Nissen (2014) developed a coping approach to deal with a state's stigma and image crisis: stigma recognition, rejection and counter-stigmatisation. Avraham and Ketter (2008), on the other hand, in their multi-step model for altering place image, suggest 24 strategies to restore place image, divided into three groups: source, audience and message (SAM strategies). The selection of the strategy to handle image crises is based on three groups of characteristics related to the crisis, audience and place (CAP) analysis.

Source strategies concentrate mainly on marketers' efforts to influence or replace the source that is perceived as being responsible for the negative image, usually the international media. Two examples include organising familiarisation tours for foreign journalists (Mair et al. 2016) and launching Internet campaigns to bypass the news media (Avraham & Ketter 2016). Audience strategies are concerned with the audience's values and perceptions; here, marketers try to high-light some of the values held in common between their destination and the target audience. Message strategies focus on tackling the negative messages reported about the destination by sending opposite messages, reducing the scale of the crisis or expanding the destination image beyond the stereotype attached to it.

National tourism boards in the Middle East

The Middle East and North Africa (MENA) has a place of honour in world history, religions, culture and international politics (Al-Mahadin & Burns 2006). From a tourism perspective, MENA makes a unique contribution, and the countries in the region offer landscapes and sites that are relatively close to their main market sources (e.g. Europe). The region's countries have long understood that tourism can contribute to economic development, create jobs, help build bridges towards peace mediation, reduce stereotypes and generalisations, and create cooper-ation between countries that have been engaged in prolonged political conflict (Al-Hamarneh & Steiner 2004; Zamani-Farahani & Henderson 2010). This is why most countries in the area have decided to develop tourism. On the other hand, conflicts, wars and socio-economic challenges have led to many crises that hamper efforts to attract more visitors. The result is that tourism to MENA is especially sensitive to crises, and each small crisis can lead to more ser-ious ones (Al-Mahadin & Burns 2006). Mansfeld (1994, 1996) and Wahab (1996) note a direct correlation between the numbers of tourists to Middle Eastern countries and the countries' level of involvement in security situations. For this reason, many Middle Eastern destination representatives have devoted considerable effort to countering the negative security stereotype of the region (Beirman 2003).

Since MENA countries have varying views about tourism, there have been significant differences between them in relation to the weight of religion in decisions that were taken, visa policies, the use of bodies to promote tourism development and marketing, strategies used, visions created and the allocation of financing for marketing. Thus, there are countries with a clear policy of tourism development and promotion, such as Tunisia, Jordan, Lebanon and Egypt, along with other countries that prefer not to engage in development or marketing such as Kuwait, Saudi Arabia, Yemen and Libya. Some countries have clearly defined visions, goals and implementation plans. Others do not, and policies are determined by ad hoc decisions. One result is that the roles and names of national tourism boards differ amongst countries.

An empirical assessment

To uncover the strategies used by MENA national tourism boards to combat tourism crises and restore positive images, three research questions were asked. First, what public relations crisis techniques and advertising campaign components, such as texts, slogans and visuals, were used by national tourism boards during tourism crises? Second, which media policies were adopted by national tourism boards to affect their destination coverage in the international media? Finally, which marketing initiatives were promoted by national tourism boards?

To answer these questions, the 'multi-step model for altering place image' (Avraham & Ketter 2008) was adopted using the SAM strategies as used by marketers and DMOs. The ana-lysis reported here utilised a qualitative content analysis of four types of data used by MENA national DMOs: advertising components (slogans, visuals and text); press interviews with national DMO officials and representatives; media policies adopted by national DMOs; and marketing initiatives.

These four tools were examined during a 14-year period from 1 January 2002 to 31 December 2016 and used Internet and video-sharing websites, such as YouTube, and countries' national tourism board websites; news reports from Middle Eastern and international newspapers; the eTurbo news (http:/eturbonews.com) website; and case studies from the academic/professional literature. The items included in the sample contain information on the marketing strategies of MENA's national DMOs, advertisements and marketing initiatives taken during or after a tourism crisis. The countries included in the analysis were Afghanistan, Algeria, Bahrain, Egypt, Iran, Iraq, Iraqi Kurdistan, Israel, Jordan, Kurdistan, Kuwait, Lebanon, Libya, Morocco, Oman, Pakistan, the Palestinian Authority, Qatar, Saudi Arabia, Syria, Tunisia, Turkey, the United Arab Emirates and Yemen.

The analysis reveals that MENA's national DMOs used three kinds of strategies to restore their countries' positive image during tourism crises: source, audience and message.

Source-focused strategies

Promoters and tourism marketers around the world understand the importance of the implications of positive media coverage. Middle East tourism ministries attempted both to influence the media and to seek alternatives to bypass the traditional foreign media in an effort to restore their positive image during or after a crisis. The analysis showed that the tourism ministries used three kinds of source strategies.

Cooperation and developing media relations

From the news reports and national tourism board websites, we learn that most Middle Eastern tourism ministries choose to cooperate with the foreign/Western media. Examples of cooperation include issuing and sending press releases, conducting press conferences and conveying information on new tourism sites, events and campaigns, and responding to journalists' queries, as well as ensuring that officials will be available for media interviews. This type of attitude by tourism ministries is understood to be helpful in promoting MENA countries' points of view on the crises being covered. In addition, tourism ministers commonly attempt to develop relations with other opinion leaders, such as travel agents, academics, religious/community leaders and tour operators.

One of the central techniques tourism ministries can employ while trying to develop media relations is to provide trips for journalists during peaceful times (Avraham 2009), as well as after a crisis, in order to let them experience the place personally. Two countries in particular, Egypt and Jordan, have both used this strategy. Egypt's tourism ministry has organised several press trips to its main cultural attractions since the beginning of the Arab Spring in 2011 (eTurbo news (eTN), 9 June 2011); the reason for these trips, according to the Egyptian Minister of Tourism, was 'so they (the journalists) can now report back how safe it is to visit Egypt' (eTN, 10 June 2011). In addition, groups of Russian consumers and journalists were invited to visit the country's resort areas (eTN, 16 September 2013). Jordan has also invited selected bloggers, travel writers and journalists from Canada and the United States (eTN, 7 April 2011). The same technique was adopted by the Pakistan Tourism Development Corporation, which arranges media familiarisation trips to various destinations in that country (eTN, 13 September 2012) with the hope of reviving positive coverage. The Syrian tourism board also hosted many opinion leaders until the civil war outbreak in 2011 (eTN, 31 October 2011).

To improve their media images, several tourism boards hired public relations companies to monitor and improve their countries' media image. For example, the Yemen Tourism

Promotion Board (YTPB) monitors foreign media to follow what is published about Yemen, particularly negative articles, and to reply to them. For those who write positive articles about Yemen, the YTPB in the past expressed its appreciation by arranging familiarisation trips to the country. In addition, the YTPB has signed contracts with public relations firms in France, Italy, Germany, the UK, Ireland, Spain, UAE, Saudi Arabia and Japan. One of the PR companies' tasks was to develop relations with reporters and public opinion leaders and to negotiate with tour operators to include Yemen in their programmes, monitor the media in their countries, arrange for activities and events, and coordinate press and familiarisation trips for tour operators and journalists. The goal of these activities was to present Yemen as a rich destination with a great deal to offer visitors (www.yementourism.com/tourism2009/aboutus/). Owing to the current escalated conflict in Yemen, however, these efforts have been suspended.

Raising complaints and reacting to negative coverage

The essence of this strategy is an expression of grievance or complaint-filing by officials about negative media coverage or towards various factors that describe the destination in a negative light, which might curtail tourist arrivals. For example, the Egyptian tourism minister, at a meeting with Italian tour operators, pointed out the negative image of his country portrayed by the Italian media during the events of the Arab Spring (eTN, 8 February 2013). Later that year he addressed some 30 Italian journalists who were hosted by the tourism ministry in Sharm El Sheikh as he struggled to convince the Italian and European governments to reconsider their travel advice not to visit Egypt (eTN, 13 September 2013).

The same strategy was used by the Tunisian tourism ministry when it voiced similar complaints about the coverage of Tunisia in the French media (eTN, 18 September 2013). In addition, after several foreign governments published travel warnings about Tunisia, the country's tourism minister said in an interview that 'the warnings have not been specific to certain parts of Tunisia, such as border areas. They instead paint the whole country as a danger zone. That's unfair and inaccurate' (Romdhani 2016). As a result, the country started to cooperate with many tourism agents abroad in an effort to remove the travel warning. In addition to the attempts to create positive media relations and raise complaints regarding a country's depiction, some governments also pressured journalists, blocked media outlets from covering crises, and threatened and arrested journalists (Avraham 2013).

Finding alternatives to the traditional media

The idea behind this source-focused strategy is the marketers' quest to find alternatives to the traditional media. As can be expected, tourism ministries are not always satisfied with their countries' international coverage, especially during crises when the media tends to increase the drama surrounding certain events. Tourism ministers would prefer the media to ignore such crises or depict them as minor events so as to prevent a tourism crisis. In their quest to find media alternatives, tourism ministries aim to bypass traditional outlets in order to reach their foreign target audiences directly without mediators' interpretations, so they can present the reality on the ground as they want the world to see it. The Internet provides a means for countries to present a crisis or even a positive event from their point of view (Gilboa 2006). In this regard, five tools used by MENA tourism ministries to improve their image and broaden support were found: Internet websites, YouTube, Facebook, Twitter, Instagram and webcams.

The Internet allows Middle Eastern countries, in the face of a lack of access to international media or a lack of funding for media campaigns, to bypass traditional media while still reaching their target audience through their own websites (Ketter & Avraham 2012). The tourism ministries have set up many websites to cast positive images and to distribute positive news about their cultures, arts, fashions, music and cuisine. For example, the Oman ministry of tourism's website (www.tourismoman.com.au/) provides information about the country's destinations, hotels and resorts, history and tradition, art, culture and shopping as well as information on how to get there, the local currency and obtaining a visa. Most of the region's countries have similar information-oriented websites.

MENA tourism ministries also use YouTube as an alternative to traditional media. The YouTube platform allows organisations to broadcast videos on demand for free. It is natural that this tool is used to send messages to target audiences and air ads and information on tourism, especially when a country believes that the traditional media is depicting it in a negative light. For example, the Iraqi government created a YouTube channel to 'fight the media's lies' (*Haaretz*, 29 November 2009). In addition, the Egyptian tourism minister appeared in a YouTube video and asked foreign travel agencies to push their governments to lift their negative travel advisories and to disseminate information necessary for recovery from the tourism crisis (eTN, 1 September 2013).

Social networks are online platforms where people gather and form relationships within a virtual space (O'Connor, Wang, & Li 2011). Social media marketing seeks to engage customers with the destination using social network websites and platforms (Ketter & Avraham 2012). There are three interests in the process: the place, the place's online marketing efforts and the customers. First, the place entails various physical interactions that are the basis for online conversations; second is the place's online marketing efforts, which aim to generate and promote the physical interaction into a virtual one; third are the customers, who engage with the place, form an online community and create the social media content. Many tourism ministries use this tool.

An example of the use of social media was a US$10 million agreement between Google and ten Jordanian entities to promote Jordan as a destination (eTN, 14 December 2010). The Jordanian tourism ministry then sponsored a social media campaign run by travel bloggers who had visited the country (eTN, 11 December 2011). Facebook was also used by Tunisia's national tourism board to highlight the country's tourism offers and which allowed visitors to share pictures and videos of the country while showcasing various tourism sites (eNT, 11 November 2011). The Egyptian tourism board encouraged Egyptians to share their favourite photos of their home country on social media as part of the ministry's 'peer-to-peer advocacy approach' (Think Marketing 2015).

Twitter and Instagram were used by Bashar Al-Assad, the Syrian president, and the Syria tourism board to show the 'other faces' of Syria. By these means Assad sought to project the image of a loved and admired leader, while no mention was made of the civil war or his acts against his own people (*Haaretz*, 3 September 2013). Tunisia's tourism board opened the Hashtag #*trueTunisia*, which describes different cities and destinations in the country in various languages, presents testimonials by previous visitors and gives advice for road trips. A Twitter account opened by the Egyptian tourism ministry with the hashtag #*ThisisEgypt* went viral on social media. Here tourists could 'start tweeting with Twitter about why you love Egypt' and receive information about events (Twitter, egypttourism@come2eg). This account was used when the Hollywood actor Morgan Freeman visited Egypt to film at the pyramids while holding a sign with this hashtag written on it (Yasser 2015). The same tool was used by the Yemen Tourism Promotion Board: @YemenTourismPB.

Webcams are another tool used in this strategy to skirt traditional media. These cameras are set up at familiar tourism locales and their images broadcast over the Internet to anyone interested. Egypt and Jordan have placed webcams at their main tourism spots in order to demonstrate to Westerners that these sites are still safe and full of activity (eTN, 6 and 11 February 2013). In November 2013, this strategy was launched by the 'Egypt Now Initiative'. The official Egypt tourism website offered a channel that streams live webcam footage of beaches at Sharm El Sheik and Hurghada (eTN, 26 September 2014). In addition to the use of webcams, the activity of Google Street View as a source of planning for tourists was also extended (Al Arabiya, 11 September 2014).

Message strategies

The second group of media strategies focuses on the message itself. While message strategies vary in emphasis, they share a common denominator in that they directly manage the possible coverage effects of crises from the tourism viewpoint, such as demonstrations, political instability, terror attacks and wars.

Ignoring the crisis or the state's problematic image

An easy solution for destination marketers is to ignore the crisis or the state's problematic image. This strategy is used by many destination marketers and was very popular in the Middle East prior to, during and after the Arab Spring. The goal was to pretend that any damage reported in the media was minor or that no serious crisis had occurred. For example, both Egypt and Turkey disregarded the terrorist attacks in several of their cities in the 2000s (Avraham & Ketter 2008) by launching tourism advertisements after the crisis, and never mentioning the attacks on their websites. Egypt continued, as a policy, to use this total disregard strategy at the beginning of the Arab Spring events (eTN, 7 February 2011). It seems like Syria took the use of this strategy to an extreme. In the summer of 2016, the Syrian tourism board issued a campaign under the slogan 'Syria—Always Beautiful', which was meant to promote its beach holidays while totally ignoring the civil war in which nearly half a million people had died (*Conversation* 2016).

Narrowing the geographical scope of the crisis

Another strategy that MENA officials have used during crises is limiting or narrowing the scale of the crisis. Here, marketers do not ignore the crisis but try to convey the feeling that they are limited to certain areas, therefore presenting no challenges to visiting other areas of the country. For example, the governor of Luxor (670 km south of Cairo) claimed that his city 'is stable and secure but suffers … problems due to the recurrent turmoil in Cairo and the Suez Canal cities …' (eTN, 3 March 2013). Using this terminology, the governor hinted that only a few cities were unsafe for visitors and the crisis was geographically limited. This limiting-the-crisis strategy was also used by the Egyptian tourism minister when he told CNN that the unrest was only in 'one square kilometer in downtown Cairo', and this should not put people off the entire country (eTN, 6 February 2013). Another example from an Egyptian official came when the tourism minister claimed that, as opposed to Cairo, other parts of Egypt were very much open for business: 'It is safe to go to Sinai, the Red Sea and Sharm El Sheik' (eTN, 1 September 2013).

Reducing the scale and the framing of the crisis event

In addition to ignoring or limiting the crisis, marketers try to portray events as insignificant, irrelevant or marginal. In other words, they try to convince their audience that the event covered is much less severe than what it seems to be from the media. This strategy is often implemented when the media demands explanations or reactions from decision makers to crisis events. Here the efforts focused on convincing journalists that the crises are local or marginal and are not connected to terror or political instability.

For example, the killing of a French tourist in the Red Sea resort city of Sharm El Sheikh was described by Egypt's minister of tourism as a 'random act' not directed against foreigners (eTN, 29 January 2012). This strategy also was adopted by the Syrian regime. After an event where the government used tanks to stop peaceful demonstrations, a government spokesperson claimed: 'These are not demonstrations and these were not even protesters. They were armed gang members, who rioted and terrorized residents' (*Haaretz*, 17 June 2011). In December 2016, a group of unknown outlaws attacked and killed five members of the security forces and a foreign tourist near a well-known attraction in southern Jordan. To prevent the framing of the event as a 'terror attack' in the international media, which could lead to a major tourism downfall, Jordanian officials immediately published a message that this incident was a result of criminal activity and not terror: 'We would encourage you to remain calm as more news unfolds in regards to this criminal incident ...' (eTN, 18 December 2016). Similarly, after a demonstration in Jordan at the beginning of the Arab Spring, the head of the Jordan tourism board tried to dismiss fears that the country could be drawn into the social unrest sweeping the Middle East:

> Protests have happened before. The maximum number of protestors was 5,000 to 10,000. There has been a revolution in Egypt, a revolution in Tunisia. But in Jordan the situation is normal—similar to London after the demonstration two weeks ago.
>
> *(Travel Weekly, 11 April 2011)*

Acknowledge the negative effect of an event's coverage and send an opposing message

Directly acknowledging the negativity of an event is not always the most convenient course of action. It is, however, the most effective course of action. This strategy maintains or regains a trustworthy image during or immediately after an event. For example, in Oman, the general director of tourism promotion understood the tendency of Western audiences to perceive Middle Eastern countries as dangerous after any small risk-related event, so he suggested 'the delivery to international markets and media of an accurate, clear and effective message about Oman remaining as safe and welcoming to tourists as ever...' (eTN, 9 July 2011). This willingness to admit the existence of a crisis prevails on many levels; the director of the Jordanian tourism board stated during a time of uncertainty, 'Jordan has a long-standing reputation as a very safe, secure and hospitable destination' (eTN, 27 March 2011). Here again the marketer knew how the destination was perceived by Westerners so he sent an opposite message: 'We are safe'. This strategy was also used by other countries' spokespersons during the Arab Spring, including Egypt (eTN, 5 August 2012) and Lebanon (eTN, 13 April 2012).

An example of Egypt's use of this strategy was found in 2014, when the tourism minister said

> Tourist destinations continue to be safe and secure and are still attracting thousands of tourists from around the world on a daily basis. We want to make it known that Egypt is a strategic, safe tourism destination for Arab and foreign visitors alike.
>
> *(eTN, 4 May 2014)*

The Egyptian minister also sent out the following message: 'The world will see tourism returning to Egypt. We have an ambitious global plan to show the world that it is safe and fun to visit Egypt anytime' (eTN, 11 May 2014). Sending the message that 'Egypt is safe' was also carried out with an advertising campaign. For example, according to a delegation from the Egyptian Tourist Authority in Saudi Arabia, the role of the famous campaign—'Egypt is where it all begins'—was to portray the fact that Egypt was a secure and safe destination (eTN, 23 May 2011).

Assuring 'a short transitional phase', a 'better future' and the beginning of 'a new era'

The strategy of acknowledging the negative image can be also applied by the tendency of tourism ministries to promote the message of a 'new era', suggesting that the country is going through a phase of changes from its problematic past to a promising present and near future. The aim of the emphasis on a short transitional phase was to ask potential tourists to accept the temporary difficulties and to convince them that the result will be worthwhile. For example, speaking in Dubai less than four weeks before the country's planned 2014 presidential election, the Egyptian tourism minister said that his country was gearing up for a fresh start with a new president and a new parliament (eTN, 11 May 2014). A similar declaration released earlier claimed that 'Things will go back to normal in Cairo within a month's time' (eTN, 16 September 2013). Sometimes this technique is mixed with one containing an opposite message: 'Egypt is safe ... and will be even more so after the elections' (eTN, 8 February 2013).

After a terror attack in Tunisia, the Tunisian tourism ministry promises a better future, saying 'Security agencies have taken the initiative. Terrorists are on the defensive ... we have pressed on with new security measures around hotels, tourism circuits and travel venues' (Romdhani 2016). Promises for a better future also came from the Egyptian tourism minister:

> We will spare no efforts in this respect. Egypt was in a transitional phase and there are many countries that experienced stages of transition, including Russia itself, but I believe we managed to pass through this phase within a relatively short period. We are now reviving all of the sectors of our country, including tourism.
>
> *(Think Marketing 2015).*

The Algerian tourism minister also employed this strategy by saying,

> I think this is an image [the conflict between government forces and Islamic militants] which is out of touch, because the black years are behind us ... all that is left in the mind is a certain number of traces, which must absolutely be rubbed out.
>
> *(eTN, 2 December 2009)*

Multifaceted promotions, exhibitions and softening hard images

Destinations involved in long conflicts and which tend to appear frequently in the news in a negative light develop a hardened image, which needs to be softened. One way to address a hard image is by enriching the destination's representation by promoting events, activities and visuals that portray opposite conditions of demonstrations, clashes and violence (Gilboa 2006). Over the years, MENA marketers have acknowledged their negative representations, while simultaneously trying to soften the effect (Avraham 2013).

Film festivals, concerts, dance performances, art exhibitions and local food fairs are examples of cultural events abroad that can be used in public diplomacy to influence countries' images. In MENA, this has been a useful technique in instilling a positive depiction into the consciousness of the potential target audiences. For example, the Abu Dhabi tourism authority initiated a multifaceted campaign in New York City that highlighted the emirate's tourist offerings and promoted the tastes and experiences of the region (eTN, 17 May 2012).

Saudi Arabia used the same strategy when marketers presented an archaeological exhibition in the US, intended to introduce the country's ancient civilisations and culture (eTN, 5 February 2012). Likewise, Pakistan's tourism authority participated in a UNWTO conference, the ITB Berlin Tourism Exhibition, the World Islamic Tourism Mart in Malaysia, the SAARC Tour Operators Conclave in India, and the SAARC Travel & Tourism Mart in Bangladesh (eTN, 13 September 2012). Kurdistan also ran a campaign to expand its image under the title 'Kurdistan: Land of Nature and History'.

To survive a crisis, destination marketers also try to expand their tourism products. For example, the Tunisian National Tourism Board (ONTT) ran a campaign to highlight the richness of the country's tourist product, especially its cultural inventory, and also to draw attention to the importance of health tourism and treatment with seawater to emphasise that Tunisia was much more than just a sea and sun destination (eTN, 3 April 2013). In 2015, a similar campaign for Tunisia was run by the tourism ministry. Called 'Vacation Tunisia', the campaign used the slogan 'Free to live it all' to promote the country's culinary delights, cultural heritage, shopping, artworks, myth and legends, traditions and opportunities for relaxation (www.youtube.com/watch?v=aUPaAfqmdXE).

Hosting spotlight cultural and sports events

One way to shift the international media's attention from a negative to a positive portrayal is by hosting spotlight events. During such events, the media's attention focuses on a particular location for a short and concentrated period of time, allowing select images to be highlighted (Avraham & Ketter 2008). This strategy can be implemented by organising events that project images of a safe place or 'business as usual'. For example, every year Bahrain hosts a Formula One Grand Prix race. Internal ethnic tensions derived from the Arab Spring led to demonstrations and riots in early 2011, which resulted in the cancellation of the race that year. In the following years the Bahraini government insisted on resuming the event to convey the message that normality had returned and to catalyse the resurgence of the country's tourism sector. Bahrain also held a number of successful events, including an international air show and concerts featuring Julio Iglesias and Andrea Bocelli, which 'allowed the marketers to showcase the security and stability in the kingdom' (eTN, 29 March 2012).

Other countries in MENA, such as Yemen, Egypt and Morocco, have similarly hosted spotlight events to shift their images. Yemen hosted an international soccer tournament, featuring eight Persian Gulf states, to refocus from an insurgent battleground and wellspring of global terrorism (Worth 2010). Morocco held a festival targeting a Western audience called the 'Gnawa Music Festival' (Wood 2012). Jordan hosted the 'first ever travel conference, supporting eco-tourism and active travel development in the Middle East and North Africa region' (eTN, 30 September 2016), and Egypt hosted the fifth Luxor Film Festival (eTN, 22 March 2016). Lebanon also hosted the Al-Bustan international festival of music and performing arts, which included various shows amongst the 'mostly Shakespeare' performances (eTN, 14 March 2016). At the same time, Lebanon promoted a live performance of the Disney movie *Frozen* in Beirut (eTN, 14 March 2016).

Ridiculing the country's existing stereotype

With this mechanism, marketers present the stereotype associated with a destination and then demolish it by showing how absurd the stereotype is. Tunisia started an interesting campaign in June 2011, which included billboards in London declaring 'They say that in Tunisia some people receive heavy-handed treatment' with pictures showing women receiving massages. While the slogan hinted at negativity during a crisis period in Tunisia, the visuals emphasised something quite contradictory. Another ad cleverly stated 'They say Tunisia is nothing but ruins' with depictions of ancient Roman remains (eTN, 15 June 2011). These are two examples of how MENA countries have tried to counter stereotypes by ridiculing them to an extreme.

Concerned with Israel's negative image as an unsafe place, the country's marketers also used this strategy. In one campaign, this strategy was used to illustrate how ridiculous Israel's unsafe stereotype was. In the commercial, a young woman tourist is walking along an Israeli seashore when she suddenly spots a handsome man sitting on the sand. As she continues walking while looking back at him, she collides with a pole. At that point the narrator declares, 'Indeed, Israel can be a dangerous place' (Avraham 2009).

Associate the country with well-known brands and celebrities

Overcoming long-term negative images can be difficult, as people do not quickly put aside their preconceptions, however erroneous they may be. In this case, instead of working to change the negative image directly, destinations sometimes try to associate with familiar brands, celebrities or cultural symbols known to their target audiences (Mair et al. 2016). The effective use of celebrities in destination image repair was shown by Walters and Mair (2012) in their research on the best strategy to attract tourism after a series of bushfires in Australia. This strategy has also been used by Middle Eastern tourism boards. For example, the Tunisian tourism and trade minister invited Kate and William, the British Royal couple, as well as Elton John, to visit post-revolution Tunisia. Egypt used this strategy when hosting American actor, Sean Penn, in October 2011; Penn was shown sightseeing at the Egyptian Museum, the Giza Pyramids and Tahrir Square (eTN, 12 November 2011). According to the newspaper *Al-Ahram Today*, the goal of Penn's tour was to show the world that the country was safe. Moreover, the Atletico Madrid team, whilst visiting the pyramids (13 November 2011) were mentioned on the Egyptian tourism ministry's Facebook page. American actor Danny Glover also was invited to serve as a judge when Egypt hosted the fifth (eTN, 22 March 2016) Luxor Film Festival in March 2016. The actor toured Luxor's historic sites and visited its attractions. In addition, the Egyptian tourism ministry hosted the singer Yanni, who performed and travelled around the country. The reason for this invitation can be understood from the words of Ayman Saad, a member of the ministry of tourism's media office: 'the tour will include visits to the Pyramids … The pictures taken from these tours will be used to promote tourism in Egypt with the hashtag #*This is Egypt* to show people the true image of Egypt' (Yasser 2015).

Audience-focused strategies

Audience strategies contain messages specific to a particular or narrow audience that is perceived as more resilient to the crisis. Audience strategies can be directed at an audience from another country on the grounds of common values, history, religion, and culture or world outlook, as well as for a local audience. Tourism ministries in MENA used two audience strategies: changing the target audience by addressing others that are seen as more resilient, and developing and marketing new niches and target audiences.

Changing the target audience by addressing other resilient ones

A destination that aims to attract different audiences needs to communicate different messages. This is important because cultural and national factors are related to an audience's reactions to crises and its perceptions of risk (Mansfeld & Pizam 2006). Markets previously treated as secondary or tertiary should perhaps become the main target of a destination (Taylor 2006). Examples include shifting the focus from sea and sun tourism, which was pitched before a crisis, to business or conference tourism, or turning the audience from international tourists to domestic visitors. Middle Eastern ministries have focused on four main target audiences in recent years: domestic tourists, regional visitors, new tourist demand from outside the region, and people of their diasporas.

In the first situation, tourism boards have tried to encourage citizens to tour their own countries, thereby replacing the declining foreign tourist market. For example, at the beginning of the Syrian civil war in 2011, the country's ministry of tourism encouraged domestic tourism (eTN, 14 August 2011). Egypt also started encouraging Egyptians to visit Sharm El Sheikh through discounted airfares and resort stays (eTN, 16 November 2015). Al-Hamarneh and Steiner (2004) show how shifts to a more local market have saved many national tourism industries from collapse long before 2010.

By emphasising regional tourism, tourism boards encourage visits from neighbouring Arab countries. For example, during the Arab Spring uprisings, several Middle Eastern countries started focusing on regional tourism and managed to re-direct their marketing efforts towards neighbouring countries to compensate for the absence of Westerners (Al-Hamarneh 2013). A few of the many examples are Jordan, Egypt, Pakistan (eTN, 13 September 2012), Oman (eTN, 30 December 2012) and Bahrain (eTN, 14 April 2013). To promote regional tourism from other Arab countries, marketers created promotional initiatives; Abu Dhabi's tourism industry, for example, ran a week-long promotion in Saudi Arabia (eTN, 29 March 2012). Libya also ran a campaign to attract tourists from the Arab world before the Arab Spring.

The third new market strategy encourages arrivals from new markets. Since the Arab Spring events, many examples exist of Middle Eastern marketers addressing new target audiences outside MENA. Syria, for example, shifted its marketing eastward to attract travellers from friendly countries such as Russia, Iran and China (eTN, 31 October 2011). Egypt sought new tourists from Japan and the BRIC countries—Brazil, Russia, India and China (eTN, 21 May 2012). The Egyptian minister of tourism also visited South Africa with a delegation to market Egypt there (eTN, 19 October 2014). During the Arab Spring, the Jordanian tourism ministry aimed its efforts at the Indian market (eTN, 14 July 2011), while Morocco's tourism machine focused on the British, German and Gulf markets (Avraham 2015). Jordan also started a campaign to attract increased numbers of tourists from Russia (AMEinfo 2015), China (Romdhani 2016) and other Asian countries (eTN, 14 August 2016).

Over the decades, many people of Middle Eastern descent have migrated to other parts of the world with huge diasporic communities located all over Europe, North America and Australia. Since the Arab Spring and other regional conflicts, this phenomenon has increased. Only in the last decade have Middle Eastern tourism ministries started to understand the huge potential of their diaspora peoples as a tourist market. In an effort to develop diaspora tourism, Lebanon, for example, targeted the Brazilian market to persuade that country's five million citizens of Lebanese ancestry to come and visit the 'old country' (eTN, 13 April 2012). Likewise, the Tunisian tourism board ran a campaign in 2011 for Tunisians living outside the country (mainly in France) under the slogan: 'This summer, I come home'.

Developing and promoting new niches

While the former strategy focuses on certain target audiences, this strategy also includes a search for new target audiences but is based less on geography and more on finding new interest-based markets. According to this strategy, marketers invest in promoting and developing new niche markets, such as golf, rural or extreme tourism—markets that were previously neglected.

Religious tourism is especially important in the Middle East and is considered less sensitive to questions of safety than other types of tourism (Collins-Kreiner, Kliot, Mansfeld, & Sagi 2006; Timothy & Olsen 2006) so it is common for destinations that suffer from prolonged image problems to try to develop this sort of tourism if they have the resources and reputation to do so (Mansfeld & Pizam 2006). Religious tourism's apparent 'immunity' to crises makes this strategy popular in MENA because of the region's chronic crises and because it boasts of so many religious heritage sites. In 2011, the Egyptian tourist authority ran a campaign titled 'Egypt—Where It All Began' to attract Arab tourists from Middle Eastern countries and included organising a Ramadan festival that year (eTN, 23 May 2011). Turkey also began developing tourism for Muslims while noting the availability of halal hotels that offered appropriate food, prayer rooms and other halal hospitality requirements (Al-Hamarneh 2013; Avraham 2013). In addition to attracting Muslim visitors, Egypt began focusing on Christian tourism during the Arab Spring crisis. According to the Christian Bible, the Virgin Mary and Jesus stayed in Egypt for 42 months, visiting 20 different places. As a result, the Egyptian Ministry of Tourism developed a tourist itinerary that ostensibly paralleled the journey of the Holy Family (eTN, 10 August 2014).

Over the years, several Middle Eastern countries, Egypt, Tunisia, Lebanon and even Syria, chose to market themselves as sun, sea and sand (SSS) destinations. This was considered a good strategy until the Arab Spring broke out. At that time, the choice of SSS branding became inappropriate for countries that consistently appeared in the global media because of various crises, as these destinations then had to compete with much safer destinations. As a result, several MENA countries began focusing on other kinds of tourism, such as green/eco-tourism, diving tourism and MICE (meetings, incentives, conferences and exhibitions) (eTN, 11 February 2014). For instance, in 2014, in a bid to preserve the environment and attract 'green tourists', a number of tourism facilities in Egypt began using cleaner or renewable energy sources (eTN, 7 January 2014). Furthermore, to increase tourist arrivals in 2013 and 2014, instead of promoting the country as a whole, Egypt started to promote various sub-brands, such as the Romantic Nile and the Land of the Pharaohs. The campaign was designed to promote Egypt's cultural heritage as an alternative to its theretofore popular beach-based tourism (eTN, 26 September 2014).

Tunisia also started diversifying its product 'away from low added-value beach-based package holidays, and to develop tourism in the interior regions' with a greater focus on ecological, cultural, spa and revolution-based tourism (Romdhani 2016). Around the same time, Jordan started to develop adventure tourism, medical and religious tourism, agritourism, and cultural and film tourism. In 2014, the Jordan Tourism Board initiated a relationship with international film producers who came to explore potential cinematic locations throughout the kingdom (eTN, 14 August 2016). Lebanon has started to promote medical tourism (eTN, 13 April 2012), and Jordan began to emphasise family tourism (eTN, 14 April 2011).

Conclusion

By utilising the 'multi-step model for altering place image' we can see that MENA's national tourism boards have used three types of strategies—source, message and audience—to deal with tourism crises, negative images and stereotypes of terrorism, violence and war. Of all the world's major geographic realms that need to adopt these anti-crisis branding tools, the Middle East is most in need. Nevertheless, only a handful of Middle Eastern national tourism boards were willing to deal with their image crises directly and seriously. Most countries have yet to decide if they want to develop tourism at all, and many of them remain unsafe destinations. Some countries have begun re-branding efforts to counter the effects of political turmoil, but this is still a major challenge for the region.

However, before actualising these re-branding efforts, these countries must first address the many barriers facing tourism development, in particular improving the security environment, integrating and involving the local community in decision-making, and addressing the basic lack of infrastructure. Thus, MENA countries need to solve some basic problems before they can begin to think about national branding (Kotler & Gertner 2002). Indeed, despite the investment of several national governments in reinventing their images, many understand that the reality on the ground must also change. For example, Jordan and Tunisia have recently begun to overhaul their tourism sites and services, such as renovating hotels and public restrooms at archaeological sites (eTN, 14 August 2016; Romdhani 2016).

Although challenging, dealing with crises will remain an important marketing issue for national tourism boards in the Middle East until such time as the region stabilises and its conflicts are resolved. Tourism is vital to MENA's various economies. It also encourages helpful intercultural dialogue and the destruction of stereotypes, prejudices and cultural misunderstanding (Al-Hamarneh & Steiner 2004; Zamani-Farahani & Henderson 2010). Future research should concentrate on which marketing initiatives, public relations strategies and advertising campaigns succeed in restoring a country's positive image following a crisis and to combat the stereotypes and generalisations that are so commonly associated with the countries of the Middle East and North Africa. 'Production research' that examines various aspects of the decision-making processes regarding the selection of marketing initiatives and media campaigns would be useful by looking at who is involved in this process and how officials understand the effectiveness of various strategies and allocation decisions for recovery campaigns.

References

Adler-Nissen, R. (2014) 'Stigma management in international relations: Transgressive identities, norms, and order in international society. *International Organisation*, 68(1): 143–176.

Al-Hamarneh, A. (2013) 'International tourism and political crisis in the Arab world—from 9/11 to the "Arab Spring"', *e-Review of Tourism Research (eRTR)*, 10(5/6): 100–109.

Al-Hamarneh, A., & Steiner, C. (2004) 'Islamic tourism: Rethinking the strategies of tourism development in the Arab world after September 11, 2001', *Comparative Studies of South Asia, Africa and the Middle East*, 24(1): 173–182.

Al-Mahadin, S., & Burns P. (2006) 'Visitors, visions & veils: The portrayal of the Arab world in tourism advertising', in R. Dahar (ed.), *Tourism in the Middle East: Continuity, Change and Transformation* (pp. 137–160). Clevedon: Channel View Publications.

AMEinfo (2015) 'Crisis-hit Jordan's tourism sector eyes Russian tourists', *AMEinfo*, 17 November 2015. Available online: https://ameinfo.com/travel/crisis-hit-jordans-tourism-sector-eyes-russian-tourists/ (Accessed 5 September, 2018).

Anholt, S. (2010) *Places: Identity, Image and Reputation*. Basingstoke: Palgrave Macmillan.

Avery, E.J., Lariscy, R.W., Kim, S., & Hocke, T. (2010) 'A quantitative review of crisis communication research in public relations from 1991 to 2009', *Public Relations Review*, 36(2): 190–192.

Avraham, E. (2009) 'Marketing and managing nation branding during prolonged crisis: The case of Israel', *Place Branding and Public Diplomacy*, 5(3): 202–212.

Avraham, E. (2013) 'Crisis communication, image restoration, and battling stereotypes of terror and wars: Media strategies for attracting tourism to Middle Eastern countries', *American Behavioral Scientist*, 57(9): 1350–1367.

Avraham, E. (2015) 'Destination image repair during crisis: Attracting tourism during the Arab Spring uprisings', *Tourism Management*, 47: 224–232.

Avraham, E., & Ketter, E. (2008) *Media Strategies for Marketing Places in Crisis: Improving the Image of Cities, Countries, and Tourist Destinations*. Oxford: Butterworth-Heinemann.

Avraham, E., & Ketter, E. (2016) *Marketing Tourism for Developing Countries: Battling Stereotypes and Crises in Asia, Africa and the Middle East*. London: Palgrave Macmillan.

Beirman, D. (2003) *Restoring Tourism Destinations in Crisis*. Wallingford: CAB International.

Benoit, W.L. (2015) *Accounts, Excuses and Apologies: Image Repair Theory and Research*, 2nd edn. Albany, NY: State University of New York.

Collins-Kreiner, N., Kliot, N., Mansfeld, Y., & Sagi, K. (2006) *Christian Tourism to the Holy Land: Pilgrimage during Security Crisis*. Aldershot: Ashgate.

Conversation (2016) 'Syria: "Always Beautiful"—can tourism be a force for peace?', *The Conversation*, 26 September. Available online: https://theconversation.com/syria-always-beautiful-can-tourism-be-a-force-for-peace-64954 (Accessed 5 September 2018).

Coombs, W.T. (2015) 'The value of communication during a crisis: Insights from strategic communication research', *Business Horizons*, 58(2): 141–148.

Dinnie, K. (2015) *Nation Branding: Concepts, Issues, Practice*. London: Routledge.

eTN (ETurboNews) (Various dates) Available online: www.eturbonews.com (Accessed 11 September, 2018).

Gilboa, E. (2006) 'Public diplomacy: The missing component in Israeli foreign policy', *Israel Affairs*, 12(4): 715–747.

Haaretz (Various dates) Available online: www.haaretz.com/ (Accessed 11 September, 2018).

Harlow, W.F., Brantley, B.C., & Harlow, R.M. (2011) 'BP initial image repair strategies after the Deepwater Horizon spill', *Public Relations Review*, 37(1): 80–83.

Ketter, E., & Avraham, E. (2012) 'The social revolution of tourism marketing: The growing power of users in social media tourism campaigns', *Place Branding and Public Diplomacy*, 8(4): 285–294.

Kotler, P., & Gertner, D. (2002) 'Country as brand, product, and beyond: A place marketing and brand management perspective', *Journal of Brand Management*, 9(4): 249–261.

Mair, J., Ritchie, B.W., & Walters, G. (2016) 'Towards a research agenda for post-disaster and post-crisis recovery strategies for tourist destinations: A narrative review', *Current Issues in Tourism*, 9(1): 1–26.

Mansfeld, Y. (1994) 'The Middle East conflict and tourism to Israel, 1967–90', *Middle Eastern Studies*, 30(3): 646–667.

Mansfeld, Y. (1996) 'Wars, tourism and the "Middle East" factor', in A. Pizam, & Y. Mansfeld (eds), *Tourism, Crime and International Security Issues* (pp. 265–278). New York: Wiley.

Mansfeld, Y., & Pizam, A. (eds) (2006) *Tourism, Security and Safety: From Theory to Practice*, 2nd edn. Oxford: Butterworth Heinemann.

Michelson, A., & Paadam, K. (2016) 'Destination branding and reconstructing symbolic capital of urban heritage: A spatially informed observational analysis in medieval towns', *Journal of Destination Marketing & Management*, 5(2): 141–153.

Muhwezi, D.K., Baum, T. & Nyakaana, J.B. (2016) 'Dealing with negative symbolism of destinations with difficult heritage: Analysis of Uganda's image', *Journal of Hospitality Management and Tourism*, 7(3): 33–42.

Murphy, P.E., & Murphy, A.E. (2004) *Strategic Management for Tourism Communities*. Clevedon: Channel View Publications.

O'Connor, P., Wang, Y., & Li, X. (2011) 'Web 2.0, the online community and destination marketing', in Y. Wang, & A. Pizam (eds), *Destination Marketing and Management: Theories and Applications* (pp. 225–243). Wallingford: CABI.

Romdhani, O. (2016) 'Tunisia's tourism ministers sees better days ahead', *The Arab Weekly*, 22 May. Available online: https://thearabweekly.com/tunisias-tourism-minister-sees-better-days-ahead (Accessed 30 December 2017).

Tasci, A.D. (2011) 'Destination branding and positioning', in Y. Wang, & A. Pizam (eds), *Tourism Destination Marketing and Management: Collaborative Strategies* (pp. 113–129). Wallingford: CAB International.

Taylor, P.A. (2006) 'Getting them to forgive and forget: Cognitive-based marketing responses to terrorist acts', *International Journal of Tourism Research*, 8: 171–183.

Think Marketing (2015) 'Egypt launches first global marketing campaign in more than 4 years', *Think Marketing*, 1 November. Available online: https://thinkmarketingmagazine.com/egypt-launches-first-global-marketing-campaign-in-more-than-4-years/ (Accessed 12 September 2018).

Timothy, D.J., & Olsen, D.H. (eds) (2006) *Tourism, Religion and Spiritual Journeys*. London: Routledge.

Travel Weekly. (2011) 'Head of Jordan tourist board dismisses fears of unrest'. 11 April. Available online: www. travelweekly.co.uk/articles/36853/head-of-jordan-tourist-board-dismisses-fears-of-unrest (Accessed 11 September 2018)

Uysal, M., Harrill, R., & Woo, E. (2011) 'Destination marketing research: Issues and challenges', in Y. Wang, & A. Pisam (eds), *Destination Marketing and Management: Theories and Applications* (pp. 99–112). Wallingford: CAB International.

Vuignier, R. (2016) 'Place marketing and place branding: A systematic literature review', *Working Paper de l'IDHE*, 5/2016.

Wahab, S. (1996) 'Tourism and terrorism: Synthesis of the problem with emphasis on Egypt', in A. Pizam and Y. Mansfeld (eds), *Tourism, Crime and International Security Issues* (pp. 175–186). New York: Wiley.

Walters, G., & Mair, J. (2012) 'The effectiveness of post-disaster recovery marketing messages: The case of the 2009 Australian bushfires', *Journal of Travel & Tourism Marketing*, 29(1): 87–103.

Wood, M. (2012) 'Gnaoua Festival D'Essaouira', *Journey Beyond Travel*, 20 June. Available online: www. journeybeyondtravel.com/blog/gnaoua-music-festival-essaouira-morocco.html (Accessed 5 September 2018).

Worth, R.F. (2010) 'Yemen loses in soccer, but scores a P.R. victory'. *New York Times*, 5 December. Available online: www.nytimes.com/2010/12/06/world/middleeast/06yemen.html (Accessed 12 September 2018).

Yasser, N. (2015) 'Morgan Freeman occupies local social media', *Daily News Egypt*, 23 October. Available online: https://dailynewsegypt.com/2015/10/23/morgan-freeman-occupies-local-social-media/ (Accessed 10 December 2017).

Zamani-Farahani, H., & Henderson, J.C. (2010) 'Islamic tourism and managing tourism development in Islamic societies: The cases of Iran and Saudi Arabia', *International Journal of Tourism Research*, 12: 79–89.

PART VI

Transportation

20

CRUISE TOURISM IN THE MIDDLE EAST

Magdalena Karolak

Introduction

Cruise tourism has become a global phenomenon in recent decades with growing passenger numbers and expansion of cruise itineraries to remote areas of the world. In a bid to develop mass tourism products, cruise companies search for new destinations to diversify their itineraries and to attract more international customers. As a result, major cruise companies operate nowadays in various parts of the world on a seasonal basis. Middle Eastern destinations offer an attractive package to cruise tourists with ancient monuments, religious sites and natural wonders that are easily accessible from ports of call. In addition, the Middle East and North Africa (MENA) is home to the longest river that is also navigable and provides access to the treasures of ancient Egyptian architecture. It comes as no surprise that the Middle East had already witnessed the beginnings of the modern cruise tourism industry in the nineteenth century. Apart from well-established tourist sites in the region, the rapid economic growth of the Arabian Gulf in the last decade opened up a new area of cruise tourism interest that today is the fastest growing cruise destination in the region.

This chapter traces the emergence of cruise tourism in MENA and examines the position of the region in relation to other cruise destinations. It emphasises the strategies and factors behind the growth of this sector of tourism but also looks at various impediments to its development. In addition, this chapter aims to analyse the geographical cruise areas within the Middle East and assess their specific patterns and reasons behind the growth of this sector. It also provides a descriptive introduction to this sector of Middle East tourism. Research devoted to cruise tourism in general is scarce (Zbuchea 2015) and is especially scarce from the perspective of Middle East tourism. The author acknowledges, however, the difficulty in providing an in-depth analysis of the subject due to the fragmented nature of data currently available. Lastly, this chapter provides recommendations and opens up new areas for further research.

Positioning MENA amongst the world's cruise destinations

The firm establishment of the cruise industry in the tourism market can be traced back to the late 1960s with the founding of modern large cruise lines (Wilkinson 2006). Despite being a recent form of leisure, the cruise industry has recorded remarkable growth since that time, in

Table 20.1 The growth of cruise passengers 2003–2013 (in millions)

Region	2003	2008	2009	2010	2011	2012	2013	10-year growth
North America	8.3	10.29	10.40	11.0	11.44	11.64	11.82	43.6%
Europe	2.71	4.47	5.04	5.67	6.15	6.23	6.40	136.2%
Subtotal	**10.94**	**14.76**	**15.44**	**16.67**	**17.59**	**17.87**	**18.22**	**66.5%**
Rest of the World	1.08	1.54	2.15	2.40	2.91	3.03	3.09	186.1%
Total	**12.02**	**16.30**	**17.59**	**19.07**	**20.50**	**20.90**	**21.31**	**77.3%**

Source: Adapted from data in Business Research & Economic Advisors (2014: 6).

terms of passenger numbers, geographic market expansion and package diversification, making it one of the fastest growing areas of tourism overall (Cartwright & Baird 1999). While between 2003 and 2013 the global tourist arrivals (mostly land-based) rose by 57 per cent to 1.087 billion, Business Research & Economic Advisors (2014) estimate that the number of cruise passengers alone increased during those years by 77 per cent to 21.3 million. As a result, in the 1990s this form of tourism became a global phenomenon encompassing markets and passengers from all over the world (Wood 2000). Although, North America has remained the most active cruise-sourcing destination, followed by Europe, other world destinations have recorded spectacular growth in the last decade as shown in Table 20.1.

The industry has experienced a rapid transformation from an exclusive product for the wealthy to a mass market one. Its growth has been prompted by, amongst others things, the expanding accessibility of cruise holidays to middle-class and budget travellers; the lowering of the average age of cruise passengers (Dowling 2006), and the emergence of new cruise destinations. The industry's success resides in the metamorphosis of cruise liners and the evolution of the packages offered. On the one hand, cruise packages have become shorter, and hence more affordable to the average consumer. Indeed, Brida and Zapata (2010) pointed out that the length of many successful packages is approximately a week or less. On the other hand, cruise ships have become in essence 'floating resorts' (Charlier & McCalla 2006: 18) and by themselves constitute tourist attractions offering more and more luxurious accommodations, increasingly varied entertainment, sports facilities and shopping venues. In the process of becoming parallel to lavish hotels ashore, cruise ships have increased in size and capacity to accommodate such facilities (UNWTO 2003) and to attract more passengers. As a result, large cruise ships have the capacity to carry over 5,000 people. Consequently, onshore resorts have become the main competition for cruise liners, not other cruise companies (UNWTO 2003: 21). Furthermore, the growth of the cruise industry was fostered by the development of theme strategies that combine cruising with specialised itineraries, activities and types of ships such as educational cruises, culinary cruises, and wine tasting cruises. Those activities gave birth to specialised cruise lines such as the Disney Cruise Line and specialised ships such as casino ships. Ultimately, from an ownership perspective, the cruise industry has grown through mergers of smaller companies. Such mergers gave rise to the three major cruise lines, namely, Carnival Corporation & plc, Royal Caribbean Cruises Ltd., & the Star Cruises Group, which together control approximately 88 per cent of all cruise supply (Business Research & Economic Advisors 2014: 14). The remaining part of the cruise segment is shared amongst minor lines that specialise in capturing mostly the North American market (UNWTO 2003). Given the high costs of entry onto the market, such as investment costs in large cruise ships that offer diverse facilities, the fast growth of the industry was immensely helped by mergers and takeovers that prevented, amongst other things, the collapse of many small cruise lines (Klein 2005).

The growth of the cruise industry is also fuelled by the potential benefits it offers to local economies. National governments have taken this opportunity seriously and began developing national and regional strategies to tap into the potential of cruise tourism (Dowling 2006). Amongst the most important economic benefits are revenue generation from sales, taxes and job creation. Like all other forms of tourism, the economic effects of cruise tourism on local economies can be classified as direct, indirect and induced (Brida & Zapata 2010b). Direct impacts result from direct sales to crew members, passengers and vessels of items such as fuel, food, maintenance, shopping and other tourist activities. Indirect effects are generated by direct suppliers providing primary materials such as supplies or laundry services. Induced effects are fuelled as increased incomes through direct and indirect earnings allow people to spend more money within a given region. Business Research & Economic Advisors (2014) estimated that in 2013, the total of these expenditures amounted to US$117.15 billion. Dowling (2006) lists the government sources of cruise-based revenue being generated through sales taxes paid by passengers, crew members and the cruise lines directly; various taxes paid through cruise line fees, such as docking charges, littering fees and other port charges; garbage disposal fees; and charges for water sales. The cruise industry also supports economies through job creation. In 2013, direct expenditures in cruises generated 417,979 full-time jobs worldwide (Business Research & Economic Advisors 2014: 23).

The growth of the cruise industry can be seen in the emergence of new regions of cruise activity. The popularity of cruise destinations is reflected in the number of passenger bed days, which entails the number of days that all berths could be 100 per cent occupied. In 2013, North America accounted for 63.1 million bed days, which is 47 per cent of the bed capacity overall (Business Research & Economic Advisors 2014: 13). The Caribbean accounted for almost 80 per cent of the North American bed capacity, making it the most popular cruise destination in the world. Europe came in second with 37 per cent (47.6 million bed days); its high scores were largely due to the popularity of the Mediterranean region. The Asia-Pacific region accounted for 13.5 million bed days, which is 10 per cent of the global capacity. The rest of the world comprised 6 per cent, with 8.3 million bed days. Within the last category, 34 per cent of bed days included the capacity of cruises in the Indian Ocean. The narrow Indian Ocean category includes cruise itineraries that cross the Red Sea, the Arabian Peninsula, coast of Africa and India; Southeast Asia and Australia/Pacific are included as separate entities within the rest of the world category. The growth of the cruise industry in this category is reflected by a 296.4 per cent increase in passenger bed days capacity (Business Research & Economic Advisors 2014: 6). Nonetheless, it is difficult to isolate data that would reflect solely cruise tourism growth in the Middle East. In fact, Charlier and McCalla (2006: 19) noted that cruise tourism statistics for the rest of the world category were simply 'educated guesses'. This constitutes the main impediment to a detailed analysis of the Middle East as a whole. In addition, data for various ports of call in the region are not available either or are severely fragmented.

Nevertheless, it is clear that the Middle East is a newly emerging cruise region and constitutes so far a minute portion of the global cruise industry, which is why it lacks scholarly research compared to major cruise destinations. Nonetheless, cruise tourism has created a new opportunity for the growth of tourism in the Middle East, a region that has been shaken by political instability and decreasing security. It has been observed, for instance, that in 2011 cruise tourism helped the region compensate for the economic downturn in the hospitality/tourism sector in general (Travel & Tourism News Middle East 2011).

The development of cruise tourism in the Middle East

MENA is characterised by hot and humid summer months with temperatures in certain locations exceeding 48°C during the daytime and remaining as high as 30°C at night but with mild and sunny winters. Given these almost constant weather patterns, the cruise season extends in the cooler months from early October to the beginnings of June. Weather is a key factor when choosing a cruise destination, and cruises worldwide operate on a seasonal basis alternating itineraries to offer the summer weather schedules to the Northern and Southern Hemispheres during their winter months, respectively (Charlier & McCalla 2006). The Middle East therefore offers an alternative to Caribbean Islands and European Mediterranean destinations in this regard.

Furthermore, the region is characterised by a great variety of natural and historical attractions that have been a magnet for tourism for centuries, which is why the Middle East is one of the earliest cruise regions in the world. MENA is home to unique monuments of ancient civilisations with the most remarkable sights in Egypt and Jordan; religious monuments, especially in Israel and Palestine; and natural wonders such as the Red Sea and deserts. Many of its monuments have been recognised on the UNESCO World Heritage List. In addition, thanks to recent economic development, the Arabian Gulf has become synonymous with extravagant modern architecture, including the tallest building in the world and a ski slope in the middle of the desert in Dubai. Nonetheless, the Middle East is also prone to violent conflicts and political instability that directly impact tourism. Repeated travel warnings have often made some areas in the region inaccessible to tourists in the past, and this trend has been clearly visible in 2016–2018 as well. In recent years, security concerns have become more serious with most of the region affected by the political upheavals during the Arab Spring, the rise of extremists groups such as ISIS, and the increase of incidents of terrorist attacks and terrorist threats in general that created a perception of insecurity, deterring tourists from travelling to the region. All of these factors have had a negative impact on tourist arrivals in the region (Strategy& 2015).

Nevertheless, the Middle East as a region presents clearly defined geographic areas of interest to cruise tourism development which, as a result, constitute separate entities from the point of view of cruise operator itineraries. The Nile in Egypt constitutes one such entity with cruises operating along the river. The Red Sea ports with an extension to the Mediterranean coast constitute the second cruise destination included within longer itineraries spanning over more than one continent. Lastly, the countries of the Arabian Gulf have emerged as the third cruise tourism area. The following overview provides details of cruise tourism patterns in each of these geographic areas.

Nile River cruises

Thanks to its rich history, Egypt has been drawing explorers and tourists for centuries as the home of the ancient Egyptian civilisation and Greek, Roman and Muslim civilisations that subsequently influenced its development (Schmitz 2010). Previous centuries have left numerous monuments of incomparable beauty and value. The country is crossed by the navigable Nile River, which links the Mediterranean coast to Aswan and further into Sudan. There are speculations that it was on the Nile itself where the first cruises in history took place in ancient Egypt (Peek 2011). The Nile marked the beginnings of modern cruise tourism in the Middle East when Thomas Cook, founder of the travel agency by the same name and precursor to the modern tour company, brought the first tourists to cruise the famous river in 1869,[1] sailing from Cairo to the Sudanese border and back (Humphreys 2015). However, tourists cruised the

Nile River even before Cook's steamships arrived using slow *dahabiya* boats (TIMEA n.d.). Nowadays, owing to safety concerns and navigational obstacles, such as the Aswan Dam, which obstructs water traffic, some areas are clearly inaccessible to cruise passengers (Samuel 2014). The cruise industry today focuses on the ancient Egyptian monuments in the southern part of Egypt, and the market is divided into international and local cruise lines with different budget options starting from basic to very luxurious (Lewis n.d.). Even though many cruise itineraries start in Cairo, after visiting the capital, the majority of tourists fly to Luxor where the actual navigation begins. From Luxor, cruise ships sail to Dendera as the furthest northern point and then return to Luxor. They then continue south to Aswan and return, stopping on the way to allow visits to the most important monuments such as Kom Ombo, Edfu and Esna (Figure 20.1). The shortest itinerary lasts three days. From Aswan, cruise passengers have the option of taking a flight to visit Abu Simbel, because the Aswan Dam creates an impediment to ship traffic. The full cruises from Cairo are less popular, because they usually take two weeks.

Since the early 2000s, poor hygiene standards aboard Nile cruise ships have improved thanks to the introduction of the Cristal Program to Nile cruises. The program, operated from the UK, provides an international hygiene and safety standards ranking of cruise vessels on the river (Check Safety First 2017). Yet, recent security concerns in Egypt have greatly affected the Nile

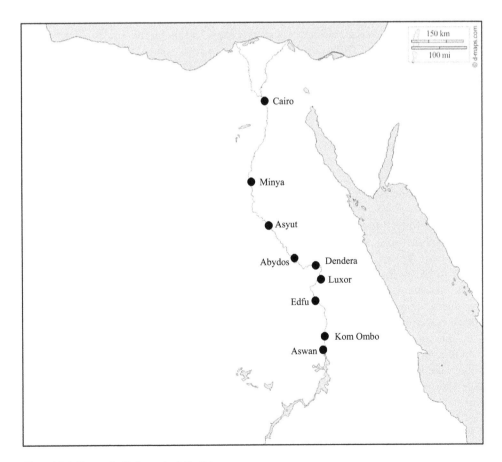

Figure 20.1 Ports of call along the Nile River

cruise industry. While it is estimated that in 2010 there were 10,000 departures on approximately 300 ships, these numbers plummeted during the Arab Spring in 2011 (Ward & Machan 2014). At that time, the majority of Western countries issued strict travel warnings against any non-essential travel in Egypt. While exact data on Nile River cruises are not available, the overall tourist arrivals to Egypt plummeted from 14 million in 2010 to roughly 9.5 million in 2014 (World Bank 2014), which more than likely also severely impacted the cruise sector. Many travel warnings were lifted for some areas of Egypt at the end of 2013 and international operators and some local cruise lines re-started operating on the Nile. Nonetheless, since then the country has been affected by major security threats. In 2015, multiple bomb attacks occurred in Cairo, a Russian Metrojet aeroplane was exploded over the Sinai just after taking off from Sharm El Sheikh, and a terrorist attack on tourists in Luxor was foiled. In 2016, three foreign tourists were stabbed in an attack in Hurghada, and an Italian student was killed in unclear circumstances while conducting research in Cairo. These incidents testify to the precarious situation of safety in Egypt that overshadows the growth of cruise tourism. The exact effects of these events on Nile cruise tourism is not known, but they most certainly affected the sector considerably.

The Red Sea and the Mediterranean shores of the Middle East

The Red Sea and Mediterranean coast boast a number of ports of call in Turkey, Jordan, Israel and Egypt which, thanks to providing access points to unique sights in the region, have been routinely included in the itineraries of cruises that begin in Europe and/or Asia crossing from one continent to another. Thanks to their overall tourist attractiveness, these ports of call have had a long history of cruise tourism, starting in the 1970s. The most opportune ports include Aqaba (Jordan) from where it is possible to take an onshore day excursion to Petra; Ashdod/Tel Aviv and Eilat (Israel), which provide access to Jerusalem; Haifa (Israel) from where religious sites such as Nazareth, the Sea of Galilee and Jerusalem are accessible; and Safaga (Egypt), which offers opportunities to visit Luxor. The Mediterranean port of Alexandria (Egypt) offers access to Cairo and various ancient monuments in both cities. Ports in Israel and Jordan provide easy day-trip access to natural wonders such as the Dead Sea and the Wadi Rum desert. Various sites along the Red Sea are accessible from Aqaba, Jordan, and from the Egyptian port of Sharm El Sheikh. Cruises also pass through the Suez Canal, with some stopping in Port Said on the way (Figure 20.2).

The cruises that currently include these ports of call pass from Europe, for instance, Italy or Spain, to Asia (India and further) or vice versa; from the Arabian Gulf to Europe; and, more recently, from Western Europe to Istanbul. In addition, the only local Middle Eastern cruise line, an Israeli small line, Mano Maritime, is based at Haifa and operates to destinations in the Mediterranean, Europe and the Black Sea, catering to Israeli tourists (Smith 2014: 211). Nonetheless, none of the ports in this area of the Middle East is a home port to large international cruise lines, or a port where cruises begin or end.

In common with the Nile situation, safety concerns are a major impediment to the growth of cruise tourism in this area. The ongoing conflict between Israel and Palestine has caused major cruise lines to drop Israeli ports of call for several years in the past (Hunter Publishing 2006: 126) and more recently in 2014 (John 2014) after a period of growth in cruise arrivals from 169,100 in 2010 to 237,000 passengers in 2011. Deterioration of security in one country often affects tourist arrivals in neighbouring countries as cruise lines change their itineraries and decide to go on to another region instead—for instance, the Greek Islands instead of the Red Sea. This trend is clearly visible in neighbouring Jordan where 2014 marked a sharp drop in cruise passengers in Aqaba from 95,724 passengers in 2013 to 35,647 in 2014 after several

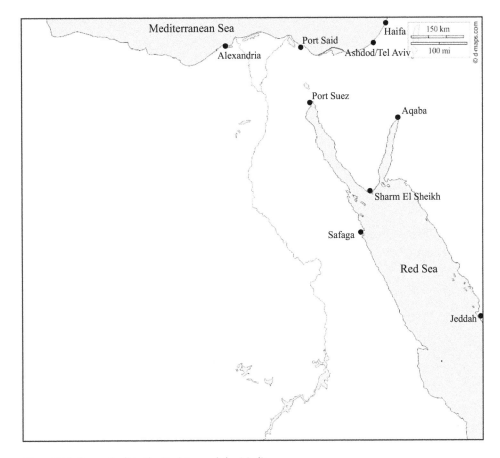

Figure 20.2 Ports of call in the Red Sea and the Mediterranean

cruise lines withdrew from Israel. Preliminary data for the first quarter of 2016 suggest that the numbers of cruise arrivals in Aqaba have rebounded with a 100 per cent increase compared to 2015 (Ministry of Tourism and Antiquities 2016). Nonetheless, the development of coastal tourism along the Red Sea coastline has already caused serious environmental concerns (Hall 2001).

The Arabian Gulf

The development of cruise tourism in the Arabian Gulf is part of a carefully crafted strategy of economic diversification put forward by some of the Gulf Cooperation Council (GCC) countries—Bahrain, Qatar, Oman, UAE, Saudi Arabia and Kuwait—that aim to reduce their dependence on oil (Karolak 2015). Thanks to government support, the cruise industry has recorded a rapid growth over the last decade, making it the fastest growing cruise region in the Middle East (Figure 20.3). In addition, the Arabian Gulf has managed to position itself as a cruise destination in its own right with short dedicated cruises in the Gulf, as well as an ending or beginning point for long cruises spanning two or more continents.

Oman and the UAE had an early start as cruise destinations in the 1990s; since that time, governments of the Gulf countries have strived to convince cruise lines to use the region as an

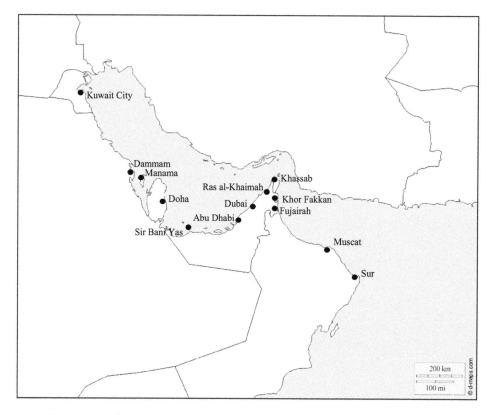

Figure 20.3 Ports of call in the Arabian Gulf

Note: Salalah in Oman and Jeddah in Saudi Arabia, while part of GCC, are located beyond the boundaries of the Arabian Gulf and were therefore not included on the map.

alternative to the overcrowded Caribbean and Mediterranean itineraries (Henderson 2006: 92). The beginnings were modest with cruise liners only sporadically visiting the region. For instance, just one cruise ship called in at the port of Dubai in 1993 (Department of Tourism and Commerce Marketing, cited in Henderson 2006). In 2000, the Gulf cruise market amounted to no more than 3,000 bookings per year (Peisley 2000). Yet, active promotion of the region and investments made in tourism development have prompted a rapid expansion of cruise tourism. The cruise industry in the Arabian Gulf received a boost thanks to the inauguration of the first cruise terminal in Dubai in 2001. However, the breakthrough came with the commitment from international cruise lines in 2006 to include the region in their cruise networks. Tourist arrivals aboard international cruise lines transformed cruise statistics as they introduced to the Gulf an international clientele, mostly Western passengers, that constitute the core of the global cruise passenger numbers overall. North Americans and Europeans constitute 75 per cent of all cruises passengers (Business Research and Economic Advisors 2014: 8). Statistics bear witness to this phenomenon. In 2003, passenger arrivals in Dubai were estimated at 10,000, but in 2013, the number of passengers had increased to 386,000. Since that time, international cruise ships have also called at other ports in the UAE apart from Dubai, namely, Abu Dhabi and Fujairah, Khor Fakkan (occasionally used for cruise activity as early as the 1980s), Ras Al Khaima and Sir Bani Yas. Other countries of the Gulf also experienced a steady rise in cruise arrivals. In Bahrain, with one port in Manama, cruise arrivals increased from 30,000 in 2006 to 130,000 in 2013. Oman, with four ports in Muscat, Khasab, Salalah and Sur, saw an especially high growth of cruise tourism in Muscat from 3,450 in 2003 to 250,000 in 2013. Less popular cruise ports of call include Qatar with one port in Doha, Kuwait with one port in Kuwait City and Saudi Arabia with two ports in Jeddah and Dammam.

Arabian Gulf ports have become a common feature in short- and long-haul cruises (Karolak 2015). The long-haul cruises that call into the Arabian Gulf ports range from round-the-world cruises to Europe to Middle East/Asia cruises and cruises that originate in the Middle East and sail in the direction of Asia, Europe or the United States. Short-haul cruises range from three to 11-day itineraries sailing in the Arabian Gulf. The five- to 11-day options include stops in UAE and Oman and sometimes a combination of the two with one stop added in Bahrain or Qatar. Furthermore, three-day options are available for cruises within the UAE only, or a combination of stops in the UAE and Oman. The growth of short-haul cruises has been facilitated by the inclusion of Dubai as a homeport to leading cruise lines in 2006. Since that time it has accommodated Costa Crociere and Aida Cruises, MSC, TUI Cruises and Royal Caribbean International. Starting from 2019, it will also become a home port for P&O Cruises. In 2015, Abu Dhabi became the second home port in the UAE, currently serving MSC Cruises and AIDA Cruises.

GCC governments have also actively sought to attract international cruise lines by expanding the existing infrastructure to accommodate cruise ships and ultimately establishing dedicated cruise terminals. The commitment to cruise industry development is seen in the Middle East's Leading Cruise Port Award, which has been awarded for nine consecutive years to Port Rashid in Dubai. Thanks to capital investments in port infrastructure, combined with a strategy to attract tourism over the last decade, these Arabian Gulf cruise ports have recorded an overall expansion of the numbers of passengers and cruise liners that call in. At the moment, it has been estimated that the Arabian Gulf captures only 1 per cent of the global cruise market, which is why the GCC countries actively seek to expand their share of the market in the future. Cruise tourism in the Arabian Gulf is expected to grow thanks to further investments and a stable economic and political climate.

Future prospects

Cruises present a tourism growth opportunity in the Middle East. First, they offer another way of visiting the region while promoting less touristy places and appeal also to a local and international clientele. Second, they have the potential to generate substantial income, especially in home ports. While various authors have discussed the economic contribution of the cruise industry, Dwyer and Forsyth (1998) stress the fact that the type of contribution depends on the type of port. They distinguish between ports of call, which are intermediate stops, and home ports where the cruises end or start. The latter experience a much greater economic impact since cruise-based tourism benefits almost all segments of the travel industry, including transportation, lodging, restaurants, attractions and shopping malls, because the majority of cruise passengers spend additional nights before or after their cruises in a home port. It comes as no surprise that Abu Dhabi has sought to become the second international home port in the region after Dubai.

The introduction of short-haul cruises in the region offers an opportunity to diversify the cruise market by appealing to the residents of the region, which is especially true in the GCC, where cruises make visiting neighbouring Gulf countries easy and convenient. The affordability of short-haul cruises also provides opportunities to attract local customers. This is also the case with local cruise companies with the best example in Israel. The Israeli cruise line Mano Maritime caters to the local market by providing lower-priced cruise tours compared to international cruise lines. In addition, the company offers entertainment, kosher food and onboard casinos, as well as packages during local holidays suitable for Israeli tourists (Rosenblum 2009). This market specialisation is seen as the reason behind the company's success, capturing half of the 100,000 annual Israeli cruise passengers (Jerusalem Post 2016). In spite of Mano's success story, another Israeli cruise line, Caspi Dream, which was established by Israeli investors in 2005 with a home port in Ashdod, ceased operations after six years. If carefully crafted, market specialisation may be an opportunity in other countries of MENA to attract more local passengers with opportunities to cater to Muslim consumers in particular with halal cruises. So far, the growth has been slow, as Arabs (local and expatriate) accounted for only 5 per cent of all cruise bookings made in the Arabian Gulf in 2014 (Cruise Arabia 2014).

Since many of the key assets for the cruise industry are managed by a variety of other industries, it is clear that the growth of cruising requires broader regional or national planning that includes a variety of stakeholders and considers issues such as port location and shore facilities, human resources, and investments in infrastructure (Manning 2006). Consequently, the medium to long-term coordination of strategies for cruise tourism development on a regional level is a must for future growth of the sector. So far, such strategies exist in the Arabian Gulf. The Abu Dhabi Ports Company, along with the Abu Dhabi Tourism and Culture Authority, the Department of Tourism and Commerce Marketing, and Oman's Ministry of Tourism established a joint initiative called Cruise Arabia at the end of 2013 to promote the Gulf region as an attractive and tourist-friendly destination. Qatar joined the initiative in March 2014. In 2014, Cruise Arabia started a promotional campaign to strengthen the appeal of the Arabian Gulf amongst the already lucrative international source markets such as Europe and North America and to open new markets such as India and China. Second, Cruise Arabia promotes this type of leisure travel amongst regional clients, Gulf nationals and expatriates. With expanding opportunities to embark on long-haul cruises out of the Middle East, the local market holds the potential for fast growth in passenger numbers. Apart from joint cooperation efforts, national governments strive to facilitate the passage of cruise passengers and tourists in general. The UAE, for instance, began to issue multiple entry visas for cruise passengers, which makes the transfer from UAE to neighbouring countries and back easier and less costly.

Despite the potential positive economic effects of the cruise industry, researchers have also highlighted the possible negative impacts on cruise destinations (Dowling 2006; Dwyer & Forsyth 1998; Klein 2005). In an attempt to evaluate the economic benefits of cruising, they point out that the transnational ownership of cruise ships may limit the positive impacts on destinations through economic leakage. Another problem is the unequal distribution of economic benefits that may be limited only to the ports. Furthermore, cruise ships are direct competitors with land-based resorts. Consequently, some stakeholders may benefit while others may not. Second, Klein (2005) evaluated the cruise sector's social and environmental impacts, including congestion, homogenisation of the port experiences and limited socio-cultural authenticity, which can outweigh potential economic gains. Several studies have pointed out the limits of the positive benefits of cruise tourism in the Pacific Islands and the Caribbean (Brida & Zapata 2010; Macpherson 2008; Pinnock 2014). As a result, governments that decide to engage with cruise tourism need to carefully coordinate their destination development strategy to maximise the benefits of cruise tourism and minimise the negative impacts to make the industry sustainable.

Based on the extensive review in this chapter, several unique observations and recommendations for future cruise tourism development in the Middle East can be made. First, regional initiatives need to be strengthened with the participation of all countries or local tourism bodies interested in cruise tourism development. Second, the image of cruise destinations in the Middle East should be managed in such a way that when an event involving violence occurs in one of the MENA countries, the world's perception of the entire region is not affected (Sönmez, Apostolopoulos, & Tarlow 1999). Cruise destinations should carefully manage their international image; stressing the security and safety of cruise destinations through counter-marketing and other means is extremely important. Nonetheless, image management will be a continuous struggle given the ongoing conflicts and volatility in many parts of the region (Avraham 2013).

The third observation is that dealing with image problems will continue to be a challenge for many MENA countries until the region stabilises and its conflicts are resolved. From this perspective, coastal cruise tourism can be portrayed as a safer way to visit areas that have suffered from security problems in the past, since cruises require less time on the ground and provide easy access to major tourist sites, unlike traditional land-based tourism.

Fourth, greater advertising efforts are needed worldwide. Guidebooks devoted to cruise itineraries, for instance Frommer's, focus on the Caribbean and the Mediterranean but do not include the Middle East's ports of call. Next, regional strategies should be developed to offer specialised itineraries and activities such as thematic cruises. Examples include heritage and culture cruises with lectures; culinary cruises with tastings and cooking lessons; fitness cruises with various recreational activities; and adventure cruises, as well as cruises specially geared towards particular groups such as families with children, couples or retirees. Similarly, a long-term strategy to retain customers and make them return to MENA for future cruises or other tourism activities should be developed. This can be done in part by providing competitive pricing strategies and ensuring high-quality shore excursions.

A seventh recommendation is to market and develop cruises to fit Middle Easterners' preferences. As there is potential for attracting a greater local market, it is necessary to offer facilities, entertainment and activities onboard that mesh better within the cultural context (Erbing & Jianyong 2013).

Another proposition is to simplify the immigration procedure for cruise passengers. Providing cruise-specific visas to ease congestion at ports of call, as well as decreasing visa fees, would go a long way towards enhancing the attractiveness of cruises in the region.

Finally, given the potential negative effects of cruise tourism (Brida & Zapata 2010; Johnson 2002), such as high environmental costs and sea floor damage, along with social exclusion and economic leakage from the port communities, developing an approach to sustainable tourism is a necessary step for future growth.

Conclusion

With the fast growth of the cruise industry worldwide, the Middle East aims to become a new hub for cruise tourism after the Caribbean and Mediterranean Europe. While the region has been able to firmly position itself on the cruise map, the industry remains in its infancy. Nonetheless, investments into this sector and new marketing strategies will likely result in a steady growth in cruising, especially in the Arabian Gulf. Despite setbacks due to past and current political unrest, the region has always been able to emerge with increased passenger growth. The continued growth, however, requires a regional strategy that would help MENA become a better-known cruise destination worldwide and tackle the obstacles to its expansion.

This chapter examined the growth of the cruise sector in MENA in recent years and provided recommendations to help achieve continued growth of the sector in the future. Further qualitative and quantitative studies are needed to understand cruise customer preferences amongst international tourists and regional residents, and to strengthen the appeal of ports of call in the Middle East. Such research should examine the factors influencing visitors' intention to return as land-based tourists, to recommend the destination to others (Brida, Pulina, Riano, & Zapata-Aguirre 2012), and the cruise experience overall.

Note

1 The cruise industry as a modern form of leisure travel began not long before this in 1844 in the US.

References

Avraham, E. (2013) 'Crisis communication, image restoration, and battling stereotypes of terror and wars: Media strategies for attracting tourism to Middle Eastern countries', *American Behavioral Scientist*, 57(9): 1350–1367.

Brida, J.G., & Zapata, S. (2010a) 'Cruise tourism: Economic, socio-cultural and environmental impacts', *International Journal of Leisure and Tourism Marketing*, 1(3): 205–226.

Brida, J.G., & Zapata, S. (2010b) 'Economic impacts of cruise tourism: The case of Costa Rica', *Anatolia*, 21(2): 322–338.

Brida, J.G., Pulina, M., Riano, E., & Zapata-Aguirre, S. (2012) 'Cruise visitors' intention to return as land tourists and to recommend a visited destination', *Anatolia*, 23(3): 395–412.

Business Research & Economic Advisors (2014) 'The global economic contribution of Cruise Tourism 2013'. Available online: www.cruising.org/sites/default/files/pressroom/Global_Cruise_Impact_Analysis_2013.pdf (Accessed 1 December 2014).

Cartwright, R., & Baird, C. (1999) *The Development and Growth of the Cruise Industry*. Oxford: Butterworth Heinemann.

Charlier, J.J., & McCalla, J.R. (2006) 'A geographical overview of the world cruise market and its seasonal complementarities', in R.K. Dowling (ed.), *Cruise Ship Tourism* (pp. 18–30). Wallingford: CAB International.

Check Safety First (2017) 'Nile cruises'. Available online: www.checksafetyfirst.com/category-result.php?Category=Nile%20Cruises&countries= (Accessed 30 November 2017).

Cruise Arabia (2014) 'Growing number of Arabs are taking cruises in the Arabian Gulf'. Available online: www.cruisearabiaonline.com/2014/10/22/Growing-number-of-Arabs-are-taking-cruises-in-the-Arabian-Gulf-say-Cruise-Arabia-partners (Accessed 14 December 2014).

Dowling, R.K. (ed.) (2006) *Cruise Ship Tourism*. Wallingford: CAB International.

Dwyer, L., & Forsyth, P. (1998) 'Economic significance of cruise tourism', *Annals of Tourism Research*, 25(2): 393–415.

Erbing, C., & Jianyong, S. (2013) 'Study of Shanghai cruise tourism product development strategy based on the balance of supply and demand', *International Journal of Business and Social Science*, 4(10): 175–183.

Hall, C.M. (2001) 'Trends in ocean and coastal tourism: The end of the last frontier?' *Ocean & Coastal Management*, 44(9–10): 601–618.

Henderson, J.C. (2006) 'Tourism in Dubai: Overcoming barriers to destination development', *International Journal of Tourism Research*, 8: 87–99.

Humphreys, A. (2015) *On the Nile in the Golden Age of Travel*. Cairo: American University of Cairo Press.

Hunter Publishing (2006) *Cruising the Mediterranean: A Guide to Ports of Call*. Edison, NJ: Hunter Publishing.

Jerusalem Post (12 September 2016) 'Cruising the open sea'. Available online: www.jpost.com/Travel/Travel-News/Cruising-the-open-sea-309452 (Accessed 14 November 2016).

John, N. (2014) 'Cruise lines cancel calls to Israel'. 7 August. Available online: cruisepassenger.com.au/cruise-lines-cancel-calls-israel/ (Accessed 5 November 2016).

Johnson, D. (2002) 'Environmentally sustainable cruise tourism: A reality check', *Marine Policy*, 26(4): 261–270.

Karolak, M. (2015) 'Analysis of the cruise industry in the Arabian Gulf: The emergence of a new destination', *Journal of Tourism Challenges and Trends*, 8(1): 61–78.

Klein, R.A. (2005) *Cruise Ship Squeeze: The New Pirates of the Seven Seas*. Gabriola Island: New Society Publishers.

Lewis, T. (n.d.) 'Nile cruise options'. Available online: http://cruises.lovetoknow.com/wiki/Nile_Cruises (Accessed 1 November 2016).

Macpherson, C. (2008) 'Golden goose or Trojan horse? Cruise ship tourism in Pacific development', *Asia Pacific Viewpoint*, 49(2): 185–197.

Manning, T. (2006) 'Managing cruise ship impacts: Guidelines for current and potential destination communities'. Available online: www.tourisk.org/content/projects/Managing%20Cruise%20Ship%20Impacts.pdf (Accessed 1 December 2014).

Ministry of Tourism and Antiquities (2016) 'Tourism statistical newsletter'. Available online: www.mota.gov.jo/contents/Tourism_Statistical_Newsletter_2016.aspx (Accessed 30 September 2016).

Peek, C.M. (2011) 'The Queen surveys her realm: The Nile cruise of Cleopatra VII', *Classical Quarterly*, 61(2): 595–607.

Peisley, T. (2000) 'The cruise industry in the Arabian Gulf and Indian Ocean', *Travel & Tourism Analyst*, 1: 3–17.

Pinnock, F.H. (2014) 'The future of tourism in an emerging economy: The reality of the cruise industry in the Caribbean', *Worldwide Hospitality and Tourism Themes*, 6(2): 127–137.

Rosenblum, I. (22 May 2009) 'Taking to the high seas', *Haaretz*, 22 May. Available online: www.haaretz.com/print-edition/business/taking-to-the-high-seas-1.276528 (Accessed 30 September 2016).

Samuel, M.G. (2014) 'Limitations of navigation through Nubaria Canal, Egypt', *Journal of Advanced Research*, 5(2): 147–155.

Schmitz, C. (2010) 'Egypt', in K.A. Appiah, & H.L. Gates (eds), *Encyclopedia of Africa, Volume 1* (pp. 398–405). Oxford: Oxford University Press.

Smith, P.C. (2014) *Cruise Ships: The Small Scale Fleet*. Barnsley: Pen & Sword Maritime.

Sönmez, S.F., Apostolopoulos, Y., & Tarlow, P. (1999) 'Tourism in crisis: Managing the effects of terrorism', *Journal of Travel Research*, 38(1): 13–18.

Strategy& (2015) 'Surviving disaster: How to reemerge as a tourism destination after a period of political instability'. Available online: www.strategyand.pwc.com/media/file/Surviving-disaster.pdf (Accessed 1 September 2016).

TIMEA (n.d.) The Nile Cruise, 1847 and 1897. Available online: http://timea.rice.edu/NileCruise.html (Accessed 15 September 2016).

Travel & Tourism News Middle East (2011) 'Middle East cruise tourism sails ahead'. Available online: www.ttnonline.com/Article/11248/Middle_East_cruise_tourism_sails_ahead (Accessed 1 November 2016).

UNWTO (2003) *Worldwide Cruise Ship Activity*. Madrid: World Tourism Organization.

Ward, D., & Machan, T. (2014) 'Nile River cruise guide'. *Telegraph*, 25 July. Available online: www.telegraph.co.uk/travel/cruises/river-cruises/Nile-river-cruise-guide/ (Accessed 11 September 2018).

Wilkinson, P.E. (2006) 'The changing geography of cruise tourism in the Caribbean', in R.K. Dowling (ed.), *Cruise Ship Tourism* (pp. 170–183). Wallingford: CAB International.

Wood, R. (2000) 'Caribbean cruise tourism: Globalisation at sea', *Annals of Tourism Research*, 27(2): 345–370.

World Bank (2014) 'International tourism, numbers of arrivals'. Available online: http://data.worldbank.org/indicator/ST.INT.ARVL?locations=EG (Accessed 11 November 2016).

Zbuchea, A. (2015) 'Framing cruise tourism', *Journal of Tourism Challenges and Trends*, 8(1): 9–26.

21

LOCAL TRANSPORTATION AND TOURISM IN THE MENA REGION

Ammar O. Abulibdeh

Introduction

Transportation is a key element of the tourism sector. Improved transportation and access have been the main driving force behind the growth of tourism. Air travel has contributed to a more interconnected world, and the motor vehicle has enabled access to distant and remote areas. Culpan (1987) identified transportation as an extremely important part of the international tourism system, acknowledging that sea, land and air modes are crucial for operations and the provision of support services such as fuel stations, auto repairs, motels and rest facilities. Transportation aims to bring tourists to destinations, moving them around the destination and departing following the trip. Transportation influences tourists' experiences and may help determine how people travel and why they select various types of holidays and destinations. The enhancement of transportation technology and capacity, coupled with low fares, has improved the accessibility of places that were previously difficult to reach. Certain factors such as the location, capacity, connectivity and efficiency of the transportation system may therefore have a major influence on the way a destination develops. At the same time, the increasing number of travellers raises challenges with respect to transport infrastructure and capacity, border crossings, inter-modality, information for travellers and compatibility of technologies with providers of tourism services.

As an integral element of tourism, transportation enables connections between regions, attractions, and commercial and housing services in destinations (Lumsdon 2000). Tourism is a significant driver in the enhancement of national and regional economies; however, it can exert pressure on transportation infrastructure, which cities and regions must address, particularly during seasonal flows. As well, while being a necessity in the modern world, transportation also has important impacts on the physical environment. Some of these congestion and environmental issues can be alleviated by encouraging people to walk or cycle as transportation alternatives, especially during peak seasons (Lumsdon 2000; Timothy & Boyd 2015).

The successful implementation of transportation involves close collaboration between local and regional authorities to provide effective infrastructure, services and information. The role of various forms of transportation in the tourism context within the Middle East and North Africa is explored in this chapter, looking at motorised and non-motorised transit, and private and public forms of mobility. Current data on local transportation in MENA are difficult to find. As a result, some of the numbers presented in this chapter are slightly outdated, but they nonetheless illustrate the trends and patterns under examination.

Critical aspects of the tourism–transport relationship

An important fact is that people travel for different reasons, over different distances through various modes of transport, and the provision of transportation is located at the core of that movement. Transportation is a necessary part of tourism because it moves people between their homes and their destinations, and provides mobility within a destination, enabling a broader dispersion of visitors and, consequently, maximum exposure to places perhaps not otherwise accessible (Page 2005).

Transport in tourism can be viewed as a series of modes functioning across large networks of points (or nodes) and routes (or vectors). Transport encompasses water, land and air, and multiple modes within these forms are possible. The networks used for day-to-day transportation function as vital economic pathways amongst destinations (Butler 1999; Duval 2007; Lumsdon 2000). Networks within a locality or country are imperative in distributing tourism's economic advantages. To achieve the goal of maximising visitor flows into a destination, it is crucial that networks on the local scale are integrated into regional and international networks. Consequently, transport and the access it provides can be viewed as the most crucial factor in determining the feasibility or success of a location's tourism industry. This is particularly the case in remote areas that are highly reliant on, for instance, international air services.

Duval (2007) argues that there is a natural 'blurriness' in the connections between tourism and transport. First, transportation itself may be a form of tourism or provide the foundations of it, such as cruises or historic railways (Orbaşlı & Woodward 2008). Second, distinguishing between non-tourist and tourist use of transportation is hard, yet not impossible, for transportation planners. Transport depends on the appeal and viability of tourism in a destination, while the destination depends on efficient transport to facilitate human mobility (Lumsdon 2000).

Connectivity and accessibility are the two most crucial factors affecting successful transport–tourism relationships (Duval 2007; Page 2005). Understanding the extent of connectivity and accessibility within a region is crucial in establishing the role of both government and private companies in enabling tourists' mobility. Accessibility is a geographic relative measure of different points within a network and the links that are possible given the current provision of transport. Connectivity is a similar measure, but it assesses the technological and practical restrictions and opportunities for increased accessibility (e.g. shorter travel time or more efficient means of transport).

The role of the government in providing transportation for tourism is unquestionable. Tourism is seen as a public product and as a result the benefits can often penetrate wide into the economy. There are compelling arguments to back the substantial involvement of local or national governments in ensuring that accessibility remains undisturbed (Butler 1999). This involvement can include government-led actions such as direct subsidies, and active ownership and control of services. Conversely, the involvement of governments may shift the market away from functioning in a free and profitable manner. Consequently, where government participation is substantial in providing transportation, the most sensible question is whether the active participation of the government limits private companies that may provide cheaper and more efficient services to important markets within the tourism industry.

Urban transportation trends in MENA

Transportation in MENA is fuelled by many factors. These include swift rates of urbanisation throughout most of the region, the subsequent boom of informal settlements resulting in urban sprawl, the inability of government-operated services to satisfy the increasing demand for urban transportation, high fatality rates for certain forms of transport, and growing rates of car ownership and earnings in certain areas of the region (Al-Geneidy, Diab, Jacques, & Mathez 2013).

Within MENA, various nations and cities have invested in facilitating capacity growth, infrastructure development, and increasing tourist arrivals and expenditures. Current estimates suggest that Middle East countries will invest more than US$3 trillion in the tourism and leisure industries, including indirect spending on improving infrastructure, over the next 20 years. Recent estimates suggest that by 2020 the region will grow its airport capacity an extra 300 million passengers, construct more than 200 hotels with more than 100,000 additional rooms, increase the number of tourist arrivals to 150 million, and achieve a growth of more than 150 per cent in the size of the regional aircraft fleet by 2025 (Al-Geneidy et al. 2013).

It is not possible to summarise the position of urban transport into a general pattern for all countries in MENA. This is largely due to the varying challenges experienced by each country, which in turn have moulded their reply to increasing demand for transportation. For example, some of the wealthier nations across the region have observed growth in the consumption of private motorised transport, in contrast with other countries that still rely overwhelmingly on public transportation. Even within the scope of public transportation, differences exist between states regarding the relative importance of formal versus informal public transportation.

The percentage share of various forms of transport in trips within MENA differs considerably across countries. In general, traffic management research has established that collective forms of transportation have substantial weight in the approximation of the modal divide amongst cities. According to 2008 data, collective modes comprise 70 per cent in Algiers, 74 per cent in Cairo, 61 per cent in Casablanca, 64 per cent in Istanbul, 59 per cent in Tehran, and 50 per cent in Tunis.

Informal forms of public transportation have developed during the past few decades within the broader context of urban public transportation. Small-scale, informal public transport differs across cities, and includes minibuses and shared taxis in Cairo, Damascus and various Moroccan cities, vans in Algiers, and similar services in Amman and Beirut. These types of transport play a vital part in the supply of public conveyance, comprising several thousand vehicles within each city and encompassing a considerable number of motorised trips (Al-Geneidy et al. 2013).

However, during the past few decades, levels of private motorisation (private vehicles per 1,000) have increased and are posing a threat to the traditional dominance of public transport, if not already superseding it. Even though ownership rates are low compared to other regions, the number of private vehicles has grown to comprise more than 50 per cent of all means of transport in cities such as Tunis and Beirut. In contrast, Algiers and Cairo have low rates of private vehicle ownership (69 and 68 respectively in 2004), while average rates were recorded in Tunis, Casablanca and Istanbul with 100 (in 2002), 110 (in 2004) and 134 (in 2006) respectively. Countries with high rates of private car ownership include Lebanon, where private transportation covers more than two-thirds of all transportation, as well as nations which generate a significant amount of revenue from oil such as Qatar, Saudi Arabia and Kuwait.

Despite the change in modal share, walking continues to be a frequent method of transportation, comprising some 30 to 50 per cent of trips surveyed in traffic management studies.

As well as being the most natural method of mobility for short trips, pedestrian activity is sometimes used for longer distances where a deficiency in the public transport system exists (Bagaeen 2015).

A wide array of social, political and economic factors affect urban mobility. Drastic differences between certain countries and minor variations within other countries need further analysis with respect to patterns, conditions and potential consequences of modal splits within intra-urban areas.

In Abu Dhabi and Dubai, urban sprawl is clearly visible, owing primarily to the swift rates of population growth and physical development (Hawas, Hassan, & Abulibdeh 2016; Parahoo, Lea Harvey, & Radi 2014). In addition, families tend to favour buying single-family homes in suburban areas. Consequently, urban and suburban development has aggravated the already dominant role of the private vehicle as a favoured form of transportation. Significant efforts are being made in the Gulf Cooperation Council (GCC) countries to develop a public transport supply within urban areas (Bagaeen 2015). Dubai is a public transportation pioneer in the Gulf area owing to the success of its metro and tram systems. Recent investments in implementing networks for the metro and bus rapid transit (BRT) systems are a step in the right direction for the development of public transportation.

Alternative forms of transportation are gradually making their way into the region. In Dubai, a car-sharing service was recently launched by a company called U-drive. Cycling is also appearing in a number of MENA's cities, including Tehran and Dubai, which already have bike-sharing schemes. In addition, civil society organisations are playing a part in promoting the bicycle as a form of transportation. An organisation called Cycle Egypt currently boasts more than 6,000 members and another organisation in Lebanon called Critical Mass hosts cycling tours on a monthly basis within the capital. With anticipated population and urban growth, public transport systems along with alternative non-motorised forms of transport will be key in tackling issues of traffic, congestion and pollution, which have already become high-priority problems in several capitals across the region.

Urban mobility has been assigned a high priority by MENA governments owing to the recent activity in metro, bus and light rail projects. This new emphasis on the provision of public transportation has brought about developments in transport demand management (TDM), fleet management and traffic control centre technology, which have enabled access to vast amounts of valuable data. These recent developments provide key opportunities for MENA to develop more technologically advanced transportation with new goals of integration and interconnectivity. Recent technological breakthroughs in areas such as geolocation, data computation and communication between objects have introduced several new applications in the field of mobility. However, companies within the IT and media industries across MENA are yet to recognise the true value of these changes in the sphere of urban mobility, and an increasing number of businesses operating in the IT and media sector can be expected to penetrate the transport market soon.

Mobile applications that provide valuable solutions in transportation can bring about challenges to transport authorities and ministries. Urban mobility is now at the heart of the modern economy, which is reliant on sharing rather than acquiring. Uber has generated billions of dollars in various countries around the world. Uber is now operational in almost all key cities in MENA with its services being offered in Qatar, Egypt, Bahrain, Lebanon, Jordan, Turkey, Saudi Arabia, Morocco and the United Arab Emirates. Uber's Middle Eastern competitor, Careem, commenced operations in July 2012 in Dubai. Since then, Careem has undergone rapid expansion in the region, registering an additional 16 cities to its network in an extraordinary timespan of less than three years. The rapid expansion of companies like Uber and Careem in MENA triggers reactions from governments to curb its impact on conventional government-owned taxi services.

The Roads and Transport Authority (RTA) of Dubai has successfully passed legislation to regulate the services of Uber and Careem such that they have practically become limousine services. In 2015, the RTA demanded all providers of limousine services, including Careem and Uber, to control their activities, including pricing in compliance with the rules and regulations set out by the RTA, to ensure that the prices of these services are 30 per cent higher than the rates of government-operated taxi services. The resolution also restricts the number of vehicles allowed in these services and their pickup locations—primarily hotels and tourist places. While enforcement has been a problem, the Dubai RTA claims to focus on improving the situation with simpler and stricter regulations and enforcement.

On the other hand, in Cairo the current situation is more chaotic. In 2015, of all the cities with Uber services, Cairo became the company's fastest-expanding market across Africa, Europe and the Middle East, in less than a year after commencing operations in Egypt. In March 2016, at a protest arranged by taxi drivers in Cairo demanding the instant closure of Careem and Uber, Egyptian security forces used tear gas to disperse the protesters who had closed off an important road in the city (CTE 2016). Recently, taxi drivers have protested the presence of Uber, as they believe Careem and Uber drivers have an unfair advantage since they are not charged the same type of fees or taxes, nor must they comply with the same licensing procedures. On the other hand, taxi passengers seem to favour the reliability of the app-based companies, sharing complaints on social media about traditional taxi drivers who frequently rig their meters or deceive customers into thinking the meter is broken with the aim of overcharging. Female users have also reported more safety and security when using the new ride services. The government of Egypt formed a legal committee in March 2016, to examine the standardisation of taxi company conditions, and a spokesperson within the cabinet recently stressed the value of these alternative modes.

Smart services and IT for urban mobility

Although ride apps such as Careem and Uber have emerged from companies operating in the private sector, cementing government intervention as a necessity, certain promising developments in the sector have been established by authorities dealing with transport activities and services. Dubai is leading the region's SMART trend where the Dubai RTA has introduced and developed 'Smart' initiatives to make the tasks of parking and paying tolls and fines much easier. In 2014, the Dubai RTA introduced a website and five new smartphone apps. Efforts in the area of SMART transportation have allowed the RTA to offer 53 smart services (CTE 2016). One of the most auspicious of these apps aims to make using public transportation easier. Initially launched as a website in 2013 and developed into an app in 2014, the Dubai RTA's first app-based journey planner, Wojhati, boasts 740,000 users. The app offers many kinds of information for residents, visitors or tourists in Dubai about diverse modes of public transport. Information from the app includes arrival and departure times, trip duration, travel costs, directions and message alerts in case of any potential or actual delay.

Other developments are occurring in innovations such as Masarak. This Qatar-based development is a composite of logistics management, intelligent transport and road safety services. Masarak depends on the instantaneous collection of traffic data from several different sources like GPS instruments installed in vehicles, Bluetooth sensors, smartphones and other sources, then feeds the unprocessed data through a platform to refine it and generate meaningful real-time traffic information, which can aid in travel and community decision-making.

Apps are key technological advancements in MENA and hence more IT companies are anticipated to penetrate the market with their effective app-based solutions in the near future (CTE 2016). To address the challenge of app-based taxi services, governments must ensure that they do not ignore the trend of app-based transportation solutions. Regulating and planning will be imperative in protecting local taxis and other transport services that generate vital revenues for transport authorities. Alternatively, government-developed SMART transport apps to collect and process data on public transit, such as Doha's Masarak and RTA's Wojhati, are truly necessary and much wanted innovations in the sphere of urban transportation within MENA.

Private motorised transportation

The role of private motorised transport as a proportion of the modal share in major urban areas in MENA is explored in this section, which also reviews the general status, patterns, conditions, and challenges and implications of private motorised transport (Hamahui, Sarkissian, El Chaarani, Aboulhosn, & Bainbridge 2010).

Private motorised transport differs significantly throughout MENA, sometimes consisting of as much as two-thirds of total trips, or as little as one tenth of all trips (e.g. Cairo) (CTE 2016). While proportions of private motorisation in nations south and east of the Mediterranean are relatively low compared to other regions in the world, fast-paced growth in urban populations has led to certain challenges that have changed travel behaviour. The failure to fulfil the growing need for public transportation services sufficiently has motivated users to look for other forms of transport, specifically private automobiles for individuals who can afford them. Although this form of transport presents benefits in terms of efficiency, speed and privacy, it also brings about disadvantages such as pollution, congestion, isolation, elevated rates of traffic-related deaths and related expenses.

Within MENA, a shift towards the liberalisation of imports, along with increasing wages and a subsequent growth in the middle class, has contributed to a greater preference for private vehicles. Many corresponding factors also determine the region's relatively low cost of car ownership, insurance and maintenance compared to other places (Abulibdeh & Zaidan 2018). For instance, Kuwait, which generates significant revenue from fossil fuel reserves, relies heavily on private motor vehicles, with 97 per cent of its residents using this mode to meet their daily travel needs. In addition, the yearly growth in the number of autos is double the growth of the overall population and the yearly expenses associated with car ownership (approximately US$4,125) (CTE 2016).

Elevated levels of private vehicle use in certain countries across MENA are strongly correlated with the low price of fuel due to government subsidies (Abulibdeh 2018). Motorisation in Egypt is particularly fuelled by the substantial subsidisation of fuel prices, providing individuals an incentive to drive their own cars. In the fiscal year 2010–2011, where 80 per cent of the budget for subsidies accounted for energy, 52 per cent comprised diesel (US$3 billion), and 23 per cent (US$1 billion) represented gasoline. Saudi Arabia, Kuwait, Libya and Iran also heavily subsidise fuel prices (CTE 2016). Owing to these deep subsidies, MENA is home to the lowest mean fuel prices.

Impacts and challenges

The growing reliance on private vehicles in MENA has important effects. In several countries, congestion is nearing dangerous levels and is further aggravated by private automobile ownership (Abulibdeh, Zaidan, & Alkaabi 2018). In the Yemeni capital, traffic surveys prior to that country's civil war reported that private cars accounted for 33 per cent of all vehicles (Sims 2009). Elevated traffic congestion in Dubai is extremely detrimental with 541 cars for every 1,000 people, incurring economic losses of approximately US$1.2 billion each year due to hours lost by employees stuck in traffic. High rates of congestion are aggravated in Lebanon by a lack of adequate road signs, failure to manage the limited supply of parking, and careless driving (Hamahui et al. 2010). Traffic congestion is also a common problem in Egypt, particularly in and around Cairo and Alexandria.

Congestion across the region is coupled with the significant problem of environmental degradation. Transport emissions in Israel are considered a significant contributor to atmospheric pollution. They comprise approximately 90 per cent of emissions originating from carbon monoxide and nitrogen oxide emissions with the range of 32 to 43 per cent. In Lebanon, about 80 fatalities, 3,000 admissions to hospitals, and 14,160 restrained days of activity are credited to air pollution linked to the widespread use of private vehicles. Similar air quality problems have been reported in Saudi Arabia, Qatar and Kuwait (Al-Geneidy et al. 2013; CTE 2016; Gray 2017). Private vehicles vary significantly, depending on the extent of economic development within each country. Within the Maghreb region—Algeria, Morocco, Libya and Tunisia—second-hand European cars dominate the roads. Algeria contains a high number of older private automobiles registered prior to 1997, resulting in higher emissions levels.

While environmental degradation and congestion present threats to sustainability on the local scale, a comparatively large rate of traffic-related deaths is a severe concern in MENA. Growing private vehicle use across MENA has contributed to an associated high level of traffic accidents. Egypt has one of the highest rates of road fatalities in the world, with 42 annual fatalities per 100,000 inhabitants; nearly half (47.5 per cent) of those deaths represent passengers or drivers of private cars. With fatalities of 40.5, 38.1, and 37.1 per 100,000 inhabitants, Libya, Iraq and the UAE lag closely behind. Private automobiles account for 70 per cent of road deaths in the UAE. Understandably, the greatest rates of road fatalities are concentrated in places that have the highest levels of motorisation. Road fatality rates in Saudi Arabia, UAE, Qatar and Kuwait greatly surpass the rates of road fatalities in Europe and the United States (Bener, Özkan, & Lajunen 2008; CTE 2016).

Formal mass transportation

This section examines the public transportation sector in MENA. Though private motorised transport has achieved popularity in certain cities and countries, public transportation continues to be a vital mode of urban mobility throughout the region.

Buses are the most popular form of transportation in many MENA countries. They provide a genuine and economical experience for tourists, although the experience may be ruined by sporadic discomfort associated with a lack of personal space, air-conditioning, quality of bus service and safety. The highest levels of bus travel can be found in Lebanon, Oman, Jordan, Qatar, Turkey, Saudi Arabia and the UAE (Belwal & Belwal 2010; Gunesch 2017). Of all Middle Eastern countries, the UAE is perhaps home to the most modern system of public bus transportation, and Turkey is known for its high-quality intercity coach services (Bener et al. 2008; Parahoo et al. 2014). In MENA, buses can be classified into three types: tourist buses, large buses operated by the government, and relatively small buses (also called micros or minibuses). Tourist buses are different than the other two types because they are bigger in size, are usually equipped with air conditioning and they sometimes come in double-decker forms.

Public buses and minibuses feature unique characteristics. For instance, fares for these types vary from country to country and city to city. When purchasing tickets or boarding buses, queuing is the expected social norm, especially when there are designated lanes for women and men (Hall, Le-Klähn, & Ram 2017). Bus etiquette usually involves people changing seats so that single travellers are not forced to sit beside people of the opposite gender.

Public transport varies across MENA according to the degree of economic, social and technological development, and can be found in formal and informal forms (Belwal & Belwal 2010). Formal types consist of buses, metros, rail and minibuses. Implementation of public transportation within MENA broadly encompasses a more versatile and cost-effective development strategy, with preferences leaning towards bus rapid transit (BRT) and light-rail transit (LRT) over more expensive, underground transportation networks (Godard 2007). However, certain nations have experienced relatively high rates of economic development and have invested their efforts in high-cost rapid transit projects. Prime examples are the Doha metro and Dubai metro (Gunesch 2017). Despite the rapid increase in private car ownership, a significant part of MENA's population still depends on public transportation to get around.

Several MENA states lag behind in the provision of public transport compared to the demand for these services. For example, Bahrain possesses a minor bus fleet of just 100 vehicles and suffers from poor service and damaged infrastructure, which have contributed to the country's failure to remain competitive with the private automobile. Likewise, Egypt's government-operated bus service lacks reliability, triggering the rapid development of informal services.

Certain forms of publicly or privately owned bus services exist in several MENA countries with varying degrees of operation. For example, the number of taxis in the Palestinian city of Ramallah is six times greater than the number of buses. On the other hand, in some countries such as Libya, there is an absence of an intra-city bus system altogether. Conversely, certain countries (e.g. Qatar) have seen positive developments in providing bus services (CTE 2016; Gunesch 2017). Qatar's bus service has witnessed impressive growth, adding 2,100 vehicles between 2005 and 2010. This significant new inventory occurred mainly due to the launch of the government-owned company Mowasalat in 2005.

Owing to the cost-intensive nature and comprehensive infrastructure requirements of underground transportation, this has seen only modest development in MENA. Only four countries possess underground transit services: Turkey, Egypt, UAE and Israel. Turkish and Israeli cities have a rather restricted metro service. Established in 1987, the Cairo metro service is the sole underground rapid transportation service in Africa. While the percentage of daily metro trips of total trips grew from 3 per cent in 1987 to 17 per cent in 2001, car and taxi trips fell from 38 per cent to 23 per cent within the same four-year period (CTE 2016). Metro use continued to increase from 2 million daily trips in 2001 to a mean of 2.35 million daily trips in 2008, reflecting a growth of nearly 15 per cent. Within the same period, the number of daily trips completed by informal types of shared taxis also witnessed an abrupt hike, hinting that formal transit services in Egypt continue to be seen unfavourably by many.

The Dubai Metro system, which cost US$7.6 billion, commenced construction in 2006 and began operating in 2009. After completion, the system is expected to house 87 driverless trains operating on two lines of more than 75 kilometres (CTE 2016). The transit authorities of Saudi Arabia, Abu Dhabi, Kuwait and Qatar have set out plans for extra underground services after observing the progress in Dubai. A metro system has also been initiated in the capital city of Algeria.

Taxi services are gaining popularity over buses amongst passengers in certain countries. Taxicabs represent a mix of private and public modes of motorised transport. Taxis in Palestine are experiencing exponential growth compared to the country's bus service. Most intra-city trips in Oman are done with 30,000 taxis or group taxis (known commonly as 'microbuses') (Belwal & Belwal 2010). Privately owned group taxis in Syria have achieved more success in intra-city transportation than their publicly owned competitors, offering a more versatile service for residents living in the central parts of Damascus and in suburban areas. In Yemen, microbuses and taxis are cheaper than intra-city buses, and offer higher efficiency and convenience in their service (CTE 2016). Taxis in Algeria tend to the transportation needs of distant places, yet the routes are selected with potential profits in mind. Championed by the government in Egypt, the Egyptian New Taxi Program was introduced with the help of various local and international funding organisations to replace old taxis with newer models.

In North Africa, there are many tramways and light-rail transit (LRT) operations (Godard 2007). Certain cities in Egypt (Cairo, Alexandria), Algeria (Oran, Algiers), Tunisia (Tunis) and Morocco (Rabat) have LRT service in the works or already in place. Services in Egypt consist of outdated trams from the late nineteenth and early twentieth centuries, and now attract less than 1 per cent of public transit motorised trips. Launched in 1985, the Métro léger de Tunis represented about 23.6 per cent of the total trips by public transport in 1998 in the city of Tunis. Just a few years ago an LRT was introduced in Morocco, and in Algeria in 2011 (CTE 2016).

Funding public transport

How can public transportation survive within MENA, given the recent economic turmoil affecting the public transport sector? In light of inadequate financial resources and tightening government budgets, can the sector achieve and maintain continued growth? These are vital questions facing the Middle East today. Despite their economic conditions, several MENA governments are steadfast in prioritising public transport. Countries of the GCC region are suffering from the recent drop in oil prices. Despite declining revenues from their prime export, the oil-rich countries of Qatar, the UAE and Saudi Arabia continue to plan large-scale urban public transportation projects. The government of Morocco on the other hand has formed a structural fund to support urban public transportation projects (CTE 2016).

Riyadh, Saudi Arabia, is currently investing US$22.5 billion on the Riyadh Metro1 project and US$12 billion on Jeddah's Metro2, along with expansions of bus fleets and road networks. The kingdom also plans to build tram, metro and bus lanes in Makkah, Medina and Dammam. This shows the value the Saudi government places on prioritising public transport. In Dubai, the RTA submits its budget approvals depending on the projected revenues for the next year. Revenue gained across the year is used to improve and expand public transportation networks (CTE 2016). A budget of Dhs 7.6 billion was approved by the Dubai RTA for 2016, which is supported by a forecasted revenue of Dhs 7.5 million. The budget for 2017 focused on the construction of 55 projects including 12 new road projects and 43 currently in the works. Abu Dhabi, which relies more on revenues from oil compared to Dubai, is continuing to invest in the expansion of the emirate's public transportation system and has added a new system of smart ticketing and a new express bus service (Parahoo et al. 2014).

Finally, with the goal of providing support to its cities, the government of Morocco has moved towards a new strategy that emphasises placing districts from the same urban area under a single financial structure (CTE 2016). Local development companies were created to deal with private operator contracts to construct routes within the public transport network with designated lanes in Marrakech, Rabat, Tangier, Agadir and Casablanca. Funding for these firms originates from the unique fund for transport reforms (FART) and the districts collectively as seed investments and loans.

Impacts and challenges

Collective transportation, including public transport and taxis, is the leading mode of motorised trips in several MENA cities, including Istanbul (64 per cent), Casablanca (61 per cent), Algiers (70 per cent), Cairo (74 per cent) and Tunis (50 per cent). Despite comparatively elevated levels of public transit use in certain cities, inefficiencies fuel the further growth of informal services. In Algiers, for example, 66 per cent of the bus stops are served less than twice per hour during the evening peak period, and several buses depart from major stations overloaded with passengers, thereby contributing to uncomfortable conditions and overcrowding, especially when drivers allow more passengers to board along the route. Bus operations along designated routes only account for 60 per cent of the total designated bus routes. In Egypt and Kuwait, the bus network is under-financed, contributing to aging fleets, overcrowding and decreasing frequencies of service. Personalised stops and versatility in service outperform the overall services offered by formal transportation (Al-Geneidy et al. 2013; CTE 2016). The supremacy of private transport threatens public transportation, mainly owing to the continued neglect of public offerings by transport authorities, planners and policymakers across the region.

Despite years of neglect, the growing number of projects being planned and implemented represents promising examples of shifting norms towards public transport. Nonetheless, Oman, Lebanon, Sudan, Yemen, Kuwait and Palestine lack policies to support the development of public transportation (Hamahui et al. 2010). In the cases of Bahrain, Iraq, Egypt, Morocco, Tunisia and Syria, the most widespread method of supporting public transport is price subsidies and enhancing accessibility and frequency of service. A striking pattern in the planned major projects of public transportation in MENA is that several of them occur in the wealthier countries of the UAE, Saudi Arabia, Kuwait and Qatar (Al-Geneidy et al. 2013; Crowther 2014).

Authorities are trying to make public transportation more appealing. They are starting to identify key areas needed to increase the use of public transport, which mainly cover safety, efficiency, comfort and ease of use and which target different population cohorts. Although there are signs of good progress, countries within MENA must still tweak the needs of their users with respect to safety, reliability, speed, ease and comfort. Transportation is a public service. Like all services, the quality of service dictates its success and hence its market share. The secret to capturing a larger share of the market is the development and implementation of effective marketing to capture potential users.

As a manifestation of this, the UAE has recently become the leader in developing user-oriented public transportation. By acknowledging the role of operator behaviour towards the assurance of passenger safety, bus and taxi drivers in Abu Dhabi and Dubai have enrolled in behavioural and psychological training programmes to improve safety (Al-Geneidy et al. 2013). Providing effective training is important in increasing standards to satisfy the expectations and needs of the consumer. The Roads and Transport Authority (RTA) in Dubai hosted numerous training workshops in 2013, covering material on corporate excellence with the aim of improving workers' performance.

Technological advancements have also helped several cities meet the modern needs of their local and tourist passengers. Dubai, Casablanca and Tehran now offer real-time information for public transportation schedules, supplying reliable information on the dates and timings, which is crucial as it enables people to plan their journeys more easily (Parahoo et al. 2014). Electronic and integrated ticketing systems have already been launched in Tehran and Dubai, while other cities continue to develop such systems. Electronic and integrated systems of ticketing make public transport easier to use by enhancing the transaction and boarding processes, making it safer and easier to board. The fundamental aim of any service is to fulfil the needs of its users, usually achieved by conducting user satisfaction surveys. Such surveys have been performed in Tehran, Abu Dhabi, Amman and Dubai to assess the quality of public transportation services and identify and understand consumer preferences (Parahoo et al. 2014).

Other examples from Dubai to fulfil the needs of consumers, include the 'Public Transport Library', which was established by the 'Read More' initiative in various metro stations to provide opportunities for users to borrow books while using the metro system. In addition, a free Wi-Fi service is offered at various metro stations. These examples cover only a few key innovative developments in the area of public transport tailored to consumer needs (CTE 2016). Nevertheless, there is still considerable room for improvement, and further investment in corresponding fields is required to shrink the gap between local and global standards. Recently, the need to fortify public transport systems achieved further attention within the Middle East. Long-term plans to achieve the development goals and expansion of the public transport sector were stressed in the region's first UITP Congress. A World Bank (2011) report indicates significant gaps with respect to capacity in the rural and urban transport infrastructure throughout MENA. Decreasing these gaps could aid in the acceleration of economic growth, integration within the region, raising living standards and job creation, as well as decreasing susceptibility to accidents and poverty.

Taxis and informal motorised transport

This section emphasises various sorts of informal transport used in MENA, describing the significance and contribution of informal services, along with the challenges and patterns linked to them. Informal motorised transport is composed of private non-regulated and regulated taxis, collective taxis and other kinds of motorised vehicles, such as those with three wheels. Based on the rules that influence their activities in different nations, private taxis may or may not be classified as an informal mode of transportation. Informal transport plays a significant role in urban mobility by filling the gaps not covered by formal public transportation. In terms of competitiveness, informal services outperform formal transit services with respect to speed and accessibility (CTE 2016). In addition, they are demand-oriented and are capable of transforming almost immediately to satisfy changes in market needs. Informal services also sometimes cost less than formal services, which is epitomised by the classic case of illegal taxi drivers who do not pay for legal fees or licence plates and therefore are able to provide the same services at a lower price. Consequently, where public transport and formal taxis are non-existent or inadequate, informal services tend to flourish. However, there are cases where private informal transport complements public transport or where the difference between the two services is small.

Taxis can be regulated, privately operated and legally monitored by the government, or unregulated altogether, operating entirely outside government influence, which is the definition of informal transport. Since the informal services are unregulated, accurate information is hard to find. For instance, taxis in Turkey are monitored at the city level, and national statistics for unofficial taxis do not exist. In 1991, a barrier to entry was put in place on formal taxis, decreasing their number to 17,416, despite the growing need for mobility. Such market penetration barriers for formal taxis in Istanbul play a significant part in the exponential growth of informal taxis owing to the 'artificial shortage' created by these entry restrictions. Such a shortage of legal taxis in Istanbul is apparent in the mode split of taxi trips, accounting for only 6 per cent of all motorised trips in 2005. An approximate number of 5,000 (22 per cent) illegally operated informal taxis existed in Istanbul in 2001, and the number has likely grown significantly since then (CTE 2016). A comparable barrier to entry was erected in Cairo in issuing new taxi licences. However, the number of taxis operating there is about twice the number of licences issued, which reveals the vitality of informal taxi operations.

A different shared form of taxi service exists in almost every country in MENA. However, the type of vehicle and service characteristics differ across the region and may include shared minibuses and taxis. Similar to taxicabs, minibuses may be classified as both public and informal transport, based on the regulations controlling their activities. Informal transport in the Kuwaiti capital is supplied by automobiles called 'one-eights'—white pickup trucks where passengers ride in the open truck bed. This mode is usually considered unsafe, and females are encouraged to avoid it.

Informal transport in Egypt, which is not planned or legally monitored by transport authorities, accounts for nearly 83 per cent of total motorised trips. These informal services cover intra-urban and inter-urban shared taxis and microbuses consisting of 7 to 17 seats, regular taxis, pickups and light vehicles (e.g. three wheelers). Also included are tourist, school and factory buses. A large number of taxis operate in Cairo with 163,300 taxis and microbuses completing 2.7 million trips every day. The proportion of informal shared taxis in Cairo to other modes has increased at a steady pace from 6 per cent in 1987 to 36 per cent and 35 per cent in 1998 and 2001, respectively, and the ratio has most likely continued to grow in the intervening 17 years. Nevertheless, these options are well known for poor service quality, since they are not organised, regulated or coordinated with other modes (CTE 2016).

In Palestine, there has been a shift towards shared taxi services, which transformed into a more preferential option since they operate with less difficulty on different roads. Taxis account for 11.4 per cent of all the automobiles in the West Bank, while in Gaza the proportion of taxis does not exceed 2.1 per cent (CTE 2016). The proportion of shared taxis and minibuses in Algiers is approximately 56 per cent of motorised transport, and the share of shared taxis in Casablanca has been estimated to constitute around 24 per cent of all motorised trips (CTE 2016).

Private taxi services are regulated internally in Qatar, Saudi Arabia, Kuwait and the UAE. In Qatar, the government is tasked with delivering taxi services via its public transportation agency. In the GCC countries, the proportion of informal forms of transport is relatively low compared to other areas in the MENA region due to stricter laws and regulations (Al-Geneidy et al. 2013; Crowther 2014). For instance, recent news reports have shown stricter enforcement of laws and regulations by the Dubai RTA to eliminate the use of illegal taxis. Elevated fines and deportation are some of the penalties against individuals who abuse the laws and regulations related to illegal taxis in several GCC countries.

Many governments have started to realise the important services privately operated taxis provide and have begun to establish new regulations or perform slight modifications to existing regulations, to enhance performance and safety amongst these informal transport services. For instance, in the Occupied Palestinian Territory, 'shared taxis' have become more organised and standardised recently in terms of their appearance, being painted a distinctive yellow and assigned easily distinguishable registration plates (Aljounaidi 2010).

In the last decade, three wheelers, small vehicles that have a maximum capacity of two passengers, have been established in certain neighbourhoods in Cairo and Alexandria. Regulations already force drivers to use three wheelers with a four-stroke engine rather than three wheelers with a two-stroke engine, because two-stroke engines release more emissions. However, despite the regulation, some drivers still use two-stroke engines on occasion. In addition, no registration or licensing regulations exist to keep track of them, and their use is spreading in a chaotic manner. In Senbelaween City, for instance, the number of three wheelers grew from zero to

3,000 between 1999 and 2005 alone (CTE 2016). In some parts of Alexandria, three wheelers are the sole form of urban transport; they provide transportation that is easy, fast, and affordable, even if they are not completely comfortable or safe.

Regardless of a country's level of economic development, informal motorised transport is significant in most MENA countries. However, in countries that have experienced rising economic growth recently, such as the UAE, the use of informal transportation is strongly discouraged. Informal transportation is at the heart of public transportation in places lacking public services. However, their operations are often not determined based on maximising advantages to society, but rather based on revenue for the operator (CTE 2016). Governments need to develop and assess regulatory options to make services offered by privately owned informal transport companies safer and more reliable, especially for women given that informal transport will continue to be a crucial service in the Middle East.

Safety is an added worry for people who use informal transport. While this mode provides a more economical substitute to private taxis, informal transportation usually only operates where the service is profitable, while reliability and safety standards are usually lower compared to public transit. In addition, in several incidents in MENA, both registered and unregistered private taxis have been linked to the harassment of female passengers. The problem of equality for females is a significant challenge in societies dominated by men, where women currently inhabit a minor presence in the public domain. To tackle this problem, a distinctive brand of taxi service has developed in certain countries. Balancing the restrictions on the public activities of women and their need for mobility, the 'pink taxi' service was launched in Dubai in 2007 and in Kuwait City in 2010. This service allows female passengers to ride in taxis operated by other female drivers, thereby increasing their mobility options and personal safety, while offering new employment opportunities for women. Owing to the newness of the service, it is still too early to discuss its success. However, services such as the pink taxi symbolise a positive development for enhancing women's transportation options across the region.

Alternative transportation

As noted so far in this chapter, motorised transport represents a considerable proportion of total urban trips in MENA. However, there is considerable potential for cities in the region to encourage non-motorised forms of urban mobility for both residents and tourists. Cycling and walking as forms of transportation are explored below, followed by a description of the restrictions that hinder the promotion of these alternative modes. The use of animals (e.g. horses and camels) for transporting tourists is not considered in this chapter.

Walking, the most fundamental means of urban mobility for all short-to-medium length travel, and cycling, play a significant role in urban transportation, especially within the majority of low-income and middle-income MENA countries. Despite the popularity of non-motorised mobility, it usually suffers from complete neglect in investment, network management and infrastructure maintenance. People usually avoid cycling or walking without safe, continuous and high-quality infrastructure (Timothy & Boyd 2015).

Non-motorised travel throughout MENA, which usually entails bicycling, walking and pushcarts, are frequently ignored, and hence are not present in several national statistics. However, traffic management research suggests that trips by foot play a crucial part in the transportation system. For instance, in Casablanca, walking accounts for 54 per cent of all urban trips (CTE 2016). Whilst almost every form of transport is accessed by walking, foot travel is usually ignored in urban infrastructure planning and implementation. Infrastructure that distinguishes various categories of road users is rare, especially in places where motorisation rates are high. In such places, the expansion of roads usually means even less designated pedestrian space, which has a negative effect on the safety and well-being of walkers.

In MENA, there are two separate categories of bicycle users: individuals who cannot afford a private vehicle and individuals who can afford a motor vehicle but choose to cycle. Those who are unable to afford a vehicle use bicycles regularly, while individuals who can afford cars use bicycles primarily for recreational purposes (CTE 2016). However, bicycle usage for leisure and recreational activities continues to be a minor activity, likely owing to the region's intense desert climate and because using bicycles as a mode of transportation is still stigmatised as being an indicator of poverty; its usage across certain countries in the Middle East and North Africa remains the domain of the less-affluent population. In areas where incomes are increasing, people appear to be replacing bicycle travel with motor vehicle travel. Several countries in the region, however, have begun promoting bicycling as a viable sightseeing and transportation option for international visitors (Hall et al. 2017).

Egypt produces the most information about the modal share of non-motorised transport. In Cairo, bicycling and walking accounted for roughly 32 per cent of total trips in 2001. Possible reasons for this high figure may be the shorter distances travelled to universities, factories and schools, as well as the expenses linked to vehicle ownership. In comparison, higher shares of walking were recorded in Tunis and Algiers, with 50 per cent in Tunis in 2006, and 56 per cent in Algiers in 2004 (CTE 2016).

The needs of cyclists and pedestrians in many countries across MENA are usually ignored, yet observed popular trends in Europe and the US, coupled with the expenses associated with vehicles, are fuelling an increasing interest in non-motorised transport. The extent of congestion in the Lebanese capital Beirut makes walking the ideal method of moving around the city, encouraging more people to walk in the process. Encouraging people to walk in the main areas of the city is one of the key priorities of a company called Solidere, which is tasked with transportation planning and development in parts of Beirut. Interest in the bicycle as a transport medium seems to be growing in Turkey as well. Though no statistics exist so far, bicycle shops are sprouting up along designated bicycle paths in Istanbul, which can be classified as part of an urban cycling movement (CTE 2016). Similarly, in the Turkish city of Konya, the nation's first public bicycle-sharing system was launched in 2012. Cycling groups (e.g. Cycle Egypt) have appeared in several cities with the help of social media. These groups promote cycling as transportation for commuting regularly to work. They also plan recreational cycling trips on a weekly basis to promote the use of bicycles.

Non-motorised transport across MENA faces several challenges. The key obstacles to growing or maintaining cycling transport are mainly poor infrastructure, followed by culture, education, funding of facilities and cycle purchases. The main issue for walkers and cyclists is safety. These people are classified as 'vulnerable road users', as they are not protected physically as vehicle passengers are. With more than 30 per cent of pedestrian deaths accounting for total road fatalities in certain countries, such as Tunisia and Israel, it is safe to suggest that pedestrian safety may potentially be a significant issue in the Middle East. Cycling is also viewed as unsafe because of inadequate road safety, and insufficient facilities expose cyclists to high-speed vehicles. While cyclist fatalities are usually underreported, they comprise a significantly lower share of traffic fatalities relative to pedestrian accidents.

Existing facilities and infrastructure remain poor in MENA. Pavement that is not maintained or constructed properly leads to pedestrians favouring the roadside, which contributes to safety problems, particularly in urban areas with high traffic density. Likewise, cycling routes, which are already extremely low in number, are inaccessible and seldom linked, partially due to the difficult and capital-intensive implementation of cycle lanes when they are not included initially in planning and traffic management.

There are an inadequate number of policies to encourage using active forms of transport in MENA. National policies to aid in promoting cycling and walking are lacking in most countries, with Syria, the UAE and the Occupied Palestinian Territory being a few exceptions. Although funding and education levels are usually low for urban areas in MENA, policies that help promote public transportation are more common. Furthermore, bicycles may prove to be a costly purchase for low-income individuals. A small number of subsidies exist to aid in financing the purchase and maintenance of bicycles, thereby incentivising the use of these alternative forms of transportation. Moreover, municipalities usually do not budget for non-motorised travel, which limits bicycle and pedestrian networks while simultaneously enhancing motorised vehicle congestion.

Conclusion

Tourism relies on the infrastructure of mobility. The history of mobility and transportation is tightly intertwined with the historical transformation of tourism. To achieve success in operating as global hubs, Middle Eastern countries need to recognise the importance of growing regional ties, infrastructure-based synergies and inter-territorial strategies (Morakabati 2013). If tourism is to play a significant role in the economic strategies of MENA nations, the region must collectively prioritise coordinated, integrated, safe, sustainable, comfortable and high-speed modes of transportation.

Aviation, hospitality and tourism represent a few important sectors that have the capacity to decrease reliance on crude in several countries that rely heavily on oil. Consequently, this sector will depend on, or highly benefit from, a cohesive system of ground transportation. However, the following factors are crucial to guide this process: easy access, functionality, comfort, value for money, high productivity and full integration. Integration also refers to coordinated services and timetables, smooth connections and cross-modal ticketing—all contributing to ensuring that ground transport is an appealing user experience. Integration is not restricted to ground transport but also covers air travel and other options, where transportation elements are included in hotel room bookings and major events. Ground transport in the destination can be integrated as part of the flat fee when purchasing air tickets. Travel offers can also be attractively priced and easy to book and purchase.

Three proposed types of integration are (1) integration of functional planning: transport and tourism, (2) integration of modes: air, rail, coaches and cruises, and (3) integration of scale: urban, local and long-distance travel. Integration calls for a systematic and holistic approach to planning tourism across many countries, particularly Egypt and the GCC countries, through a directive that is 'built on a comprehensive analysis of the urban fabric, land availability and its best use, environmental issues, mobility, infrastructure and urban services' (Alameri & Wagle 2011: 29). An interconnected multi-modal ground transport network, serving all destinations of interest, could encourage travel to create inimitable experiences linked to an appreciation of the distinct attributes of the region (e.g. desert, coastal and mountain landscapes, and Arabian architecture). Such a network would make individual tourist attractions part of something greater, linking them to one continuous experience instead of dissecting them into separate (disrupted) events. An effectively designed transportation system could help showcase many countries in the region, particularly in the context of an 'open world', compliant with the customs of international tourism yet respectful of the region's strong social and religious heritage.

Combining the heritage, traditions and values of MENA, which possesses modern, up-to-date technology, is also crucial in accepting an integrative system of ground transportation by local users. This is a requirement for modern touristic use that also includes product and service quality, aesthetics, comfort and economic value as primary factors of success in the long term. Constructing infrastructure for transportation systems from the beginning enables effective planning and design for integrated tourism and transportation, which should also satisfy the needs of a sustainable, environment-friendly and easy-to-use system of transport. More importantly, local strategies to establish environmentally friendly transportation within the region and to advocate the use of public transportation should be high on the list of key objectives of MENA countries (see Batzner 2015).

Certain MENA nations are amongst the wealthiest in the world with a lifestyle highly centred around cars, affecting the spatial development of urban, peri-urban and non-urban areas. Time-consuming traffic jams and long gridlocks are common problems of car dependency and its effects on daily life. The prevalence of road accidents symbolises the 'fastest way to die in the region' (Ghazal 2012). For instance, in Saudi Arabia, there are roughly 526,000 annual road accidents and up to 17 daily fatalities, with estimated economic expenses of US$5.6 billion annually (Saudi Gazette 2016).

In Dubai, where road traffic density has reached saturation levels, the success of the Dubai Metro rail network demonstrates the feasibility and acceptance of the public sector approach to transport in the region. Operating since 2009 and popular with both locals and tourists, the Dubai Metro doubled its 2011 passenger number to 138 million in 2013 (Thomas 2014). Along with Dubai Tramway and the Road and Transport Authority transit bus network, Dubai Metro proved that innovative and integrated solutions can encourage transformations in the behavioural patterns of tourists and mobile persons. In fact, in the first quarter of 2016, the Dubai Metro served 49,913,698 passengers, and the Dubai Tram served 1,338,601 passengers (Khaleej Times 2016). The Dubai Tram is the first tramway project in the GCC region powered by a ground-based electric supply system. Operating from 2014 and involving 11 stations, the tramway encourages passengers to travel the full length of the 10.6 km route for only DH3 (US$0.82) (Badam 2015). Dubai's urban transport network is an example for other countries in the region. In Qatar, for example, the first phase of the Doha Metro is scheduled for completion in 2019, with two further phases scheduled for completion prior to the 2022 FIFA World Cup (Railway Gazette 2013). Although Kuwait City acknowledged the need to develop a metro system as early as 2006, the planned 160 km network, including 66 stations, should surpass the procurement stage by the end of 2018. Around 60 per cent of the network will be underground, with an anticipated cost of around US$7 billion (Railway Gazette 2015). Within the past five years, metro networks have also been announced in major cities in Saudi Arabia.

Light rail and highly flexible dial-a-ride systems can operate locally in inner-city areas and around major tourist attractions. It is essential that new destinations are designed for efficient transportation. The chaos affecting Dubai's 2013 Sandance Festival on Palm Island illustrates how inadequate and unaccustomed transport infrastructure can be, where a surge in visitor demand can seriously compromise the tourism product (Trenwith 2014). Well-developed, scalable and expandable ground transport networks allow easier access to sites of interest, which can have an obvious impact on the customer's perception of the nature and quality of the transportation product and service. Consequently, it is in the interests of many countries in the region, particularly the GCC countries, to take heed of the need for a good internal transport network.

References

Abulibdeh, A. (2018) 'Implementing congestion pricing policies in a MENA region city: Analysis of the impact on travel behaviour and equity', *Cities*, 74(3): 196–207.

Abulibdeh, A., & Zaidan, E. (2018) 'High-occupancy toll (HOT) lanes on the main highways of the city of Abu Dhabi: The public's willingness to pay', *Journal of Transport Geography*, 66: 91–105.

Abulibdeh, A., Zaidan, E., & Alkaabi, K. (2018) 'Empirical analysis of the implementation of cordon pricing: Potential impacts on travel behaviour and policy implications', *Transportation Research Part F: Psychology and Behaviour*, 53(3): 130–142.

Al-Geneidy, A., Diab, E., Jacques, C., & Mathez, A. (2013) *Sustainable Urban Mobility in the Middle East and North Africa*. Nairobi: United Nations Human Settlements Programme.

Alameri, A., & Wagle, G. (2011) 'Abu Dhabi efforts in facing global warming challenges through urban planning', in C.A. Brebbia, & E. Beriatos (eds), Sustainable Development and Planning (pp. 29–38). Southampton: WIT Press.

Aljounaidi, L (2010) 'Gender and transport in MENA: Case studies from West Bank, Gaza and Yemen', *MENA Knowledge and Learning, Quick Notes Series*, 21: 1–4.

Badam, R.T. (2015) 'Special report: Dubai tram's on the right track'. *The National*, 14 February. Available online: http://thedubaitram.com/special-report-dubai-trams-right-track/ (Accessed 30 July 2017).

Bagaeen, S. (2015) 'Saudi Arabia, Bahrain, United Arab Emirates and Qatar: Middle Eastern complexity and contradiction', in G. Squires, & E. Heurkens (eds), *International Approaches to Real Estate Development* (pp. 100–121). London: Routledge.

Batzner, A. (2015) 'Greening urban transport in the Gulf Cooperation countries: Localised approaches to modal integration as key success factors', in M.A. Raouf, & M. Luomi (eds), *The Green Economy in the Gulf* (pp. 161–180). London: Routledge.

Belwal, R., & Belwal, S. (2010) 'Public transportation services in Oman: A study of public perceptions', *Journal of Public Transportation*, 13(4): 1–21.

Bener, A., Özkan, T., & Lajunen, T. (2008) 'The driver behaviour questionnaire in Arab Gulf countries: Qatar and United Arab Emirates', *Accident Analysis & Prevention*, 40(4): 1411–1417.

Butler, R.W. (1999) 'Sustainable tourism: A state-of-the-art review', *Tourism Geographies*, 1(1): 7–25.

Crowther, L. (ed.) (2014) *Qatar Residents' Guide* (6th edn). Dubai: Explorer.

CTE (Center for Transport Excellence) (2016) *MENA Transport Report 2016*. Dubai: UITP and RTA.

Culpan, R. (1987) 'International tourism model for developing economies', *Annals of Tourism Research*, 12(4): 541–552.

Duval, D.T. (2007) *Tourism and Transport: Modes, Networks and Flows*. Clevedon: ChannelView Publications.

Ghazal, R. (2012) 'Road accidents in the Gulf: Fastest way to die in the region', *The National*, 10 September. Available online: www.thenational.ae/uae/road-accidents-in-the-gulf-the-fastest-way-to-die-in-the-region-1.478770 (Accessed 3 January 2017).

Godard, X. (2007) 'Some lessons from the LRT in Tunis and the transferability of experience', *Transportation Research Part A: Policy and Practice*, 41(10): 891–898.

Gray, M. (2017) 'Theoretical approaches to the political economy of tourism in the GCC states', in M.L. Stephenson, & A. Al-Hamarneh (eds), *International Tourism Development and the Gulf Cooperation Council States: Challenges and Opportunities* (pp. 29–44). London: Routledge.

Gunesch, K. (2017) 'Bus travel, Middle East', in L.L. Lowry (ed.), *The SAGE International Encyclopedia of Travel and Tourism* (pp. 192–195). Thousand Oaks, CA: SAGE.

Hall, C.M., Le-Klähn, D-T., & Ram, Y. (2017) *Tourism, Public Transport and Sustainable Mobility*. Bristol: ChannelView Publications.

Hamahui, C., Sarkissian, E., El Chaarani, H., Aboulhosn, N., & Bainbridge, M. (2010) *At Home in Beirut: A Practical Guide to Living in Beirut*, 4th edn. Beirut: Turning Point Books.

Hawas, E.Y., Hassan, N.M., & Abulibdeh, A.O. (2016) 'A multi-criteria approach of assessing public transport accessibility', *Journal of Transport Geography*, 57: 19–34.

Khaleej Times (2016) 'Al Rigga, Al Fahidi busiest metro stations in Dubai'. *Kaleej Times*, 18 April. Available online: www.khaleejtimes.com/nation/transport/al-rigga-al-fahidi-busiest-metro-stations-in-dubai (Accessed 20 November 2017).

Lumsdon, L. (2000) 'Transport and tourism: Cycle tourism—a model for sustainable development?', *Journal of Sustainable Tourism*, 8(5): 361–377.

Morakabati, Y. (2013) 'Tourism in the Middle East: Conflicts, crises and economic diversification, some critical issues', *International Journal of Tourism Research*, 15(4): 375–387.

Orbaşlı, A., & Woodward, S. (2008) 'A railway "route" as a linear heritage attraction: The Hijaz Railway in the Kingdom of Saudi Arabia', *Journal of Heritage Tourism*, 3(3): 159–175.

Page, S.J. (2005) *Transport and Tourism: Global Perspectives*, 2nd edn. London: Pearson.

Parahoo, S.K., Lea Harvey, H., & Radi, G.Y.A. (2014) 'Satisfaction of tourists with public transport: An empirical investigation in Dubai', *Journal of Travel and Tourism Marketing*, 31(8): 1004–1017.

Railway Gazette (2013) 'More Doha metro contracts awarded'. *Railway Gazette*, 11 June. Available online: www.railwaygazette.com/news/single-view/view/more-doha-metro-contracts-awarded.html (Accessed 30 August 2017).

Railway Gazette (2015) 'Kuwait metro and rail procurement to begin next year'. *Railway Gazette*, 9 October. Available online: www.railwaygazette.com/news/single-view/view/kuwait-metro-and-rail-procurement-to-begin-next-year.html (Accessed 30 August 2017).

Saudi Gazette (2016) 'Report: Saudi Arabia records 526,000 road accidents annually'. *Saudi Gazette*, 1 January. Available online: http://english.alarabiya.net/en/News/middle-east/2016/01/01/Report-Saudi-Arabia-records-526-000-road-accidents-annually.html (Accessed 30 August 2017).

Sims, D. (2009) *Sana'a: A City Development Strategy*. Washington, DC: World Bank.

Thomas, B. (2014) 'Dubai Metro doubles number of users in 2 years'. *Arabian Business*, 23 February. Available online: www.arabianbusiness.com/dubai-metro-doubles-number-of-yearly-users-in-2yrs-539894.html (Accessed 30 August 2017).

Timothy, D.J., & Boyd, S.W. (2015) *Tourism and Trails: Cultural, Ecological and Management Issues*. Bristol: Channel View Publications.

Trenwith, C. (2014) 'Sandance organisers offer refunds amid traffic chaos'. *Arabian Business*, 1 January. Available online: www.arabianbusiness.com/sandance-organisers-offer-refunds-amid-traffic-chaos-533065.html (Accessed 30 August 2017).

World Bank (2011) *Urban Transport Projects: Patterns and Trends in Lending, 1999–2009*. Washington, DC: World Bank.

22

AIR ROUTE DEVELOPMENT AND TRANSIT TOURISM IN THE MIDDLE EAST

Bojana Spasojevic and Gui Lohmann

Introduction

Air route development is a key industry process and, in many respects, is related to transit tourism. The growing interest in the relationship between air transport and tourism is, in general, also supported in the academic literature where the number of publications on this topic has tripled between 2000–2014 (Spasojevic, Lohmann, & Scott 2018). Air route development involves not only the development and maintenance of routes, but also, on a strategic level, the opportunity to exploit gateway or transit tourism opportunities. Previous studies (Lohmann, Albers, Koch, & Pavlovich 2009; Warnock-Smith & O'Connell 2011; Zhang & Findlay 2014) have identified the Middle East and Southeast Asia as places that have successfully exploited transit air transport tourism opportunities.

Transit air transport tourism development parallels the transformation of airports from transportation hubs to tourist destinations. This transformation has only been possible through well-orchestrated stakeholder engagement exercises. According to Chen and Lee (2012), the successful transformation from an air hub to a tourism destination depends on the following four key elements: improved international airport terminal facilities; aviation market liberalisation; improved aviation competitiveness; and effective tourism marketing. Lohmann et al. (2009) compare two successful examples: Singapore and Dubai. In both cases, the geographical location of the hub was an attractive factor for further integration of government policy, destination marketing organisations (DMOs), airports and airlines, who foresaw the benefits of transforming these air transport hubs into world-leading tourism destinations. In both cases, the close stakeholder collaboration amongst airlines, airport, DMOs, and other aviation-related companies is controlled by government agencies. Led by these successful examples, other countries and regions are exploring the potential benefits of closer collaboration between air transport and tourism to foster transit tourism. For example, Taiwan, whose location makes it a desirable potential air hub for East Asia, has recognised the opportunity for transformation into a leading tourist transport centre.

When examining the growth of passengers transported within and between the continents and regions of the world during the ten-year period from 2006 to 2015 (see Table 22.1), passenger traffic through the Middle East had the highest increase amongst all regions, with an average 98 per cent growth. This result is followed by Asia with a 95 per cent growth rate, well ahead of South America with a 66 per cent growth rate. In comparison with the rest of the world, Asia had a very high average increase of passenger traffic, particularly from the Middle East (166 per cent). Only Central America and the Middle East have obtained similar trends. Nevertheless, no other region has obtained such impressive growth as the Middle East (see Table 22.1). For example, passenger traffic growth from the Middle East to South America grew, on average, 1,559 per cent, to Australasia 350 per cent and to North America 256 per cent in the period 2006–2015. Given that the Middle East proportionally has a much smaller population than other parts of the world, a significant part of the region's passenger traffic growth mainly consists of transit passenger traffic from outside the region, passing through emerging hubs such as Abu Dhabi, Doha and Dubai. Thus, it is worth examining in more detail air route development in the Middle East and how transit tourism has flourished in this part of the world.

Air route development and transit tourism

The air transport industry has experienced numerous changes and rapid development since the first scheduled passenger airline service between St. Petersburg and Tampa (Florida) in 1914 (Sharp 2012). Airports, a key element of any air transport network, were traditionally considered public service spaces. However, after the process of airline deregulation in the late 1970s in the US and in the mid-1980s in other countries (Oum, Adler, & Yu 2006), a number of airports were transformed from public service entities into commercial enterprises (Halpern & Graham 2015). The commercialisation, or privatisation, of airports and airlines led to an increase in cooperation amongst various stakeholders to exploit commercial opportunities within airport spaces. Retail outlets, banks, hotels, rental car companies, insurance companies (Graham 2013) and local government tourism agencies and other tourism organisations were incorporated into airport spaces.

In 2013, the number of air passengers worldwide reached over 3 billion for the first time, with that figure expected to have grown to 3.6 billion in 2016 (IATA 2012, 2013). At the same time, the number of international tourists worldwide grew by 4.4 per cent between 2014 and 2015, reaching a total of 1.184 billion tourists (UNWTO 2016). Furthermore, in 2014, 54 per cent of the total number of international tourists travelled by air (UNWTO 2015). Presented data show that the modern tourism industry is hardly imaginable without air transport, sophisticated airport infrastructure, efficient and safe airline services and worldwide air transport networks. In addition, a high number of international tourists travelling by air represent an important part of the overall number of air passengers, evidencing the co-dependence of the air transport and tourism industries. In many cases, the development of new routes is a result of increased tourism traffic. Between 2005 and 2011, 79 per cent of international air traffic growth was created by new routes, while only 21 per cent occurred from existing routes (Thelle, Pedersen, & Frederik 2012). Air traffic growth influences economic growth, an important element of tourism economic development.

Air route development

As noted earlier, air route development is a well-known industry process that has received little attention in both the academic and professional literature (Halpern & Graham 2015). Persuading airlines to operate new routes between two airports is a complex process, involving a number of key business partners and commercial decisions. In addition to the airlines and airport decision makers, this process might require the engagement of government agencies

Table 22.1 Percentage of inter- and intra-continental passenger route growth in the period 2006–2015

Destination	Origin								
	Caribbean	South America	Europe	Africa	Middle East	Asia	Australasia	North America	Central America
Caribbean	−19	69	7	–	–	–	–	2	247
South America	64	65	23	45	1,559	–	61	67	184
Europe	6	19	6	47	122	54	–	14	237
Africa	–	69	45	163	161	61	25	101	–
Middle East	–	1,638	122	60	69	166	351	256	–
Asia	–	–	53	25	169	96	49	46	–
Australasia	–	60	–	77	350	50	3	32	–
North America	−5	66	14	53	256	43	32	−13	67
Central America	208	186	208	–	–	–	–	67	16
Total traffic	**−9**	**66**	**9**	**53**	**98**	**95**	**5**	**−12**	**34**

Source: Compiled from data provided by AirportIS (2016).

and other stakeholders either directly or indirectly involved in tourism (e.g. regional development agencies, chambers of commerce, non-government organisations (NGOs), and other business associations). Numerous industry reports aim to explain the complexity of the air route development process. Route development can be defined as the 'marketing activities undertaken by airports with the aim of attracting new routes, for example through participation in route development conferences, offering incentive schemes, meetings with airlines, producing bespoke reports for airlines, etc.' (Thelle et al. 2012: 81). Furthermore, air route development is a relatively new process which started after the airport privatisation process began in the 1980s. It consists not only of persuading airlines to fly from a particular airport, but also to increase the capacity of an existing route by adding flight frequency or using larger aircraft (STRAIR 2005).

Seminal studies on air route development (e.g. Goodovitch 1996; Swan 2002; Weber & Williams 2001) are mostly concerned with the identification of the air route development process and the factors that are necessary for its success. Even though this part of the literature emphasises deregulation, aircraft manufacturing, economic stability and passengers' preferences as the key factors for air route development, it fails to provide a clear explanation of the process. A number of questions still need to be addressed by the literature, including: How is this process being established? Who is leading it? Whose partnership is the most important for the route's success? What is the role of transit tourism in air route development?

Early studies on air route development have identified route development as a significant component in the air transport development process (Goodovitch 1996). The air transport development model (Figure 22.1) was created in 1996 and includes the following six phases: (1) 'scattered airports' where pre-existing service points (airports) are linked with sporadic and disorganised networks; (2) 'penetration routes' which represent the beginning of scheduled services; (3) 'maximum connectivity' where all involved city-pairs are linked; (4) 'fully-connected networks' as a more efficient operating system; (5) a 'hub-and-spoke network' with a central hub which enables rerouting of all flights; and (6) 'dehubbing' as a more efficient network, with feeder routes and stopover flights (Goodovitch 1996). The model shows different characteristics of air service within each of the six phases. Air routes, an operational part of the air service

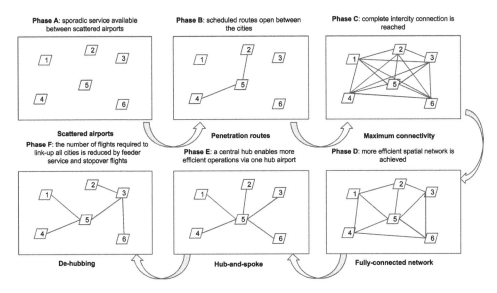

Figure 22.1 Air transport development model
Source: Adapted from Goodovitch (1996).

network, can be modified and improved to follow market demand. Interestingly, this model ana-lyses the development of air service networks purely from the perspective of airlines. According to this model, the main role of the airport is its geographical position, while airlines are respon-sible for developing air service networks through the six phases described above. This is one of the key differences between the so-called 'earlier stage' and 'recent research'.

Recent studies on this topic (Halpern & Graham 2015, 2016; Lohmann et al. 2009; Lohmann & Vianna 2016) address the role of airports in fostering air route development. In their study, Halpern and Graham (2016) list four stages for the air route development process from the air-port perspective:

1. Setting the objectives for route development;
2. Undertaking market research, often in association with potential stakeholders;
3. Conducting strategic marketing activities; and
4. Managing implementation, including resources, procedures and evaluation.

The ASM report (2009, as cited in Halpern & Graham 2016), found that 94 of 100 surveyed airports undertake active marketing campaigns vis-à-vis the airlines, including websites devoted to air route development and attending air route development meetings and conferences as well as tourism-related trade exhibitions to promote their targeted routes. In addition to airports, tourism authorities have also been identified as important partners for route development (87 per cent), followed by local and city authorities (56 per cent), chambers of commerce (50 per cent), regional governmental organisations (47 per cent), and NGOs (22 per cent) (ASM 2009, as cited in Halpern & Graham 2016). Many airports also use other techniques to attract new airlines, including special agreements and incentive schemes. Some of the common incentive schemes include direct payments per flight/passenger (where the airport pays an agreed amount to the carrier for each departing passenger or flight); joint marketing support for airlines (the so-called 'Co-OP Marketing Funds', where route development agencies or tourism boards promote new routes at the same time as promoting the region itself); discounted charges for landing, parking, security and air bridges; discounted or rent-free offices and parking; and risk-sharing where the airport guarantees the airline's occupancy or revenue levels during the agreed period (STRAIR 2005). An airport competition study (Thelle et al. 2012) identified the participation at the Annual World Routes conference as the most common air route development activity both in Europe and worldwide, followed by meeting airlines in their own offices and targeting airlines, inviting them to visit the airport.

Even though both air route development studies conducted by Halpern and Graham (2015, 2016) have included only airports, they present some valuable conclusions that can be used to advance research on this topic. For example, the need to collaborate was identified as one of the most important development activities, an observation which also supports the findings from an air routes suspension study (Lohmann and Vianna 2016) where the lack of cooperation between aviation and non-aviation stakeholders was stated as one of the main reasons for air route suspension.

Transit air transport and tourism

Any tourist's travel plan contains at least two geographic places: the tourist's place of origin and the tourist destination. The origin, also known as the tourist's 'permanent place of residence' in Mariot's (1983) model, is the tourist's home. Although there are many definitions of tourism, the tourist generally must travel to and stay 'in places outside their usual environment for not more than one consecutive year for leisure, business and other purposes' (UNWTO 2007). The number of tourists originating in a given area will in large part depend on the number of people living in that certain area, but other factors can also influence a region's status as a supplier of tourists including the average income, the local cost of living (a high cost in the region of origin can encourage travel to places with lower costs of living to maximise the benefits of a strong currency), the existence of political factors (e.g. bans on leaving the country, as was the case in many communist countries) and environmental considerations (i.e. climate, due to a desire to go someplace warmer) (Pearce 2001).

Networks comprised of various modes of transport suited to different geographic scales interconnect places of origin and places of destinations. These networks are interconnected by terminals or nodes that, in many cases, fulfil special functions within the network. The four types of nodal functions that are relevant to transit tourism and air route development are origins, destinations, hubs and gateways. To demonstrate these concepts, Figure 22.2 graphically illustrates a theoretical example of the nodal functions which are relevant to transit tourism

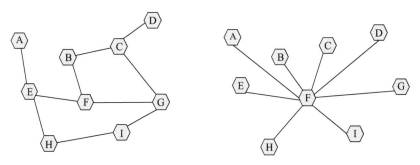

Figure 22.2 A theoretical example of a grid network (left), converted to hub-spoke (right)

and air route development. Initially, all nine dots (A to I) shown in each scheme of Figure 22.2 can be considered potential origins and tourism destinations. However, point F on the right side of the figure has a privileged location in the transport network because all the traffic that connects the various nodes of the network pass through it, thus characterising F as a hub. More theoretically, hubs have been defined as exhibiting 'centrality and intermediation spatial qualities [which] increase the importance and levels of traffic hubs strategically located within the transport system' (Hoyle & Knowles 1998: 2).

A number of transportation hubs, particularly airports, are associated with air travel. Compared with road and rail networks, the implementation or displacement of an air hub from the node of one network to another is much easier, given that air transport uses airways that do not require surface construction. Amongst the advantages of hubs is the possibility of interconnecting multiple points in a network with few connecting pairs (compare the number of connecting pairs that are required to travel from point A to point D in the diagrams of Figure 22.2). The major disadvantage of the hub is that the travel time increases considerably because not only can the distance travelled increase (compare the increase in the distance travelled when connecting points B and C in both diagrams of Figure 22.2), but also, substantial layover time may accrue at the hub between two travel segments because of, for example, the schedules relating to onward connections, required minimum connection times, required security clearance times or other reasons.

Another special feature illustrated in Figure 22.2 (see the scheme with the grid network on the left) is represented by tracing the path between nodes C and E given that the entire connection to/from node A occurs through E and all connections to/from node D occur through C. This makes node E the gateway to node A and, consequently, the exit from A to the rest of the network (the same is true for the C–D relationship). According to Burghardt (1971, cited in Pearce 2001: 30), there are four attributes of gateway cities. First, these cities are in charge of the connections between the tributary area and the outside world and they develop in positions that have the potential to control the flow of goods and people. Second, they usually develop in their contact zones different intensities and types of production.

Third, although local ties are important, the gateways are best characterised by long distance commercial connections. Fourth, they are strongly committed to transport and trade.

One aspect of the gateway is the notion of intermediateness—a place in between two extremes, which can be 'expanded by an association with a function of stopover, from where visitors are sent to other centres or resorts' (Pearce 2001: 31). Gateways can generally be compared to a funnel through which travellers converge from different routes to gain access through a certain point and from where they can either disperse or converge, depending on the function of the other node. Intermediateness provides gateways with the advantage of capturing the passing traffic, with some travellers stopping and becoming tourists. Two examples of hubs that have taken advantage of the flow of passengers to expand their tourist destinations are Singapore (Asia) and the United Arab Emirates (UAE). In both cases, the national airlines (Singapore Airlines and Emirates, respectively) created internationally recognised in-flight services that increasingly captivated new and old passengers (Lohmann et al. 2009). With the significant flow of passengers who currently use both the Changi (Singapore) and Dubai (UAE) airports as hubs, numerous incentives have been created to encourage these passengers to take advantage of passing through the hub region by becoming acquainted with those hubs as tourist destinations. Amongst these incentives are shopping tour packages which include the purchase of airfares combined with hotel stays at significantly reduced rates, in addition to a range of services provided by the existing infrastructure of the airports, such as movie theatres, pools, etc. (Lohmann et al. 2009). For example, at Changi Airport, passengers waiting for more than five hours between flights can take a free bus from the terminal to tour the city; moreover, customers can choose between two different itineraries.

Air transport growth in the Middle East

While this book identifies many countries in MENA, this chapter focuses primarily on the Middle East area, particularly the Persian Gulf region, where transit tourism and air travel development has been especially notable in recent years. The number of flights in the ten-year period between January 2006 and December 2015 were gathered, using the database AirportIS in 2016. However, because of the political or military instability of some of the countries listed above, air transport was significantly impacted either because they were recovering from war (e.g. Iraq) or were affected by conflict (e.g. Libya and Syria) during this period. For example, Iraq experienced astronomic growth (4,330 per cent) in flight numbers in this period, while Libya (60 per cent growth) and Syria (6.4 per cent growth) experienced much smaller increases in flight numbers in comparison with the other countries listed (see Figure 22.3). However, these three countries were excluded from further analysis because of the acute political instability that they experienced. Several countries were also excluded because the total number of international flights in the year 2015 was very small, that is, fewer than 18,250 in a year, or 50 flights a day. These countries include Afghanistan (with growth of 552 per cent, but with only 13,673 flights in 2015), Libya (7,158 flights in 2015), Syria (1,086 flights in 2015) and Yemen (113 per cent growth in the period 2006–2015, but only 10,436 flights in 2015). Libya and Syria were also included in this list with 7,158 and 1,086 flights, respectively. The indexed growth in international flights for the remaining 15 countries is presented in Figure 22.3.

According to the indexed growth of international flights during this period (i.e. 2006–2015), the Middle East countries experiencing the highest growth include Turkey (454 per cent growth, Qatar (342 per cent), UAE (310 per cent), Oman (282 per cent) and Saudi Arabia (248 per cent). More specifically, the growth of international flights in Turkey (the country with the highest growth of international flights) displays important seasonality fluctuation, where Q3 of every year represents the peak season, and Q1 the off-peak season. This result is highly influenced by the summer tourism season in Q3 (from June to September) and demonstrates the seasonality of Turkish tourism and the air transport network in general. Similar seasonality fluctuations are also evident in other countries such as Morocco and Tunisia, whose tourism relies on leisure sun-lust travellers. However, their growth is not as substantial as the Turkish example. Two other leading countries, Qatar and UAE, have shown continuous growth in international air traffic. In the case of Qatar, which had 97,489 flights in 2015, there is hardly any fluctuation during the year because tourism is less dependent on the weather and because Qatar's main target is transit traffic. UAE had even more consistent growth with 301,932 flights in 2015, with the exception of an 11 per cent decrease in the number of international flights in Q2 2014. This decrease was primarily due to the temporary reduction of flights experienced during an 80-day runway refurbishment project between May and July, and the shift of freighter operators and general aviation to Al Maktoum International at Dubai World Central (DWC) in May 2014. The transit passenger traffic at some of the leading countries will be analysed in the following section.

Transit passenger traffic and tourism opportunities at major Middle East hubs

In this section, we examine the transit passenger traffic at major airport hubs in the Middle East, particularly Abu Dhabi (AUH), Doha (DOH), Dubai (DBX), Jeddah (JED), Istanbul (IST),

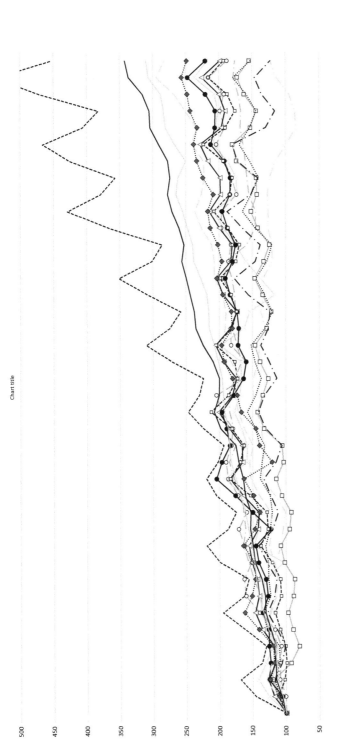

Chart title

Figure 22.3 Air transport passenger growth for 15 airports in the Middle East during the period January 2006 to December 2015

Source: AirportIS 2016.

Kuwait (KWI), Muscat (MCT) and Tel Aviv (TLV). Primary data about transit passenger traffic were extracted from the AirportIS database. Bi-directional (total) data were selected for the period 2010 and 2015. Only origin–destination (OD) combined country data that represented more than 0.5 per cent of the airport passenger traffic are presented in order to identify the main OD transit markets. The 0.5 per cent threshold was considered in order to obtain only the strongest routes available within a particular airport, this value being the highest one available for the AirportIS database. It is crucial to have a threshold considering the efforts required by airports and tourism organisations to develop particular marketing strategies. The following number of routes with a market share of at least 0.5 per cent were identified for each airport: AUH (17 routes), DOH (13), DXB (18), JED (2), IST (2), KWI (22), MCT (18) and TLV (22).

JED and IST both had only two routes attaining at least 0.5 per cent of their passenger traffic data: Pakistan–UK and India–US; and Iran–Germany and Iraq–UK, respectively. The average number of reported and estimated transit passengers for JED is very small, nearly 18 passengers per day for these two routes in the six-year period analysed. IST has a much stronger average with over 177 passengers per day. Because of the combination of few routes with a strong market share and, in the case of JED, experiencing a low number of transit passengers, neither airport can be considered established transit points. However, IST is developing a number of strategies to become a transit point, including the construction of a new airport at a cost of more than €10 billion, aiming to serve 150 million passengers in the first phase (Clark 2016).

Other airports such as KWI, MCT and TLV have a much larger number of transit routes representing at least 0.5 per cent of their market shares in comparison to JED and IST. However, what is evident in the case of these three airports is that the absolute number of transit passengers is very small. The 22 routes at KWI had a six-year average of 24 passengers per day, MCT with an average of 28 passengers per day, and TLV with an average of fewer than five passengers per day. In terms of the most important routes for these three airports, out of the combined 62 routes identified in this study, only five routes (8 per cent) had an average daily traffic of more than 50 passengers per day in the six-year period 2010–2015. They were India–US and UK–Philippines for KWI; and India–UK, Thailand–Germany, and Germany–Maldives for MCT. The remaining routes for these airports were quite weak in terms of passenger traffic. When compared with the major airports in the Middle East—AUH, DOH and DXB—their daily average passenger numbers for the routes with at least 0.5 per cent of the market share were respectively 155, 190 and 493. Aggregating the 48 routes analysed for these three airports yielded an average of at least 90 passengers per day per route from 2010 to 2015.

On the basis of using a combined level above 0.5 per cent for transit traffic market share and the higher average of daily passengers for AUH, DOH and DBX in comparison with other major airports in the Middle East, further analysis will be provided only for these three airports. In many respects, the strategy initially developed by Dubai, so-called 'Dubaisation' (Elsheshtawy 2010; Steiner 2010) involved a local airline offering outstanding in-flight and ground services linking a large number of airports around the world. In fact, Emirates is one of the few airlines in the world to serve all continents. This strategy, providing outstanding services, has been supported by promoting local attractions, events and other tourism initiatives to international passengers to foster stopover visitors. AUH and DOH, in many aspects, have followed strategies similar to those originally developed by Dubai/Emirates. Secondary data were obtained from the AirportIS to illustrate some of these strategies.

As discussed earlier in this chapter, airlines are playing an important role in introducing new routes and creating possibilities for increasing the number of transit passengers/tourists. The major Gulf carriers, Etihad, Emirates and Qatar Airways, are usually mentioned as the leading

Middle East airlines, but Turkish Airlines is also following this development part (Carrington 2014). All four carriers are expanding their network towards the US, while Turkish Airlines has positioned itself as a leading international carrier in Africa. Furthermore, Turkish Airlines and the Gulf carriers (i.e. Etihad, Emirates and Qatar Airways) have been increasingly developing their networks across Brazil, Russia, India and China (BRICs), countries considered to be the most promising developing markets in the twenty-first century (Carrington 2014). As confirmation of this successful strategy, Dubai's Department of Tourism and Commerce Marketing (DTCM) announced an 18 per cent increase in the number of Chinese tourists between 2014 and 2015, while the number of Russian tourists declined due to the current political situation (AmeInfo 2016).

Dubai (DXB)

Dubai has emerged as a key intercontinental hub in recent decades. A small number of countries are amongst the top main origin–destination markets, including Australia, France, Germany, Hong Kong, India, Italy, Pakistan, South Africa, Thailand, the UK and the US. Figure 22.4 shows the OD markets which have more than 0.5 per cent of the passenger traffic through Dubai, including India–US (4.8 per cent), India–UK (3.7 per cent), Australia–UK (2.9 per cent), UK–Pakistan (1.4 per cent), UK–Thailand (1.2 per cent), Australia–Italy (1.1 per cent) and UK–South Africa (1.0 per cent).

The countries with the highest market share for transit travel through DXB (see Figure 22.4), are the UK (with ten pairs or 52 per cent of the 19 routes with more than 0.5 per cent market share), India (six pairs or 31.6 per cent), Australia (four pairs or 21 per cent), Germany (three pairs or 15.8 per cent), Italy, South Africa and Thailand (two pairs each or 10.4 per cent of the aggregated whole) and China, France, Hong Kong, Kuwait, Malaysia, Mauritius, Singapore and the US with only one pair (5.2 per cent of the aggregated whole).

The rise of Dubai is a modern phenomenon widely studied from different academic perspectives. Dubai is directly connected with 238 destinations and has 6,500 direct flights per week (Dubai International Airport 2016). The number of international tourists has reached 12 million in 2016 (Visit Dubai 2016), with India, Saudi Arabia and the UK as leading source markets. The average length of stay in Dubai in 2016 was 3.6 days (Visit Dubai 2016). From the tourism perspective, Dubai has built its leading tourism and hub position through a strong brand based on the consecrated '6S model': stable, strategic, superlative, sophisticated, sustainable and successful (Lawton & Weaver 2017). Data obtained from Dubai Airport and DTCM support the '6S model'.

Abu Dhabi (AUH)

When comparing DXB and AUH in respect of the major originating country markets, similar patterns can be observed amongst those transit routes with more than 0.5 per cent of the market share (see Figure 22.5). As in the case of DXB, and also DOH, India–US is the most important OD market, with 3.4 per cent of the market share. Other dominant routes for both DXB and AUH (with at least 1 per cent of the market share) include Australia–UK (2.5 per cent), Thailand–UK (1.9 per cent), India–UK (1.3 per cent), UK–Pakistan (1.1 per cent)—all percentages for the AUH market. The remaining routes with at least 1 per cent of the market share through Abu Dhabi are Germany–Thailand (1.9 per cent), US–Pakistan (1.3 per cent) and Australia–Ireland (1 per cent). Markets that are particularly relevant to AUH, but not to DXB, are Ireland, Greece, Lebanon and Belgium (with at least 0.5 per cent of the market share).

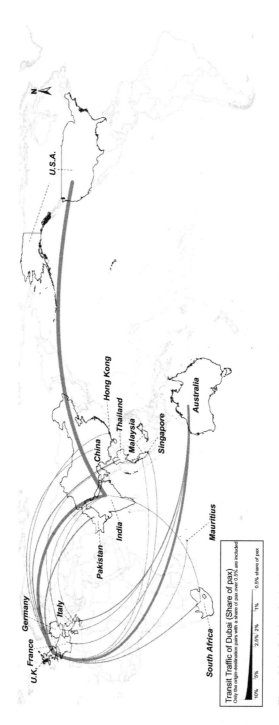

Figure 22.4 Origin–destination air transport passenger country market using Dubai as a transit airport

Note: Average 2010–2015 data for routes with more than 0.5% of the market share.

Source: AirportIS 2016.

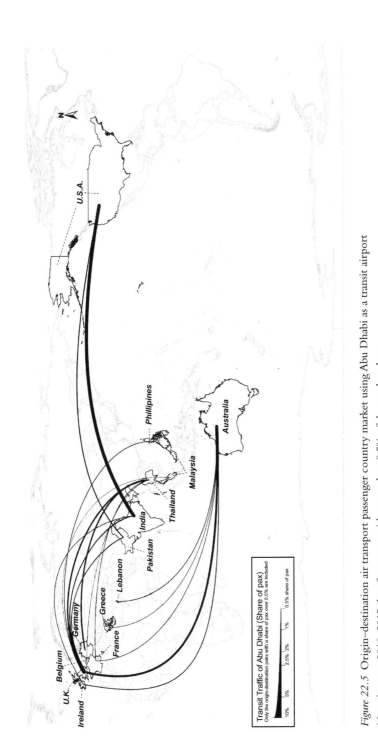

Figure 22.5 Origin–destination air transport passenger country market using Abu Dhabi as a transit airport

Note: Average 2010–2015 data for routes with more than 0.5% of the market share.

Source: AirportIS 2016.

The countries with the highest market share for transit travel through AUH include the UK (six pairs or 31.6 per cent of the 19 routes with more than 0.5 per cent market share), Australia (five pairs or 26.3 per cent), India and Thailand (four pairs each or 21 per cent), US (three pairs or 15.8 per cent), France, Ireland and Pakistan (two pairs each or 10.4 per cent) and Belgium, Germany, Lebanon, Malaysia and the Philippines with only one pair each (5.2 per cent).

Similar patterns appear to exist between Dubai's and Abu Dhabi's transit routes, with these two destinations deploying similar tourism development models. Although both Dubai and Abu Dhabi are targeting the same markets, they do not compete, but rather complement each other (Lawton & Weaver 2017). Abu Dhabi is creating its image as a more traditional and cultural destination compared to Dubai, which is an ultra-modern, luxury destination and trading hub. Abu Dhabi does not intend to imitate Dubai, even though both cities are creating their attractions based on their unique architecture and an atmosphere of luxury and a superlative tourism product. Abu Dhabi's development as a transit tourism destination is highly dependent on the cooperation of Etihad Airways, Abu Dhabi International Airport and the Abu Dhabi Tourism and Culture Authority. It is expected that Abu Dhabi will reach 7.5 million tourists by 2030, a target which will boost significant air route development opportunities (Abu Dhabi Airports 2016).

Doha (DOH)

Doha (DOH) airport presents a total of 13 OD country pairs of transit markets, six fewer than AUH and DXB (see Figure 22.6). DOH only has two routes that comprise at least 1 per cent of the market share, that is, India–US (2.5 per cent) (which also comprises the most important markets for AUH and DXB), and India–UK (2.2 per cent). They are followed by Thailand–UK (0.9 per cent), UK–Pakistan, UK–Australia, Germany–Thailand, US–Pakistan and India–Italy, all of which have a market share of 0.8 per cent. The remaining five top pair of markets are China–Nigeria (0.7 per cent), Sri Lanka–UK, Thailand–France and UK–Nepal (all with 0.6 per cent), and Spain–China (0.5 per cent).

The countries with the highest market share for transit passengers through DOH, are the UK (six pairs or 46.1 per cent of the 13 routes with more than 0.5 per cent of the market share), India and Thailand (three pairs or 23 per cent), Pakistan and the US (two pairs or 15.4 per cent), and Australia, China, France, Germany, Italy, Nigeria, Spain and Sri Lanka with only one pair each (7.7 per cent).

Currently, Doha represents the biggest competitor for Dubai and Abu Dhabi. In terms of air route development, Doha has built a strong and successful strategy with Qatar Airways operating more than 160 different routes, with an additional seven to be added in 2017 (Qatar Airways 2016). Many of these routes are served exclusively by Qatar Airways, such as some to Africa and Eastern Europe (Mayasandra 2011), thereby distinguishing Qatar from its competitors, Emirates and Etihad. Furthermore, a new-build airport in Doha, which is especially designed to accommodate A380 planes, suggests that Qatar is paving its way to becoming a serious world hub in the Middle East (O'Connell 2011). Some of the strategies that Doha has deployed to attract higher numbers of tourists have already proven to be successful in Dubai, Singapore and Abu Dhabi. For example, Qatar Airways offers free tours of Doha for all transiting passengers staying between five and 12 hours (*Gulf Times* 2014) while, since 2016, Qatar has offered a 96-hours visa-free pass for all transiting passengers regardless of nationality (Badawi 2016). As for other Middle East destinations, Doha transit tourism heavily depends on air route development, as well as aviation and tourism authorities working together to continue to develop Doha as a hub and tourism destination.

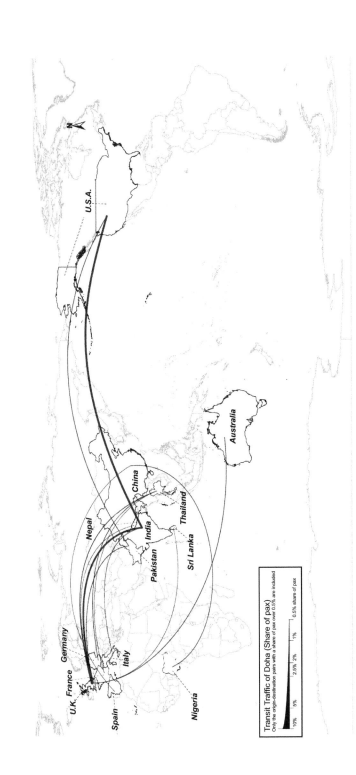

Figure 22.6 Origin–destination air transport passenger country market using Doha as a transit airport

Note: Average 2010–2015 data for routes with more than 0.5% of the market share.
Source: AirportIS 2016.

Conclusion

The close partnership between air transport providers and tourism authorities is creating new air routes and opening unforeseen opportunities for transit tourism and economic growth. The fulfilment of this growth depends on the successful engagement of a large number of stakeholders, an area which requires the consolidation of the academic research conducted so far.

The Middle East has positioned itself as one of the fastest growing tourism regions in the world. As discussed earlier in this chapter, this development is led by the UAE, followed by Qatar, with Turkey aspiring to become a transit destination. The constant growth in tourist numbers, including transit passengers, has been influenced by the introduction of new routes and strategic and partnership promotion of the Middle East cities as 'must see', high-class destinations.

Initial research on this topic, conducted predominantly between 1985 and 2000 (Swan 2002), identified the increase in air route frequency as the predominant way of developing air traffic worldwide. Frequency has been increased through a variety of methods, including the economic deregulation of the air transport sector, and has boosted the development of new routes; advances in technology have allowed for higher capacity aircraft and better performance; and finally, the overall global economic climate has created more potential for the establishment of new routes. The Middle East carriers have capitalised on this favourable environment, enabling them to attain the highest goal in the air transport industry: the development of long-haul routes (Weber & Williams 2001). Some of the key, specific factors that enable them to achieve this goal include their geographical location, liberal regulations, the use of a modern fleet and innovative airlines (Weber & Williams 2001). It is within this context that the Gulf States' three main carriers, Emirates, Etihad and Qatar Airways, were analysed in this chapter, considering their impressive achievements in traffic growth.

Despite the growth in new international flights within the overall Middle East region, some countries have been affected by unstable political environments and terrorism threats. For example, Israel experienced a consistent decrease in the number of flights between 2006 and 2010. Similarly, Iran and Tunisia experienced a significant decline in 2014 and 2015. In contrast, research on the Arabian travel market conducted by Global Futures and Foresight (2007) has forecasted that Saudi Arabia will overtake the leading position in the number of international arrivals by 2020 with almost 45 million tourists arriving or transiting by air, followed by Turkey, UAE, Egypt and Jordan. However, in today's world of constant political and economic turmoil, it is very difficult to predict the future of tourism destinations. Furthermore, it will take countries such as Syria, Libya and Iraq, whose infrastructure has been severely destroyed or damaged, a long time to recover in order to support a prosperous tourism industry. Technological developments may also threaten the future of air hubs and transit tourism destinations as new generation aircraft are capable of flying longer distances, thereby eliminating the need to make stopovers en route. For example, Qantas recently announced the commencement of a direct service between Perth (Australia) and London (18 hours) in 2018, with additional, similar flights to be launched in the future (Eddie & Peters 2016). This would allow the airlines to bypass the Middle East as a connecting transit point. Thus, the turbulent political situation and rapid technological progress are posing the following question to all Middle East countries: Do they have a strong and innovative strategy for developing new routes and tourism income?

References

Abu Dhabi Airports (2016) 'Abu Dhabi—Economy & Destination'. Available online: www.adac.ae/english/doing-business-with-us/airline-development/abu-dhabi-economy-destination (Accessed 12 January 2017).

AirportIS (2016) *IATA Airport Intelligence Services (AirportIS) Database*. Available online: www.iata.org/services/statistics/intelligence/airportis/Pages/index.aspx (Accessed 10 December 2016).

AmeInfo (2016) 'Dubai tourism numbers: DTCM reveals top 3 countries'. 17 November. Available online: http://ameinfo.com/travel/dubai-tourism-numbers-dctm-reveals-top-3-countries/ (Accessed 10 January 2017).

ASM (2009) 'Industry trends and climate survey: Interim research results'. Live Webinar, July.

Badawi, N. (2016) 'New free four-day transit visa now available in Qatar'. Available online: https://dohanews.co/new-free-four-day-transit-visa-now-available-in-qatar/ (Accessed 12 January 2017).

Burghardt, A.F. (1971) 'A hypothesis about gateway cities', *Annals of the Association of American Geographers*, 61(2): 269–285.

Carrington, D. (2014) 'How new airline routes are reshaping the world'. Available online: http://edition.cnn.com/2013/11/12/business/looking-for-an-emerging-market-airline-routes/ (Accessed 10 January 2017).

Chen, C.A., & Lee, H.L. (2012) 'Developing Taiwan into the tourist transport centre of East Asia', *Tourism Economics*, 18(6): 1401–1411.

Clark, J. (2016) 'Istanbul New Airport shaping up as a hub for the 21st century'. Available online: www.thenational.ae/business/the-life/istanbul-new-airport-shaping-up-as-a-hub-for-the-21st-century (Accessed 12 January 2017).

Dubai International Airport (2016) 'Dubai International Airport'. Available online: www.dubaiairports.ae/docs/default-source/airline-development-microsite/doc1_dxb-airport-and-market-facts.pdf?sfvrsn=6 (Accessed 11 January 2017).

Elsheshtawy, Y. (2010) *Dubai: Behind an Urban Spectacle*. London: Routledge.

Eddie, R., & Peters, D. (2016) 'Will we soon be able to fly Australia to London DIRECT? Qantas predicts non-stop 18-hour flights to Europe "within a year" after taking delivery of new Dreamliners'. Available online: www.dailymail.co.uk/news/article-3740892/First-direct-flights-Australia-Europe-new-Dreamliners- Qantas.html (Accessed 13 January 2017).

Global Futures and Foresight (2007) 'The future of travel and tourism in the Middle East—A vision to 2020'. Available online: www.thegff.com/Articles/109671/Global_Futures_and/Reports/Travel_and_Tourism/Travel_and_Tourism.aspx (Accessed 10 January 2017).

Goodovitch, T. (1996) 'A theory of air transport development', *Transportation Planning and Technology*, 20(1): 1–13. doi:10.1080/03081069608717576.

Graham, A. (2013) *Managing Airports: An International Perspective*, 4th edn. London: Routledge.

Gulf Times (2014) 'Qatar Airways offers free Doha city tours for transit passengers'. Available online: www.gulf-times.com/story/383460/Qatar-Airways-offers-free-Doha-city-tours-for-tran (Accessed 12 January 2017).

Halpern, N., & Graham, A. (2015) 'Airport route development: A survey of current practice', *Tourism Management*, 46: 213–221. doi:10.1016/j.tourman.2014.06.011

Halpern, N., & Graham, A. (2016) 'Factors affecting airport route development activity and performance', *Journal of Air Transport Management*, 56, Part B: 69–78. doi:10.1016/j.jairtraman.2016.04.016

Hoyle, B., & Knowles, R. (eds) (1998) *Modern Transport Geography*. 2nd edn. Chichester: Wiley.

IATA (International Air Transport Association) (2012) 'Airlines to welcome 3.6 billion passengers in 2016'. Available online: www.iata.org/pressroom/pr/pages/2012-12-06-01.aspx (Accessed 13 April 2016).

IATA (2013) 'New Year's Day 2014 marks 100 years of commercial aviation'. Available online: www.iata.org/pressroom/pr/Pages/2013-12-30-01.aspx (Accessed 13 April 2016).

Lawton, L., & Weaver, D. (2017) 'Destination brands Dubai and Abu Dhabi: Bitter rivalry or strategic partnership?' in H. Almuhrzi, H. Alriyami, & N. Scott (eds), *Tourism in the Arab World: An Industry Perspective* (pp. 161–174). Bristol: Channel View Publications.

Lohmann, G., & Vianna, C. (2016) 'Air route suspension: The role of stakeholder engagement and aviation and non-aviation factors', *Journal of Air Transport Management*, 53: 199–210. doi:10.1016/j.jairtraman.2016.03.007

Lohmann, G., Albers, S., Koch, B., & Pavlovich, K. (2009) 'From hub to tourist destination: An explorative study of Singapore and Dubai's aviation-based transformation', *Journal of Air Transport Management*, 15(5): 205–211.

Mariot, P. (1983) *Geografia Cestovného Ruchu* [Tourism Geography]. Bratislava: Veda.

Mayasandra, V. (2011) 'Qatar Airways expands via niche markets, opening 24 new routes in 2 years' time'. Available online: www.airlinetrends.com/2011/12/11/qatar-airways-niche-markets/ (Accessed 29 September 2016).

O'Connell, J.F. (2011) 'The rise of the Arabian Gulf carriers: An insight into the business model of Emirates Airline', *Journal of Air Transport Management*, 17(6): 339–346.

Oum, T.H., Adler, N., & Yu, C. (2006) 'Privatization, corporatization, ownership forms and their effects on the performance of the world's major airports', *Journal of Air Transport Management*, 12(3): 109–121.

Pearce, D.G. (2001) 'Towards a regional analysis of tourism in Southeast Asia', in P. Teo, T.C. Chang, T.C., & K.C. Ho (eds), *Interconnected Worlds: Tourism in Southeast Asia* (pp. 27–43). Oxford: Pergamon.

Qatar Airways (2016) 'Going places together: Fly to more than 150 destinations with Qatar Airways'. Available online: www.qatarairways.com/en-qa/destinations.html (Accessed 19 January 2017).

Sharp, T. (2012) 'World's First Commercial Airline—The Greatest Moments in Flight'. Available online: www.space.com/16657-worlds-first-commercial-airline-the-greatest-moments-in-flight.html (Accessed 13 April 2016).

Spasojevic, B., Lohmann, G., & Scott, N. (2018) 'Air transport and tourism–a systematic literature review (2000–2014)', *Current Issues in Tourism*, 21(9): 975–997.

Steiner, C. (2010) 'From heritage to hyper-reality? Tourism destination development in the Middle East between Petra and the palm', *Journal of Tourism and Cultural Change*, 8(4): 240–253.

STRAIR (2005) *Air Service Development for Regional Agencies: Strategy, Best Practice and Results*. Brussels: STRAIR.

Swan, W.M. (2002) 'Airline route developments: A review of history', *Journal of Air Transport Management*, 8(5): 349–353. doi:10.1016/S0969-6997(02)00015-7

Thelle, M.H., Pedersen, T.T., & Frederik, H. (2012) *Airport Competition in Europe*. Copenhagen: Copenhagen Economics Ed.

UNWTO (2007) 'International Recommendations on Tourism Statistics (IRTS)'. Available online: http://unstats.un.org/unsd/tradeserv/EGTS/IRTS%20-%20the%20provisional%20draft.pdf (Accessed 19 January 2017).

UNWTO (2015) 'International tourist arrivals up 4% reach a record 1.2 billion in 2015'. Available online: http://media.unwto.org/press-release/2016-01-18/international-tourist-arrivals-4-reach-record-12-billion-2015 (Accessed 19 January 2017).

UNWTO (2016) 'Tourism highlights'. Available online: www2.unwto.org/publication/unwto-tourism-highlights-2016-edition (Accessed 19 January 2017).

Visit Dubai (2016) 'Dubai Tourism 2016: Performance Report'. Available online: www.visitdubai.com/en/tourism-performance-report (Accessed 19 January 2017).

Warnock-Smith, D., & O'Connell, J.F. (2011) 'The impact of air policy on incoming tourist traffic: The contrasting cases of the Caribbean Community and the Middle-East', *Journal of Transport Geography*, 19(2): 265–274.

Weber, M., & Williams, G. (2001) 'Drivers of long-haul air transport route development', *Journal of Transport Geography*, 9(4): 243–254. doi:10.1016/S0966-6923(01)00018-7.

Zhang, Y., & Findlay, C. (2014) 'Air transport policy and its impacts on passenger traffic and tourist flows', *Journal of Air Transport Management*, 34: 42–48.

PART VII

Contemporary trends

23

HALAL TOURISM

A growing market on a global stage

Asad Mohsin and Chris Ryan

Introduction

The tourism industry's uniqueness, dynamics and resilience are evident from data that show it continues to record growth despite adverse events like the Gulf War, terrorism attacks, health scares and other crises. The *Tourism 2020 Vision* of the World Tourism Organization (UNWTO 2014) forecasts that tourism will generate 1.56 billion international arrivals by the year 2020. This figure represents a growth rate of 4.1 per cent from 1995 to 2020. In 1995, long-haul travel accounted for 18 per cent; by 2020 it is expected to increase to 24 per cent (UNWTO 2014). It is worth noting where the growth in tourist numbers is being generated and what the industry's level of preparedness is to attract those markets.

A report titled *Global Muslim Lifestyle Travel Market* published by the Dinar Standard and Crescent Rating (2012) notes that Muslim travellers are a major niche market. Their characteristics, according to the report, represent a young and affluent segment that has seemingly spent some US$126.1 billion in outbound expenditures on leisure and business; a figure that excludes spending on religious travel for the annual hajj or umrah. The expansion in Muslim travel and related growth in expenditures is largely from the Muslim majority countries of the Middle East (Battour, Ismail, & Battor 2010, 2012; Dinar Standard and Crescent Rating 2012). From an industry perspective, a key concern is how best to meet the demands of this market in a way that is profitable and sustainable (Timothy & Ron 2016).

People's religious needs have implications for the hospitality and tourism industries (Weidenfeld 2006; Weidenfeld & Ron 2008). The unique requirements of Muslim travellers fundamentally relate to halal food, a family-friendly environment, gender-related nuances, prayer needs and leisure activities accepted within the Islamic norms. Many of these issues, however, are not inconsistent with the needs of non-Muslims, and indeed halal food can meet the dietary requirements of many regarding assurances as to quality and freshness.

Before exploring halal tourism, it is important to understand fundamental characteristics of Muslim consumers to win their trust and provide for their needs. This chapter examines their consumption patterns, and seeks to address how service providers can gain their patronage. The chapter considers tourism industry opportunities and challenges associated with this segment as they travel for business or leisure. In particular, the chapter examines the Islamic world and Muslim consumers' beliefs, practices and consumption patterns; halal regulations and certification; Muslims' consumption patterns; halal tourism's definition and development; and opportunities and challenges related to developing halal tourism.

The Islamic world and Muslim consumers' beliefs, practices and consumption

The current population of Muslims is around 1.5 billion, and it is expected to reach 2.2 billion by 2030 (Carboni, Perelli, & Sistu 2017). Though the word Islam means peace, from the spiritual perspective it also means peace and complete submission to Allah (God). Muslims are widely distributed around the world, representing different ethnicities, cultures, nationalities and languages. Their core beliefs are the oneness of Allah; His angels; His messengers (e.g. Abraham, Moses, Jesus and Mohammad, peace be upon them all); and His books, *The Day of Judgement* and *Divine Destiny: good or bad*. The core practices of Muslim consumers include prayers five times a day; *zakat* (charity); fasting during the month of Ramadan; pilgrimage (the hajj); and being a good person (i.e. being a good neighbour and an honest businessperson). Sources of beliefs and practices for Muslims are the Qur'an; the traditions of the Prophet; the consensus of learned Muslims on emerging issues derived from the Qur'an and traditions of the Prophet (Peace be Upon Him), and compliance with the laws of the land as long as they do not contradict God's laws. Muslim consumers see Islam as a complete way of life, and everything they do within the norms of their faith, including eating, doing business, travel, politics and even entering the toilet can be seen as acts of worship.

Muslims' dietary needs adhere to several concepts and practices, such as food being *halal* (lawful), *haram* (unlawful), *makrooh* (discouraged) and *mashbooh* (suspect). In brief, *halal* dietary consumption refers to properly slaughtered cattle, sheep, goats, deer, camels and chickens based upon Islamic teachings. Not all seafood needs to be slaughtered, and all non-poisonous vegetables and fruits are considered *halal*. In contrast, carrion, swine including all products and ingredients derived from pork, flowing or congealed blood, foods dedicated to idols, intoxicants of all types, carnivorous animals with fangs, and birds of prey with sharp claws are *haram*. Religious regulations have had a significant influence on food consumption since the dawn of time. In contemporary society, however, Dugan (1994: 80) suggests that 'Being able to adhere to religious groups' food-service requirements could become a marketing tool for those operators who are willing to learn about food prohibitions, preparation, and service'.

Though dietary requirements are straightforward, some debate and confusion surrounds other tourism-related consumption patterns amongst Muslims, such as entertainment, dress and touristic activities. Carboni, Perelli and Sistu (2017) highlight that the application of Islamic beliefs to particular markets and products is extremely complex and dynamic. The levels of acceptance of dress codes vary from the use of the *hijab* (a headscarf worn by Muslim women that is widely worn in the West and comes in many styles and colors) and the *niqab* (a veil for the face that leaves the area around the eyes clear, which may be worn with a separate eye veil with an accompanying headscarf) to the *burqa* (the most concealing of all Islamic veils), which is a one-piece veil that covers the face and body, often leaving just a mesh screen to see through. Equally, it is not uncommon to observe Muslim women wearing trousers, loose-fitting shirts, and a hijab in the West. While participating in individual sports and other activities they often wear dresses like the *burqini* (a dress with head cover used for surfing or swimming), or other appropriate attire, but usually with a hijab. Business operators will need to assess Muslim consumers' needs based on the heterogeneity they reflect, which usually is the case with most consumers, whether Muslim or non-Muslim.

What is more important for Muslim consumers is the assurance of genuineness of the products and services they are expected to consume, especially food. The two major components of halal tourism are food and accommodation, and travellers from Muslim countries frequently look for guarantees that they will be able to access halal products or specific Muslim-friendly services. This assurance is often achieved through halal certification. Indeed, for his part, Stephenson (2014) states that the hospitality industry needs to play a proactive role in working with designated international bodies to develop criteria for global certifications.

Halal regulation and certification

Halal certification is issued by an established incorporated body in any country or city that draws knowledge and decisions based on the following sources of Islamic law: the Qur'an, Sharia law, the *hadith* (traditions of the Prophet), and the consensus of learned Muslims on emerging issues derived from the Qur'an and the traditions of the Prophet (PBUH).

While the words of God were revealed to other prophets such as Moses, Jesus and Adam, the Qur'an contains the word of God (Allah SWT) as revealed to the Prophet Mohammad (PBUH). Followers of Islam adhere to religious practices as an integral part of life as described in the Qur'an. Islam encourages leading a good life and the well-being of all humans through socio-economic justice and brotherhood. A balance between humankind's spiritual and material needs is also stressed (Rice & Al-Mossawi 2002). Sharia law is derived from the *hadith* and the Qur'an (Esposito & Donner 1999). Muslims practice ethics derived from divine revelations based on *quh* (ugliness, unsuitable) versus *husn* (beauty and suitability). Although the Qur'an and the *hadith*, as the primary sources of law, address most human actions, any variance or contextual differences are resolved through the *fiqh*, which represents the consensus of Muslim scholars and covers various aspects of law, including civil law, political, social, constitutional and procedural law as well as religious law (Mohsin, Ramli, & Alkhulayfi 2016).

Halal certification is a critical factor that enables Muslim consumers to make informed decisions. It provides evidence that products and services follow what is permitted for consumption based on Islamic ethics. It is the religious obligation of the issuing authority to ensure compliance on the part of suppliers of foodstuffs and services seeking certification. The significance of halal certification has grown internationally as the halal market is one of the fastest growing segments in several non-Muslim countries with a global estimated expenditure volume of US$580 billion a year and an annual growth of 7 per cent (Henderson 2016; Ismaeel & Blaim 2012). While certification is common in the food and financial industries, it is spreading to other sectors such as cosmetics and pharmaceuticals, in addition to tourism and entertainment (Ismaeel & Blaim 2012). The hotel sector is eager to cater to travellers from the Middle East and other Muslim-majority countries, as figures cited by the UNWTO (2014) report that residents of Arabian Gulf countries spend US$20 billion on vacations every year, led by Saudi tourists whose expenditures top US$8.5 billion. In a bid to encourage travellers from the Gulf to visit its hotels in Germany, Hyatt issued a press release focused solely on promoting the fact that its four properties in the country offer Arabic-speaking staff, authentic culinary specialities and prayer carpets (Henderson 2003). Certainly, in the last decade, there has been an increase in awareness about Islamic hospitality and the need for Sharia-compliant lodging and food services. Stephenson (2014: 157) summarises what is required for a hotel to acquire Sharia compliance to obtain halal certification, stating there are normally five essential key components:

1. Human Resources: traditional uniforms for hotel staff; dress code for female staff; prayer time provision for Muslim employees; restricted working hours for Muslim staff during Ramadan;

staff (and guest) adherence to moral codes of conduct; and guest-centric strategies underpinning service delivery.

2. Private Rooms (bedrooms and bathrooms): separate floors with rooms allocated to women and families; markers (i.e., Qibla stickers) indicating the direction of Mecca; prayer mats and copies of the Qur'an; conservative television channels; geometric and non-figurative patterns of decoration (e.g., calligraphy); beds and toilets positioned away from facing Mecca; toilets fitted with a bidet shower or health faucet; and halal-friendly complementary toiletries.

3. Dining and Banqueting Facilities: halal food with no pork; soft beverages only (i.e., no provision or consumption of alcohol); dining quarter provision for women and families in addition to public area provision; art that does not depict human and animal form; and no music expressing seductive and controversial messages.

4. Other Public Facilities: no casino or gambling machines; separate leisure facilities (including swimming pools and spas) for both sexes; female and male prayer rooms equipped with the Qur'an (also available at the front desk); built-in wudhu facilities located outside prayer rooms; toilets facing away from Mecca; and art that does not depict human and animal form.

5. Business Operation: ethical marketing and promotion; corporate social responsibility strategies (linked to Islamic values) and philanthropic donations; and transactions and investments in accordance to principles and practices associated with Islamic banking, accounting, and finance.'

Given that the outbound halal market is not limited to the Middle East, for it can also originate from the Asia Pacific, Europe, the US or the UK, it is pertinent that authentic and certified halal tourism and hospitality services and products are available and promoted to attract this segment. Several countries such as Australia, New Zealand, India, Indonesia, Malaysia, Singapore, South Korea, Japan, Taiwan, Thailand, Turkey, the US, the UK, France and Germany have all established authorised associations or government bodies, or are currently working to do so, to issue halal certification and protect Muslim consumers from the consumption of *haram* products (Mohsin et al. 2016; Razzaq, Hall, & Prayag 2016; Samori, Md Salleh, & Khalid 2016). In comprehending Muslim consumers' beliefs, practices and consumption patterns, and the role halal certification plays in winning their trust and business, it is also worth exploring their consumption patterns to assess the volume of business that this segment could generate.

Muslim travellers' consumption patterns

Muslim consumers' expenditures are driven by the desire to ensure that they spend only on halal products and earn the blessings of the Almighty. This approach has generated an Islamic economy that now encompasses several industries including finance and banking, food, family-friendly vacations and activities, fashion and clothing, cosmetics and personal care, pharmaceuticals, and media and recreation. The rest of this chapter concentrates on the consumer patterns applicable to food, travel and tourism and related activities.

Halal food consumption

Some verses from the Qur'an relate to food consumption, including:

> O mankind, eat from whatever is on earth [that is] lawful and good and do not follow the footsteps of Satan. Indeed, he is to you a clear enemy.
>
> *(Al-Quran 2:168)*

He has only forbidden to you dead animals, blood, the flesh of swine, and that which has been dedicated to other than Allah. But whoever is forced [by necessity], neither desiring [it] nor transgressing [its limit]—then indeed, Allah is Forgiving and Merciful.

(Al-Quran 16:115)

O you who have believed, indeed, intoxicants, gambling, [sacrificing on] stone alters [to other than Allah], and divining arrows are but defilement from the work of Satan, so avoid it that you may be successful.

(Al-Quran 15:90)

Guided by the Qur'an and Sharia law, Muslim consumers are mindful of what foods they consume. A report by Thomson Reuters and Dinar Standard (2013) states that Muslim consumers globally spent US$1.088 billion on food in 2012, or 16.6 per cent of global expenditures. The report also estimates that by 2018, the figure is expected to reach US$1.626 billion, representing 17.4 per cent of global expenditures. On the other hand, awareness about this huge food market grows at a much slower rate than the market itself. As yet, however, any move towards a globally accepted halal certification remains fragmented and a challenge that could have implications for improving awareness about the potential of this market. Having said that, the progress made in generating Sharia-compliant hotels in several Muslim countries needs to be acknowledged (Battour et al. 2010; Smith & Hindley 2017). Halal restaurants, cafés and fast-food outlets are also becoming a more common sight in many non-Islamic countries as businesses respond to the commercial opportunities the Muslim market presents (Timothy & Ron 2016; Zannierah, Marzuki, Hall, & Ballantine 2012). Thomson Reuters and Dinar Standard (2013) acknowledge that despite halal food being a one trillion dollar market, as yet there are no global brands representing or being dedicated to it.

Travel and tourism consumption

Some Qur'anic verses that discuss travel and considerations incumbent on Muslims are as follows:

Say, [O Muhammad], 'Travel through the land and observe how He began creation. Then Allah will produce the final creation. Indeed Allah, over all things, is competent.'

(Al-Quran 29:20)

And proclaim to the people the Hajj [pilgrimage]; they will come to you on foot and on every lean camel; they will come from every distant pass. That they may witness benefits for themselves and mention the name of Allah on known days over what He has provided for them of [sacrificial] animals. So eat of them and feed the miserable and poor. Then let them end their untidiness and fulfil their vows and perform Tawaf around the ancient House.

(Al-Quran 22:27–29)

Though the relationship between travel and religion has been widely addressed in the tourism literature, theoretical perspectives in the context of Islam remain scarce (Battour et al. 2010). Sharia teachings about tourism, on the one hand, encourage Muslims to travel the world, subject to the caveat that they are forbidden to travel to places where sins are committed through alcohol consumption, corruption and immoral acts.

As previously noted, Muslim consumers are identified as one of the fastest growing market segment. Of the total number, approximately 42 per cent are under the age of

30 years. This makes it an important group for businesses and global marketers looking for potential opportunities in the youth market (Stephenson 2014). The growth and increasing disposable income of this group has also helped generate growth in outbound tourism as they become better educated, acquire well remunerated jobs and increasingly access the world through smartphones like their counterparts in the West and Asia (UNWTO 2014). Despite these trends, it appears that (akin to the market for halal food) awareness about the specific needs of Muslim travellers remains low and unclear for most tourism businesses. Given the more than US$120 billion in expenditures by Muslim travellers, it appears that many have yet to grasp the opportunities being presented. Thomson Reuters and Dinar Standard (2013) also estimate that by 2018, spending on travel by this market will have grown to approximately US$181 billion.

The Qur'an encourages Muslims to travel to visit friends and relatives and appreciate the beautiful world of God (Allah SWT). From a more secular perspective, it can be noted that the Islamic Development Bank with its 53 Muslim member countries has also expressed support for tourism for social and economic reasons (Henderson 2003). Hence, the recommendation for Muslims to travel as tourists is both religious and social.

Halal tourism: Definition and increased visibility

While there may be variations in its meaning, halal tourism is defined here as 'a tourism product and service that meets the needs of Muslim travellers to facilitate their worship and dietary requirements based on Islamic teachings and values'. An alternative view is suggested by Battour and Ismail (2016: 151) who defined it as '...any tourism object or action which is permissible according to Islamic teachings to use or engage by Muslims in [the] tourism industry'. Generally, the majority of definitions offered by scholars (e.g. El-Gohary 2016) state that the core of halal tourism rests in an adherence to Muslim religious practices. While this is understandable, Ryan (2016) comments that this process of differentiation has both a positive and a negative aspect. Processes of differentiation are the basis of any market segmentation policy, but he notes that in the minds of many there remains an entanglement between halal tourism and the wider issues that surround some parts of the Islamic world:

> In a world where differences have become so important, (especially in the tangled aftermath of Western intrusion into the Arab world that has placed the Middle East into positions of stark contrast with mainstream western democracies), research that looks at both difference and similarity may well have value. To quantify the extent to which members of the Islamic faith share their human condition with those of other religious or secular belief systems would not go amiss in this world of the second decade of the twenty-first century. So perhaps now researchers need to progress from just description and observation of halal tourism to more analytical processes to achieve better understanding of this phenomenon.
>
> *(Ryan 2016: 123)*

In short, there is a need also to note the similarities between this form of tourism and the wider context of tourism or that which focuses on the needs of other faiths. Alsawafi, Ryan and Mohsin (2016) noted in a study of Muslim tourists in New Zealand, that one notable aspect was that they wished to visit the same places and attractions as non-Muslim visitors, and equally it is the same characteristics of New Zealand's attractions (notably its landscape) that appealed to them as to other tourists. One criticism of this perspective is that it fails to distinguish between observed behaviour and the motivation for the behaviour and the interpretation attributed to it (Ryan 2002), but the observation should assure that the tourism industry focuses not only on this group but also other groups.

Ryan (2016) also provides a review of the evolution of halal tourism and notes that the early literature tended to focus on the physical requirements of the hajj. The works of Morrison (1979) and Khogali and Al-Khawashk (1980) are examples where, for instance, the impacts of heatstroke on pilgrims were studied. Equally, Ryan notes the changes of terminology, in that writers up to about 2009 (e.g. Henderson 2009) tended to use the phrase 'Islamic tourism', but with the appearance of the paper by Battour, Ismail and Battor (2010) and the work of Islamic scholars being published in English, the term 'halal tourism' has become more accepted amongst researchers and the industry.

While the term 'halal tourism' is relatively recent, it is gaining visibility and clout in both academic and industry circles. In terms of symposia, conferences and conventions that specifically address the concerns of halal tourism, as far as the writers are aware, the first were the New Zealand Halal Tourism Conference in 2013 (and subsequently in 2015 and 2016), the World Tourism Organization's First Regional Seminar on the Contribution of Islamic Culture and its Impact on the Asian Tourism Market held in Bandar Seri Begawan, Brunei, in November 2015 (held jointly with the Ministry of Primary Resources and Tourism of Brunei Darussalam). Again, in late 2015, the First World Halal Travel Summit and Exhibition was held in Abu Dhabi, UAE, which also hosted the Second Summit in November 2016. This summit is planned to become an annual event.

Halal tourism: Opportunities and challenges

If we consider the commercial context of halal tourism, there are implications for both Muslim and non-Muslim tourism business operators. As noted above, the growth and expenditure patterns of Muslim travellers provide significant commercial opportunities. Indeed, the global halal market or potential market is larger than that of outbound expenditures originating in the US, Germany, China or the UK in 2012 (Thomson Reuters & Dinar Standard 2013). As service providers recognise the opportunity, there is a growing trend in Muslim majority countries, such as the UAE, Turkey, Egypt, Malaysia and Indonesia, for hotels to promote commercial accommodations based on Islamic values to address the needs of Muslim tourists better (Samori et al. 2016). This is also occurring in other countries. For example, as noted earlier, the Hyatt's properties in Germany offer Arabic-speaking staff, Muslim-friendly food, and prayer carpets (Henderson 2003). The potential to develop halal tourism in diverse destinations is significant (Hassan & Hall 2003). Stephenson (2014) also suggests that the appeal may not be restricted to Islamic travellers, but such campaigns may also attract non-Muslim guests who are seeking different cultural experiences and a healthy lifestyle. The halal market traditionally seeks a family-oriented environment in commercial accommodations based on Islamic values that may appeal to a wider family market. Additionally, the growth of core and potential supplementary markets, such as families, may also trigger opportunities to establish an internationally applicable halal concept in commercial accommodations that could be certified and monitored by recognised government and/or religious community organisations.

The current challenge for halal tourism is the perception that it is some form of religious tourism that is different to normal leisure types of travel and tourism. This clearly is not the case. As previously noted, in the present circumstances of the Middle East and North Africa, and poor relations between the West and especially that part of the Muslim world located between the Gulf countries and Pakistan, these circumstances have complicated and inhibited interest in halal tourism. Islam has become associated with conservatism, oppression, terrorism and anti-Western sentiment (Armstrong 2001). These perceptions are not aided by limited research on what Muslim tourists are really looking for, how different they are to other tourists and what those differences are. Appropriate promotion of halal tourism should help overcome serial misconceptions and become a means of building bridges.

Conclusion

This latter observation leads to the first conclusion, which is that the development of halal tourism just might become a means whereby misconceptions might be corrected. Differences in dress and customs, however, require open-mindedness on both sides, and for this to succeed, people must get past shallow perceptions based on perceived dissimilarities. Some within the tourism academy believe that tourism can be a force for peace (D'Amore 2009; Moufakkir & Kelly 2010), and it is hoped that both tourist and host can better learn about each other as more Muslims travel and similarities are shared more than differences accentuated.

A second conclusion is that the halal market is significant with strong spending power. The halal and haram items listed earlier should indicate that hospitality towards Muslim tourists is not overly onerous or difficult to achieve. Equally, as in any belief system, some people are more conservative than others. It is relatively easy to meet the dietary needs of many Muslims. If food providers are uncertain about whether their meats are halal, salads and vegetables are generally acceptable, and for many, most fish is equally acceptable. Hotels with fitness rooms and pools might be able to consider temporal zoning so that there are women-only times—something some non-Muslim women might also appreciate. The requirement here is that the times are announced well in advance if the hotel has only one pool, which most do. As well, in today's Internet age, it seems unnecessary for hotels to offer 'adult TV' channels.

Third, as is increasingly recognised by different countries in their promotional efforts aimed at the halal market, the provision of information is a key requirement. Not every Muslim will pray five times a day or go to a mosque on Fridays when travelling (and indeed many Islamic authorities recognise that concessions can be made when members of the faith are travelling, are fatigued, may not be well or are pregnant), but by providing information as to the direction of Mecca, the location of the nearest mosque, where halal food is available, or where a prayer room may be provided, service providers permit Islamic travellers to make their own decisions regarding how they will fulfil their religious obligations. In this way, services will meet their obligations as hospitable hosts and win customer loyalty.

Fourth, one potential challenge to developing halal tourism is that such an Islam-friendly 'brand' might deter other, non-Muslim travellers from utilising services or avoiding a destination altogether. As Battour and Ismail (2016: 153) noted:

> The marketing of Halal tourism is not an easy task because of the variance between the demands of non-Muslim tourists and Muslim tourists. The non-Muslim tourist may decide not to travel to a particular destination in the absence of certain attributes (Battour et al. 2011; Battour et al. 2017). Therefore, the challenge for Muslim destinations is how to cater for the non-Muslim tourist and satisfy their needs without clashing with Islamic teaching. For example, some hotels declare on their website that they are a Shariah-compliant hotel and this may not be attractive to non-Muslim guests. Therefore, Halal tourism practises could be seen as constraints to tourism destination development. These constraints are a critical and big challenge to tourism planning and destination marketers. However, this could be an opportunity

for businesses to use their creativity and flexibility in catering to the different needs of Muslim and non-Muslim.

The answer is satisfying the needs of a growing market segment of significant economic importance. Halal tourism presents an opportunity to engage with more people and to learn about their stories and ways of seeing the world. It offers a chance to diversify products in ways that may also appeal to non-Muslims. It introduces variety to restaurant food and from a purely commercial perspective, like any market segment, halal tourism presents other consumers with unique culinary and lodging experiences. In some cases those tastes are congruent with other markets while simultaneously being incompatible with others. These types of marketing strategies are well recognised in other spheres of tourism, and the industry has proven many times that it can be successful based on branding, spatial and temporal zoning and promotional messaging to cater to the needs of many different market niches.

References

Alsawafi, A.M., Ryan, C. & Mohsin, A. (2016) 'The role of Islamic belief in determining choice of destination and behaviour at a destination: Data from Omanis holidaying overseas', 3rd Halal Marketing and Tourism Research Symposium, 3 December, University of Canterbury, Christchurch, New Zealand.

Armstrong, K. (2001) *Islam: A Short History*. London: Phoenix Press.

Battour, M.M., & Ismail, M.N. (2016) 'Halal tourism: Concepts, practises, challenges and future', *Tourism Management Perspectives*, 19: 150–154.

Battour, M.M., Ismail, M.N., & Battor, M. (2010) 'Toward a halal tourism market', *Tourism Analysis*, 15(4): 461–470.

Battour, M.M., Ismail, M.N., & Battor, M. (2011) 'The impact of destination attributes on Muslim tourists' choice', *International Journal of Tourism Research*, 13(6): 527–540.

Battour, M.M., Ismail, M.N., & Battor, M. (2012) 'The mediating role of tourist satisfaction: A study of Muslim tourists in Malaysia', *Journal of Travel & Tourism Marketing*, 29(3): 279–297.

Battour, M., Ismail, M.N., Battor, M., & Awais, M. (2017) 'Islamic tourism: An empirical examination of travel motivation and satisfaction in Malaysia', *Current Issues in Tourism*, 20(1): 50–67.

Carboni, M., Perelli, C., & Sistu, G. (2017) 'Developing tourism products in line with Islamic beliefs: Some insights from Nabeul–Hammamet', *The Journal of North African Studies*, 22(1): 87–108.

D'Amore, L. (2009) 'Peace through tourism: The birthing of a new socio-economic order', *Journal of Business Ethics*, 89(4): 559–568.

Dinar Standard and Crescent Rating (2012) 'Global Muslim lifestyle travel market: Landscape & consumer needs study for airlines, destinations & hotels/resorts'. Available online: www.dinarstandard.com/travel-study/ (Accessed 11 September 2018).

Dugan, B. (1994) 'Religion and food service', *Cornell Hotel and Restaurant Administration Quarterly*, 35(6): 80–85.

El-Gohary, H. (2016) 'Halal tourism: Is it really halal?' *Tourism Management Perspectives*, 19: 124–130.

Esposito, J.L., & Donner, F.M.G. (1999) *The Oxford History of Islam*. Oxford: Oxford University Press.

Hassan, M.W., & Hall, C.M. (2003) 'The demand for halal food among Muslim travelers in New Zealand', in C.M. Hall, L. Sharples, R. Mitchell, B. Cambourne, & N. Macionis (eds), *Food Tourism around the World: Development, Management and Markets* (pp. 81–101). Oxford: Butterworth Heinemann.

Henderson, J.C. (2003) 'Managing tourism and Islam in Peninsular Malaysia', *Tourism Management*, 24: 447–456.

Henderson, J.C. (2009) 'Islamic tourism reviewed', *Tourism Recreation Research*, 34(2): 207–211.

Henderson, J.C. (2016) 'Halal food, certification and halal tourism: Insights from Malaysia and Singapore', *Tourism Management Perspectives*, 19: 160–164.

Ismaeel, M., & Blaim, K. (2012) 'Toward applied Islamic business ethics: Responsible halal business', *Journal of Management Development*, 31(10): 1090–1100.

Khogali, M., & Al-Khawashk, M. (1980) 'Heat stroke during the Makkah pilgrimage (hajj)', *Saudi Medical Journal*, 2(2): 85.

Mohsin, A., Ramli, N., & Alkhulayfi, B.A. (2016) 'Halal tourism: Emerging opportunities', *Tourism Management Perspectives*, 19: 137–143.

Morrison, D. (1979) 'Heatstroke on the Hajj', *The Lancet*, 315(8174): 935.

Moufakkir, O., & Kelly, I. (eds) (2010) *Tourism, Progress and Peace*. Wallingford: CAB International.

Razzaq, S., Hall, C.M., & Prayag, G. (2016) 'The capacity of New Zealand to accommodate the halal tourism market—or not', *Tourism Management Perspectives*, 18: 92–97.

Rice, G., & Al-Mossawi (2002) 'The implications of Islam for advertising messages: The Middle Eastern context', *Journal of Euromarketing*, 11(3): 71–96.

Ryan, C. (2002) *The Tourist Experience*. London: Continuum.

Ryan, C. (2016) 'Halal tourism', *Tourism Management Perspectives*, 19: 121–123.

Samori, Z., Md Salleh, N.Z., & Khalid, M.M. (2016) 'Current trends on halal tourism: Cases on selected Asian countries', *Tourism Management Perspectives*, 19: 131–136.

Smith, M.K., & Hindley, C. (2017) Halal tourism: Definitions and developments. In H. Almuhrzi, H. Alriyami, & N. Scott (eds), *Tourism in the Arab World: An Industry Perspective*, pp. 118–130. Bristol: Channel View Publications.

Stephenson, M.L. (2014) 'Deciphering "Islamic hospitality": Developments, challenges and opportunities', *Tourism Management*, 40: 155–164.

Thomson Reuters and Dinar Standard (2013) *State of the Global Islamic Economy Report*. Dubai: Global Islamic Economic Summit.

Timothy, D.J., & Ron, A.S. (2016) 'Religious heritage, spiritual aliment and food for the soul', in D.J. Timothy (ed.), *Heritage Cuisines: Traditions, Identities and Tourism* (pp. 104–118). London: Routledge.

UNWTO (2014) UNWTO Facts and Figures. *Tourism 2020 Vision*. Available online: www.unwto.org/facts/menu.html (Accessed 11 September 2018).

Weidenfeld, A. (2006) 'Religious needs in the hospitality industry', *Tourism and Hospitality Research*, 6(2): 143–159.

Weidenfeld, A., & Ron, A. (2008) 'Religious needs in the tourism industry', *Anatolia*, 19(2): 357–361.

Zannierah, S., Marzuki, S., Hall, C.M., & Ballantine, P.W. (2012) 'Restaurant managers' perspectives on halal certification', *Journal of Islamic Marketing*, 3(1): 47–58.

24

MUCH ADO ABOUT HALAL TOURISM

Religion, religiosity or none of the above?

Omar Moufakkir, Yvette Reisinger and Dhoha AlSaleh

Introduction

Much of the literature on Arab/Muslim tourism revolves around the importance of religion in this group's tourist behaviour. Subsequently, the contemporary literature in the field has gravitated around halal tourism. Halal tourism is a recent phenomenon that has attracted the attention of tourism and hospitality academics and the industry. This form of tourism is defined in relation to activities and behaviours that are Islamic and Sharia-compliant. It identifies numerous rules and principles that guide the behaviour and activities of Muslims. Consequently, Muslims are expected to participate in that which is *halal* (allowed) and dissociate from that which is *haram* (forbidden) (Battour & Ismail 2015). All Muslims are to be guided by those principles.

However, the heart of the matter is that there is Islam (religion) and there are Muslims (individuals), which means that not all that Muslims do is religious. There are religious Muslims, but there are Muslim people who are not religious; some are part-time religious. This being said, there has been much ado about halal tourism in the tourism industry and in academic research. Like Battour and Ismail (2015: 3), we are of the opinion that the term 'Muslim-friendly holidays' and Muslim-friendly destinations are more appropriate to be used instead of 'halal holidays' and halal destinations. The word halal in halal destinations is catchy and trendy, yet it is inappropriate, deceptive and misleading. Not only is halal tourism confused with Islamic tourism (Battour & Ismail 2015; Smith & Hindley 2017), it is also, mistakenly associated with, for example, 'Travellers who wish to maintain Muslim principles (i.e. prayer, food, cultural norms) while travelling' (a definition of halal travellers proposed by Context Consulting (2016)). Nonetheless, not all Muslim tourists are halal tourists.

For halal tourism to exist there must be halal tourists. Indeed, reports indicate that the demand for halal tourism has been growing. For example, according to the Amadeus report,

> The Halal Tourism sector was estimated to be valued at $145 billion in 2014 … Halal travel is one of the fastest growing travel sectors in the world, with an estimated growth rate of 4.8% against the 3.8% industry average.
>
> *(Context Consulting 2016: 8)*

However, while more is known about the supply side of halal tourism, little is known about its demand side. In reality, little is known about halal tourists' behaviours. Much of what is known about halal tourists is that they prefer to patronise halal establishments. Indeed, a few hotel accommodations and eating-places have been 'halalised' to attract this market. However, there is more to tourism and to what is halal and what halal tourists do than selecting accommodations and restaurants based on some halal principles. This chapter offers a light critique of halal tourism with the purpose of dissipating certain confusion about the relationship between Muslims, Islam, halal tourism and halal tourists, and advance an understanding about this tourism phenomenon (also see Battour & Ismail 2015).

Halal tourism and religiosity

Halal tourists represent a segment of the Muslim tourism market. Associating Arab and Muslim tourists with religion or, for that matter, with what is haram and what is halal is misleading. This association disregards between and within group differences in motivation, preference, experience, constraints and expectations. Furthermore, automatically associating halal tourism with Islam and halal tourists with religion is myopic and deceptive.

Studying the travel behaviour of Arab/Muslim people in light of religion alone is a thorny and challenging academic exercise for many reasons. First, the complexity lies in failing to realise the differences within the Arab world, between Arab and Muslim, religious and secular, fundamentalist and atheist, believer and agnostic, young and old, female and male, married and single or divorced, married with children or empty nester, or educated or otherwise. It is a reality that the religiosity of a Muslim individual can be measured on a scale from -10 to 10, where -10 represents not religious at all and 10 represents very religious. If we look closely into this proposition, only then does it become necessary to (re)consider the tourism motivations of Arab/Muslim tourists and to consider their complex tourism behaviours, outside of what is halal and what is haram. Hence, what is halal tourism becomes secondary to the travel behaviour of Muslim and Arab tourists. Second, not all Arabs are Muslims, and neither are all Muslims religious.

Failure to acknowledge such differences may result in a misunderstanding of not only Muslim tourists but also Arab and Muslim people in general. Prayag and Hosany (2014) are right in saying that Arab and Muslim tourists *tend* to travel to friendly/halal-oriented destinations, but that surely there are also Arab/Muslim tourists who prefer to visit destinations regardless of their halal orientation. Many Muslim and Arab travellers seek novelty in their tourism experiences. For example, in a study about recreational travel motivations of Kuwaiti citizens, Moufakkir and AlSaleh (2017) identified 105 motivational items. This plethora of items emphasises the complexity of Arab tourists' motivation and is a clear indication that treating Arab and Muslim tourists as one homogeneous market and disregarding intra-group differences can automatically lead to fallacious reasoning.

The Arab and Muslim tourism market is under-studied and hence misunderstood. The reasons why little is known about this market can be summarised as follows. First, there is a lack of interest in the Arab and Muslim tourism market by international and domestic academics. Second, there is a lack of funding for this type of research. Third, the exploratory nature of the research, although needed, can be perceived as descriptive and hence simplistic. Fourth, descriptive research is not easily accepted by mainstream academic journals, and finally, academics are pressured to publish in high-ranked journals. In addition, non-English speaking academics encounter language difficulties in publishing in English academic journals, and funding for proofreading and editing is not always available (Reisinger & Moufakkir 2015). This creates a dearth of literature authored by Arab and Muslim researchers on this topic. This neglect not only affects the whole field of tourism, hospitality and leisure studies, but also contributes to perpetrating stereotypical images of the Arab/Muslim tourist and his or her world.

Arabs and Muslims

Sometimes, scholars experience confusion in differentiating between the Arab World, the Islamic World (Jafari & Scott 2014), the Middle East (Feghali 1997), and North Africa. Arab is an ethnic term, Arabic is a language, Islam is a religion, and the Middle East and North Africa refer to geographical areas. Darity (2008) explained that the term 'Arab' is an ethno-national term. Geographically, Arab states stand on two continents: Asia and Africa. In 2010, there were 1.6 billion Muslims in the world, representing 23.2 per cent of an estimated population of 6.9 billion (Reisinger & Moufakkir 2015). More than 61 per cent of Muslims live in the Asia-Pacific region and about 20 per cent in the Middle East and North Africa (Pew Resource Center 2011). In 2010, five of the ten countries with the largest Muslim populations were in Asia: Indonesia (209 million), India (176 million), Pakistan (167 million), Bangladesh (133 million) and Iran (74 million). Of the remaining five, three were in North Africa (Egypt, Algeria and Morocco), one in Europe (Turkey) and one in Sub-Saharan Africa (Nigeria). Russia, China and the US also have sizeable Muslim populations. The world's Muslim population is projected to grow by about 35 per cent between 2010 and 2030 to 2.2 billion (Pew Resource Center 2011).

It is obvious that considering Muslims and Arabs as one homogeneous consumer market presents research and reasoning fallacies, subsequently leading to policies based on misleading recommendations. Therefore, future tourism research about Arab and Muslim consumers needs to be dismantled into specific units of analysis with considerations for respective countries and between and within group differences. Nassar, Mostafa and Reisinger (2015) rightly argued that there is little understanding of how destinations can best market themselves and cater for Muslim/Arab guests. There are many challenges to overcome in order to respond to the needs and desires of this complex and fast-growing visitor market.

Islam, Muslims and travel

Muslims are required to observe Islamic commitments when travelling (Timothy & Iverson 2006; Zamani-Farahani & Henderson 2010). The Islamic sets of codes strictly determine Muslims' destination choice, purpose of travel, hotel selection, preferences for amenities, food consumption, participation in activities, and service expectations that need to follow Islamic-friendly criteria (Stephenson 2014). Muslims are commanded to travel to Mecca to perform Hajj (pilgrimage) and Umrah (minor Hajj), and visiting the three mosques: al-masjid al-Haram, the Mosque of the Messenger, and the Mosque of al-Aqsa in Palestine (Alsawafi 2017). Muslims are not allowed to travel to places where sins are committed. They are not allowed to travel to non-Muslim countries, except for medical treatment, for business purposes that require travel, or to learn knowledge that cannot be obtained in a Muslim country, and to call people to Islam and spread the faith (Islam Q&A 2010). Likewise, Muslim women are not allowed to travel without a Mahram (i.e. a companion from amongst their relatives) (Hashim, Murphy, & Hashim 2007; Islam Q&A 2010). It is extremely important to consider these propositions cautiously.

Muslims are commanded to travel for religious purposes. However, in the Arab world, there is a mishmash and, to a certain extent, confusion between religion and tradition. To what extent each one is impregnated by the other and to what degree is a huge debate. This is why discussing Islam in tourism and tourism in Islam is a thorny intellectual issue (Reisinger & Moufakkir

2015). The teachings of Islam emanate from the interpretation of the holy book, the Qur'an, and from the Sunna or the exemplary life of Prophet Mohammad (Peace Be Upon Him) and his teachings. There are things that are clearly and strictly haram (forbidden) in Islam and which have a strong bearing on travel, including drinking alcohol, eating pork, gambling, nudity, fornication and adultery. The concepts of haram (unlawful) and halal (lawful) strongly affect the way of life of the Muslims, including their travel behaviour, to a certain extent. Al Jallad (2008: 77) explains:

> These concepts [Haram and Halal] are deeply rooted in the Arab-Muslim tradition and history, affecting the Arabs' way of thinking and acting. Therefore, accurate definitions of these concepts may help to understand the Arab-Muslim identity that is vaguely or poorly understood by non-speakers of Arabic. Furthermore, to non-speakers of Arabic, these notions are often misunderstood, inadequately explained, and inaccurately translated into other languages.

Muslim travel motivations originate from Islamic motivations. Islam connects travel motivation to worship, conveying the message of God to people, enabling one to appreciate the wonders of God's creation and enjoy the beauty of his great universe (Henderson 2003; Islam Q&A 2010; Stodolska & Livengood 2006). Several authors noted that Islamic travel has important religious and social functions (Al-Hamarneh 2008; Henderson 2003, 2009; Timothy & Iverson 2006; Zamani-Farahani & Henderson 2010). For example, Laderlah, Rahman, Awang and Mann (2011) noted that Islam motivates its followers to visit and immerse themselves in places that strengthen their appreciation of creation and faith in Allah (Battour, Ismail, & Battor 2011; Sanad, Kassem, & Scott 2010; Yusof & Muhammad 2013; Zamani-Farahani & Henderson 2010). Bhardwaj (1998) stressed the importance of visiting shrines that relate to the cultural traditions of Islamic populations. Eickelman and Piscatori (1990) argued that Muslims travel to appreciate the beauty of God's world, and foster unity amongst the Muslim community. Laderlah et al. (2011) emphasised the role of travel in Islamic teachings. Din (1989) reported that Muslims travel to Islamic historical places as a way to learn about the history of Islam. In order to attract more Muslim tourists Jordan promotes visitation to the shrines of the pre-Islamic prophets and the companions of Prophet Mohammed (PBUH) (Neveu 2010). Certainly, there are a few Muslim tourists who belong to this type of spiritual tourism. These tourists seek spirituality in nature and at natural and religious sites. The quest for spirituality, however, does not necessarily make a spiritual tourist a religious person, or all Muslims religious people.

Perhaps, according to some commentators' observations, a Muslim person should not travel at all to Western destinations, and even visiting an Arab/Islamic destination becomes problematic as many, if not all of them, are speedily 'Westernising'. Surely, if it were the case that Muslims should not travel, the word travel and its significance would be omitted from the holy Qur'an or limited to Islamic pilgrimage. Travel, however, is well covered in the Holy Book. For example, in Surah (verse) Al-Imran, God says: 'Many were the Ways of Life that have passed away before you: travel through the earth, and see what was the end of those who rejected Truth' (Surah Al-Imran 137) (Quran Index 2017e). Travel in the Qur'an is about observation, discovery, learning, and amazement about God's works; travel shows the right path to God. In Surah Al-Hajj, God says:

> Do they not travel through the land, so that their hearts (and minds) may thus learn wisdom and their ears may thus learn to hear? Truly it is not their eyes that are blind, but their hearts, which are in their breasts.
>
> *(Surah Al-Hajj 46) (Quran Index 2017d)*

And, 'Travel through the earth and see how Allah did originate creation; so will Allah produce a later creation: for Allah has power over all things' (Surah Al-'Ankabut 20) (Quran Index 2017a). Clearly, Muslims are encouraged to travel and wander the earth in wonder of God's work and his creation to learn about and from the peoples of the world, regardless of their religion. Thus, religion is not a travel motivation *per se.* Certainly, travel to Mecca *is* a religious duty for those who can afford it, and it is a religious motivation in itself.

Halal tourism, on the other hand, only offers certain conditions that contribute to the experience of the tourist. Tourism motivation is multifaceted and tourists' motives can overlap, depending on the type of experience sought and the destination selected (Sirakaya, Uysal, & Yoshioka 2003). Muslim tourists do not travel to London for spiritual fulfilment or for a religious duty. They visit London for different reasons and for different experiences, including shopping and culture (Moufakkir & AlSaleh 2017).

The Arab tourist market, influence of religion and halal tourism

The literature indicates that Arab travellers are characterised by longer stays (between two and eight weeks), larger travel party size, higher spending and a preference for cooking their food themselves (e.g. Michael & Beeton 2007; Michael, Armstrong, Badran, & King 2011; Sulaiman 2008). Arab travellers have the highest average travel expenditure (Wells 2012). The average spending per capita for Arab travellers is around US$250 and higher than the world average of US$134 (ETC & UNWTO 2012). Citizens of Arabian Gulf countries spend around US$3000–4000 per day when travelling internationally. Gulf travellers spend four times more than others on accommodation and almost three times more on airfares, and business class seats preference is higher amongst Arabs (Wells 2012).

Arabs tend to travel with their families, stay longer, and spend more money than the average tourist. This being acknowledged, not much is known about the other trip characteristics of Arabs. For example, the travel behaviour of an Algerian tourist compared to that of the Emirati tourist is very different. Most Algerians' international tourism is VFR-oriented (visiting friends and relatives), as many have family members and friends living in European countries. Research about the GCC tourists is progressing, but our understanding about other Arabs and Muslims is lagging behind (Stephenson & Al-Hamarneh 2017).

According to Almuhrzi, Scott and Alriyami (2017), more than 60 per cent of the population in the Arab world is represented by young people who are familiar with new technology and are more exposed to new online media. Their behaviour, like any other youth segment, is dynamic and needs to be monitored for a better understanding and to cater better to their tourism needs. Certainly, their travel preferences and consumption patterns are affected by many factors in addition to religion, including universal, societal and individual values, gender roles, country politics, family relationships, lifestyles, traditions, modernity, education, history, language, media use and entertainment, and exposure to the world. Therefore, it is important not to neglect understanding the travel behaviour of non-religious Arabs, non-religious Muslims, and Christian Arabs. Religion should not be uncritically accepted as a determining variable affecting their tourism behaviour and destination choice. Religiosity, rather than religion, might be an important indicator of customer attitudes, behaviours, and satisfaction. Moreover, businesses need to understand the different ways in which other values, lifestyles and practices influence their consumers. For example, Muhamed and Mizerski (2013) suggested that labelling religious affiliation, such as Muslim, does not consider commitment to a religion. Religiosity is better captured in the lifestyles, values, attitudes and practices that are influenced by religion (Eid & El-Gohary 2015).

Commentators have argued that Islam as a religion cannot easily be separated from everyday life practices (e.g. Eid & El-Gohary 2015). This statement can be misleading for the above-mentioned reasons. Thus, millions of Muslims travel to non-Muslim destinations and to non-Islamic destinations for leisure purposes. Of these, some observe religious practices at the destination, while some do not. Muslims can pray in a space that is clean, and as such they do not need to be in a mosque to engage in prayers. Muslim tourists also have the choice not to eat meat and to eat fruits and vegetarian meals. From this perspective, it is nonsensical to suggest that Muslim tourists who travel to non-halal-oriented destinations are not Muslim, or is it? Certainly, halal tourism is a choice, but it is not the choice of all Muslim tourists. Dean (2014) argued that catering to Muslim guests is not the same as dealing with 'preferences'. According to him, dealing with Muslim guests is dealing with religious 'values'. This statement is simplistic and misleading: Muslim tourists have different preferences— their preferences can be based either on religious values, personal values, universal values, or on all of the above.

As already noted, the global Muslim population is estimated to be around 1.6 billion and is expected to increase to 2.2 billion by 2030 (Healey 2015). An increase in the Muslim population does not necessarily mean an increase in the level of demand for Halal-oriented tourism destinations or Islamic-oriented tourism. Again, *true* Islamic tourism can be found only in relation to the pilgrimage to Mecca (the Hajj). In Mecca, Muslim pilgrims perform the religious rituals of Hajj. In other Muslim destinations, Muslim tourists visit religious sites and shrines, in combination with many other non-religious tourist activities (Timothy & Iverson 2006). Therefore, homogenising the Arabs and Muslims into one tourism market tends to fall into the false stereotyping of tourist behaviour—that is, that all Arabs are Muslims, that all Muslims are religious, and therefore that halal tourism is Islamic and that all Muslims adhere to halal tourism practices and are all likely to buy halal tourism products.

Islam is the main religion in many Arab and non-Arab societies (i.e. Sub-Saharan, Asian, Persian, Turkish and Kurdish societies). These societies have different cultures (Hassan 1991; Hourani 1992) and many cultural differences exist between Arab-Islamic and non-Arab-Islamic societies in their way of living and societal traditions (Hassan 1991; Hourani 1992). Jafari and Scott (2014: 2) explained, 'there is diversity of religion, culture, politics and historical influences within the global Muslim community'. As such, there is no single label or categorisation one can use to characterise the Muslim world (Almuhrzi, Scott, & Alriyami, 2017). For these and similar reasons, the travel behaviours and experiences of Muslim and Arab tourists need to be interpreted cautiously, and with sensitivity.

The main challenge for destinations wishing to attract tourists from the Arab and Muslim worlds is to understand the differences that exist between the needs, wants, and desires of Muslims and non-Muslim tourists amongst the broader Arab/Muslim tourist market. Most tourism destinations are targeting tourists with a different culture, religion, and with distinct needs and wants. Destinations that show in their promotional ads their attractions and the hospitality and friendliness of the locals are the winning destinations in the long run. Perhaps, halal-oriented tourism is only a contemporary and trendy fad. In this case, it is interesting to know more about the tourism behaviour and preferences of halal tourists, especially outside the halal environs or outside the 'environmental bubble' of halal-oriented tourism.

Halal tourism and its 'environmental bubble'

Despite the growing interest in halal tourism, it has not been subject to criticism in the social sciences. The more one knows about halal tourism the more questions should be raised. For example, considering Cohen's (1972) typology of tourists, a legitimate question to ask might be: are halal tourists really tourists? What other halal-oriented activities do they participate in during their halal vacations? Is all of their vacation 'halalised'? What becomes of tourism if and when tourists live their tourism activities in a tourism bubble? Cohen (1972: 162) believes that

> tourism as a cultural phenomenon becomes possible only when man develops a *generalised* interest in things beyond his particular habitat, when contact with and appreciation and enjoyment of strangeness and novelty are valued for their *own* sake.

Cohen sees novelty and strangeness as essential elements in the tourist experience. Analogically, the halal tourist is a tourist who lives his tourism experience in an 'environmental bubble' (Cohen 1972: 166). Halal hotels are institutionalised establishments that sell the illusion of halal to the tourist. They sell an experience enrobed in an 'ecological bubble' (Cohen 1972: 169), wherein decorations and activities are 'halal-washed'. Both the halal tourists and the halal tourism establishments are compartmentalising religion in a halal make-belief of places and things—the lavatories are halal, the swimming pools are halal, the hotel rooms are halal, the foods and drinks are halal, and hotel personnel are halal. Halal is guaranteed indoors, and surely we have no control of whether or not the outdoors is halal. Hotel entrances and lobbies are not halalised yet, but the management is likely working on it.

The ecological bubble of halal tourism may not only lead to distorted views of the Arab/Muslim market, but it may also portray a negative image of Islam and convey a distorted understanding of Islam and Muslims. Religion is not for sale, neither can a Muslim be Islamic in one place because it is a halal place and not in another place because it is not a halal place. Halal in Islam is not only a state of being but also a state of mind. God says in the Holy Qur'an: 'Say to the believing men that they should lower their gaze and guard their modesty: that will make for greater purity for them: And Allah is well acquainted with all that they do' (Surah An-Nur 30) (Quran Index 2017b). God also says: 'And say to the believing women that they should lower their gaze and guard their modesty; that they should not display their beauty and ornaments except what (must ordinarily) appear thereof' (Surah An-Nur 31) (Quran Index 2017c). Lowering the gaze is clearly an important behavioural principle in Islam, a mental capability of human beings, an encouraging commandment of God for humans to be in the crowd, and a social code on how to behave in that crowd.

The paradox of halal tourism, using Cohen's (1972: 172) explanation of institutionalised and standardised tourism facilities, is that 'though the desire for variety, novelty, and strangeness are the primary motives of tourism, these qualities have decreased as tourism has become institutionalised'. He further explains, 'the sad irony of modern institutionalised tourism is that, instead of destroying myths between countries, it perpetuates them' (Cohen 1972: 174) in that the tourists learn nothing about the native culture and the natives learn nothing about the tourists' culture. Ironically, the halal tourist remains isolated from the host society, the very same society he or she has selected to visit and encounter. Do all halal tourists live in a halal environmental bubble? Can halal tourists be clustered based on their indoor and outdoor activities? Can they be segmented based on their religiosity, familiarity or novelty? These are all crucial questions that remain unanswered.

From another angle, giving too much academic and industry importance to halal tourism, an importance even greater than how the majority of Muslims see it, is to blindly support the 'clash of civilisations' thesis, which presents Western and Islamic religions and social traditions as incompatible. To put it simply, halal tourism exaggerates the difference between Islam and the West. Yet, many Muslims live in the West and many Westerners live in Muslim countries, respecting each other's values and sharing the same universal values. That most people in the Western and Muslim worlds have similar needs and wants is undeniable, and the same can be said about their travel motivations.

Muslim tourists travel to Western destinations for many reasons, most of which are not motivated by religion but by curiosity and discovery. Furthermore, the Westerners who sojourn in Arab and Muslim countries dress in Western cloths and do not cover their heads with a scarf (*hijab*) or wear an abaya or burka. Even Muslim women in the majority of Muslim countries do not cover their heads. There are also Muslim women who half-cover their heads and wear American jeans. Furthermore, the majority of businesses, services and entertainment venues in the Arab and Muslim worlds are not gender segregated. Several Muslim countries have casinos and serve alcohol to the public in local bars, restaurants and franchised hotels. Hence, the important questions to delve into in this regard are: how did halal tourism start and how will it further develop in an increasingly globalised world? Is it more religion-driven, politics-driven, or economy-driven? What external factors, and socio-cultural, and religious variables discriminate the most between halal tourists, Muslim tourists, and Western tourists? Such questions can advance our understanding of halal tourism, halal tourists and the relationship between religion and tourism in the global village.

Conclusion

In general, knowledge about the Arabs and Muslims is limited in so many domains, including travel and tourism. There has been, however, an increasing demand for halal amenities, which has encouraged research about halal tourism and halal tourists. Nevertheless, there is now too much focus on this form of tourism in the tourism literature. This chapter discussed halal tourism, in relation to religion and travel motivations, from a critical perspective. The purpose was to offer a positive criticism of halal tourism to disentangle our understanding about the relationship between Islam and tourism.

The Arab and Muslim tourist market is a heterogeneous market with differences between and also within consumer groups. Their travel motivations are multifaceted and depend on several factors other than religion or in relation to religiosity. That is, not all Muslims are Islamic and neither are all Arabs similar in behaviour, attitudes and expectations. The focused concentration in the past few years on halal tourism has confused the understanding about what Islam is and what Muslims should do. A discussion of halal tourism is complicated and complex because it *should* deal with what is allowed (halal) and what is forbidden (haram) in Islam. At the heart of the matter is that Muslims do negotiate what is haram and what is halal in their lives. This negotiation should be taken into consideration when discussing halal tourism.

Religion is not a motivation per se, except with regard to pilgrimages or visits to religious sites. Muslim tourists select certain destinations because they are perceived as Muslim-friendly. They also select certain tourism accommodations because they see them as compliant with *specific* religious beliefs. Muslim people thus do not travel to London for religious purposes in the same manner they travel to Mecca or to visit the Al-Aqsa Mosque. Their motivation to visit Mecca is pilgrimage. Their motivation to visit London is to see the city's famous historical sites, museums, to shop and to enjoy city life.

Halal establishments, in London or in Sydney, offer halal tourists a certain (yet pseudo) familiarity. Unlike pilgrimage sites, halal establishments do not embody spirituality or lead to spiritual fulfilment. Thus, one should not simplistically confuse halal tourism with religion, spirituality, Muslims or Islam. Indeed, certain halal establishments have become the choice of many non-Muslim families. Halal establishments have become a matter of lifestyle and not a matter of religion.

To conclude, halal tourism has been overly emphasised in contemporary tourism literature. Yet, our understanding of this phenomenon remains descriptive and simplistic, and it lacks clarification and contextualisation. For example, we do not know how halal tourists negotiate between their international tourism destination selection and their religious convictions or practices, or how they manage to 'lower their gazes' when they are outside their religious environmental bubble. It is also important to understand the religiosity of halal tourists and the extent to which they patronise halal-friendly establishments in their own Muslim countries.

There are, therefore, many unanswered, yet critical, research questions. Is halal tourism a fad that results from religious convictions or political orientations? What is the recreation and leisure behaviour of halal tourists at home? How do they respond to the Westernisation of their respective countries? What do they think about the non-Muslim people they encounter during their international trips and those who are residents of their own countries? How do they define Islam and what do they think about Muslim people and non-Muslims? How do they reconcile the Islamic and the non-Islamic in their lives and in their trips? What is Islamic about halal tourism when halal tourists venture outside their hotels, if they venture outside at all? What are their experiences, attitudes and behaviours when they stroll around the city? Which social practices could be perceived as the antithesis to all that is perceived as Islamic by halal tourists? Can halal tourism exist in other destinations other than Mecca? Or, what does halal mean in international halal tourism? Is halal preserved only in hotels and hotel rooms? What is halal about the hotel lobbies, restaurants and service employees? Does halal tourism correspond to how travel is outlined in the Qur'an? Is there room to talk about 'halal-washing' in the social sciences? It is our hope that this discussion and critique will serve as a background for further studies, and will generate positive reactions to further our understanding about the intricacies of halal tourism and so many other factors that have contributed to its development.

Halal tourism has received much attention from tourism academics and practitioners in the past few years, while relatively little is known about the tourism behaviour of Arab and Muslim tourists. Halal tourism has been defined in relation to Islamic Sharia law, which prescribes rules and codes of conduct for Muslims. A few tourism destinations have implemented some Sharia-compliant activities in their tourist establishments to accommodate the wants of the halal tourism market. The discourse on halal tourism, however, conflates this phenomenon with religion, Muslims, Arabs, Islam, Sharia and the tourism behaviour of Arabs and Muslims. This confusion not only leads to a myopic understanding of Muslim tourists, but also perpetuates stereotypical images of Islam and Muslims. This chapter constitutes the first critical review of halal tourism. The travel motivation of this market segment is multifaceted, and religion plays only a small, if not a subsidiary role in their destination choice and tourist activities.

References

Al-Hamarneh, A. (2008) 'Islamic tourism: A long-term strategy of tourist industries in the Arab World after 9/11', *Centre for Research on the Arab World*. Available online: www.ceraw.uni-mainz.de (Accessed 15 December 2017).

Al Jallad, N. (2008) 'The concepts of al-halal and al-haram in the Arab-Muslim culture: A translational and lexicographical study', *Language Design*, 10: 77–86.

Almuhrzi, H., Scott, N., & Alriyami, H. (2017) 'Introduction', in H. Almuhrzi, H. Alriyami, & N. Scott (eds), *Tourism in the Arab World* (pp. 1–15). Bristol: Channel View Publications.

Alsawafi, A. (2017) 'The role of Islam in Omani tourists' travel behaviour', in H. Almuhrzi, H. Alriyami, & N. Scott (eds), *Tourism in the Arab World* (pp. 235–253). Bristol: Channel View Publications.

Battour, M., & Ismail, M. (2015) 'Halal tourism: Concepts, practices, challenges and future', *Tourism Management Perspectives*, 19: 150–154.

Battour, M., Ismail, M., & Battor, M. (2011) 'The impact of destination attributes on Muslim tourist's choice', *International Journal of Tourism Research*, 13(6): 527–540.

Bhardwaj, S. (1998) 'Non-hajj pilgrimage in Islam: A neglected dimension of religious circulation', *Journal of Cultural Geography*, 17(2): 69–87.

Cohen, E. (1972) 'Toward a sociology of international tourism', *Social Research*, 39(1): 164–182.

Context Consulting (2016) 'Halal travellers', *Atto Report: An Amadeus-commissioned Report*. Available online: www.amadeus.com/web/binaries/blobs/864/164/halal-travel-report-2016.pdf (Accessed 6 December 2017).

Darity, W. (2008) 'Arabs', in W. Darity (ed.), *International Encyclopedia of the Social Sciences, Volume 1*, 2nd edn. Detroit, MI: Macmillan.

Dean, J. (2014) 'Muslim values and market values: A sociological perspective', *Journal of Islamic Marketing*, 5(1): 20–32.

Din, K. (1989) 'Islam and tourism: Patterns, issues, and options', *Annals of Tourism Research*, 16(4): 542–563.

Eickelman, D., & Piscatori, J. (eds) (1990) *Muslim Travelers: Pilgrimage, Migration, and the Religious Imagination, Volume 9*. Berkeley, CA: University of California Press.

Eid, R., & El-Gohary, H. (2015) 'The role of Islamic religiosity on the relationship between perceived value and tourist satisfaction', *Tourism Management*, 46: 477–488.

European Travel Commission (ETC) and World Tourism Organization (UNWTO) (2012) *The Middle East Outbound Travel Market with Special Insight into the Image of Europe as a Destination*. Madrid: UNWTO.

Feghali, E. (1997) 'Arab cultural communication patterns', *International Journal of Intercultural Relations*, 21(3): 345–378.

Hashim, N.H., Murphy, J., & Hashim, N.M. (2007) 'Islam and online imagery on Malaysian tourist destination websites', *Journal of Computer-Mediated Communication*, 12(3): 1082–1102.

Hassan, K. (1991) *Studies in the History of Arab Society*. Beirut: Dar Beirut Almhrosah.

Healey, M. (2015) 'How halal tourism is travelling in the right direction'. *The National*, 13 August. Available online: www.thenational.ae/arts-culture/how-halal-tourism-is-travelling-in-the-right-direction-1.71737 (Accessed 6 November 2015).

Henderson, J. (2003) 'Tourism promotion and identity in Malaysia', *Tourism, Culture and Communication*, 4: 71–81.

Henderson, J. (2009) 'Islamic tourism reviewed', *Tourism Recreation Research*, 34(2), 207–211.

Hourani, A. (1992) *A History of the Arab Peoples*. New York: Warner Books.

Islam Question and Answer (2010) 'Travel and tourism (Siyaahah) in Islam: Rulings and types'. 9 October. Available online: www.islamqa.com/en/ref/islamqa/87846 (Accessed 9 October 2010).

Jafari, J., & Scott, N. (2014) 'Muslim world and its tourisms', *Annals of Tourism Research*, 44: 1–19.

Laderlah, S., Rahman, S., Awang, K., & Man, Y. (2011) 'A study on Islamic tourism: A Malaysian experience'. Paper presented at the 2nd International Conference on Humanities, Historical and Social Sciences, Singapore.

Michael, N., & Beeton, S. (2007) 'Exploring the cultural transferability of western-derived tourist motivation theories in Arabic culture: A preliminary discussion'. Paper presented at the *CAUTHE 2007* conference, Sydney, Australia.

Michael, N., Armstrong, A., Badran, B., & King, B. (2011) 'Dubai outbound tourism: An exploratory study of Emiratis and expatriates', *Journal of Vacation Marketing*, 17(1): 83–91.

Moufakkir, O., & AlSaleh, D. (2017) 'A conceptual framework for studying recreational travel motivation from an Arab perspective', *Tourism Recreation Research*, 42(4): 522–536.

Muhamed, N., & Mizerski, D. (2013) 'The effects of following Islam in decisions about taboo products', *Journal of Psychology and Marketing*, 30(4): 357–371.

Nassar, M., Mostafa, M., & Reisinger, Y. (2015) 'Factors influencing travel to Islamic destinations: An empirical analysis of Kuwaiti nationals', *International Journal of Culture, Tourism and Hospitality Research*, 9(1): 36–53.

Neveu, N. (2010) 'Islamic tourism as an ideological construction: A Jordan case study', *Journal of Tourism and Cultural Change*, 8(4): 327–337.

Pew Resource Center (2011) 'The future of the global Muslim population'. 27 January. Available online: www.pewresearch.org/topics/muslims-and-islam/2011 (Accessed 30 November 2017).

Prayag, G., & Hosany, S. (2014) 'When Middle East meets West: Understanding the motives and perceptions of young tourists from United Arab Emirates', *Tourism Management*, 40: 35–45.

Quran Index (2017a). Surah Al-'Ankabut, 20. Available online: www.quranindex.net/index.php (Accessed 13 October 2017).

Quran Index (2017b). Surah An-Nur, 30. Available online: www.quranindex.net/index.php (Accessed 13 October 2017).

Quran Index (2017c). Surah An-Nur, 31. Available online: www.quranindex.net/index.php (Accessed 13 October 2017).

Quran Index (2017d). Surah Al-Hajj, 46. Available online: www.quranindex.net/index.php (Accessed 13 October 2017).

Quran Index (2017e). Surah Al-Imran, 137. Available online: www.quranindex.net/index.php (Accessed 13 October 2017).

Reisinger, Y., & Moufakkir, O. (2015) 'Cultural issues in tourism, hospitality and leisure in the Arab/Muslim world', *International Journal of Culture, Tourism and Hospitality Research*, 9(1): 1–6.

Sanad, H., Kassem, A., & Scott, N. (2010) 'Tourism and Islamic law', *Bridging Tourism Theory and Practice*, 2: 17–30.

Sirakaya, E., Uysal, M., & Yoshioka, C. (2003) 'Segmenting the Japanese tour market to Turkey', *Journal of Travel Research*, 41(3): 293–304.

Smith, M.K., & Hindley, C. (2017) 'Halal tourism: Definitions and developments', in H. Almuhrzi, H. Alriyami, & N. Scott (eds), *Tourism in the Arab World: An Industry Perspective*, pp. 118–130. Bristol: Channel View Publications.

Stephenson, M. (2014) 'Deciphering "Islamic hospitality": Developments, challenges and opportunities', *Tourism Management*, 40: 155–164.

Stephenson, M., & Al-Hamarneh, A. (eds) (2017) *International Tourism Development and the Gulf Cooperation Council States: Challenges and Opportunities*. London: Routledge.

Stodolska, M., & Livengood, J. (2006) 'The influence of religion on the leisure behavior of immigrant Muslims in the United States', *Journal of Leisure Research*, 38(3): 293–320.

Sulaiman, Y. (2008) 'Malaysian tourism targeting big spenders next'. *eTurbonews*. Available online: www.eturbonews.com/706/malaysian-tourism-targeting-big-spenders-next (Accessed 5 October 2017).

Timothy, D.J., & Iverson, T. (2006) 'Tourism and Islam: Considerations of culture and duty', in D.J. Timothy, & D.H. Olsen (eds), *Tourism, Religion and Spiritual Journeys* (pp. 186–205). London: Routledge.

Wells, R. (2012) *Tourist Numbers Set to Soar to 195 Million in 2030*. London: TME Media 21 Ltd.

Yusof, M., & Muhammad, M. (2013) 'Introducing Shariah compliant hotels as a new tourism product: The case of Malaysia'. Paper presented at the 20th International Business Information Management Association Conference (IBIMA). International Business Information Management Association, 2 March 2013, Kuala Lumpur.

Zamani-Farahani, H., & Henderson, J. (2010) 'Islamic tourism and managing tourism development in Islamic societies: The case of Iran and Saudi Arabia', *International Journal of Tourism Research*, 12: 79–89.

25

TOURISM, MIGRATION AND AN EXPATRIATE WORKFORCE IN THE MIDDLE EAST

Kevin Hannam and Cody Morris Paris

Introduction

In the Middle East, migration, employment and labour market dynamics contrast with those documented in Western contexts (Ewers & Dicce 2016). This includes the widespread use of an expatriate labour force, the *kafala* system of labour sponsorship and the influence of state-mandated nationalisation initiatives on the labour market (Ewers & Dicce 2016; Rees, Mamman, & Bin Braik 2007). In the Gulf States, in particular, the 1960s and 1970s brought a construction boom stimulating large in-flows of international labour covering a wide range of occupations and skill levels. These in-flows have consisted of both high-skilled, high-wage knowledge workers from Europe and North America, often referred to as expatriates, and lower-skilled, lower-wage construction and service workers initially from other Arab countries but increasingly from South Asia, often referred to as migrants (Brand 2006; Kapiszewski 2001). However this dichotomy between highly skilled expatriates and lower skilled migrants is, in fact, complicated. Indeed, there are increasingly many highly skilled people moving to the Middle East from South Asia, and there are also migration processes within the Middle East itself despite labour mobility restrictions; for example, a Jordanian living in Dubai might self-refer as an expatriate rather than a migrant.

Nevertheless, foreign workers comprise the majority of the total labour force in each of the Gulf States, while the local population relies on high-wage, public sector jobs as a benefit of citizenship. These divisions are formally enshrined in the kafala system of labour sponsorship—a complex regulatory system 'governing the mobility and employment of migrant workers in the Gulf States which ensures their status as foreign, temporary, and separate from the region's elite minority and without access to any of the benefits citizenship entails' (Ewers & Dicce 2016: 2452).

This division of labour is also manifested spatially within the urban landscape and across the residences and lived spaces of foreign and local populations, producing distinct sub-urban communities where different groups of migrants live, work and socialise (Sidaway 2007). Indeed, both Dubai and Abu Dhabi have been criticised as 'divided cities', consisting of, on the one hand, wealthy Western expatriates secluded within gated communities with exclusive spaces of consumption (Buckley 2013), and, on the other hand, low-wage, low-skill service and construction workers, primarily of South Asian origin. Furthermore, Ewers and Dicce (2016: 2453) point out that: '[w]hile the division between poor and wealthy migrants demonstrates a stark contrast, further and more prominent divisions exist between highly skilled expatriate workers and the region's citizens'.

Elsewhere in the wider Middle East and North Africa region, migration often makes more reference to the historical migration of the population out of the country and into the West. Thus, countries such as Morocco, Tunisia, Algeria, Lebanon and Jordan, for instance, may reference their own highly skilled migrant expatriates that live and work in France but who return to visit their country of origin for 'visiting friends and relatives' (VFR) tourism. This chapter provides a critical review of the literature regarding the role of expatriates and migrants within the Middle East in relation to the tourism sector. We begin with a broader discussion of the expatriate/migrant nexus before focusing on, first Western expatriate behaviour and, second, MENA expatriate behaviour. We then examine the employment issues concerning expatriate and migrant labour in the context of the tourism industry. Finally, we conclude by arguing that the contemporary migration of workers to and within the Middle East needs also to recognise the figure of the refugee and consider wider geopolitical mobilities.

Expatriates or migrants?

The concept of the 'expatriate' is politically laden and contested, as it has often referred to mostly white, Western and class-privileged elites moving to work temporarily in poorer countries due to their expertise and capital affordances (Kopnina 2007; Kunz 2016). In contrast, citizens from less economically developed regions are typically termed immigrants or migrant workers (Yeoh & Willis 2005). The very term 'expatriates' has been used by elite or privileged migrants themselves as a self-identifier as well as having more pejorative nuances as a signifier of neo-colonial attitudes (Coles & Walsh 2010; Fechter & Walsh 2010; Kunz 2016). Indeed, the term originally referred to an intra-company transfer of a member of staff abroad for a finite period of time but has become associated more broadly with transnational professionals or highly skilled workers (Kunz 2016).

Intermediary agencies frequently dictate the mobility of skilled international workers through deployment of information and resources through what Findlay and Li (1998) call 'migration channels', including the recruitment and expatriation practices of international firms, project-based work in small and medium-sized firms with international contracts, the social networks of individual expatriates, international recruitment agencies and national immigration policies (Ewer & Dicce 2016). Nevertheless, expatriates are seeing significant changes, as many international businesses change their operating practices away from the use of expatriates towards the use of indigenous labour forces as these become more highly skilled and connected within the global economy (Fechter & Walsh 2010).

Indeed, McNulty and Brewster (2017: 32) have defined business expatriates as:

> legally working individuals who reside temporarily in a country of which they are not a citizen in order to accomplish a career-related goal, being relocated abroad either by an organization, by self-initiation or directly employed within the host-country.

Nevertheless as Kunz (2016: 92) has argued, 'while there is considerable ambiguity around who is considered an expatriate, the category is firmly linked to the realities of global power relations and inequality'. Thus the concept's continuing widespread usage also has important moral and political implications despite studies showing the diversity of expatriates (Fechter

& Walsh 2010). Individual agency to participate and move across 'global production networks' reflects the intersection of a person's gender, class, race, ethnicity, nationality, education and age (Rodriguez & Mearns 2012).

The interplay between international patterns of mobility, globalisation and internationalisation of business has resulted in increased complexity and multidimensionality of the conceptualisation of expatriates (Rodriguez & Scurry 2014). Traditionally, expatriate managers, towards the end of their careers, were assigned by their company to work in other countries and often had little or no previous international experience. However, Hutchings, Michailova and Harrison (2013: 292) argue that over the past decade the profile of the typical expatriate has shifted to individuals who tend more likely to be 'early in his/her career, with a strong disposition towards learning about other cultures and also maybe having had prior international experience from personal and professional travel'. This 'new generation' of expatriates is also more likely to seek global professional opportunities beyond a single organisation, embrace an identity characterised by cosmopolitanism and nomadic mobility and be self-initiated (Howe-Walsh & Schyns 2010).

Self-initiated expatriates (SIEs) are individuals who independently and voluntarily pursue global careers. Research into SIEs suggests that many are driven by career development, learning and progression opportunities, increased financial earnings, increased quality of life, and adventure (Baruch & Forstenlechner 2017; Hutchings, Michailova, & Harrison 2013). The greater ease of the movement of labour across borders, developments in information and communication technologies, and sizeable shortages of both skilled and unskilled labour in particular regions of the world have contributed to the increase in self-initiated expatriation (Baruch & Forstenlechner 2017). While SIEs may share certain characteristics, the motivations, attitudes and experiences of SIEs can be quite different for individuals from different backgrounds. In their study of self-initiated expatriate motivations, Baruch and Forstenlechner (2017) found that financial remuneration was a primary motivation for SIEs from all regions included in their study regardless of whether they came from Western, Asian, African or Middle Eastern countries, to the UAE. However, beyond the financial motivation, other main motives for expatriation differed. For example, for Westerners, the second most important factor to expatriate to the UAE was for career opportunities, whereas for expatriates from MENA and other predominantly Muslim countries, the second most important factor was the cultural fit.

Within MENA, and in particularly the GCC, SIEs, and other foreign workers, fill demands for foreign labour that are driven by ambitious development plans. The demand has resulted in a heavy reliance on a foreign workforce to alleviate staff shortages and/or provide technical expertise. Within most Gulf countries, the number of expatriates greatly exceeds the number of local citizens. To counter the reliance on foreign workers and unemployment within the growing local youth populations, most GCC governments have established labour localisation policies. These policies aim to increase local participation in the private sector as part of larger national strategies for economic diversification and sustainability.

The tourism and hospitality sector, in particular, has low levels of local employment in much of the region. According to the Abu Dhabi Tourism and Culture Authority, Emiratis account for only 1 per cent of employment in tourism and hospitality. Low participation in the sector has been attributed to a lack of capacity and skills needed, a lack of awareness of the range of opportunities available, low salaries offered in comparison to public sector jobs, and a lack of prestige (Sadi & Henderson 2005; Stephenson, Russell, & Edgar 2010). To address these challenges recent initiatives have sought to provide training and spread awareness about career opportunities for nationals in the tourism and hospitality industry. In the UAE, Emiratisation programmes for the tourism sector have focused on education and training for youth. For example, the Dubai Department of Tourism and Commerce Marketing recently launched the Dubai Tourism College as a means of recruiting and training Emirati youth for tourist-facing roles and to become role models within the industry. The focus on knowledge and education development as a means of localisation will help to overcome some of the challenges in the region in previous localisation attempts. For example, previous policies in countries like Oman and Saudi Arabia set quotas for local employment that were not aligned or sustainable with overall growth and development plans. With this realisation, policies now are focused on more gradual and organic growth in local skills, management competencies and participation in the private sector.

Western expatriates in the Middle East

Western expatriates may effectively exist vicariously between two different worlds: their original home environment and their new home environment (Thieme 2008). As a result, it may be thought that their experiences and expectations may become blurred as they move from one living space to another. Studies have observed the adaptation techniques of expatriates to new foreign surroundings and the mediation techniques required to enable a suitable recalibration of their desired experiences and expectations (Smith 2001; Tung 1998; Walsh 2006, 2007, 2011, 2012, 2014). However, the use of the term adaptation does not necessarily imply that these individuals become assimilated into their new countries of residence. Instead, studies contest that expatriates opt simply to avoid the problems they encounter and as a consequence, contact with locals will be reduced or avoided (Beaverstock 2002).

It has been shown that expatriates may find stability in the form of firmly established networks, cultural practices and social relations, which are already deeply embedded in the particular urban enclaves where they choose to reside (Beaverstock 2002; Smith 2001). Indeed, Beaverstock (2002: 527) has argued that the spaces of global cities are frequently arranged around the Western expatriate and that they are permitted to live in environments or enclaves that revolve around their own occupational and social needs. Expatriate enclaves are a notable feature of many global cities and have been identified as bubbles or 'safety zones' that have the power to 'shelter' or 'hide' Westerners from the myriad sensations of the host society. As Stephenson and Ali-Knight (2010: 284) have argued in the context of Dubai:

> The social distinctions within the ethnic strata of expatriate communities are indeed conspicuous when it comes to issues of urban residency. European communities generally occupy more salubrious surroundings near to the tourist locations, hotels and restaurants, and sport and recreational complexes. The tourism environment has, in many ways, cemented the ethnic distinctions within the expatriate communities.

Conversely, however, while many expatriates who choose to work abroad may be motivated by the employment advantages foreign placements offer and reside in such enclaves, the affordances of location and the opportunity to venture out and travel and experience their new locations as tourists are also significant factors for their overall mobile lifestyles (Butler & Hannam 2014).

Moreover, gender has been recognised as a key aspect of Western expatriate migration and fundamental to the organisation of expatriate communities and identities (Coles & Fechter 2008; Yeoh & Willis 2005). Coles and Fechter (2008) show that men's careers are often prioritised over those of their wives, which are put on hold or discontinued as women adopt the infamous role of the 'trailing spouse', engaging in the socialising and pleasure-seeking lifestyles of leisure and tourism. Indeed, economic and institutional factors as well as administrative rules governing immigration often present hurdles to women's employment. Women are often automatically issued dependents' visas that do not allow paid work, and some transnational corporations have been found to insist on the female spouse's non-employment (Fechter 2007; Lehmann 2014; Yeoh & Khoo 1998). Indeed, women's domestic and emotional labour, and especially their social activities, can be essential for advancing their husbands' careers (Beaverstock 2005; Fechter 2007).

Hannam (2017) has further demonstrated, however, that in the context of Saudi Arabia everyday mobility restrictions for migrant women may be structured in order to keep a woman within strictly defined limits. Thus, travel and the freedom to use both public and private means of transport for women within Saudi Arabia was highly constrained for both local women and also female expatriates, thus limiting their independent use of the tourism and leisure infrastructure. With the recent legalisation for women to drive in Saudi Arabia, some of these mobility restrictions will be alleviated.

Hutchings, Michailova and Harrison (2013) examined the perceptions of gender and cultural stereotyping of Western women in the UAE. Their study found that many expatriates did not perceive gender or cultural stereotyping in the workplace, but rather perceived it in non-working contexts. The experiences are clearly different from the experiences of Arab women expatriates working in Dubai, who noted having experienced gender stereotyping in the workplace (Miller, Kyriazi, & Paris 2017). Interestingly, the study found that in non-work environments, some respondents engaged in auto-stereotyping, particularly in settings away from the 'expatriate ghettos'. A third key finding of the study, was that expatriates' working and living experiences need to be understood along a continuum from completely segregated to 'cosmopolitan'.

In the UAE, the expatriate labour market has become further segmented along lines of race, gender, occupation and country of origin, partly due to the rapid pace of urbanisation, but also due to changes in the employment regulations of the UAE (Ewers & Dicce 2016). In Dubai, for example, 'the status distinction between various nationalities of migrants is taken for granted' and indeed carefully policed (Walsh 2014: 7). Moreover, British expatriates' leisure encounters with and discourses about other low-skilled migrants from and within the Middle East can be seen as having neo-colonial overtones or even involve Orientalising or racist discourses (Walsh 2007, 2012, 2014).

MENA expatriates

In her seminal book, *Citizens Abroad*, Laurie Brand (2006) offers a rather different perspective on the notion of expatriates in the Middle East from the one discussed above. Rather than focus on white, Western expatriates in the Gulf States of the Middle East, she analyses expatriates from Morocco, Tunisia, Jordan and Lebanon who move both to Europe and within the Middle East, often supported by state institutions. She argues that expatriates need to be considered within the complex of regional and/or international relations and notes that many 'sending states have developed the impression, rightly or wrongly, that their expatriates can push for special consideration of their needs by the host state' (Brand 2006: 16). Indeed, there is a substantial history of European state involvement in the affairs of foreign nationals in the Middle East. Nevertheless, while tourists are expected to obey or abide by the laws of the lands they are visiting, expatriates are subject to a wide range of host state laws, and their work and extended residence do not qualify them for political membership in the receiving states. Conversely, sending states frequently offer their expatriates favourable taxation regimes (for example, on second homes) in order to foster a sense of loyalty to their home country. For expatriates from and within the Middle East, remittances also perform an important element in their motivations and relationships and thus reinforce VFR tourism.

Jordan has had a growing expatriate population abroad, overwhelmingly in the Gulf States. Brand (2006) discusses the identity of Jordanian expatriates as being particularly 'problematic' as, for many Jordanian expatriates, the relationship to Jordan was one of an imposed nationality. In the case of Lebanon, with its significant diaspora, the majority of Lebanese descendants are no longer Lebanese citizens, and many 'have never been to Lebanon, do not speak Arabic, and have even changed their family names to integrate more easily into their host societies' (Brand 2006: 134). Although referred to as a 'bird with two wings', expatriate and resident, Lebanese expatriates have been romanticised by the Lebanese state as being entrepreneurial. Successive Lebanese governments have been concerned with maintaining or rebuilding ties between expatriates (and/or their descendants) and the homeland, particularly in terms of encouraging tourism development (Brand 2006).

Furthermore, the Lebanese diaspora has been described as:

> a diaspora of dispersal in which the recovery of identity reflects the experience of cross-generational attrition in assimilating societies … The recovery of the imaginary homeland for many Lebanese resembles the broader predicament at present time, social impermanence, fluid identities and individual uncertainty.
>
> *(Humphrey 2004: 17)*

Nevertheless, this has not meant that Lebanese migrants forget their identity, as they took their traditions with them when they migrated, similar to other diasporic groups (Abdallah & Hannam 2016; Coles & Timothy 2004). Abdelhady (2007) has also identified how notions of solidarity, democracy and rights are central to many members of the Lebanese diaspora and thus their emphasis on cosmopolitan citizenship informs their participation in public events through which they can express their identities.

The Lebanese diaspora in London, for example, embodies the Lebanese homeland through the social construction of its hospitality and food, much the same way other diasporic groups do throughout the world (Chhabra, Lee, Zhao, & Scott 2013; Kaftanoglu & Timothy 2013). They have adapted Lebanese culinary heritage with a degree of Western 'exoticness' in order to form a socially constructed cultural diaspora that would be welcomed and embraced in a Western world. Expatriate Lebanese entrepreneurs have thus achieved success by developing a hybrid Lebanese Middle Eastern cuisine; however, this cuisine is based upon a largely quixotic sense of past events and places (Abdallah & Hannam 2016).

Similarly, in her analysis of Moroccan expatriates based in Europe, Wagner (2017) argues that their identities are also constructed through an engagement with tourism practices. Moroccan expatriates on holiday in Morocco sought elite leisure spaces in ways that were predicated on both their familiarity with Morocco as a homeland and their access to a car, intentionally avoiding certain kinds of public spaces whilst consuming more Westernised food and hospitality.

Employment in tourism

In the discussion above we have highlighted the role of expatriates and migrants mainly in terms of leisure and tourism consumption. However, migrants' actual tourism work and management practices also need to be recognised. Research on expatriates is frequently considered within the field of human resource management, reflecting its significance for international business and elite mobilities (McNulty & Brewster 2017). In the Middle East it has further been recognised that Human Resource Management (HRM) practices have many differences from those in the West. As Rodriguez and Scurry (2014: 1051) have noted, 'HRM is acknowledged to be a challenge for both international and local organisations in the Middle East'. Research in the Middle East has thus made reference to the

> challenges resulting from organizations' lack of investment in HR development, which arises from the combined challenges of having a large number of temporary (and in some cases itinerant) migrant workforce and the limited professionalization of the HR function.
>
> *(Rodriguez & Scurry 2014: 1051)*

With the recognition of the role that expatriates and migrants play in the tourism industry there is greatly increased competition within the Middle East to recruit and retain high quality frontline service workers—talent management: 'an organisational mindset that seeks to assure that the supply of talent is available to align the right people with the right jobs at the right time, based on strategic business objectives' (Baum 2008: 720). Strategic talent management in the hospitality industries is not just about systematically recruiting staff with a particular technical skill set but also with particular emotional and aesthetic outlooks (Baum 2008). Further, the strategic talent management in the GCC in particular requires companies to achieve a balance between local adaptation to legal localisation rules and global assimilation that enhances their economic sustainability (Sidani & Al Ariss 2014.)

Hence, various Middle Eastern countries have sought to develop different strategies to overcome their shortage of tourism workers. Qatar, for instance, with the upcoming Football World Cup in 2022, has attempted to develop a Human Capital Tourism Development Strategy (HCTDS) which should be in harmony with local traditions and values—encouraging family values and social cohesion; should align with the national agenda by contributing to economic, social and human development, and reduce Qatar's reliance on energy by diversifying the economy; should create a positive economic impact by enhancing productivity and creating employment in tourism and non-tourism sectors, encourage SME activity and private initiative and entrepreneurship, spreading tourism offerings to all parts of Qatar not just Doha; and should also be environmentally responsible, preserving Qatar's delicate and valuable ecosystems. Many Gulf States currently struggle to staff their tourism industry adequately in terms of numbers and quality—and that struggle will only continue to increase with growth in the sector—with low indigenous participation and low service quality continuing to be issues even as the number and size of tourism-related events continue to grow.

Multi-national enterprises within the tourism and hospitality sector in MENA also have to consider their own HRM practices in the context of local settings given the diversity of the expatriate and local workforces and the differences in local labour laws and markets. In examining American Hotels HRM practices in Saudi Arabia, Al Khaldi (2016) found that organisational learning in regards to the local cultural and institutional contexts is significant for transferring HRM practices and policies. Some practices may be localised, while others may need to fully adapt according to local labour laws and markets. Al-Khaldi (2016) also found that many of the multinational hotels were actively investing and promoting Saudi HR managers to more senior positions in order to facilitate organisational learning, adaptation and talent management.

There is an increasing number of MENA expatriates employed in management and upper management positions in the tourism industry in the region. Managers, many with more than five or ten years of experience, from Lebanon, Syria, Palestine and Egypt are increasingly common in international hotel chains. Steiner (2007) argued that the integration of MENA expatriates into the management structures can increase the companies' local embeddedness with local knowledge and experience. Companies with a higher degree of local embeddedness are able to moderate perceptions during crises, a key for both resilience and destination recovery in countries like Egypt, Lebanon and Tunisia.

Conclusion

In this chapter we have attempted to provide a critical review of the literature regarding the role of expatriates and migrants within the Middle East in relation to the tourism sector. Conceptualising the expatriate/migrant nexus in the context of the Middle East demonstrates that both Western expatriates and MENA expatriates demand engagement in different types of tourism both as consumers and as employees.

Thinking beyond the expatriate/migrant nexus, however, we also need to consider the precarious position of the refugee within and beyond the Middle East, particularly in the context of conceptualising Islamic hospitality (Abdallah & Hannam 2013). Expatriates and migrants are subject to wider geopolitical changes within and outside the Middle East in terms of their status; however, the position of refugees who may subsequently become expatriates and/or migrants is also significant given the ongoing conflicts in the region. Mason (2011) has explored the experiences of Iraqi refugees in Jordan, demonstrating that while their mobility has largely been shaped by pan-Arab ideologies concerning 'hospitality'—refugees are seen as 'guests'—this mobility is highly dependent on their socioeconomic position. Hence, there is a need to think about the expatriate, the migrant and the refugee in terms of wider mobilities.

References

Abdallah, A., & Hannam, K. (2013) 'The Lebanese diaspora and hospitality in the UK', *E-Review of Tourism Research*, 10(5/6): 19–37.

Abdallah, A., & Hannam, K. (2016) 'Food as a quixotic event: Producing Lebanese cuisine in London', in K. Hannam, M. Mostafanezhad, & J. Rickly (eds), *Event Mobilities: Politics, Place and Performance* (pp. 133–143). London: Routledge.

Abdelhady, D. (2007) 'Cultural production in the Lebanese diaspora: Memory, nostalgia and displacement', *Journal of Political and Military Sociology*, 35(1): 39–62.

Al-Khaldi, A.H (2016) 'The transfer of HRM policies and practices in American multinational hotels in Saudi Arabia', (doctoral dissertation). Available online: https://espace.curtin.edu.au (Accessed 11 September 2018).

Baruch, Y., & Forstenlechner, I. (2017) 'Global careers in the Arabian Gulf: Understanding motives for self-initiated expatriation of the highly skilled, globally mobile professionals', *Career Development International*, 22(1): 3–22.

Baum, T. (2008) 'Implications of hospitality and tourism labor markets for talent management strategies', *International Journal of Contemporary Hospitality Management*, 20(7): 720–729.

Beaverstock, J.V. (2002) 'Transnational elites in global cities: British expatriates in Singapore's financial district', *Geoforum*, 33(4): 525–538.

Beaverstock, J.V. (2005) 'Transnational elites in the city: British highly-skilled inter-company transferees in New York city's financial district', *Journal of Ethnic and Migration Studies*, 31(2): 245–268.

Brand, L. (2006) *Citizens Abroad: Emigration and the State in the Middle East and North Africa*. Cambridge: Cambridge University Press.

Buckley, M. (2013) 'Locating neoliberalism in Dubai: Migrant workers and class struggle in the autocratic city', *Antipode*, 45: 256–274.

Butler, G., & Hannam, K. (2014) 'Performing expatriate automobilities in Kuala Lumpur. *Mobilities*, 9(1): 1–20.

Chhabra, D., Lee, W., Zhao, S., & Scott, K. (2013) 'Marketing of ethnic food experiences: Authentication analysis of Indian cuisine abroad', *Journal of Heritage Tourism*, 8(2/3): 145–157.

Coles, A., & Fechter, A.M. (eds) (2008) *Gender and Family among Transnational Professionals*. London: Routledge.

Coles, T., & Timothy, D.J. (eds) (2004) *Tourism, Diasporas and Space*. London: Routledge.

Coles, A., & Walsh, K. (2010) 'From "Trucial state" to "postcolonial" city? The imaginative geographies of British expatriates in Dubai', *Journal of Ethnic and Migration Studies*, 36(8): 1317–1333.

Ewers, M., & Dicce, R. (2016) 'Expatriate labor markets in rapidly globalising cities: Reproducing the migrant division of labor in Abu Dhabi and Dubai', *Journal of Ethnic and Migration Studies*, 42(15): 2448–2467.

Fechter, A.M. (2007) *Transnational Lives: Expatriates in Indonesia*. Aldershot: Ashgate.

Fechter, A.M., & Walsh, K. (2010) 'Examining "expatriate" continuities: Postcolonial approaches to mobile professionals', *Journal of Ethnic and Migration Studies*, 36(8): 1197–1210.

Findlay, A., & Li, F. (1998) 'A migration channels approach to the study of professionals moving to and from Hong Kong', *The International Migration Review*, 32(123): 682–703.

Hannam, K. (2017) 'Gendered automobilities: Female Pakistani migrants driving in Saudi Arabia', in J. Rickly, K. Hannam, & M. Mostafanezhad (eds), *Tourism and Leisure Mobilities: Politics, Work, and Play* (pp. 54–63). London: Routledge.

Howe-Walsh, L., & Schyns, B. (2010) 'Self-initiated expatriation: Implications for HRM', *International Journal of Human Resource Management*, 21(2): 260–273.

Humphrey, M. (2004) 'Lebanese identities: Between cities, nations and trans-nations', *Arab Studies Quarterly*, 26(1): 15–17.

Hutchings, K., Michailova, S., & Harrison, E. (2013) 'Neither ghettoed nor cosmopolitan: A study of Western women's perceptions of gender and cultural stereotyping in the UAE', *Management International Review*, 53(2): 291–318.

Kaftanoglu, B., & Timothy, D.J. (2013) 'Return travel, assimilation and cultural maintenance: An example of Turkish-Americans in Arizona', *Tourism Analysis*, 18(3): 273–284.

Kapiszewski, A. (2001) *Nationals and Expatriates: Population and Labor Dilemmas of the Gulf Cooperation Council States*. Reading, MA: Ithaca Press.

Kopnina, H. (2007) *Migration and Tourism: Formation of New Social Classes*. New York: Cognizant.

Kunz, S. (2016) 'Privileged mobilities: Locating the expatriate in migration scholarship', *Geography Compass*, 10(3): 89–101.

Lehmann, A. (2014) *Transnational Lives in China: Expatriates in a Globalizing City*. New York: Palgrave Macmillan.

Mason, V. (2011) 'The im/mobilities of Iraqi refugees in Jordan: Pan-Arabism, "hospitality" and the figure of the "refugee"', *Mobilities*, 6(3): 353–373.

McNulty, Y., & Brewster, C. (2017) 'Theorising the meaning(s) of 'expatriate': Establishing boundary conditions', *International Journal of Human Resource Management*, 10.1080/09585192.2016.1243567.

Miller, K., Kyriazi, T., & Paris, C. (2017) 'Arab women employment in the UAE: Exploring opportunities, motivations and challenges', *International Journal of Sustainable Society*, 9(1): 20–40.

Rees, C.J., Mamman, A., & Bin Braik, A. (2007) 'Emiratisation as a strategic HRM change initiative: Case study evidence from a UAE petroleum company', *The International Journal of Human Resource Management*, 18(1): 33–53.

Rodriguez, J.K., & Mearns, L. (2012) 'Problematising the interplay between employment relations, migration and mobility', *Employee Relations*, 34(6): 580–593.

Rodriguez, J.K., & Scurry, T. (2014) 'Career capital development of self-initiated expatriates in Qatar: Cosmopolitan globetrotters, experts and outsiders', *International Journal of Human Resource Management*, 25(1–2): 190–211.

Sadi, M., & Henderson, J. (2005) 'Local versus foreign workers in the hospitality and tourism industry: A Saudi Arabian perspective', *Cornell Hotel and Restaurant Administration Quarterly*, 46(2): 247–257.

Sidani, Y., & Al Ariss, A. (2014) 'Institutional and corporate drivers of global talent management: Evidence from the Arab Gulf region', *Journal of World Business*, 49(2): 215–224.

Sidaway, J.D. (2007) 'Enclave space: A new metageography of development?' *Area*, 39(3): 331–339.

Smith, P.M. (2001) *Transnational Urbanism*. London: Routledge.

Steiner, C. (2007) 'Political instability, transnational tourist companies and destination recovery in the Middle East after 9/11', *Tourism Hospitality Planning & Development*, 4(3): 167–188.

Stephenson, M., & Ali-Knight, J. (2010) 'Dubai's tourism industry and its societal impact: Social implications and sustainable challenges', *Journal of Tourism and Cultural Change*, 8(4): 278–292.

Stephenson, M., Russell, K., & Edgar, D. (2010) 'Islamic hospitality in the UAE: Indigenisation of products and human capital', *Journal of Islamic Marketing*, 1(1): 9–24.

Thieme, S. (2008) 'Sustaining livelihoods in multi-local settings: Possible theoretical linkages between transnational migration and livelihood studies', *Mobilities*, 3(1): 51–71.

Tung, R.L. (1998) 'American expatriates abroad: From neophytes to cosmopolitans', *Journal of World Business*, 33(2): 125–144.

Wagner, L. (2017) 'Viscous automobilities: Diasporic practices and vehicular assemblages of visiting "home"', *Mobilities*. DOI: 10.1080/17450101.2016.1274560

Walsh, K. (2006) 'British expatriate belongings: Mobile homes and transnational homing', *Home Cultures*, 3(2): 123–144.

Walsh, K. (2007) 'It got very debauched, very Dubai!' Heterosexual intimacy amongst single British expatriates', *Social & Cultural Geography*, 8(4): 507–533.

Walsh, K. (2011) 'Migrant masculinities and domestic space: British home-making practices in Dubai', *Transactions of the Institute of British Geographers*, 36(4): 516–529.

Walsh, K. (2012) 'Emotion and migration: British transnationals in Dubai', *Environment and Planning D: Society and Space*, 30(1): 43–59.

Walsh, K. (2014) 'Placing transnational migrants through comparative research: British migrant belonging in five GCC cities', *Population, Space and Place*, 20(1): 1–17.

Yeoh, B.S.A., & Khoo, L.M. (1998) 'Home, work and community: Skilled international migration and expatriate women in Singapore', *International Migration*, 36(2): 159–186.

Yeoh, B.S.A., & Willis, K. (2005) 'Singaporeans in China: Transnational women elites and the negotiation of gendered identities', *Geoforum*, 36(2): 211–222.

26

BUSINESS TRAVEL AND THE MICE INDUSTRY IN THE MIDDLE EAST

Joan C. Henderson

Introduction

This chapter is concerned with business travel in the Middle East and examines selected aspects of the market. After some comments on the defining features of business travel in general, the scale of demand and differences amongst countries in the region are considered before an assessment of trends and underlying determinants. Attention is then given to supply issues, future prospects and the challenges that lie ahead before a final conclusion. There is evidence of a significant amount of existing activity and commercial opportunities, but these are not evenly distributed across the region. Economic and political forces operating internally and externally are critical influences on performance. Formidable obstacles must be overcome regarding the tourism industry and wider conditions if the region's overall potential as a destination for business travellers is to be realised.

Business travel defined

Business travel describes travel in which the primary purpose is business of multiple sorts and can encompass meetings, incentives, conventions and exhibitions (Swarbrooke & Horner 2001). A distinction is sometimes made and the acronym BTMICE used, but the term 'business travel' is employed in this chapter to refer to these types of tourism collectively unless otherwise specified. It includes travel by officials and people working for non-governmental organisations as well as those involved in trade and commerce. Unlike much leisure tourism, business travel is usually non-discretionary and funded by employers or other agencies. Frequency is often high and being constantly on the move may be deleterious to health and personal life (Espino, Sundstrom, Frick, Jacobs, & Peters 2002). Such travellers require various modes and standards of transport and accommodation and some are able to complete their work in a day so do not need a place to stay. Superior services and facilities offering efficiency and comfort, enabling business to be conducted without distractions in transit and on arrival, are often favoured. There is likely to be little interest in attractions, although these can play a role when business is combined with leisure or organisers are making decisions about conference venues and take into account the general appeal of destinations (Yu & Weber 2005).

Levels of business travel have risen substantially in recent decades as a result of increased international flows of goods, money, people and information. Business has become more geographically dispersed and workforces more mobile. Easier movement, especially by air, is another manifestation and driver of these globalisation processes linked to business travel (Beaverstock, Derudder, Faulconbridge, & Witlox 2010). The market is perceived to be lucrative because of its spending power and the fact that it is less affected by seasonality than many forms of tourism (UNWTO 2014). It is thus a target for destinations and service providers, but has possible disadvantages of a comparatively short average length of stay and vulnerability to economic and trade fluctuations (Ka & Kan 2016). Public spending on conference and exhibition sites can be controversial because of opportunity costs and disappointing returns, although benefits are not readily quantifiable (Jones & Li 2015). Business travel is also distinguished by its organisational complexity whereby numerous parties are involved and this underlines the need for proper management (Gustafson 2012). Demand continues to be robust, suggesting the importance still attached to personal contact irrespective of the virtual alternatives afforded by modern communication technologies; indeed, the two can be complementary as demonstrated by hybrid meetings which unite face-to-face and remote exchanges (Sox, Kline, & Crews 2014).

Demand in the Middle East

The Middle East and North Africa have a relatively small share of the world's international tourism with 4.6 per cent (54.1 million) and 1.6 per cent (18.8 million) respectively in 2015; the former was an increase of around 3 per cent over 2014, but the latter was a decline of 8 per cent (UNWTO 2016). Akin to the rest of the world, most tourism is intra-regional and there is a great deal of domestic travel. Of the global receipts from overseas visitors of US$1.5 trillion in 2014, the Middle East earned 4 per cent whereas the figure for North Africa was 0.8 per cent. Israel is classed as part of the Southern European/Mediterranean sub-region for statistical purposes by UNWTO and recorded 2.8 million visitors in 2015, the same as in 2010 (UNWTO 2016). Tourism growth in the Middle East and North Africa has been uneven in the past few years, reflecting its vulnerability to adverse conditions, which are returned to in later sections.

Statistics are not broken down by purpose, but UNWTO (2015) estimates that 14 per cent of all international travel around the world was for business reasons in 2014. Another report calculates business travel spending of US$1.156 trillion worldwide in 2014 (Dubai World Trade Centre 2016). As many as 41.3 million trips for business were made to the Middle East and Africa in 2011, or 2.1 per cent of the world's total (Euromonitor International 2012). Despite recent uncertainties, advances in Middle East business travel are observable in the MICE sector. International association meetings tripled in the decade prior to 2014 (Alpen Capital 2014), and it is currently the location for an estimated 2 per cent of the world's exhibitions (Dubai World Trade Centre 2016). The rising number of meetings and business events has been made possible by the development of a supporting infrastructure and the tourism industry generally (TTG MENA 2016a). In another sign of progress, the 2014 Arabian Travel Market attracted 2,800 exhibitors from 86 countries and 26,000 visitors, generating US$2.4 billion in deals; in comparison, the first gathering in 1994 drew 300 exhibitors from 52 nations and 7,000 trade visitors (Arabian Travel Market 2016).

Country contrasts

Regional data obscure often marked variations by country. Given the diversity of economies and stages of development, as well as political systems, it is not surprising that the volume and value of business travel ranges widely. It is generally less significant than leisure travel and accounts for around one-third of tourist spending in the Gulf Cooperation Council (GCC) zone which comprises Bahrain, Kuwait, Oman, Qatar, Saudi Arabia and the UAE. The highest share of 70 per cent is recorded in Qatar followed by Oman (35.1 per cent), Saudi Arabia (25 per cent) and Kuwait (23 per cent) (Alpen Capital 2014). Nevertheless, the UAE is a popular MICE destination and especially the emirates of Dubai and Abu Dhabi. A 2014 survey disclosed that major UAE origin markets are India, the US, Eastern Europe, Scandinavia and the Benelux area. Most travellers are from the pharmaceutical, IT and automotive industries (Gulf Business 2015). Saudi Arabia and Qatar are also up-and-coming venues and have been joined by Oman (Euromonitor International 2012). The UAE was ranked 40 in the world in terms of meetings in 2015 and Dubai and Abu Dhabi were amongst the world's most visited cities for meetings with rankings of 46 and 73 respectively. Turkey surpassed GCC members, however, with a country rating of 18, while Istanbul was placed 8th in the city list (ICCA 2016). One of the travel and tourism competitiveness measures devised by the World Economic Forum (2015) is the average annual number of international associations meetings hosted over the previous three years. Country scores confirm contrasting performances and range from 20th position out of 141 for Turkey to 120th for Kuwait.

Dubai's achievements in the field are noteworthy, and it has effectively positioned itself as a premier regional business travel destination, aspiring to occupy a global role. Authorities cite ten reasons for choosing Dubai that yield insights into prerequisites of success. The selling points are its global aviation hub, world-class infrastructure, meetings and convention facilities, hotels, business growth opportunities, knowledge hub function, safety, adventure and experiences, restaurants and entertainment, and experienced industry support (Visit Dubai 2016). Dubai is also less rigid about the implementation of Sharia law, practised by the Islamic governments that define most of the region, within a tourism context. The approach differs from the austere Wahhabist interpretation of the religion in Saudi Arabia, for example, where very strict rules and penalties for non-compliance apply to visitors and residents. Although perhaps the envy of certain states in the region and beyond, Dubai's economic and tourism development strategies may be unsustainable because of the heavy reliance on credit and real estate for funding which prevails in the UAE as a whole. Drawbacks became apparent in Dubai after the onset of the global financial crisis in 2008 when several projects were delayed. Expo 2020, to be held in Dubai, has incurred escalating costs and debt burdens with warnings of a property surplus (Euromonitor International 2014a).

The omission of several countries from the World Economic Forum's competitiveness index is indicative of weaknesses in their tourism industries, which are attributable mainly to wider circumstances. The worst instance is Syria where the civil war, which started in 2011, has caused devastation and crippled the economy. International airlines have suspended services and many hotels have been destroyed. Resolution seems very far off and will be a long-term process with business travel severely depressed in the interim (Euromonitor International 2014b). Sudan is also deemed extremely unstable and dangerous for visitors (Euromonitor International 2014c) alongside Yemen since the revolution in 2011; kidnappings of foreigners in the latter have aggravated fears about personal safety for all travellers (Euromonitor International 2013). Efforts to rebuild Afghanistan after years of turmoil have led to more business travel illustrated by the introduction of first and business class on Dubai's Emirates airline flights to the Afghan capital of Kabul in 2013 (Euromonitor International 2014d). Stability has not been restored, however, and hotels patronised by business travellers are targets for insurgent groups. There are similar worries in Iraq where any recovery has stalled and business travel is unlikely to grow much in the immediate future. Possibilities in Kurdistan, which is relatively peaceful (Euromonitor International

2014e), have inspired some optimism, in spite of its 2017 referendum backing independence, albeit an independence that has not been recognised by Iraq or other states. It is also difficult to be positive about prospects in Palestine in view of the country's situation and constraints on doing business, including restrictions on physical movements and border crossings. Inbound arrivals in Israel have been adversely affected by regional instability and violent clashes between Israelis and Palestinians (BMI Research 2016).

Destinations with ongoing serious conflicts face continuing threats to government authority, transport disruption, damaged infrastructure, economic dislocation and interruption to regular trade and commerce. These all impact negatively on business travel and investors look to alternatives in the region believed to be safer and more secure, exemplified by the UAE. In some cases, advisories against visiting are issued by official agencies in generating nations which are detrimental to the restoration of confidence and may invalidate insurance coverage if ignored. At the same time, except in the direst situations, there will be travel to struggling nations by people such as diplomatic staff, aid workers from assorted formal and non-governmental organisations, and journalists. Some countries with a history of upheaval that appears to be abating may be considered in transition and thereby more appealing, prompting travel for the purposes of renewed business operations and investment. Recovering states also need foreign assistance and expertise, leading to an inflow of personnel engaged in reconstruction and rehabilitation.

Underlying drivers

Political stability emerges as one key determinant of business travel demand and distribution. Its absence in several territories has created dangerous realities and discouraging perceptions, which inhibit business and related travel; in contrast, certain destinations where politics are more settled have flourished. Official backing for tourism is evident across much of the region and has acted as another stimulus of overall destination development. Governments such as those of Kuwait and Oman have long-term tourism strategies and many have set ambitious targets for international tourism. Emphasis is commonly given to leisure markets, but MICE travellers have a place in plans for Jordan, Oman (Global Futures and Foresight 2007) and Saudi Arabia (Monshi & Scott 2017; SCTH 2016) amongst others. Dubai's intention is to be a 'leading destination for global travel, business and events by 2020' (DTCM 2015), a vision shared by Abu Dhabi and Qatar (QTA 2015; TCA 2015). Units within tourism administrations promote business travel; for example, the Abu Dhabi Convention Bureau, Dubai Business Events, the Saudi Exhibition and Convention Bureau and convention and visitor bureaux in Turkish urban centres of Istanbul, Antalya and Izmir. Authorities in Israel, where tourism contributes an estimated 6.8 per cent of total GDP, recognise the dilemmas for conference organisers caused by the geopolitical situation and introduced a scheme in 2015 that provides compensation in certain cases of cancellation (Israel Ministry of Tourism 2016).

Economic factors are equally important and tied to matters of politics with business travel partly determined by the health of national, regional and global economies. Oil and gas have tended to dominate economically and catalysed urbanisation, industrialisation and development in parts of the region. These have involved massive projects and construction booms, all of which has boosted business travel. Large communities exist of expatriate workers from manual labourers to professionals who are consumers of both business and leisure travel. Geographically, the region is strategically located between Europe and Asia Pacific, which is conducive to trade, and has seen very heavy spending on airports and airlines as well as ports. International connectivity has facilitated business travel and, alongside improvements in information communications technologies, encouraged commercial organisations to move to the region (Insights Management Consultancy, h2c & Amadeus 2007). Several GCC states have business-friendly environments and corporate taxation regimes that have also favoured inward investment and the opening of foreign enterprises (Alpen Capital 2014).

Nevertheless, weaknesses in the global economy since the turn of the century have resulted in slowdowns in trade and industrial production which, in turn, have had negative consequences for some business travel—so, too, has the deceleration in China's growth. Oil producing nations are at risk from the so-called resource curse whereby the economy is distorted and damaged as a consequence of over-reliance (Gelb & Turner 2008). Public sectors are often large, bureaucratic and inefficient and private enterprise is hampered. Much labour is imported and there are now insufficient jobs for local populations, which are growing in size and increasingly well-educated (Hvidt 2013). Sharp falls in oil prices commencing in 2014, and expected to be prolonged, are another concern that is elaborated upon later. The International Air Transport Association noted sluggish sales of business and first class air travel in early 2015 and commented on how volumes of such premium passenger traffic are sensitive to the health of global financial markets, world trade and business confidence (IATA 2015).

There are thus several factors and forces in operation that shape the size, scale and character of business travel in the Middle East, and its future is a matter for some debate. Prospects are discussed below, together with obstacles to surmount, after a more detailed account of the region's current supply of the facilities and services that are essential to business travel.

Current supply

Meeting, conference and exhibition spaces

An appropriate stock of amenities is critical for a thriving MICE industry, and all countries advertise conference and exhibition centres, usually in capital or major cities, and are frequently state-owned and operated. Hotels provide additional MICE space, albeit on a smaller scale. Dedicated centres are of varied size and standard, and a 2014 study acknowledged 'state of the art' MICE infrastructure in the GCC zone (Alpen Capital 2014). Conference and exhibition centres have been built or expanded with the UAE offering the grandest and most up to date, which can cater for larger events such as Dubai Expo 2020. Examples are the doubling in capacity of the Dubai World Trade Centre and opening of the Abu Dhabi National Exhibition Centre. The Riyadh International Convention and Exhibition Centre is being enlarged and Oman launched a new Convention and Exhibition Centre in 2016, hailed as an iconic landmark of the capital and Sultanate (TTG MENA 2016b). Developments are not confined to the Gulf: the government in Algiers is building a Centre International de Conferences, due to be completed in 2016. Major Israeli cities of Tel Aviv, Jerusalem and Haifa have modern conference facilities able to accommodate 50 to 10,000 as do several universities. Costs can be very high, as demonstrated by the Doha Exhibition and Conference Centre, which opened in late 2015 after an investment of US$631.81 million. Such funding may be beyond the means of authorities in poorer countries and could incite opposition of a sort previously mentioned due to the diversion of scarce resources away from areas believed to be of greater direct benefit to citizens.

Specialist services

Business travel and especially the MICE component rely on assorted enterprises to assist in arranging and delivering products and services. Specialists include business travel agents in the country of origin, a few of which have an international network of offices. Event planners and meeting organisers, based in both generating and destination countries, liaise with the venues as well as accommodation and transport sellers. Expertise of this type is found in much of the region and numerous operators promote themselves; for example, at the time of writing, 19 specialist conference and incentive enterprises are listed on the official website for Israel. Degrees of professionalism are, however, not uniform and are lacking in some instances. Support is also given by official agencies, which proffer advice and practical aid encompassing help with marketing and logistics and occasionally financial incentives.

Accommodation and foodservice

Unless their work is finished in sufficient time to return home, business travellers require food and overnight accommodation. Many such visitors have budgetary constraints and cannot afford costly accommodation, so a balanced supply from modest to deluxe properties is desirable. Nevertheless, there is often a preference for familiar brands and middle and upscale hotels by arrivals from outside the region. International chains such as Accor, Hilton, IHG and Marriot/Starwood have increased their portfolios in the region accordingly (The Hotel Show 2016). The focus tends to be on the GCC, and commercial interest is often greater in coastal resorts in North Africa, but business destinations in the latter are reasonably well served. Regional chains are active and independent hotels should not be overlooked. Hotels provide dining, the largest at a selection of restaurants with cuisines from around the world, and there is a miscellany of other foodservice options. Islamic rules and regulations about permissible foodstuffs and modes of preparation, however, have ramifications for all caterers and certain items are denied consumers. The drinking and selling of alcohol is restricted and sometimes banned, although controls may be loosened in hotels and at additional outlets in some of the more liberal states. Adherence to Sharia law also affects other aspects of hotel operation in ways that impinge on the guest experience (Henderson 2003; Weidenfeld & Ron 2008).

Transportation

Access by air is vital to much business travel and the Gulf region in particular has seen great expansion in airport capacity (Derudder, Bassens, & Witlox 2013; Murel & O'Connell 2011), with Dubai overtaking London Heathrow as the world's busiest airport with around 78 million passengers in 2015. Emirates, Abu Dhabi's Etihad and Qatar Airways have introduced new routes and frequencies, especially on long haul journeys (Henderson 2014). Modern aircraft have been purchased such as the Airbus 380 and Boeing 777, which can carry high volumes and cover lengthy distances (Strickland 2015). The airlines are thus seeking to take advantage of the Middle East's strategic position and rising traffic amongst emerging markets of Asia, Latin America and Africa. The phenomenon is also evident in Turkey where Istanbul's Ataturk Airport is at the heart of an increasingly comprehensive route network flown by Turkish Airlines, allowing it to compete with the Gulf carriers. Israel's open-skies agreement with Europe, due to be implemented between 2014 and 2018, is improving accessibility and a new international airport is expected to open at Eilat in mid-2018. The low-cost carrier industry is still immature, but companies such as Fly Dubai and Air Arabia (founded in the emirate of Sharjah with bases in Egypt and Morocco) operate on short and medium haul routes within and outside the region. Surface transport infrastructure has not progressed as rapidly as that of civil aviation, and alternatives of high-speed rail travel, for example, are rarely found. Road systems are, however, generally satisfactory and permit movement by private or hire car outside cities.

Attractions

Much business travel is dictated by the location of public sector organisations and private firms engaged in the production of goods and services, shaped also by events specific to the particular sphere of business and in the wider world. Considerations such as climate and conventional tourist attractions are less relevant. However, as noted in the introduction, these place attributes may be influential when there is an element of discretion and choices have to be made; for example, regarding some conferences and exhibitions and meetings. Generalisations are complicated by the diversity within the region, but there are numerous sightseeing and entertainment possibilities derived from fascinating histories and unique cultural heritages. Deserts are interesting natural landscapes, the scene of a mix of leisure activities, and many countries have stretches of sandy coastlines with resorts and seaside amenities. Cities are centres of contemporary and traditional cultures and many offer cosmopolitan dining and nightlife as well as shopping and assorted events. These features can be packaged to create appealing programmes for incentive travellers and conference delegates, combining promises of Arabian exoticism with modern efficiency in certain instances.

Future prospects

There are grounds for optimism about the future, indicated by predictions that global shares of international tourism of all types will reach 8.2 per cent for the Middle East and 2.5 per cent for North Africa by 2030 (UNWTO 2015). Middle East airline traffic is also forecast to rise by over 6 per cent annually between 2013 and 2031, above the world average, with the highest rates in the UAE (Boeing 2013). Annual increases of worldwide business travel are expected to average 3.7 per cent up until 2024 (Dubai World Trade Centre 2016) and grow at a fast pace in the Middle East (Global Futures and Foresight 2007). It is anticipated that MICE visitors to Dubai will double to between 1.7 and 1.9 million by 2020 and Abu Dhabi's MICE annual earnings, currently around US$1.4 billion, will reach US$2.4 billion that year (Alpen Capital 2014). More business and non-business events, especially those of a prestigious character, are also likely (Weber & Ali-Knight 2012) and both will generate business travel. Hosting is a tool in the rebranding exercises undertaken by some states, exemplified by Qatar's successful bid for the FIFA 2022 World Cup (Henderson 2016).

Positive outlooks are attributed in part to the levels of investment in the tourism industry overall. An estimated US$3 trillion is being spent over the next 20 years in the Middle East on MICE facilities as well as museums, retail outlets, theme parks and sports stadia, which will complement business travel offerings in ways already explained. An additional 694 hotel projects were underway in the Middle East and Africa in 2015, due to add over 188,800 rooms. Dubai accounted for 96 of the schemes followed by Morocco (46), Riyadh (43) and Doha (38) (The Hotel Show 2016). Hilton, IHG and Marriot reportedly had 34, 29 and 28 properties respectively in the pipeline in 2013 in GCC countries (Alpen Capital 2014) and Starwood Hotels and Resorts announced in 2015 that it would be doubling its Middle East hotels with the opening of 50 by 2019 (Business Wire 2015). The supply of mid-priced accommodation is set to grow and thereby give business travellers more affordable choices (Gleksman 2015). Airports are planning further expansion, and Turkey is intending to build a third airport at Istanbul to handle 150 million passengers by 2028 (Zalewski 2015), more than any in Europe. Dubai will be able to deal with 90 million passengers and Doha and Abu Dhabi are doubling their capacity to 50 million and 20 million respectively within the next decade. There are additional plans to extend and upgrade surface transport networks, mainly in the GCC area.

In terms of wider conditions, the emergence of powerful economies in Asia and notably China and India has already created new trade and business opportunities. The region is expected to continue to exploit these and consolidate its position as a gateway to Asia and Sub-Saharan Africa. Analysts conclude that many Middle Eastern economies should remain robust and some might see significant real GDP growth (EIU 2016a), although the re-imposition of some sanctions in 2018 was a setback. Economic progress in less advanced countries will fuel intra-regional business travel alongside the anticipated resurgence of Iran after the lifting of international sanctions at the beginning of 2016. Ongoing diversification efforts to reduce dependence on the hydrocarbon sector could lead to more development projects and commercial ventures, stimulating demand for business travel. For example, Saudi Arabia launched its ambitious Vision 2030 in 2016, which incorporates a National Transformation Plan to modernise aspects of society and diversify the economy (Saudi Vision 2030 2016). Government policies in Israel to promote competition, increase foreign trade and investment, exploit large gas deposits in the Mediterranean, and upgrade infrastructure (EIU 2016b) are likely to stimulate business travel. Opportunities have been identified related to the sizeable start-up sector, which favours more international conferences (Euromonitor International 2016a). Many of the start-ups are located in Tel Aviv, which is increasingly a centre of international business and its hotels have more business guests than any other city in Israel (Euromonitor International 2016b).

Challenges ahead

Forecasts for tourism as a whole are positive with ambitious targets having been proposed, but these will not necessarily be attained given the challenges that lie ahead and indeed may constitute possible impediments. A key current and future concern is instances and perceptions of political insecurity, not least terrorist actions, and their effects. The EIU (2016c) anticipates heightened intra-regional rivalries (for example the 2017 boycott of Qatar by several of its MENA neighbours), dangers of external interventions and 'widespread social unrest, war and terrorism' in the Middle East and North Africa in the period from 2016 to 2020. Syria is an especial cause for anxiety as well as Lebanon and Iraq. Although a greater barrier to leisure travel, actual and perceived instability affects levels of economic activity and investor confidence with a dampening effect on business and related travel demand. Even destinations such as Dubai can be tainted and rejected as too risky for event organisers and meeting planners in the West. Turkey is not immune and its tourism may be damaged by disturbances in Syria, with which it shares a border, and terrorist outrages as well as domestic political dissension. Much business travel is intra-regional and participants are perhaps better informed about and more resistant to regional volatility, but drawing visitors from outside is vital. However, it is not easily achieved in light of deleterious images cultivated by chronic upheaval in some places and eruptions of violence elsewhere.

There are additional economic uncertainties to contend with which have implications for business travel. Despite the optimistic projections made reference to earlier, the region is responsible for around one-quarter of the world's oil production, and prolonged downward pressure on prices will have harmful consequences for economies and undermine business confidence. Some revisions in economic and social policies may be forced on governments which will no longer have such substantial financial reserves at their disposal (EIU 2016d), acting as a brake on planned developments. The results of diversification programmes may be disappointing, as they have been in the past (Flamos, Roupas, & Psarras 2013). Inefficiencies pertaining to administration persist and, writing about tourism at large in the Middle East and North Africa, a World Bank commentary calls for greater official commitment to tackle the 'strategic, operational and regulatory bottlenecks' which hinder competition and growth.

Obstacles identified are the absence of a 'strategic focus ... outdated regulatory and administrative structures' and 'undeveloped infrastructure' (Bell, Malinska, McConaghy, & Al Rowais 2012: 3).

Regarding civil aviation, and while centres in the region are striving to be global hubs, there are inadequacies in regulatory regimes and cross-border collaboration. Many governments adopt a protectionist stance and are unenthusiastic about moves towards deregulation and liberalisation (Timothy 2017). Congestion in the air, airspace constraints for military reasons and over-burdened air traffic control are other issues that must be addressed (Strickland 2015). Low-cost carriers have a comparatively small market share, narrowing options for business travellers on a budget. Air and surface transport systems in poorer countries are also less efficient and under-funded, inhibiting access and mobility, and the new investment required may not be forthcoming. Shortcomings in the range and type of tourist attractions must be recognised and can impinge directly and indirectly on business travel. Service standards and staffing are additional matters for attention, as there are difficulties of recruitment, retention and ensuring a labour force with suitable skills and professionalism. Information communications technology innovations could also result in more virtual meetings and conferences, eroding demand for business travel services regionally and around the world (Euromonitor International 2012). Finally, worldwide and regional competition is strong and parts of the region are at a disadvantage when targeting certain elements of the business travel market. Wealthier states that are longer-established destinations and in possession of the necessary facilities tend to be preferred.

Conclusion

The extent and characteristics of business travel in the Middle East are thus an outcome of prevailing economic, political and socio-cultural conditions within individual countries, the region and globally. Factors and forces operate to create opportunities that are being pursued by governments and private industry, but also create challenges that must be appreciated and surmounted if untapped potential is to be realised. Growth and evolution of the market is occurring, yet experiences are not uniform. More affluent oil-rich Gulf States have led the way, especially as places to host business-related gatherings of various sorts after very costly investments in facilities and supporting infrastructures. However, the old economic order is changing and spending may be constrained hereafter by shrinking oil revenues, with the effectiveness of efforts at diversification to offset losses remaining to be seen. Other countries attract some business travel, depending upon their amenities and economic and industrial activity, but are held back by the stage of development and adverse political circumstances, both of which have ramifications for the performance of economies and business. Widely held notions of instability and religious fanaticism also negatively affect the image of the whole region as a destination for selected forms of business travel. Future prospects are inextricably linked to the bigger picture and broader trends and perhaps look brighter in the longer term given the shorter- and medium-term dilemmas and problems awaiting resolution.

References

Alpen Capital (2014) 'GCC hospitality industry: Alpen Capital Investment Banking'. Available online: www.alpencapital.com/industry-reports.html (Accessed 14 February 2016).
Arabian Travel Market (2016) 'History'. Available online: www.arabiantravelmarket.com/About/History/ (Accessed 6 February 2016).

Beaverstock, J.V., Derudder, B., Faulconbridge, J., & Witlox, F. (eds) (2010) *International Business Travel in the Global Economy*. Farnham: Ashgate.

Bell, S.C., Malinska, J., McConaghy, P., & Al Rowais, S. (2012) 'Tourism in MENA: A strategy to promote recovery, economic diversification and job creation', *World Bank MENA Knowledge and Learning. Quick Notes Series*, January, No. 78.

BMI Research (2016) 'Economic analysis: Domestic and regional instability preventing tourism recovery'. Available online: https://bmo-bmiresearch (Accessed 14 August 2016).

Boeing (2013) 'The Boeing Company 2013 Annual Report'. Chicago, IL: Boeing Corporate Headquarters.

Business Wire (2015) 'Starwood hotels and resorts to double Middle East portfolio in the next five years'. *Business Wire*, 5 June. Available online: www.businesswire.com/news/home/20150505006509/en/Starwood-Hotels-Resorts-Double-Middle-East-Portfolio (Accessed 14 September 2018).

Derudder, B., Bassens, D., & Witlox, F. (2013) 'Political-geographic interpretations of massive air transport developments in Gulf cities', *Political Geography*, 36: A4–7.

DTCM (2015) 'About us'. Available online: www.visitdubai.com/en/department-of-tourism_new/about-dtcm (Accessed 1 May 2016).

Dubai World Trade Centre (2016) 'The GCC MICE market: Growth trends, opportunities and challenges'. Available online: www.dwtc.com/en/media-centre/Pages2015%20Features (Accessed 8 February 2016).

EIU (Economist Intelligence Unit) (2016a) 'Middle East and Africa growth and inflation'. EIU Global Forecasting Service, 20 January.

EIU (2016b) *Israel Country Forecast*. London: Economist Intelligence Unit.

EIU (2016c) 'Troubles in the Middle East and North Africa are spilling over regional borders'. EIU Global Forecasting Service, 20 January.

EIU (2016d) 'Low oil prices are compelling the region's governments to reform'. EIU Global Forecasting Service, 20 January.

Espino, C.M., Sundstrom, S.M., Frick, H.I., Jacobs, M., & Peters, M. (2002) 'International business travel: Impact on families and travellers', *Occupational and Environmental Medicine*, 59(9): 309–322.

Euromonitor International (2012) *Business Travel: A Challenging Recovery*. London: Euromonitor International.

Euromonitor International (2013) *Travel and Tourism in Yemen*. London: Euromonitor International.

Euromonitor International (2014a) *Travel and Tourism in the United Arab Emirates*. London: Euromonitor International.

Euromonitor International (2014b) *Travel and Tourism in Syria*. London: Euromonitor International.

Euromonitor International (2014c) *Travel and Tourism in Sudan*. London: Euromonitor International.

Euromonitor International (2014d) *Travel and Tourism in Afghanistan*. London: Euromonitor International.

Euromonitor International (2014e) *Travel and Tourism in Iraq*. London: Euromonitor International.

Euromonitor International (2016a) *Travel in Israel: Industry Overview*. London: Euromonitor International.

Euromonitor International (2016b) *Lodging in Israel: Category Briefing*. London: Euromonitor International.

Flamos, A., Roupas, C., & Psarras, J. (2013) 'GCC economies diversification: Still a myth?' *Energy Sources*, Part B(8): 360–368.

Gelb, A., & Turner, G. (2008) 'Confronting the resource curse', in B. Desker, J. Herbst, G. Mills, & M. Spicer (eds), *Globalisation and Economic Success: Policy Lessons for Developing Countries* (pp. 36–75). Johannesburg: The Brenhurst Foundation.

Gleksman, A. (2015) 'American Express forecasts business travel 2016'. Available online: www.travelmarketreport.com/articles/Amercian-Express-Forecasts-Business-Travel-2016 (Accessed 4 February 2016).

Global Futures and Foresight (2007) 'The future of travel and tourism in the Middle East: A vision to 2020'. Available online: www.thegff.com/Articles/75959/Global_Futures_and/Reports/The_Future_of.aspx (Accessed 5 February 2016).

Gulf Business (2015) 'UAE among most popular global MICE destinations in 2014: Study'. Available online: www.gulfbusiness.com/articles/industry/uae-among-most-popular-global-mice-destinations-in-2014-study/ (Accessed 8 February 2016).

Gustafson, P. (2012) 'Managing business travel: Developments and dilemmas in corporate travel management', *Tourism Management*, 33: 276–284.

Henderson, J.C. (2003) 'Managing tourism and Islam in Peninsular Malaysia', *Tourism Management*, 24(4): 447–456.

Henderson, J.C. (2014) 'Global Gulf cities and tourism', *Tourism Recreation Research*, 39(1): 107–114.

Henderson, J.C. (2016) 'Hosting the 2022 FIFA World Cup: Opportunities and challenges for Qatar', *Journal of Sport and Tourism*, 19(3/4): 281–298.

Hvidt, M. (2013) 'Economic diversification in GCC countries: Past record and future trends'. Kuwait Programme on Development, Governance and Globalisation in the Gulf States. London School of Economics and Political Science Research Paper.

IATA (International Air Transport Association) (2015) 'Premium Traffic Monitor. November 2015'. Available online: www.traveldailynews.com/post/iata-premium-traffic-monitor---november-2015-51422 (Accessed 10 February 2016).

ICCA (International Congress and Convention Association) (2016) *ICAA Statistics Report 2015*. Amsterdam: ICCA.

Insights Management Consultancy, h2c and Amadeus (2007) 'Securing the prize for the Middle East'. Available online: www.amadeus.com/web/amadeus/en_ID-ID/Amadeus-Home/News-and-events/Media-centre/Media-gallery/Video---Securing-the-prise-for-the-Middle-East/1319477792357-AmadeusMedia_C-AMAD_VideoDetailPpal-1259082628909 (Accessed 5 February 2016).

Israel Ministry of Tourism (2016) 'Conventions and incentive'. Available online: www.goisrael-conference-and-incentive.com/ (Accessed 15 August 2016).

Jones, C., & Li, S. (2015) 'The economic importance of meetings and conferences: A satellite account approach', *Annals of Tourism Research*, 52: 117–133.

Ka, W.H., & Kan, M. (2016) 'Causality between business travel and trade volumes: Empirical evidence from Hong Kong', *Tourism Management*, 52: 395–404.

Monshi, E., & Scott, N. (2017) 'Developing event tourism in Saudi Arabia: Opportunities and challenges', in H. Almuhrzi, H. Alriyami, & N. Scott (eds), *Tourism in the Arab World: An Industry Perspective* (pp. 33–55). Bristol: Channel View Publications.

Murel, M., & O'Connell, J.F. (2011) 'Potential for Abu Dhabi, Doha and Dubai airports to reach their traffic objectives', *Research in Transportation Business and Management*, 1: 36–46.

QTA (2015) 'Qatar Tourism Authority'. Available online: http://portal.www.gov.qa/wps/portal/directory/agency/qatarourismauthority (Accessed 30 April 2015).

Saudi Vision 2030 (2016) 'Vision 2030'. Available online: http://vision2030.gov.sa/en (Accessed 2 August 2016).

SCTH (2016) 'Product development programs'. Available online: https://scth.gov.sa/en/Programs-Activities/Pages/default.aspx (Accessed 17 May 2016).

Sox, C.B., Kline, S.F., & Crews, T.B. (2014) 'Identifying best practices, opportunities and barriers in meeting planning for Generation Y', *International Journal of Hospitality Management*, 36: 244–254.

Strickland, J. (2015) 'From modest beginnings: The growth of civil aviation in the Middle East', *Journal of Middle Eastern Politics and Policy*. Available online: http://hksjmepp.com/from-modest-beginnings-the-growth-of-civil-aviation-in-the-middle-east/ (Accessed 10 February 2016).

Swarbrooke, J., & Horner, S. (2001) *Business Travel and Tourism*. Oxford: Butterworth-Heinemann.

TCA (2015) 'Abu Dhabi Tourism and Culture Authority: About us'. Available online: http://tcaabudhabi.ae/en/about/Pages/about-us.aspx (Accessed 2 May 2015).

The Hotel Show (2016) 'Dubai leads Middle East and Africa hotel construction with over 100,000 rooms forecast for 2020'. Available online: www.thehotelshow.com/press (Accessed 11 February 2016).

Timothy, D.J. (2017) 'Tourism and geopolitics in the GCC region', in M.L. Stephenson, & A. al-Hamarneh (eds), *International Tourism Development and the Gulf Cooperation Council States: Challenges and Opportunities* (pp. 45–60). London: Routledge.

TTG MENA (2016a) 'Middle East MICE sector poised for unrivalled growth'. Available online: www.ttgmena.com/middle-east-mice-sector-poised-for-unrivalled-growth/ (Accessed 6 February 2016).

TTG MENA (2016b) 'Long-term commitment'. Available online: www.ttgmena.com/long-term-commitment/ (Accessed 6 February 2016).

UNWTO (2014) *Global Report on the Meetings Industry*. Madrid: World Tourism Organization.

UNWTO (2015) *UNWTO Tourism Highlights 2015*. Madrid: World Tourism Organization.

UNWTO (2016) *World Tourism Barometer, Volume 14*. Madrid: World Tourism Organization.

Visit Dubai (2016) 'Dubai: Top ten reasons'. Available online: www.visitdubai.com/en/event-planning/why-dubai/top-10-reasons (Accessed 8 February 2016).

Weber, K., & Ali-Knight, J. (2012) 'Events and festivals in Asia and the Middle East/North Africa (MENA) region: Opportunities and challenges', *International Journal of Event and Festival Management*, 3(1): 4–8.

Weidenfeld, A., & Ron, A.S. (2008) 'Religious needs in the tourism industry', *Anatolia*, 19(2): 357–361.

World Economic Forum (2015) *The Travel and Tourism Competitiveness Report*. Davos: World Economic Forum.

Yu, J., & Weber, K. (2005) 'Progress in convention tourism research', *Journal of Hospitality and Tourism Research*, 29(2): 194–222.

Zalewski, P. (2015) 'Istanbul third airport plan ruffles feathers'. *Financial Times*, 15 November. Available online: www.ft.com/intl/cms/s/0/72b834f8-7753-11e5-a95-27d368e1ddf7.html (Accessed 22 February 2016).

27

MEDICAL TOURISM

In search of an economic niche

John Connell

Introduction

It is sometimes said that the Mesopotamians originally established medical tourism when, as far back as the fifth millennium BP, they travelled to the temple of healing gods or goddesses at Tell Brak in Syria, perhaps in search of a cure for eye disorders. Thousands of years later, Greeks and Romans travelled to spas and Mediterranean coasts in search of respite and cures from the stresses of daily life. The very earliest global ventures into tourism were thus to gain access to some basic therapies associated with the curative properties of particular places, usually associated with water. Over the centuries, coasts and spas became health tourism destinations. Rather later a distinctive, less passive medical tourism developed.

While any definition of medical tourism is inconclusive, it has typically been associated with long-distance, international travel for some kinds of invasive procedures, notably cosmetic surgery. In practice, much of medical tourism is relatively short distance, over adjacent borders and involves procedures as basic as check-ups (Connell 2013, 2015). Definitions of medical tourism are linked to duration, volition, who pays and what is involved. Stem cell therapies have sometimes been excluded, whereas mobility for fertility treatment has been included. While reproduction appears a private and intimate affair, it is bound up in national policies (for example, towards abortion, adoption, provision of contraception, family sizes and one-child families), in what has been described as a 'global market of commercial fertility' or 'cross-border reproductive care' (Inhorn 2011, 2015). Here and elsewhere medical tourism is inextricably related to national policies.

Long-distance travel for medical care has existed for centuries in the Middle East and elsewhere, but it developed in a more modern form in the nineteenth century with the movement of patients to such cities as London, Berlin and New York. Relatively well-off individuals travelled from the countries of the south, including the Middle East, to those of the north. Rather later, Beirut and Cairo also became attractive destinations for Middle Eastern travellers, but the less well-off travelled to India.

What is now generally regarded as medical tourism is an inversion of this structure, with patients moving from the wealthier countries of the north to those of the south. Its recent growth is largely associated with the rise of travel to South and Southeast Asia, notably to Thailand, Malaysia, Singapore and India (Connell 2011a). The established pattern of movement

of wealthy individuals, travelling northwards from regions such as the Middle East, has fundamentally remained in place because of the status attached to European medicine, while multiple movements also exist across European Union borders, and between the countries of the
south; however, most conventional usage of 'medical tourism' relates to movement from richer
countries towards poorer countries. Indeed, quintessential medical tourism was often that of
mobility from relatively rich Gulf states, notably UAE and Saudi Arabia, to the emerging Asian
destinations.

Relationships with tourism and leisure, as sources of pleasure and relaxation, may be
tenuous or simply absent for sick, anxious and stressed patients, yet frequent repetition and
industry support, for obvious marketing reasons, ensure that international medical travel
remains 'medical tourism'. Nonetheless, since mobile patients (and accompanying kin and
carers) must travel and stay somewhere, and take advantage of the facilities designed for
tourists—principally hotels, restaurants and transport services—and perhaps avail themselves
of a range of activities, often during periods of convalescence, such as shopping, medical
travel is intricately linked to the tourism industry (Connell 2011a), and is widely marketed
and advertised as a pleasurable experience. In a sense, medical tourism constitutes a particular
example of niche tourism, though more normative tourism is only exceptionally an intentional part of medical tourism.

Medical travel represents a dynamic transnationalisation of healthcare, once assumed to be
highly localised, but now transformed through new knowledge, communications, aspirations,
affluence, transport and biotechnology (Ormond 2013). This is part of a wider globalisation of healthcare—involving the mobility of skilled health workers, technology transfer,
pharmaceuticals (and diseases and lifestyles), hospital chains, public–private partnerships, and
global governance—and of travel. Medical tourism is uneven because of intense competition, political instability and, like the related tourism industry, is subject to shifts in economics,
fashion, flight paths and technology, the fluctuations of personal and national economies, and
the stability of destinations. It has added one more component to the commodification and
globalisation of 'intimate industries' such as adoption, retirement, marriage, sex tourism, and
sex work (e.g. Constable 2009; Yeates 2009). Medical tourism is particularly complex in the
Middle East as many countries and corporations aspire to be involved and flows of medical
tourists are into, out of and within the region.

Because of the competitive nature of the industry, boosterism, the range of procedures,
institutions and places involved, the privacy of medical records and the need for success,
accurate data are rare and numerical data are rarely anything more than generous guesstimates
(Connell 2015a). Even much-quoted and repeated 'data' often prove to be merely derived
from newspaper articles or press conferences. That is complicated further since, even more than
other facets of tourism, medical tourism is particularly susceptible to political unrest, since sick
patients are especially unwilling to travel to dangerous places. Unrest, violence and volatile
politics in the Middle East have slowed the growth of medical tourism, discouraging diasporic
medical tourism (so significant elsewhere) and even restricted mobility from the region to distant sources of medical care.

This chapter seeks to review recent trends in medical tourism in the Middle East, so
covering the rationale for and pattern of travel outside the region, attempts by Middle Eastern
locales (notably Dubai) to reverse the outflow of medical tourists by developing more cost-
effective local facilities, and the impact of medical tourism in various states. It emphasises the
high costs of medical care within much of the region, and especially the Gulf, the ethical
concerns attached to giving priority to overseas patients and the constraints to developing an
effective industry.

Patients and procedures

People engage in medical tourism for a range of reasons. Patients seek out treatments unavailable, inadequate, too delayed or unaffordable at home, especially by moving to places where health care is relatively cheap. Where insurance does not cover such procedures as dentistry and cosmetic surgery, medical tourism offers an option. Demand for relatively rare or complex procedures may involve more distant travel than for straightforward procedures.

A significant component of medical travel is of diaspora patients returning to familiar, usually cheaper circumstances. Such travellers have been poorly documented, being perceived of as having limited economic significance (although that is rarely true) and difficult to distinguish from local patients. The return migration of Indians effectively instigated medical tourism in India. Cultural and linguistic familiarity, proximity, speed, effectiveness and cost are all advantages. In Turkey and Jordan, returning overseas nationals are a significant proportion, perhaps a majority, of medical travellers, which may be true elsewhere (Connell 2011a), and it has accounted for a part of medical tourism elsewhere in the Middle East.

Costs are important and many procedures in the Middle East are routinely stated to cost about a tenth of those in the United States, but they are similar to those in South and Southeast Asia, providing no real global comparative advantage for developing medical tourism. The Middle East must therefore compete on quality (and accessibility) in an amenable cultural context. Turkey, like other countries, thus promotes high quality and low price services, internationally accredited hospitals, educated and experienced human resources and short waiting times, while stressing its general popularity as a tourist destination, where health (wellness) tourism is also possible and popular (Kaya, Karsavuran, & Yildiz 2015). Turkey has also signed agreements with a number of countries, including Sudan, Afghanistan, Yemen, Albania and Kosovo, for the planned treatment of their patients, provided financial support for promotion and marketing and given tax exemptions on half the income earned from medical tourism (Kaya et al. 2015). Few other Middle Eastern states have directly supported the medical tourism sector or developed effective strategies to support it.

Medical tourism involves a range of procedures. The very limited data from Turkey suggest that international patients came primarily because of eye diseases, followed by orthopaedics, internal diseases and ear-nose-throat problems (Kaya et al. 2015). Despite cultural conservatism, demand for cosmetic surgery, especially rhinoplasty and breast augmentation, has substantially increased in the region. Here medical tourism is a want rather than a need, an exercise in empowerment and the discovery of self, distinct from physical notions of 'cure'. Relatively poor regional patients are more likely to travel shorter distances across adjacent borders for quite straightforward procedures and economic reasons (Connell 2016), coming from large parts of the world where basic treatments are expensive or simply absent, because of national policy failures and practices, sometimes because of civil unrest, and often because of the emigration of skilled health workers. Thus, Afghanistan provides a regular flow of medical tourists to Iran, as does Yemen to Lebanon.

Despite the images and aspirations promoted by the industry, much mobility is across nearby borders, with social networks facilitating choice of procedure and destination, and is also often of the diaspora, drawn by cheaper prices, cultural and linguistic familiarity and familial support. Libyan and Afghan medical travellers go mainly to Tunisia and Iran respectively. Azerbaijanis and Iraqis from Kurdish areas travel to Iran (Jabbari, Kavosi, & Gholami 2014; Noubar, Heidarzadeh, & Bahador 2014) while other Iraqis go to Jordan. More than 80 per cent of medical tourists in Shiraz, the main Iranian destination, come from Oman, Bahrain, UAE, Kuwait and Iraq, with a few from Canada and France, significant centres of the Iranian diaspora (Safaeepour,

Goodarzi, & Rostami Kondari 2015). By contrast, Turkey claims that most of its medical tourists come from European countries like Germany, the Netherlands and Belgium (Medical Tourism Magazine 2013); if that is so, it is likely that most were of Turkish ancestry. In 2012, most medical tourists in Turkey came from Libya, Germany, Iraq, Azerbaijan and Russia (Kaya et al. 2015): a mix of neighbours and the diaspora. For the more specialised case of reproductive travellers in Dubai, these came from a grand total of 50 countries, the largest group being from India and the second largest from Lebanon (Inhorn 2012).

At every scale and in every region, word of mouth concerning quality of care is of crucial importance (e.g. Kangas 2007; Yeoh, Othman, & Ahmad 2013). Despite the rise of the Internet, in Oman more than 70 per cent of medical travellers got their information from friends and a further 19 per cent from family (Al-Hinai, Al-Busaidi, & Al-Busaidi 2011). Word of mouth and precedent are more valuable than international recognition. The most significant global accreditation is by JCI (Joint Commission International) but, while well understood within the industry, it is of little significance to most potential travellers contemplating destinations. Nonetheless, in 2014 Turkey had 43 JCI-accredited hospitals, Jordan had ten, Egypt seven and Lebanon four. The UAE had even more than Turkey—a crude and limited measure of the strength of health services in the region.

In quest of niches

Medical tourism emerged in Asia after the Asian financial crisis of 1997 and in this century has become particularly competitive as new countries and transnational corporations have sought to enter the market. International mobility has become more probable and feasible as privatisation of medical care continues, discontent with public care increases, cosmetic procedures are marketed and disposable capital is available. Medical tourism is consumer-oriented and competitive, centred on price and quality, since some procedures do not need to be undertaken, and most are possible in many countries, usually including home countries.

Medical tourism is a source of foreign exchange and employment; earnings from incoming patients are potentially greater than from domestic patients, especially where the public sector dominates healthcare, while the expenditure of medical tourists can be greater than that of standard tourists (partly because of the duration of stay). It therefore appears an attractive option for many countries despite ethical questions centred over its relationship to national health care provision. In 2003 in Tunisia, the only country where reasonable income estimates exist, medical tourists spent rather less than average tourists, but medical tourism created more than 10,000 jobs, over half of which were in the tourism sector (Lautier 2008). Patients rarely travel alone, preferring family groups for friendship and reassurance (Connell 2011a), thereby making a larger contribution to destination incomes.

National and institutional interest in economic development and diversification have instigated both 'strategic' investment to encourage inward flows of medical travellers and 'defensive' investment to discourage outbound travel and capital flight. Both situations exist in the Middle East. Many countries and hospitals have sought to develop medical tourism, despite the challenges of breaking into a crowded market, where experience is invaluable and word of mouth vital. Several Asian states, such as Malaysia and Korea, have been vigorous national proponents of the industry, as a modern, strategic growth strategy, with hospitals subsidised through advertising, tax reduction or infrastructure support (Connell 2011a). Outside Turkey, such support and promotion has been rare in the Middle East. However, various improbable claimants have emerged. Some countries have geographical and cultural advantages, are adjacent to a large market, have a reasonable tourist reputation, political stability, and a significant diasporic population. Others lack the necessary skilled human resources, sometimes as out-migration has created shortages. Success requires an existing health industry, investment, a positive image, identity and political stability, somewhat difficult to create in a volatile competitive context where some countries are barely known, even in what they perceive as future markets, or are known as places of turbulence rather than tranquillity.

Despite widespread assumptions that medical tourist numbers are increasing, there is no particular reason to assume that this is so, nor that new countries might easily establish an industry. Indeed, success in following the leaders has been rare. Korea, having oriented itself to a growing Russian and Chinese market, is a rare example of belated success, but otherwise no great diversification from the established players has occurred.

For much of recent history, the countries of the Middle East have been suppliers of medical tourists to other parts of the world, especially as oil wealth made this feasible for greater numbers of people. Much of this has been associated with the movements of patients to Europe and, more recently, to Southeast Asia and India, an established destination for less well-off patients from Oman and the UAE particularly. At the same time there have been some significant flows within the Middle East from relatively poor countries such as Yemen. After 11 September 2001, when Middle East residents became, and perceived themselves to be, more unwelcome in the United States, medical tourists became rather more likely to travel to Asia. Falling oil prices and thus revenues from the mid-2010s have slowed medical tourism from the region, and encouraged more 'defensive' investments.

The outwards flow of medical tourists from the Middle East has been a function of the affluence of many patients from states such as Saudi Arabia and the UAE, but also of the willingness of the state, in countries like the UAE, Kuwait, Qatar, Bahrain and, formerly, Libya, to foot the bills of overseas patients and, in many cases, of their close kin. Many formal, documented medical travellers in major Thailand metropolitan hospitals are thus from the UAE and other Gulf states. They are reputed to come with more family members, and spend more both on healthcare and beyond; hence, hospitals in South and Southeast Asia have sought to emphasise their being Arab and Muslim-friendly, with halal food, Arabic-speaking staff, and distinct wings and floors of hospitals (Ormond 2013). Symbolically, images of Gulf patients typify popular coverage of medical tourism in Thailand.

Violence in the Middle East has also had implications for medical tourism from the region. Indian hospitals lost patients from Iraq and Syria in mid-2014 when increased insurgency resulted in medical travellers' inability to secure plane tickets, the Iraqi government being unable to fund them, while visa restrictions and security concerns prevented Indian doctors travelling to the region to engage in preliminary consultations (Anon. 2014).

Developing medical tourism

Most regions have one or more countries that have sought to position themselves as medical tourism hubs. Some such regional hubs have succeeded; in the Middle East there has been only partial success, because of the inadequacies of some national health care systems and nearby violence, rather than the attractions and benefits of cross-border mobility. Beneficiaries of violence in parts of the region have been those neighbours that have remained largely stable and peaceful. Iran has drawn medical travellers from nearby troubled countries (after initially entering the industry for 'defensive' reasons), as has Tunisia for the Maghreb, while Jordan has targeted both the Arab diaspora and nearby Iraq and Syria. Symptomatic of the challenges that face medical tourism in the Middle East are those that beset Turkey in 2016, seen as 'the falling star of medical tourism' as 'it faces a battle to combat the impact of terrorism, Syria, human rights issues, embargoes, refugees and civil war' (Youngman 2016: n.p.), even before a decline in Russian tourism (because of political differences between Ankara and Moscow), bombings in Ankara and Istanbul, and an attempted military coup.

Medical tourism has grown slowly in MENA, often assisted by diaspora patients. Jordan, Tunisia and Turkey have been relatively successful. Jordan serves patients from some parts of the Middle East, and at least in 2005 its low costs made it a regional hub, especially for patients from nearby Iraq, Palestine and Syria, without the resources to travel to more distant locations (Alsharif, Labonté, & Zuxun 2010). Unlike several states which, largely unsuccessfully, targeted better-off patients, from as early as the 1990s Jordan sought to become a popular destination for less well-off patients from Yemen, Libya, Algeria, Sudan, Iraq and Syria. It has also specialised in, and become recognised for, reproductive medicine.

It was said that in 2007, including some health and wellness visitors, over 250,000 patients from around 84 Arab and other foreign countries were treated in Jordan (Vequist, Bolatkale, & Valdez 2009). No data corroborated that and exactly the same number was given for 2012 with patients said to be accompanied by more than 500,000 companions with a total revenue exceeding US$1 billion. A year later it was claimed that 210,000 patients came from some 48 countries, and US$1 billion—some 4 per cent of GDP—was again suggested (Kronfol 2015; Stephano 2014). Political stability and an existing tourism infrastructure have been beneficial, though, as elsewhere, neither numbers nor revenue are likely to have been so substantial. Indeed, Jordan's ability to provide health care for foreigners has been challenged by the influx of refugees from Iraq and Syria, and the need to provide for them, and a shortage of health workers, especially nurses.

In North Africa, Tunisia claims dominance with as many as 250,000 foreigners said to have visited the country for medical treatment in 2009. If true, that would represent a massive increase from 2003 when 42,000 foreigners, more than three-quarters from Libya, were said to have arrived for medical treatment, generating a revenue of US$55 million and providing an estimated 10,500 jobs (Connell 2011a; Lautier 2008). By 2013, an estimated 155,000 foreign patients visited Tunisia, again mainly from Libya. Most medical tourists in 2009 came from adjoining Libya (perhaps up to 70 per cent) and Algeria, but also from Sub-Saharan Africa (about 12 per cent), notably from Francophone and Muslim states. Some medical tourists are said to be Westerners (from France, Germany and elsewhere in Europe). Thus, Tunisia has drawn patients from nearby, either from the more affluent parts of Western Europe, some of whom are migrant Tunisians, from adjoining Libya and from other Francophone sources—a range of countries greater than for most other MENA destinations. Recently, Tunisia has faced terrorist actions that have devastated its tourism industry, and Morocco has provided growing competition as a somewhat similar destination, close to Western Europe, with an extensive tourism infrastructure, and such specialisms as cosmetic surgery, laser eye surgery and dental tourism. It has attracted older patients from Francophone European countries, but especially Moroccan migrants in Europe.

Turkey, like Tunisia, until recently relatively peaceful and with a modern health care system, has had some success with cosmetic surgery, and has sought to promote both health and medical tourism (Sugorakova 2014). Turkey grandly claimed to have received 300,000 medical tourists in 2013 (although this included health tourism) and was seeking to double that total by 2023. That was an advance on the equally dubious figure of 270,000 in 2012 who were said to have produced a net revenue of US$1 billion (Kaya et al. 2015; Medical Tourism Magazine 2013). Once again, diaspora medical tourism was common (Nielsen, Yazici, Petersen, Blaakilde, & Krasnik 2012). Turkish medical tourism has had relatively strong government support and promotion, links with the national airline and public–private partnerships, and a strong tourist industry. It has had some success with hair transplants and, somewhat improbably, a niche within a niche: moustache transplants. Unlike most Middle Eastern countries, Turkey has actively sought a Sub-Saharan market, directed at the many travellers leaving Kenya and Nigeria, with the Medical Park Hospital Group, a consortium of 19 hospitals in Turkey, orienting to Kenya (quoted in Medical Tourism Magazine 2014: 22). Little African success has yet been reported.

Even such limited successes have largely eluded other states. Israel caters to Jewish patients and others from nearby countries, through specialising in female infertility, IVF and high-risk pregnancies. It has also sought to market medical tourism in combination with the perceived therapeutic and restorative qualities of the Dead Sea, one of the rare examples in the Middle East where medical tourism had been combined with a broader restorative health tourism. In 2010, Israel is said to have received 30,000 medical tourists, many of whom were from Russia, and Russia remains a key source.

Egypt and Lebanon, once the major tourism destinations of the Middle East, have sought to break into medical tourism. Making Lebanon the 'hospital of the East' has been the ambition of its Tourism Council for over a decade, and a relatively modern health care system otherwise offers opportunities, especially for cosmetic surgery, but Lebanon has been hampered by the lack of a durable peace in Beirut. As elsewhere, Iraq has been a source of many medical travellers, whether in need of basic care or seeking cosmetic surgery, with continued warfare in places and the breakdown of the national health care system (after the departure of military health care services and the migration of skilled professionals). A significant proportion has gone to Lebanon for cancer treatment. While the growth of medical tourism was predicted to average an annual 30 per cent between 2009 and 2011 (Connell 2011a), there was a steady decline in numbers as political tensions increased, so that only Jordanians and Iraqis go to Lebanon. Lebanon is one of the very few countries that has ever admitted to an actual decline in medical tourism numbers.

Egypt claimed in the first decade of this century to receive 50,000 medical tourists a year from other Arab countries, including perhaps 40,000 from Libya, and was seeking to build medical tourism around rehabilitation and recuperation alongside its existing tourism industry (Helmy & Travers 2009; Johnson 2010). But that was before the 'Arab Spring' became a bleak autumn, and tourism numbers plummeted.

In Iran, the health minister claimed in 2004 that 'No Middle East country can compete with Iran in terms of medical expertise and costs', comparing the cost of open heart surgery at US$18,000 in Turkey, US$40,000 in UK and US$10,000 in Iran so that patients 'can afford the rest on touring the country' (quoted in Connell 2011a: 55). However, such arguments have not enabled steady development of a medical tourism industry in a country where diasporic tourism is minimal, and political tensions and religious differences with neighbours discourage regional travel. It is claimed that some 30,000 people went to Iran in 2012 for medical treatment but the figures are impossible to verify. Most medical tourists are from relatively poor neighbouring countries including Azerbaijan, Turkmenistan, Iraq and Turkey, or they are less affluent residents of Kuwait and Oman.

Even high-cost Saudi Arabia has sought to link medical tourism, and especially cosmetic surgery and dentistry, with pilgrimage (*hajj*) visits to the country, with most patients being from other Gulf countries (Connell 2011a). That was never likely to lead to an industry. Bahrain, too, has considered medical tourism as a means of diversifying away from the oil industry (Ebrahim and Ganguli 2017) but is unlikely to be competitive in the near future.

By 2016, relatively low-cost Jordan remained the main medical tourism destination in the Middle East, with Israel an emerging but limited success story, and Tunisia and Turkey fading in the face of violence. Compared with other regions of the world, medical tourism in the Middle

East has been limited, and is characterised by patients leaving the region, or crossing regional borders, rather than visiting from more distant countries, despite a small flow from the diaspora.

Reversing the flow?

While such countries as Tunisia, Lebanon and Iran were actively promoting medical tourism as a national revenue-generating exercise, a second phase became more evident towards the end of the 2000s when some Middle Eastern states, notably the UAE, centred on Dubai, began to discourage medical tourism, because of the significant loss of income, and instead to develop more adequate and accessible local facilities, that might also play a role in attracting medical tourists from elsewhere in the region, who might have otherwise gone elsewhere. While Lebanon and Jordan have drawn patients from the Gulf States, most medical tourists from there have gone to Asian or high-cost European destinations. The huge loss of medical tourists overseas has prompted Gulf States to develop better national services with the intention of redirecting flows of medical tourists. Enormous variations exist in the extent to which countries have given financial support to health services, and contributed to a regional medical tourism industry by easing the entry of foreign capital and corporations, removing visa restrictions or establishing public–private partnerships.

After 2002, Dubai began to build Dubai Healthcare City (DHCC) in order to capture the Gulf and Middle Eastern market and discourage Gulf medical tourists from going to Asia. DHCC was intended to be a small city, centred on a 'medical mall' offering a range of services. Unable to compete on price, the Gulf now largely seeks to compete on quality, with Dubai bringing in German doctors to guarantee high skill standards, and hiring many foreign specialists to build expertise in the medical field and become a regional hub. It has also extended the visas of medical tourists and their carers from one to three months.

In 2014, the Dubai medical tourism strategy was aiming at building expertise in orthopaedics, sports medicine and a range of other specialisms and had a target of bringing half a million medical tourists a year to the city's hospitals by 2020. In 2015, the city reported 135,000 foreign visitors using its hospitals, and this was expected to increase to 150,000 in 2016. However, a majority were expatriate residents in the UAE, rather than travelling there for medical care. A minority, however, were infertile men from various parts of the Middle East, notably Lebanon and other parts of the UAE, and elsewhere, especially India, travelling for Dubai's particular specialisation (Inhorn 2012, 2017). Since prices for cosmetic surgery are similar to those in London, and thus much more than in Asia, Dubai must otherwise compete on quality, and by 2015 there was very little evidence that it had been able to do that (Kronfol 2015). Moreover, Dubai continued to struggle to provide the basic healthcare needs of its own rapidly growing population.

As medical tourism has grown in the Gulf, rich world countries have become more involved. Thus, the Bavaria Medical Group (BMG) has developed links with Oman and Qatar Airways, with some patients being taken from Oman to Germany, and specialist BMG doctors visiting Oman, the latter of which may have contributed to better national health, and reduced some flows, but has not reversed them. Such developments are yet to attract medical tourists to high-cost destinations. The Gulf States have not stemmed the tide.

Ethics and equity

The language of contemporary international, corporate healthcare involves public relations prose, aggressive marketing, profitability, business models and trade fairs. In Asia especially regional and global networks of hotel chains have extended, with packages linking tourism, airlines and healthcare (Toyota, Chee, & Xiang 2013) and 'hospitels'—hospitals that resemble hotels—but that phase with its elaborate linkages has yet to occur in the Middle East. That has not displaced some concern over the impacts of medical tourism.

Healthcare is labour intensive yet many countries where medical travel has emerged, or is proposed, have existing skilled health labour shortages, uneven access to healthcare, and an internal brain drain of skilled health workers, hence the emergence of two-tier systems—a private sector serving better-off local and international patients, where medical tourism is established, and a public sector that may be underfunded and short of skilled workers, especially in regional areas. Concern exists in several Asian destinations (Chen & Flood 2013; Connell 2011b), and in Israel and Jordan, skilled health workers (doctors, nurses and technical staff) may be drawn into the medical tourism sector (where wages are higher) at some cost to the national system, without real national benefits from taxation. By contrast, in Tunisia entry in the medical tourism industry was stimulated by the overcapacity of private clinics (Lautier 2008). Although this does not necessarily mean an effective public sector, there was no evidence that medical tourism had disadvantaged the Tunisian health system, either through an internal brain drain or the diminished availability of healthcare for the poor. The costliest medical tourism is a metropolitan phenomenon, rarely evident outside capital cities (because of preferences for direct flights and JCI-accredited hospitals), hence concerns exist over urban bias and the marginalisation of remote regions. In Lebanon at least, medical tourism has been perceived as attractive enough to draw in fake providers, often of 'alternative' medicine, and of counterfeit drugs and medicines (Anon. 2015). That too has failed to boost the image of the industry in the region.

In Israel, particular attention has been given to notions of national need and equity: an indication that medical tourism has been significant enough to attract wider health policy interest. Some Israeli hospitals give preferential treatment to medical tourists at the expense of locals, and medical tourism revenue goes directly to doctors rather than being reinvested in equipment or hiring staff. A two-tier system has emerged where hospitals provide the best facilities to affluent patients from Russia and elsewhere, resulting in a general shortage of beds and nurses (Anon. 2016a; Connell 2015b). That prompted Israel, in 2016, to pass a Medical Tourism Bill, supported by the Minister of Health, at the core of which were three principles: quality of and access to treatment for Israeli citizens must not be lowered and should be improved (perhaps anticipating some trickledown benefits); income received from the medical tourism sector must be directed to improving the public health system (a rare recognition of national health care provision in association with medical tourism); and the need to ensure that medical tourists must be 'protected', by receiving ethical, professional and fair treatment. To enable these three principles to be achieved, it was intended, first, that restrictions be put on the total number of medical tourists in a particular hospital, to ensure that the quality of care for Israeli citizens would not be compromised. Second, hospitals interested in attracting medical tourists must develop infrastructure to send adequate data to the Ministry of Health so that procedures could be properly monitored. Third, income from medical tourists must be utilised to improve the public healthcare system, and fourth, hospitals must show economic flows in a transparent manner in order to properly track the revenues gained from medical tourism (Anon. 2016b).

More than any other Middle Eastern state, Israel has consciously considered how medical tourism might fit into the national health care system and, more importantly, not compromise (but rather improve) overall health care. More frequently, medical tourism has not been conceptualised within the national system. Concern for any negative consequences of medical tourism has been largely absent elsewhere. That may be a partial reflection of the relative insignificance of the industry, but there is reason for concern over the extent of tax exemptions offered to the Turkish industry, and the promotion of a private sector that is unusually advantaged relative to the public sector. Moreover, Israel's national health care system, where medical tourism exists within the public sector, enables a greater degree of regulation and the possibility of generating more useful data on its economic significance, than is occurring elsewhere. Beyond Israel and, to a limited extent, Tunisia, no analyses have been made of the wider impact of medical tourism, although, other than in Turkey and Jordan, it is unlikely to have had a significant impact.

Nonetheless, even Israel has experienced a situation where

> attempts over several years by the government and politicians to find out if medical tourism affects the health services offered to locals have been stymied by hospitals flatly refusing to cooperate and argue that information on numbers, spend or profit are all commercial information that no state organisation or politician can have access to.
> *(Anon. 2016a: n.p.)*

This is even more indicative of the situation elsewhere and emphasises the scepticism that must be attached to all data.

Little solid research has been undertaken on the industry in the Middle East, hence conclusions over its economic and social impact, and the extent to which it has influenced the national health system or the tourist industry are conspicuous by their absence. Attempts to develop medical tourism plans have often been frustrated by the lack of data and the unwillingness of hospitals and other organisations to release relevant data, as in Egypt (Helmy & Travers 2009). There is some risk that should medical tourism in the Middle East grow, its ethical and equitable impacts will be ignored in the pursuit of economic growth, as is presently occurring in Jordan and Dubai.

Conclusion

Political instability, weak and fragile states, inability to deliver services adequately, and wealthy individuals, ensure there will always be sources of medical tourists, but impecunious travellers attract little interest in the industry, where ability to pay and stay is welcomed. With many countries unable to meet the basic health needs of all their people, medical travel is relatively common, but often for simple procedures across regional borders. By contrast, medical tourism in the Middle East is symbolised by relatively well-off patients and their families travelling in some degree of style to Europe and Southeast Asia. That better-off patients choose to travel overseas, and lack trust and confidence in national systems, has been a significant brake both on developing health care systems in the Middle East and making the region a destination for medical tourism. Consequently, despite attempts to reduce flows from the region and build more effective local and national health care systems, catering for both national and overseas needs has yet to occur. Even relatively successful nations, such as Jordan and Turkey, have been held back by considerations of regional violence and distrust, while developments such as DHCC are out of economic reach for most of the population of the region.

Medical tourism is particularly susceptible to political unrest, and global images of a region seemingly constantly fraught with internecine warfare and unending instability have discouraged all forms of medical tourism. That has been well summed up for Lebanon: 'The problem is how to change the image of the country and get more medical tourists from a wider range of countries. As yet the government has no solution' (Anon. 2016c: n.p.). That has consequently stimulated more interest from countries such as Germany to attract medical tourists from the region (Stephano 2015). Diaspora medical tourism has helped keep Lebanon and Turkey afloat. Bombing, an attempted coup and subsequent repression have almost destroyed contemporary Turkish aspirations. Medical tourism is fragile and fluid. Intra-regional competition is strong. Violence has deterred corporate interest and limited successful linkages with the travel industry. Inadequate health services in several countries and the loss of skilled health workers have done much to stimulate the regional medical travel of both the poor and the wealthy. Much travel is of the most needy, themselves often affected either directly by violence or by its outcome. Only rarely can it be seen as tourism; for such travellers, despite their expenditure on travel, food and accommodation, tourism has no relevance.

Much dubious data is centred around grandiose expectations of growth that are barely based in reality. Only Kangas (2002, 2007, 2011) and Inhorn (2012) have studied medical tourism from the perspective of the travellers themselves and their welfare. With the partial exception of Tunisia, no published source examines the economic impact of medical tourism anywhere in the region. Ethics have been avoided. Effective forward planning will require more accurate data.

Quite different national strategies, alongside those of hospital chains, are indicative of the increasingly complex globalisation of healthcare, the multi-directional flows of patients and investment, the extent of corporatisation, the centralisation of profits, and orientation towards those who can pay (rather than those in need). Some Middle Eastern governments have strongly promoted medical tourism, occasionally in association with health tourism. Others, such as Iraq and Syria, have more immediate objectives. Border crossers and basic needs are absent from all such strategies. Here, even more than elsewhere, mobility for healthcare has little to do with tourism, and is centred on needs rather than wants, and far from dominant images of global trajectories in search of expensive and indulgent cosmetic surgery. However, without a lasting peace in the region, medical tourism may well remain that of the relatively poor from nearby, and the distant departure of the better off—a distinctive regional two-tier system, rather than an industry that fills a niche and comes close to rivalling that in other parts of the world.

References

Al-Hinai, S., Al-Busaidi, A., & Al-Busaidi, I. (2011) 'Medical tourism abroad: A new challenge to Oman's health system—Al Dakhilya region experience', *Sultan Qabus University Medical Journal*, 11: 477–484.

Alsharif, M., Labonté, R. and Zuxun, L. (2010) 'Patients beyond borders: A study of medical tourists in four countries', *Global Social Policy*, 10: 315–335.

Anon. (2014) 'Iraq crisis hits Indian medical tourism'. *International Medical Travel Journal*, 14 July. Available online: www.imtj.com/news/iraq-crisis-hits-indian-medical-tourism/ (Accessed 12 September 2018).

Anon. (2015) 'Lebanon seeks to clean up health care provision'. *International Medical Travel Journal*, 25 August. Available online: www.imtj.com/news/lebanon-seeks-clean-healthcare-provision-0/ (Accessed 12 September 2018).

Anon. (2016a) 'Israeli hospitals must record medical tourism statistics'. *International Medical Travel Journal*, 6 October. Available online: www.imtj.com/news/israeli-hospitals-must-record-medical-tourism-statistics/ (Accessed 12 September 2018).

Anon. (2016b) 'Israel makes headway in medical tourism legislation'. *Medical Tourism Magazine*, November. Available online: www.medicaltourismmag.com/israel-medical-tourism-legislation/ (Accessed 12 September 2018).

Anon. (2016c) 'Medical tourism a priority for Lebanon'. *International Medical Travel Journal*, 30 October. Available online: www.imtj.com/news/medical-tourism-priority-lebanon/ (Accessed 12 September 2018).

Chen, Y., & Flood, C. (2013) 'Medical tourism's impact on health care equity and access in low- and middle-income countries: Making the case for regulation', *Journal of Law, Medicine and Ethics*, 41(1): 286–300.

Connell, J. (2011a) *Medical Tourism*. Wallingford: CAB International.

Connell, J. (2011b) 'A new inequality? Privatisation, urban bias, migration and medical tourism', *Asia Pacific Viewpoint*, 52: 260–271.

Connell, J. (2013) 'Contemporary medical tourism: Conceptualisation, culture and commodification', *Tourism Management*, 34(1): 1–13.

Connell, J. (2015a) 'Medical tourism: Concepts and definitions', in N. Lunt, D. Horsfall, & J. Hanefeld (eds), *Handbook on Medical Tourism and Patient* Mobility (pp. 16–24). Cheltenham: Edward Elgar.

Connell, J. (2015b) 'From medical tourism to transnational health care? An epilogue for the future', *Social Science and Medicine*, 124: 398–401.

Connell, J. (2016) 'Reducing the scale? From global images to border crossings in medical tourism', *Global Networks*, 16(4): 531–550.

Constable, N. (2009) 'The commodification of intimacy: Marriage, sex, and reproductive labour', *Annual Review of Anthropology*, 38: 49–64.

Ebrahim, A., & Ganguli, S. (2017) 'Strategic priorities for exploiting Bahrain's medical tourism potential', *Journal of Place Management and Development*, 10(1): 45–60.

Helmy, E., & Travers, R. (2009) 'Towards the development of Egyptian medical tourism sector', *Anatolia*, 20(2): 419–439.

Inhorn, M. (2011) 'Globalisation and gametes: Reproductive "tourism", Islamic bioethics and Middle Eastern modernity', *Anthropology and Medicine*, 18(1): 87–103.

Inhorn, M. (2012) 'Reproductive exile in global Dubai: South Asian stories', *Cultural Politics*, 8(2): 283–306.

Inhorn, M. (2015) *Cosmopolitan Conceptions. IVF Sojourns in Global Dubai.* Durham, NC: Duke University Press.

Inhorn, M. (2017) 'Medical cosmopolitanism in global Dubai: A twenty-first-century transnational intracytoplasmic sperm injection (ICSI) depot', *Medical Anthropology Quarterly*, 31(1): 5–22.

Jabbari, A., Kavosi, Z., & Gholami, M. (2014) 'Medical tourists' profile in Shiraz', *International of Health System & Disaster Management*, 2(4): 232–236.

Johnson, J. (2010) 'Egypt: Where it all begins', *Medical Tourism Magazine*, 15: 36–38.

Kangas, B. (2002) 'Therapeutic itineraries in a global world: Yemenis and their search for biomedical treatment abroad', *Medical Anthropology*, 21: 35–78.

Kangas, B. (2007) 'Hope from abroad in the international medical travel of Yemeni patients', *Anthropology and Medicine*, 14: 293–305.

Kangas, B. (2011) 'Complicating common ideas about medical tourism: Gender, class and globality in Yemenis' international medical travel', *Signs*, 36(2): 327–332.

Kaya, S., Karsavuran, S., & Yildiz, A. (2015) 'Medical tourism developments within Turkey', in N. Lunt, D. Horsfall, & J. Hanefeld (eds), *Handbook on Medical Tourism and Patient Mobility* (pp. 332–338). Cheltenham: Edward Elgar.

Kronfol, N. (2015) 'Medical tourism developments within the Middle East', in N. Lunt, D. Horsfall, & J. Hanefeld (eds), *Handbook on Medical Tourism and Patient Mobility* (pp. 307–312). Cheltenham: Edward Elgar.

Lautier, M. (2008) 'Export of health services from developing countries: The case of Tunisia', *Social Science and Medicine*, 67: 101–110.

Medical Tourism Magazine (2013) 'Medical tourism providing needed Band-Aid to Turkish debt', *Medical Tourism Magazine*, 28: 16–17.

Medical Tourism Magazine (2014) 'Out of Africa: Cures for ailing health systems found in foreign lands', *Medical Tourism Magazine*, 30: 21–22.

Nielsen, S., Yazici, S., Petersen, S., Blaakilde, A., & Krasnik, A. (2012) 'Use of cross-border healthcare services among ethnic Danes, Turkish immigrants and Turkish descendants in Denmark: A combined survey and registry study', *BMC Health Services Research*, 12: 390.

Noubar, H., Heidarzadeh, N., & Bahador, B. (2014) 'Evaluating strategies for promoting health tourism', *Journal of Political and Social Sciences*, 1(1): 15–19.

Ormond, M. (2013) *Neoliberal Governance and International Medical Travel in Malaysia.* London: Routledge.

Safaeepour, M., Goodarzi, M., & Rostami Kondari, N. (2015) 'Planning and developing medical tourism in megalopolis Shiraz', *Management Science Letters*, 5: 123–136.

Stephano, R. (2014) 'Just doing it: Jordan making a name for itself in medical tourism', *Medical Tourism Magazine*, 32: 61–63.

Stephano, R. (2015) 'Germany's designs on Arab patients', *Middle East Health*, September: 28–32.

Sugorakova, D. (2014) 'Turkey: Renaissance of thermal therapy', *Medical Tourism Magazine*, 32: 103–105.

Toyota, M., Chee, H., & Xiang, B. (2013) 'Global track, national vehicle: Transnationalism in medical tourism in Asia', *European Journal of Transnational Studies*, 5(1): 27–53.

Vequist, D., Bolatkale, E., & Valdez, E. (2009) 'Health tourism economic report—Jordan', *Medical Tourism Magazine*, 2: August.

Yeates N. (2009) *Globalising Care Economies and Migrant Workers: Explorations in Global Care Chains*. Basingstoke: Palgrave.

Yeoh, E., Othman, K., & Ahmad, H. (2013) 'Understanding medical tourists: Word-of-mouth and viral marketing as potent marketing tools', *Tourism Management*, 34: 196–201.

Youngman, I. (2016) 'The falling star of medical tourism'. *International Medical Travel Journal*, 15 April 2016. Available online: www.imtj.com/news/falling-star-medical-tourism/ (Accessed 11 September 2018).

28

SHOPPING, TOURISM AND HYPER-DEVELOPMENT IN THE MIDDLE EAST AND NORTH AFRICA

Esmat Zaidan

Introduction

Tourism has the potential to drive growth and economic diversification in the Middle East and North Africa (MENA) (UNWTO 2016). However, maximising the influence of the industry needs increased cooperation within the region, prioritisation of tourism within national agendas, and building resilience and sustainable growth. Despite the challenging global situations the world is facing due to geopolitical conflicts, economic crises, and travel health notices, the tourism industry in MENA continues to thrive, remaining one of the world's fastest growing tourism regions (Kovjanic 2014; UNWTO 2016). Until relatively recently, tourism was only an afterthought in the high-income countries of the Arabian Gulf where economic development and fiscal policy have depended overwhelmingly upon the 'rent' acquired from the exploitation of natural resources, such as hydrocarbons (Becken 2015; Bill & Springborg 1994; Ross 2001). These other so-called 'rentier states' (e.g. the UAE), however, have recently placed tourism at the forefront of their economic development plans with the goal of achieving diversification and fiscal strength while reducing their reliance on fluctuating oil prices (Zaidan 2016a).

One of the preeminent forms of tourism taking greater hold in the Middle East is shopping. As a visitor attraction and revenue-generating activity, shopping is a fundamental element of tourism, and there is a growing literature on its importance in the travel experience (Henderson, Chee, Mun, & Lee 2011; Timothy 2005). Shopping is an essential part of the tourist trip and frequently an influencing factor in destination choice (Moscardo 2004), with a distinction between shopping as the prime goal of travel and where it is a secondary activity (Timothy 2018). Even with less emphasis, shopping is a salient tourist hobby enjoyed universally, and opportunities to get involved in it can improve the appeal of a destination (Butler 1991). A range of factors affect the extent and nature of tourists' commitment to shopping, such as age, gender, socio-economic position and family status (Kozak 2001), all of which have consequences for tourist satisfaction (Henderson et al. 2011). Currency conversion rates, lifestyles, reasons for travel, accommodation and transportation types, and exposure to attitudes towards destination cultures are also influential factors, not to mention the origin of the shopper. The acknowledgement of tourists' enthusiasm for shopping and its actual and potential contribution to local and national economies has resulted in its adoption as a 'tourism policy and promotional strategy' (Timothy 2005: 72) in many places; and destination marketing material worldwide mentions the wide-ranging shopping attractions awaiting potential visitors (Henderson et al. 2011).

Although the literature on shopping tourism is growing, much of it is North American and European in orientation (Henderson et al. 2011). There is still much to learn about different parts of the emerging world, particularly amongst the developing and newly developed countries of North Africa and the Middle East where shopping studies are limited (Cohen & Cohen 2015). This chapter explores aspects of shopping and tourism in MENA with specific reference to cities that advertise themselves as retail destinations and the factors that enable their success. The chapter demonstrates how tourism and shopping are closely connected and emphasises how shopping destinations in the Middle East are a suitable setting for exploring this inextricable and dynamic relationship. The emerging shopping–tourism nexus in certain MENA cities is becoming a highly profitable prospect with a large and diverse supply of retailers being developed. These matters are discoursed within the geographic framework of MENA and specifically the cities that are leading international tourist centres where shopping is crucial to the visitor experience.

Shopping as a tourist activity

Shopping is an important leisure activity at home and tourist activity while away from home. The pervasiveness of shopping reflects how consumerism 'pervades modern capitalism' (Bocock 1993: 50). Shopping is an extremely important part of the economy and has several purposes beyond the utilitarian, being a leisure activity that satisfies a variety of psychological and social needs (Henderson et al. 2011; Timothy 2005).

The World Tourism Organization (UNWTO 2017) estimates that the number of individuals travelling globally more than doubled in the past 20 years, to 1.24 billion in 2016. A significant driver of domestic and international travel has been shopping. While not the principal reason for travel in most cases, shopping is a significant activity for tourists in a destination. The impact of tourist shopping on the development of the retail industry in destinations and, more broadly, to the development of local economies, is strong and the role of retail in increasing the appeal of tourist destinations has been widely acknowledged (McIntyre 2012; Timothy 2005; Zaidan 2016b).

Overall, shopping is valued as the second most vital onsite expenditure after accommodation; however, when it comes to prominent retail destinations (e.g. Hong Kong), shopping tends to be tourists' primary expenditure item (Turner & Reisinger 2001). Retail purchases continue to account for about one-third of total tourist expenditures, but the proportion differs from nation to nation and from one market segment to another (Chang, Yang, & Yu 2006; Jin, Moscardo, & Murphy 2017; Keown 1989; Kim & Littrell 1999, 2001; Wong & Law 2003). For instance, shopping has traditionally comprised approximately half of the total budget of tourists visiting Hong Kong (Mak, Tsang, & Cheung 1999; Wong & Law 2003). Tourists shop for a variety of goods, ranging from handicrafts to luxury items (Park, Reisinger, & Noh 2010) and may even include utilitarian purchases (Timothy 2005). Thus, tourist shopping plays a considerable role in the development of the retail industry in destinations and has a major impact on the economy (Lin & Lin 2006).

Despite extensive recognition that shopping is a key tourist activity and destination attraction, the role of shopping in tourism has only recently started to receive substantial academic attention (Choi, Heo, & Law 2016; Jin et al. 2017; Moscardo 2004; Timothy 2005). Not surprisingly, given its economic potential, many destinations have sought to exploit tourists' retail tendencies by developing shopping malls and precincts as tourist attractions and by providing numerous incentives such as tax-free shopping programmes (Butler 1991; Shim & Santos 2014; Timothy & Butler 1995; Zaidan 2016b). Moscardo (2004) examined shopping as a factor in tourist destination choice and how retail areas can develop into prime attractions. She suggested that tourist shopping is a multidimensional phenomenon that should receive more attention by researchers. Moscardo concluded that traditional tourists' consumption concentrated on particular goods and services (hotels, restaurants, cultural or leisure and entertainment offers), while modern tourists' expenditures reflect high purchasing power, focused on broader goods, such as fashion, crafts or design.

For tourists, shopping tends to take on a more leisurely aura compared to shopping at home. Foreign customers often purchase more items and spend more per item than domestic customers do when offered the same retail environment (UNWTO 2014). Timothy (2005: 11) added, 'consumption is not just about products. It is about consuming places, spaces and time', which is inherent in the definition of tourism. The World Tourism Organization (UNWTO 2014: 13) defines shopping tourism as 'a contemporary form of tourism fostered by individuals for whom purchasing goods outside of their usual environment is a determining factor in their decision to travel'. This exemplifies the notion that shopping is becoming an increasingly salient motivation for travel and marker of destination attractiveness.

This has resulted in an increasing number of destinations focusing on shopping and providing retail opportunities. In their marketing efforts, many destinations have come to emphasise their retail services as they realise that many tourists consider unique shopping experiences when selecting their holiday destinations. Travellers nowadays tend to focus on what they can do rather than on what they can see. Accordingly, whether cities can become destinations of choice relies significantly today on the quality of their retail offerings (UNWTO 2014).

Urban change, retail and tourism development in the Middle East

The exponential physical growth of cities in several hubs, such as Dubai, raises a plethora of issues pertaining to local marketplaces and the development of urban landscapes and tourism. In most cases, this Westernised approach to urban development and tourism does not consider local environments, human scales, cultural values, or the historical urban fabric, as the call for 'iconic high-rise buildings' tends to ignore the fundamental conditions of producing sustainable structures and comfortable living spaces (Ogaily 2015). Since the 1970s, the Gulf Cooperation Council (GCC) countries have seen immense urban population growth. Because of this, there has been considerable pressure to transform the region's cities rapidly by using imported Western technology and designs. Up until then, urban transitions had occurred much more slowly, allowing cultural values and identities to adapt to change and to be conserved and reinforced during the development process. However, since the 1990s, and particularly in the GCC countries, the normative transitional phase was superseded as speed, abundance and quantity drove development. Consequently, modern, world-class skylines appeared incongruously in traditionally conservative areas.

The 1930s saw the unconventional expansion of culturally and traditionally conservative areas into extraordinary cities based on blueprints of wide highways and roads with unusually large plot sizes, starting an era of major urban and social transformation. The following few decades, especially the 1950s and 1960s, brought about major structural changes promoted by governments and famous architects and based on Western styles. The result has been a rapid growth in international-style buildings and tourism-related infrastructure (e.g. retail outlets, large-scale shopping malls, hotels, amusement parks, and event and entertainment venues) superimposed upon very traditional environments (Stephenson 2014). The new urbanscapes had little to no connection with traditional Arab cultural landscapes.

Indeed, urban development is closely aligned with retail development. Trending growth in hotel, leisureplex and mall construction is directly linked to growing trends in tourism. Waterfront development in the form of urban gentrification and construction of new waterfronts through land reclamation are part of this new urbanscape development. Waterfront renewal and urban growth in general in the modern world are intrinsically connected to growing leisure opportunities, including recreational shopping.

The influence of shopping environments on retail experiences and purchase decision-making has been well studied (Michon, Chebat, & Turley 2005; Wakefield & Blodgett 2016). MENA's shopping environments, which range from high-end malls to street markets and beaches served by mobile vendors, also affect shopping experiences and decision-making. Shopping centres have undergone major transformations in their forms and functions during the past three decades. They have gone from being boxy, generic establishments containing a random collection of retailers to now having more distinctive personalities, appealing designs and controlled tenants. Perhaps the most prevalent change has been from purely non-descript shopping venues to malls becoming mixed environments replete with recreational facilities, entertainment complexes, and lodging under one roof, oftentimes with a specific underlying theme (Nelson 1998; Simmons 1991; Vester 1996). While this experiment in 'shoppertainment' was pioneered in North America (Timothy 2005), related changes are occurring throughout the world, nowhere more evident than in MENA, especially in the Gulf States.

Many companies have resorted to integrating hotels and malls, especially in the Gulf States, to exploit the booming shopping tourism sector (Shankman 2012). Some hotels in Saudi Arabia and the UAE have also begun offering multi-mall shopping tours. Lodging establishments in Dubai achieve a nearly 90 per cent occupancy rate during shopping festivals, which attract millions of tourists annually (DTCM 2016).

Parallel to these developments is a boom of large-scale projects that are fundamentally reshaping tourism landscapes across parts of the Middle East (Steiner 2010). For instance, in Dubai, the construction of iconic hotels such as the Burj al Arab and the Palms, a fabricated island network designed to resemble a palm tree, have come to represent Dubai as a destination. The proliferation of shopping malls and the remarkable design of buildings complement these efforts. Due to their striking scale, these projects have evolved and come to define the touristic image of numerous cities, areas and countries in the Middle East (Table 28.1).

Tourists are enticed by such venues and share the spaces with residents, although they may use them in contrasting ways (Snepenger, Murphy, O'Connell, & Gregg 2003). Commentators have cautioned about focusing too heavily on tourists while neglecting the cultivation of a loyal local customer base (Henderson et al. 2011). Overwhelmingly luxurious in style and iconic in design, new hotels complement the large-scale landscaped waterfront developments and the restructuring of tourism spaces throughout the Gulf countries (Steiner 2010). These projects along with skyscrapers such as the Burj Khalifa (currently the tallest building in the world), shopping malls such as Qatar Mall in Doha, the Ibn Battuta Mall (a retail outlet designed in various 'traditional' oriental architecture styles), the Dubai Mall (with 450,000 m2 gross leasable area, or GLA) and the recently planned Mall of Arabia (which will be the largest shopping mall in the world with 600,000 m2 GLA), and leisure and fun projects such as the Ski Dubai hall (which offers a 400 metre ski slope in a desert environment) are increasingly shaping the international image of Dubai and the UAE. All of these integrated tourist resorts, iconic buildings,

Table 28.1 A selection of current waterfront development projects in the Middle East

Name	Country	Estimated investment cost (€ billions)	Facts
The Pearl	Qatar	2.0	400 ha; 8000 residential units; 3 hotels, 4 marinas; 60,000 m² retail
Bahrain Bay	Bahrain	2.5	Business, retail and residential areas, yacht club, hotels
Two Seas Islands	Bahrain	2.5	1100 ha; residential clusters; luxury hotels; schools; hospitals; retail
The Wave	Oman	3.0	7 km beachfront; 200 ha; 18-hole golf course; marina; hotels; villas; apartments
Palm Islands	UAE (Dubai)	100.8	Two man-made islands in the shape of palm trees with a beach front of 120 km; 5000 villas; 3600 apartments; 100 hotels; 4 marinas; theme parks; restaurants; shopping malls; sports facilities
The World	UAE (Dubai)	11.0	300 Islands in the shape of the world
Waterfront Dubai	UAE (Dubai)	Not specified	World's largest waterfront project with 81 million m² beachfront; mixed use destination encompassing
Saadiyat Island	UAE (Abu Dhabi)	21.0	3 marinas; 29 hotels; 8,000 private villas; 38,000 apartments; 2 golf courses; various museums, including branches of the Louvre and the Guggenheim; 1 concert hall; various galleries

Source: Steiner (2010).

massive shopping malls, leisure and sport facilities, and waterfront projects have become tourist destinations and attractions in their own right.

The recent phenomenon of integrating shopping and entertainment complexes has been used to create a universal retail experience, especially in popular tourist destinations. This innovative trend has been dubbed 'retailtainment' (Stephenson 2014) or 'shoppertainment' (Timothy 2005) and is derived from the ubiquitous shopping environments of several tourist havens in MENA, specifically Dubai. Retailtainment and shoppertainment reflect the new trend of combining retail and entertainment into a single venue, and is widespread in Dubai. Malls are no longer only a shopping venue, but also an entertainment complex and total holiday destination in some cases.

While the number of retail centres, malls, leisure and entertainment complexes, iconic buildings, and waterfront projects continue to grow across the Arab world, these projects increasingly lack spatial, historical and social embeddedness. Rather, architectural and interior design styles are eclectically combined and may be incongruous with traditional architecture and urban forms. They often showcase architectural features and forms from other building styles and cultural and historical contexts that have minor practical significance to the functionality of the building (Steiner 2010). The Balbaa Hotel in Sharm El Sheikh, Egypt, is constructed in an exaggerated and fantastical 'Pharaonic' style, combining large papyrus columns with Asian-style bamboo huts. The Royal Mirage hotel in Dubai merges Moroccan, Egyptian, Syrian and Gulf

Arab architecture and interior design. These eclectic blends can be viewed as an 'orientalisation of the Orient' (Al-Hamarneh 2006; Steiner 2010) in an effort to accentuate the exotic, orientalist image of the Arab world. In comparison, a shopping mall like the Mall of the Emirates in Dubai, the fourth largest shopping centre in the world, includes an indoor ski hall that resembles materialised paradoxes of hyperreality (Henderson et al. 2011). The integration of shopping with snow skiing in a desert society does not reflect an expressed 'genuineness' but offers a new hyperreal experience of the Orient that is clean, calculable, reliable and streamlined. Here, the hyperreal Orient has been transformed into a complete commodity for tourism, reflecting the sentiment of Henderson and her colleagues (2011) that in the Arab world, a lot must change for everything to remain the same.

Dubai—the shopping haven of the Middle East

Dubai is well recognised globally as the shopping haven of MENA (Alhosani & Zaidan 2014; Sharpley 2008). Shopping centres in Dubai are not just simple venues to purchase products but are much more than that (Zaidan 2016b). For instance, the Dubai Mall, the world's largest shopping centre spanning over 12 million square feet, has an Olympic-size ice rink and an indoor aquarium. The Mall of the Emirates accommodates bars and hotels, as well as an indoor ski slope with artificial snow (Stephenson, Russell, & Edgar 2010). Horner and Swarbrooke (2005: 110) note that Dubai, as a shopping destination, has 'pioneered a new, almost postmodern, style of recreational tourism incorporating entertainment, shopping, and strikingly designed luxury hotels'. Dubai, similar to Las Vegas and Honolulu, has become a critical shopping zone to which many tourists travel to capture the shopping experience for themselves. Dubai offers a wide range of luxury retail services (Anwar & Sohail 2004), trailing only slightly behind London in number of retailers. Tourist shopping opportunities have spread beyond the malls to include outdoor shopping districts, official retail shops, luxurious cruise liners and hotels, airports and famous shopping festivals. All international brands can be found in Dubai's 95-plus shopping centres and major retail outlets. The Dubai Mall is popularly known to house every international fashion brand, and is soon expected to emerge as an international fashion capital thanks to the 440,000 square feet of fashion space. As part of the city's growing commercial landscape, Dubai has developed a year-round programme of shopping festivals, such as the Dubai Shopping Festival (DSF) and Dubai Summer Surprises (DSS) (Stephenson et al. 2010).

The growth of self-contained and gated corporate parks, residential communities, and giant multipurpose shopping malls may be described as a source of mega-physical 'damming'. In fact, these three types of projects are increasingly merging into enormous developments that combine residential, entertainment, retail and tourism functions. These projects may be called, collectively, 'late capitalist phalansteries' because of their 'symbolism of size, interiority or self-sustainability, and hybridity' (Kanna 2005: 66).

Airports are unconventional shopping environments whose customers are largely transit travellers and other tourists, at least in the departure lounges where retailers exploit passengers' spare time and boredom (Choi et al. 2016; Chung 2015; Timothy 2005). Major airports are no longer defined simply as travel hubs, but are also venues for shopping that compete with city centres and one another. Numerous international airports run intensive advertising campaigns and feature prominent shopping facilities. In MENA, Dubai International Airport stands out amongst airports in this regard. Airport retail revenues rely heavily on duty-free shopping, which is estimated to comprise approximately 30 per cent of all spending by travellers (Henderson et al. 2011). Such shopping activity tends to focus on high-end brands, has its own pricing system, caters to a captive audience and is contingent on special taxation rules.

Established in 1983, Dubai Duty Free generated sales of US$20 million in its first year and has matured into one of the largest travel retail operators with worldwide sales of US$1.85 billion in 2016. Currently employing some 6,000 workers, the company has consistently raised the bar for airport retailing, and it continues to grow. Dubai Duty Free currently operates over 35,400 square metres of retail space at Dubai International Airport and 2,500 metres at Al Maktoum International, which is expected to grow in conjunction with the immense development plans of Dubai South and will ultimately cover some 80,000 square metres of retail space (Dubai Duty Free 2017).

Dubai has innovatively created a unique combination of shopping and entertainment to revolutionise a universal shopping experience that appeals to volumes of global customers (Zaidan 2015). It is one of the only places where tourists can swim with dolphins and sharks, while remaining close to the most popular international brand retail outlets. Consumers in Dubai can wander around traditional Arabian markets and browse through spices and gold the same way people have done for centuries, and then head for the modern, world-renowned fashion district in downtown Dubai. The 'retailtainment' experience of Dubai is unique in the world and continues to attract tourists from all over the globe (Zaidan, Taillon, & Lee 2016). This is especially so during the peak season when Dubai hosts its shopping festivals. Apart from its unprecedented shopping experiences, the malls in Dubai also provide a wide range of recreational opportunities.

On most sightseeing tours of Dubai, the malls are the main attraction. Named after the famous Arab explorer, the Ibn Battuta Mall has country-themed sections representing Andalucia, China and Egypt. Tourists can also view the Egyptian pyramids at the Wafi Mall, stroll through the Italian village at Mercato Mall, and see the largest Chinese-based market outside China at DragonMart, which is shaped like a dragon. The Mall of the Emirates enables tourists to watch Gentoo and King Penguins or enjoy a zip line ride down the snowy bank of Ski Dubai inside the mall.

Tourists and other shoppers visit local *souqs* (markets) to experience traditional Arab marketplaces. Two famous marketplaces are the Souq Al Bahar and the Madinat Souq, which aim to conserve the traditional souq heritage only steps away from five-star hotels and eateries. Tourists can walk through the famous Gold Souq or stroll through the Spice Souq to enjoy the tastes and fragrances of the Middle East.

In contrast to the local experience, tourists can visit Global Village where over 65 countries and their native products are represented in luxurious pavilions. Products such as Iranian carpets, Yemeni honey, African wood pots and Thai dried fruits are amongst the most popular commodities.

Qatar—an emerging shopping destination

Like Dubai and some other UAE locales, Qatar is becoming a key venue of world-class facilities, aesthetic buildings, entertainment complexes and diverse cultural activities. The State of Qatar began focusing on tourism in 1989; however, not until recently has it become a major destination. It is becoming increasingly known as an emerging destination for leisure and business tourism. The small peninsula boasts a coastal area of more than 700 kilometres with several areas having shallow enough waters for tourists to enjoy. In addition, the country is home to several islands.

Qatar shot to fame after it successfully bid and won the rights to host the World Cup in 2022, which cemented its spot in the sport tourism sector. The country is up to date with the latest technology, including 12 air-conditioned stadiums, which will harness solar energy to provide the electricity for each stadium's operations. When the stadiums are not in use, the harnessed power will be transferred to the national grid. This is Qatar's initiative to reduce its carbon footprint while maintaining carbon-neutrality. To prepare for the upcoming World Cup, Qatar's government has funded several high-end projects to expand its social and tourism infrastructure, in addition to constructing new cultural and event venues. A larger number of world-class four- and five-star hotels and leisure facilities have been included in the bid to attract global visitors, helping to place Qatar at the centre of international sports. In the meantime, regional tourists from the Gulf States and other Arab countries are attracted by the implementation of new festivals and entertainment opportunities. Up to the end of 2011, US$25 billion had already been invested, according to Ahmed Abdullah Al Nuaimi, the chairman of the Qatar Tourism Authority. A further US$11 billion investment had been secured to develop and construct a new international airport to accommodate up to 50 million passengers annually, alongside another massive investment of US$5.5 billion for a mega-seaport to facilitate cruise ships and offshore residential facilities. Qatar currently has approximately 30,000 rooms in a wide range of world-renowned hotel and residential properties.

Like the UAE, Qatar is a major shopping destination in the Middle East. It sports traditional marketplaces, such as Souq Waqif, which has undergone huge renovations to preserve cultural and traditional architectural values. Boasting authentic cafés and restaurants, antique shops, craft vendors, and textile and metal merchants, Souq Waqif remains an extremely favourable tourist attraction (Adham 2008). It is built over an area of 20,000 square metres and houses over 1,200 shops, which sell a wide array of products. It sees over 7,000 visitors each day, with figures skyrocketing as high as 20,000 during busy weekends. Apart from Souq Waqif, there are several other textile and gold souqs that offer items including clothes, fragrances, shoes, household goods and carpets at unbeatable prices, especially on Thursdays and Fridays.

There are also several modern shopping complexes in Doha, such as the new Mall of Qatar and Al Hazem Mall, alongside the classic City Centre Doha, Landmark Mall, and Mall of Villagio, which is based on an Italian theme and provides Venetian-style canals which can be travelled through the mall in a gondola. The Mall of Qatar, which was inaugurated in 2017, covers a 500,000 square metre area with a US$1.4 billion price tag. This mall sports 500 shops, a five-star hotel, an indoor amusement park for children and an oasis area with restaurants, fountains and live entertainment. Doha Festival City was also inaugurated in 2017, and is located 1 kilometres north of downtown Doha. It spans 477,837 square metres and includes an IKEA store, an entertainment park and two major hotels. The complex provides over 400 shops and services, alongside restaurants featuring multinational cuisines, an Angry Birds theme park, a snow park, and an F1 simulator. The cost of the project was approximately US$1.7 billion.

Doha also saw a rise of GCC visitors by nearly 40 per cent during the first half of 2017, a result of Qatar's policies easing access by GCC citizens. This statistic is forecasted to rise further due to a six-week festival planned to run after the Islamic month of Ramadan, until Eid al Adha, in Doha Park. Spanning over 30,000 acres of open land close to the Doha Exhibition Centre, the festival includes over 100 entertainment events, amusement centres, shopping areas, restaurants, internationally known circuses, an electronic video gaming arena, theatrical productions, art exhibitions, and sporting contests and prizes.

The 2006 Asian Games torch stands as a monument to the success of Qatar's sporting ambitions. Lifestyle-based projects are complex to implement as they present a difficult stakeholder environment for the project teams. 'When developing a traditional mall, you have multiple users with their own agendas, but they are all retail-, dining- and entertainment-driven,' says Karen M. Scott (cited in Burba 2016: 12), senior project manager, Skye Group, Orlando,

Florida, US. The primary niche of Skye Group is managing shopping centre projects and coordinating tenants. 'Mixed-use projects are more complicated because all the uses have different requirements. They do not always easily coexist.' The complications are visible in several ways, such as nearby residents who want a quiet atmosphere near their residences; however, some lifestyle centres promote live music to attract customers, which is contradictory to residents' desires.

Qatar's policymakers and leaders have identified and stressed the need for a highly developed and diversified economy capable of meeting the needs of, and establishing a high standard of living for, current and future generations (General Secretariat for Development Planning 2008). Tourism plays a key role in Qatar's pursuit of achieving a highly competitive and diversified economy. As a result, the Emir of Qatar announced the Qatar National Tourism Strategy 2030 with the aim of developing the country's tourism industry. Since the strategy was put into motion, various shopping campaigns have been launched to provide unique retail experiences for tourists and residents. Held annually, the Summer Festival is a major attraction with live shows and concerts, shopping promotions and raffle draws in several malls. The Qatar Summer Festival has proven to be a successful shopping campaign launched by the Qatar Tourism Authority (QTA), with an estimated contribution of QAR 630 million to the economy in its third year alone (Qatar Tourism Authority 2017). Another successful campaign launched by the QTA to boost shopping and tourism is the Shop Qatar festival. Designed to offer the best shopping and entertainment experiences for tourists and residents, the inaugural 2017 Shop Qatar festival generated about QAR 1.06 billion (Qatar Tourism Authority 2017).

Other shopping contexts

Mega-malls, gold souqs and shopping festivals are not the only retail contexts of interest to tourists in the Middle East, even though they dominate the GCC region. Tourists look for a variety of merchandise, ranging from luxury items to handicrafts, and they are not always seeking to be surrounded by hyperreal urban landscapes. Handicrafts are an important source of income for local artists, and they are an important tourism resource as they increase the retail appeal of the destination in the eyes of the tourists (Kozak & Baloglu 2011; Swanson & Timothy 2012). In addition, handicrafts comprise a vital part of the tourist experience as they often signify the traditions and cultures of indigenous populations. The Middle East region is blessed with a variety of handicrafts that play a key role in offering a touch of culture to curious tourists. This is important, as culture plays a vital part in displaying a positive image of the destination (Al Refaie, Ko, & Li 2012).

A good example of this situation is Jordan, which is rich in cultural heritage with historical sites, festivals, performances and handicrafts. Tourism is an important part of Jordan's economy, comprising 14 per cent of the country's GDP (Mustafa 2011). The handicrafts sector in Jordan is diverse with products such as handmade glass, mosaics, woodcarvings, pottery and ceramics leading the craft market (Abuamoud, Libbin, Green, & Al Rousan 2014; Mustafa 2011, 2014). Handicrafts in Jordan generate approximately 30 million Jordanian Dinars every year (Qattan 2009).

Turkey also has a strong and diverse handicrafts sector that appeals to international tourists. The handicrafts industry in Turkey consists of traditional handicrafts such as ceramics, embroidery, carpet-making, rug-making, cloth-weaving and woodwork (Traditional Arts and Crafts n.d.). Tourists in Turkey spend generously on Turkish handicrafts, especially on carpets and rugs with a total spending of US$46 million between the months of January and June in 2017 (Daily Sabah 2017). Empirical research shows how these handicrafts are an important part of the

Turkish experience for foreign visitors and how they contribute to tourists' overall satisfaction (Tosun, Temizkan, Timothy, & Fyall 2007).

Religion has been and continues to be a significant motivator for travel to the Middle East (Egresi 2012; Stausberg 2011). Religious tourism is big business with an estimated value of US$18 billion and an annual market of 300 million dedicated travellers (Tourism and More 2014). In addition, religious tourism is less prone to fluctuations in demand incurred by unstable economic and political conditions (Collins-Kreiner, Kliot, Mansfeld, & Sagi 2006; Tourism and More 2014). Shopping plays a key role in pilgrimage tourism experiences in the Middle East. A prime example of this is Palestine, which has important historical significance for Christians, Jews and Muslims in Jerusalem, Bethlehem, Nazareth, Hebron and Jericho (Abahre & Suleiman 2016). Bethlehem, which is believed to be the birthplace of Jesus, attracts more than 80 per cent of tourists who come to visit the Palestinian territories (Rabinowitz 2010). Around Christmas time, Christian pilgrims from all around the world spend generously on olivewood carvings—the most profitable tourist product in Bethlehem (Bethlehem Christian Families 2017).

The streets of Bethlehem and Old Jerusalem are lined with handicraft vendors selling a wide variety of locally produced and imported products. What the majority of these products have in common is their focus on the life of Jesus, but they also depict biblical scenes and images of the Holy Land more broadly. Outside of Palestine, Holy Land Christian tours frequently include Egypt and Jordan on their itineraries, and Christian-themed tours of Turkey are becoming more popular. Wherever Christian tours circulate, vendors have set up shop, selling olivewood carvings and other regional crafts that allow spiritual visitors to take home a physical reminder of their sacred experience. These vendors and the crafts they sell, especially in Bethlehem and Jerusalem, are prominent fixtures in those cities. They have become, through the years and generations, an integral part of the physical urban form and a striking part of the religious tourism landscape.

Conclusion

Postmodern development may be a plausible explanation for the success of new shopping tourism destinations in the Middle East owing to conditions of hyperreality in urban design and related shopping landscapes. The total simulation of various realities is a basis for their attractiveness, and these simulations ideally fit postmodern consumers' demands and expectations in hyper-McDisneyised ways (Ritzer & Liska 1997). Postmodern hyperreality's economic value is based on places' value as shopping capitals in a global race for recognition and retail consumers. Official tourism marketing and development strategies in some MENA destinations recognise the positive economic influence of shopping, which plays a vital part in future growth strategies. Shopping 'paradises' within MENA possess both weaknesses and strengths, and the tourism authorities in retail destinations should consider both perspectives as the question of global competitiveness in tourism becomes more critical.

Shopping and tourism are unmistakably linked. Retail destinations in MENA are an interesting and suitable setting for investigating this close and dynamic relationship. Official marketing and development strategies point to the increasingly important role of shopping-based tourism, in many forms, in the broader goals of economic development. As cities in the Middle East continue to grow, and as economic development continues to subsume tourism, shopping will remain a major feature to attract international tourists and an ancillary activity to occupy those who may be visiting for other reasons.

References

Abahre, J.S., & Suleiman, A.S. (2016) 'Religious tourism: Experience of Palestine', *International Journal of Advanced Academic Research*, 2(2): 1–6.

Abuamoud, I.N., Libbin, J., Green, J., & Al Rousan, R. (2014) 'Factors affecting the willingness of tourists to visit cultural heritage sites in Jordan', *Journal of Heritage Tourism*, 9(2): 148–165.

Adham, K. (2008) 'Rediscovering the island: Doha's urbanity from pearls to spectacle', in Y. Elsheshtawy (ed.), *The Evolving Arab City: Tradition, Modernity & Urban Development* (pp. 218–258). London: Routledge.

Al-Hamarneh, A. (2006) 'Orientalising the orient: Postmodern geographies of tourism in the Arab World'. Paper presented at the Second World Congress of Middle Eastern Studies, Amman, Jordan, June.

Alhosani, N., & Zaidan, E. (2014) 'Shopping tourism and destination development: Dubai as a case study', *The Arab World Geographer*, 17(1): 66–81.

Al Refaie, A., Ko, J.H., & Li, M.H. (2012) 'Examining the factors that affect tourists' satisfaction, loyalty, WOM and intention to return using SEM: Evidence from Jordan', *International Journal of Leisure and Tourism Marketing*, 3(2): 179–197.

Anwar, S.A and Sohail, M.S. (2004) 'Festival tourism in the United Arab Emirates: First-time versus repeat visitor perceptions', *Journal of Vacation Marketing*, 10: 161–170.

Becken, S. (2015) *Tourism and Oil: Preparing for the Challenge*. Bristol: Channel View Publications.

Bethlehem Christian Families (2017) 'Bethlehem Christian Families: The Olive Wood'. Available online: www.bcfmission.com/olive-wood-history.html (Accessed 20 November 2017).

Bill, J., & Springborg, R. (1994) *Politics in the Middle East*. New York: Harper Collins.

Bocock, R. (1993) *Consumption*. London: Routledge.

Burba, D. (2016) 'The mall life: A new kind of mall presents project managers with a more complex stakeholder environment', *PM Network*, 30(8): 12–13.

Butler, R.W. (1991) 'West Edmonton mall as a tourist attraction', *The Canadian Geographer*, 35: 287–295.

Chang, J., Yang, B.T., & Yu, C.G. (2006) 'The moderating effect of salespersons' selling behavior on shopping motivation and satisfaction: Taiwan tourists in China', *Tourism Management*, 27: 934–942.

Choi, M.J., Heo, C.Y., & Law, R. (2016) 'Progress in shopping tourism', *Journal of Travel & Tourism Marketing*, 33: 1–24.

Chung, Y. (2015) 'Hedonic and utilitarian shopping values in airport shopping behaviour', *Journal of Air Transport Management*, 49: 28–34.

Cohen, E., & Cohen, S.A. (2015) 'A mobilities approach to tourism from emerging world regions', *Current Issues in Tourism*, 18(1): 11–43.

Collins-Kreiner, N., Kliot, N., Mansfeld, Y., & Sagi, K. (2006) *Christian Tourism to the Holy Land: Pilgrimage during Security Crisis*. Aldershot: Ashgate.

Daily Sabah (2017) 'Tourists in Turkey spend $1.2 billion on clothes, shoes'. Available online: www.dailysabah.com/tourism/2017/08/03/tourists-in-turkey-spend-12-billion-on-clothes-shoes (Accessed 10 January 2018).

Department of Tourism and Commerce Marketing [DTCM] (2016) 'Dubai welcomes 4.1 million overnight visitors in Q1 2016, up 5.1% year on year'. Available online: www.visitdubai.com//media/presskits/prs-april-2016/atm-day-1-announcement-2016-q1-visitorresults.pdf. (Accessed 25 September 2016).

Dubai Duty Free (2017) 'Media Center-News'. Available online: www.dubaidutyfree.com/media_center/news (Accessed on 15 June 2017).

Egresi, I. (2012) 'Tourism at religious sites: A case from Mardin, Turkey', *Geographica Timisiensis*, 21(1): 5–15.

General Secretariat for Development Planning (2008) *Qatar National Vision 2030*. Doha: General Secretariat for Development Planning.

Henderson, J.C., Chee, L., Mun, C.N., & Lee, C. (2011) 'Shopping, tourism and retailing in Singapore', *Managing Leisure*, 16(1): 36–48.

Horner, S., & Swarbrooke, J. (2005) *International Cases in Tourism Management*. London: Butterworth-Heinemann.

Jin, H., Moscardo, G., & Murphy, L. (2017) 'Making sense of tourist shopping research: A critical review', *Tourism Management*, 62: 120–134.

Kanna, A. (2005) 'The "State Philosophical" in the "Land without Philosophy": Shopping malls, interior cities, and the image of utopia in Dubai. *Traditional Dwellings and Settlements Review*, 16(2): 59–73.

Keown, C.F. (1989) 'A model of tourists' propensity to buy: Case of Japanese visitors to Hawaii', *Journal of Travel Research*, 27(3): 31–34.

Kim, S., & Littrell, M. (1999) 'Predicting souvenir purchase intentions', *Journal of Travel Research*, 38: 153–162.

Kim, S., & Littrell, A.M. (2001) 'Souvenir buying intentions for self versus others', *Annals of Tourism Research*, 28(3): 638–657.

Kovjanic, G. (2014) 'Islamic tourism as a factor of the Middle East regional development', *Tourism*, 18(1): 33–43.

Kozak, M. (2001) 'Comparative assessment of tourist satisfaction with destinations across two nationalities', *Tourism Management*, 22: 391–401.

Kozak, M., & Baloglu, S. (2011) *Managing and Marketing Tourist Destinations: Strategies to Gain a Competitive Edge*. New York: Routledge.

Lin, Y.H., & Lin, K.Q.R. (2006) 'Assessing Mainland Chinese visitors' satisfaction with shopping in Taiwan', *Asia Pacific Journal of Tourism Research*, 11(3): 247–268.

Mak, B.L.M., Tsang, N.K.F., & Cheung, I.C.J. (1999) 'Taiwanese tourists' shopping preferences', *Journal of Vacation Marketing*, 5(2): 190–198.

McIntyre, C. (ed.) (2012) *Tourism and Retail: The Psychogeography of Liminal Consumption*. London: Routledge.

Michon, R., Chebat, J.C., & Turley, L.W. (2005) 'Mall atmospherics: The interaction effects of the mall environment on shopping behavior', *Journal of Business Research*, 58(5): 576–583.

Moscardo, G. (2004) 'Shopping as a destination attraction: An empirical examination of the role of shopping in tourists' destination choice and experience', *Journal of Vacation Marketing*, 10(4): 294–307.

Mustafa, M.H. (2011) 'Potential of sustaining handicrafts as a tourism product in Jordan', *International Journal of Business and Social Science*, 2(2): 145–152.

Mustafa, M.H. (2014) 'Tourism development at the baptism site of Jesus Christ, Jordan: Residents' perspectives', *Journal of Heritage Tourism*, 9(1): 75–83.

Nelson, E. (1998) *Mall of America: Reflections of a Virtual Community*. Lakeville, MA: Galde Press.

Ogaily, A. (2015) 'Urban planning in Dubai: Cultural and human scale context'. Paper presented for the Council on Tall Buildings and Urban Habitat.

Park, K.S., Reisinger, Y., & Noh, E.H. (2010) 'Luxury shopping in tourism', *International Journal of Tourism Research*, 12(2): 164–178.

Qatar Tourism Authority (2017) 'QTA begins writing next chapter of National Tourism Sector Strategy'. Available online: www.visitqatar.qa/corporate/media/corporate-news-release/2017/may/qta-begins-writing-next-chapter-of-national-tourism-sector-strategy.html (Accessed 20 November 2017).

Qattan, A. (2009) *Handicrafts Market Demand Analysis*. Amman: USAID Jordan Economic Development Program.

Rabinowitz, G. (2010) 'Palestinians aim to push tourism beyond Bethlehem'. *The Telegraph*, 11 February. Available online: www.telegraph.co.uk/expat/expatnews/7214355/Palestinians-aim-to-push-tourism-beyond-Bethlehem.html (Accessed 5 January 2017).

Ritzer, G., & Liska, A. (1997) '"McDisneyization" and "post-tourism": Complementary perspectives on contemporary tourism', in C. Rojek, & J. Urry (eds), *Touring Cultures: Transformations of Travel and Theory* (pp. 96–109). London: Routledge.

Ross, M. (2001) 'Does oil hinder democracy?', *World Politics*, 51(3): 325–361.

Shankman, S. (2012) 'Trend alert: Shopping tourism to drive growth as east invades west's shopping malls'. Available online: http://skift.com/2012/11/05/trend-alert-shopping-drives-tourism-inthe-middle-east-europe-and-asia/ (Accessed 29 August 2014).

Sharpley, R. (2008) 'Planning for tourism: The case of Dubai', *Tourism and Hospitality Planning and Development*, 5(1): 13–30.

Shim, C., & Santos, C.A. (2014) 'Tourism, place and placelessness in the phenomenological experience of shopping malls in Seoul', *Tourism Management*, 45: 106–23.

Simmons, J. (1991) 'The regional mall in Canada', *The Canadian Geographer*, 35: 232–240.

Snepenger, D.J., Murphy, L., O'Connell, R., & Gregg, E. (2003) 'Tourists and residents use of shopping space', *Annals of Tourism Research*, 30: 567–580.

Stausberg, M. (2011) *Religion and Tourism: Crossroads, Destinations and Encounters*. London: Routledge.

Steiner, C. (2010) 'From heritage to hyper-reality? Tourism destination development in the Middle East between Petra and the Palm', *Journal of Tourism and Cultural Change*, 8(4): 240–253.

Stephenson, M.L. (2014) 'Tourism, development and "destination Dubai": Cultural dilemmas and future challenges', *Current Issues in Tourism*, 17: 723–738.

Stephenson, M.L., Russell, K.A., & Edgar, D. (2010) 'Islamic hospitality in the UAE: Indigenisation of products and human capital', *Journal of Islamic Marketing*, 1: 9–24.

Swanson, K.K., & Timothy, D.J. (2012) 'Souvenirs: Icons of meaning, commercialisation, and commodit-isation', *Tourism Management*, 33(3): 489–499.

Timothy, D.J. (2005) *Shopping Tourism, Retailing and Leisure*. Clevedon: Channel View Publications.

Timothy, D.J. (2018) 'Shopping tourism', in S. Agarwal, G. Busby, & R. Huang (eds), *Special Interest Tourism: Concepts, Contexts and Cases* (pp. 132–142). Wallingford: CAB International.

Timothy, D.J., & Butler, R.W. (1995) 'Cross-border shopping: A North American perspective', *Annals of Tourism Research*, 22(1): 16–34.

Tosun, C., Temizkan, S.P., Timothy, D.J., & Fyall, A. (2007) 'Tourist shopping experiences and satisfaction', *International Journal of Tourism Research*, 9(2): 87–102.

Tourism and More (2014) 'The importance of the religious tourism market'. Available online: www.tourismandmore.com/tidbits/the-importance-of-the-religious-tourism-market/ (Accessed 5 January 2018).

Traditional Arts and Crafts. (n.d.). 'Handicrafts'. Available online: www.kultur.gov.tr/EN,98709/traditional-arts-and-crafts.html (Accessed 11 September 2018).

Turner, L.W., & Reisinger, Y. (2001) 'Shopping satisfaction for domestic tourists', *Journal of Retailing and Consumer Services*, 8: 15–27.

UNWTO (2014) 'Global report on shopping tourism'. Available online: http://dtxtq4w60xqpw.cloudfront.net/sites/all/files/pdf/am9-shopping-report_v2.pdf (Accessed 29 August 2017).

UNWTO (2016) *Tourism Annual Report*. Madrid: World Tourism Organization.

UNWTO (2017) *Tourism Highlights 2017*. Madrid: World Tourism Organization.

Vester, H.G. (1996) 'The shopping mall: A tourist destination of postmodernity', *Gruppendynamik*, 27: 57–66.

Wakefield, K.L., & Blodgett, J. (2016) 'Retrospective: The importance of servicescapes in leisure service settings', *Journal of Services Marketing*, 30(7): 686–691.

Wong, J., & Law, R. (2003) 'Difference in shopping satisfaction levels: A study of tourists in Hong Kong', *Tourism Management*, 24(4): 401–410.

Zaidan, E. (2015) 'Dubai as a first-choice destination for Saudi tourists: Analysis of socio-economic characteristics, travel behaviour, and perceptions of Saudi visitors to Dubai', *The Arab World Geographer*, 18(4): 262–281.

Zaidan, E. (2016a) 'The impact of cultural distance on local residents' perception of tourism develop-ment: The case of Dubai in UAE', *Tourism*, 64(1): 109–126.

Zaidan, E. (2016b) 'Tourism shopping and new urban entertainment: A case study of Dubai', *Journal of Vacation Marketing*, 22(1): 29–41.

Zaidan, E., Taillon, J., & Lee, S. (2016) 'Societal implications of UAE tourism development', *Anatolia*, 27(4): 543–545.

29

CONCLUSION

Future research directions

Dallen J. Timothy

That the Middle East and North Africa is an attractive region with considerable tourism potential is undeniable. This book examines many of the natural and cultural characteristics that make MENA an attractive destination but also realistically looks at the many complications that keep much of the region from flourishing. These include geopolitical turmoil, religious contention and environmental challenges. There are many recent opportunities and industry trends, however, that are unique in this region and have the potential to stimulate tourism growth. Supplementing the traditional pilgrimage and religious tourism, as well as cultural heritage-based tourism, new products and spaces have emerged in recent years to take centre stage.

The cruise sector, for example, is growing, even though it is not accepted across the board the way it often is in other realms. Nevertheless, more coastal states are becoming involved in it and see it as a viable tourism alternative (Karolak 2015). Recent recommendations suggest that cruises should be considered in MENA as a vacation opportunity for the growing Muslim leisure market, who often travel in larger family groups and who desire a wider array of Muslim-friendly destinations and products (Dowling & Weeden 2017). Likewise, the upward trend in halal tourism reflects increasing numbers of Arabs and Muslims from other areas choosing to spend their holidays in MENA. This is in large part a result of fears of a perceived growing post-September 11 Islamophobia in the West.

The association between medical tourism and the Middle East has long centred on the notion of affluent Middle Easterners travelling to Europe or Southeast Asia for treatment and recovery. Malaysia has been a favoured destination owing to its competent and Muslim physicians and staff members who will practise according to Islamic requirements (Ormond 2013). However, medical tourism is on the rise in certain MENA countries that are becoming known for high-quality health care and well-qualified medical staff (Connell 2011). Shopping tourism is thriving in several countries, especially in the Gulf States, where retail is an inseparable part of the hyper-urban development still unfolding in the UAE, Qatar, Bahrain and Kuwait. Traditional Arab *souqs* have long been sought out by visitors from abroad throughout MENA and continue to be an important part of the urban heritage milieu of the region (King-Irani 2006; Zaidan 2016), but they are in many cases becoming pigeonholed against the proliferation of the mega shopping mall. Business travel, or MICE tourism, is increasing in stature in the Middle East as well, particularly paralleling the development of high-end tourism and hyper-urbanisation in the Gulf States (Al-Hamarneh 2005). Since the discovery of fossil fuels, business travel has been an important part of the tourism repertoire, even in countries where 'tourism' did not officially exist. Now, however, it is becoming an increasingly important market segment targeted by several countries in the region.

Domestic and intra-regional travel

The majority of chapters in this volume have used a reasonably persuasive supply-side approach to describe tourism assets and issues. This largely reflects the availability of information on resources, products and places in MENA. Fewer meta-data are available about tourism demand on a regional level, and some countries provide no statistics at all. Most academic studies focus on inbound tourism to the region and to individual countries, yet we know that domestic tourism and intra-regional travel are also an important part of human mobility in both the Middle East and North Africa. More than a decade ago, Robinson (2007) lamented that very little research had been done up to that point on domestic and intra-regional tourism in MENA and that knowledge about it was scarce. This reality remains the same in 2018–2019, although a handful of case studies since the early 2000s have looked at domestic tourism in individual countries in very descriptive ways (e.g. Abu Tayeh & Mustafa 2011; Al-Badi, Tarhini, & Al-Sawaei 2017; Alipour, Kilic, & Zamani 2013; Ghaderi 2011; Mustafa 2012; Shemma 2014; Singh & Krakover 2015; Soliman 2011).

Conceptually rich and theoretically grounded studies have yet to be undertaken on subnational travel in MENA. Despite the growing collection of published case studies, there is still a vital need to understand domestic tourism and cross-national patterns throughout the region that make it different from other parts of the world. While domestic tourism manifests in many ways, it generally concentrates on family visits to beaches and coastal areas, shopping, religious tourism, cultural festivals, and visiting friends and relatives (VFR) (Al-Hamarneh & Steiner 2004; Bogari, Crowther, & Marr 2003; Daher 2007; Sönmez 2001; Timothy 2005).

Other manifestations of domestic tourism remain under-researched, although they certainly exist. The larger states, such as Morocco, Turkey, Iran and Saudi Arabia have vast natural and cultural reserves and distant localities that appeal to their citizens. These countries possess bountiful getaway opportunities in the domestic context, but what about the smaller countries? Still unknown in MENA (and everywhere throughout the world actually) is how residents of the geographically smallest states (i.e. Bahrain, Qatar, Israel, Palestine, Tunisia, Lebanon and Kuwait) perceive domestic tourism. Leisure activities that might not be reckoned strictly as domestic 'tourism' in the larger countries (e.g. day trips to the coast or visits to amusement parks, shopping malls and museums) because they do not conform to the 'official' UNWTO definition of overnight stays, may necessarily be the only configuration of 'domestic tourism' in the geographically challenged small states. In this instance, distance and scale are the only variables differentiating between small-state domestic tourism and that in larger nations.

Outbound tourism from MENA has also been comparatively neglected by researchers, and far fewer data are available. Traditionally, most incoming tourists headed to the poorer countries of the region with few interested in visiting the rentier countries of the Gulf (Daher 2007). Citizens of the wealthier Gulf States, however, have long dominated outbound travel. During the 1970s, the countries of the Arabian Gulf became wealthy by selling their petroleum resources, and systems were established to share that prosperity amongst their citizenry. This newfound affluence enabled Kuwaitis, Saudis, Emiratis, Qataris and Bahrainis to travel extensively throughout the entire world, with Europe and North America being their preferred destinations. Most outbound travel from the Gulf was geared towards high-end experiences for shopping, beach vacations, casinos and even health care. MENA's wealthy became accustomed to visiting Europe on lavish vacations, and families travelled regularly to exotic and faraway places. Even visits to other countries in the Middle East entailed highly frolicsome and leisure holiday choices (Daher 2007; Mumuni & Mansour 2014).

The terror events of 11 September 2001 were a major turning point for Middle Eastern tourists. Right away, many cancelled their journeys abroad or changed their plans to visit other Muslim countries in Asia or the Middle East that appeared to be more welcoming. Owing to perceptions of an escalating climate of Islamophobia in non-Muslim countries, largely exacerbated by the media, many people chose not to visit Europe or North America for fear they would be unwelcomed in the Western world and might face retaliatory action (Robinson 2007; Steiner 2010). These avoidance behaviours lasted several years into the 2000s, and in fact, they still continue today, albeit to a much lesser degree.

This event prompted a re-evaluation of Arabs' travel decisions, destination choices and expectations. Many people reoriented their travel interests to focus on Muslim-friendly holiday destinations, especially those closer to home. While there is a long history of intra-regional tourism, for example Algerians, Libyans and Moroccans visiting Tunisia (Carboni, Perelli, & Sistu 2014), regional travel benefited considerably from the downturn in long-haul outbound journeys. This hastened the development of halal tourism and Islamic tourism in response to the growing demand for Muslim-friendly vacations and Sharia-compliant services (Zamani-Farahani & Henderson 2010). In their minds, Middle Easterners can have the leisure experiences they desire, even in their own region in a Muslim-friendly environment (Battour, Ismail, & Battor 2010; Henderson 2010)—something on which they might have earlier had to compromise in visiting Europe and the Americas. By staying in MENA, they can even enjoy beach vacations, which many more conservative Muslims are reluctant to do in the West. For the most part, the beaches of MENA are safe spaces where modesty is honoured and where women can wear modest beach attire (e.g. burkinis) without standing out from the crowd or receiving undue attention.

Regional travel is often cheaper than long-haul trips, but not always. In fact, sometimes cross-border travel may be less expensive than vacationing in the homeland. For example, in some of the wealthier countries, lodging, food and transportation can be quite expensive. Thus, journeying to cheaper countries in the region, including Egypt, Syria and Lebanon, can be a cost-effective alternative to domestic holidays (Mustafa 2012). Thus, even within MENA, there is a 'north–south' pattern of development and tourist flow.

Religion and tourism

Several chapters in this book have addressed the market(s) for the products of Middle East tourism. Per capita, it is the most visited realm in the world amongst religious tourists/pilgrims of several different faiths (Timothy & Olsen 2006). Israel, Palestine, Egypt, Jordan, Lebanon, Turkey and formerly Syria, are extremely important destinations for Christian travellers. Saudi Arabia plays a special part in Islamic pilgrimages as a required destination, while Iraq, Iran and Syria are also prominent Muslim destinations. While few Jews travel specifically for religious pilgrimage (Cohen Ioannides & Ioannides 2006), there are several types of tourism that attract them to Israel from throughout the global diaspora, and there are Jewish heritage sites throughout MENA that could feature more prominently as destinations if political conditions allowed it.

Much has been written about Islamic, Jewish and Christian travel to and within the Middle East. Yet, as Chapter 3 indicated, the region is home to other religions and many subsects beyond these three. Understanding the religious travel patterns amongst Hindu, Sikh and Buddhist guest workers could help expatriate associations better serve the needs of immigrant employees. Raising such questions can also place these religions' adherents into the mainstream population of MENA and provide insight into how they might use Middle Eastern religious assets as attractions as they themselves undertake regional holidays.

There are other homegrown faiths whose beliefs, practices, structures and festivities have relationships to tourism. Druze, Samaritanism, Zoroastrianism and the Bahá'í Faith all originated in MENA and remain strongest there. All of these belief systems have shrines and historic sites that devotees revere and to which they travel for adulation or celebratory purposes. They also contribute to the overall cultural milieu that helps make this region inimitable amongst regions. Aside from the Bahá'í World Center in Haifa, Israel, which is a major UNESCO and religious attraction in that city (Collins-Kreiner & Gatrell 2006), these faith-based heritages have all but been ignored by scholars, even if the faiths wish not to be part of tourism beyond their pilgrimage mandates. Although of secondary importance in tourism, or having no relationship at all, these other faiths contribute to a diverse cultural landscape that gives the Middle East its flavour and sense of identity.

Diasporas

MENA is the source of many significant diasporas. Diaspora tourism, sometimes referred to as return travel, represents emigrants and/or their descendants travelling back to the original motherland for a variety of purposes—visiting relatives, religious ceremonies, festivals and events, reunions, genealogy and family history research, and more. This can involve first-generation emigrants (those who migrated) or any of their progeny of subsequent generations (Coles & Timothy 2004b). The most prominent diaspora is the Jews. They are more widespread around the world than any other nationality or group from the region, and they have one of the most noteworthy histories. There are far more Jews outside of Israel than there are within. Outside of Israel, the United States, France, Canada, the United Kingdom and Russia have the largest Jewish populations, but Jews dwell in most countries of the world including many in Asia, Africa and Latin America. Return visits to Israel have many purposes, including bar/bat mitzvah celebrations, holiday observance, family visits, religious rites, funerals, and visits to tombs, temples and holy sites (Collins-Kreiner & Olsen 2004; Ioannides & Cohen Ioannides 2004). Birthright Israel is a unique type of diaspora tourism that enables Jewish youth to visit their native soil in order to learn about the state, Israeli identity and Jewish traditions. The journeys are funded by various private organisations and the State of Israel as a means of educating and building solidarity with Israel amongst diasporic youth (Brin 2006; Cohen 2004; Kelner 2010).

There are many other Middle Eastern diasporas that receive less academic attention. The Lebanese diaspora includes millions of people of Lebanese descent living in numerous countries. Most, however, are concentrated in South and North America, Australia and other Middle Eastern countries. While the majority of Lebanese emigres are Christians, there are also large populations of Muslim, Druze and Jewish Lebanese living outside the homeland.

There are people of every MENA descent living in various parts of the world, many driven from their homeland by war and violence, others by economic necessity or family ties. Several, however, such as Jews and Lebanese, stand out amongst the most populous and influential. Additionally, there is a sizeable Moroccan diaspora across Europe, an Algerian community in France, and a Palestinian diaspora scattered throughout the Middle East and the Americas. There is a large Turkish diaspora in neighbouring countries and throughout Europe, especially Germany, and Iranians can be found dispersed throughout most of the world with the highest concentration in the United States. These and many smaller ones contribute significantly to their motherland economies through remittances and return tourism. For example, much of Lebanon's tourism industry is sustained by diasporic Lebanese returning to visit relatives and the motherland (Abdelhady 2011; Hourani 2007). In the same way, much of Israel's tourism economy is dependent on Jewish tourists visiting Israel from every corner of the globe.

The idea of diasporas and tourism raises many questions that scholars have yet to address adequately. Many diasporic populations endure prejudice and intolerance in their adopted lands. Perhaps even more common, however, is a 'hyphenated identity' (e.g. Lebanese-American, Moroccan-Dutch, Iranian-Canadians), which causes many people, including downline younger generations, to feel unrooted and in a perpetual state of in-betweenness, belonging neither to the homeland of their roots nor to the adopted land where they were born or to which they immigrated (Coles & Timothy 2004a). How does this condition play out in their travel choices? Can visiting the homeland help heal the chasm in their identities? Does tourism help them preserve their former national identity or widen the hyphen that already exists?

Political boundaries are an important consideration here, despite their colonial origins. Perhaps not every emigrant ensemble defines itself by the state boundaries from which it originated, which may add another layer of identity or lack thereof. The Druze, for instance, are an ethno-religious community that inhabit Syria, Lebanon, Israel and Jordan. Most diasporic Druze (the largest population being in Venezuela, followed by the United States) identify as Druze-Venezuelans or Druze-Americans before relating to a specific Middle Eastern state (Radwan 2009; Swayd 2006). Lebanon, for example, is a multi-faith country, with current representative populations of Christians, Muslims and Druze. Large numbers of both Christian and Muslim Lebanese emigres live outside MENA, yet as regards their social identity, both tend to identify first as being of Lebanese descent. In their case, the state borders matter more than for the Druze, whose identity is more transnational, religious and cultural rather than bounded by the frontiers of their country of origin. How do different groups that originated from a single country reconcile their identity 'crisis' and how might this affect their return travel patterns? Do different types of diasporas (e.g. victim, labour, imperial) kindle different connections to the motherland? Countless questions such as these could be fruitfully addressed, and many more raised, through additional research.

Environmental issues

The ecological problems facing MENA are manifold and troublesome. The Arabian Peninsula's continued economic overdependence on fossil fuels has salient implications not only for those countries but also for the rest of the world. While oil and natural gas are finite resources, they are often treated as infinite reserves with little forethought for the future. A few countries are beginning to consider tourism as a potential alternative to their rentier economies, but they have yet to decelerate petroleum exploring and tapping on a perceptible scale. Clearly, a region with such an abundance of alternative natural energy sources (e.g. wind and sunshine) and technological expertise could bring its best minds together to devise solutions to global climate change and escalating aridity.

Desertification continues throughout the region but especially in North Africa and the Sahel. Here the Sahara continues to spread southward into the Sahel, brought about by natural processes but quickened in part through overgrazing and global warming. Similar patterns have occurred on the Arabian Peninsula, but the Sahel's desertification is expanding faster than in any other desert on earth. This has clear implications for continued poverty, famine and the destruction of cultures and environments. Increased aridity throughout MENA means that countries are having to find alternative water sources (e.g. desalination and imports) and import a higher quantity of their food. This has clear economic implications, just as it does for biosecurity and food security, which may or may not be directly connected to political stability and turmoil (Hall, Timothy, & Duval 2003; Timothy 2006). It also has obvious implications for heavy energy-, construction- and food-dependent tourism (Lew, Hall, & Timothy 2015), but there is much work to be done to examine these phenomena in this regional setting.

MENA's natural environment—its topography, natural landscapes and biotic systems— while vast and ancient, are fragile and irreplaceable. While nature-based tourism was not the core of any chapter in this book, it was implied in several. This form of tourism is growing in popularity in the region and logically concentrates on desert landscapes and mountain ecosystems. Four-wheel drive activities and camel caravans are amongst the most popular activities in the Arabian Desert and the Sahara. While deserts are more resilient to human recreation than some other ecosystems (e.g. arctic tundra and rainforests), they can nonetheless be over-utilised, contributing to desertification processes. Likewise, desertification can influence tourism and how it is planned, carried out and managed, especially in the long term. While 'ecotourism' is often perceived to be an activity exclusively for tropical biomes, it actually has little to do with where it happens but rather how it happens. In addition to providing low-impact and small-scale activities in natural areas, its goals are to help protect the natural environment and contribute to the well-being of residents. It also tends to have an educative element and is pro-conservation. This raises many questions for the deserts of MENA, especially as regards indigenous people who roam the deserts, the use of oases as water sources, and the potential environmental impacts of off-road vehicles. How sustainable are these activities and how well do they benefit the communities where they occur? In the absence of nearby settlements, what communities are involved and which are best empowered by these 'responsible' forms of tourism? The physical and cultural environments of MENA are unique enough to merit extensive additional research about ecotourism and other manifestations of 'responsible' tourism.

Geopolitics

Political discord and religious contention underpin many tourism relationships in MENA. The constant state of war and malcontent keeps tourism from developing in ways that it has in other regions of the world. Tourism is extremely sensitive to geopolitics, terrorism and war and reacts quickly and durably. State travel warnings have played a major part in spreading the word of caution about travel to many Middle Eastern countries. These warnings provide useful travel information regarding security situations, but they may also be used as a political pawn to threaten insecure states into complying with the wishes of more powerful players. Many countries in the Middle East and North Africa are on the travel warning lists of Western countries and have been for years, even though there are safe places to visit. There are safe places for tourists in Iraq and Syria, for example, yet government travel warnings in major source markets continue to dissuade people from visiting out of an abundance of caution. While many MENA states have made valiant efforts to manage crises and recovery marketing during difficult times, the majority of countries have not realised their full tourism potential.

Since 2017, there has been a constant salvo of political events that have a bearing on the region's security and tourism. The Trump administration's December 2017 recognition of all of Jerusalem as the capital of Israel, and the 14 May 2018 relocation of the US embassy to the contested city, incited violence in Jerusalem and other occupied parts of Palestine, resulting in extended firefights along the Israel–Gaza border. A handful of other countries followed suit and moved their embassies at the same time. The United States' pulling out of the Iran Nuclear Deal in 2018 erected additional obstacles to Middle East peace.

The steady stream of refugees from Syria, Iraq, Libya and Tunisia into Europe has caused major security and political problems in the European Union and led, in part at least, to the enfranchisement of several conservative governments that hope to curtail cross-Mediterranean migration. The economic and political blockade of Qatar in 2017–2018 by Saudi Arabia, Bahrain, the UAE and Egypt also has implications for tourism, not least of which were required air route changes into and out of Qatar and stalled intra-regional tourism. Turkey's ongoing quarrels with the EU and the United States are proving problematic. The Kurdish vote for independence from Iraq may have long-term implications we do not yet know about. The division of Libya between belligerent leaders and ongoing civil wars in Syria and Yemen continue to destabilise the region in every way, not just for tourism.

Volumes could be written about social, cultural, political, economic and ecological conditions in the Middle East and North Africa, and how these influence tourism or are influenced by tourism. This book is a step in the right direction and has provided a great deal of insight into these and other issues. However, there is much more work to be done to understand the dynamics of this unique realm and how they contrast with those in other parts of the world. Tourism will continue to rise and fall with every change and whisper of discontent, yet MENA will continue to wield a sense of awe, mystique and curiosity for generations to come.

References

Abdelhady, D. (2011) *The Lebanese Diaspora: The Arab Immigrant Experience in Montreal, New York and Paris.* New York: New York University Press.

Abu Tayeh, S.N., & Mustafa, M.H. (2011) 'Toward empowering the labor Saudization of tourism sector in Saudi Arabia', *International Journal of Humanities and Social Science*, 1(3): 80–84.

Al-Badi, A., Tarhini, A., & Al-Sawaei, S. (2017) 'Utilising social media to encourage domestic tourism in Oman', *International Journal of Business and Management*, 12(4): 84–94.

Al-Hamarneh, A. (2005) 'New tourism trends in the Islamic world', *Islamic Tourism*, 16: 50–54.

Al-Hamarneh, A., & Steiner, C. (2004) 'Islamic tourism: Rethinking the strategies of tourism development in the Arab World after September 11, 2001', *Comparative Studies of South Asia, Africa and the Middle East*, 24(1): 173–182.

Alipour, H., Kilic, H., & Zamani, N. (2013) 'The untapped potential of sustainable domestic tourism in Iran', *Anatolia*, 24(3): 468–483.

Battour, M.M., Ismail, M.N., & Battor, M. (2010) 'Toward a halal tourism market', *Tourism Analysis*, 15(4): 461–470.

Bogari, N.B., Crowther, G., & Marr, N. (2003) 'Motivation for domestic tourism: A case study of the Kingdom of Saudi Arabia', *Tourism Analysis*, 8(2): 137–141.

Brin, E. (2006) 'Politically oriented tourism in Jerusalem', *Tourist Studies*, 6(3): 215–243.

Carboni, M., Perelli, C., & Sistu, G. (2014) 'Is Islamic tourism a viable option for Tunisian tourism? Insights from Djerba', *Tourism Management Perspectives*, 11: 1–9.

Cohen, E.H. (2004) 'Preparation, simulation and the creation of community: Exodus and the case of diaspora education tourism', in T. Coles, & D.J. Timothy (eds), *Tourism, Diasporas and Space* (pp. 124–138). London: Routledge.

Cohen Ioannides, M., & Ioannides, D. (2006) 'Global Jewish tourism: Pilgrimages and remembrance', in D.J. Timothy, & D.H. Olsen (eds), *Tourism, Religion & Spiritual Journeys* (pp. 156–171). London: Routledge.

Coles, T., & Timothy, D.J. (2004a) '"My field is the world": Conceptualising diasporas, travel and tourism', in T. Coles, & D.J. Timothy (eds), *Tourism, Diasporas and Space* (pp. 1–19). London: Routledge.

Coles, T., & Timothy, D.J. (eds) (2004b) *Tourism, Diasporas and Space*. London: Routledge.

Collins-Kreiner, N., & Gatrell, J.D. (2006) 'Tourism, heritage and pilgrimage: The case of Haifa's Bahá'í Gardens', *Journal of Heritage Tourism*, 1(1): 32–50.

Collins-Kreiner, N., & Olsen, D.H. (2004) 'Selling diaspora: Producing and segmenting the Jewish diaspora travel market', in T. Coles, & D.J. Timothy (eds), *Tourism, Diasporas and Space* (pp. 279–290). London: Routledge.

Connell, J. (2011) *Medical Tourism*. Wallingford: CAB International.

Daher, R.F. (2007) 'Reconceptualising tourism in the Middle East: Place, heritage, mobility and competitiveness', in R.F. Daher (ed.), *Tourism in the Middle East: Continuity, Change and Transformation* (pp. 1–69). Clevedon: Channel View Publications.

Dowling, R., & Weeden, C. (2017) 'The world of cruising', in R. Dowling, & C. Weeden (eds), *Cruise Ship Tourism*, 2nd edn (pp. 1–39). Wallingford: CAB International.

Ghaderi, Z. (2011) 'Domestic tourism in Iran', *Anatolia*, 22(2): 278–281.

Hall, C.M., Timothy, D.J., & Duval, D.T. (eds) (2003) *Safety and Security in Tourism: Relationships, Management and Marketing*. New York: Haworth.

Henderson, J.C. (2010) 'Sharia-compliant hotels', *Tourism and Hospitality Research*, 10(3): 246–254.

Hourani, G. (2007) *Lebanese Diaspora and Homeland Relations*. Cairo: The American University.

Ioannides, D., & Cohen Ioannides, M. (2004) 'Jewish past as a "foreign country": The travel experiences of American Jews', in T. Coles, & D.J. Timothy (eds), *Tourism, Diasporas and Space* (pp. 95–110). London: Routledge.

Karolak, M. (2015) 'Analysis of the cruise industry in the Arabian Gulf: The emergence of a new destination', *Journal of Tourism Challenges and Trends*, 8(1): 61–78.

Kelner, S. (2010) *Tours that Bind: Diaspora, Pilgrimage and Israeli Birthright Tourism*. New York: New York University Press.

King-Irani, L. (2006) 'The millennial medina: Discourses of time, space and authenticity in projects to market and renovate Beirut and Nazareth', *Studies in Culture, Polity and Identities*, 7(1): 1–23.

Lew, A.A., Hall, C.M., & Timothy, D.J. (2015) *World Regional Geography: Human Mobilities, Tourism Destinations, Sustainable Environments*, 2nd edn. Dubuque, IA: Kendall-Hunt.

Mumuni, A.G., & Mansour, M. (2014) 'Activity-based segmentation of the outbound leisure tourism market of Saudi Arabia', *Journal of Vacation Marketing*, 20(3): 239–252.

Mustafa, M.H. (2012) 'Improving the contribution of domestic tourism to the economy of Jordan', *Asian Social Science*, 8(2): 49–61.

Ormond, M. (2013) 'Claiming "cultural competence": The promotion of multi-ethnic Malaysia as a medical tourism destination', in C.M. Hall (ed.), *Medical Tourism: The Ethics, Regulation, and Marketing of Healthy Mobility* (pp. 187–199). London: Routledge.

Radwan, C.K. (2009) 'Assessing Druze identity and strategies for preserving Druze heritage in North America'. Unpublished master's thesis, University of South Florida.

Robinson, M. (2007) 'Preface', in R.F. Daher (ed.), *Tourism in the Middle East: Continuity, Change and Transformation* (pp. vii–ix). Clevedon: Channel View Publications.

Shemma, M. (2014) 'Tourist destination: Demand-motivating factors in Israel's domestic tourism', *Journal of Tourism Challenges and Trends*, 7(2): 65–86.

Singh, S., & Krakover, S. (2015) 'Tourist experience at home: Israeli domestic tourism', *Tourism Management*, 46: 59–61.

Soliman, D.M. (2011) 'Exploring the role of film in promoting domestic tourism: A case study of Al Fayoum, Egypt', *Journal of Vacation Marketing*, 17(3): 225–235.

Sönmez, S. (2001) 'Tourism behind the veil of Islam: Women and development in the Middle East', in Y. Apostolopoulos, S. Sönmez, & D.J. Timothy (eds), *Women as Producers and Consumers of Tourism in Developing Regions* (pp. 113–142). Westport, CT: Praeger.

Steiner, C. (2010) 'Impacts of September 11: A two-sided neighborhood effect?', in N. Scott, & J. Jafari (eds), *Tourism in the Muslim World* (pp. 181–204). Bingley: Emerald.

Swayd, S. (2006) *The A to Z of the Druzes*. Lanham, MD: Scarecrow Press.

Timothy, D.J. (2005) *Shopping Tourism, Retailing and Leisure*. Clevedon: Channel View Publications.

Timothy, D.J. (2006) 'Safety and security issues in tourism', in D. Buhalis, & C. Costa (eds), *Tourism Management Dynamics: Trends, Management and Tools* (pp. 19–27). Oxford: Elsevier/Butterworth Heinemann.

Timothy, D.J., & Olsen, D.H. (eds) (2006) *Tourism, Religion and Spiritual Journeys*. London: Routledge.

Zaidan, E.A. (2016) 'Tourism shopping and new urban entertainment: A case study of Dubai', *Journal of Vacation Marketing*, 22(1): 29–41.

Zamani-Farahani, H., & Henderson, J.C. (2010) 'Islamic tourism and managing tourism development in Islamic societies: The cases of Iran and Saudi Arabia', *International Journal of Tourism Research*, 12: 79–89.

INDEX

For Product Safety Concerns and Information please contact our EU
representative GPSR@taylorandfrancis.com
Taylor & Francis Verlag GmbH, Kaufingerstraße 24, 80331 München, Germany

www.ingramcontent.com/pod-product-compliance
Ingram Content Group UK Ltd.
Pitfield, Milton Keynes, MK11 3LW, UK
UKHW011454240425
457818UK00021B/827